The
Edinburgh Critical History
of
Nineteenth-Century
Philosophy

The Edinburgh Critical History of Philosophy
General Editors: Howard Caygill and David Webb

Titles available
The Edinburgh Critical History of Nineteenth-Century Philosophy
Edited by Alison Stone

Forthcoming volumes in the series
The Edinburgh Critical History of Greek and Roman Philosophy
Edited by Giuseppe Cambiano and Alexandra Lianeri

The Edinburgh Critical History of Islamic Philosophy
Edited by Ilham Ibnouzahir and Nigel Tubbs

The Edinburgh Critical History of Middle Ages and Renaissance Philosophy
Edited by Richard A. Lee and Andrew LaZella

The Edinburgh Critical History of Early Modern and Enlightenment Philosophy
Edited by Gary Banham

The Edinburgh Critical History of Early Twentieth-Century Philosophy
Edited by Andrew Benjamin

The Edinburgh Critical History of Contemporary Philosophy
Edited by Alberto Toscano

Visit the Edinburgh Critical History of Philosophy website at
www.euppublishing.com/series/echp

The
Edinburgh Critical History
of
Nineteenth-Century
Philosophy

Edited by Alison Stone

Edinburgh University Press

Edinburgh University Press Ltd
22 George Square, Edinburgh

www.euppublishing.com

Typeset in 11 on 13 Ehrhardt

actually
10/13
Goudy

ourne

m the British Library

)88.

I am very grateful to the Leverhulme Trust for awarding me a Philip Leverhulme Prize in 2008. This funded a period of research leave that expedited my editorial work on this volume. I also thank Judith Menzel for help with German, and John Varty for the many kinds of help that he has provided during the editing process.

Contents

General Editors' Preface   vii

Introduction: Philosophy in the Nineteenth Century
    Alison Stone   1

1. *The New Spinozism*   13
    George di Giovanni

2. *The Absolute in German Romanticism and Idealism*   29
    Dalia T. Nassar

3. *The Question of Romanticism*   47
    Judith Norman and Alistair Welchman

4. *The Hermeneutic Turn in Philosophy of Nature in the
    Nineteenth Century*   69
    Philippe Huneman

5. *Idealism and Naturalism in the Nineteenth Century*   89
    Sebastian Gardner

6. *Darwinism and Philosophy in the Nineteenth Century:
    The 'Whole of Metaphysics'?*   111
    Gregory Moore

7. *Faith and Knowledge*   128
    George Pattison

8. *Philosophising History: Distinguishing History as a Discipline*   145
    James Connelly

9. *Genealogy as Immanent Critique: Working from the Inside*   168
    Robert Guay

10. *Embodiment: Conceptions of the Lived Body from
    Maine de Biran to Bergson*   187
    Mark Sinclair

11. *The Unconscious in the German Philosophy and Psychology of the*
    Nineteenth Century   204
    Günter Gödde (translated from the German by Ciaran Cronin)

12. *Individuality, Radical Politics and the Metaphor of the Machine*   223
    Alex Zakaras

13. *The Rise of the Social*   242
    William Outhwaite

14. *Theory and Practice of Revolution in the Nineteenth Century*   259
    Paul Blackledge

15. *Nihilism in the Nineteenth Century: From Absolute*
    Subjectivity to Superhumanity   278
    Michael Gillespie

16. *Repetition and Recurrence: Putting Metaphysics in Motion*   294
    Clare Carlisle

17. *Nineteenth-Century Philosophy in the Twentieth Century and Beyond* 314
    Andrew Bowie

Notes on contributors   330
Index   333

General Editors' Preface

All forms of inquiry are enriched by an appreciation of their own history, and this seems especially true in the case of philosophy. The study of past thinkers and their works continues to sustain and to renew philosophical thought, shaping the way that even the most concrete of contemporary problems are seen, and how they are tackled. If one of the hallmarks of philosophy is a reflection on the limits of what it is possible to think at any time, then the history of philosophy is at once an indispensable resource, a testing ground, and a reminder that we are never really done with thinking.

The Edinburgh Critical History of Philosophy places itself in the European tradition of philosophy, without being bound to any single vision of what philosophy should be. It treats the history of philosophy from its beginnings in Ancient Greece to the present day as composed of many threads, breaks, borrowings and intrigues that cannot be unified in a single narrative. Often, the orthodox classification of philosophy into themes and sub-disciplines has been set aside, since it does not always reflect the way problems and themes first emerged. In turn, consideration of this emergence has sometimes allowed for the inclusion of figures who may not be well known outside specialist circles, but whose work was significant in shaping later developments.

Although the idea of critical philosophy properly speaking has passed through many reformulations since originating with Kant, the idea of philosophy as an ongoing reflection on its limits has become almost commonplace, and goes beyond any adherence to this or that methodology, school or tradition. The aim of the series is to present a historical perspective on philosophy that matches this broad critical outlook. As such, it recognises that 'Western Philosophy' has developed through exchanges across its geographical borders; that historically speaking, not only are limits hard to define, but periods are sometimes linked in multiple and unexpected ways; and that what is taken to define a given period, movement, or sub-discipline within philosophy is often not indigenous to it. In the same way, philosophy has often taken up problems from other disciplines, transforming them, and sometimes being transformed by them, in the process. Ignoring these movements across and along borders can obscure the multifaceted development of problems and themes as they feed into, and off, one another. It can also tempt one to regard the subject matter of philosophy as simply given, as though its history were merely a record of increasing clarification. Similarly, although there are essays in this series dedicated to individual philosophers, this is not the default choice. Instead, the critical perspective adopted in this series tries to keep in view how the problems and themes of a given period took shape, and in turn gave shape to the philosophical work around them. Wherever possible, we have encouraged volume editors and authors to consider that links may exist between different essays within volumes, and across volumes. However, for good reasons, this could not become their central preoccupation, and so many of these links remain implicit, and even unintended. It is our hope that this may add to the richness of the work as a whole and that the reader will take pleasure in their discovery.

As general editors of the series, we have enjoyed working with volume editors who are outstanding subject specialists, and who have brought great imagination and dedication to the task. The series as a whole owes a great deal to all of them. Special thanks goes to Carol Macdonald at Edinburgh University Press, whose patience, care and determination has made all the difference.

Howard Caygill
David Webb

Introduction

Philosophy in the Nineteenth Century

Alison Stone

Nineteenth-century philosophy can be broadly characterised by several themes: the conflict between metaphysics and religious faith on the one hand and the empirical sciences on the other; a new focus on history, progress and evolution; new ideas of individuality, society and revolution; and ever-increasing concerns about nihilism.[1] This volume provides a re-examination of nineteenth-century philosophy in terms of these and other themes distinctive of the period.

It is worth remembering that this was the period in which much of the fundamental structure of modern society took shape in Europe, North America and beyond. At the beginning of this development, the French Revolution of 1789 sparked political and social modernisation across Europe and spread ideals of freedom and equality, inspiring a generation with hopes for a new moral, social and spiritual world. Market economies were established and the industrial revolution took off. In their wake came rapid urbanisation, the industrial proletariat, urban poverty and the so-called 'social question'. Enlightenment and French Revolutionary ideals spurred waves of revolutionary activity and insurrection, followed by waves of reaction and restoration. The empirical sciences advanced dramatically and their success was visibly linked to practical applications in technology and industry. This advance threw traditional religious beliefs and attitudes into crisis. (It is revealing that the word 'secularism' entered the English language in 1846.) In the wake of this religious crisis and of the rise of bureaucracy and mass society, concerns grew about modern life's supposed conformism and mediocrity and its lack of any guiding moral or religious framework.

Nineteenth-century philosophy is marked by and feeds into this broader social context, even when philosophers do not directly address it. Earlier in the century, philosophical and intellectual life was dominated by the German idealism of J. G. Fichte, F. W. J. Schelling, G. W. F. Hegel and others. German idealism has its starting point in Kant. For this reason, the publication of Kant's *Critique of Pure Reason* (1st edn 1781, 2nd edn 1787) marks one of the two key events after which we may take nineteenth-century philosophy to begin. The other event is the French Revolution, of which many people saw Kant's philosophy, with its emphasis on autonomy, as the theoretical correlate (see Pinkard 2002). 'Nineteenth-century' philosophy as an intellectual rather than strictly chronological phenomenon thus actually begins in the later 1780s and the 1790s, in response to Kant's Critical philosophy and the French Revolution.

Kant sought to defend Enlightenment values of freedom, reason and science against the threat that he thought they faced from the Enlightenment's own metaphysics (sometimes materialism, sometimes ideas of a rational and divinely grounded cosmos) and epistemology (sometimes empiricism, sometimes rationalism). For Kant this metaphysics and epistemology led inexorably to insoluble sceptical problems (see Stern 2004). F. H. Jacobi added urgency to these worries by suggesting that Enlightenment reason, which for him was embodied in Spinoza's philosophy above all, led straight to nihilism – an attitude of corrosive rationalism, atheism, determinism and scepticism. In response to concerns of this kind, the German idealists continued and radicalised Kant's line of thought. They sought not only to preserve his emphasis on autonomy and the moral and political values of the Enlightenment but also to overcome what they saw as unacceptable dualisms in his thinking – dualisms between things-in-themselves and appearances, freedom and nature, sensibility and understanding. In different ways, this project led the idealists back to pre-Kantian metaphysics – Platonism, Spinozism. But this was no naïve return to positions that Kant had discredited. The German idealists tried to rethink these traditions to defend them against scepticism, to make them compatible with modern values of freedom, equality and reason and to integrate them with new discoveries in empirical science (this was the project of *Naturphilosophie*, 'philosophy of nature'). Thus we can see them as trying to produce a new kind of metaphysics appropriate to the modern world. How successful they were remains open to question.

Another dominant current in the earlier nineteenth century and beyond was Romanticism. In fact Romanticism and idealism were intertwined. This was especially so in Germany: the Early German Romantics were heavily involved in the philosophical debates of the time. In the US, too, idealism and Romanticism merged in the 'transcendentalism' of Ralph Waldo Emerson, Henry David Thoreau and others and in England S. T. Coleridge popularised German idealist ideas in his *Biographia Literaria* of 1817. Despite – or perhaps in resistance to – the industrialisation, urbanisation and class divisions of the time, nineteenth-century thought became decisively shaped by Romantic ideas about the value and uniqueness of individual and cultural self-expression. The intellectual climate was likewise shaped by Romantic re-evaluations of nature, sentiment and art and by Romantic preferences for the organic over the mechanical, the concrete over the abstract, unique individuality over uniformity.

A key issue on which Romanticism and idealism converged was the all-pervasiveness of history. In Hegel's version of this view, everything in human life is historical – morality, culture, society, modes of thought and belief, religious doctrines and practices and even nature insofar as it is the object of human thought and practice. All these are historical in that they are fully shaped by human activity, which for Hegel is rational, self-critical and self-reflexive and so continually transforms and redefines its own guiding norms. This means that the practices, institutions and forms of life which human activity produces are also subject to continual transformation. These Hegelian ideas were perhaps the most important expression of the broader 'historical turn' that took place in the philosophy and intellectual life of the time.

Nineteenth-century insights into the all-pervasiveness of history and culture have become premises for much if not all subsequent thought. But the idealist metaphysical framework in which these insights were often embedded has survived less well. Twentieth-century philosophers have often disparaged German idealism as outmoded metaphysical and religious speculation. This attitude has roots in the reaction against idealism by Bertrand Russell and his co-workers in the early twentieth century. However, the complaint that German idealism is misguided metaphysics was already heard in the nineteenth century. In this as in other ways, twentieth-century thought has often continued nineteenth-century discussions even when professing to reject the nineteenth century.

After Hegel's sudden death in 1831, German idealism rapidly unravelled and a variety of anti-idealist lines of thought came to dominate. One of these was positivism. In its decisive formulation by Auguste Comte, positivism relegated theology and metaphysics to the status of pre-modern modes of thought and took science as the paradigm of knowledge, advocating its extension to society and history. Scientific advance and its application were expected to produce not only progress in understanding but also improvements in social conditions and wellbeing. In a similar vein in the UK, John Stuart Mill developed Bentham's utilitarianism, again taking science as the model of knowledge, while understanding science to be specifically empirical and inductive. In Germany, Russia and elsewhere, many scientists and scientifically informed philosophers championed materialism, which centred on a mechanistic and deterministic view of nature. The materialists inveighed against the hangovers of theology and teleology which they thought had held back earlier nineteenth-century science, especially due to the malign influence of *Naturphilosophie*. Elements of these diverse anti-idealist currents coalesced in Karl Marx, who, in explicit opposition to Hegel, developed his theory of history which he saw as both empirically based and materialist.

These various anti-idealist developments coincided with and drew support from the rapid theoretical and practical advances in the sciences at this time. These advances led to such achievements as Charles Darwin's theory of evolution, expressed in *The Origin of Species* of 1859. The developments in science lent new weight to a naturalistic view of the world: a view that denies the existence of any supernatural forces or beings and that treats human beings as completely natural creatures, including in their capacities for reason, creativity and moral and practical agency. These capacities, it now seemed, could in principle be completely understood by the empirical sciences. Increasingly, naturalism was supplanting Christianity as the reigning outlook, at least amongst intellectual elites.

There was of course resistance to this trend, but it did not always take the form of a return to idealism. A very different non-naturalist and anti-idealist line of thought of the 1830s and 1840s was Søren Kierkegaard's proto-existentialism. He sought to recover individual subjectivity and the individual's subjective relation to God from (what he saw as) their obliteration within idealist philosophical systems that subordinated individuals to the whole. From Kierkegaard's perspective, naturalism and idealism are in fact alike – and at fault – in adopting a purely objective, third-person stance, overlooking or denying subjectivity and the first-person viewpoint.

Nevertheless, naturalism became the dominant outlook in the mid-to-later century. In a sense, its proponents sought to keep alive eighteenth-century Enlightenment ideas of progress through scientific knowledge. As Robert Stern has remarked, 'the "fight between the nineteenth century and the eighteenth" runs like a thread through the philosophical debates in the period' (Stern 2004; this image goes back to John Stuart Mill's autobiography). Indeed, the fight went on as much within the thought of individual philosophers as between different individuals or schools. Many thinkers combined elements of idealism and naturalism. For instance, Arthur Schopenhauer construed Kant's thing-in-itself as a boundlessly creative will – but a purposeless, godless, ultimately meaningless will. In this way he gave a distinctly naturalistic slant to a view that otherwise might have seemed idealist and Romantic. Figures who today are largely forgotten, such as Hermann Lotze and Gustav Fechner, devised new idealist metaphysical systems with which they intended to 'do justice to the mechanical view of nature' (Mandelbaum 1971: 7). Others who eagerly embraced new developments such as Darwinism in effect reinterpreted them within the terms of older styles of religious and metaphysical thought. We see this in Herbert Spencer, for instance, but also – in more sophisticated form – in others such as Charles Sanders Peirce.

Such compromises reflect the fact that many would-be naturalists still struggled to extricate themselves from idealism, or devised naturalistic theories that remained indebted to idealism – or both, as in Marx's case, whose theory of history owes so much to Hegel's. Indeed, the very orientation to history that typified the whole century – and which, with Darwinism, entered into science itself – reflected the legacies of idealism and Romanticism. However, from a naturalist perspective the all-pervasiveness of history takes on a different character. Chains of social, psychological, biological determination run everywhere and the human agency that feeds into these chains is itself a natural phenomenon. On one reading of Friedrich Nietzsche's *On the Genealogy of Morals* of 1887, this work represents the ultimate extension of this line of thinking to morality. Moral ideals and standards have no absolute validity; they are merely contingent products of human affects and desires that have been shaped by power relations over the centuries.

The fact that moral ideals and standards could become subject to naturalistic critique and deflation exposes one reason why so many thinkers of this time sought to combine idealism and naturalism – or in some cases, such as the British idealists of the late nineteenth century, returned to idealism. These thinkers doubted that naturalism in itself could do justice to value. This doubt was part of a wider, not exclusively philosophical, set of concerns about the spiritual emptiness of modern life. More specifically, as Sebastian Gardner (2007) has argued, naturalist approaches seemed either – pessimistically – to explain value away by accounting for it in psychological, social, biological, etc., terms (as, perhaps, in Nietzsche's *Genealogy*) or – in the spirit of Enlightenment optimism – to account for values, in terms of sensations, desires or pleasures, in an unpalatably crude and shallow way. Nietzsche raised a further worry: that naturalism is incoherent, because any attempt to give a true account of the causal genesis of morality, religion, etc., presupposes acceptance of at least one absolute value – truth. And this, Nietzsche suggested, presupposes a deeper-rooted but unacknowledged debt not only to idealism but also, through it, to the whole Platonic-cum-Christian metaphysical tradition.

Many thinkers of the time thus believed that values could only be accommodated by a return to more idealist or Romantic ideas. Mill's synthesis of utilitarianism with Romantic ideas of individuality and culture can be seen as indicative of this, as can the spread of British idealism. Others, such as Kierkegaard, sought alternative ways to address religious and moral concerns. Others again, notably Nietzsche, seemed only to conclude that the European intellectual inheritance was hopelessly conflicted and debased. But whatever route was adopted, as the century went on it seemed more and more that wholesale naturalism could not but collapse into nihilism. Nietzsche distilled this thought when he redefined nihilism as the event that the 'highest values devalue themselves' (Nietzsche [1887] 1968: 9). In part, he means that because of the 'death of God', the decline of religious faith and authority and the rise of naturalism in their place, we have been left without any normative horizon. But moreover, having destroyed all other normative foundations, naturalism is proceeding to self-destruct as well, producing a dangerously total void of grounds for belief and action. At the century's end as at its beginning, nihilism still appeared to be the great danger, now in the sense of an all-encompassing cultural and spiritual crisis – yet one that appeared inescapable.

These nineteenth-century preoccupations remain to varying degrees our own – whether and how science and religion can be reconciled; whether and how value can be accommodated in a naturalistic world-view; what scope the modern world allows for individuality and individual self-realisation; what form, if any, metaphysics can appropriately take in modernity; how, if at all, to ward off the danger of nihilism, supposing that it remains real. To understand how such issues arise for us today – and how some of them have ceased to arise or come to look very different – we need to understand the nineteenth-century background that has shaped subsequent thought.

The aim of this volume is to re-examine nineteenth-century philosophy in terms of concepts, issues and themes which are distinctive of the time or which take on new prominence and significance at this time. These include history, nihilism, individuality, society, nature (in the philosophy of nature) and embodiment (in the French 'spiritualist' tradition). This volume, then, is organised around neither current philosophical sub-disciplines nor individual thinkers. Rather, the focus is on themes, or on broader lines of thought within which continuities and discontinuities of theme emerge, such as Romanticism, naturalism and Darwinism. The volume also has a particular but not exclusive focus on themes that will become important in relation to later Continental European philosophy. Evidently, not all the chapter topics are specifically philosophical – some address general preoccupations in the intellectual life of the time. This reflects another aim of this volume, which is to look at the relations between philosophical and non-philosophical thinkers and between canonical and lesser-known figures. After all, this was a time when specialisation was much less advanced than it is today and when many disciplinary boundaries were still quite fluid. (It was only during this period that many current disciplines formed: for example, psychology and sociology became separated from philosophy over the century; the separation was essentially completed by the 1890s.)

The volume begins in the 1780s and 1790s, with the heated climate of discussion in which German idealism and Early German Romanticism took shape. The volume extends, through the decline of idealism in the 1830s and 1840s, into themes from late in the century. However, many of these later developments continue well into the twentieth century – for example, debates about the nature of history and historical method and concepts of the unconscious mind as they feed into Freudian psychoanalysis. This volume therefore cannot cover these developments fully, but instead will primarily address how these late-century issues arise out of and transform earlier nineteenth-century thinking.

The chapters are arranged around a combination of chronological and thematic links. Broadly, we move from themes in epistemology and metaphysics, to scientific and religious issues, to history, to philosophy of mind, to society and politics and finally back to the intersection of metaphysical, religious, cultural and moral questions in the nihilism issue. This organisation is not meant to suggest that epistemology and metaphysics are 'first philosophy'. After all, much nineteenth-century thinking in metaphysics and epistemology is already informed by normative and practical concerns – with warding off nihilism, carrying forward the liberatory heritage of the Enlightenment and the French Revolution, or improving society through the application of science.

In Chapter 1, George di Giovanni traces German idealism's roots in the crisis of the Enlightenment in 1780s and 1790s Germany. He distinguishes this from an earlier crisis (from 1650 onwards) that traditional religious authority had undergone at the hands of the Enlightenment. The new crisis affected the Enlightenment itself, as it became threatened by the very currents – faith and emotion – which Enlightenment thinkers had cast as irrational and against which they had defined themselves. This crisis crystallised in Jacobi's warnings about nihilism. Specifically, Jacobi argued, Spinoza's view of the world as a rationally intelligible chain of causal determinations denies human freedom and neglects the sheer immediate givenness of things which precedes any conceptual understanding. However, as di Giovanni shows, Jacobi's emphases on immediate existence and human freedom suggested the need for an expanded reconception of reason that could do them justice. Fichte and Schelling sought to provide this reconception. Thus, these first German idealist systems arose not out of an absurd inflation of the powers of reason but out of an effort to rethink and expand Enlightenment reason so as to defend it against the threat of irrationalism.

Arguably, the concept most central to these idealist systems is that of the Absolute, often ridiculed as the height of metaphysical obscurity. Challenging this judgement, Dalia T. Nassar in Chapter 2 shows how this concept arose to resolve difficulties in Kant's philosophy. For Kant, reason must seek completeness and therefore a unity of nature and freedom, subject and object. But, for Kant, this unity can only ever be regulative: a methodological postulate that does not refer to any ontological reality. Ultimately, however, to ground knowledge and overcome scepticism, this unity must be assumed to be real – or so Kant occasionally conceded and the German idealists generally concluded (according to Nassar). For the idealists and Romantics, this subject–object unity – the Absolute – is known in intuition (*Anschauung*). This raises several questions. What is the relation between intuition and reason? How can reason retain the insights of intuition? And does the Absolute really differentiate itself into the plurality of empirical things, or do these manifold things only appear to exist under a narrowly reflective form of understanding?

Nassar's chapter reflects an important trend in recent scholarship, the trend to recognise the Early German Romantics – Novalis, Friedrich Schlegel and others – as having been to a significant extent philosophical thinkers and not only poets. Judith Norman and Alistair Welchman also adopt this view in Chapter 3, in which they consider Romanticism – which, as they note, is notoriously hard to define. They re-examine its meaning by looking at how the Romantics themselves, both English and German, took up this initially pejorative label and 'transformed it into a self-conscious movement'. To be romantic, they thought, was to be self-consciously nostalgic for the lost unity, social solidarity and lack of alienation attributed to the pre-modern world – sometimes classical, sometimes medieval. Paradoxically, though, this nostalgia was fuelled by the progressive ideals of the French Revolution, which the Romantics supported. Progressively, they sought to create a new reconciled world; but, conservatively, they construed this in terms of returning to a former unity that modernity had lost. Norman and Welchman argue that this idea of a return was related to an idea of returning to the subject as the ground of experience, thought and creative imagination. Yet since this subject could be present only in its productions and writings, language after all took priority over the author and the subject proved to be empty or missing – hence the widespread romantic interest in meaninglessness, nonsense, musicality and irony, all of which prefigures modernism.

Philosophy of nature has been another often-reviled aspect of German idealism. As we have seen, objections to it had already become commonplace in the later nineteenth century. As Philippe Huneman shows in Chapter 4, these dismissive objections misunderstand what kind of project philosophy of nature was. It was not anti-scientific but arose in the same epistemological space as the modern sciences. This space resulted from the breakdown of the pre-modern unity of theology, metaphysics and inquiry into nature's divinely grounded economy. Philosophy of nature was thus a specifically modern project, Huneman argues: the project of interpreting the meaning of nature as a whole – an immanent, not a divinely grounded, meaning. This was different from the scientific project of explaining natural phenomena with reference to laws. Philosophy of nature was a distinctly hermeneutic project, whose proponents sought not to challenge or replace scientific theories but to reinterpret them. Huneman argues this with respect to Schelling, Hegel, Schopenhauer and, in the US, Thoreau.

The decline of philosophy of nature may be seen as forming part of idealism's longer-term retreat before the advance of naturalism, as Sebastian Gardner suggests in Chapter 5. He takes this retreat as a guiding thread for re-examining nineteenth-century philosophy as a whole. He traces the conflict between idealism and naturalism back to Kant's dualism of nature and freedom. One way of overcoming this dualism was to return to nature, the other – the way taken by the German idealists – was to put freedom first and re-interpret nature in its light, as pure productive activity and as approximating and leading up to free subjectivity. Within the breakdown of German idealism, Gardner looks at (*inter alia*) Schopenhauer's important intervention and specifically the pessimistic direction in which he took naturalism. Against classical Enlightenment optimism that science would end superstition, drive social improvements and maximise happiness, Schopenhauer stressed the will's endless, goal-less, futile striving and the consequent omnipresence of suffering – effectively pushing naturalism's theoretical against its practical side. Thus Gardner suggests that the various attempts made in the period to combine naturalism with idealism had an overwhelmingly practical and value-related motivation: 'idealism', he writes, 'conceive[d] itself . . . in the terms supplied by classical German philosophy, that is, as practically . . . motivated and as giving metaphysical expression to what must at all costs be preserved . . . from our theological and humanistic heritage'. Idealist optimism lined up against naturalist pessimism. Yet many late-century thinkers – the neo-Kantians, Nietzsche – sought to avoid this opposition and in doing so they ultimately contributed to the broader process by which idealism ceased to be compelling.

Another major factor in the rise of naturalism from the mid-century onwards was Darwin's theory of evolution. Yet Darwin had less impact on nineteenth-century philosophy and thought than one might have expected, Gregory Moore argues in Chapter 6. *Prima facie*, Darwin's theory should have decisively discredited old views of nature as a harmonious, divinely grounded order and of reason and morality as divine or supernatural faculties. But actually Darwin's theory displaced neither traditional systematic, speculative philosophising nor traditional Christian beliefs and moral teachings. Instead most later nineteenth-century philosophers – Moore concentrates on English and US figures – reinterpreted Darwin's theory within those pre-existing frameworks. In England, Spencer spearheaded this trend, weaving elements of Darwin's theory into his essentially pre-Darwinian theory of 'Evolution' as the universe's progression to ever more complex levels of organisation – an Evolution that he saw as manifesting God. If developments such as Darwinism dealt potentially fatal blows to traditional Christianity, then, those blows tended to be softened by filtration through Christianity's pre-existing moral and metaphysical fabric.

Even so, the tensions between new challenges and old assumptions reanimated questions about the epistemic status of Christian religious claims. As George Pattison discusses in Chapter 7, these questions were framed in 1830s and 1840s Germany in terms of whether or not faith was knowledge. This framing of the issues derived from Kant and Hegel. Whereas Kant spoke of delimiting knowledge to make room for faith, for Hegel, faith seemingly *was* knowledge, since he saw philosophical knowledge as the conceptual articulation of religious belief and experience – although this left a major ambiguity as to whether conceptually articulated knowledge itself retained any distinctively religious content or character. Hence Hegel created the conceptual space for successive, increasingly atheistic, forms of 'Left Hegelianism' in David Strauss, Ludwig Feuerbach and Marx. These Left Hegelian developments are relatively well known. But Pattison aims to restore to their place in history the often neglected theological (or 'Right') Hegelians. He focuses on J. E.

Erdmann, who held that lived Christian faith and theological knowledge ultimately converge in speculative knowing, which is God's becoming in thought. It is against just such views, Pattison argues, that Kierkegaard stresses the finitude, temporality and incompleteness of human existence and the partial, incomplete, character of human thinking. For Kierkegaard, human beings can reach unity with God only through God's gift, not through their own intellectual efforts. Thus out of theological Hegelianism arises Kierkegaard's reaction against it and thence, ultimately, the existentialist currents that have exerted such influence in twentieth-century philosophy and theology.

In Chapter 8 James Connelly looks at the historical turn in the nineteenth century and the attendant debates amongst philosophers and historians about historical method. The historical turn crystallised in Hegel's conception of history as the progressive, rational and dialectical process through which the principle of human freedom gradually works itself out in thought and practice. Hegel's treatment of history in connection with freedom, reason and spirit (*Geist*), as opposed to nature, fed into the emerging distinction between the historical and natural sciences. For some, historical study was necessarily of unique individuals (persons or cultures) and contexts of meaning and hence required methods distinct from those of the natural sciences, which subsume particulars under general laws. Such views conflicted with the positivist approach to history espoused by Comte, J. S. Mill and Henry Thomas Buckle amongst others. This conflict motivated a range of attempts to distinguish the natural sciences, purportedly centred on explanation (*erklären*), from the human sciences, purportedly centred on interpretative understanding (*verstehen*). Connelly also looks at the British idealists, who in the nineteenth century paid surprisingly little attention to issues of historical method, with the exception of an important essay by F. H. Bradley which Connelly discusses. Bernard Bosanquet, in particular, disparaged history as the 'doubtful story of successive events' – but in a way, Connelly argued, that compromised Bosanquet's own theory of 'concrete universals', which he ultimately needed to identify with historical individuals (such as the Renaissance, the Catholic Church or the Athenian marketplace).

An important form of historical inquiry that arose in this period was 'genealogy'. This was the method that Nietzsche professed to use for his critical inquiry into morality. Today, as Robert Guay notes in his account of genealogy in Chapter 9, many scholars in the humanities and social sciences also claim to practise genealogy, but they understand this method in very varied ways. Moreover, Guay argues, Nietzsche was not the unique originator of this method. He was only building on a long-running nineteenth-century tradition, within which (even if the word was not always used) genealogy was an approach to human cultural and moral phenomena with four key features: (1) it was cosmopolitan and (2) it rooted these phenomena in collective human agency; (3) it was critical, typically tracing how normative ideals and practices have failed by their own standards, undermining themselves from within; and (4) it was historical and hermeneutic, identifying these ideals and practices as being entirely constituted by and in their history. Guay sees this approach emerging in Rousseau and Kant, coming to full fruition in Hegel and entering into more materialist and more Humean variations in Marx and J. S. Mill, respectively. Nietzsche's version of genealogy, Guay argues, was distinctive chiefly in its pessimism: Nietzsche saw no exit from the history of ascetic ideals, in which we remain entangled even (or especially) when we try to escape it.

In the next two chapters we turn to philosophy of mind. In Chapter 10 Mark Sinclair examines ideas of embodiment in the often neglected French 'spiritualist' tradition, which runs from Maine de Biran through to Henri Bergson. Challenging mind–body dualism,

Maine de Biran and his successor Félix Ravaisson developed the idea of the lived body as an intelligent corporeality which is identical to the self. This idea notably anticipates Merleau-Ponty's phenomenology of embodiment. Sinclair argues that, of the French spiritualists, it was Ravaisson who most consistently advanced beyond mind–body dualism. This is because Bergson reintroduced a form of dualism and, although Maine de Biran argued that our immediate first-person apprehension of our bodies in the exercise of the will precedes any third-person conception of the body as an object, nonetheless Biran also suggested that prior to volition bodies really exist as physiological objects. Ravaisson, in contrast, focused on the significance of habit and he argued that the habituated body has become animated from within by tendencies and ideals and therefore no longer exists as a purely physiological system. Thus, Sinclair concludes that Ravaisson's work 'represents the summit of nineteenth-century philosophical reflection on embodiment'.

In Chapter 11 Günter Gödde looks at nineteenth-century ideas of the unconscious mind. Freud is often credited with the discovery of the unconscious. But in fact he brought together (and transformed) various strands of a large and highly diverse body of pre-existing, especially German, nineteenth-century philosophising about the unconscious. Re-examining this body of work, Gödde identifies three main 'lines of tradition' within it. The first, that of the 'cognitive' unconscious, he links to Johann Friedrich Herbart. Herbart's approach to the mind was empirical and mechanistic. Yet his work opened up a path to study of the unconscious because it highlighted the causal effects of mental representations that fall below the 'threshold' of consciousness. The second tradition is that of the 'Romantic-vital' unconscious, which emerges from ideas in Romantic medicine about a 'vital power' regulating organic life and distinct from both mind and body. The third and most developed tradition is that of the 'compulsive-irrational' unconscious, which emerges in Schopenhauer, Eduard von Hartmann and Nietzsche and which – in Schopenhauer and Nietzsche especially – focuses on instinctual drives and their internal power struggles. Gödde shows how Freud took up various elements of these traditions and how this fed into his successive models or topographies of the mind.

The next chapters address political and social questions. In Chapter 12 Alex Zakaras examines the ideals of individuality and individual self-realisation which originated with the Romantics, especially Wilhelm von Humboldt. Humboldt's ideal was for individuals to cultivate their unique natures, fostering social bonds based on active association and solidarity with others. Individuality so understood was often contrasted, at least in Europe, to individualism – which was equated with narrow egoism and atomism. However, as Zakaras explores, Humboldt thought that individuality would be best promoted by (what we now call) a minimal state, whereas liberal socialists such as Pierre Leroux in France favoured an active state. For them, the state was to promote equality of individual self-realisation through redistributive and interventionist strategies. John Stuart Mill tried to synthesise these conflicting approaches to individuality. Yet as the century advanced, support for individuality increasingly tended to combine (as it did in Mill himself) with pessimism about the conformism imposed by modern society and the tyranny of the majority. Zakaras explores this tendency, suggesting that it eventually led some, such as Nietzsche, to pit individuality (for the select few) against equality altogether.

Alongside these developments in thinking about individuality went increasing theoretical and practical attention to 'society', the many strands of which are explored by William Outhwaite in Chapter 13. By the early nineteenth century, he notes, some had already conceptualised society as an association of separate and in principle equal individuals, moving away from prevailing earlier 'images of hierarchical complementarity'; and the new conception gathered force as the century went on. The impact of the French Revolution spurred this development on, as did the rise of the Hegelian and more broadly historicist view that political and legal structures are aspects of broader social and economic processes and hence are subject to historical change. Further consequences of the new view of society were the rise of movements for social reform, which reflected growing concerns about poverty and class inequality, and the associated rise of the social sciences, which had become largely separate from philosophy by 1900. However, Outhwaite suggests, this separation meant that many major questions at the intersection of philosophy and society remained unanswered.

In Chapter 14 Paul Blackledge examines the decisive role that the contested concept of revolution played in nineteenth-century political thought. He focuses on three main currents of thought and activity. The first is anarchist rejection of the state as an external imposition upon society, a current represented especially by Pierre-Joseph Proudhon and Mikhail Bakunin (in France and Russia respectively). The second current consists of socialist projects for reform of the state, represented *inter alia* by Louis Blanc and Eduard Bernstein. The third current consists principally of Marx's attempt to steer a middle course between the first two, an approach that Blackledge broadly defends. Marx, he argues, rejected the bourgeois state – which Marx saw as characterised, amongst other things, by a split between universal laws and everyday egoism. In its place Marx advocated a proletarian state. This, however, was to be a wholly different kind of state, not imposed upon social life from the outside. Rather, Marx saw its lineaments emerging directly from and within the everyday social life of the working class insofar as this increasingly embodied a practical, anti-egoistic, spirit of community and of individuality-in-society. It did so, Marx thought, insofar as the working class engaged in political struggle, for instance, over the length of the working day. Being rooted in everyday life, this kind of state would after a period of transition dissolve away as a distinct formation. In this way, Blackledge argues, Marx sought to understand how revolution could emerge from below, against the model of revolution imposed from above which had been made so familiar by Robespierre.

Reminding us that these political issues were inextricable from metaphysical and religious debates, Michael Gillespie in Chapter 15 traces the roots of these conceptions and practices of revolution back to debates about nihilism within Early German Romanticism and German idealism. Jacobi detected nihilism not only in Spinoza but also, more importantly in this connection, in Fichte. Jacobi found Fichte's conception of the subject egoistic and Promethean in its exaltation of human freedom and he found it nihilistic in that it seemed to dissolve the reality of the outer world and of God into that of the solitary subject. Hegel, in response, sought to convert negativity into a moment within the overall positive process of the realisation of reason and freedom in history. Gillespie shows that Hegel's approach was taken in a socially critical direction by the Left Hegelians and others, who reclaimed nihilism by linking it to practical, non-egoistic, reformism. In Russia, however, nihilism took a more radical – and destructive – turn, culminating in the revolutionary nihilism of Bakunin and Nechaev. Meanwhile, Gillespie argues, the tradition of opposition to nihilism was continued in Russia by Dostoevsky, who famously denounced nihilism as entailing that everything is permitted.

Nietzsche too, as we have seen, grappled with the question of nihilism, to which his doctrine of 'eternal recurrence' was in part a response. In Chapter 16, Clare Carlisle re-examines this doctrine in conjunction with Kierkegaard's related idea of repetition. One feature that these ideas share, she argues, is that they are not simply theoretical but are intended to be practically thought through, appropriated and incorporated in ways that are transformative of those who think these ideas – and where the nature of this transformation cannot be predicted or known in advance. Repetition is transformative above all because it involves the movement of opening oneself to receive God's gift, which comes to the self from the outside. For its part, the doctrine of eternal recurrence brings to a head the conflict in modern thought between freedom and determinism. The doctrine thereby throws reason into outright crisis and this creates a potential opening to a radically new future. In their emphases on personal transformation, then, the 'ideas' of repetition and eternal recurrence both foreground lived subjectivity in opposition to the prevailing historicism of the nineteenth century. As such, both ideas resonate beyond their immediate contexts, heralding existentialism and more recent continental thinking concerning the gift and event.

This returns us to the question of the relations between nineteenth- and twentieth-century philosophy, on which Andrew Bowie reflects in Chapter 17 in connection with debates about the history of philosophy. Challenging the idea of looking for ways in which nineteenth-century anticipates twentieth-century philosophy, he reminds us that philosophy is not a discipline in which progress straightforwardly occurs. On the contrary, Bowie suggests, many philosophers – particularly in the analytical tradition – rejected or ignored nineteenth-century philosophy for much of the twentieth century and yet have recently returned to certain of its key elements. Notable examples are John McDowell's recovery of Hegel's critique of empiricism and Quine's questioning of the analytic/synthetic distinction, which effectively recovers themes that were already present in Friedrich Schleiermacher's hermeneutics. Bowie concludes that the history of philosophy might be most helpfully studied not in terms of progressive resolution of problems but rather of problems that come and go in response to broader tensions in their intellectual and social contexts – tensions to which philosophical problems give 'unresolved expression'. For example, Bowie suggests, philosophy of nature may no longer seem a viable project, but we can recognise – perhaps now more than ever – the validity of the concerns that motivated it: concerns about the moral appropriateness and the harmful consequences of treating nature as a mere set of objects or limitless resources.

To read and re-examine the texts and contexts of nineteenth-century philosophy and thought, then, is not to engage in a narrowly historical exercise. In rediscovering the past that has shaped our current intellectual horizons, we rediscover ourselves. When we engage with nineteenth-century ideas and theories that initially seem strange and unfamiliar, we often discover profound challenges to contemporary ways of conceiving of and addressing philosophical problems. Nineteenth-century ideas can then become the source of new questions and ways of philosophising in the present.

Note

1. I thank Graham Smith, John Varty and Garrath Williams for responses to earlier drafts.

References

Gardner, Sebastian (2007), 'The limits of naturalism and the metaphysics of German idealism', in Espen Hammer (ed.), *German Idealism: Contemporary Perspectives*, London: Routledge, pp. 19–49.

Mandelbaum, Maurice (1971), *History, Man, and Reason: A Study in Nineteenth-Century Thought*, Baltimore: Johns Hopkins University Press.

Nietzsche, Friedrich (1968), *The Will to Power*, trans. Walter Kaufmann and R. J. Hollingdale, New York: Vintage.

Pinkard, Terry (2002), *German Philosophy 1760–1860: The Legacy of Idealism*, Cambridge: Cambridge University Press.

Stern, Robert (2004), 'Nineteenth-century philosophy', in Edward Craig (ed.), *Routledge Encyclopaedia of Philosophy*, London: Routledge (retrieved 17 November 2009, from <http://www.rep.routledge.com/article/DC100>).

1

The New Spinozism

George di Giovanni

Our world is the material of our duty made sensible. (Fichte, *On the Basis of Our Belief in a Divine Governance of the World*)

The objective world is simply the original, as yet unconscious, poetry of the spirit; the universal organon of philosophy . . . *is the philosophy of art.* (Schelling, *System of Transcendental Idealism*)

1. Introduction: Crises of Reason

In 1935 Paul Hazard famously spoke of a 'crisis of the European mind' to describe the transition from the earlier confessional era – when reason was still taken to be subservient to faith and political power to the rule of God and the Church – to the Enlightenment, when reason reversed that relation by asserting its autonomy with respect to religious belief and philosophers began to look to reason's rule for the authentication of political power. Hazard himself dated that transition to around 1680 (Hazard [1935] 1953: xv–xvi). Recent scholarship has pushed this date back to 1650 and has also refined the layout of the crisis. The tendency now is to consider it as a global European phenomenon rather than to break it down into the various lands and linguistic groups that made up seventeenth-century Europe (see Israel 2001: 20, 22). There is also a greater sensitivity now to the variety of the strands of thought that caused it. Some of these strands were especially reluctant to forge compromises with the tradition of the past and, among these, the one of which Spinoza was both the spiritual father and the continuing inspirational force – the so called 'radical Enlightenment' – was especially uncompromising (Israel 2001: 11–13; Jacob 1981: 20–3, 93).

But, although greatly refined, Hazard's thesis remains essentially unchallenged. It is tempting indeed, if we consider the course that philosophy took in Germany in the final decades of the eighteenth century during the so-called High Enlightenment, to take the year 1800 as the signal date for another crisis – a crisis this time of the very reason that had originally made the Enlightenment.

Evidence of such a crisis is abundant, especially within the limits of the German *Aufklärung*. In general, a new awareness of the limits of reason had taken hold of philosophers and poets alike – a new willingness to grant to the irrational an irreducible place in experience. But did this new awareness, this new willingness, mark a retrenchment on the part of the hitherto triumphant reason – was reason's crisis one of self-confidence? Or, on the contrary, was this crisis the effect of a new *prise de conscience*, of reason's recognition that the faith and the irrationality that it had been fighting all the while had been in fact an inevitable product of its own rationality – that its past struggle had been in fact a struggle with itself and that the forces that it had demonised were the indirect effect of its own power? If taken in this sense, then the crisis was one more episode in the radicalisation of the Enlightenment: the final episode that brought it to an end as a recognisable cultural phenomenon. The *prima facie* evidence that this was indeed the case is twofold. On the one hand, there is the fact that Spinoza, the father of the Radical Enlightenment, was the one who presided in spirit over the chain of events that finally precipitated the crisis. On the other hand, it is also a fact that Friedrich Heinrich Jacobi,[1] the most perceptive critic of the *Aufklärung*, saw the new interest of the philosophers in faith and the irrational precisely in this light – namely, as reason's final attempt to pre-empt whatever grounds were still left for the faith of old. Reason did this by recreating that faith from within after its own image, a creature of its needs as reason.

2. Jacobi and Spinozism

I have just mentioned Jacobi. Although Spinoza was already everywhere present in the intellectual Germany of the second half of the eighteenth century, Jacobi was to be the one responsible for giving to this presence the peculiar significance that it assumed in the concluding years of the *Aufklärung* and also for implicating it in the reception of Kant's Critique of Reason (as Kant's critical project was at the time referred to as a whole). As we shall soon explain, that presence was to be, paradoxically enough, curiously non-Spinozistic in character. But then, from the beginning Spinoza had worked his magic in Germany in unique ways. Moses Mendelssohn had tried to domesticate him, so to speak, as early as 1761, by interpreting all that he had said about the relation of substance to attributes and modes as directly applying only to the internal life of God – to God's knowledge of himself, in other words. It did not in any way preclude the possibility of a created and finite world that would be distinct from the divine life itself. On this reading of Spinoza, his otherwise offending monism could be brought well in line with more common and more orthodox ways of thinking (Mendelssohn 1761). This was indeed Mendelssohn's intention, pre-occupied as he was with the prospect that the charge of impiety normally brought against Spinoza would be automatically extended to the Jewish community at large with which Spinoza was associated in everybody's mind.

But for a younger generation of intellectuals the charge posed no threat. Goethe was a notable case in point. To him the same monism of Spinoza that had brought the charge of impiety provided instead the required philosophical language for expressing the divinisation of nature that fuelled his *Sturm und Drang* art. The young Goethe considered himself a Spinozist and Spinoza had been the subject of the emotionally charged discussion that took place between him and Jacobi (his senior contemporary) on the occasion of his visit at the latter's Pempelfort country house in 1774.

For the events that were to follow, that visit was fateful. For we can safely surmise that it was during that visit that Goethe had handed over to Jacobi the manuscript of his poem *Prometheus*. This is the same poem with which Jacobi was then to confront Lessing during his own visit at the latter's Wolfenbüttel house in the summer of 1780, allegedly exposing his host's Spinozism. And it was still the same poem, unnamed and without attribution to Goethe (see di Giovanni 1994: 70–1), which Jacobi included in 1785 in his famous little book, *Concerning the Doctrine of Spinoza in Letters to Herr Moses Mendelssohn*, published in that year (a much enlarged second edition was published in 1789: for an English translation of the first edition and excerpts from the second, see Jacobi 1994). *Concerning the Doctrine of Spinoza* is the book that brought to public attention the controversy that had been brewing in private between Jacobi and Mendelssohn, after the death of Lessing in 1781, on the subject of Spinozism. Jacobi claimed to have evidence that Lessing had been a Spinozist; Mendelssohn denied that he had ever been such. In the still deeply religious culture of the day, Jacobi's allegation was especially serious because, since Lessing was the acknowledged foremost representative of the *Aufklärung*, his supposed Spinozism would have reflected on what Jacobi claimed to be the Spinozism implicit in the whole of the *Aufklärung*. 'Spinozism', 'pantheism' and 'atheism' were widely accepted at the time to be synonymous terms.

Now in 1785, when Jacobi's book was published, Kant's Critique of Reason had already made inroads into the German intellectual landscape. Karl Leonhard Reinhold – a sometime Viennese priest who had sought refuge in Protestant Germany and was eager to forge a philosophical career for himself – had the idea of using it as the basis of a possible reconciliation between what was taken to be Jacobi's fideism and Mendelssohn's rationalism – a way of granting the logical force of Spinozism while metaphysically and morally disarming it at the same time.[2] Reinhold's idea, as developed in a series of letters published in the *Teutscher Merkur*, proved to be highly successful in attracting public attention. And so Spinoza became implicated in the new idealism that followed upon Kant's transcendental form of it.

This is, of course, only a one-sided way of telling the story. Spinoza had been part of the German intellectual landscape long before Kant. As we have just said, the young Goethe had already made of his pantheism the intellectual manifesto for the new and more tragic sense of the human situation to which his art gave expression. This sense was directly opposed to the florid, but stylised and psychologically well-ordered, cult of feeling which was still fashionable at the time, itself only the sensuous counterpart of the rationalism of the age. In the Germany of the time, this cult had centred around figures such as C. M. Wieland and W. L. Gleim. Jacobi and his brother Georg belonged to the circle of those gravitating around them. Indeed, especially remarkable about the friendship that suddenly sprang into being in 1774 between Jacobi and Goethe (soon cooling off and having a thorny history of ups and downs) is that Goethe had recently lampooned this Wieland circle, taking explicit aim at the Jacobi brothers in his 1773 satires *Das Unglück der Jacobis* and *Götter, Helden, und Wieland*. To what extent, therefore, in raising the issue of Lessing's alleged Spinozism, Jacobi was also aiming his attack at Goethe and Goethe's vision of humanity is a possibility well worth pondering.

Be that as it may, the point now is that one can think of Kant as being implicated and interfering with the reception of Spinoza just as much as one can think of Spinoza as being implicated and interfering with the reception of Kant and that in either case, whether one takes Kant or Spinoza as the main point of reference, Spinozism was being reinterpreted in line with interests that would have been totally foreign to Spinoza himself. These interests reshaped Spinozism in ways that to him would have made it unrecognisable. What these new interests were and what difference they made to Spinozism can be seen in two works that were both published in 1800 and which, viewed retrospectively, were to set up the intellectual tone in Germany for the century to come. One was by Fichte and the other by Schelling – both self-professed disciples of Kant, both claiming to have brought his idealism (and, in the case of Schelling, Spinoza's monism as well) to a logical conclusion. But even more important is the historical and conceptual context that made these works possible in the first place. The problem that motivated them had already been set up for them by Goethe's *Prometheus* and Jacobi's reaction to it.

Just how Goethe's poem could possibly have been taken as a statement of Spinozism was a question that at least one reviewer of Jacobi's book raised immediately upon its publication (see di Giovanni 1994: 68). But the public did not know at the time that the poem was Goethe's, nor did it yet know of the new sense in which the name of Spinoza had become a shibboleth for both Goethe and Jacobi. The poem itself was a *cri de coeur* – the heroic testimony of a man who, as a child, used to revere the immortal gods on high, but now, whetted by the experiences of life, felt nothing but contempt for them. They too, like him, are subjected to Fate, to the anonymous course of Time. But they, feeding as they do on the fat sacrifices that foolish men offer to them, lack one advantage that he enjoys – namely, that he, though seeing the 'budding dreams' of his youth shattered, can none-theless go on striving, suffering and weeping and yet, in these travails, still rejoice and boldly shape a race of Men in his likeness. 'Here sit I, shaping Men/ In my likeness:/ A race that is to be as I am,/ To suffer and weep./ To relish and delight in things' (see Jacobi 1994: 186).

The mention of Fate, which evokes the idea of determinism, was the note in the poem that brought Spinozism into play. Of course, the belief that all that happens in the universe is preordained and works for the perfection of the whole – in other words, that everything is as it must be – was typical of the German Enlightenment. It was shared by such contrasting personalities as the theologian J. J. Spalding, the first to raise the issue of the vocation of humankind (in his *Die Bestimmung des Menschen* of 1748) and Adam Weishaupt, the founder of the *Illuminati*.[3] But in the minds of most, this determinism was still taken to be personal in nature, simply the metaphysical counterpart of the Christian belief in Providence. What made it specifically Spinozistic in Goethe's poem was the impersonalism that attached to it precisely by being associated with Fate and Time. Spinoza had clearly severed whatever ties still held between metaphysics and Christian religious beliefs. It was in the shared recognition of this fact that Goethe and Jacobi could have found in their 1774 meeting not only a true meeting of minds but also, because of their differing reactions to it, a profound emotional discord. At least, this is what we can surmise from the way in which Jacobi was to use Goethe's poem to challenge Lessing in 1780.

Jacobi's Spinoza differed in two ways from how Spinoza was normally received at the time (apart from the fact that Jacobi had a truly scholarly acquaintance with the texts). For one thing, when Spinoza was not simply dismissed as a perfidious Jew, the tendency was to show that his pantheism was in fact a conceptually unnecessary variant of the accepted metaphysics that respected God's transcendence. Mendelssohn's already noted attempt in this vein was especially imaginative. Jacobi took instead a directly contrary view. According to him, Spinoza's pantheism was rather the logical conclusion of the assumption that underlay classical metaphysics. This assumption – as stated in the classical formula, *gigni de nihilo nihil, in nihilum nil potest reverti* (nothing can arise from nothing, nothing can revert to nothing) – in fact pre-empted the possibility that anything genuinely new would ever occur in reality (Jacobi 1994: 204–5). In one way or another, classical metaphysics had either denied the reality of becoming or had reduced it, at best, to a phenomenon *bene fundatum*. Spinoza deserved admiration, according to Jacobi, precisely because he had had the mental clarity and the courage to recognise this consequence. The classical assumption, according to Jacobi, was itself the product of reason's natural desire to attain perfect explanation. But to explain means to reduce particular representations to more universal ones that contain them. And since this reduction can be performed only by abstracting from the determinations that otherwise individuate the more particular representations, it inevitably entails a loss of representative content. The process of explanation, if allowed to follow its inner logic, thus necessarily culminates in a perfect abstraction (such as Spinoza's 'substance') that explains everything *in toto* but by the same token nothing in particular. *That* there are particular determinations is itself reduced to an irrational surd. Each determination is only explainable by being externally referred *ad hoc* to another in a series that, since it proceeds *ad infinitum*, must ultimately fail to secure the being of any of them. It must fail precisely because it lacks an ultimate term, both *a quo* and *ad quem*. Each individual determination is thus reduced to a disappearing event. This, according to Jacobi, was the general outline of Spinoza's system. The system had brought to a logical conclusion the tendency already at work in all metaphysics to subordinate the requirements of existence to those of explanation, thus forcing upon reality a structure that in truth belongs only to the realm of representation.

The other way in which Jacobi's criticism of Spinoza differed from commonly accepted views logically followed from the first. Existence, according to Jacobi, requires irreducible individuation. Spinoza's system, according to Jacobi, undermined the possibility of human agency because it compromised the individuation of any presumed subject of action. Since it reduced the identity of any such subject to a mere semblance, it made impossible the attribution of action – at least, in a way that would make the subject truly responsible for it. As Jacobi was to say to Lessing, when confronting the latter with the implications of what he took to be his sympathies for Spinoza, in a Spinozistic universe one cannot say that anyone in particular painted the 'School of Athens' but must say, rather, that a sequence of anonymous events resulted in an appearance which we call 'the School of Athens' and which we choose to attribute to someone called 'Raphael' as its author (Jacobi 1994: 189). In other words, it was not primarily the fear of denying *God's* transcendence vis-à-vis nature that motivated Jacobi's criticism of Spinoza, as it had motivated the criticisms of many before him, but rather the fear of denying *Man's* transcendence vis-à-vis *nature*. Actually God's and Man's transcendence vis-à-vis nature went hand in hand in Jacobi's mind. For significant individuation requires opposition. There is no 'I' without a 'Thou' confronting it, according to the formula which Jacobi was the first to articulate in his *Letters to Herr Moses Mendelssohn* (1994: 230–1). It is, therefore, only to the extent that finite Man is confronted by the utter otherness of God, and defines himself precisely with reference to this otherness, that he stands as an irreducible individual and hence also as a responsible agent, both before God and in contrast with mere nature.

Jacobi was a deeply pious man. Nothing could have been further removed from Goethe's paganism than Jacobi's religiosity – nothing more dissonant than their respective emotional reactions to Spinoza. Yet one can see how in 1774 the two men would not only have had a meeting of minds but also, at an emotional level, would have felt, if not sympathy for each other, at least a certain affinity – an affinity at a distance, so to speak. Intellectually, they both understood that the Spinoza type of determinism had nothing to do with the determinism which was part and parcel of the Enlightenment's vision of the universe. This universe was pervaded by rational intentions that assured that all things would work to the perfection of the whole and the appropriate good of each of its parts. It was on the supposed efficacy of these intentions that those such as Spalding and Weishaupt, to whom we have already referred, rested their hopes for happiness. In the universe of Spinoza there were, on the contrary, no such intentions at work. Events happened just because they happened, all equally driven by an infinite power that worked its efficacy without the encumbrance of either preordained plan or preordained limits – all equally caught up in a concatenation of other events and all only externally linked together. Spinoza's determinism was truly a form of Fatalism. Both Goethe and Jacobi understood this much. But the young Goethe had accepted this Fatalism enthusiastically, for it suited his at the time heroic view of Man. The *amor fati* that his poem expressed, the rebellious pride with which the protagonist accepted his situation and even took joy in it – this was his way of rescuing Man from the impersonalism of Spinoza's universe. Jacobi's religious piety did not allow him this solution. And since Jacobi could not fall back upon the sophisms of classical metaphysics, which he believed to be a self-deceiving form of Spinozism, his reaction was rather to reject the false reason which he took to lie behind both that metaphysics and Spinoza's Fatalism – a reason that subordinated existence to explanation.

Accordingly, in 1780, when Jacobi met Lessing, what he proposed to him as an antidote to his perceived Spinozistic inclinations was an act of faith that would reverse precisely that order.[4] Whereas explanation requires the rule of the universal, Jacobi was to declare himself the champion of the exception. Now, in 1774, no two attitudes could have been more opposed than Goethe's and Jacobi's. The affinity lay nonetheless in the fact that both men made the dignity of the human individual the centrepiece of their humanism and that both based it, not on any vocation presumably preappointed for humankind in general within the greater scheme of nature's mechanism, but on the existential attitude that the individual himself assumed with respect to the latter – on his capacity to disentangle himself from it, whether in pride (as for Goethe) or faith in a personal God (as for Jacobi) and however much (at least in the case of Goethe) nature itself was divinised or Man himself seen to be *in fact* inextricably bound to it. In this, both Goethe and Jacobi set the tone of much that was to come. Spinoza himself would not have recognised himself in the *persona* he was made to assume in this new set of historical circumstances. Spinozism was donning a new mask. But then, there were aspects of his thought that logically lent him to this *persona*. As we shall see, these same aspects were responsible for an element of affinity even between Spinoza and Jacobi.

3. The Primacy of Existence

To see the nature of this affinity and how it facilitated the transition to the idealism of Fichte and Schelling, one must recognise how Reinhold's intervention in the Jacobi–Mendelssohn dispute, despite its wide public acceptance, was strangely anachronistic. Kant had used his professed 'critical ignorance' about the 'thing in itself' to make available to reason an ideal space where the latter could introduce conceptual constructs for which no objective truth could be claimed. These constructs could nonetheless be subjectively justified on the basis of moral or other interests of reason. It must be said that to justify truth claims pragmatically was in line with the generally practical bend of mind of the Enlightenment. But Reinhold was now using Kant's strategy of critical ignorance in effect to reintroduce beliefs about the order and rationality of things which were still typical of the Enlightenment, except that they now came indexed as subjectively required for moral praxis. As Schelling bitterly wrote to Hegel in a letter of 1795: 'Here there are Kantians in droves . . . All imaginable dogmas have been stamped as postulates of practical reason' (Schelling 1961: 1: 13).

Reinhold was to extend this practice of reintroducing Enlightenment beliefs as practical requirements to the point where he reintroduced issues and disquisitions which only a faint obeisance to critical ignorance saved from old dogmatic modes of thought. A case in point was the bitter dispute regarding the nature of human freedom in which he became involved with his Jena colleague, C. C. Schmid, around 1790. The dispute became all the more bitter as others joined it, until a halt was put to it by the intervention of public authority.

At issue was whether freedom of choice requires that the will has the capacity, first to remain indifferent to two possible alternatives of choice and then to determine itself *on its own* for either one or the other. Reinhold argued for this capacity, accordingly rejecting Kant's identification of will and reason. Schmid argued instead for a strict determinism. He made freedom rest instead on the spontaneity with which the will makes its choices on the strength of tendencies naturally inherent in it, according to a preappointed order of things. There was no question of an original indeterminacy, the presence of which would have disturbed, in his opinion, precisely the assumption of such an order. This position, which went under the title of 'comparative freedom', was the common one at the time.

This debate was nothing new. It had a long metaphysical pedigree. What made it strangely anachronistic is that, whether one took Reinhold's position or Schmid's, it still raised the issue of human freedom in physical terms, as if the human will were one more cause among many others and its effects part and parcel of the general order of the cosmos. It still entangled human freedom with the causality of nature – this at a time when Goethe and Jacobi had instead transposed the whole issue of freedom to an altogether different order of reflection by raising it in existential terms. This term might sound anachronistic when used in connection with the late eighteenth century, but Jacobi had explicitly raised the issue in terms of what comes first – requirements of existence or requirements of explanation (Jacobi 1994: 194–5).

Goethe and Jacobi, then, had raised the issue of freedom as one concerning the attitude that the human individual should personally assume before nature – whatever the material constitution of the latter – precisely in order to assert his transcendence before it. This was a new tone that was being injected into philosophical debate (but one, it must be added, that had abundant precedents in the religious culture of which Jacobi himself was a product). Reinhold and Schmid might have been forgiven for missing it in the 1785 controversy. Mendelssohn himself had missed it. But they had no excuse for not having noticed how Kant himself, of whom they both professed to be disciples, had also recently redefined the issue of freedom in ways which, albeit in more scholastic modes of expression, made the human individual's stance towards nature the centrepiece of moral doctrine.

We can forget Schmid. He is only a marginal figure. We can also leave Reinhold aside, even though his philosophical influence was immense. The fact is that from beginning to end – from his early days in Vienna, where he led the double life of cleric and member of the *Illuminati*, to his activities in Kiel where his professorial career was to extend well into the nineteenth century – Reinhold remained committed to the rational programme of the *Aufklärung*. He eventually repudiated idealism, joining a group that gravitated around the now ageing Jacobi and included such figures as Jakob Friedrich Fries and Friedrich Schleiermacher. As for Goethe, he would make an improbable figure in any philosophical debate, however much Jacobi had tried to drag him into one. The point of interest is the intricate conceptual connection that bound Spinoza, Jacobi and Kant. Jacobi is again the one to give us the clue to where the point of connection lay – even though, as we shall see, he was soon to become aware of the threat that this connection posed to his own personalism.

In 1787, in an autobiographical digression in his *David Hume on Faith or Idealism and Realism*, Jacobi recounted how excited he had been by two early essays of Kant. We now call such essays 'pre-critical'. In both, the point that Kant made, to quote his words *verbatim* as Jacobi also did, is that

existence is not a predicate or a determination of a thing, but is rather the absolute positing of the thing . . . Inner possibility always presupposes existence . . . If all existence were removed, nothing would be posited absolutely and nothing would therefore be given either. (Jacobi 1994: 284–5)

Jacobi also reminisced (281) that in two parallel essays published at the same time by Kant and Mendelssohn the latter had instead privileged 'possibility' over 'existence',[5] thus following Leibniz in taking the concept of a perfect possibility as the starting point of his proof for the existence of God. Kant had reversed that order, taking the thought of an absolute existence as his starting point. But that is exactly what Spinoza, to whom Jacobi also referred in the same context, had done in his *Cartesian Meditations*. From the beginning Jacobi admired and respected Spinoza for that. Even at the time of his controversy with Mendelssohn, he had praised Spinoza, no less than he had criticised him, precisely because from Spinoza he had learned that truth is ultimately to be grasped, not through any ratiocinative process, but intuitively. The conceptual reflection of reason is secondary to and dependent upon the immediate apprehension of existence in intuition. Spinoza's mistake was to express the content of that intuition in the medium of the concept of 'substance', which was in fact the product of an abstraction of reason. The consequent fall into what Jacobi believed to be the 'nihilism' of classical metaphysics was therefore inevitable.

The critical Kant, whom Jacobi was openly criticising in 1787, denied that *we*, human beings, are capable of intellectual intuition. Yet he had this much in common with Spinoza, that the possibility of such an intuition, as available to a being other than the human, had to be conceded at least in principle. It *had* to be conceded precisely as the conceptual counterpiece of his professed critical ignorance that made the claim to this ignorance meaningful. But whether it was conceded *realiter* or hypothetically, the possibility of an intuition that transcends the limits of the discursive determinations of reason had the same effect of reducing the latter to a secondary and even relative order of cognition – for Spinoza, to attributes or modes of substance that have validity only from a finite point of view; in Kant's critical system, to merely subjective intentions. But *that*, according to Jacobi, was all that philosophical reflection had *in fact* ever been able to achieve. In other words, despite the different interests and the differing speculative commitments that divided them, the link connecting the three – Spinoza, Jacobi and Kant – was the very belief on which Jacobi had made his stand in philosophy, namely, that existence precedes essence and that, consequently, any conceptual determination of reality has to have only relative status.

Therein lay the threat for Jacobi. For one cannot consistently privilege existence over essence without also privileging efficient over final causality. But, as the pre-critical Kant had already pointed out, 'surely, without knowledge and purpose [God] would be only a blind necessary ground of other things and even of other minds, distinguished not at all from the eternal fate of some of the ancients' (cited by Jacobi in the 1789 edition of his *Letters to Herr Moses Mendelssohn*; see Jacobi 1994: 366, n. 10). In 1789, citing this same passage, Jacobi was to gloss:

> I deny that there can be an in-between system (such as conceived by us men) between the system of final causes and the system of purely efficient ones. If intellect and will are not the first and highest powers . . . they are not original springs of movement but a clockwork. (1994: 366)

Under threat was the possibility of the same freedom and personalism which Jacobi had championed when confronting Lessing's alleged Spinozism. The critical Kant was to try to preserve some room for it transcendentally – with, however, more than a measure of dissemblance. He openly admitted in the *Critique of Judgement* (Kant [1790] 1987: 284–6, §76) that, if one could just see things as they are in themselves, the modal categories would lose all meaning, since all *that is* would simply *be there*. But it is the modal categories, notably the distinction between the possible and the *de facto* actual, that are at the basis of the moral *ought*. In other words, Kant was indirectly admitting that, if we could see things as they really are (but fortunately we cannot), we would discover that the whole moral order is in fact, from an absolute standpoint, only a subjective phenomenon – exactly what Spinoza would say. One can understand, therefore, Jacobi's incapacity, after his dispute with Mendelssohn and in response to the charges of irrationalism that were being laid against him, to come up with a positive yet conclusive philosophical position of his own. Conceptually, he was conflicted – just as he had been emotionally conflicted in his first encounter with Goethe. He felt intellectual affinity for the existentialism of both Spinoza and Goethe but was conceptually unable to see himself clear of the fatalism, which he attributed to the abstractions of reason, that motivated it. Short of rejecting reason altogether and thus making good the charges of irrationalism levelled against him, could he come up with an idea of rationality which, while still playing an explanatory function, would allow the individual to count within the world and before his God as an exception? This was precisely the problem.

By the end of the eighteenth century, Jacobi was to restate altogether his position on a new conception of reason. But he had unwittingly defined the problem that was to motivate Fichte's redoing of Kant's transcendental idealism. Fichte, by far Kant's most perceptive interpreter, was repeatedly and ardently to declare himself a disciple of Jacobi – despite the latter's just as often repeated and ardent rebuff of him. Could one establish precisely what Jacobi had said was impossible, namely, an in-between system of final causes and purely efficient ones – in effect, a system that would respect the primacy of existence over essence while at the same time validating the objective status of reason? And could one accomplish this feat while also respecting Jacobi's deeply personalist religious faith? This was still the problem of reconciling Spinoza and Mendelssohn (which Reinhold had thought Kant had already resolved). But the issue was whether and how faith would come into the picture in the very emergence of reason and rationality and not, as was the case for Kant, only when human happiness is at issue. Or again, the issue was also how to conceive freedom as an event emerging at the intersection of existence and rational discursiveness and not – as in the Reinhold–Schmid dispute – as some sort of extra-phenomenal, yet still physical, cause.

4. Fichte's *Vocation of Man*

This is the conceptual and historical context in which Fichte and Schelling composed their two works in 1800. Fichte's work came at a time when he had taken refuge in Berlin after fleeing Jena, accused of atheism and politically suspected of Jacobinism. The work's title – *The Vocation of Humankind*, where 'Vocation' (*Bestimmung*) in German means both 'determination' and 'vocation' – reprised the title of Spalding's book, mentioned above, which over fifty years earlier had been a statement of *Aufklärung* rational faith. This circumstance was significant, for although Fichte hoped that his spokesman in the book would stand for *Mensch* in general, there was no doubt that the experience that he related was his own in the first place and for him such an experience had begun as that of an *Aufklärer*. In both books, the protagonist is engaged in a reflection on who he is and why; in Fichte's, the conclusion at which he arrives at the end of the first part is exactly the same that the protagonist of Spalding's reaches at the end – namely, that the universe where he finds himself is an ordered whole, of which every part has its well-appointed determination. The special vocation within it that defines his identity is precisely to reflect this order through his conceptual representations. It is by fulfilling this vocation that he can hope to attain the perfection, and the consequent happiness, that gives meaning to his many present travails.

This was indeed the belief on which the rational optimism of the *Aufklärung* was based and it had apparently also been Fichte's original belief. But much had happened since the days of Spalding's original manifesto to disturb this optimism; this is now also reflected in Fichte's book. First, there was the recognition that Spalding's naturalistic vision of the universe brought with it the fatalism of Spinoza in train. The posthumous intervention of Spinoza had caused this disturbance. Criticism, itself a product of the Enlightenment, intervened second, raising the doubt whether Spalding's vision might not after all be but a subjective projection of reason with no foundation in reality. This doubt could have saved Spalding's *Mensch* from the fatalism of Spinoza, but only at the price of undermining the conceptual framework within which the question itself of a 'who' and a 'why' could be objectively raised – in effect replacing one form of what Jacobi had called nihilism with another. In other words, whether at the hand of rational dogma or rational criticism, the *Aufklärung*'s quest for personal identity and meaning was being frustrated.

Therefore we see Fichte's protagonist fall into deep despair, the very antithesis of Enlightenment optimism, twice in the book – at the end of the first part, where he fears that his feeling of being free is only a delusion (Fichte [1800] 1956: 30–4), then again at the end of the second part, where his fear is that the very 'I' to whom he attributes that feeling is itself a delusion (79). But redemption is fortunately at hand. It comes in a hint dropped with the parting words of an ethereal figure who has been in dialogue with him in the second part of the book. This figure, vaguely reminiscent of Descartes's evil spirit, has personified in the book the voice of criticism and he now reminds Fichte's protagonist that his quest so far was for knowledge and that he (the spirit) had simply guided him to where this quest would finally lead him. Indeed, Fichte's protagonist, not unlike the Enlightenment *Mensch* of Spalding, had sought knowledge of reality in an effort to justify the belief, which inescapably accompanied all his actions, that there was a meaningful place within it for both him and his actions. In other words, he had sought *knowledge* in order to validate *belief*. The suggestion now is that this order is wrong and that it is the cause of the despair into which Fichte's protagonist has fallen: 'You wanted to *know* and you took a wrong road' (81). Existentially, it is *belief* – or the immediate feeling of being an effective agent – that motivates the quest for *knowledge* and validation in the first instance.

The suggestion, in other words, is that, rather than validating belief in 'who' we are and 'why' in terms of 'what is', we should instead take this belief as the norm of what counts as effectively *being there*. It is not 'what is' but 'what ought to be' that is the measure of reality. Should it happen that 'what is the case' does not measure up to 'what ought to be', it is then incumbent on the one who acts to reshape the former in order to make it conform to the latter. The ultimate norm that defines the 'ought' in question is precisely that the purely existential requirement 'that there be action' is both respected and promoted. To create a world where one can be a free agent is indeed the vocation of the human being, the answer to the question of 'who' and 'why' we are.

This is the suggestion that Fichte's protagonist follows in the third part of the book. And, behold, all that he thought he possessed in the first and second part, but which had then been lost, the ordered universe of the first and the subjectivity of the second – all this is now given back to him, a hundredfold, as it were, because now invested with a new meaning. It is not just that all things, the putative subject of experience included, turn out to be mere appearances. They *must be interpreted* as mere appearances precisely in order that they can be remade – intentionally first and physically eventually – into the manifestation of a transcendent freedom at work in the universe. Or again, it is not that this universe simply happens to be mechanically organised. It must be so organised, because the self-given lawfulness that freedom generates requires that it be so. The third part of the book is thus like a manifesto of *homo faber*, a visionary account of an earth, the product of human work, where there shall be no more diseases, no more putrid swamps, but where 'the wolf also shall dwell with the lamb' (Isaiah 11: 6). Fichte writes:

> There is but one world possible – a thoroughly good world. All that happens in this world is subservient to the improvement and culture of man and, by means of this, to the promotion of the purpose of this earthly existence. It is this higher Worldplan which we call Nature when we say: Nature leads men through want to industry; through the evils of general disorder to a just constitution; through the miseries of continual wars to endless peace on earth. (Fichte [1800] 1956: 142–3)

Of course this is only an ideal which, *ex hypothesi*, will never be realised in real time. For, however expansive and detailed the work achieved at any time, it never exhausts all that 'might be the case': it is, in other words, a *determinate* and, therefore, only *limited* manifestation of freedom, never the thing itself. Nonetheless, a system of ends is thereby introduced within the domain of human actions – one, however, which is not physically preappointed but is generated instead by the requirements of action itself. It is the kind of system that Goethe's *Mensch* would have to set up for himself, in defiance of the gods and in full responsibility for his Fate.

There was nothing that Fichte said in popular style in 1800 that he had not already said in more technical language in the various shapes of his *Wissenschaftslehre*, his new Science of Knowledge, which he had presented up to that point and which had brought upon him the suspicion of atheism.[6] Fichte had begun his system by interpreting the otherwise undefined feeling of self-awareness that accompanies all experience and which Kant had straightaway conceptualised as a reflective 'I', as the intimation of an action which is intended as pure act of freedom – a thought thinking itself simply for the sake of thinking itself – but results instead in the thought of something determined, namely, an objective 'other'. The presence of the latter in experience is at once an *unintended result*, which in fact frustrates the original attempt at infinite freedom, *and a necessary result*. For without the determination that it brings to the intended freedom, neither would the latter acquire a name (that of a subjective 'I') nor would this 'I' be conscious of itself. Accordingly, Fichte proceeds to interpret the whole of experience as an attempt on the part of this 'I' to transform the 'other', which it otherwise *feels* as an obstacle to its intended freedom, into an objective presence of itself – to manifest 'nature', in other words, as *in fact* a work of freedom. The *Wissenschaftslehre* did this work of transformation intellectually. The 1800 book was to make explicit its pragmatic consequences in the form of a manifesto for moral and social action. Fichte could have believed indeed that he had thereby achieved the 'in-between system' that Jacobi had declared impossible – a system where 'efficacy' stood on the one side in the form of a freedom understood as *causa sui* and 'nature' stood on the other, subjectively invested with determinate purposes, all intended to demonstrate the effectiveness of the other side. And the connection between the two lay precisely in the need on the part of freedom to let itself go – to loose itself into the finitude of nature, so to speak – in order to realise itself *consciously*.

All this was well and good. But there was a problem and a sign of it was that Fichte's system ultimately held together on the strength of a metaphor – that of a fall of freedom into the finitude of nature. The presence of the metaphor was a clear indication that the system's closure could be achieved only on the strength of extra-conceptual means. There was no conceptual ground on which ultimately to defend it. Competing positions drawing inspiration from alternative metaphors were possible. And to prove the point, thus rendering the problem all the more pressing, there was Schelling's system of 1800.

To Fichte's credit, he both saw and confronted the problem. He openly recognised that it takes an act of faith, indeed a deliberate choice, to place the origin of experience in an act of freedom and, accordingly, to interpret the whole of experience as a protracted moral commitment (see his first *Einleitung in der Wissenschaftslehre* of 1797; Fichte 1994: 12–20). As Fichte openly acknowledged, one may just as well take the origin of experience as an event of mere nature. For since such an origin is *ex hypothesi* preconscious, it is resistant to reflective comprehension and univocal reflective determination. Fichte made the apprehension of this origin the object of an intuition, but, as he also acknowledged, even the fact that we have such an intuition must itself be accepted on faith.[7] For intuition escapes conceptualisation. It is at best a feeling and, therefore, its dominance at the opening of the *Wissenschaftslehre* injected into the latter a moment of irrationality that could only be contained (though never dissolved) through extra-logical means. It was temperament – personal interest in freedom, as Fichte declared (1994: 18–20) – that gave the system its convincing force. But for others of different temperament the system's moralism was singularly distasteful. Such were the early Romantics, notably Schiller, Hölderlin, Novalis and the Schlegel brothers – and Schelling was there to meet their special interests.

5. Schelling and the Unity of Self and Nature in Art

Despite overlap of language, Schelling's *System of Transcendental Philosophy* of 1800 was radically different both in spirit and construction from anything that Fichte had attempted in his Science. The difference was clearly visible at three levels. First, at the very beginning. Schelling assumes an original perfect equipoise of subject and object in the immediate self-awareness that precedes (as he also assumes) reflective consciousness ([1800] 1978: 49–50). The net result is that the 'other' which is the object of consciousness is not straightaway construed, as it is in Fichte's *Wissenschaftslehre*, as a fall from an act that would have been, if it had just been possible, an expression of pure subjectivity. The second difference is in the unfolding of the System itself. As the assumed original equipoise is disturbed, two series of ever-more complex configurations of existence are made to arise according as the one or the other of its sides predominate: one series is of natural configurations, the other of conscious ones. In Schelling's System these two series are continuous and – even more significant – the series of conscious configurations simply repeats the natural configuration in conscious mode, that is, ever more reflectively and deliberately (at a higher power, to use Schelling's own language). Natural existence is thus granted an independent status as the prehistory of spiritual existence.[8] This is the third difference.

With the emergence of reflection there occurs a *falling apart* of nature and spirit that gives rise, on the part of spirit, to a sense of loss of innocence and also a longing to recover a once natural past. But this 'falling apart' is not a fall of nature from spirit or, for that matter, of spirit into nature – as it is for Fichte. To use a later image of Hegel, it is rather an '*upward* fall' of spirit from nature – a 'rise' above the latter that brings unique evils with it and also the need to recover the original immediate unity with nature. The problem is that immediacy cannot be retrieved reflectively. Here Schelling, like Fichte, turns to intellectual intuition. Is there a way of retrieving this union with nature consciously, yet in a medium which is non-reflective – at once expressive (like the concept) yet blindly spontaneous (like nature)? Now there is, according to Schelling, a type of human individual who manages precisely this feat. This is the Genius, the artist whose works are the product at once of blind nature and conscious *Besinnung*. In his intuition and in his artistic witness to it, the original unity of self and nature is both retrieved and expressed in works of beauty (Schelling [1800] 1978: 312–16).

Schelling's Genius was clearly a philosophical reprise of the young Goethe's *Mensch*. The Spinozistic inspiration motivating this aesthetic vision of humanity was just as obvious. One need only replace Schelling's two series of constructs with Spinoza's *res cogitans* and *res extensa* to see the Spinozistic template that Schelling was retracing in his System. The difference is that Schelling was post-Kantian and that he therefore took his starting point, not dogmatically from the concept of substance but from the problem of a finite mind aware of, yet incapable of expressing, the unity underlying all experiences. Of course, this type of *ascensus intellectus ad Deum* that the System provided could itself be taken as a form of Spinozistic mental discipline, a kind of *medicina mentis*. But this is all the more reason to believe that Schelling's Romanticism was indeed a kind of Spinozism – an aesthetic version of Spinoza's monism that better accorded with the temperament of the time.

But was Fichte's system any different? Of course, Fichte could not accept Schelling's System because he rightly thought that it was a kind of naturalism. Indeed, Fichte had made the choice of rejecting this possible interpretation of the presence of the 'other' in experience the condition for entering into his own Science. But the fact is that the choice *had* to be made because he, just like Schelling, had made the validity of his Science – which like Schelling's was the product of reflective reason – dependent on an intuition that escaped logical means of comprehension; because, like Schelling, he had made essential determination secondary to existence; like him, therefore, he found himself caught up in that indeterminate zone between Spinoza's *causa sui* and the presence of infinitely finite modes that could only be traversed through extra-logical commitments. His commitment happened to be different from Schelling's; his way of providing a face for the *causa sui* accordingly different. But none of this detracted from the fact that, whether Fichte wanted it or not, his *Wissenschaftslehre* was itself the attempt of a mind, itself a finite mode, to find its way back to the source of its existence.

Jacobi saw the Spinozism of both Fichte and Schelling and condemned both.[9] What he apparently did not see was the embarrassing position in which he had landed himself. He had insisted on the primacy of existence over essence, of intuition over conceptual determination. The problem was that, to the extent that one granted that primacy, one also forced conceptualisation into the very formalism that he had decried in classical metaphysics. One forced it to an endless play of thought determinations which could only intend, but never achieve, the individuality of experience of which Jacobi had declared himself to be the champion. Of course, when Jacobi spoke of existence, he had primarily in mind the religious experience of a subject who stands alone before his God, an 'exception' before God that transcends any universal order of being. Philosophical reflection matters little, if at all, to this experience. But Jacobi had raised the issue of existence philosophically and he could not now blame those such as Fichte, or the early Romantics, for having wanted also to resolve it conceptually. In the process, they had demonstrated that an element of irrationality, and the need to contain it through extra-logical means, necessarily arises within experience precisely in the effort at constituting an 'I' reflectively out of what would otherwise simply be blind efficacy. They had also given an object lesson that it is possible to contain that irrationality by means that were other than Jacobi's religiosity. As of 1799, in his reaction to Fichte and to the charges of atheism that were being brought against him, Jacobi chose to fall back upon religious rhetoric, limiting himself simply to attacking the play of empty conceptual determinations that he now declared all science – but Fichte's in particular – to be. He was soon to have occasion to level the same charge against Schelling. But, I repeat, Jacobi had originally raised the issue of existence philosophically, expecting philosophers to deal with it to his satisfaction. As of 1800, the issue still remained unsolved.

6. Aftermaths

Much was to happen after 1800. Jacobi restated his position regarding reason. He now opposed to it another faculty which he called (following Kant) the 'understanding' and reserved for the latter the work of comprehending reality which is typical of the sciences of nature. As for reason itself, he now identified it with a type of 'feeling' which, he now claimed, provides immediate access to such eternal moral/religious values as motivate specifically human action.[10] Together with Fries and Schleiermacher, Jacobi was thus to initiate the tradition of moral/religious positivism, the counterpart of the scientific positivism based on the understanding, which had its history in the new century. But the earlier Jacobi, the champion of the 'exception', still had his influence. He was to find an artistically much more articulate and powerful voice in that of Kierkegaard.

As for Fichte, in Berlin he presented new versions of the *Wissenschaftslehre* in a more religious mode, but only orally. The young Schopenhauer attended his lectures. One can easily recognise, in his *World as Will and Representation*, the same interplay of transcendent freedom and mechanistic manifestation of it in particularised experience that we find in the *Wissenschaftslehre* (for the Fichte/Schopenhauer connection, see Zöller 2006). The essential difference is that Fichte's dissembling religious language now gives place to open myth-making. Schelling, for his part, continued to pursue his Romantic agenda but, like Fichte, in a different and more religious mode. In late life he switched from the earlier reflective reconstructions of experience to a more positive examination of it, delving into the history of myths in order to find evidence there of the presence of the Absolute.

It was Hegel who clearly recognised the problems that positing the primacy of intuition over conceptualisation posed for any theory of experience. He deliberately broke with both Fichte and Schelling on this score. He did away with the infinite and atemporal distance that in both Fichte's and Schelling's Systems *ex hypothesi* separates the assumed original act of sheer efficiency and the presumed first conscious representation of it. Hegel replaced it with a historical process through which reason gradually emerges out of an only inchoately intelligent natural existence in order to take explicit possession of itself. This process does not culminate in any immediate intuition of the Absolute – be this intuition either moral or aesthetic – but, on the contrary, in a totally discursive Idea which is absolute only in the sense that through it reason fully comprehends, although reflectively and therefore necessarily abstractly, the structure of the universe of meaning which it has itself generated and which constitutes the matrix of all experience. Hegel also restated the problem of individuality in social terms, as the problem of creating the kind of society that allows an individual truly to come into his own precisely as an irreducible individual. On both counts, his was an interesting conceptual project, but his legacy was quickly dispersed into the various attempts at pressing this project either in the service of naturalism in the shape of anthropology or in the service of orthodox Protestant theology.

Many, then, were the ways in which the intellectual situation in Germany as of 1800, as reflected by Fichte and Schelling, was to work itself out in the century to come. But it must be remembered that it had been Spinoza who had finally carried the assumptions on which classical metaphysics was based to their logical conclusion; Jacobi who had given fair warning to his contemporaries that they could not have it both ways – subscribe to those assumptions but also hold on to the ethos of Christian personalism that still inspired their humanism. Their universe of reason was based on fragile premises and it did indeed shatter. The early post-Kantians, we have argued, were the first to face up to this fragmentation. Their various efforts were motivated by different interests and were pursued along radically different conceptual patterns. But they were all directed at re-establishing, albeit on new premises, the organic unity of reason which for the Enlightenment had been axiomatic. Those who followed them were to pursue a different course altogether. Theirs was rather an effort at capitalising on individual fragments of that unity of reason which once was. Yet, presiding over all these thinkers, whether the early post-Kantians or their nineteenth-century successors, there still stood the figure of Spinoza, the father of the radical Enlightenment.

Notes

1. For a study of Jacobi in English, see di Giovanni 1994.
2. Reinhold's letters were originally published in *Der Teutscher Merkur* from 1786–87. A much augmented version was later published as a two-volume book, *Briefe über die Kantische Philosophie*, in 1790 and 1792. For an English translation of the first eight letters and additions from the 1790 version, see Reinhold 2005.
3. On Spalding and his place in the German Late Enlightenment, see di Giovanni 2005: ch. 1. On Weishaupt, see di Giovanni 2005: 104–5.
4. Jacobi did not think himself an irrationalist – and with good reasons. As far as he was concerned, the philosophers were the ones who generated irrationality because of their formal rationalism. They walked on their heads. Only a *salto mortale* would have allowed them to walk again with their feet on the solid ground of common sense. For the image of the *salto mortale* (a kind of somersault), see Jacobi 1994: 189.
5. The relevant essays are Kant's *The Only Possible Ground of Proof for a Demonstration of God's Existence* of 1763; Kant's *Untersuchungen über die Deutlichkeit der Grundsätze der natürlichen Theologie und Moral* (Enquiries Concerning the Principles of Natural Theology and Morality) of 1764; and Mendelssohn's *Über die Evidenz in metaphysischen Wissenschaften* (Concerning Evidence in Metaphysical Sciences) of 1764.
6. Fichte gave several versions of this Science, starting in 1794/5, some never published in his lifetime. The most accessible texts are two early 'Introductions', the first intended for the general philosophical public, the second for his critics, both from 1797. See Fichte 1994: 7–35 and 36–105.
7. 'We have here presupposed the fact of this intellectual intuition so that we could then proceed to explain its possibility . . . It is, however, an entirely different undertaking to confirm, on the basis of something even higher, the *belief* in the reality of this intellectual intuition' (Fichte 1994: 49). As Fichte goes on to say, the 'something even higher' is the 'ethical law within us'. The intuition must be comprehended in concepts.
8. The first series had already been developed by Schelling in previous works, notably in *Ideen zu einer Philosophie der Natur* (see Schelling [1797] 1994). The *System of Transcendental Idealism* – see Schelling [1800] (1978) – documents a second series of configurations that reflectively retrieve

and consciously repeat the natural ones – at first as forms of subjective experiences and eventually in the reflectively more complex forms of social existence. The *System* is itself the highest expression of this reflective retrieval of otherwise unconscious configurations – the point at which the emergence of consciousness from its preconscious past becomes itself an object of reflective reconstruction. To borrow an expression of Hegel's dating from when he was still Schelling's follower, at this point 'the absolute substance first gives a sketch of itself in the idea' (Hegel 1998: 262, line 7). Exactly how this is possible, or what it might mean, is a problem of all Romantic idealism of Schelling's type.

9. Jacobi attacked Fichte in his open letter to him of 1799 and attacked Schelling a decade later when both were members of the Royal Academy in Munich. This was the third of the three public disputes in which Jacobi was involved in his lifetime. His position was stridently declared in *Von den Göttlichen Dingen und ihrer Offenbarung* (see Jacobi 1811) (Of Divine Things and Their Revelation). At this time, in the outcry that ensued, Goethe definitely broke with Jacobi.

10. This development was documented in the Preface to the 1815 second edition of the dialogue *David Hume* which served also as Preface to the author's *Collected Works*. See Jacobi 1994: 539–45, 556.

References

di Giovanni, George (1994), 'The unfinished philosophy of Friedrich Heinrich Jacobi', in Friedrich Heinrich Jacobi, *The Main Philosophical Writings and the Novel 'Allwill'*, trans. and ed. George di Giovanni, Kingston and Montreal: McGill-Queen's University Press, pp. 1–167.

di Giovanni, George (2005), *Freedom and Religion in Kant and His Immediate Successors: The Vocation of Humankind, 1774–1800*, Cambridge: Cambridge University Press.

Fichte, Johann Gottlieb [1800] (1956), *The Vocation of Man*, trans. and ed. Roderick M. Chisholm, New York: Bobbs-Merrill.

Fichte, Johann Gottlieb (1994), *J. G. Fichte, Introductions to the Wissenschaftslehre and Other Writings (1797–1800)*, trans. and ed. Daniel Breazeale, Indianapolis: Hackett.

Hazard, Paul [1935] (1953), *The European Mind*, trans. J. Lewis May, London: Hollis & Carter.

Hegel, Georg Wilhelm Friedrich (1998), *Gesammelte Werke*, vol. 5: *Schriften und Entwürfe (1799–1808)*, ed. Theodor Ebert, Manfred Baum and Kurt Rainer Meist, Hamburg: Meiner.

Israel, Jonathan I. (2001), *Radical Enlightenment: Philosophy and the Making of Modernity 1650–1750*, Oxford: Oxford University Press.

Jacob, Margaret (1981), *The Radical Enlightenment*, London: Temple Publishers.

Jacobi, Friedrich Heinrich (1811), *Von den Göttlichen Dingen und ihrer Offenbarung*, Leipzig: Fleischer.

Jacobi, Friedrich Heinrich (1994), *The Main Philosophical Writings and the Novel 'Allwill'*, trans. and ed. George di Giovanni, Kingston and Montreal: McGill-Queen's University Press.

Kant, Immanuel [1790] (1987), *Critique of Judgment*, trans. Werner S. Pluhar, Indianapolis: Hackett.

Mendelssohn, Moses (1761), *Philosophische Gespräche*, Berlin: Voß.

Reinhold, Karl Leonhard (2005), *Letters on the Kantian Philosophy*, trans. James Hebbeler, Cambridge: Cambridge University Press.

Schelling, Friedrich Wilhelm Joseph von (1961), *Briefe Von und An Hegel*, ed. Johannes Hoffmeister, Hamburg: Meiner.

Schelling, Friedrich Wilhelm Joseph von [1800] (1978), *System of Transcendental Idealism*, trans. Peter L. Heath, Charlottesville, VA: University Press of Virginia.

Schelling, Friedrich Wilhelm Joseph von [1797] (1994), *Ideen zu einer Philosophie der Natur. Werke. Historisch-Kritische Ausgabe* vol. 5, ed. Manfred Durner with the assistance of Walter Schieche, Stuttgart: Frommann-Holzboog.

Zöller, Günther (2006), 'Kichtenhauer: Der Ursprung von Schopenhauers *Welt als Wille und Vorstellung* in Fichtes *Wissenschaftslehre* 1812 und *System der Sittenlehre*', in Lore Hühn and Philipp Schwab (eds), *Die Ethik Arthur Schopenhauers im Ausgang vom Deutschen Idealismus (Fichte/Schelling)*, Würzburg: Ergon, pp. 365–86.

2

The Absolute in German Idealism and Romanticism

Dalia T. Nassar

1. Introduction

One of the most obscure, yet significant, concepts in early nineteenth-century philosophy is that of the Absolute. As a word, the Absolute came into philosophical discourse with Schelling to mean the ontological ground of and point of identity between subject and object. In this sense Hegel adopted the term in his early works, while in his later writings he came to identify the Absolute with the process and final conclusion of reason. Although it is these figures who employed the words 'the Absolute' (*das Absolute*), the idea of the Absolute as the ontological ground in which subject and object are identical, and out of which they arise, was central in much philosophy of the early nineteenth century.

While the notion of the Absolute has been criticised and even dismissed as metaphysical nonsense, its significance in nineteenth-century philosophy cannot be underestimated. Following the publication of the first and second editions of the *Critique of Pure Reason* in 1781 and 1787 and the critiques levelled against the Kantian project, it became apparent to philosophers of the time that a system which rests on fundamental dualisms – between self and nature, sensibility and understanding, noumena and phenomena – cannot provide an adequate response to scepticism. Only a philosophical monism, based on an original identity and harmony between subject and object, thing and its presentation, could overcome scepticism. Such a monism, however, was neither naïve nor dogmatic. Rather, the philosophers of the early nineteenth century attempted to establish the phenomenological reality of this principle of identity and to develop it on a sound epistemological ground. As the principle which underlies and thus precedes all difference and dualism, the Absolute, they reasoned, could not be given through discursive reflection. Rather, the Absolute can be gleaned only through an immediate insight which does not divide or separate in order to present. They termed this insight 'intuition' (*Anschauung*).

In the *Critique of Pure Reason* Kant introduces the idea of an unconditioned ground, identifying it with reason's goal. In the *Critique of Judgement* (1st edn 1790; 2nd edn 1793) he speaks of a supersensible basis underlying nature and unifying mechanism and teleology. However, following the restrictions he had placed on reason, Kant could not provide a positive conception of this ground and concluded that it is 'a matter that does not admit of explanation . . .' (Kant 1900–: 5: 413).[1]

'Reason', Kant writes, 'is a faculty of principles and the unconditioned is the ultimate goal at which it aims' (Kant 1900–: 5: 401). The unconditioned, as *unconditioned*, must lie beyond or outside of all determination (Kant identifies the unconditioned with the 'things in themselves' in the second Preface to the *Critique of Pure Reason*) and therefore cannot be sensibly intuited (Kant 1900–: 3: B xx). According to Kant, because the human intellect is discursive, it can gain knowledge only through the cooperation of sensible intuition and understanding.[2] For this reason, the unconditioned, being outside of all determination, can never be cognised by the human intellect. Yet, while the unconditioned remains unknown, the *idea* of the unconditioned is necessary – for it makes our experience coherent, as well as reconciles our moral experience with our experience of nature.

Kant thus grants the unconditioned a regulative status. However, as ultimately unknowable and unprovable, the tenability and philosophical coherence of his understanding of the unconditioned came under heavy criticism. The notion that we must assume but can never know the unconditioned became perhaps the most significant question of the time. Thus Novalis (Friedrich von Hardenberg) remarked of his time, 'We search everywhere for the unconditioned [*das Unbedingte*], but we always only find things [*Dinge*]' (Novalis 1960– 88: 2: 413). Without a fundamental principle or ground that could be proven (not simply posited and assumed, as Kant had done), the coherence and truth of knowledge could not be guaranteed. It therefore became necessary for any systematic attempt to ground knowledge to consider the nature of this unconditioned ground and to prove its reality. In fact, it is precisely the epistemological concern with knowing the unconditioned and the attempt to explicate the unconditioned systematically that distinguish the nineteenth-century formulations of the Absolute from its various predecessors and influences – whether Platonic, Christian, mystical or Spinozistic.[3]

In this essay, I provide a brief account of Kant's understanding of the unconditioned and his restrictions on reason, establishing the origins of the nineteenth century conception of the Absolute. I then briefly reconstruct the move from Kant's critical system to an ontological understanding of the Absolute, by way of Fichte. This is followed by a consideration of the meaning of the Absolute in the works of Schelling and Hegel. I will also draw on the ideas of the Early German Romantics, Novalis, Friedrich Schleiermacher and Friedrich Schlegel, whose conception of the Absolute played a significant role in the development of Schelling's thinking, especially in his works on nature and art.[4] My analysis of Schelling begins with his understanding of the Absolute in his philosophy of nature and *System of Transcendental Idealism*, published in 1800. I will then consider the shift in Schelling's thinking which took place in 1801, initiating the period of his thinking known as 'identity philosophy'. The writings from this period serve as the foundation for Hegel's critique of Schelling in his 1807 *Phenomenology of Spirit*, a critique that I then examine. I explicate Hegel's understanding of the Absolute as formulated in the *Phenomenology* and in his later writings on logic. I conclude with an account of the roles of intuition and reflection in knowing the Absolute, arguing that Hegel's and Schelling's diverging conceptions of knowledge were inherently connected to their opposing views on the nature of the Absolute.

2. Dualism and Monism in Kant

Although dualism in modernity begins with Descartes, it is equally at home in Kant. In the first edition of the *Critique of Pure Reason*, Kant argues that the transcendental idealist is a dualist, since he admits that there is an unbridgeable divide between our consciousness and things-in-themselves, a divide which permits no knowledge of anything other than representations or appearances (Kant 1900–: 4: A370).

Kant's dualism is a fundamental aspect of his system, dating back to his letter of 21

February 1772 to Marcus Herz. In this letter, Kant distinguishes between intuitive and discursive thinking. Whereas intuitive thinking is the source of its own objects, discursive thinking receives objects from an external source. 'Our understanding', he writes, 'through its representations is neither the cause of the object (save in the case of moral ends), nor is the object the cause of our intellectual representation in the real sense' (Kant 1900–: 10: 130). The knowledge given to the discursive intellect is never of the objects themselves, but of representations. In contrast, intuitive thinking is the productive ground (in the ontological sense) of its objects and therefore has a direct grasp of them as things-in-themselves. In this way, Kant acknowledges a difference between our understanding, on the one hand, and the object of our understanding, on the other.

Alongside the dualism between the thing-in-itself and the representation or appearance is the dualism between sensibility and reason, the finite and the infinite, or, in Kantian terms, between the phenomenal world and the noumenal world. While sensibility receives data from within the finitely intelligible forms of time and space, reason demands the infinite intelligibility of the principle of sufficient reason. There are therefore two worlds, the world that can be known by finite intelligence through discursive thinking – sensible intuition and concepts – and the world which can only be known by the infinite intelligence, intuitive thinking, but can only be presupposed by us.

In the *Critique of Judgement* Kant acknowledges that his 'two world' theory runs into difficulty and sets out to overcome the 'gap' between the two domains, the sensible and the supersensible. Kant introduces the dilemma at hand: the objects of nature present themselves to us in intuition as appearances and not as things-in-themselves; the objects of freedom present themselves as things-in-themselves, but not in sensible intuition. 'Hence', he writes,

> an immense gulf is fixed between the domain of the concept of nature, the sensible, and the domain of the concept of freedom, the supersensible, so that no transition from the sensible to the supersensible is possible, just as if they were two different worlds, the first of which cannot have any influence on the second; and yet, the second *is* to have an influence on the first, i.e., the concept of freedom is to actualise in the world of sense the purpose enjoined by its laws. (Kant 1900–: 5: 175)

For this reason, he concludes, 'there must be a basis *uniting* the sensible that underlies nature and the supersensible that the concept of freedom contains practically'. The question is whether this basis refers to an ontological reality, which in turn constitutes nature and our experience of it, or to a regulative idea, a methodological principle that we assume in order to make our experience coherent.

Throughout the work, Kant is clear that this unity is regulative and cannot refer to an ontological reality in nature or in reason. Therefore he writes, 'this transcendental principle must be one that reflective judgement gives as a law, but only to itself: it cannot take it from somewhere else . . . nor can it prescribe it to nature . . .' (Kant 1900–: 5: 180). This principle, he goes on, 'can be given by an understanding (even though not ours)', that is to say, by an intuitive intellect.

In the 'Critique of Teleological Judgement', Kant argues for reason's regulative role in the same way that he did in his letter to Herz (Kant 1900–: 5: 401). Understanding restricts the validity of the ideas of reason to the subject because of 'the nature of our (human) cognitive ability, or . . . any concept *we can form* of the ability of a finite rational being as such'. For human cognition requires 'two quite heterogeneous components', namely, 'understanding to provide concepts and sensible intuition to provide objects corresponding to these' and if this were not the case, he goes on, 'our understanding would be intuitive rather than discursive, i.e., conceptual'.

The necessary basis that unites the sensible and supersensible, the representation and the thing-in-itself, is – for our understanding – a regulative idea. This is because of the nature of our thinking. Because it is discursive, it cannot have an intuition of the unifying ground of the two worlds. We cannot have any experience of this unity and can therefore never know whether a uniting basis exists, but can only presuppose that it does and act accordingly. According to Kant, human nature itself – the finitude of human thinking – necessarily leads to a dualism in knowing.

With the separation of the thing-in-itself from its representation, the supersensible from the sensible and the mere assumption of a unity between the two that can never actually be known, the question of true knowledge becomes critical and the road to scepticism seems inevitable. Kant appears to have recognised this himself when he states in the 'Appendix to the Transcendental Dialectic' that a *regulative* systematic unity of reason is simply not enough. He asserts that we must assume that there *is* a systematic unity in reason and in nature in order to arrive at a 'sufficient criterion of empirical truth' (Kant 1900–: 4: A651; 3: B679).

Kant explains that it is necessary to assume a transcendental principle of rational unity. Lacking such a principle, he argues, reason has no claim 'to treat the manifoldness of the powers which nature gives to our cognition as merely a concealed unity and to derive them as far as it is able from some fundamental power', that is, reason has no right to assume coherence in nature. If this were the case, however, then reason 'would proceed directly contrary to its vocation, since it would set as its goal an idea that entirely contradicts the arrangement of nature'. Reason seeks unity and lacking unity there would be no reason. In turn, without reason, there would be no 'coherent employment of the understanding' and, lacking that, no 'secure empirical criterion of truth'. Therefore, Kant concludes, 'we have no option save to suppose the systematic unity of nature as objectively valid and necessary'. In other words, the very fact of reason and the understanding necessarily leads us to assume a systematic unity in nature.

The claim that there is an objectively valid and necessary unity in nature appears to run counter to Kant's teachings. In this case, Kant is not claiming that we must remain agnostic about the unity's ontological status. Rather, we must presuppose that such a unity actually exists. Further, in speaking of the systematic unity of nature in these terms – that is, in terms of the unity of reason – he is drawing a significant parallel between reason and nature, suggesting even a conformity between reason and nature. Throughout the third *Critique*, in contrast, Kant is clear about the regulative status of any claims made about the natural organism. Accordingly, we are justified in treating an organism *as if* it were spontaneous and reflective – as if it were like reason. In the 'Appendix' to the first *Critique*, however, the 'as if' aspect is eliminated, replaced by the assertion that there *is* a systematic unity in nature and therefore a conformity between reason and nature. Finally, insofar as this unity precedes the subject–object distinction and is the necessary condition for the coherent use of the understanding, it is a point of identity of the subjective and objective that lies outside of or prior to the dualism engendered by discursive thinking. What Kant takes as the starting point of his investigation – the discursive intellect – presupposes a unity which enables it to function, a unity, moreover, that cannot merely be assumed, for it is on the basis of this unity that the entire operation of knowing, as outlined by Kant, is possible.

Although Kant tacitly assumes a monism, a point of unity prior to the subject–object distinction and prior to the duality that arises out of the difference between concept and intuition, reason and nature, he does not explicitly state this monism, nor does he pursue it any further. In fact, just a few pages after suggesting this unity as a necessary conformity between reason and nature, Kant returns to the claim that any such unity is only regulative (Kant 1900–: 4: A671; 3: B699). The tension in Kant's thinking thus remained unresolved.

Kant's first critics noticed this tension, accusing Kant of scepticism. If things-in-themselves could not be known, then how could we be sure that our knowledge actually reflects truth and is not merely illusory? (The first review of the *Critique of Pure Reason*, co-authored by Johann Georg Heinrich Feder and Christian Garve, published in 1782 and now known as the 'Feder/Garve Review', levelled precisely this critique against Kant, arguing that his philosophy was a full-blown idealism.) Or, how can a priori forms agree with or correspond to a posteriori matter? (This was the principal critique made by Salomon Maimon in his *Versuch über die Transcendentalphilosophie* of 1789.) Or, given Kant's basic premises, how can we know that sensibility is indeed receptive and that things-in-themselves exist at all? (This was the essence of Jacobi's argument, in which he claimed that Kant inconsistently argued that objects are the causes of our representations. For, on the one hand, *empirical* objects cannot be the causes of our representations since they are mere appearances or representations. And, on the other, *transcendental* objects cannot be the causes of our representations, since they are beyond our grasp. The question then is, what exactly is causing our representations? Thus Jacobi famously stated that: 'I need the assumption of things-in-themselves to enter the Kantian system; but with this assumption it is not possible for me to remain inside it'; Jacobi 1846: 2: 304.)

The challenge of scepticism was great. How was the gap between the understanding and sensibility, between noumena and phenomena, to be bridged? If such a gap could not be bridged, Kant's critics argued, then scepticism could not be overcome.

3. Fichte and the Ontological Absolute

These early critiques led Kant's first interpreters – Fichte and Reinhold – to reconsider the dualism in the Kantian system. Reinhold maintained that it was only on the basis of an original unity, a first principle of consciousness from which sensibility, understanding and reason are derived, that the necessary correspondence between sensibility and understanding (cognitive matter and form) could be achieved and knowledge made possible. Similarly, Fichte claimed that an unconditioned ground of knowledge which was absolutely certain was necessary in order to save Kantian philosophy from the infinite regress of scepticism. Fichte's most important contribution, however, came in his reinvigoration of the concept of intellectual intuition.

Fichte saw that the only way to save Kantian philosophy was not simply by unifying the various cognitive faculties but by eliminating the duality between self and world – that is, eliminating the unknown thing-in-itself. This did not mean a denial of the existence of the thing-in-itself but rather the critical claim that the existence of the thing-in-itself is not only uncognisable but also unthinkable (see Beiser 2002: 269). The concern of critical philosophy can only be that which is radically immanent: what is 'for the self', as opposed to 'in itself'. There is therefore no need to presuppose or assume a reality outside of the self, for all that is – all that concerns philosophy – is what is given to the self. The duality between self and world, between knowledge and thing-in-itself, is in this way overcome.

For Kant, however, the reality of the noumenal realm establishes the possibility of freedom; therefore, its elimination may appear to be the elimination of freedom (Kant

1900–: 3: B xxvii). By subjugating all reality – including the self – to the realm of determination (to the 'for the self'), Fichte, it seems, made freedom impossible. But this was certainly not Fichte's goal, nor was it his conclusion.[5]

As noted above, Kant differentiates the human and divine intellects on the basis of intellectual intuition. Only the divine intellect can have immediate (that is, non-conceptual, non-sensible) insight into the object of knowledge because only the divine intellect does not *receive* its object of knowledge but *produces* it. Fichte agreed with Kant's definition of intellectual intuition. However, he regarded Kant's denial of intellectual intuition to the human intellect as wrong, especially in the case of self-knowledge.

Upon close inspection of the self, specifically of self-consciousness, it becomes evident that the act of self-consciousness is immediate and intuitive in the sense outlined by Kant. The experience of self-consciousness is indemonstrable – each individual must undergo this experience for her- or himself – and is therefore immediate. Furthermore, in this experience, the I is absolutely active and spontaneous (as opposed to passive) and cannot therefore be determined or subsumed under any concept or principle. It is its own principle. Finally, the act of self-consciousness not only involves self-*knowledge* but also self-*production*, or, as Fichte terms it, the self *posits* itself in self-consciousness. So self-consciousness is not solely an epistemological act but also an ontological one.

Fichte explains this as follows. The self is necessarily self-conscious, that is, only a self-conscious being is a self. Therefore, the self *is* a self only through the act of self-consciousness. Prior to this act, there is no self. The self, then, *is* only insofar as it *knows* itself. In other words, in knowing itself, the self *brings itself forth*. To put it in Kant's terms, the knower produces the object of knowledge. Self-consciousness, therefore, is an act which involves not only the knowledge of the self but also the creation of the self and, in this way, fulfils Kant's definition of intellectual intuition.

As Fichte continued to develop his theory of self-consciousness, he came to realise that the self as subject, as the infinite *act*, was dependent on a finite, opposing object, an object that is necessarily *not* the product of the self (what he calls 'check'). It is only through an opposing principle that is independent of the self's activity, Fichte came to argue, that the self becomes active. In other words, activity (in contrast to non-activity) emerges only out of opposition or restriction. Lacking opposition, there is no activity.

The Romantics and idealists were familiar with the Reinholdian-Fichtean line of defence and agreed that an absolute first principle or ground was necessary. They also agreed with Fichte that such a first principle is not simply a regulative ideal but an ontological, productive reality. They were not convinced, however, by Fichte's claim that this reality is limited to the activity of self-consciousness, nor were they convinced by what they took to be Fichte's reintroduction of Kant's thing-in-itself. By asserting the need for an opposing principle, a check, Fichte appeared to be reinstating the Kantian dualism of self and world. Therefore, instead of establishing the necessary correspondence between the subject and the object, Fichte returns to an absolute dichotomy between subject and object. What needed to be demonstrated, therefore, was not the principle or ground of the self, in opposition to the not-self, but the unity which precedes the division between self and not-self. This original unity is the Absolute.[6]

4. The Absolute

The Absolute could not be merely regulative, as Kant argued, because as the Absolute it cannot be anything other than the *ontological ground* of reality. In turn, as the ground of reality, the Absolute is necessarily active and productive. Furthermore, as Absolute, it cannot be opposed to anything – there can be nothing outside of or other than the Absolute. Therefore, the Absolute is the underlying productive ground of the world as well as its totality. The Absolute is all that is.

Previous philosophies ran into difficulties (hence were criticised by Kant) because they misunderstood the nature of the Absolute. Kant is right, the Romantics and idealists maintained, to claim that the Absolute cannot be given as an *object* in experience (Kant 1900–: 4: A308; 3: B364). However, this is not because the Absolute is an unknown unconditioned that is beyond determinate experience. Rather, it is because the Absolute *is not* an *object*, a substance, a thing that can be given or predicated or, as Schelling puts it, the Absolute cannot be 'said to be' (Schelling 1976: 7: 77).

As the ground of all beings, the Absolute necessarily precedes all beings – and, in turn, precedes all difference and determination. Yet the Absolute is not a first cause, in the sense of a substance that brings both itself and other substances forth. Rather, as Novalis puts it, it is a ground characterised by a 'relation with the whole' (Novalis 1960–88: 2: 269). He explains what he means with an illuminating metaphor: the Absolute is that whole which 'rests more or less like persons playing without a chair, merely sitting one on the knee of another and forming a circle' (2: 242). The Absolute is not a substance that precedes the circle that is formed; it is in fact not there, in any traditional meaning of the term 'there'. Yet, it is there, as the principle which underlies and informs the circle, without which the circle would not have formed and would have remained – as Schlegel often reminds his readers – nothing.[7] In essence, the Absolute is the constituting principle of the whole; it *is* or can be said to be *only in its parts*, which, as part of the whole, mutually support and bear one another. Therefore, the Absolute is neither inaccessible nor fundamentally distinct from that which it grounds. Rather, the Absolute presents itself both in the whole and in its various parts.

The question remains, however, regarding the exact relation between the Absolute and the world that it brings forth. What does it mean to say that the Absolute 'presents' itself in the whole and in parts? On this particular point – the exact relation between the Absolute as the ground that informs and sustains the world and the Absolute as the totality, as the world in its various manifestations – disagreement arose.

Some Romantic and idealist thinkers conceived the relation as one of *mediation*, wherein the Absolute 'goes out of itself' and thus brings forth the world, as Schlegel put it. Others – most notably Schelling during his 'identity philosophy' period – argued that the notion of mediation necessarily implies opposition but that the Absolute, as all that is, cannot be opposed to anything, not even itself. Based on this fundamental difference Hegel famously wrote in the Preface to his *Phenomenology of Spirit* that a certain perspective conceives of the Absolute 'as the night in which all cows are black' (Hegel 1968–: 9: 17). Hegel denounced this contemporary 'formalism', which, with its 'single insight, that in the Absolute everything is the same', overlooks 'the full body of articulated cognition'.

Hegel's remark has led to a misunderstanding of Schelling's philosophy as a whole and of the direction of philosophy at that time, as well as to an avoidance of the inherently difficult task of conceiving the Absolute. For one, it was only during the period between 1801 and 1809 (his 'identity philosophy' period) that Schelling's conception of the Absolute could be interpreted as simple and immediate. In his earlier works Schelling developed a conception of the Absolute much closer to the one Hegel put forth in the *Phenomenology*. Moreover, Schelling's move toward a philosophy of identity was occasioned by a continued struggle with his earlier conception of the Absolute. If the Absolute is all that is, then all that is must exist within the Absolute and must be absolutely identical with it. Therefore, to speak of the Absolute as an entity that 'goes out of itself', in the sense that the Absolute brings itself forth through an act of self-negation and thus develops itself, seems unjustified. If the Absolute *is*, then why must the Absolute *become*?

Before examining Schelling's identity philosophy and Hegel's critique of it, then, we must consider Schelling's earlier philosophy, wherein his views are much more in concert with those of Hegel and the Romantics.

5. Schelling

In his works on the philosophy of nature (especially his 1799 *First Outline of a System of the Philosophy of Nature*) and in the 1800 *System of Transcendental Idealism* Schelling attempts to develop what he sees as nothing other than two sides of the Absolute: nature (objective) and self (subjective). In the philosophy of nature, he shows how the Absolute develops unconsciously, from inanimate matter to complex organisation, while in the *System* he traces the conscious development of the Absolute. In both cases, Schelling understands the Absolute in terms of development or becoming, that is, the Absolute is not a stationary substance but the principle of formation that underlies the growth of nature as well as the development of self-consciousness. His goal is to illustrate that in both instances one and the same Absolute underlies and informs the objective and the subjective developments and that consciousness is nothing other than a more developed manifestation of unconscious nature.

The relation between the Absolute and its parts is understood as a relation of presentation, or self-presentation. The Absolute (like Fichte's self) *is* only in its various self-presentations (self-consciousness). Each presentation is a moment or a stage in the development of the Absolute. There are therefore 'higher' and 'lower' (more complete and less complete) manifestations of the Absolute. Whatever the case, however, the manifestations are not other than the Absolute nor is the Absolute in any way outside of the manifestations. Rather, each manifestation is a manifestation of the Absolute – only in a different stage of its development.

In turn, the development of the Absolute, whether in nature or in consciousness, is dependent upon opposition. Therefore in the same way that the self must first intuit itself as an object, must oppose itself to itself in order to become itself, so an original opposition, in both nature and consciousness, is necessary to drive the Absolute toward becoming itself. That the Absolute must *become* itself implies that the Absolute involves difference, opposition and finitude.

The Absolute attains to its highest manifestation only when it comes to see itself as the ground of both itself (subject, conscious) and the world (object, unconscious), that is, as the original identity of self and world. In essence, the Absolute must arrive at the point at which it sees itself as the Absolute. This, according to the 1800 *System*, can be achieved only in the work of art, in which the opposition between the conscious intuiting subject and unconscious intuited object is overcome (Schelling 1856–61: 3: 617).

In these earlier works Schelling's understanding of the Absolute stands very close to that of Schlegel, Schleiermacher and Novalis, who agreed that the Absolute is inherently mediated and, as such, essentially constituted by opposition. Because the Absolute is constituted, that is, because it is the result or the outcome of opposition, it is neither simple and immediate nor complete in its beginning. Rather, it necessarily arises out of various stages of opposition and either attains fulfilment (as in Hegel) or does not (as in Schlegel's understanding of a universal progressive poetry).

In this way these various thinkers – including Hegel – clearly align themselves with the general direction of Fichte's notion of the self-positing I. Hegel's claim in the 'Preface' to the *Phenomenology* that the Absolute is not merely substance but also subject harkens back to the Fichtean structure of the subject's self-opposition. Similarly, though with a less subjective tone, Schlegel conceives of the Absolute as having 'gone out of itself and made itself finite' (*aus sich herausgegangen und hat sich endlich gemacht*) (Schlegel 1958–: 12: 39). Schleiermacher, in turn, conceives of the universe as an 'uninterrupted activity', which has come about through the infinite opposition of two forces – attraction and repulsion (Schleiermacher 1984: 2: 191). Novalis elaborates that being is not an unmediated, self-identical reality, but 'an absolute relation . . . being does not express identity [*Seyn . . . ist eine absolute Relation . . . Seyn drückt nicht Identität aus*]' (Novalis 1960–88: 2: 247).

Schelling's contrasting view was first introduced in the 1801 essay 'Presentation of My System'. The goal of this essay, as the title betrays, is to distinguish his system from Fichte's.[8] To do this, Schelling does not believe that he needs to make any changes to his previously outlined systems but that he simply needs to explicate what he had, up to that point, left unsaid (Schelling 1856–61: 4: 107). Despite this self-presentation, there are important differences between the 'Presentation' and Schelling's earlier works. For one, he adopts the geometrical method used by Spinoza, where he begins by postulating definitions. Second, he puts forth a Platonic view of the Absolute as an eternal unchanging reality, which does not enter into the temporal sequence of the world and thus cannot be said to develop. This leads him to adopt his third and most controversial claim (which Hegel criticises in the 'Preface' to the *Phenomenology*), namely, that *difference* can only exist *outside* of the Absolute and that, insofar as the Absolute is all that is, difference cannot be real but is merely ideal. Difference, he explains, arises out of the perspective of reflection, a perspective that is inadequate for conceiving the Absolute. Finally and most significantly with regard to Hegel's critique, Schelling explains that the Absolute is not something that is 'constructed' or 'produced' but is the point of *indifference* prior to any division and construction.

Up to 1801, Schelling had presented his philosophy from two different angles: the philosophy of nature, on the one hand, and, on the other, transcendental philosophy. The goal of the 1801 essay, in contrast, is to present the 'point of indifference' of the two angles – the point prior to the division between the philosophy of nature and transcendental philosophy. It is neither to 'realism' nor to 'idealism' that Schelling turns – nor even to 'some third combination of them' – but to 'a system of identity' of the two. This system cannot be grasped from the standpoint of reflection, which 'works only from oppositions and rests on oppositions', but only from the standpoint of reason (Schelling 1856–61: 4: 113).

By reason Schelling means 'the absolute reason, or reason insofar as it is thought as the total indifference of subjective and objective' (4: 114). Usually reason is understood subjectively, that is, as inherently tied to a thinking subject. This is a mistake because 'reason's thought is foreign to everyone' and thus, to arrive at reason as the absolute, 'one must abstract from what does the thinking'. In abstracting reason from a thinking subject, one is also freed from the objective, 'since something objective or a thought item is only possible in contrast to a thinking something, from which we have completely abstracted' (4: 115). In this way, reason 'becomes the true *in-itself*', the point of absolute identity between the subjective and objective.

As the Absolute, reason is neither subjective nor objective but their identity. As such, the law of identity is the 'highest law for the being of reason' (4: 116). Reason, then, 'is simply one and simply self-identical'. Schelling then elaborates on the relation between the essence and existence of reason. The essence of absolute identity, he writes, is its existence: as the absolutely true, it necessarily exists. In other words, its essence implies its existence. This holds for reason as well, insofar as it is identical with absolute identity. Thus, Schelling concludes, '*the being of reason is just as unconditioned* as that of absolute identity, or: **Being** *belongs equally to the essence of reason and to that of absolute identity*' (4: 118).

Essence, however, should be distinguished from *form*. While the essence of absolute identity is simply that it is, its form is A = A. The difference is decisive because the form of A = A implies difference, that is, it implies A as subject and A as object, whereas the essence of absolute identity does not imply difference but only the existence of one absolute identity. Therefore, *the essence of absolute identity remains indifferent while its form contains difference*. What this means, significantly, is that absolute identity is not constituted by A as subject and A as object (that is, by the difference or opposition between the two) but rather *is* the indifference of the two.

Difference therefore does not lie in the essence of absolute identity but in its form. While the form A = A implies a distinction between A as subject and A as object, it does not imply that there are (in essence) two distinct As – rather, the same A is posited. The difference, therefore, is entirely formal. Schelling surmises that this difference cannot be qualitative, since it is one and the same A – the same essence. Rather it is a quantitative difference. In other words, the difference has to do with a predominance of one A (whether the subjective or the objective) over the other. Schelling explains:

> since the same A is posited in the predicate and in the subject position in the proposition A = A, without doubt there is posited between the two utterly no difference at all, but an indifference. In this situation, difference . . . would become possible only if either predominant subjectivity or predominant objectivity were posited, in which case A = A would have changed into A = B. (4: 124)

Quantitative difference, therefore, says nothing about the essence or being of A (the essence of A remains absolutely indifferent), but refers to the amount of being in A as subject as different from the amount of being in A as object. It is therefore not a difference in kind (A *is* absolutely) but in degree (in quantity).

As the indifference of subject and object, absolute identity is not a synthesis of the two. This is because absolute identity is outside of the realm of distinction and synthesis implies an original difference. This means that quantitative difference 'is only possible *outside* absolute identity', that is, it is outside the Absolute. The Absolute, however, is in everything, is everything, is totality and the universe (4: 125). Where, then, is quantitative difference?

Quantitative difference is in the individual, because individuals are not 'in themselves' (their essence does not imply their existence) and therefore are not absolute. Insofar as they are not in themselves, individuals, however, are also not real. Therefore, in asking the question: where is quantitative difference?, we are led to a second significant question regarding the status of individuals. If everything that is is in absolute identity and if quantitative difference must exist outside of absolute identity, then what are individuals, which are the outcome of quantitative difference? To make the case that his claims are not contradictory, Schelling returns to an earlier distinction between that which is in itself and that which is not in itself. Thus, he writes that 'there is no individual being or individual thing in itself' and in fact only the absolute totality is in itself (4: 125). This can only mean, therefore, that 'there is nothing in itself outside of totality and if something is viewed outside of totality, this happens only by an *arbitrary separation of the individual from the whole effected by reflection*' (4: 126; emphasis added).

Thus, difference is the outcome of perspective, namely, reflection and individuals are not real entities, but born out of the perspective of one 'who finds himself outside indifference, who fails to view absolute identity itself as primary and original' (4: 128). Rather than recognising the Absolute as the point of original indifference, such a person views the Absolute as something 'produced' (*producirt*). This viewpoint is false, Schelling concludes, because it relies on a separation that is 'intrinsically impossible' – namely, a separation between absolute totality and its parts.

It is in Schelling's writings of this period that the struggle to understand the relation between the Absolute and its parts is most intense. For, as just noted, if the Absolute is all that is, then there can in fact be no separation between the Absolute and its parts, for nothing other than the Absolute exists. Furthermore, if the Absolute is all that is, then the Absolute is not an outcome of oppositions born out of separation. Or: if the Absolute is absolutely, then why must it become?

In the 'Presentation', Schelling is neither concerned with the process of the Absolute's development nor with its appearances, but with the Absolute as such – as reason. Reason is the Absolute thinking itself *immediately* – neither as subject nor as object, neither as thought nor as being, but as original indifference. In turn, there is no movement of reason in which it develops and manifests itself but rather things are to be conceived of as they are 'in themselves', that is, as 'they are in reason' (4: 128). In the earlier writings, in contrast, the Absolute is considered to be somewhat lacking in its first appearance and thus needing to go out of itself and develop itself; in the 'Presentation', reason as the Absolute is conceived of as absolutely self-sufficient and, ultimately, unmoving and unchanging. Schelling thus writes, 'The basic mistake of all philosophy is the presupposition that absolute identity actually goes out of itself and the attempt to conceptualise in which way this going out of itself takes place' (4: 119–20).

6. Hegel

In the 1801 essay 'The Difference Between Fichte's and Schelling's System of Philosophy', Hegel's sympathies are clearly with Schelling. Nevertheless, Hegel's later critiques are not far from some of the poignant remarks he makes at this earlier stage. First, Hegel maintains that difference is *real*, writing that:

> because both subject and object are Subject–Object, the opposition of subject and object is real; for both are posited in the Absolute and through it they have reality. The reality of opposites and real opposition only happen because of the identity of the opposites . . . (Hegel 1968–: 4: 35)

For Hegel the opposition between the subject and object is essential and inherent to the Absolute.

This leads to the second way in which Hegel distinguishes himself from Schelling, in that he sees the principle of becoming as inherent to the Absolute. Thus Hegel describes the Absolute as 'an infinite self-begetting' (Hegel 1968–: 4: 40). Such self-begetting, he emphasises, arises out of real opposition. Hegel contrasts this with what he considers to be a merely formal philosophy. A formal philosophy recognises opposition as merely ideal (that is, an opposition that arises out of a perspective). In such a system, the overcoming of the opposition is also merely ideal, that is, formal. The only way by which a real (as opposed to ideal) identity is attained is through the overcoming of a real opposition, that is, an opposition in being (35). He thus concludes that 'it is only in real opposition that the principle of identity is a real principle'.

In the light of these early differences, Hegel's critique of Schelling in the *Phenomenology* gains substance. The differences within the Absolute are real – the Absolute is not absolute indifference, but 'the identity of identity and difference' (34). In the same way that the Romantics and the early Schelling conceived of the Absolute as inherently active and developing, so Hegel writes in the Preface to the *Phenomenology* that the Absolute 'is in truth actual only in so far as it is the movement of positing itself, or is the mediation of its self-othering with itself' (Hegel 1968–: 9: 20, §18).[9] Because the Absolute is 'subject', it negates itself and thus creates a bifurcation in the simple substance. The subject, Hegel continues, 'is the doubling which sets up opposition and then again the negation of this indifferent diversity and of its antithesis [that is, immediate simplicity]'. This process of self-restoration, 'this reflection in otherness within itself', is what Hegel calls 'the true'. The Absolute, therefore, is not a simple, immediate or original identity but 'the process of its own becoming, the circle that presupposes its end as its goal, having its end also as its beginning; and only by being worked out to its end is it actual' (Hegel 1968–: 9: 20, §18).

The Absolute is in this sense clearly purposive – its result is already implied in its beginning; however, it is only in its end that its purpose is actualised. It is therefore self-moving and in this motion it unfolds and becomes itself. The motion of the Absolute arises out of the original opposition between subject and object. In this opposition, consciousness (as subject) is negated (by the object of consciousness). Consciousness then comes to realise that the disparity between itself and its object is only a seeming disparity and that in fact the object (the negation) does not arise externally to itself but from within itself – that is, it is its 'own doing'. Thus, Hegel concludes,

> When it has shown this completely, Spirit has made its existence identical with its essence; it has itself for its object just as it is and the abstract element of immediacy and of the separation of knowing and truth is overcome. Being is then absolutely mediated; it is a substantial content which is just as immediately the property of the I, it is the self-like or the concept (*Begriff*). (9: 29)

Such a self-moving subject can only be thought, Hegel realises, by reconfiguring the meaning of the subject-predicate relation in judgement. Rather than conceiving the subject as a 'fixed' entity, a passive substance that 'inertly supports the accidents', which, despite its relation to the predicate through the copula, remains opposed to the predicate, Hegel conceives of the subject and predicate as fundamentally transformed through the copula. This means, first, that the movement of the proposition is not something external to the subject and predicate but rather expresses their internal relation. The copula, therefore, is not an empty form imposed upon them but is the expression of their inherent unity. In turn, while the subject is transformed such that it dissolves in the predicate, the predicate is transformed such that it is no longer an empty universal but a concrete universal which contains within itself the subject. This does not imply, however, a dissolution of the difference between subject and predicate, but a transformation of both such that what emerges out of their relation is a harmonious unity (9: 43–5).

In this way the Absolute transforms itself in its appearances throughout the *Phenomenology*, beginning with simple self-identity, a 'pure abstraction', which necessarily negates itself and thus transforms itself, concluding in absolute knowing. Absolute knowing is not simply self-consciousness but the point at which the object of self-consciousness is no longer external to itself, indeed no longer an *object*, but is incorporated into it and thus transformed into a unity higher than either subject or object alone.

The *Phenomenology* was conceived by Hegel as the 'introduction' to his logic, in that it traces the Absolute in its *appearance*, and it is the conclusion to the *Phenomenology* – wherein appearance (objectification) ceases and absolute knowing arises – that forms the first step in pure knowing (*reines Wissen*) or pure science (*reine Wissenschaft*). In the *Logic*, the first part of the *Encyclopedia of the Philosophical Sciences in Outline*, of which successive editions appeared in 1817, 1827 and 1830, the goal is to identify and work through the three categories of pure knowing – being, essence and the concept. For Hegel the concept (*Begriff*) is the culmination of logic, as of thought. He writes,

> since thought seeks to form a *concept* of things, this concept (along with judgment and syllogism as its most immediate forms) cannot consist in determinations and relationships that are alien and external to things . . . thinking things leads over to what is *universal* in them; but the universal is itself one of the moments of the concept. (Hegel 1968–: 20: 67, §24A)

The concept therefore has ontological implications – it is the 'objective thought' that constitutes the purpose of objects (by 'objective thought', Hegel means the concept of the object, the determining ground of the object). Thus in the same way that he describes the spirit at the end of the *Phenomenology* as having attained to its concept ('the self-knowing spirit, just because it grasps its concept, is the immediate identity with itself' (1968–: 9: 432)), so in the *Logic* he understands the concept to be the *truth* and the *living reality* of its object, such that every object that attains to its concept (its inner purpose) has become a true object (1968–: 20: 67, §24A).

The concept first develops its subjective side, which concerns the usual logical data such as judgement and syllogism, then its objective side, the reality or being of an object and finally attains to the idea, which is nothing other than the concept coming to grasp itself as concept. In grasping itself as a concept, the concept sees itself as identical with itself. For this reason, the structure of the idea, Hegel concludes, is that of 'subjectivity, thinking, infinity' (1968–: 20: 218, §215A). What takes place at this final stage in the development of the concept is not only an objectification of the concept but also a *recognition* of this objectification as objectification of the concept. It is for this reason that only subjectivity (the I) is an adequate representation of Hegel's understanding of the concept. Or, as Hegel puts it, the idea is 'the course in which the concept . . . determines itself . . . into *subjectivity*' (20: 218, §215).

The idea is absolute because it is the purpose of the world thinking itself. The reason that the idea is the purpose of the world is that it is the concept conscious of itself – in other words, it is the concept that has attained to its own concept. While the concept is the constitutive ground of beings in the world, the concept of the concept – the idea – is the self-aware constitutive ground of the world. It is thus the Absolute – the ground of all that is raised to self-consciousness.

While for Hegel the construction of the Absolute out of opposition led to his conclusion that the Absolute is ultimately subjective – formed in accordance with the structures of self-consciousness – for Schelling in the identity philosophy the Absolute is indifferent, neither subjective nor objective. However, Schelling's attempt to provide a non-objective, non-subjective Absolute, an Absolute that is not determined in accordance with the structures of self-consciousness, led him to the conclusion that the Absolute must exclude opposition and difference, as well as particularity and finitude. The disagreement in their conceptions of the Absolute reveals the complexity of the matter at hand: the Absolute cannot be designated either subjective or objective, for as Absolute it furnishes the very possibility of such an opposition. Yet, the Absolute must in some significant way account for the existence of the non-Absolute, such that the relation between the Absolute and the relative is a real, not solely ideal, relation. Ultimately, the question of the Absolute in its relation to the non-Absolute is the question of the one and the many, intimately tied to the question of being and becoming. How can the one be many, how can that which *is* absolutely *become* something other than itself?

7. Knowing the Absolute

Despite the differences in their conceptions of the Absolute, Schelling and Hegel, as well as the Romantics, agreed in one fundamental way: intellectual intuition was central to knowing the Absolute. They viewed Kant's elimination of intellectual intuition based on his conception of the discursive intellect as unjustified. As Novalis put it, 'The most arbitrary prejudice of them all is that man is denied the capacity to get outside himself and to have consciousness beyond the realm of the senses' (Novalis 1960–88: 2: 421, #22). Although not entirely in agreement with Fichte, Novalis and his fellow Romantics and idealists were influenced by Fichte's insight into the mind and his implicit critique of the Kantian understanding of the human discursive intellect.

With some modifications, the Romantics and idealists more or less agreed with Fichte's understanding of intuition. The most significant modification they undertook was to extend the scope of the intuiting mind, such that in the same way that the I is able to perceive itself as a non-sensible reality so it is also able to perceive the underlying and non-sensible laws which unify, structure and constitute the universe. Even Hegel, who was critical of the notion of an 'immediate intuition' agreed that the human mind was *intuitive*, stating in 1830 that 'the notion of an *intuitive understanding*, of *inner* purposiveness, etc., is the *universal* concurrently thought of as *concrete* in itself' (1968–: 20: 94, §55A). Only through an intuitive insight, according to Hegel, can the particular be determined through the universal and the universal made concrete.

Having established the necessity of an intuiting mind, all that was needed was to show how this mind intuited or perceived non-sensible realities other than the I. From within a natural-scientific, Kantian framework, it makes no sense to speak of a non-material reality that underlies and constitutes the world. However, it was precisely this point that the Romantics and idealists contested, claiming, in contrast, that there was no distinction between inward and outward intuition. Thus, for them, what can be given to the mind when it reflects upon itself (the intelligible reality of the I) can also be given to the mind as it considers nature (the intelligible reality of the world).

Underlying this conception of an intelligible outer reality is the notion – discussed above – of an *objective* concept or idea. In other words, what determines and forms beings in the world is a concept that underlies their development and grants them existence. In his philosophy of nature, Schelling explains the meaning of an *objective idea*. Nature, he begins, is an organic whole, in that in it 'all things mutually bear and support each other' (Schelling 1856–61: 3: 278–9). This implies that nature as a whole, as an idea, must precede and inform its parts. For only as such is nature not the outcome of its parts, but that which forms its parts and thus informs their relations. The idea, therefore, is not a concept or category imposed upon nature but is nature itself – the constitutive ground of the parts and their relations.

The goal of intellectual intuition is to grasp this ground and the relations among the parts, that is, the whole. It is only through intuition, however, that the whole can be given. Discursively, only the parts are known and the whole is patched together out of the parts. This, however, culminates in a mechanistic vision of reality – a reality assembled out of parts – which violates nature as an organic, living reality which informs its parts.

The question arises as to what is involved in intuiting the whole. The idealists and the Romantics agree with the Kantian (and Fichtean) premise that we know only what we make or construct (see, for example, Novalis 1960–88: 2: 589, #267).[10] The meaning of construction, however, must be clarified. Following Fichte, construction is what is involved in intuition: the self constructs itself in intuiting itself. Schelling develops construction further, such that it extends beyond the self-construction of the I in intuition to the construction of nature. This, however, seems contradictory – how can the self construct nature? Here Schelling introduces experimentation – for in experimentation we create phenomena (Schelling 1856–61: 3: 275–6).

Schelling is cautious about experimentation, however, noting that it does not produce phenomena absolutely but only within specific circumstances. Therefore, although experimentation grants insight into nature's inner workings, it does so to a limited degree. For this reason, it must be supplemented by an 'absolute hypothesis' that directs one's gaze toward nature, thus revealing nature's laws as they are given in experiment and experience.

The 'absolute hypothesis', Schelling explains, is the principle from which the entire system of nature can be deduced. However, such a hypothesis must conform to the phenomena of nature; otherwise it is invalid. Given that nature is an organic whole, whose parts mutually support and bear one another, the absolute hypothesis is the notion that nature is an inherently and interdependently connected whole. With this hypothesis in mind, the experimenter is aware of and looking out for the connections, the mutual support and, ultimately, the ways in which each part is a transformation and manifestation of the other parts (and of the whole) of nature. What the experimenter seeks is the original and underlying organising idea of nature as it is given in its various parts.

Although this principle of organisation underlies and constitutes the material reality of nature, it is itself not material. It is the concept or idea, which, in spite of its ideality, is nevertheless a real and formative element that develops and sustains the material reality and which cannot be divorced from it. In essence, the material being cannot exist without this formative principle. And it is this objective idea or organising principle that only the intuiting mind can grasp.

While among the Romantics and idealists Hegel appeared to be critical of intuition, he was also keenly aware of the necessity of intuitive knowledge, arguing that mere reflection is incapable of attaining to the unity of all opposites for it 'stubbornly holds fast to being against non-being' (Hegel 1968–: 4: 95). Reflection, according to Hegel, undertakes the significant task of differentiating. Intuition, however, grants insight into the whole without which knowledge would be impossible (4: 28). Reflection on its own, or intuition on its own, concludes in formalism, 'for thing as well as concept is, each taken by itself, just a form of the Absolute'. In this sense, Hegel's understanding of the task of knowledge echoes Schelling's as construed in the latter's philosophy of nature – wherein experimentation and comparative reflection are supplemented by intuitive insight. Yet Hegel is critical of Schelling's understanding of intuition as it was developed in the identity philosophy.

In the 'Presentation of My System', Schelling explains that 'truly absolute knowledge' is possible only 'where thought and being come together absolutely, where there is no longer the question of a connection between concept and object, where the concept itself is at the same time the object and the object the concept' (Schelling 1856–61: 4: 345–6). This is the case when there is a coincidence of the two, such that the concept need not go out of itself in order to attain the object and the object need not strive for a concept external to itself.

On account of this immediacy in knowledge, Schelling emphasises intuition – for it is only through intuition that such immediacy is attainable. He begins his explication by likening philosophy's method to that of geometry and arithmetic. Demonstration in geometry is not based on causal derivation but on 'proof'. In the same manner that a geometer does not explain a triangle by explaining its parts, so a philosopher does not derive one thing by subordinating it to another – that is, by deriving it from the other and hence seeing it as caused by the other. Rather, the philosopher comes to see that 'everything in the universe is unconditioned in its own way . . . nothing is to the other a true cause, rather everything is grounded in the unconditioned in the same way' (Schelling 1856–61: 4: 344). To seek the cause of one thing from that of another is to fall into an endless 'chain', which, he continues, is nonsense that concludes with a 'complete nothing [Unding]' for a science (343).

Reflection is precisely that method which, because it continues to rely on subordination and causal derivation, concludes in an Unding. Intuition, in contrast, grasps the original and immediate identity. The insight given through intuition escapes the chains of causality and arrives at the unmediated identity of reality. Hegel's critique of Schelling's emphasis on intuition goes hand in hand with what he sees as a formalism in Schelling's conception of the Absolute. According to Hegel, intuition which does not work alongside reflection is inarticulate and, ultimately, incapable of presenting the Absolute to consciousness. The Absolute cannot be grasped through intellectual intuition alone, which may simply 'fall back into inert simplicity and does not depict actuality itself in a non-actual [that is, merely formal] manner' (Hegel 1968–: 9: 20, §18). The Absolute is not an immediate original unity or identity, but the process and the result of its becoming itself. Simple intuition cannot grasp the development of the Absolute as it negates itself and then becomes itself again. Reflection is also necessary. However, reflection is not to be viewed as a mere necessary step toward grasping the Absolute but as an essential characteristic of reason, which enables the development of the Absolute. It is reflection, in fact, which *brings the Absolute forth*. Thus, Hegel writes,

> Reason is therefore misunderstood when reflection is excluded from the True and is not grasped as a positive moment of the Absolute. It is reflection that makes the True a result, but it is equally reflection that overcomes the antithesis between the process of its becoming and the result, for this becoming is also simple and therefore not different from the form of the True which shows itself as *simple* in its result; the process of becoming is rather just this return into simplicity. (9: 19–20, §21)

Schelling, in contrast, concludes that the Absolute, as all that is, does not 'go out of itself', does not bring forth a world distinct from its absolute infinitude. In fact, he considers this perspective of the Absolute to be inherently flawed and based on a misunderstanding of the relation between the infinite and the finite as a causal relation. Thus, he states in the 'Further Presentation of My System' that the fact:

that the going out of itself of the absolute . . . is absolutely unthinkable, is, in the same way as the unity and the inner relatedness of all things among themselves and with the god-like essence, a further axiom of the true philosophy. (Schelling [1802] 1856–61: 4: 390)

What is needed, then, to grasp the Absolute is immediate, non-discursive insight into this original, undifferentiated identity. Reflection, in contrast, distracts from the true immediacy of the Absolute.

8. Conclusion

Although the Absolute as a term fell out of philosophical parlance in the second half of the nineteenth century, its historical and systematic significance cannot be overlooked. As I have tried to show, the notion of the Absolute was developed as an attempt to overcome scepticism and nihilism and to affirm the possibility of philosophical knowledge. Furthermore, the Absolute was neither dogmatically asserted nor naïvely assumed. Rather, the philosophers of the early nineteenth century attempted to establish the phenomenological reality of the Absolute. Insight into the Absolute cannot be given through discursive thinking, which can only grant knowledge of the parts and not of the whole that underlies and precedes the parts. Only intuition can offer insight into the whole and adequately explain its relation to its parts. Lacking such insight, the relation of the Absolute and its parts can only be conceived mechanistically and hence incompletely.

The difficulties of conceiving and formulating a philosophy around the notion of the Absolute should by no means be viewed as reason to criticise or dismiss the attempt to philosophically draw out the Absolute. Rather, these difficulties should serve as insights into the complexity of the questions at hand. The notion of the Absolute was developed out of sound philosophical judgement, as a response to fundamental philosophical problems – of dualism, scepticism, nihilism and the possibility of knowledge – that cannot be ignored.

Notes

1. All translations are the author's own unless otherwise indicated.
2. Kant famously distinguishes between the human *discursive* intellect and the divine *intuitive* intellect in his letter to Marcus Herz of 21 February 1772. While the discursive intellect cannot create its object of knowledge but must be given it by external means, the intuitive intellect does create its object of knowledge and therefore has direct insight into its object, that is, the insight is not mediated by either the forms of sensibility or the concepts of the understanding. In other words, the intuitive intellect knows the object as it is 'in itself'.
3. Schelling, for example, although sympathetic to Spinoza, repeatedly criticised him on this ground: Spinoza does not explain how the self is to know the Absolute. He writes, 'Spinoza was unable to make it intelligible how I myself in turn become aware of [the] succession [of my presentations]' (Schelling 1976–: 5: 90).
4. My account of the German Romantic tradition and its relation to the Kantian legacy differs from Judith Norman's and Alistair Welchman's in Chapter 3 of this volume. Although I would not want to eliminate all differences between the individual thinkers, I do not think that one of these differences rests in their varying responses to Kantianism. Rather, as I see it, the Romantics were just as dissatisfied with the Kantian dualisms and the sceptical outcomes of the Kantian system as the idealists. Thus, although one can perhaps trace a kind of Kantian scepticism in some of the earliest writings of the Romantics, this scepticism is soon discarded in favour of an idealist

monism, on the basis of which the knower can have insight into the known – whether immediate or mediated. See Nassar 2006.

5. Fichte's defence of idealism is based on his belief that only idealism (as opposed to dogmatism) can grant human freedom. See for example his 1797 'Second Introduction' to the *Wissenschaftslehre* (Fichte 1964–: 4 (2): 23).

6. The Romantics and idealists saw themselves as combining Fichte's emphasis on the productive self with Spinoza's emphasis on the Absolute, or the Infinite. While the former too narrowly focused on the self, the latter could not adequately respond to the epistemological question.

7. The question underlying much of Schlegel's thinking, as he puts it in his Jena *Lectures on Transcendental Idealism* of 1800–1, is: 'why has the infinite gone out of itself and made itself finite [*aus sich herausgegangen und hat sich endlich gemacht*]? In other words: why are there individuals? Or, why doesn't the game of nature run out in an instant, so that nothing would exist at all?' (Schlegel 1958–: 12: 39; see also 12: 221 and 17: 281, #1033). (When applicable, references to Novalis and Schlegel include fragment or note number (indicated #) after page number.)

8. This essay was followed by the 'Further Presentation of My System', which was written directly after the first but published in 1802.

9. When applicable, references to Hegel's works include paragraph number (§) after page number. 'A' (for example §55A) indicates a reference to Hegel's 'addition' to the paragraph.

10. Thus Novalis writes, 'We know [*wissen*] something only insofar as we can express [*ausdrücken*] it, i.e., make [*machen*] it. The more readily and manifold we are able to produce [*produciren*] it, to execute it, the better do we know it – we know it completely when we are to mediate [*mitteilen*] it, to cause it everywhere and in all manner – to effect an individual expression of it in every organ' (Novalis 1960–88: 2: 589, #267).

References

Beiser, Frederick (2002), *German Idealism: The Struggle against Subjectivism 1781–1801*, Cambridge, MA: Harvard University Press.

Fichte, Johann Gottlieb (1964–), *Gesamtausgabe der Bayerischen Akademie der Wissenschaft*, ed. Reinhard Lauth, Hans Jacob and Hans Gliwitsky, 40 vols, Stuttgart-Bad Cannstatt: Fromann.

Frank, Manfred (1997), *Unendliche Annäherung*, Frankfurt: Suhrkamp.

Hegel, Georg Wilhelm Friedrich (1968–), *Gesammelte Werke*, Hamburg: Meiner.

Jacobi, Friedrich Heinrich (1846), *Werke*, ed. Friedrich Heinrich Jacobi and Friedrich Köppen, 6 vols, Leipzig: Weidmann.

Kant, Immanuel (1900–), *Kants gesammelte Schriften*, Akademie Ausgabe, ed. Wilhelm Dilthey et al., Berlin: de Gruyter.

Nassar, Dalia (2006), 'Reality through illusion: presenting the Absolute in Novalis', *Idealistic Studies*, 36 (1): 27–46.

Novalis (Friedrich von Hardenberg) (1960–88), *Novalis Schriften*, ed. Richard Samuel et al., 6 vols, Stuttgart: Kohlhammer.

Schelling, Friedrich Wilhelm Joseph von (1856–61), *Sämmtliche Werke*, ed. Karl Friedrich August Schelling, 14 vols, Stuttgart: Cotta.

Schelling, Friedrich Wilhelm Joseph von (1976–), *Werke. Historisch-Kritische Ausgabe*, ed. Hans Michael Baumgartner, Wilhelm G. Jacobs and Hermann Krings, Stuttgart: Frommann-Holzboog.

Schlegel, Friedrich (1958–), *Kritische Friedrich Schlegel Ausgabe*, ed. Ernst Behler, Jean Jacques Anstett and Hans Eichner, 35 vols, Munich: Schöningh.

Schleiermacher, Friedrich Daniel Ernst (1984), *Kritische Gesamtausgabe*, ed. Günter Meckenstock, Berlin and New York: de Gruyter.

3

The Question of Romanticism

Judith Norman and Alistair Welchman

1. What is Romanticism?

1.1 Beginning

'Romanticism' is one of the more hotly contested terms in the history of ideas. There is a singular lack of consensus as to its meaning, unity and historical extension and many attempts to fix the category of Romanticism very quickly become blurry. In his *Conversations with Eckermann*, Goethe says that the concept of Romanticism 'is now spread over the whole world and occasions so many quarrels and divisions' (Goethe [1836] 1984: 297) and this situation has not rectified itself in the 180 years since then. But the term was poorly defined from the start. Friedrich Schlegel, frequently claimed as the progenitor of European Romanticism, wrote to his brother August Wilhelm Schlegel, widely acknowledged as its most important populariser: 'I can hardly send you my explication of the word Romantic because it would take – 125 pages!' (Lacoue-Labarthe and Nancy 1988: 6). In 1866 Alfred de Musset writes of the search for the meaning of Romanticism: 'No, my dear sir . . . you may try in vain to seize the butterfly's wing; the dust that colours it will be all you can hold in your fingers' (De Musset [1866] 1908: 209).

As a result, the great historian of ideas, Arthur Lovejoy, famously concludes that: 'the word "romantic" has come to mean so many things that, by itself, it means nothing. It has ceased to perform the function of a verbal sign' (Lovejoy 1948: 232).[1] But his pessimistic advice has not stopped scholars from trying to define Romanticism. If anything, it has brought renewed vigour to the determination with which critics try to pinpoint the term. There are several approaches to take, for those who attempt to do so. One class of critics tries to enumerate the features shared by the authors and texts generally considered romantic. According to René Wellek's classic rebuttal of Lovejoy:

> They [scholars of Romanticism] all see the implication of imagination, symbol, myth and organic nature and see it as part of the great endeavour to overcome the split between subject and object, the self and the world, the conscious and the unconscious. This is the central creed of the great romantic poets in England, Germany and France. It is a closely coherent body of thought and feeling. (Wellek 1963: 220)[2]

This description certainly includes a number of elements that many of the writers generally thought to be romantic have in common. But there is something unsatisfying about this approach, which presupposes a sort of pre-theoretical grasp of Romanticism which it then tries to formulate. The theory rarely completely conforms to the pre-theoretical grasp. (Wellek admits that Byron fits poorly into his description.) Do these lists of empirical commonalities really indicate some underlying profound and essential identity and if so what? An alternative approach would try to identify the fundamental unity that informs Romanticism and gives rise to the empirical commonalities. But what would this essential feature be? The French Revolution? Manic depression? Fichte's *Wissenschaftslehre*? Attempts like this are sometimes problematically reductive and also fail to capture figures whom we might want to include: A.W. Schlegel was no depressive, Wordsworth was unmoved by Fichte and so on.

Both of these approaches take an external perspective on Romanticism, seeing it as the *object* of inquiry. An alternative approach, which we will pursue, looks at romantic *subjects* and Romanticism as a self-constituting category, rather than merely as an externally imposed one. In other words, we will take as basic neither an (empirical) array of candidate properties constituting Romanticism nor a supposed underlying (rationalist) essence from which properties can be derived, but rather we will focus on how the romantics themselves took up the idea of Romanticism and transformed it into a self-conscious movement. We will treat the question of Romanticism with respect to England but above all Germany. Although romantic movements arose and flourished elsewhere in Europe (and in France in particular), German and English Romanticism were uniquely theoretically sophisticated and philosophically nuanced.

The transformation of the idea of Romanticism into a movement is by no means easy to account for. When Friedrich Schlegel, in his essay *On the Study of Greek Poetry*, written in 1795 and published in 1797, made his own contribution to the long-standing quarrel between the ancients and the moderns, he described much of what would come to be associated with the romantic sensibility without either using the term or even liking modernity very much. His category of modernity was broad, including Dante and Shakespeare. He called their art 'interesting' and described it as subjective, opposing it to the objectivity of the ancients. He went on to characterise it as a fusion (or confusion) of genres, a tendency to combine philosophy with aesthetics, a valorisation of the striking and novel over the traditional and a desire to depict what is characteristic and individual rather than what is universal. Modern art rejects the aesthetic ideal of self-contained, harmonious beauty in favour of different ideals, such as the sublime, the interesting and even the ugly. It valorises striving over achievement, the imagination over reason. As Schlegel writes: 'if a faint hint of perfect beauty is found [in modern art], it is experienced not so much in serene enjoyment as in unsatisfied longing' (Schlegel [1797] 2001: 18).

This characterisation was not novel, nor was Schlegel's dislike of this modern tendency. It took an additional manoeuvre (which he had accomplished by 1797) for him to begin positively valorising the art of the moderns: a historicist recognition of the definitive end to classicism and of the fact that his nostalgia was no longer *just* nostalgia but was itself something distinctively modern. According to Arthur Lovejoy's classic study, it was Schiller who converted Schlegel to the modern ideal, which Schlegel only now christened 'romantic', making Schiller a sort of 'spiritual grandfather of German Romanticism' (Lovejoy 1948: 220).

The term 'romantic' had been used before; it was associated with the courtly romances of medieval literature, the legend of Roland and the Arthurian myths (as well as the tales they inspired) and thus denoted a tradition separate from that of classical antiquity, with particular affinities to the Middle Ages. The word gradually came to signify certain more specific features of this literature such as its exoticism, its valorisation of amorous passions and excessive states of emotion and its stylistic departures from neo-classical form. What Schlegel does is to start using it as a broad characterisation of a distinctively modern sensibility.

The structure of this event deserves closer scrutiny: Schlegel was initially repelled by the restless dissatisfaction and incompleteness of modern art – its failure to emulate the naïve harmony of the ancients. But we could say that he came to a self-awareness of his own Romanticism by virtue of his very nostalgia, of his feeling of distance from the classical ideal. He later berated his own, earlier work on antiquity as lacking sufficient irony, which is to say (minimally) a lack of critical distance from his own nostalgic affect (Schlegel [1797] 1970: 144, #7).[3] In other words, his 'Romanticism' was not constituted by nostalgia but by the realisation that his nostalgia is both itself distinctively modern and hence that it is not *about* the past but about the present. Incompleteness became emblematic of modernity and a certain ironic nostalgia became its sensibility. Both are brought together in the paradoxical notion of an intentional ruin or fragment, since this embodies the notion of a self-conscious nostalgia. Schlegel would later write 'Many of the works of the ancients have become fragments. Many modern works are fragments as soon as they are written' (Schlegel [1798] 1970: 164, #24). And indeed this remark was published in one of the Schlegel brothers' collections of fragments, a literary form that they cultivated and that would become something of a signature style for the group that was beginning to gather around them in Jena in the late 1790s.

It was this group that would come to be retrospectively designated as the *Jena Frühromantiker*, the Early German Romantics. It included the Schlegel brothers, Friedrich Schlegel's wife, Dorothea (daughter of the Enlightenment philosopher, Moses Mendelssohn, and aunt of the composer Felix Mendelssohn), and A. W. Schlegel's wife, Caroline, who would soon divorce him – amicably, it seems – for the philosopher Schelling, who was also associated with the group. Friedrich von Hardenberg was an active participant (writing under the assumed name of Novalis), as was the playwright Ludwig Tieck, the writer Wilhelm Wackenroder and the theologian Friedrich Schleiermacher. They were all young – when the group broke up around 1800 (and stopped publishing their journal, *Athenäum*), they were all under 40, mostly under 30 and Novalis and Wackenroder were already dead. A. W. Schlegel then went on to publicise the group's ideas in a series of lectures, first in Berlin (1801–4) and then in Vienna (1808–9, published in 1809–11). The Vienna lectures were translated almost immediately into several languages and proved to be the primary mechanism for the dissemination of the German romantic theories to the rest of Europe, both on their own as well as through the works of intermediary expositors such as Madame de Staël (whose children he tutored), Simon de Sismondi and Friedrich Bouterwek.

In 1805, a second and similar group began to form, this time in Heidelberg, around Clemens Brentano (who had been in Jena and was familiar with the group there), Achim von Arnim, Josef Görres and Friedrich Creuzer. They were authors, classicists, orientalists and philosophers of mythology. Brentano and Arnim produced the significant anthology of German folksongs, *Des Knaben Wunderhorn* (1805–8) and their friends, Jacob and Wilhelm Grimm, also collected stories. This group incurred the personal and professional enmity of a group of more conservative thinkers and principally the classicist J. J. Voß, who attacked and parodied them in 1808, referring to both the Heidelberg and Jena groups as *Romantiker*. This was the first systematic use of the term in reference to contemporary writers (see: Eichner 1972; Wellek 1963) – the Jena group had used the term to refer to post-classical art in general and particularly literary models such as Cervantes and Shakespeare. It was in this vituperative context that the group first acquired a label and a historical destiny as a unified movement.

Romanticism, then, had something like a double origin. As we saw, Schlegel achieved an implicit self-recognition of himself as romantic at the moment that he both named and valorised the concept and soon after that he was tagged with the label by those who still regarded it as a negative term. His own positive understanding of Romanticism extended back at least as far as Giovanni Boccaccio, while the critics' hostile but ultimately victorious category limited the scope of the term to the Jena and Heidelberg groups – in other words, those in whom the nostalgia had become self-conscious. Hegel famously preserves this duality: in his *Lectures on Fine Art* he labels the entirety of the post-classical, Christian world 'romantic' (retaining the resonance between Romanticism and Rome as the site of the disintegration of the classical form and the beginning of the Christian world) and sees the Romanticism of his contemporaries as only the end and logical (and shameful) conclusion of this broader movement.

1.2 Returning

Hegel was not the only one to see the contemporary romantic movement as a degraded repetition of specifically post-classical themes. In his frankly hostile account of the (German) romantic school, intended as a dampening corrective to Madame de Staël's more enthusiastic assessment, Heine writes that Romanticism:

> was nothing other than the revival of the poetry of the Middle Ages as manifested in the songs, sculpture and architecture, in the art and life of that time. This poetry, however, had had its origin in Christianity; it was a passion flower rising from the blood of Christ . . . (Heine [1833] 1985: 3)

The romantic school, for Heine, was a secularised form of medieval Christianity, a return to both its themes and its styles. This notion of Romanticism as a secularisation of Christian themes was the subject of a highly acclaimed study by M. H. Abrams, *Natural Super-naturalism*. Although he certainly did not view Romanticism as a degradation, Abrams joins Heine in claiming that the 'characteristic concepts and patterns of Romantic philosophy and literature are a displaced and reconstituted theology' (Abrams 1973b: 65), the theology of Christianity. The specific theological element taken up and secularised by Romanticism is the narrative of a circuitous journey, a *Bildungsreise* (paradise lost and regained, the prodigal son) that attempts to recapture a lost unity or sense of identity. The distinctive contribution of Romanticism is to secularise this notion and make the journey a search for personal – or even social – fulfilment rather than a quest for God. '*Wo gehen wir denn hin?*' Novalis asks in *Heinrich von Ofterdingen* (written in 1799–1800) – 'Where are we going?' '*Immer nach Hause*' – we are always going home, trying to work our way out of our present alienation and return to the comfort and harmony we have lost.

Although Abrams's thesis takes in German Romanticism, its primary object is English Romanticism and so we must briefly consider the historical relationship between the two. There were some channels of influence from Germany to England, particularly in the figure of Samuel Taylor Coleridge, who had been to Germany and studied with Schelling, whom he plagiarised shamelessly in his 1817 *Biographia Literaria*. But Coleridge did not have much success in transmitting his enthusiasm for these ideas: Wordsworth was certainly restrained and once announced, '[I have] never read a word of German metaphysics, thank Heaven!'

(quoted in Abrams 1973b: 278). Byron, for his part, was famously dismissive of the distinction between Romanticism and classicism. Indeed, although there was an early recognition of the novel and distinctive character of the English poets we now know as romantic, it was only much later, in literary histories from the 1860s and 1870s, that the term Romanticism gradually came to be applied to English authors (see Whalley 1972). On the whole, English Romanticism seems to have developed out of largely autonomous, or autochthonous, factors (see Butler 1981).

Why then have we come to classify the Jena and Heidelberg groups under the same heading as the English Lake Poets?[4] Without using the term romantic, Percy Bysshe Shelley wrote that all the major poets derive:

> from the new springs of thought and feeling, which the great events of our age have exposed to view, a similar tone of sentiment, imagery and expression. A certain similarity all the best writers of any particular age inevitably are marked with, from the spirit of that age acting on all. (Shelley [1819] 1964: 2: 127)

Looking beyond the mystification of the notion of a *Zeitgeist*, Shelley cites as a common cause 'the great events of our age'. By this he means, primarily, the French Revolution, which he had called 'the master theme of the epoch in which we live' (Shelley 1964: 1: 504). We will return to the master theme of the Revolution in Section 3, but here we will look more closely at his claim as to its effect, the 'similar tone of sentiment, imagery and expression'.

We have already indicated a candidate notion for a distinctively romantic sentiment, that of a sort of self-conscious nostalgia. Although lacking the element of self-consciousness (a problem we will return to shortly), Abrams's notion of a circular journey is in line with the notion of nostalgia, the expression of a desire to return to our point of origin (in terms of the historical past as well as childhood), tinged heavily with melancholy (Wordsworth writes: 'it is not now as it hath been of yore' in the poem 'Ode: Intimations of Immortality from Recollections of Early Childhood', line 6). It accounts for many of the sentiments indicated by Friedrich Schlegel and now frequently seen as emblematic of Romanticism: a longing for wholeness, a craze for fragments and ruins, the theme of the wanderer, a penchant for millenarian fantasies of founding a 'new Jerusalem' or, in Shelley's case, 'another Athens' (in the poem *Hellas*). A range of romantic literature from Novalis's *Heinrich* to Wordsworth's *Prelude* retraces the clearly and often explicitly lapsarian idea that a prior age, generally identified as classical Greece, had enjoyed a sort of naïve, unreflective unity, a sense of wholeness or belonging that has since been lost. The present age, according to this scheme, is characterised by an overriding sense of alienation, expressed in various dichotomies, between freedom and necessity, subject and object, duty and inclination, mind and nature and so on. A. W. Schlegel announces in his Vienna lectures:

> The Grecian ideal of human nature was perfect unison and proportion between all the powers, – a natural harmony. The moderns, on the contrary, have arrived at the consciousness of an internal discord which renders such an ideal impossible; and hence the endeavour of their poetry is to reconcile these two worlds between which we find ourselves divided and to blend them indissolubly together. (A. W. Schlegel [1808] 1879: 27)

As Schlegel articulates it, the romantic project is to overcome these dichotomies and recover a unity, although hopefully on a higher plane (the fall was a fortunate one). This desire informs a scientific programme as well, as the passage from Schlegel immediately above suggests. German romantic science and *Naturphilosophie* are strongly motivated by a rejection of Enlightenment mechanistic models of nature in favour of organic ones and a wish to re-enchant nature. Hence the interest in alchemy, medieval science and the esoteric doctrines of Jacob Boehme that the universe is driven by opposed forces, polarities of a quasi-sexual nature, which Schelling takes up and systematises in his philosophy of nature. Politically and with respect to the 'great events of the age', this conception of the problem and project of Romanticism can be associated with attitudes towards the French Revolution, which were in general characterised at first by a sense of hope for the establishment of genuinely liberatory social institutions. This then often evolved into a restitutionist longing to refound the institutions (of the Middle Ages, for instance) which made possible certain types of human solidarity (Novalis's 1799 *Christentum oder Europa* is a model of this): for instance, a paternalistic monarchy, chivalric social code and a shared religion. The dream of liberation represents the progressive side of Romanticism and the restitutionist fantasy its reactionary side, but both shared a diagnosis of the present as somehow broken or deficient and a desire or even plan to recreate a sense of past unity that has been lost. This structure is not absent from Marx himself, who for this reason has been considered, in this one aspect at least, romantic.[5]

These romantic themes can be seen throughout the philosophy and literature of the late eighteenth and early nineteenth centuries. In fact, the danger might lie in casting our net a bit too wide: Hegel and Marx both fall into this generic, circular model of alienation/reconciliation. In his *English Fragments* of 1828, Heine himself looks for a New Jerusalem in post-revolutionary Paris. Even Nietzsche has his share of classicist nostalgias and futural longings, as well as a theory of return. These are figures, it must be said, who revile Romanticism and yet Abrams has no trouble absorbing them into his conception of Romanticism which, in fact, he happily extends into the present day. In addition to the question of when Romanticism starts, we have the question of when – or even whether – it ends.

In their seminal text on the Jena romantics, the French philosophers Philippe Lacoue-Labarthe and Jean-Luc Nancy write:

> [W]hat interests us in Romanticism is that we still belong to the era it opened up. The present period continues to deny precisely this belonging, which defines us (despite the inevitable divergence introduced by repetition). A veritable romantic unconscious is discernable today, in most of the central motifs of our 'modernity'. Not the least result of Romanticism's indefinable character is the way it has allowed this so-called modernity to use Romanticism as a foil, without ever recognising – or in order not to recognise – that it has done little more than rehash Romanticism's discoveries. (Lacoue-Labarthe and Nancy 1988: 15)

We cannot recognise Romanticism and cannot have done with it; modernism is an (unconscious) return of Romanticism, which, according to Abrams at least, was already a return of Christian themes and specifically the theme of return. We seem to be in the grip of a genuine repetition compulsion. Abrams is pleased with what he sees as the ubiquity of romantic concerns in modernism – he embraces the romantic project and believes that it represents the best in us. Lacoue-Labarthe and Nancy also see romantic themes in the present, but unlike Abrams they see this as a 'genuine degeneration' – not the best but rather the worst of us. Romanticism is a 'fascination and a temptation' (Lacoue-Labarthe and Nancy 1988: 16) that we have to understand in order to resist.

We have quite a few questions on the table, about the scope, content and even desirability of Romanticism. To begin to address them, we need to look much more critically at the theme of return; specifically, we need to return to the notion of critical self-consciousness that Abrams omitted. We will see that what begins (conceptually) as an already complicatedly self-conscious but clearly empirical conception of nostalgia for a lost past quickly assumes the Kantian character of a return to a transcendental rather than empirical ground. On this account, which will occupy us in Section 2, the past is a cipher for a return to the *subject* as the locus of logical rather than chronological priority in transcendental constitution. This moment of romantic thought elaborates an underlying Kantian framework centred in particular on the concepts of the transcendental imagination and the genius. But as we will see, the Kantianism of the romantics extends further than to an account of the (romantic) subject. The romantics are also *critical* of the epistemic optimism of the classical idealists (Fichte and Hegel) and emphasise instead the extent to which the lost subject to which Romanticism returns is impossible to recover. Finally, we will also consider the extent to which the romantics begin to break apart the notion of the subject of return entirely by exploring other potential transcendental operators that bypass the subject, most notably language.

But however compelling and critical the romantic notions of return might be, it is perhaps odd that this compulsion to return to origins should arise at a historical moment of unprecedented interest in the future, the time of the French Revolution. We will end by suggesting, in Section 3, some points of connection between Romanticism and this master theme.

2. Backwards or Forwards?

2.1 Kant

The concept of return does not necessarily involve going backwards and wanting to retrieve what was past; it can be conservative and melancholic, but it can also be radical and self-critical, an affirmation of distance from the point of departure, or even the discovery of uncanny origins. One cannot simply return to the primitive harmony, as Hölderlin's *Hyperion* testifies. Accordingly, Romanticism is at times radical and at times conservative; it generated (and celebrated) a considerable amount of reactionary nostalgia, but it was also the site for crafting some of the more perceptive tools for taking this nostalgia apart.

In Section 1, we saw that Friedrich Schlegel discovered the nature of Romanticism by looking critically at his own nostalgia for classical antiquity. More strongly, he began to claim that the idea of Greece was patently fantasy construction: 'To believe in the Greeks is only another fashion of the age' he writes in one of his fragments (Schlegel 1970: 201, #277). A.W. Schlegel writes that 'up to now everyone has managed to find in the ancients what he needed or wished for: especially himself' (Schlegel 1970: 181, #151). Romantic nostalgia is not so concerned with the past, its putative object, as it is with itself: the longing for the past becomes a mirror for discovering one's self. We see this in the probable ending of Novalis's unfinished *Novices at Sais* of 1798–9 – a young initiate into the mysteries of Isis tears the veil from the statue of the goddess to achieve enlightenment – and sees only himself. This is the romantic *Weg nach Innen*, the path inward, and the romantics' own consensus as to the essential nature of their own literary ideal, that it was subjective as opposed to classical objectivity. The past (or, in another tendency of Romanticism, the exotic) functions as a self-conscious projection by which the subject comes to understand primarily *itself*.

But we must take this further and conceive the idea of projection transcendentally rather than in terms of empirical psychology. Indeed, the theme of the return to the subject brings Romanticism into close proximity with problems current in the philosophy of the time and specifically with Kant. The first *Critique* is an investigation of how experience is conditioned by structures of subjectivity and how the nature of the subject of experience can only be found through an investigation into the nature of the experience it conditions. 'The conditions of the possibility of experience in general are at the same time conditions of the possibility of the objects of experience', Kant writes (Kant [1781/1787] 1998: A158/ B197) and the nature of subjectivity is essentially bound up with (and discoverable through) the objects it conditions. But Kant famously goes further and finds that the self that is discovered is a peculiarly empty one – a formal category, the condition for unified experience and nothing more. And as we shall see, German Romanticism follows his lead.

We see a related movement in English Romanticism, which has its own thematic of projection and pursues its own *Weg nach Innen*. For instance, Coleridge argues for the essential 'subjectivity' of Shakespeare's works – that the figure of the artist himself is indelibly present in all his language and descriptions. It is not a personal subjectivity that Shakespeare expresses, Coleridge argues, it is an impersonal, quasi-divine subjectivity – but a subjectivity none the less. But more essentially, we see in the texts of English Romanticism nostalgia reaching the point where the object becomes merely a cipher for understanding the subject. There are passages where, as Paul De Man writes, the romantic 'vision almost seems to become a real landscape' (De Man 1984: 7). On the one hand, this pathetic 'fallacy' can be referred to the familiar, reassuring blending of psychology and landscape, or imagination and perception, and can thus be read as a typically romantic attempt to overcome the dichotomy between subjective and objective. But as with German Romanticism, this apparently unsophisticated projective structure is actually self-consciously critical. Poetic language is taking over the landscape, contesting, as De Man puts it, the ontological primacy of the sensible object. Perhaps (as critics have argued with respect to Wordsworth) poetic language even wins this contest and dispenses with the object entirely.[6]

Affinities with Kant are palpable here (we speak of affinities to avoid the difficult question of influence). In the third *Critique*, Kant discusses aesthetic experience as a site for the reconciliation of subject (the faculty of understanding) and object (or at least the intuition of the object). But he conceives of this reconciliation as merely subjective, a feeling rather than an experience. He is particularly insistent that the feeling of the sublime is merely subjective – we cannot discuss sublimity in nature, but only our feelings of sublimity in response to experiences of nature. This theory was of great interest and importance to Coleridge (and, through him, to Wordsworth; see Modiano 1983), who used it to emphasise the subjective character of the distinctively romantic affect.

The romantic tendency to emphasise the subject of creative production is popularly associated with the idea of genius and it is certainly true that romanticism brings in a distinctive conception of the artistic consciousness in particular and the mind in general, a conception that stresses creativity and activity over passivity and receptivity. Romanticism takes seriously the *poesis* of the poem. Wordsworth famously stated in the Preface to the *Lyrical Ballads* (1800) that 'All good poetry is the spontaneous overflow of powerful feelings' (19). This emphasis on the subject of artistic production weakens and even displaces a mimetic conception of art: the work is essentially an expression of artistic powers rather than an image of nature. The mind, accordingly comes to be seen as a lamp – or even fountain, wind-harp or plant – rather than a mirror (see Abrams [1953] 1973a). As we pointed out before, the romantic conception of subjectivity tended to be based on transcendental philosophy rather than empirical psychology and one issue that makes Romanticism the adversary of the Enlightenment is their quite divergent theories of mind. The romantics reject the Lockean notion of a passive mind that receives impressions in favour of a Kantian notion that stresses the spontaneity and creative powers of the understanding and, above all, the imagination.

Kant's notion of the imagination was of inestimable significance for the development of romantic theories of creativity. Of particular importance was the distinction between transcendental and empirical imagination, which Coleridge recast as the distinction between imagination and fancy. Imagination for Coleridge is organic (vital), while fancy is mechanical (a conception derived from eighteenth-century empiricist theories of imagination). Coleridge developed this theory in the context of a critical analysis of Wordsworth, as a way of accounting for Wordsworth's distinctive poetic achievement. Fancy merely reproduces the contents of memory in a variety of different arrangements; the imagination, in contrast, is productive of genuine novelties. As such, it is modelled on divine production: 'The primary imagination I hold . . . as a repetition in the finite mind of the eternal act of creation in the infinite I AM' (Coleridge [1817] 1975: 167). John Keats even stated (with reference to *Paradise Lost*) that: 'The Imagination may be compared to Adam's dream – he awoke and found it truth' (Keats [1817] 2009: 102).

2.2 Hegel

Kant's conception of the transcendental imagination can be and has been pushed in the direction of intellectual intuition, the notion of a creative intelligence whose thoughts are productive of reality. Kant strictly denied that such a faculty was possible for humans: for Kant, our intuition is receptive and not spontaneous. But the idealists found enough encouragement in the critical corpus to resuscitate the (essentially pre-critical, theological) idea. Fichte and the early (romantic) Schelling revised Kant's notion of the transcendental unity of apperception into the transcendental ego, no longer the highest condition of knowledge but in fact its author, wielding intellectual intuitions to generate (in Fichte's case at least) not only the form but also the substance of experience.

The theme of the artist as second creator is expressed here in the idea of the artist as transcendental ego, creating its own little reality through intellectual or (as Schelling often glosses it in his *System of Transcendental Idealism* of 1800) aesthetic intuitions. The operation of this faculty is certainly well described by Keats in the quote above: the contents of Adam's dream becoming reality. As such, the prominence of the figure of the author in Romanticism bears a clear relation to the development of idealist theories of the role of the transcendental ego. This is the basis of Hegel's critique of the Jena romantics in his *Lectures on Fine Art* (delivered in 1820–1). He claims that they elided the figure of the genius/author with that of the transcendental ego, conceiving of the genius as an over-inflated ego, a monster of self-will capable of creating reality as he wishes it to be. This, Hegel believes, accounts for the bizarre dreamscapes of some of the romantic novels and fairytales, the liberties with form and chronology. Most significantly, in Hegel's mind, this explains the romantics' signature device of irony, the effect of mockery and self-distance from a reality that the author knows to be a figment of his caprice.

Hegel's distinctive interpretation of the nature of genius and irony was well suited to the dialectical position that German Romanticism was assigned within his system, as the limit case of the modern emphasis on subjectivity in art, the empowerment of the subject and its divorce from the rapidly atrophying object. But his reading of the romantics was highly misleading. He overemphasised Fichte's influence on the movement, a piece of mischief that it has taken scholars generations to undo. The fact is that the Jena romantics did not share the post-Kantian German idealists' confidence about the attainment of absolute knowledge.[7] Rather, they remained with Kant on what Hegel would call the perspective of reflection and most specifically with respect to what Kant considered limitations to self-knowledge. Their interest in subjectivity did not entail a commitment to the possibility of transparent (or even dialectically mediated) self-cognition. Rather, part of what we might consider the pathos of Romanticism was bound up with the impossibility of just such knowledge, with the rejection of the Cartesian cogito (see Norman 2000; 2007) and hence with the thought that 'the self is no longer the master in its own house', as Manfred Frank puts it (Frank 2004: 173).

Frank has documented how the romantics were in contact with former students of Reinhold, who shared an anti-foundationalist critique of Fichte's system. They were sceptical not only about the epistemic availability of first principles but also about their reality. In place of something like an idealist intellectual intuition or direct positing of the self-identical subject (or subject/object) as an absolute ground, the Jena romantics affirmed the infinite approximation of the ground. Nor was the ground considered real, if elusive. Rather, they considered it something like a Kantian Idea, playing a heuristic or merely regulative role in systematising knowledge. Frank shows that in the absence of philosophical demonstration, Novalis, at least, thought that we needed to assume an inventive attitude towards the ground, treating it as not merely heuristic but down-right fictional (Frank 2004: 51 and 174). Indeed, as Novalis writes: 'if the character of the given problem is irresolution, then we resolve it when portraying its irresolution [as such]' (Novalis 1960–88: 3: 376). It is no wonder that we find Hamlet put forward by the Schlegels as emblematic of modernity.

This marks a subtle but significant distinction between English and German Romanticism – German Romanticism develops its own philosophical path in contrast to post-Kantian idealism. The philosophical basis of German Romanticism is distinct from that of idealism and the two represent competing programmes in the landscape of post-Kantian German philosophy. English Romanticism, in contrast, did not define itself in relation to this idealism and more readily absorbed (or resembled, since questions of influence are difficult here) trends in idealist thought. Accordingly, we do see shades of German idealism in English Romanticism – Byron's narcissism has been rightly considered Fichtean and the idea of the imagination in Coleridge (and, as we saw, Keats) can take on overtones of a Schellingean intellectual intuition. But we should not over-emphasise the philosophical influences on English Romanticism. Its poetic achievements stand on their own and the elements of philosophical scaffolding can be disregarded by readers uninterested in this issue.

German Romanticism is quite different in this regard. It takes a subtle, complicated and significant set of philosophical positions and these are the inspiriting force behind its productions. The theory matters and it matters that their conception of subjectivity is in greater proximity to Kant's notion of the transcendental unity of apperception than it is to Fichte's transcendental ego. Kant's apperceptive unity was hollow, a mere form of subjectivity. So, while Romanticism does involve a return to the subject, this is neither triumphal nor reassuring, not the proper object for a tidy nostalgic fantasy of a comfortable homecoming. Rather, in German Romanticism at least, the subject is often missing, dead, or deeply depressed. Tieck's plays explore what he calls 'the vast emptiness, the terrible chaos' at the heart of the subject (quoted in Lokke 2005: 146). Far from an affirmation of the self-present cogito, his *Weg nach Innen* resembles the path of Freudian psychoanalysis, to a fractured, displaced subject. (Nor was this conception absent from English Romanticism: introspection often reveals demons, as in Coleridge's *Kubla Khan*. Keats too writes that the poet 'has no Identity . . . he has no self': Keats [1818] 2009: 295. We even see this in French romantic poetry, where, as one commentator writes, 'the subject of these works is obsessed by its incompleteness, which takes the specific form of loss': Strauss 2005: 193.)

It is instructive, in this context, to look at how the Jena romantics criticised and appropriated Fichte. We noted earlier that, for Kant, subjectivity is only apparent in the object it conditions: the unity of the subject is only evident in the unity of the object. But the same can be said of literature when the subject *of* a text (that is, the author) is conceived as being merely an object *in* a text. With obvious and explicit reference to the method of Kantian critique, Schlegel sees this as the task of literary criticism. 'The true task and inner essence of criticism', Schlegel wrote in 'On the Essence of Criticism', 'is to characterize' (Schlegel [1804] 1958–: 3: 60) – which means to provide a character sketch of the author, to make the author into a character. But this is a project not only for literature but also for philosophy: criticism of philosophy consists of characterising the philosopher. Indeed, Schlegel has designs on Fichte, as he makes clear:

> [T]o use the jargon that is most usual and appropriate to this kind of conception, [I will] place myself on Fichte's shoulders, just as he placed himself on Reinhold's shoulders, Reinhold on Kant's shoulders, Kant on Leibniz's and so on infinitely back to the prime shoulder. (Schlegel [1797] 1970: 264)

Schlegel intends to criticise Fichte as Fichte criticises Kant and by effecting a similarly transcendental move. Kant showed that experience is in fact conditioned by a set of subjective structures; Fichte showed that the structures were conditioned by a transcendental subject and Schlegel will show that the transcendental subject is conditioned – by Fichte. The *Wissenschaftslehre* is 'as rhetorical as Fichte himself . . . with regard to individuality, it is a Fichtean presentation of the Fichtean spirit in Fichtean letters' (Schlegel 1958–: 18: 33). A double fictionalisation is in effect. The transcendental ego is exposed as a character of Fichte's (an invention, as Novalis had pointed out) and Fichte himself is exposed as 'rhetorical' – becoming, perhaps, a character of Schlegel's.[8] The author is indelibly inscribed within the text.

2.3 Linguistic Turns

The notion of unintended textual consequences is of great importance here. Indeed, if the author is inside the text rather than behind it, we might pose the question of who is in control. One characteristically romantic answer points to the role of the unconscious in textual production. Again the locus for this conception is Kant, who writes:

> [T]he author of a product for which he is indebted to his genius does not know himself how he has come by his ideas; and he has not the power to devise the like at pleasure or in accordance with a plan. (Kant [1790] 1987: 174–6, §46)

In line with this conception, Friedrich Schlegel writes that 'a poem is only a product of nature which wants to become a work of art' (Schlegel [1797] 1970: 145, #21). But the notion of unconscious creation was not a consensus view within Romanticism. A. W. Schlegel, Coleridge and Schelling all emphasise the cooperation of conscious and unconscious productive forces in the creative process. And A. W. Schlegel criticises Kant for not giving more scope to conscious processes in creativity.

However, this notion of conscious control was not necessarily in the service of a theory of the individual artist. In fact, we see in German Romanticism an interesting and subtle set of theories of collective authorship, in which it is not nature but a social collectivity that is the ultimate locus of creativity. Schlegel describes 'antiquity' as a 'genius', the collective author of ancient texts (Schlegel [1797] 1970: 197, #248). Or the productive social collective could be a small community – *The Athenaeum* explored the concept of 'symphilosophy' as a mutual endeavour among a small group of friends, the plan of constituting a secret alliance. Authorship is, on this model, quite strictly a collective act, not an individual one. The idea of the productive social collective could also be used in the service of nationalism, as with the romantic fixation on folk arts, folksong, or even fairy tales, as the collective expression of a people, a *Volk*. (We must note at once that this is not nationalism in a chauvinistic sense – the romantics supported a resurgence of all regional traditions without claiming the superiority of their own – a point on which Herder, for one, sharply criticised the Enlightenment. In this sense, the romantics might be considered the first multiculturalists; see Blechman 1999: 9.)

Schlegel suggests, however, a distinctive response to the question of who is in control of his texts:

> [In my writings] I wanted to demonstrate that words often understand themselves better than do those who use them . . . there must be a connection or some sort of secret brotherhood among philosophical words that, like a host of spirits too soon aroused, bring everything into confusion in their writings and exert the invisible power of the World Spirit on even those who try to deny it . . . (Schlegel 1970: 260)

Language has a mind of its own and will lead the supposed author along lines he or she hardly intended to follow. For instance, Schlegel wrote of Goethe's *Wilhelm Meister* that: 'surprised by the tendency of its genre, the work became suddenly much greater than its first intention' (Schlegel 1958–: 2: 346–7). Here it is the structure of the *genre* that is doing the work: in this case, it is not the unconscious that is in control, but language itself.

Novalis thematised this in an essay called *Monologue*: 'One can only marvel at the ridiculous mistake that people make when they think that they speak for the sake of things. The particular quality of language, the fact that it is concerned only with itself, is known to no one . . .' As the monologue progresses, it becomes progressively self-reflective (or progressively conscious of its inherent self-reflexivity): 'What if I were compelled to speak? What if this urge to speak were the mark of the inspiration of language, the working of language within me? . . . Could this in the end, without my knowing or believing, be poetry?' (Novalis 1997: 83).

This introduces a conception of language as an autonomous and self-expressive rather than representational or communicative structure. We have already seen what De Man describes as the tendency of poetic language to displace the primacy of the object in English Romanticism. In *The Order of Things*, Michel Foucault pinpoints the early nineteenth century as the moment when 'words ceased to intersect with representations and to provide a spontaneous grid for the knowledge of things . . . language may sometimes arise for its own sake in an act of writing that designates nothing other than itself' (Foucault 1970: 304). Wilhelm von Humboldt would write that language is a world of its own, distinct from reality or subjective intention. This conception is a significant factor in the development of modern hermeneutics: if the author is not the ultimate (or even proximate) locus for the intelligibility of the work of art (and neither is nature, as we saw earlier), then a new interpretative science is necessary to tell us what it means. As Friedrich Schlegel writes: 'the question of what the author intends can be settled; not, however, the question of what the work is' (Schlegel 1958–: 18: 318).

It is interesting but somewhat counter-intuitive to regard language as a formal system without reference to anything extrinsic – but it is hardly unusual or startling to say the same thing about music. Music accordingly came to be seen not only as the basis for language (a return to Vico's idea that we sang before we spoke) but also as a model for thought and reason. Schlegel speaks of 'a certain tendency of pure instrumental music toward philosophy' (Schlegel [1797] 1970: 239, #444). And we frequently find in romantic texts language being referred to in musical terms. Music's (previously problematically) non-mimetic character now became its mark of superiority and elevated it to a supreme position in the system of the arts.

In fact romantic music theory typically held that music was the dominant element in song and opera, with the lyrics of songs relegated to the role of merely repeating and embellishing the music. In Schumann's *Lieder* for instance, the piano has an autonomous and in many ways more musically interesting role than the voice (see Rosen 1995: 68). And the idea continues into late Romanticism as well. Nietzsche notes that Schopenhauer's arguments in favour of the priority of music eventually convinced Wagner to put aside his conception of the *Gesamtkunstwerk*, an ideal synthesis of the arts, to give music the lead role. Accordingly, in the (post-Schopenhauerian) Wagnerian music drama, the music speaks an independent and primary language that is only echoed by the speech and action on stage. Wagner's attitude towards this shift in thinking was characteristically romantic too. As he describes it, it was (Nietzsche notwithstanding) factors intrinsic to the music drama itself that brought music to the fore – Schopenhauer's theory was just the outward stimulus forcing him to recognise this ineluctable fact. Thus, Wagner wrote of his earlier theory: 'I didn't dare to say that it was music which produced drama, although inside myself I knew it' (quoted in Magee 1983: 351). We can say of Wagner's *Tristan* what Schlegel said of Goethe's *Meister*, that it was 'surprised by the tendency of its genre'.

It is perhaps surprising for music to be held up as a model for thought precisely because it is devoid of extrinsic meaning. But, to the extent that the romantics embraced the non-referential nature of language, they called for literature to be meaningless. Or rather, as philosophers such as Maurice Blanchot, Foucault, Lacoue-Labarthe and Nancy claim, this conception of the meaninglessness of language – the notion that language is concerned only with itself – marks the beginning of what we know of as literature. We can refer this again to the transcendental function of language.[9] According to an argument familiar to all transcendental philosophers, we cannot describe a transcendental condition in terms of what it conditions (the category of causation cannot itself be involved in a causal sequence, etc.). Consequently, language as a condition for meaning is itself devoid of meaning: the ground for sense must itself be nonsensical. As the philosopher Winfried Menninghaus writes in his study of the romantic fairytale: 'Nonsense is a way in which "the non-hermeneutical" . . . still appears within the horizon of the hermeneutical field' (Menninghaus 1999: 8). The appearance of nonsense in a text, then, fulfils Schlegel's criterion for proper critical philosophy as the intimate unity of a determining structure, in this case language, together with the sense it determines (see Norman 2009).

Accordingly, Novalis calls for

> tales, without logic, nevertheless with associations, like dreams. Poems – simply sounding well and filled with beautiful words – but also without any sense or logic – at most single stanzas intelligible – they must be like mere broken pieces of the most varied things. At best, true poetry can have . . . an indirect effect like music, etc. (Novalis 1960–88: 3: 572)

The romantics were particularly attracted to the genre of the fairy tale, considering it to be a model of meaninglessness in this sense (see Novalis 1960–88: 3: 438, 449; Schlegel 1958–: 16: 475; Menninghaus 1999). They praised its disconnected dream logic, its ability to explore the confusion of liminal states of consciousness. But beyond the fairy tale we see in German romantic literature a persistent valorisation of chaos, confusion, chance and caprice, on the level of language, style and plot. The art of meaninglessness extended to the visual arts, with Constable's landscapes criticised for 'meaning nothing' – having a paucity of reference (quoted in Rosen 1995: 75). The landscape is supposed to speak for itself. Indeed, the romantic playwright Ludwig Tieck formulates his literary ideal in painterly terms, praising paintings that 'delight' solely by their 'dazzling colours without coherence' (quoted in Menninghaus 1999: 37).

2.4 Irony

This is already a form of proto-modernism: we are in the neighbourhood of Archibald MacLeish's modernist dictum from his *Ars Poetica* that 'A poem should not mean / but be' (lines 23–4) – and the transition from narrative painting to pure landscapes to painterly abstraction is a fairly clear one. We will take up the question of the proximity of romantic theory to modernism (and even post-modernism) shortly, but we need to look first at the stylistic device on which the romantics might most reasonably stake their claims to modernity (should they wish to do so): their emblematic trope of irony. While (also characteristically) never defining just what irony is, Friedrich Schlegel wrote in his *Dialogue on Poetry*:

> Every poem should be genuinely romantic and every [poem] should be didactic in that broader sense of the word that designates the tendency toward a deep, infinite meaning. Additionally, we make this demand everywhere, without necessarily using this name. Even in very popular genres – the theater, for example – we demand irony; we demand that the events, the people, in short, the whole game of life actually be taken up and presented as a game as well. (Schlegel 1958–: 2: 323)

Irony persistently blocks the referential function of language (or perhaps demonstrates language at work blocking our attempts to make it referential) – it undermines whatever serious (meaning-bearing) work language is supposed to be doing and turns everything into a game. We see this in many of the literary works of Jena Romanticism: an insistent irony that does not let you forget that the text is fiction. For instance, a character in Brentano's *Godwi* of 1801 tells the narrator: 'there is the pond into which I fall on page 266' (Brentano 1995). In a scene from Tieck's *The World Turned Upside Down* (*Die verkehrte Welt*) of 1798, the character of the innkeeper says:

Few guests stay with me now and, if this keeps up, in the end, I'll just have to take down my sign. – Ah, yes, once things were good: there was scarcely a play then without an inn and its innkeeper. I still can recall the hundreds of plays in which the greatest intrigues were prepared right in this very room . . . (Tieck 1996: I, iv)

The play is taken up and presented as a play and, as with language, refusing to countenance the illusion that it refers to anything beyond itself. Of course this sort of self-referential device is hardly distinctive of the period that we call Romanticism, but one of the ways that the Jena authors are distinguished from earlier models is that, as the critic Peter Szondi notes about Tieck, the *actor* is not 'stepping out of his role' (a standard comic device at least since Aristophanes) – rather, the *character* is asserting its self-consciousness as a character (Szondi 1986: 72). The character knows itself as such – it becomes self-conscious of its fictional status.

This in fact brings us to the heart of the German romantic philosophy of literature: the idea of a literature that contains a moment of critical self-consciousness. Schlegel famously writes, the 'theory of the novel would itself have to be a novel' (Schlegel 1958–: 2: 337). Like Tieck's innkeeper, the novel will know itself as such and reflect on what it can and should be as a work of art. The fairy tale reveals its own meaning as nonsense, the naked presence of language working its perverse arabesque. Moreover, this points back to the romantic 'death of the author' as discussed earlier – the work is spawning its own intrinsic level of theory (this is precisely the 'tendency' of the novelistic genre that took Goethe by surprise). In this sense, the work even can do without the author – although the properly 'characterised' author could always join the fun within the text itself (as in the romantic's beloved *Tristram Shandy*).

2.5 Some Recent Appropriations

Needless to say, twentieth-century philosophers have found the romantic conceptions of language and literature both prescient and congenial to their own ideas. De Man writes:

There is a machine there, a text machine, an implacable determination and a total arbitrariness, *unbedingter Willkür* . . . which inhabits words on the level of the play of the signifier, which undoes any narrative consistency of lines and which undoes the reflexive and the dialectical model, both of which are, as you know, the basis of any narration . . . (De Man 1996: 181)

According to De Man, romantic wordplay (and in particular irony) play a deconstructive role, undermining any consistent narrative. Deconstructive critics like to cite Friedrich Schlegel's famous adage: 'it is equally fatal for the mind to have a system and to have none. It will simply have to combine the two' (Schlegel 1970: 167, #53). Although deconstructive readings usefully foreground the notion of language as a transcendental operator, it would be misleading to push Romanticism too far in this direction: Romanticism had an expansive tendency and a creative optimism foreign to deconstruction. The romantics were concerned not with what they were tearing down but with what they were building up, their projects and poetry. The romantics refer texts to the conditions of their possibility by characterising the author, letting language come to the fore and so on, but this is no deflationary technique. They did not dwell on the simultaneous inevitability and impossibility of the traditional narrative form. They wanted to explore alternatives: to write fairy tales and poetry and play with their 'dazzling colours'.

It remains the case, however, as the deconstructive critic will be quick to point out, that the Jena romantics generally failed to do so, often quite spectacularly. Most of their works remained fragmentary. Intentionally or not, their projects were never completed and many of them even died young; all in all, they left an infamous legacy of the partial and incomplete. Maurice Blanchot takes up this theme and suggests that perhaps Romanticism isn't simply unfulfilled, but rather introduces a new mode of fulfilment: 'the works' power to be and no longer to represent . . .' (Blanchot 1993: 353). The project of Romanticism, for Blanchot, is pure self-assertion, a pure act of self-conscious declaration of independence of literature, the 'theoretical wing of the French Revolution'. Blanchot writes:

> [T]o write is to make (of) speech a work, but that this work is an unworking . . . to speak poetically is to make possible a non-transitive speech whose task is not to say things (not to disappear in what it signifies), but to say (itself) in letting (itself) say . . . (Blanchot 1993: 357)

In other words and strictly in keeping with themes that we have discussed above, language is the subject and language is in control. It does not speak for the sake of anything but itself. Blanchot considers this 'the work of the absence of (the) work; a poetry affirmed in the purity of the poetic act . . . ' (Blanchot 1993: 353) The presentation of language itself and by itself is the revelation of the now rather impersonal act of *poesis* and all this abstracted from content or meaning. Again, we return to the theme: Romanticism is the presentation of transcendental subjectivity and nothing other than this presentation, according to Blanchot, but the subject is simply language itself.

3. Revolutions

The notion of the literary text which the romantics developed appears remarkably self-absorbed and does not seem to leave much room or role for an audience or readership. And in fact we see in many romantic pronouncements a mixture of indifference and contempt for the audience, or at least a sense that it is superfluous, as J. S. Mill wrote: 'All poetry is of the nature of soliloquy' (Mill [1833] 1897: 205). And Keats declared his independence too: 'I never wrote one single Line of Poetry with the least Shadow of public thought' (Keats [1818] 2009: 138).

In fact, the late eighteenth and early nineteenth century are marked by a dramatic change in the nature and significance of the audience for the arts. This is perhaps most striking in the case of music, where the system of patronage (by the Church or court) was coming to an end; musicians were left to compose for a much more impersonal public. But the same transition was taking place in all the arts, where the growing importance of the marketplace was helping to create a new social role for artists and intellectuals as salesmen for their manuscripts, paintings and compositions (see Löwy and Sayre 2001: 48). This change in social function was registered in the art itself, as the artist became much more lonely and isolated a figure. One historian writes of British Romanticism that

> the new conditions, an art marketed rather than an art commissioned, also imposed upon the artist-intellectual the symptoms of disorientation. The necessity to communicate with a large public to which no individual could relate created large problems, of form and tone, and also imposed peculiar strains such as alienation and 'modern literary *Angst*'. (Butler 1981: 71)

But the situation in Germany at the end of the eighteenth century was even more problematic, because the reading public barely existed. The narrow size of even the potential pool of readers was further reduced because the German aristocracy still preferred to read French writers – the market for German books was perhaps a twelfth the size of that for books in French (Brunschwig 1974: 140). Whether or not the romantic authors desired an audience, they did not have one.

But the romantic malaise went deeper than this. As one historian writes about the situation in late eighteenth-century Prussia:

> Thus, wherever he turns, the middle-class young man graduating from the university cannot find what he is seeking. He cannot always make a career in the civil service; and the state of society is not such as to enable him to earn a living purely as an intellectual. The consequence is that the ranks of the dissatisfied swell; petty officials, theological candidates, tutors, briefless barristers, doctors with no practice and writers with no readers come to the bitter conclusion that society has not furnished them with a place worthy of their deserts. (Brunschwig 1974: 146)

So the romantics had no effective outlet for their ambitions. This suggests a new angle on Romanticism, as a sort of *ressentiment* (or, minimally, frustration) in the face of an unpropitious social situation. No less an expert than the French romantic Chateaubriand claims that the ideas characteristic of Romanticism derive from the 'irritation of the stifled passions fermenting all together'. As he writes: 'our imagination is rich, abundant and full of wonders; but our existence is poor, insipid and destitute of charms' (Chateaubriand [1802] 1856: 296–7). Nor have critics hesitated to link these stifled passions to feelings about the French Revolution. Political conditions in England and Germany were simply not favourable to revolution; for instance, there was no unified polity in Germany. Reinhold, accordingly, commented that: 'Germany, of all European countries, is most inclined to revolutions of the spirit, least inclined to political revolutions' (quoted in Abrams 1973: 349). Henri Brunschwig reconstructs Reinhold's observation according to the logic of *ressentiment*: 'Excluded from active life much against their will, [the romantics] take refuge in literature' (Brunschwig 1974: 163) – and even there they are denied a means of effective expression. Romanticism on this reading is the privatisation of revolution, an involuntary retreat into a dream of illusory self-realisation after the possibility of real transformation has been rendered impossible.

The diagnosis of Romanticism as *ressentiment* was taken up, perhaps most famously, by Nietzsche. He echoed Goethe in declaring that Romanticism was 'sick', in contrast with 'healthy' classicism (although Goethe was thinking about French Romanticism). What Nietzsche had in mind was that the lack of rigour and resolution in Romanticism – the sentimentality and appeal to affect – had an attraction for and affinity with bodies in a state of decline or decadence. Not being capable of acts of genuine strength and intellectual rigour, romantics valorise inaction and fuzzy-headed sentiment.

The romantics make no secret of their interest in and (at least initially) sympathy for the French Revolution, 'the master theme of the epoch in which we live', as we have seen Shelley say. Wordsworth had wanted to lead the Girondin faction in Paris in 1792 and harboured explicitly revolutionary goals for poetry (Hindle 1999: 69); and, although only Caroline Schlegel among the Germans was directly involved in revolutionary political activities, the Early German Romantics embraced a republican ideal and wanted to radically rethink literary conventions and social norms – the role of the author and the status of women. Nor did the romantics hesitate to connect and compare their ideas with the great events in Paris. Hazlitt writes of the Lake Poets:

> [T]his school of poetry had its origin in the French Revolution, or rather in those sentiments and opinions which produced that revolution; and which sentiments and opinions were indirectly imported into this country in translations from the German about that period. (Hazlitt [1818] 1970: 215)[10]

For his part, Friedrich Schlegel famously declares that the three 'tendencies' of the age are Fichte, the French Revolution and Goethe and continues:

> Whoever is offended by this juxtaposition, whoever cannot take any revolution seriously that isn't noisy and materialistic, hasn't yet achieved a lofty, broad perspective on the history of mankind. Even in our shabby histories of civilization . . . many a little book, almost unnoticed by the noisy rabble at the time, plays a greater role than anything they did. (Schlegel [1797] 1970: 190, #216)

So books, even if they are unnoticed when written, can be more important than revolutionary deeds. German idealism took this notion as central, as we clearly see from the elevated historical role Hegel gives to philosophy, in addition to Schelling's pronouncements on the subject in 1804:

> The golden age . . . is to be sought, not by an endless and restless progress and external activity, but rather by a return to that point from which each of us has set out – to the inner identity with the Absolute . . . This will not be a gradual progress, it will be the true revolution, the idea of which is utterly different from that which has been called by that name. (Schelling 1856–61: 6: 564)

Again, the true revolution will be in ideas and not deeds.

This certainly elevates the role of intellectuals – or perhaps radically overestimates it, according to Marx, now very distant from Romanticism when he insists in the *German Ideology* that 'liberation is a historical and not a mental act' (Marx and Engels 1976: 44). There is, of course, no reason (even on Marx's terms) why it cannot be both, but there is still a question of priority and the passages above establish pretty clearly where the romantics stand. Jerome McGann comments critically on this notion in his seminal study *The Romantic Ideology*:

> The idea that poetry, or even consciousness, can set one free of the ruins of history and culture is the grand illusion of every Romantic poet. This idea continues as one of the most important shibboleths of our culture, especially – and naturally – at its higher levels. (McGann 1983: 91)

We are back to the theme of Romanticism as a spectre haunting our modern consciousness. According to McGann, we are still in Romanticism's trap, to the extent that we believe in the transformative power of consciousness and locate solutions to human problems in a realm of ideas.

McGann's position is a helpful corrective to a tendency in some of the scholarship to accept the romantics' own insistent self-mythologising. But at the same time it is too facile to dismiss Romanticism as ideological. Culture might be ideology, but it is not *merely* ideology.[11] So what are we to do? One approach is to understand the material factors as such as distinct from Romanticism proper; they have an impact, but only insofar as they are taken up by the movement (and this taking up can be in the manner of repression). The French Revolution can and did occasion a wildly disparate set of responses and so cannot be considered to play any decisive role in determining the specific and interesting nexus of ideas and impulses that we know as Romanticism. Moreover, the changing social relations of patronage and the lack of an audience cannot be said to determine the existence or nature of Romanticism. Rather, these factors are occasions – they open up the space – for a new intellectual and artistic relationship between the writer and the public. So there are more nuanced ways of viewing the relation between romantic culture and its material base than simply one of ideology. Nor do we need to accept McGann's contention about the ideological function of romantic thought. Rather than viewing the dominant impulse of Romanticism as an impotent retreat from active life into the narcissism of interiority, we might, perhaps, view it rather as a productive and inventive set of protests against the depredations of an increasingly alienating society. The nostalgia for homecoming and wholeness, the project of re-enchantment, imply (at the very least) a criticism of a reality that is alienating. The romantic resistance was not necessarily of an exclusively progressive nature – Romanticism has reactionary impulses as well, looking to the Middle Ages as much as (if not more than) to the future for signs of how to solve the problems of the present, the increasingly apparent horrors of capitalist modernity.[12] But much more radically, as we have been arguing throughout this paper, romantic nostalgia is no simple escapism, but is in fact highly complicated and self-critical. It is a call to self-examination and the self that is discovered – when one is discovered – is hardly reassuring. More likely it is ironic, decentred, impersonal, transcendentally inaccessible, a conclusion that under-mines any reassuring ideology of the well-centred individual as a subjective locus of control. Romanticism often refuses to portray a fantastic solution to alienation because it refuses to portray any solution at all. Marx, at times, seems more utopian than Schlegel.

Whether or not our modernity is recognisably romantic, we undeniably are still working through a set of problems that Romanticism was the first to raise – not least the identity of Romanticism itself. Perhaps Lacoue-Labarthe and Nancy were right to say: '[L]iterature, as its own infinite questioning and as the perpetual positing of its own question, dates from Romanticism and as Romanticism. And therefore . . . the romantic question, the question of Romanticism, does not and cannot have an answer' (Lacoue-Labarthe and Nancy 1988: 83). But Schlegel, characteristically, merely deferred the moment of truth: designating his age not the Age of Romanticism but rather the 'Age of Tendencies', he wrote:

> As to whether or not I am of the opinion that all these tendencies are going to be corrected and resolved by me, or maybe by my brother or by Tieck, or by someone else from our group, or only some son of ours, or grandson, great-grandson, grandson twenty-seven times removed, or only at the last judgment, or never: that I leave to the wisdom of the reader, to whom this question really belongs. (Schlegel 1970: 264)

And it still does.

Notes

1. Lovejoy doesn't reject the term completely; he pluralises it and urges us to recognise the existence of multiple romantic movements.

2. Michael Ferber (2005: 6) usefully summarises the history of lists of characteristics proposed for a definition of Romanticism.

3. When applicable, references to Schlegel include fragment number (indicated #) after page number.

4. The Lake Poets (Wordsworth, Coleridge and Robert Southey) were first identified as a group in a vituperative context as well, by a contemporary critic, Francis Jeffrey, who branded them revolutionary dissidents (for discussion, see Hindle 1999: 66).

5. Marx relies theoretically both on a contrast with the medieval era (in which exploitation is present but directly visible) and with a notional era of primitive communism. See Löwy and Sayre 2001: 95; Welchman 1995.

6. See, for instance, Michael Riffaterre's analysis of Wordsworth's *Yew-trees* (Riffaterre 1981).

7. However, see Dalia Nassar's contribution in Chapter 2, for an alternative reading of the relationship which emphasises the continuity between Romanticism and idealism.

8. O'Brien sees the *Fichte-Studien* as the 'decisive point . . . in the history of German Romanticism: the point at which Romanticism turns away from idealistic philosophy, or more precisely, turns back upon it in order to analyze it as language and ultimately, as a fiction' (O'Brien 1995: 78).

9. This is in line with the ideas of the *Sturm und Drang* philosopher Johann Georg Hamann (considered by Isaiah Berlin to be the progenitor of German Romanticism: Berlin 2000). Hamann had already attempted a linguistic interpretation of Kant, considering the categories of the understanding from Kant's first *Critique* to be essentially categories of language.

10. Indeed, this is a leading and perhaps one of the more plausible theories of the unity of Romanticism: it is not the case the Germany spread its theories abroad (a theory that has little empirical support) but rather that comparable social conditions in different countries (and specifically comparable responses to the French Revolution) produced a similar sort of literature. See Butler 1981: 74.

11. Recent scholarship has challenged McGann's thesis; see Malpas 2000.

12. Löwy and Sayre (2001) argue that Romanticism is essentially a critique of capitalism.

References

Abrams, Meyer H. ([1953] 1973a), *The Mirror and the Lamp*, Oxford: Oxford University Press.

Abrams, Meyer H. (1973b), *Natural Supernaturalism*, New York: Norton.

Berlin, Isaiah (2000), *Three Critics of the Enlightenment: Vico, Hamann, Herder*, Princeton: Princeton University Press.

Blanchot, Maurice (1993), *The Infinite Conversation*, trans. Susan Hanson, Minneapolis, MN: University of Minnesota Press.

Blechman, Max (1999), 'The revolutionary dream of early German Romanticism', in Max Blechman (ed.), *Revolutionary Romanticism*, San Francisco: City Lights Books, pp. 1–34.

Brentano, Clemens (1995), *Godwi oder Das steinerne Bild der Mutter*, ed. Ernst Behler, Stuttgart: Reclam.

Brunschwig, Henri (1974), *Enlightenment and Romanticism in Eighteenth Century Prussia*, trans. Frank Jellinek, Chicago: University of Chicago Press.

Butler, Marilyn (1981), *Romantics, Rebels and Reactionaries: English Literature and Its Background 1760–1830*, Oxford: Oxford University Press.

Chateaubriand, François Reneé, Vicomte de (1856), *The Genius of Christianity*, trans. Charles I. White, Baltimore: John Murphy & Co.

Coleridge, Samuel Taylor [1817] (1975), *Biographia Literaria*, ed. George Watson, New York: Dent.

De Man, Paul (1984), *The Rhetoric of Romanticism*, New York: Columbia University Press.

De Man, Paul (1996), 'The concept of irony', in Paul De Man, *Aesthetic Ideology*, ed. Andrzej Warminski, Minneapolis: University of Minnesota Press, pp. 163–84.

Eichner, Hans (1972), 'Germany/Romantisch – Romantik – Romantiker', in Hans Eichner (ed.), *'Romantic' and Its Cognates*, Toronto: University of Toronto Press, pp. 98–156.

Ferber, Michael (2005), 'Introduction', in Michael Ferber (ed.), *A Companion to European Romanticism*, Oxford: Blackwell, pp. 1–9.

Foucault, Michel (1970), *The Order of Things: An Archaeology of the Human Sciences*, trans. Alan Sheridan, London: Tavistock.

Frank, Manfred (2004), *The Philosophical Foundations of Early German Romanticism*, trans. Elizabeth Millán-Zaibert, Albany, NY: SUNY Press.

Goethe, Johann Wolfgang von [1836] (1984), *Conversations with Eckermann: 1823–1832*, trans. John Oxenford, San Francisco: North Point Press.

Hazlitt, William (1970), 'Lectures on the English Poets', in *William Hazlitt: Selected Writings*, ed. Ronald Blythe, Harmondsworth: Penguin.

Heine, Heinrich [1833] (1985), 'The Romantic School', trans. Helen Mustard, in Jost Hermand and Robert C. Holub (eds), *The Romantic School and Other Essays*, New York: Continuum, pp. 1–127.

Hindle, Maurice (1999), 'Revolting language: British romantics in an age of revolution', in Max Blechman (ed.), *Revolutionary Romanticism*, San Francisco: City Lights Books, pp. 65–82.

Kant, Immanuel [1790] (1987), *Critique of Judgment*, trans. Werner S. Pluhar, Indianapolis: Hackett.

Kant, Immanuel [1781/1787] (1998), *Critique of Pure Reason*, ed. and trans. Paul Guyer and Allen W. Wood, Cambridge: Cambridge University Press.

Keats, John (2009), *Keats's Poetry and Prose*, ed. Jeffrey N. Cox, New York: Norton.

Lacoue-Labarthe, Philippe and Jean-Luc Nancy (1988), *The Literary Absolute*, trans. Philip Barnard and Cheryl Lester, Albany, NY: SUNY Press.

Lokke, Kari (2005), 'The romantic fairy tale', in Michael Ferber (ed.), *A Companion to European Romanticism*, Oxford: Blackwell, pp. 138–56.

Lovejoy, Arthur (1948), *Essays in the History of Ideas*, Baltimore: Johns Hopkins University Press.

Löwy, Michael, and Robert Sayre (2001), *Romanticism against the Tide of Modernity*, trans. Catherine Porter, Durham, NC: Duke University Press.

McGann, Jerome J. (1983), *Romantic Ideology: A Critical Conversation*, Chicago: University of Chicago Press.

Magee, Bryan (1983), *The Philosophy of Schopenhauer*, Oxford: Oxford University Press.

Malpas, Simon (2000), 'In what sense "communis"? Kantian aesthetics and romantic ideology', *Romanticism on the Net*, 17 <http://users.ox.ac.uk/~scat0385/17kant.html>

Marx, Karl, and Friedrick Engels (1976), *The German Ideology*, trans. W. Lough, in Karl Marx and Friedrick Engels, *Collected Works*, vol. 5, London: Lawrence and Wishart.

Menninghaus, Winfried (1999), *In Praise of Nonsense: Kant and Bluebeard*, trans. Henry Pickford, Stanford, CA: Stanford University Press.

Mill, John Stuart (1897), 'What is Poetry?', in *Early Essays of John Stuart Mill*, ed. J. W. M. Gibbs, London: Bell.

Modiano, Raimonda (1983), 'The Kantian seduction: Wordsworth on the Sublime', in Theodore G. Gish and Sandra G. Frieden (eds), *Deutsche Romantik and English Romanticism*, Munich: Fink, pp. 17–26.

Musset, Alfred de (1908), *The Complete Writings of Alfred de Musset: A Medley of Literature and Criticism*, trans. Mary Artois, privately printed in New York.

Norman, Judith (2000), 'Squaring the romantic circle: Hegel's critique of Schlegel's theories of art', in William Maker (ed.), *Hegel and Aesthetics*, Albany, NY: SUNY Press, pp. 131–44.

Norman, Judith (2007), 'Hegel and the German romantics', in Stephen Houlgate (ed.), *Hegel and the Arts*, Evanston, IL: Northwestern University Press, pp. 310–36.

Norman, Judith (2009), 'The work of art in German Romanticism', in *Internationales Jahrbuch des Deutschen Idealismus 6, Romantik/Romanticism*, ed. Karl Ameriks, Berlin: De Gruyter, pp. 59–79.

Novalis (Friedrich von Hardenberg) (1960–88), *Novalis Schriften*, ed. Richard Samuel et al., Stuttgart: Kohlhammer.

Novalis (Friedrich von Hardenberg) (1997), *Novalis: Philosophical Writings*, ed. and trans. Margaret Mahonie Stoljar, Albany, NY: SUNY Press.

O'Brien, William Arctander (1995), *Novalis: Signs of Revolution*, Durham, NC: Duke University Press.

Riffaterre, Michael (1981), 'Interpretation and descriptive poetry: A reading of Wordsworth's "Yew Trees"', in Robert Young (ed.), *Untying the Text: A Post-Structuralist Reader*, New York: Routledge, pp. 103–32.

Rosen, Charles (1995), *The Romantic Generation*, Cambridge, MA: Harvard University Press.

Schelling, Friedrich Wilhelm Joseph von (1856–61), *Sämmtliche Werke*, ed. Karl Friedrich August Schelling, 14 vols, Stuttgart: Cotta.

Schlegel, August Wilhelm ([1808] 1879), *Lectures on Dramatic Art and Literature*, trans. John Black, London: George Bell and Sons.

Schlegel, Friedrich (1958–), *Kritische Friedrich Schlegel Ausgabe*, ed. Ernst Behler, Jean Jacques Anstett and Hans Eichner, 35 vols, Paderborn: Schöningh.

Schlegel, Friedrich (1970), *Friedrich Schlegel's* Lucinde *and the Fragments*, trans. and ed. Peter Firchow, Minneapolis, MN: University of Minnesota Press.

Schlegel, Friedrich [1797] (2001), *On the Study of Greek Poetry*, trans. Stuart Barnett, Albany, NY: SUNY Press.

Shelley, Percy Bysshe (1964), *The Letters of Percy Bysshe Shelley*, 2 vols, ed. Frederick L. Jones, Oxford: Clarendon Press.

Strauss, Jonathan (2005), 'The poetry of loss: Lamartine, Musset, and Nerval', in Michael Ferber (ed.), *A Companion to European Romanticism*, Oxford: Blackwell, pp. 192–207.

Szondi, Peter (1986), *On Textual Understanding and Other Essays*, trans. Harvey Mendelsohn, Minneapolis, MN: University of Minnesota Press.

Tieck, Ludwig (1996), *Die verkehrte Welt: Ein historisches Schauspiel in fünf Aufzügen*, Stuttgart: Reclam.

Welchman, Alistair (1995), '"Wild above rule or art": Creation and critique', PhD Dissertation, University of Warwick.

Wellek, René (1963), *Concepts of Criticism*, New Haven, CT: Yale University Press.

Whalley, George (1972), 'England/romantic–Romanticism', in Hans Eichner (ed.), *'Romantic' and Its Cognates*, Toronto: University of Toronto Press, pp. 157–262.

4

The Hermeneutic Turn in Philosophy of Nature in the Nineteenth Century

Philippe Huneman

1. Introduction

In the nineteenth century the natural sciences underwent a radical transformation. The paradigms of many of the disciplines that we know today, such as geology, chemistry, thermodynamics, cell biology or evolutionary biology, were established in this period. Prior to this period, knowledge of nature was a part of philosophy, as the examples of Leibniz or Descartes show. Moreover, the Kantian critique of metaphysics from the *Critique of Pure Reason* onwards had a profound impact on philosophers, especially in Germany. Kant dismissed the traditional objects of philosophical inquiry such as God, the world and the soul, which for Kant were to be replaced by reason's investigation of our faculty of knowledge and its limits. Philosophical discourse about nature therefore had to take a different form to the classical and Enlightenment 'natural philosophy' of which figures such as Galileo were practitioners.

Amongst post-Kantian philosophers, Schelling, at the beginning of the nineteenth century, developed a theory of nature called *Naturphilosophie* which had an important influence upon his contemporaries. At the same time Schelling systematised inspirations from thinkers and scientists like Goethe and Herder, who had already called for a novel philosophical reappraisal of nature shaped by artistic values. Followers of *Naturphilosophie* such as Lorenz Oken and Henrik Steffens and critics such as Hegel agreed on the necessity of rethinking the philosophy of nature. These developments and debates were harshly criticised by the scientific materialists whose approach became dominant in the second part of the century. Nonetheless, the whole movement of philosophy of nature proved important for the emergence of radically new ways of philosophising about nature.

After 1830, many scientists came to think that *Naturphilosophie* and philosophy of nature in general were irrelevant programmes compared to the sciences. However, the very idea of a philosophy of nature is, as I will argue, clearly related to the new status that the natural sciences gained in this period. The present chapter will show how a particular philosophical project was embedded in the approaches to nature adopted by otherwise disparate authors such as Schelling, Schopenhauer, Nietzsche and Henry David Thoreau. Section 2 traces the conceptual conditions of this project by pointing out how it became possible within the new epistemological structure within which modern science was produced and which was reflected by Kant's critique. Section 3 characterises the aim and method of the project as a hermeneutic one. Section 4 describes the relationship of this project to the natural sciences. Section 5 considers some of the main themes that this project introduced into the modern philosophical agenda. Section 6 sketches how the project impinged upon later philosophical views of nature.

2. From Natural Philosophy to the Natural Sciences

For Leibniz, there was a continuum between logic, the sciences and theology. He stated that metaphysics, logic and theology were the same thing. Metaphysics uncovers the elementary essences of which everything in the possible worlds is constituted; logic studies the connections between these essences; and theology understands the connections between the divine understanding and the divine will that, by computing the optimal quantity of reality in the range of possible worlds, chose which possible world came into existence (Leibniz [1696] 1978: 86). God's existence itself is proven through logic by an analysis of the elementary essences and the requirements for their combination. The actual world can be known though empirical investigation, although an infinite understanding would see how the empirical determinations of things instantiate a priori determinations. The truth of scientific investigation rests on metaphysical a priori truths, which in the last instance are grounded in the existence of God – since his calculus is the ultimate reason why this world exists rather than another one and hence why there are the laws of nature proper to our world. Theology, investigation of nature and logic as the grammar of essences instantiated in nature are therefore continuously related; and mathematics, as grounded in logic (for Leibniz) is the natural language for these investigations of nature. Philosophy is one single discourse: theology when applied to God; metaphysics or logic when applied to the possible worlds or the very general determinations of the actual world and the reasons for them; and natural philosophy, or natural history, when inquiring into the laws and details of this world. In the general economy of classical knowledge about nature as it is reflected in Leibniz's major philosophical synthesis, natural philosophy tries to explain by seeking general laws, while natural history classifies the species to be found in nature.[1]

Leibnizian doctrine is an easy way to describe the continuity between natural history, natural philosophy and natural theology. The notion of *mathesis*, clearly dominant in how philosophers from the seventeenth and early eighteenth century talked about science, embodies this structure of continuity: *mathesis* is a way of organising knowledge that pervades all regions of nature and uses mathematics, or at least elementary logic. The main assumption of the project of a *mathesis universalis* is that the same logic underlies all sectors of knowledge. And this is ultimately grounded on metaphysical assumptions about the foundation of all laws of nature resting in God's divine understanding, this understanding being ruled by logic (Rescher 1981). Leibniz was the most prolific contributor to the idea of *mathesis universalis* (Belaval 1978). Interestingly, this idea disappears in nineteenth-century philosophy: this disappearance signals a change in the regime of science. Natural *philosophy* (singular) is replaced by natural *sciences* (plural) and the plurality of the latter makes it problematic to assume a *mathesis*.

This is not to say that all pre-nineteenth-century natural philosophers were Leibnizian – clearly not, but Leibniz gives the clearest expression of a structure of knowledge pervasive until the 1800s. Natural philosophy was the quest for laws and natural history was the description of essences instantiated by the species and genera of natural things (biological and mineral alike). Both could ultimately prove the existence of God because they displayed perfection in nature. Both assumed that fundamental connections – between substances and properties or between causes and effects – were grounded in the system of essences in some transcendent existence. When Hume elaborated his devastating critique of natural religion in the *Dialogues Concerning Natural Religion*, posthumously published in 1779, he assumed that this view of nature and investigation was taken for granted by his contemporaries. What is crucial is the connection between *mathesis* as a structure of knowledge, metaphysics as investigation of its foundations and theology as the place of the ultimate a priori warrants of knowledge. This connection organises the solidarity between natural philosophy, natural history and natural theology, in the context of which controversies about the natural sciences during the classical age and the Enlightenment took place.

Kant's work does not share this structure and was decisive in changing it. In particular, the meaning of the 'a priori' changed in his philosophy (Strawson [1966] 1995; Allison 2003). For Kant this refers no longer to God but rather to the very possibility of experience, which is called the 'transcendental' domain. Kantian criticism was decisive at two levels. First, the *Critique of Pure Reason* disconnected knowledge of nature from knowledge of theology, since the a priori warrants of knowledge were no longer to be found in an infinite understanding. No infinite understanding can contain essences, because any thought of essence, as far as it is thought by us, is related to our finite thinking. In our cognitive faculty concepts and intuition are separated and this constitution of ours is a contingent fact (since another kind of cognitive faculty is conceivable; see Lebrun 1970). Moreover, in the Dialectic of the *Critique of Pure Reason* Kant's three critiques of the three proofs of God's existence broke the continuity between natural philosophy and natural theology. Nature does not lead to God. On a second level, a pervasive distinction runs through Kant's work between *nature*, as the set of objects ruled by the transcendental principles of possible experience (see Kant [1783] 1997: 47) and the *order of nature*, a system of (mostly) empirical laws that regulate nature and which is not given by the transcendental principles. The third *Critique*, the *Critique of Judgement* of 1790, is devoted to the idea of order, in general in the whole of nature and in particular within those ordered entities that are organisms. Kant argued that the knowledge of order in nature does not lead to any transcendent warrant and is not grounded on one.

More precisely, the traditional architecture of discourses was defeated by a major criticism, the rejection of an *economy of nature*. The Linnaean school plainly expressed the conviction, pervasive throughout the whole of seventeenth- and eighteenth-century natural history, that in nature any organism and any species has a role and contributes to the wellbeing of the whole (see Linnaeus [1748] 1972). Criticising the idea of relative purposiveness, Kant destroyed the metaphysical basis of this conviction. From Kant onwards, purposiveness came to mean only and principally internal purposiveness; it concerned wholes and parts within an organism (Kant [1790] 1987: 244–7, §63). No one can say that plants are there to serve herbivores: organic creatures serve no function in relation to one another. Function and adaptation, as teleological concepts, are an internal matter and do not allow us to deduce any divinely grounded economy of nature. Defining natural purposes, Kant shifts from the vocabulary of means/ends to the lexicon of wholes/parts. This shift indicates his essential departure from the traditional metaphysics of purposiveness. It does so because he no longer assumes that utility is the *primary* meaning of purposiveness and that human technological practice (adjusting means and ends) provides its principal measure (Huneman 2007b).[2]

Kant thus neutralises the ontological use that was made of the concept of economy of nature by traditional natural historians such as Linnaeus. In the structure sketched above linking natural history and natural philosophy with theology, organisms were the nodal point because their manifest design (which proved God's existence) was such because it fulfilled its role in the economy of nature (which also proved God's existence). Physiology, natural history and theology were thus tightly linked through this idea of purposiveness as utility and design, which the third *Critique* deconstructed.

This Kantian breakthrough was not universally accepted, but it coheres with the change from the triad natural philosophy/natural history/natural theology to the modern framework of the natural sciences. This change had many causes, of course, and Kant's philosophy both reflected and contributed to the change. Arguably, a major factor in this emergence of the plurality of natural sciences was the rise of biology as an autonomous science in the second half of the eighteenth century, on the basis of advances in physiology (for example, Albrecht von Haller, the Montpellier vitalists: see Rey 1987; Wolfe 2008), embryology (for example, Wolff's treatises: see Wolff [1764] 1966) and comparative anatomy (see: Coleman 1979; Barsanti 1995; McLaughlin 2002; Huneman 2008). Kant's assessment of biology in the third *Critique* intrinsically concerned this epistemological transformation. Accordingly, we notice that within science the refutation of relative purposiveness took place simultaneously. In his comparative anatomy, Cuvier (1801) expressed the idea that adaptation is a matter of internal relationships between parts of an organism allowing the entity to survive in its environment. But this organism does not accomplish any role defined previously by God in the whole of nature. In his morphology, Goethe too expresses the same idea, saying that no one could tell that the fish is made for water (Goethe [1790] 1995: 54–5).

In his Preface to his *Metaphysical Foundations of Natural Science*, published in 1786, Kant claims that nothing can count as science unless it is grounded on a priori principles and stated in mathematical language. Few sciences correspond to Kant's requirements and in the nineteenth century most scientific breakthroughs – cell theory, evolutionary theory or thermodynamics, for example – were not scientific in his sense. But, plausibly, we cannot understand Kant's own interest in the life sciences unless we assume that 'science' had several meanings for Kant, which are not wholly exhausted by the *Metaphysical Foundations*. These meanings reveal a conception of science which Kant inherited from earlier Leibnizian metaphysics, even if his own transcendental philosophy challenged it. Sloan (2006) convincingly distinguishes between *Naturwissenschaften* and *Naturlehre* in Kant's discourse; only the former is encompassed by the *Metaphysical Foundations*'s narrow definition. But the latter is knowledge of nature too and sometimes Kant seems to see chemistry and biology in this latter way.

Later philosophers would go further than Kant in rejecting the classical a priori view of science and they would put *Lehre* and *Wissenschaft* on a par in order to assess the specificity of the emerging natural sciences. In this new framework, within which the natural sciences acquired a novel status which was at the same time reflected and reinforced by the critical philosophy, a new kind of philosophical discourse on nature appeared, of which the *Naturphilosophie* of Schelling and his disciples is the best illustration. It was to be a discourse *distinct* from the natural sciences (since it would not be mathematically expressed), but it was to interpret nature in an *immanent* way, without tracing its order back to a transcendent foundation.

3. The Hermeneutics of Nature and its Genealogy

In its radical formulation by Schelling, philosophy of nature is intended to *construct* nature: 'To know an object is to determine the principles of its possibility and to determine these is to be able to construct it, to reproduce its activity in thought' (Schelling [1799] 2004:

196).[3] Its method consists in interpreting in a systematic manner the contents and findings of the natural sciences. Although less radical, Hegel's project is characterised in a related way by Westphal:

> One of Hegel's aims in his *Philosophy of Nature* is to systematically order our most basic ontological and natural-scientific concepts and principles . . . beginning with the most abstract, undifferentiated and universal . . . and working through a finely-grained series of steps . . . towards the most complex, the organic life of animal species. (Westphal 2008: 306)

As a philosophical discourse, philosophy of nature aims to conceive of nature in an immanent but non-mathematical way. That is, it aims to grasp a *meaning* immanent in nature, a meaning that the sciences of nature cannot capture because they express *laws* – but a meaning which does not lead to or presuppose a creative God. This project parallels that of the critical philosophy, which considers thoughts and meanings as immanent to finite thinking, without relating them to a divine understanding that would circumscribe the thinkable a priori. Yet this new programme was not Kantian, because, as defined in the *Metaphysical Foundations of Natural Science*, the natural sciences for Kant were self-sufficient and had no immanent meaning left for philosophers. The new programme can be called a *hermeneutics of nature*, since its aim is to unveil a specific meaning immanent to nature and to be deciphered in the discourse of the natural sciences.

Kant's metaphysics of nature was decisive for the *Naturphilosophen*: Schelling defined his first programme of philosophy of nature with reference to Kant's deduction of the two forces of nature. In the *Metaphysical Foundations of Natural Science*, Kant had argued that all matter was constituted from the two forces of attraction and repulsion. In the *Einleitung zu dem Entwurf eines Systems der Naturphilosophie* (Introduction to the First Outline of a System of the Philosophy of Nature, of 1799), Schelling sought to reconcile these forces in a third one. The quest for a pair of original forces was a crucial part of Schelling's *Naturphilosophie* program, which was perpetuated in various successive forms. One of these forms was that of the *Von der Weltseele* (On the World-Soul), in which we find at the very beginning the partition between two absolute forces (Schelling [1801] 1911: 3–4). Goethe's ideas of a unity of plans in nature and of a unity between poetry and science (Richards 2002), as well as Herder's views of the history of nature and of organisms in particular as realising a progressive plan (see Herder [1784] 1967), were also decisive for the elaboration of a philosophy of nature.

Yet we must also emphasise the role of the third *Critique,* in which Kant's project was to understand that which overwhelms the universal a priori laws of nature, transcendentally understood in the *Critique of Pure Reason* as conditions of possibility of experience. The *lawfulness* of nature was warranted by such transcendental principles, but not the *systematicity* of empirical laws, the laws that rule particulars and allow naturalists to classify them into species and genera. In this sense, Kant in the *Critique of Judgement* recognises that the lawfulness of nature, which makes natural science possible, does not exhaust the whole of nature. The whole topic of the work is what is in excess of laws of nature – on the one hand, this includes the excess of the empirical laws themselves insofar as they cannot be deduced from the general laws of nature; on the other hand, it includes the excess of the norms of organisation since they cannot be derived from the mechanical laws of nature. Life is – epistemologically speaking – in excess of nature pure and simple and therefore life must be made intelligible in a different way.

Embryology is a case in point: knowledge of embryological processes cannot be inferred from the physical laws that condition these processes. These inferences, indeed, could not allow us to make the distinction we make between normal and abnormal development (i.e. development leading to a monster) since both happen according to the same laws. So here we presuppose that development aims at a goal, namely, the type of the animal. This presupposition is peculiar to the knowledge of life and since it is justified not by objective reasons but by the requirement to make our knowledge of embryology possible, it is 'reflective'. Beauty and life are two forms of this excess with respect to the rules of the understanding which Kant tried to analyse in the third *Critique*.[4] The acknowledgement that the laws that are the subject-matter of the natural sciences do not encompass the whole of nature defines the territory of a discourse on nature that will not involve the mathematical unveiling of laws but rather the deciphering of meaning: hence, a hermeneutics of nature.

4. The Relationship Between Philosophy of Nature and the Natural Sciences

Kant elucidated the possibility of the concepts of the natural sciences by confronting them with the requirements of human thought as such. In contrast the hermeneutics of nature, as practised by Schelling, Hegel or Schopenhauer, has to interpret these concepts to decipher what they reveal about the meaning of nature. From this perspective, the science of nature is a discourse the meaning of which is to be recovered by philosophy. These three authors, however, accomplish the hermeneutic stance towards nature in different ways.

For Schelling, philosophy does not aim to produce a theory, but deduces the object of the scientific theory. He states in his *Philosophy of Revelation* of 1841 that:

> the great revolution brought about by the period (following classical metaphysics) consists in no longer dealing with the search for predicates (therefore creating a true theory about some objects) but in getting an insurance about the objects themselves. Still now, lots of people come to philosophy thinking that there are some statements or propositions that one can take home as a reward. But it is no more the case. The current philosophy consists in a deduction of the objects themselves, those objects that the old metaphysics presupposed simply in experience or ordinary conscience. (Schelling 1856–61: 13: 102)

That is why Schelling speaks of the 'construction' of objects – but this term, which Kant used to denote mathematical activity in sensible intuition, for Schelling refers to the activity of a kind of thought that is no longer finite: a kind of thought for which understanding and sensibility are no longer separated.[5] Through this activity, philosophers can grasp nature as the infinite and structured productive power from which nature arises as the sum of objects investigated by the natural sciences. This production – often expressed by Schelling through an appeal to the Spinozist difference between *natura naturans* and *natura naturata* – is the immanent meaning of nature which science cannot reach and which is the object of hermeneutics. Thus, Peter Hanss Reill describes how Schelling and the *Naturphilosophen* used science as follows: they 'populated the phenomenal world with bipolar oppositions, supposedly recapitulating the *Ur-polarity*, drastically revising the content of the "normal" sciences from which they borrowed some of their individual concepts' (Reill 2005: 211). This 'construction' of science by philosophy is reflected in

Schelling's recurring phrase 'philosophical X', where X might be chemistry, mathematics or physiology. Here, *Naturphilosophie* is thought to duplicate science with the meaning of science, which can only be delivered from the viewpoint of the philosopher. As such, this project has been caricatured and criticised, by Jakob Friedrich Fries, for example, as 'a duplicating narration of the experiences themselves in a modified language' (Fries [1803] 1978: 24: 188). But, in principle, this transformation of science through philosophy is made possible by the gap between lawful regularity and meaning – chemistry pertaining to the former, 'universal chemistry' to the latter – a gap that already opened up within Kant's third *Critique*, as we have seen.

The concept of 'finite science' yields Hegel's own position. Science as such presupposes *the object as given*, therefore it is finite. So Hegel shares Schelling's idea that philosophy proceeds to the point where the object of science is no longer presupposed as given. Only philosophy can confer on science its real status and bearings, since philosophy exposes the meaning of the object, which is constituted as a result. To be sure, Kant also deduced meanings and their limits – for example, the meaning of 'natural purpose' – but for Kant, philosophy halts before the *content* of science, whereas for Hegel, this scientific content too is thought by philosophy. To this extent, Hegel's philosophy of science could be seen as a hyper-Kantianism, a Kantianism that gives up the major Kantian distinctions (form/ matter, regulative/constitutive, etc.) and therefore reaches conclusions very different from those of Kantianism.

However, because of nature's own status as the *entfremdet* (self-alienated) Idea, nature cannot exactly match the rational determinations of the Concept: nature has an essential lack of power, an *Ohnmacht* (impotence). This term indicates that because nature is the immediate realisation of the Idea, *the Idea in exteriority* (time and space), it is therefore somehow external to itself (Hegel [1831] 1970: 3: 211–13, §376A).[6] But this finitude of nature is, ultimately, the exteriority of the particular vis à vis the universal. The kind is not the individual – think of a zoological species – hence the concept lies always outside its object. Hence for Hegel the impossibility of bringing the facts of nature, the facts established by natural science, back to the Idea, does not indicate a weakness of science or a finitude of our understanding, but rather this *Ohnmacht* of nature itself.

On this basis, the philosopher can interpret the finite sciences – and this interpretation is the hermeneutics of nature. She makes the inverse gesture to the scientist's; she begins with the concept – exactly as Hegel's *Encyclopädie* begins with the science of logic. While the naturalist claims to proceed from the empirical animal forms to the concept, the philosopher reconceives science by beginning from the concept – which is the truth of the scientist's knowledge. Thus Hegel writes:

> The infinity of the animal forms is not to be taken so that the necessity of the orders in nature should be constant. This is the reason why one, on the contrary, must take as a rule the universal determinations of the Concept and then compare the natural formations to those determinations. (Hegel [1831] 1970: 3: 180, §368A)[7]

In Chapter VI of the *Phenomenology of Spirit*, when Hegel shows how reason looks for itself within organic nature, he explains that the organic forms are contingent: they cannot be ordered in a rational progressive series, since every time a species is realised in a given environment this milieu causes some singular traits to occur in the individuals that instantiate the species. What Hegel calls 'Earth as an individual' alters the individuals attempting to realise a universal type. So philosophers cannot demand too much of the natural sciences. This marks the difference between Hegel's philosophy of nature and *Naturphilosophie*, especially that of Schelling. Schelling is more committed to the contents of the natural sciences because he has greater confidence in the possibility of a rational interpretation of nature.

For this reason, Schelling speaks in terms of real forces and natural moments (see Steigerwald 2002), whereas Hegel has in his own way already de-naturalised these contents of the natural sciences. This is because, for him, their intelligibility refers to logical moments (chemism, mechanism) of the *Science of Logic*. That is why Schelling is compelled to find real correspondences between natural moments, such as light and life, or chemism and digestion, whereas for Hegel these correspondences are mere arbitrary abstractions (mere formalism, as he objects in the Preface to the *Phenomenology of Spirit*). What for Schelling would be universal chemistry, as the proper concept of philosophy of nature, indeed pertains for Hegel to *logic* in the first place rather than to philosophy of nature – and that is why, for Hegel, chemism is a concept that concerns both natural and spiritual phenomena. Finally, the anteriority of logic to philosophy of nature in the *Encyclopedia* indicates the finite status of nature for Hegel and distinguishes his project of a philosophy of nature from Schelling's.

For Schopenhauer, the correspondence between matters of fact investigated by science and philosophical concepts is necessarily required. He thinks that science by itself converges towards Schopenhauerian philosophy, so that when one approaches scientific content in light of our philosophical intuition (given primarily in our experience of the lived-body) that the *In-sich* of the world is the will, then one finds that the scientist is saying the same thing as the philosopher, whether he knows it or not. Science thus corroborates philosophy: while science and philosophy proceed in an independent manner, they also meet up and the results of the empirical sciences can be translated into the Schopenhauerian metaphysics of the will:

> My metaphysics proves itself as being the only one that possesses a genuine common boundary with the physical sciences in the sense that these come to meet it *by their own means*, so that they really encounter it, and that establishes their juncture. (Schopenhauer [1836] 1901: 215–16)

Schopenhauer's position on natural science is close to Schelling's, because for Schopenhauer philosophy has to reinterpret natural science without any logical prerequisites. It was with this intention that he wrote *On the Will in Nature*, published in 1836. But since science should confirm philosophical conclusions, so that philosophy works by itself towards these conclusions, there are no guarantees that the whole of natural science can provide such a confirmation. Schopenhauer's *On the Will in Nature* is therefore less confident than Schelling's *Naturphilosophie*, although close to it in intention; while, like Hegel, Schopenhauer seeks to find, through the natural sciences, traces within nature of its core of truth: the Will (rather than the Concept).

The kind of relationship entertained by hermeneutics to natural science is exemplified in the case of the categories of mechanism and organism. In the third *Critique*, Kant argues that besides mechanism, which is the principle of causation specified as explanation of behaviour of wholes on the basis of explanations of the behaviour of parts,[8] some entities require another principle, 'teleology', to be understood. This specific intelligibility of life is defined by the principle of purposiveness, which every researcher must assume in addition to the general principle of mechanism, in order to be able to ask the philosophical questions which are required if organisms are to be explained. These entities are organised beings *qua* self-organising and they cannot be understood unless we appeal to an explanatory principle which explains the parts from the wholes.

The interpretation of the status of these two kinds of explanation is highly controversial. A particularly controversial issue is whether mechanism is a regulative principle or whether it is constitutive, since it is certainly based on the principle of causality which is a requirement for any kind of knowledge (see Huneman 2007a: 9–11). Teleology, at least, is clearly a regulative principle for the 'reflective faculty of judgement': 'regulative' means for Kant that teleology only gets its meaning in relation to our project of understanding organisms – whereas constitutive principles are required for any kind of knowledge and for experience as such. To this extent, the model of a *mathesis* can no longer be assumed to be valid for the whole of nature and this represents a departure from the traditional model of natural philosophy.

The philosophers who followed Kant, as well as the life scientists (although for different reasons), overcame this distinction between the statuses of teleology and mechanism. Scientists such as Karl Ernst von Baer, Christian Heinrich Pander (see Larson 1979), or even the earlier Blumenbach (see Richards 2001) may have simply had no interest in Kant's main concern in stating these distinctions. This concern was metaphysical, in that Kant tried to understand the meaning of order and purposiveness within the structure of knowledge established by transcendental philosophy. Philosophers of nature were dissatisfied that Kant simply opposed these principles. Admittedly, in the Dialectic of the *Critique of Judgement*, Kant assumed that the two principles may be identical in the supersensible substrate of nature (since both are related to the necessities of our finite thought). His Methodology, too, stated that in practice both principles could be articulated together in the study of organisms, basically by the teleological principle leading us to ask about the functions of certain parts and by the mechanistic principle grounding our investigation of the mechanisms through which such functions are carried. But this conjunction seemed too extrinsic to Hegel or Schelling, because it did not relate the principles themselves in terms of their meaning. Philosophy of nature had to show how the principle of mechanism itself gives rise to that of teleology, otherwise there was an arbitrary gap in our science of nature.

For Schelling, then, there is only a difference of degree between inorganic and organic entities and the intellectual operations for understanding mechanisms are entrenched in organismic schemes. He states in *Von der Weltseele*: 'The organism is so little to be explained from the mechanism that mechanism is to be explained from organism . . . a *world*, an *organisation* and a *general organism* are the *condition* (and as such the *positive*) of the *mechanism*' (Schelling [1801] 1911: 349). He contends that 'as soon as our conceptions rise to an idea of nature as a whole, the opposition between mechanism and organism vanishes, this opposition which delayed for too long the progress of natural science' and that 'the succession of all the organic beings happened by the progressive development of a unique organisation'.

For Hegel, considering the category of mechanism itself leads dialectically to the category of teleology, which appears as mechanism's truth – according to a scheme of process that pervades all of Hegel's logic and encyclopaedia of philosophical science. Mechanism does indeed construe the behaviour and structure of wholes on the basis of the parts, but in order to be singled out *as* parts, it must already be presupposed that these parts are included in a whole and hence they inherit their meaning as parts from the whole. This prior assumption of the whole means that we are already adopting a teleological stance.

The general conception of explanation, as it is drawn from the practices of the empirical sciences, is therefore inverted in hermeneutics. On the received view, mechanism is the easiest and clearest kind of explanation and this makes organisms difficult to understand – a motivation for Kant's concern with organisms in the third *Critique*. On the alternative hermeneutic view, the organism provides the complete explanatory scheme, so it becomes clearer and easier to understand than mechanism. This is clear when we consider the Hegelian theory that life is the Concept existing for-itself for the first time (which means: life is the Idea but in its immediate state, opaque to itself). The same view is expressed no less clearly by Schelling. Notwithstanding all their differences, Hegel, Schelling and Schopenhauer all agree on the priority of organism to mechanism. The reason for this shift is that we have switched from the viewpoint of lawful regularity to the viewpoint of meaning, which is proper to the hermeneutics of nature.

The philosophy of nature, then, effected a general synthesis of the natural sciences of the time, aiming to give a philosophical interpretation of a meaning that was immanent to nature and was likely to be decipherable in the concepts necessary to the natural sciences. Two things are worth mentioning about this synthesising project.

In the eighteenth century, some naturalistic philosophies had emerged which viewed nature as a whole realising the same property to various degrees in a succession of stages: for example, the theory that sensibility is latent in atoms of matter and expressed in its highest form in the human mind. Diderot, for instance, in the *Rêve de d'Alembert*, written in 1769, articulated such views. Even if these philosophers' insistence on continuity in nature and their focus on life and organisms may remind us of *Naturphilosophie*, however, they are structurally different syntheses of the natural sciences. Naturalistic philosophies mostly rest on vitalism, in the form of the claim that all vital phenomena are based on an irreducible property of sensibility present in the elementary bases of life (Rey 1987; Wolfe 2008). These philosophies extrapolated a continuous gradation of this property up to psychology (in the form of sensations and sentiments) and down to matter (in the form of gravity). Ultimately, they favoured a kind of materialism of 'feeling matter' (Huneman 2008). The *Naturphilosophen* did not start with ontological assertions about elementary entities and their properties but with the structure of natural science, namely, the categories of organism and mechanism. Although they often sounded vitalist, it was not the same vitalism as the Enlightenment vitalism of Diderot or others (see Reill 2005).

The fact that *Naturphilosophie* often sounded idealistic, in contrast to the materialist-sounding views of Enlightenment naturalist philosophers, results from this difference in structure, which ultimately stems from the difference in the space of knowledge about nature that occurred at the time of Kant. However, the relationship between the hermeneutics of nature and the natural sciences, especially in Schellingian *Naturphilosophie*, is complex. While the main project of philosophers like Schelling or Hegel was to unveil immanent meaning in nature, they saw themselves as likely to do useful research in the empirical sciences, especially in those fields that were new and that were appealing to Newtonian-style forces (Darnton 1968) such as animal magnetism, galvanism, etc. Indeed, Schelling's *Naturphilosophie* is full of experiments in magnetism, chemistry and other topics.

In fact, in the 1800s, *Naturphilosophie* could be seen as 'normal science' in the Kuhnian sense. Technologies such as microscopes and concepts such as galvanism as the energy proper to nerve transmission were recent and controversies were raging about their proper scope and *Naturphilosophen* such as Johann Wilhelm Ritter or Steffens made important contributions to these discussions, often by experimenting themselves. L. S. Jacyna (1990) argued that one of the main achievements of the biological sciences in the nineteenth century, namely, cell theory, owed a great debt to *Naturphilosophie*. This is because the general aim of uncovering universal primitive elements of life relied on the idea, supported by the *Naturphilosophen*, that something general should unify all aspects of life so that a single form underlies all living phenomena.

At another level, *Naturphilosophie* was strongly entangled with morphology, since the notion of a unity of plan across animal taxa, put forth by Goethe and then developed in the context of comparative anatomy by Geoffroy Saint Hilaire (Rehbock 1983; Huneman 2006), was foundational for the very project of a philosophy of nature. The so-called 'transcendental morphology' school, represented by Johann Friedrich Meckel, Étienne Serres and Joseph Henry Green, aimed at understanding the few major plans of organisation under which all organisms were thought to fall. These scholars were influenced by Carl Friedrich Kielmeyer's teaching and unpublished discourse (Bach 2001), which in 1800 initiated the project of understanding the scale of living species according to the types of forces which these species instantiated, a hierarchy of forces which was in turn grounded in a metaphysical hierarchy of concepts (Schmitt 2007; Pross 1994). This project, although explicitly using Kant's notion of purposiveness, clearly resonated with *Naturphilosophie*'s idea of generating the major concepts of the special sciences. It is noteworthy that Richard Owen, author of a major achievement in comparative anatomy by theorising the vertebrate archetype, confessed to having been deeply influenced by Oken, one of the most speculative *Naturphilosophen* (Owen [1837] 1992; see Sloan 2003).

These close relations between *Naturphilosophie* and the sciences undermine the still-widespread view that *Naturphilosophie* was metaphysical delirium which was clearly detrimental to science. It can even be argued (see Rueger forthcoming) that, beyond the case of cell theory, the systematic views of *Naturphilosophen* such as Oken were translated into a materialist framework even by those who were its most virulent adversaries, such as Emil du Bois Reymond or Justus von Liebig, while physiologist Johannes Müller was inspired by *Naturphilosophie* to forge his theory of the proper energy of the senses. However, Timothy Lenoir (1982) argued that a line can be drawn between (1) biologists who undertook the Kantian project of a life science ('teleomechanism'), of articulating functional-teleological questions with mechanistic explanations of teleological features and who therefore were serious scientists and (2) philosophers of nature, especially Schelling, who conferred dogmatic metaphysical status on Kantian regulative principles. Yet pace Lenoir, transcendental morphology, whose main works (such as those of Owen or Meckel) were important achievements within the life sciences, cannot simply be subsumed under the 'Kantian tradition', because it involves ideas such as that of a unity of plan across organisms, ideas that are alien to teleomechanism. The morphologist Joseph Henry Green extensively drew on ideas from Schellingian *Naturphilosophie* to construct his hierarchy of types and their relationships, although he presented it in a rather Kantian way (Sloan 2007). This calls into question a clear-cut boundary between *Naturphilosophie* and 'teleomechanism'; rather, the theoreticians in these fields belong to a continuum.

Through their unravelling of the formal relationships between the plans of organisations, transcendental morphologists as well as some embryologists like Von Baer conceived of a temporality proper to the biological reign, since they thought that the various plans of organisation emerged one after the other, according to relationships of logical presupposition and conditioning. The scholium of Von Baer (1828) explicitly considers this successive appearance of ideal major types of animals. This peculiar kind of evolutionism influenced Darwin, as Richards (1992; 2002) has convincingly argued – even if Darwinian history is conceptually distinct from this kind of temporal succession which merely instantiates formal logical relationships. The subtle relationships between *Naturphilosophie* and Darwinism – through transcendental morphology and descriptive embryology – illustrate the rather complex scientific status of the philosophy of nature.

5. The Content of a Hermeneutics of Nature

Although there are many different philosophical positions within the project of a hermeneutics of nature, their common descent from Kantian themes in the *Critique of Judgement* and the situation of these projects within the same epistemological space mean that the work of Schelling, Hegel and Schopenhauer (and others) shares some common themes.

One is an emphasis on the notion of the organism. Previously, in the classical configuration of natural philosophy, the concept of *order* provided the link between natural history, theology and metaphysics: organisms exhibited an *internal* order and were part of a *general* order which was evidence of divine design. After Kant, however, life as a self-organising process, grounded on the biological teleology implemented by organic parts (Ginsborg 2004; Zumbach 1984; Huneman 2007b), replaces the concept of order as a clue to the articulations and transitions within the general structure of knowledge, especially between metaphysics and natural history. The organism becomes a *general scheme for conceiving nature*. Schelling refers to Kant's concept of the organism to sketch out the consequences for our general understanding of nature of this reversal in the explanatory roles of organism and mechanism:

> Since, in any organism everything reciprocally holds and supports everything else, this organisation must as a whole pre-exist its parts and the whole cannot stem from the parts, but the parts have to stem from the whole. It is not that we *know* nature a priori, but nature *is* a priori, namely all that is singular within it is determined from the whole or from the idea of a nature in general. (Schelling [1799] 2004: 198–9)

Through the notion of the organism, Schelling tries to overcome the opposition between dualism and materialism: we can be naturalists (that is, we are never to explain things in nature by referring to anything outside nature) and not dualists, yet we must not embrace materialism (since mechanism is not the real scheme of explanation).

On the basis of this scheme, Schelling was able – contrary to Kant – to claim that nature itself is an organism, and Oken will equate life and being. In Schelling's 1802 work *Bruno*, we read: 'The universe embraces itself and . . . constitutes a living being organised in such a way that it cannot perish' (Schelling 1907: 2: 482). In *Von der Weltseele* too, nature is an evolving organism, constituted by higher and higher degrees of a general organisation – whose highest point is consciousness. This crucial status of life in the philosophy of nature partly comes from the Kantian claim that purposiveness is a concept that we human beings, with our finite power of thought, *necessarily have*; as a consequence, the concepts used to conceive life express what is essential to human thinking. Therefore, for Kant, life is distinctive within nature because it relates to the finitude of the human thought that apprehends living creatures. Organisms, which we conceive as purposive, are that in which the very structure of our finite thinking is reflected.[9] In this way Kant demonstrated a close and immanent relationship between finite thought and life. The hermeneutics of nature inherited this claim, so that the *main concepts used to decipher immanent meaning in nature referred to the phenomenon of life*. Therefore, when Schelling writes that for *Naturphilosophie* 'nature is nothing else than the organ of self-consciousness' (Schelling 2004: 194), or when Hegel conceives of nature as the mind opaque to itself, they both rely on this interpretation of life as a reflexive concept, proper to the necessities of finite thought, elaborated in the third *Critique* (Kant [1790] 1987: 283–94, §§76–7).

In this context the boundary between the organic and the inorganic in nature, which was fundamental for Kant, disappears (Zammito 1992: 215–22). For example, Schelling writes:

> There is a productivity with no consciousness, but which is conscious productivity originally transformed, the simple reflection of which is seen in nature and which, from the viewpoint of the natural perspective, must appear as one and the same blind instinct that acts at various levels from crystallisation to the heights of organic formations (from which it returns again to crystallisation through the formative drive [*Kunsttrieb*]) . . . (2004: 194)

This completely reverses Kant's argument in the *Critique of Judgement* that crystallisation must not be conceived on the same lines as the organic *Bildungstrieb* (see Huneman 2006; Sloan 2006).

A second *leitmotif* of the hermeneutics of nature is conflict, absurdity and tragedy. Given Kant's criticisms of physical theology and of the economy of nature, the hermeneutic approach to nature cannot regard it as an area in which order and harmony are guaranteed by a transcendent reference point. Rather, conflict and disharmony are pervasive features of the meaning of nature. Schelling writes in *Von der Weltseele*:

> The negative condition of the vital process is an antagonism of negative principles, which is entertained by the continuous influence of the positive principle (the first cause of life). If this antagonism is to be permanent in the living being, the equilibrium of principles has to be continuously disturbed inside it. (Schelling [1801] 1911: 202; see also Bowie 1993)

The privileged status of life within nature means that there is a constant possibility of conflict between life and non-living nature. This reactivates a conceptual motif to which vitalist physicians continuously referred up until Xavier Bichat famously stated that 'life is the set of the forces which resist death' (Bichat 1800).[10] It is therefore not surprising that Bichat's work is a major reference point for Schopenhauer and for Hegel (Schopenhauer [1818/1844] 1966: 2: 261–8; Hegel [1831] 1970: 3: 126–7, §355; 3: 150, §362A).

Schopenhauer describes the process by which the inorganic gives rise to the organic as follows:

> There is no victory without fight: the highest idea, or objectification of the will, cannot arise without overcoming the lower ones and it has to triumph over the resistance of those forces which, while reduced to slaves, still aspire to manifest their essence in an independent and complete manner. ([1818/1844] 1966: 1: 146)

In Hegel's philosophy of nature, life, as the immediate form of the Idea, realised in nature, is in itself negativity; hence, it carries in its essence its own conflictual opposition to brute matter. Hegel draws the consequences of this: 'the elementary powers of objectivity . . . are

. . . continuously ready to jump to begin their process within the organic body and life is the constant fight against this possibility' (Hegel [1831] 1991: 293, §218). So:

> [T]he living body is always on the edge of falling into a chemical process: acid stuff, water, salt, are always about to rise up, but are always suppressed and it is only in death, or in illness, that this chemical process can appear for itself. (Hegel [1831] 1970: 3: 10, §337A)

Schopenhauer and Hegel conceive of this conflict in the same terms: subordination of non-living stuff to living things, together with living creatures undergoing continuous harassment by chemical processes through which they eventually perish. And for both authors, the living and the non-living are moments of the same process: for Schopenhauer, both are stages of the objectification of the will, whereas, for Hegel, both are stages of the logical process of the Concept realised within nature. Both agree that this process is not a temporal one and both contend that life has an intelligibility different to that of the non-living realm. However, for Hegel, physical phenomena pass into organic phenomena because in a way the former are the *same* as the latter and therefore the former are defeated by the latter. As we saw earlier, life is the truth of nature pure and simple and that is why life can destroy and appropriate brute nature. Schopenhauer says something different: life has an intrinsically higher force than non-living nature because life is a higher degree of the objectification of the will (Schopenhauer [1818/1844] 1966: 1: 139–52).

The *leitmotif* of conflict goes beyond this vitalistic conflict. Hermeneutics inherits the radical critique of natural economy in the third *Critique*, a critique that fitted in perfectly with the trends in comparative anatomy at this time. 'Everywhere in nature', says Schopenhauer, 'we see fight, war and alternative victories and therefore we better understand the divorce of the will with itself' ([1818/1844] 1966: 1: 146). Conflict in nature is *pervasive* and does not lead to any stable order. Schopenhauer acknowledges that species are stable and co-exist (1: 153–61), although individuals fight eternally. But this is no longer the Linnaean idea of an order through conflict. What is emphasised now, if we read Schopenhauer, is not the resulting order, but the *infinity and absurdity* of the eternal fight which divides the will from itself:

> It is an unending, never satisfied, effort that is the essence of the plant, a continuous effort through more and more noble forms, until the seed which is, then, a new beginning and this is repeated infinitely. *Never a true goal, never a final satisfaction, nowhere a place to rest.* (1: 309)

This picture of nature is very close to the Hegelian idea of the bad infinite, which for Hegel is pervasively present within nature – for example, in the genera of living creatures which exist as successive infinite series.

A third and final *leitmotif* of the hermeneutics of nature is that of *gender* (*Geschlecht*) as a major sign of nature's finitude – as nature's attempt and failure to overcome such a finitude. For Hegel, reproduction is the highest moment of the living being's process. Here the living being relates to another living being and so it recognises itself in an Other; and the Universal – that is, its species – exists for it through the mediation of this Other. However, because a species exists as the bad infinite of the sequence of generations, the universal and the particular can never accord: the living being dies (Hegel [1831] 1970: 3: 175–6, §369). This death, nevertheless, means that life – and therefore nature itself, whose final end consists in life – leaves room for the moment of Spirit (3: 210–11, §376). This relationship between nature and spirit which comes about through the failure of the gender process is properly Hegelian (see Beiser 2002; Westphal 2008). However, the special status of sexuality is a general feature of the hermeneutics of nature at this time.

For Schelling, the genders are nature's attempt to overcome its own separation, as well as its inability to overcome it insofar as these genders are themselves this very separation that they perpetuate. 'Nature *hates* gender and, where it arises, it arises against nature's will. The separation into genders is an unavoidable fate, with which nature has to cope and which nature cannot overcome insofar as it is organic' (Schelling [1799] 2004: 231). Peter Hanss Reill (2005: 229) has recently made a convincing case that for the *Naturphilosophen*, unlike the Enlightenment vitalist thinkers, gender differences were a crucial intellectual focus because they could be interpreted in terms of polarities, oppositions and meaningful schemas. Thus, Schopenhauer gave a long analysis of these matters in the Supplement XLIV to the *World as Will and Representation*, entitled 'The metaphysics of sexual love'. This is surely the best example of a system placing the theme of sexual lust at the heart of its conception of nature.

6. The Fate of the Hermeneutics of Nature

Philosophical reflection about nature in the nineteenth century was deeply influenced by the hermeneutic project. However, from the 1830s onwards with the rise of critiques of idealism in general and of Hegelianism and *Naturphilosophie* especially, the kind of post-Kantian philosophy of nature which I have described here was progressively dismissed. We can distinguish two sources of criticism: philosophical, coming from thinkers such as Feuerbach, Marx and Nietzsche; and scientific. The former source of attacks on philosophy of nature was the side-effect of a general rejection of Hegel and of post-Kantian idealism. Within this, philosophy of nature was sometimes understood – by Marx, for example – as paradigmatic of the idealist privileging of ideas over reality.

The other line of criticism came from scientists themselves, especially chemists. The synthesis of urea by Friedrich Wöhler in 1828 provided materialists with a strong argument that vital properties were reducible to plain matter. The rise of Darwinism, especially in Germany, involved a materialist interpretation of the succession of species which had interested the *Naturphilosophen* and the transcendental morphologists. The prospect of unifying physics and biology within a general science of evolving matter, a synthesis later advocated by Ernst Haeckel, was far removed from the kind of universal organicism endorsed by the hermeneuticists of nature. The conjunction of Darwinism and chemical materialism in the second half of the nineteenth century may explain why almost all philosophers gave up programmes in the philosophy of nature of the same ambition as Schelling's.

Yet the hermeneutics of nature remained alive in several philosophical works about nature. Distinct from the natural sciences which developed within Darwinian and/or materialist frameworks and also distinct from the kind of scientifically oriented philosophy which understood philosophical discourse on science to be mainly methodological or epistemological – for example John Stuart Mill and William Whewell (see Whewell 1840) – there was a philosophical trend which took up many elements of the hermeneutic stance. Since Schopenhauer shared this post-Kantian hermeneutic stance, the Nietzschean project of interpreting nature as the antagonism of various irreducible wills – a project directly stemming from Schopenhauer's metaphysics of will – belonged to this trend. The later idea of *Lebensphilosophie*, developed by Wilhelm Dilthey amongst others at the end of the century, rested on an insistence that the very fact of being alive provided human beings with hermeneutic capacities through which they could understand themselves and the world in which they live, in a way different to that of the explanatory natural sciences (see Dilthey [1883] 1959). This project reactivates important dimensions of the hermeneutic stance.

The general idea of uncovering a meaning in nature that is immanent to it and yet is not exhausted by the natural sciences constitutes the point of connection between the philosophy of nature (as I have described it here) and important philosophical views of nature which developed outside the German area. Thoreau and Emerson, authors of two major philosophical works on nature, were aware of some of the mostly German developments sketched here. Coleridge introduced Schelling's thought into English-speaking countries (Modiano 1985; Wellek 1931) and Emerson and Thoreau, as well as the group who called themselves 'transcendentalists', were exposed to this teaching. So it is unsurprising that Thoreau's views on nature, famously presented in his 1854 work *Walden*, resonate with aspects of the hermeneutics of nature. Nature according to him has intrinsic value and significance; rightly approached, it is spiritual as much as physical, not the symbol of spirituality, but deity and spirituality itself, 'without metaphor', which we can experience. Science can help to foster this experience, as in the case of entomology, as Thoreau writes in his *Natural History of Massachusetts*: 'Entomology extends the limits of being in a new direction, so that I walk in nature with a sense of greater space and freedom' (Thoreau [1842] 1906: 5: 107).

In particular, the philosopher of nature is supposed to take the natural sciences into account while producing a discourse on nature of a different kind. Stanley Cavell regarded Thoreau as a Kantian transcendentalist because he highlighted the role of the form of our knowledge in our acquisition of science. But the view of nature and science which Thoreau developed stems much more from the hermeneutics of nature that Coleridge had made familiar to the American transcendentalists. While Thoreau relies on science to know nature, since the 'true man of science . . . [will have] a deeper and finer experience than other men' (Thoreau 1906: 5: 131), he insists that science by itself does not carry the meaning of nature: the scientist 'studies nature as a dead language', he writes in his *Journal* entry for 10 May 1853 (11: 135). So philosophy integrates the natural sciences – but, contrary to the philosophers of nature, it does not bring about systematic knowledge, since it proceeds from a 'a sudden revelation of the insufficiency of what we called knowledge before' (5: 241). This is in the sense that the very meaning of what we knew according to the sciences now appears in an experience where it displays an essential aspect different from the previous content of our knowledge. The truth about nature is not genuinely accessible through scientific methodologies: 'We do not learn by inference and deduction and the application of mathematics to philosophy, but by direct intercourse and sympathy' (5: 131) – although scientific facts and recollections are necessary to fuel this learning, as is exemplified by Thoreau's reading of botanists and naturalists in order to write about his excursions.

Thoreau is not committed to any form of idealism. Yet his general position on nature and the natural sciences to some extent replicates the hermeneutic stance that had developed at the beginning of the century. Thoreau affirms that there is an immediate relationship of meaning between nature and humanity – an immediate relationship that the scientific knowledge of nature could not exhaust, although some scientific knowledge is needed for any grasp of nature. Thoreau's position contrasts with the German materialism that was increasingly shaping the whole of physical and chemical scientific theory.

As a theory, *Naturphilosophie*, as well as Hegel's philosophy of nature, became outdated after the middle of the nineteenth century. But the theoretical matrix elaborated through the critical reappraisal of Kant's *Critique of Judgement*, and defined here as a hermeneutic stance towards nature, continued to produce philosophical theories and views of nature in the writings of Thoreau or Nietzsche. A genealogy could trace important philosophical interpretations of nature in the twentieth century back to this theoretical matrix – interpretations such as those of Alfred North Whitehead or Henri Bergson.

7. Conclusion

Kant's analysis of purposiveness opened up a space for philosophical interpretations of nature because it created a gap between nature's lawful regularity and nature's meaning. Within German idealism, philosophy of nature was the research programme of this hermeneutics of nature; *Naturphilosophie*, Schopenhauer's theory of the will in nature and Hegel's philosophy of nature were three divergent realisations of this programme. Due to its Kantian genealogy, the hermeneutics of nature gave special status to life, stressed the overwhelming character of conflict and disorder and the importance of gender and was sensitive to a kind of tragic meaning in nature.

These elaborations of course do not exhaust all the various conceptions of nature in nineteenth-century philosophy – interpretations of Darwinism, Anglo-Saxon theories of science such as those of Whewell or Mill and large-scale syntheses such as Comte's positivism, Antoine Cournot's (1875) rational analysis of the natural sciences and Herbert Spencer's general doctrine of evolution were important and influential throughout the century and sometimes these thinkers were not aware of the developments underlined in this chapter. My intention has been to delineate an important alternative philosophical stance regarding nature, a stance that continued to be pursued by various philosophers later in the century. This hermeneutic stance marks an alternative to the epistemological or positivist views which emerged later in the century and which, several decades later, gave rise to what is now known and practised as philosophy of science. To this extent, the historical importance of this hermeneutic stance goes beyond its main achievements such as *Naturphilosophie* and bears on the genealogy of contemporary ways of philosophising about nature.

Notes

1. Foucault (1966) famously understood knowledge of nature in the classical age as natural history. However, what metaphysicians such as Leibniz made clear is the fundamental connection between natural history and natural philosophy.
2. In the third *Critique* (Kant [1790] 1987: 257–61, §67), Kant reintroduces relative purposiveness and therefore a hierarchy of organisms serving one another, but this reintroduction is conditional. Only on the basis of assessing internal purposiveness can one make use – mainly as a heuristic tool – of the idea that one organism fulfils a role for another. Hence, the system of nature that can be drawn up on this basis is, so to speak, *more* regulative than is the use of internal purposiveness. We can conceive of organisms without conceiving a purposive system of nature, whereas we cannot conceive of the latter without presupposing the former.
3. All translations from Schelling 2004 are modified in light of Schelling 2001.
4. Schelling recognises that the project of a philosophy of nature is motivated by the need to give a philosophical account of these two excesses. In the *Entwurf*, he identifies two ways in which philosophy overcomes the opposition between conscious and unconscious intelligence: imme-

diately in the activity of genius, mediately in 'some products of nature, to the extent that within them the co-penetration [*Verschmelzung*] of the ideal and the real is perceived' (Schelling 2004: 193).

5. See Schelling 2004: 196. Since this paper is not a study of Schelling, I will be quoting from various stages of his thought. However, although his several versions of *Naturphilosophie* are quite different (see Richards 2002; Beiser 2002; Bowie 1993), his general position on philosophy's relation to science remains constant.

6. Translations from Hegel and Schopenhauer are sometimes modified by the author without special notice. References to Hegel's works include paragraph number (§) after page number. 'A' (e.g. §55A) indicates a reference to Hegel's 'addition' to the paragraph.

7. In Petry's translation, which on this point is based on the first and second editions, this passage appears as §370A.

8. On the interpretation of mechanism in Kant see McLaughlin 1990, Ginsborg 2004.

9. Kant does not identify organisms and life and the *Critique of Judgement* deals only with the science of organisms as objects of biological judgement, whereas life is identified by self motion (rather than by a kind of organisation) and the concept occurs mostly in psychological contexts, as the lowest level of the faculty of desire. Yet the philosophers of nature will conflate life and organisms, precisely because they will no longer take purposiveness to be a merely regulative concept and will confer on organisms the same metaphysical status as any other natural being, so that *organism* becomes just as metaphysical a concept as *life*.

10. On Bichat's work in the history of physiology see Huneman 1998.

References

Allison, Henry (2003), *Kant's Transcendental Idealism*, New Haven, CT: Yale University Press.

Bach, Thomas (2001), *Biologie und Philosophie bei C. F. Kielmeyer und F. W. J. Schelling*, Stuttgart: Frommann-Holzboog.

Barsanti, Guilio (1995), 'La naissance de la biologie: Observations, théories, métaphysiques en France, 1740–1810', in Roselyne Rey, Claude Blanckaert and Jean-Louis Fischer (eds), *Nature, Histoire, Société: Mélanges offerts à Jacques Roger*, Paris: Klincksieck, pp. 196–228.

Beiser, Frederick (2002), *German Idealism: The Struggle against Subjectivism*, Cambridge, MA: Harvard University Press.

Belaval, Yvon (1978), *Leibniz: Critique de Kant*, Paris: Gallimard.

Bichat, Xavier (1800), *Recherches physiologiques sur la vie et la mort*, Paris: Béchet.

Bowie andrew (1993), *Schelling and Modern European Philosophy*, London: Routledge.

Coleman, William (1979), *Biology in the Nineteenth Century: Problems of Form, Function and Transformation*, Cambridge: Cambridge University Press.

Cournot, Antoine Augustin (1875), *Matérialisme. Vitalisme. Rationalisme. Essai sur l'emploi des données de la science en philosophie*, Paris: Hachette.

Cuvier, George (1801), *Anatomie comparée*, Paris.

Darnton, Robert (1968), *Mesmerism and the End of the Enlightenment in France*, Cambridge, MA: Harvard University Press.

Dilthey, Wilhelm [1883] (1959), *Einleitung in die Geisteswissenschaften. Versuch einer Grundlegung für das Studium der Gesellschaft und der Geschichte*, in Wilhelm Dilthey, *Gesammelte Schriften*, 12 vols, Stuttgart: Teubner.

Foucault, Michel (1966), *Les mots et les choses*, Paris: Gallimard.

Fries, Jakob Friedrich (1978), *Sämtliche Schriften*, ed. Gert König et al., 33 vols, Aalen: Scientia.

Ginsborg, Hannah (2004), 'Two kinds of mechanical inexplicability in Kant and Aristotle', *Journal of the History of Philosophy*, 42 (1): 33–65.

Goethe, Johann Wolfgang von [1790] (1995), 'Toward a general comparative theory', in Johann Wolfgang von Goethe, *Scientific Studies*, ed. and trans. Douglas Miller, Princeton: Princeton University Press.

Hegel, Georg Wilhelm Friedrich [1831] (1970), *Philosophy of Nature (Part Three of the Encyclopaedia of Philosophical Sciences)*, 3 vols, ed. and trans. Michael John Petry, London: Allen and Unwin.

Hegel, Georg Wilhelm Friedrich [1831] (1991), *The Encyclopaedia Logic*, trans. T. F. Geraets, W. A. Suchting and H. S. Harris, Indianapolis: Hackett.

Herder, Johann Georg [1784] (1967), *Ideen zur Philosophie der Geschichte der Menschheit*, ed. Bernhard Suphan, Hildesheim: Olms Verlag.

Huneman, Philippe (1998), *Bichat: La vie et la mort*, Paris: Presses Universitaires de France.

Huneman, Philippe (2006), 'From comparative anatomy to the "adventures of reason"', *Studies in History and Philosophy of Biological and Biomedical Sciences*, 37 (4): 649–74.

Huneman, Philippe (ed.) (2007a), *Understanding Purpose? Kant and the Philosophy of Biology*, Rochester: University of Rochester Press.

Huneman, Philippe (2007b), 'Reflexive judgement and Wolffian embryology: Kant's shift between the First and Third *Critiques*', in Philippe Huneman (ed.), *Understanding Purpose? Kant and the Philosophy of Biology*, Rochester: University of Rochester Press, pp. 75–100.

Huneman, Philippe (2008), 'Montpellier vitalism and the emergence of alienism in France (1750–1800): The case of the passions', *Science in Context*, 21 (4): 1–33.

Jacyna, Leon S. (1990), 'Romantic thought and the origins of cell theory', in Andrew Cunningham and Nicholas Jardine (eds), *Romanticism and the Sciences*, Cambridge: Cambridge University Press, pp. 161–8.

Kant, Immanuel [1790] (1987), *Critique of Judgment*, trans. Werner S. Pluhar, Indianapolis: Hackett.

Kant, Immanuel [1783] (1997), *Prolegomena to Any Future Metaphysics*, ed. and trans. Gary Hatfield, Cambridge: Cambridge University Press.

Larson, James (1979), 'Vital forces: Regulative principles or constitutive agents? A strategy in German physiology, 1786–1802', *Isis*, 70 (2): 235–49.

Lebrun, Gérard (1970), *Kant et la fin de la métaphysique*, Paris: Armand Colin.

Leibniz, Georg Wilhelm [1696] (1978), *De l'origine radicale des choses, et autres opuscules*, ed. Paul Schrecker, Paris: Vrin.

Lenoir, Timothy (1982), *The Strategy of Life: Teleology and Mechanism in Nineteenth Century German Biology*, Dordrecht: Reidel.

Linnaeus ([1748] 1972), *L'équilibre de la nature*, ed. C. Limoges, Paris: Vrin.

McLaughlin, Peter (1990), *Kant's Critique of Teleology in Biological Explanation: Antinomy and Teleology*, Lewiston, NY: Edwin Mellen Press.

McLaughlin, Peter (2002), 'Naming biology', *Journal of the History of Biology*, 35 (1): 1–4.

Modiano, Rachel (1985), *Coleridge and the Concept of Nature*, London: MacMillan.

Owen, Richard [1837] (1992), *Richard Owen's Hunterian Lectures, May–June 1837*, ed. Phillip R. Sloan, Chicago and London: University of Chicago Press/British Museum of Natural History.

Pross, Wolfgang (1994), 'Herders und Kielmeyers Begriff der organischen Kräfte', in Kai Torsten Kanz (ed.), *Philosophie des Organismus in der Goethezeit: Studien zu Werk und Wirkung des Naturforschers Carl Friedrich Kielmeyer (1765–1844)*, Stuttgart: Steiner, pp. 81–99.

Rehbock, Phillip (1983), *The Philosophical Naturalists: Themes in Early Nineteenth-Century British Biology*, Madison: University of Wisconsin Press.

Reill, Peter Hanns (2005), *Vitalising Nature in the Enlightenment*, Chicago: Chicago University Press.

Rescher, Nicholas (1981), *Leibniz's Metaphysics of Nature*, Boston: Reidel.

Rey, Roselyne (1987), 'Naissance et développement du vitalisme en France, de la deuxième moitié du 18ème siècle à la fin du Premier Empire', Thèse de l'université de Paris I.

Richards, Robert J. (1992), *The Meaning of Evolution: The Morphological Construction and Ideological Reconstruction of Darwin's Theory*, Chicago: Chicago University Press.

Richards, Robert J. (2001), 'Kant and Blumenbach on the *Bildungstrieb*: A historical misunderstanding', *Studies in History and Philosophy of Biology and Biomedical Sciences*, 31 (1): 11–32.

Richards, Robert J. (2002), *The Romantic Conception of Life: Science and Philosophy in the Age of Goethe*, Chicago: Chicago University Press.

Rueger, Alexander (forthcoming), 'Conceptions of the natural world', in Allen Wood and Songsuk

Susan Hahn (eds), *Cambridge Companion to Nineteenth Century Philosophy*, Cambridge: Cambridge University Press.

Schelling, Friedrich Wilhelm Joseph von (1856–61), *Sämmtliche Werke*, ed. Karl Friedrich August Schelling, 14 vols, Stuttgart: Cotta.

Schelling, Friedrich Wilhelm Joseph von (1907), *Werke*, ed. Otto Weiss, 3 vols, Leipzig: Eckhardt.

Schelling, Friedrich Wilhelm Joseph von [1801] (1911), *Von der Weltseele*, Leipzig: Meiner.

Schelling, Friedrich Wilhelm Joseph von [1799] (2001), *Erster Entwurf eines Systems der Naturphilosophie. Werke. Historisch-Kritische Ausgabe* vol. 7, ed. Wilhelm G. Jacobs and Paul Ziche, Stuttgart: Frommann-Holzboog.

Schelling, Friedrich Wilhelm Joseph von [1799] (2004), *First Outline of a System of the Philosophy of Nature*, trans. Keith R. Peterson, Albany, NY: SUNY Press.

Schmitt, Stéphane (2007), 'Succession of functions and classification in post-Kantian *Naturphilosophie* after 1800', in Philippe Huneman (ed.), *Understanding Purpose? Kant and the Philosophy of Biology*, Rochester: University of Rochester Press, pp. 123–36.

Schopenhauer, Arthur [1836] (1901), *On the Will in Nature*, trans. Karl Hillebrand, <http://en.wikisource.org/wiki/On_the_Will_in_Nature>.

Schopenhauer, Arthur [1818/1844] (1966), *The World as Will and Representation*, 2 vols, trans. E. F. J. Payne, New York: Dover.

Sloan, Phillip (2003), 'Whewell's philosophy of discovery and the archetype of the vertebrate skeleton: The role of German philosophy of science in Richard Owen's biology', *Annals of Science*, 60: 39–61.

Sloan, Phillip (2006), 'Kant on the history of nature: The ambiguous heritage of the Critical Philosophy for natural history', *Studies in History and Philosophy of Biological and Biomedical Sciences*, 37 (4): 627–48.

Sloan, Phillip (2007), 'Kant and British bioscience', in Philippe Huneman (ed.), *Understanding Purpose? Kant and the Philosophy of Biology*, Rochester: University of Rochester Press, pp. 149–70.

Steigerwald, Joan (2002), 'Epistemologies of rupture: The problem of nature in Schelling's philosophy', *Studies in Romanticism*, 41 (4): 545–84.

Strawson, Peter [1966] (1995), *The Bounds of Sense: An Essay on Kant's* Critique of Pure Reason, London: Routledge.

Thoreau, Henry David (1906), *The Writings of Henry David Thoreau*, 20 vols, Boston: Houghton Mifflin.

Von Baer, Karl Ernst (1828), *Entwicklungsgeschichte der Thiere: Beobachtung und Reflexion*, Königsberg: Göttingen.

Wellek, René (1931), *Immanuel Kant in England, 1793–1838*, Princeton: Princeton University Press.

Westphal, Kenneth (2008), 'Philosophising about nature: Hegel's philosophical project', in Frederick Beiser (ed.), *The Cambridge Companion to Hegel and Nineteenth Century Philosophy*, Cambridge: Cambridge University Press, pp. 281–310.

Whewell, William (1840), *The Philosophy of the Inductive Sciences*, London: Parker.

Wolfe, Charles (ed.) (2008), *Vitalism without Metaphysics? Medical Vitalism in the Enlightenment*, special issue of *Science in Context*, 21 (4).

Wolff, Caspar Friedrich [1764] (1966), *Theorie von der Generation in zwei Abhandlungen erklärt und bewiesen*, reprint edn, Hildesheim: Olms.

Zammito, John (1992), *The Genesis of Kant's* Kritik der Urteilskraft, Chicago: Chicago University Press.

Zumbach, Clark (1984), *The Transcendent Science: Kant's Conception of Biological Methodology*, The Hague: Nijhoff.

5

Idealism and Naturalism in the Nineteenth Century

Sebastian Gardner

1. Introduction

The nineteenth century may be regarded as comprising the first chapter in the story, as it must appear to us now, of idealism's long-term decline and of the eventual ascent within the analytic tradition of a confident and sophisticated naturalism.[1] The chief landmarks of both developments are fairly clear. The former begins with Kant's Critical Philosophy and the great systems of Fichte, Schelling and Hegel, a rich legacy which is re-explored continuously over the course of the century and provides the basis for myriad novel positions, leading in the final quarter of the nineteenth century to a renaissance of absolute idealism in Anglo-American philosophy. The story of the growth of naturalism may be taken to begin with Auguste Comte and to develop through John Stuart Mill and Herbert Spencer to Richard Avenarius and Ernst Mach, receiving an important impetus from the mid-century German materialism of Karl Vogt, Ludwig Büchner, Jacob Moleschott and Heinrich Czolbe (see Gregory 1977), as well as of course, after the publication of *The Origin of Species* in 1859, Charles Darwin's theory of natural selection, which found forceful advocates in figures such as Thomas Henry Huxley and Ernst Haeckel. The neo-Kantian development which established itself in Germany from the 1860s and 1870s onwards has a place in the trajectories of both idealism and naturalism.

Both of these narratives, sketched here in the briefest outline, require elaboration not merely through the addition of numerous other and less salient figures and movements but also through an account of their context: namely, the exponential growth of scientific knowledge witnessed in the nineteenth century, especially in physics, physiology and experimental psychology, together with the profound cultural shift accompanying the achievements and industrial applications of modern science, to which belongs the erosion of the institutional bases of Christian theism and demise of its intellectual authority. Closely bound up with these developments is the cultural dissemination of what might be called 'practical naturalism' – the view, reborn with the Enlightenment, that the true Good is of an exclusively worldly nature and its realisation fostered by scientific modernity.

What I propose to do in this chapter, in place of attempting to fill out the historical detail of each of the developments independently, is to concentrate on instances where they interact or come into significant contact. More exactly, my focus will be on philosophers of the period who did not simply and straightforwardly pursue either of the two tendencies but instead regarded the relation of natural scientific knowledge to metaphysical speculation as posing a problem not to be solved by coming down simply on one side rather than the other and so advanced positions which responded in a creative fashion to the competing claims of idealism and naturalism, in some cases offering a kind of fusion. This approach, I will suggest, allows us to identify what it was that formed for nineteenth-century philosophy, to the extent that one can generalise over such a period, the crux of the opposition of idealism and naturalism. Because the main locus of developments at the intersection of idealism and naturalism was Germany, the figures I shall discuss belong chiefly to German philosophy. The order of discussion is loosely chronological but I shall depart from the strict historical sequence where doing so helps to give the historical territory a clearer systematic shape.

2. Nature *versus* Freedom: Classical German Philosophy

Although anticipations can be located in early modern and even ancient philosophy, the opposition of idealism and naturalism, as it was understood in the nineteenth century, had its origin in classical German philosophy. Kant famously asserts in the Introduction to the *Critique of Judgement* of 1790 that 'there is an incalculable gulf fixed between the domain of the concept of nature, as the sensible, and the domain of the concept of freedom, as the supersensible' (Kant [1790] 2000: 63). While conceding that something must be done by way of constructing a connecting link from the one domain to the other – the overarching aim of the third *Critique*, Kant says, is to show that 'nature must be conceived in such a way that the lawfulness of its form is at least in agreement with the possibility of ends that are to be realised in it in accordance with the laws of freedom' – Kant regards it as inconceivable, for human as opposed to divine reason, that Nature and Freedom should be cognised as comprising two parts of a single unified reality.

This opposition of ontological realms – or, to the extent that our concern is with representations rather than their objects, of two domains of concepts and judgement – corresponds to and underpins the opposition of idealism and naturalism as philosophical or metaphilosophical positions. In so far as Nature and Freedom are considered to be not contiguous, mutually cohering realities but rather – by virtue of the principles and forms of explanation which they mandate – in metaphysical competition, they provide the basis for an exclusive disjunction: *either* we take the side of Nature, yielding the thesis that all existents are subject to natural law and that all true explanation is natural scientific in form; *or* we take that of Freedom, yielding the denial that Nature, as conceived in the terms of empirical natural science, is ontologically or explanatorily comprehensive and the affirmation that human subjectivity is non-natural yet irreducibly real. A more ambitious form of idealism will add that subjectivity itself supplies the grounds, if not ontological then at least conceptual, of Nature. On each alternative, the competition of Nature and Freedom is resolved by taking one of the pair to encompass the other.

Kant himself does not draw up the philosophical geography in exactly these terms. The highest opposition of (meta)philosophical positions recognised by Kant is that of transcendental idealism, his own standpoint, to transcendental realism, whose forms are legion and of which naturalism is only one. Nor is naturalism, in the sense that the term has for us now, regarded by Kant as of special interest and importance. Kant concerns himself variously with materialism, scepticism, empiricism and other standpoints which deny validity to pure reason and so annul the reality of Freedom and he in addition recognises an entrenched tendency in human reason (at the level of natural consciousness as much as that of philosophical reflection) to assimilate all objects of thought to empirical objects, but he does not envisage a position which seeks to appropriate philosophically the epistemological prestige of the natural sciences in the manner characteristic of naturalism as we now know it. In large part this is because Kant took his own position to accommodate as fully as can reasonably be demanded the distinctive epistemic authority of natural science: subsequent to the *Critique*, in the *Metaphysical Foundations of Natural Science* of 1786 and in the notes published as *Opus Postumum*, Kant attempted to show that his transcendental analysis of the conditions of experience could be extended to provide natural science with its basic concepts and principles.

Kant's organisation of the field of philosophical debate makes sense to the extent that one keeps in view and wishes to take issue with the huge number of 'dogmatic' but non-naturalistic pre-Kantian metaphysical positions, from Plato to Leibniz, in order to be able to present transcendental idealism as a novel, comprehensive and final solution to the problems of philosophy. But once the lesson of Kant's critique of supersensible metaphysics has been absorbed – once it has been accepted that metaphysics as an enterprise of theoretical reason is a vain endeavour, which can survive only in the attenuated form of transcendental idealism's system of principles of possible experience – and when in addition it is recognised that Kantian idealism is open to challenge from proto-naturalistic, Humean and Spinozistic quarters, as had been demonstrated in the early reception of Kant's *Critique of Pure Reason* and *Critique of Practical Reason*, the philosophical landscape changes. We then arrive at a view according to which the philosophical options divide cleanly and exhaustively between idealism and naturalism.

This is the picture presented by Fichte, whom we find maintaining in 1797 that at the ultimate limit of philosophical reflection an opposition is confronted between 'idealism' – which, according to Fichte, is necessarily transcendental in character and treats the free non-empirical subject as the universal philosophical *explanans* – and 'dogmatism', defined by its commitment to explaining subjectivity in terms of 'things', *Sachen*, these being either empirically real natural objects or modelled closely on them (see Fichte [1797] 1994: 12–25; and Martin 1997: 36–42). Fichte argues that the choice between these two standpoints, which comprise the only ones possible, is all-decisive, that is, it determines the results that we will reach in all other contexts of philosophical reflection. And it cannot, according to Fichte, be made on grounds of theoretical reason, for it is entirely possible to construe the world on the basis of mere *Sachen* – doing so will fail to reconstruct the self-positing *Ich* affirmed by idealism, but the significance of this failure cannot, by means of purely theoretical reflection, be communicated to the dogmatic standpoint, which must consequently be granted internal consistency.

In the course of German idealism's further development, which interweaves with German Romanticism, Fichte's disjunction is held to have been overcome. Schelling's more comprehensive idealism or *Real-Idealismus* obviates the need for an original choice of standpoints by refusing to grant in the first place the coherence of the naturalist's conception of natural phenomena as *Sachen*. Within Schelling's idealism, nature is treated in terms of idealist categories, and the a priori reflection which, he holds, establishes that Nature in the sense of *natura naturans* is infinite pure activity joins seamlessly with scientific enquiry, which reveals natural phenomena, from the most basic forces of light, electricity and magnetism up to the complex functions of natural organisms, to be stages belonging to a single unified process which culminates in – for it is directed towards – the coming-into-existence of self-consciousness. The *Naturphilosophie* of Hegel's *Encyclopaedia*, although proceeding in terms of a different set of philosophical categories from Schelling – Hegel's emphasis is on the immanent rationality, in the sense defined by his Logic, of Nature – borrows its pattern from Schelling.

Clearly, such philosophy had gone strikingly far beyond Kant. The 'system of natural causes' affirmed in the third *Critique* permitted judgements about nature to be *regulated* by teleological ideas, but by no means did Kant allow the very existence of Nature to be 'deduced' from Freedom: Kant's aim had been merely and modestly to coordinate Nature and Freedom, without implying their knowable ontological unity, let alone that Freedom is constitutive of Nature and that it is possible for us to explain the existence of mechanism in teleological terms.

At the time of Hegel's death in 1831 – when his system, though subject to much dispute, had no rival of equal strength – the most original, progressive and widely endorsed philosophical developments in Germany embraced, therefore, an idealistic resolution of the antinomy of Nature and Freedom. The *Naturphilosophie* of absolute idealism thus joined with the tradition of romantic science, indebted to Johann Gottfried Herder and enjoying the prestigious sanction of Goethe, pursued by such creative figures as Lorenz Oken, Franz von Baader, Karl August Eschenmayer and Gotthilf von Schubert. Had natural science in the nineteenth century followed the course projected for it by *Naturphilosophie*, the idealism/naturalism opposition would have disappeared from view and the notion that natural science threatens the reality of autonomous subjectivity would have come to be regarded as an error belonging to a more limited stage of philosophical understanding.

This was not, of course, how things turned out; the union of idealist philosophy and a posteriori enquiry into nature did not endure. It is important, however, to get this fact into focus. Romantic ideas about nature did not disappear or lose currency abruptly or at any clearly determinable point. They remained strongly influential, to such an extent that from the point of view of many nineteenth-century figures – Alexander von Humboldt, Gustav Theodor Fechner and Haeckel provide examples – the elements of their thought that we would consider genuinely 'scientific' join inseparably with those that we would call 'romantic'. This was not because the notion of a line of demarcation between science and pseudo-science was alien to the nineteenth century. Nineteenth-century thought about nature, even in the early decades, was not credulous or undisciplined and thinkers for whom the schemas and speculations of *Naturphilosophie* had intellectual appeal were not ignoring the evidence of their senses. The question of what counts as genuine empirical explanation had been a preoccupation of early modern philosophy ever since the over-throw of Aristotelianism, and Kant had affirmed the epistemological priority (for human minds) of mechanical over teleological explanation, and even laid down mathematisation as a stringent condition of natural scientific status. The extensive debates about vitalism and galvanism showed how fiercely the empirical credentials of theoretical entities could be contested. The crucial point, rather, is that even for those thinkers to whom it was as clear as it is to us now that science does not consist in grasping divine ideation and for whom the systems of German idealism represented so much verbal fabrication, the accumulated body of scientific knowledge did not determine sharply, in the way that it presumably does for us now, the scientificity of a given theoretical proposal.

That said, it remains the case that, for a variety of reasons, the notion that philosophical reflection can reach all the way down to empirical particularity and contribute to the content of natural science fell by the wayside: Hegel's system failed to retain its power of conviction for the following generation, *naturphilosophisch* forms of explanation came to seem fruitless and over the course of the century nature increasingly shook itself free of romantic attributes. In so far as nineteenth-century thinkers rejected the programme of uniting romantic speculation about nature with a theory of the Absolute and thereby abandoned the German idealist integration of Nature and Freedom, the opposition of idealism and naturalism re-presented itself.

3. After Hegel

If we ask where the earliest instance of a confrontation between idealism and naturalism is to be found, an obvious candidate is Ludwig Feuerbach, who provides an important bridging element in the transition from Hegel's idealism to Marx's materialism. In his first book, *Thoughts on Death and Immortality* of 1830, Feuerbach attacked the Christian doctrine of personal immortality, insisting on the bodily existence of the self, and naturalistic elements became increasingly prominent in the course of his critical appropriation of Hegel's thought for emancipatory humanist purposes, in particular in his introduction of the foundational concept of man's 'species-being', *Gattungswesen*.

Feuerbach's writings gave powerful encouragement to the German materialists, with whom Feuerbach later associated himself. It should be emphasised, however, that the naturalism of Feuerbach and that of the Young Hegelians more generally was of a tempered sort. It involved of course repudiation of the supernatural entities of Christian theology, but, once those had been expelled, there was little more to be gained for the purposes of radical social theory by emphasising man's embeddedness in the natural order; on the contrary, if human self-realisation constitutes the ideal for our endeavours, then man needs to be well distinguished from the rest of nature. Thus Feuerbach declared, in terms that a thorough-going naturalist would scarcely be able to accept, that: 'Man is not a particular being, like the animals, but a universal being . . . an unlimited and free being . . . this freedom and universality extend themselves over man's total being' ([1843] 1986: 69).

In addition, although foundational issues of epistemology and metaphysics were implicated in its attempt to provide an account of the conditions for human self-realisation – Feuerbach himself was committed to an unrefined empiricist identification of the real with the 'sensuous' ([1843] 1986: 49–51) – Young Hegelianism fought its battles chiefly not on the terrain of general metaphysics but rather of theology, Biblical criticism, philosophy of history and political thought. The materialist theory of history advanced by Marx, which locates man's original distinction from animals in his production of his means of subsistence and implies a strong continuity of human development with natural history, is not typical of Young Hegelianism but rather signalled his break from it (see Marx and Engels [1845–46] 1970: 37–52).

It is notable more generally that a number of the positions which pitted themselves explicitly against idealism in the first half of the nineteenth century were neither motivated by, nor pointed in the direction of, a naturalistic world-view. To take two central instances which have had lasting influence, Schelling's critique in his late 'positive' philosophy of Hegel's rationalism and Søren Kierkegaard's repudiation of the Hegelian System were both directed, on the contrary, to religious ends. Schelling and Kierkegaard both maintained the irreducibility of being to conceptuality and so affirmed that reality outstrips idealist comprehension, but for neither was being in the relevant sense a possible object of natural scientific investigation. Schelling's dark reflections on *Seyn*, inspired by Jacob Boehme, were intended to explain how the existence of Nature is related to that of God and to reconcile the unity of a necessary being with the multiplicity of the contingent phenomenal world. For Kierkegaard the value of the thought that Being eludes conceptualisation lay in the opening that it gave to recognition of the individual's 'existing subjectivity' as philosophically ultimate. The possibility of undertaking a critique of idealism without endorsing naturalism was facilitated by an identification of idealism with Hegel's system, rejection of which was compatible with embracing other forms of (idealistically inclined) anti-naturalism. Thus Schelling may be described, it has been suggested, as providing a 'self-critique of idealism', while Kierkegaard is standardly regarded as heralding twentieth-century existentialism.

4. Schopenhauer

To locate a more pointed expression of the naturalistic vision – untrammelled by emancipatory social concerns and free from any taint of Hegelian idealism – we should look before Feuerbach to Schopenhauer.

When the term German idealism is employed in its broadest sense, Schopenhauer is himself included within that movement. This has a plain justification, for the very title of his main work informs us that the world is to be regarded, in one of its two aspects, as mere 'representation', and Kant's theories are drawn on liberally by Schopenhauer in his account of phenomenal reality. But of deeper importance for the purpose of tracking long-term, underlying tendencies of philosophical development is the fact that the thought which stands at the centre of Schopenhauer's philosophical system is profoundly in accord with the outlook of modern naturalism.

The thesis that the world in its second, ontologically basic aspect is *Wille* contradicts Kant's conception of the order of things no less than it does those of Fichte, Schelling and Hegel. Kant had defined 'will' as the faculty of practical reason and the final architecture of Kant's Critical system locates man, on account of his capacity for pure practical reason, that is, morality, at the very pinnacle of creation. Kant tells us in the third *Critique* that the whole of nature may be regarded as having a *telos*, as constituting 'a system in accordance with the rule of ends, to which idea all of the mechanism of nature in accordance with principles of reason must now be subordinated' (Kant [1790] 2000: 250). Schopenhauer, while agreeing that man occupies a distinctive and privileged position in the order of things, departs from Kant on two key points.

First, Schopenhauer holds that there is fundamental metaphysical continuity between human beings and other organisms, indeed, empirical entities in general. Kant had reasoned in such a way that only rational subjects come to be regarded as possessing, in addition to their 'empirical character', an 'intelligible character' falling outside the bounds of empirical causality. Schopenhauer, in contrast, asserts that all empirical entities are to be regarded as manifestations of an intelligible character (Schopenhauer [1818/1844] 1966: 1: 156): persons and stones are equally objectifications of *Wille*, differing merely in the 'adequacy' of the 'grade' of objectivity possessed by the 'Idea' which defines the natural kind to which they belong; the 'deliberate conduct of man' differs from 'blindly acting forces of nature' only in 'degree' (1: 110).

Second, although Schopenhauer accepts the teleological description of natural phenomena and even agrees with Romantic-idealist *Naturphilosophie* that the natural world in its entirety must be considered a teleological whole (1: 153–61), there can be no sense in which the existence of man or anything else instantiates genuine purposiveness for Schopenhauer, for the very nature of *Wille* is inconsistent with the ultimate reality of any *Zweck*. That nature exhibits teleological order merely reflects the fact that nature expresses 'the identity of the *one* and indivisible will in all its very varied phenomena' (1: 119) and this One Will is 'a striving without aim', *ein Streben ohne Ziel* (1: 321), the inner nature of which is not characterised by purposiveness, which presupposes determination and so is internal to the sphere of representation: 'willing as a whole has no end in view' (1: 165). It is true therefore, as Kant says, that nature must be considered a system, but it is subordinated to no 'principle of reason'.

In accordance with this schema, Schopenhauer, recalling Hume, treats reason as a mere capacity for abstraction and man's intellect as a tool of the will, regarding human motivation in general as strictly subservient to natural drives and human action as strictly necessitated: knowledge 'enters as an expedient required at this stage of the will's objectification for the preservation of the individual and the propagation of the species' (1: 150). Schopenhauer's anticipations of Freud, with respect to the general tenor of his anthropological view as well as particular psychological hypotheses, have received frequent comment (and see Chapter 11 in this volume).

Although the final basis of the metaphysics of will is a priori, in so far as it derives from a necessary component of inner self-awareness, Schopenhauer maintains that, once we are in possession of this essential cognitive key, knowledge of the non-purposive character of *Wille* becomes available also a posteriori, through examination of the 'physiognomy' of natural phenomena (see Schopenhauer [1836] 1992), not least the quality of human experience – the predominantly painful, conflictual and pointless character of what proceeds in the phenomenal world is merely our apprehension a posteriori of the fact that purposiveness is a priori categorially alien to *Wille*.

In so far as idealism is defined less by a thesis of objects' mind-dependence than by the assertion that reality is ultimately akin to man's rational mind and therefore congenial to his exercise of capacities of freedom and reason which transcend his merely animal nature, Schopenhauer's philosophy is aggressively anti-idealistic: his system amounts to an assertion of the truth of naturalism in the language and terms of modern idealism. This becomes clear when it is reflected that all that is required in order to give Schopenhauer's metaphysics a bona fide naturalistic character is the naturalisation of *Wille*: if this ontological substrate is brought within the scope of natural science and thus the line between science and metaphysics pushed back, then the 'world as will' becomes the scientific image of a fully naturalised world and the 'world as representation' its manifest image.

Schopenhauer's philosophy did not draw attention or exert its influence until the middle of the nineteenth century and, when it did so, this consisted not in the direct fostering of naturalistic philosophical doctrine – the metaphysical idealistic character of his system ruled that out – but rather in making it an urgent topic of philosophical debate whether the nature of reality warrants optimism or pessimism. The connection with idealism and naturalism was, however, close to the surface. The genius of Schopenhauer's position lay in its suggestion that when Kantian idealism is properly thought through it agrees on fundamental points with naturalism, pace Hegel and rationalistic German idealism, just as naturalism, pushed to the limit, must acknowledge that empirical explanation needs to be completed with a metaphysical thesis; and that the upshot of this union is a practical and axiological outlook which merits the title of pessimism or, as Nietzsche later termed it, nihilism.

The challenge set by Schopenhauer was, therefore, to discover a way of sustaining optimism or at least avoiding pessimism without returning to Christianity or its Hegelian variant or subscribing to the programme of Comtean positivism, the naïvety of which Schopenhauer had exposed. Ever since the Enlightenment, the promise of naturalism, trumpeted by materialist *philosophes* such as Julien Offray de La Mettrie and Baron d'Holbach, had been to deliver unprecedented quantities of human happiness through the elimination of false supernaturalisms and the effective instrumentalisation of natural causes. This practical dimension was regarded not as an incidental gain but as integral to the rationality of the naturalistic world-view: it is no less pronounced in nineteenth-century British figures such as Mill and Spencer and naturalists with intentions of radical social and political reform such as Marx, Mikhail Bakunin and Eugen Dühring. But if, as Schopenhauer maintains, analysis reveals the very structure of Nature in man to be counter-hedonic, then naturalism is undermined on its own axiological territory and must accordingly restrict its claims of justification to the theoretical sphere. In this respect Schopenhauer, just as he turned idealism upside down, did the same with naturalism, pitting its own metaphysical implications against its self-association with practical fulfilment.

5. Hartmann

I now turn to consider a set of thinkers from the second half of the nineteenth century who engaged with the dichotomy of idealism and naturalism.

The first of these is Eduard von Hartmann, whose reception in academic quarters was generally unfavourable, but who enjoyed extraordinary popularity with the general public after the appearance in 1868 of his *Philosophy of the Unconscious*, a work which passed through eleven editions in its author's lifetime and continued to generate commentary well into the early twentieth century.

Hartmann's overarching description of his philosophy is that of a synthesis of the philosophies of Hegel and Schopenhauer (Hartmann [1868] 1931: 1: 4–5, 27–32, 117–25). The aim of uniting the optimistic arch-rationalist Hegel with the irrationalist arch-pessimist Schopenhauer may appear an extreme case of the nineteenth century's tendency to syncretistic eclecticism, but we can begin to appreciate why Hartmann's project is not arbitrary by considering the points at which Schopenhauer's differentiation of his position from that of Hegel betrays weaknesses.

Schopenhauer's basic dualism of, on the one hand, undifferentiated, impredicable, pre-empirical *Wille* and, on the other, a realm of spatio-temporal objects individuated and locked into mechanical causal relations with one another according to principles embedded in transcendental subjectivity is insufficient for metaphysical purposes. In order to account for the actual form of organised nature, Schopenhauer needs in addition, as noted, his theory of Ideas, which determine the essence or natural kind of individual phenomena. These Ideas may be thought of, Schopenhauer tells us, as distinct 'acts' by which *Wille* becomes objectual. But how is this objectification to be thought of and why does it occur at all? It cannot be merely the result of the subject's imposition of representational form, but if its explanation does not derive from the subject then it seems that it must lie in *Wille* – in which case there must be more to *Wille* than the bare blank dynamic of striving allowed by Schopenhauer. If *Wille*'s expression in the form of a world of objects is a metaphysically real event, not merely a matter of subjective representation, then this must have its explanation, which cannot appeal to mechanical causality, since this is confined to the world as representation, and neither, if *Wille* exhausts trans-empirical reality, can it be due to some external action upon it. By elimination, then, *Wille* must contain *within itself* the ground of its disposition to self-expression and if the concept of 'will' is to retain any meaning in this context it would seem that this ground can only be an *end* which *Wille* seeks to realise through expression.

This is exactly Hartmann's inference – a purpose must be attributed to *Wille*. And with purpose comes the attribution of conceptual content, forcing the union, Hartmann claims, of Schopenhauer with Hegel: it is precisely the Hegelian *Idee*, Hartmann suggests, that furnishes the ideational material which informs *Wille*. *Idee* gives the world its form and content, *Wille* its existence. The *telos* of the world – the ultimate realisation of which it is left as the task of humanity to complete, through collective abnegation of the will to life – is to undo the primordial metaphysical confounding of Will and Idea, restoring reality to a state of pre-lapsarian innocence. The world itself, having run its teleological course, will then disappear from existence. To that extent, Hartmann favours Schopenhauer's vision over Hegel's – salvation does not lie in rational social life – but at the same time he shows Schopenhauer's anti-teleological, anti-Hegelian conclusion to be the result of a failure to push philosophical explanation to its proper limit.

Thus far, Hartmann appears to have devised a new, baroque form of absolute idealism, one which resolves the antinomies of Hegel and Schopenhauer, optimism and pessimism, reason and will and which in that sense has to its credit a greater comprehensiveness than Hegel's system and may perhaps claim some advantage over Schelling's late philosophy, from which Hartmann borrows heavily. The associated and deeper sense in which Hartmann unites idealism with naturalism emerges when we consider his methodology.

I presented Hartmann as proceeding from the Schopenhauerian premise that the ontological substrate of the phenomenal world is *Wille*. Hartmann rejects, however, Schopenhauer's account of its epistemology and indeed all claims to a priori knowledge. The basis on which we can know the world to be *Wille*, Hartmann holds, is strictly inductive and his *Philosophy of the Unconscious* bears the sub-title: '*Speculative Results According to the Inductive Method of Physical Science*'. Hartmann describes his philosophy as one that '*takes full account of all the results of the natural sciences*' ([1868] 1931: 2: 63).[2] In direct contradiction to Kantian doctrine – and to the whole trajectory of modern scientific reflection – Hartmann defends the view that empirical inference warrants the positing of acts of will, which remain unconscious until the stage of animal existence is reached, as the explanatory ground of all natural events and kinds, organic and inorganic. The first two volumes of *Philosophy of the Unconscious* encompass a painstaking journey through the natural world, thick with references to contemporary scientific publications, in which Hartmann argues, with respect to everything from ganglions to gravity, that the hypothesis of an immanent will having as its content the representation of an end to be achieved enjoys the highest degree of probability. Finally, the overall unity and coherence of nature is argued to warrant a further inference, to a ground of unity of the plurality of acts of volition displayed in nature: the world, Hartmann concludes, consists of a single, cosmic *Unbewußte*.[3]

6. Lotze

The fact that Hartmann's reduction of mechanical causality to the teleology of volition contradicts the accepted modern view of mechanistic explanation as primary and self-sufficient is itself, arguably, no argument against his view. That said, one cannot fail to be struck by the poverty of Hartmann's case for a teleological explanation of natural phenomena and in consequence thereof the great under-motivation of the speculative by the *a posteriori* elements in his system.

The view that natural scientific explanation is exhaustively mechanistic was upheld – and indeed applied, in major contributions to medical science – by Rudolph Hermann Lotze, who was nonetheless one of the great late absolute idealists. The challenge for one who grants mechanism full sway over natural processes – and who also agrees that reflection on human knowledge must start with the facts of experience, as Lotze does, rejecting German idealism's attempt to 'deduce' Nature – and yet wants to uphold the truth of idealism is to explain why anything more than mechanism is needed.

Lotze has an essentially simple argument for the necessary incompleteness of the mechanical view (see Lotze [1856–64] 1888: Bk. IX, Ch. I; [1883] 1884: §§38–49; and [1883] 1892: Ch. I, Sects. XIV–XXI). Ordinary experience presents a world of Things, which have properties, stand in relations with one another and effect changes in one another's states. Naturalism affirms the adequacy of this schema, which natural science fills out and elaborates. Supposing that the basic conception of a propertied thing is granted, the question arises as to how it is possible for Things to act on one another (Lotze [1883] 1884: 56; [1883] 1892: 28). The answer, Lotze argues, requires us to reject the assumption of the independence of Things: in place of 'a multiplicity of self-subsisting Things' which become 'combined subsequently' – a conception which, Lotze argues, involves the incoherent conception of relations as entities located 'between' Things – we must suppose 'the self-subsisting existence of some background, or some medium [. . .] in which the relations of one real thing to another pursue their course' ([1883] 1884: 77; see also Lotze [1856–64] 1888: Bk. IV, 443–5, Bk. IX, 602–3). Instances of efficient causality between Things must be conceived, Lotze argues, as events *internal* to a self-subsisting One, 'modifications of a single whole' ([1883] 1884: 116).

This holistic view provides Lotze with the basis for further regressive inferences. Because, Lotze argues, the only identifiable source of the conceptual forms applied in ordinary apprehension of the world lies in the experience that we have of ourselves – specifically, the relation of our selves to our mental states is the only thing that can provide the basis for our conception of the unity of a Thing with its properties ([1883] 1884: 138–42; [1883] 1892: 47) – and because in addition there is no other way of giving content to the thought that individual Things enjoy real independent existence ([1856–64] 1888: Bk. IX, 644–7; and [1883] 1884: 137–8), we must suppose the underlying character of the world to be 'spiritual', *geistig*. This thesis in turn allows a careful reintroduction of teleology: although final causes can have no place within the world of natural science, teleology may be postulated, Lotze contends, in order to complete natural scientific explanation, on the basis that nature conceived scientifically fails to account for itself in the strongest sense and on the condition that purposiveness is taken to be wholly realised in lawful efficient causation, not an alternative or supplement to it. Moreover, Lotze supposes, we can postulate the final ground of the world to be the highest Good – meaning that, although necessarily fact and value remain distinct in our apprehension of the world, the distinction can be regarded as overcome at the point where reality achieves, as Lotze argues that it must, total unity ([1856–64] 1888: Bk. III, Ch. V and Conclusion and Bk. IV, Chs I–III; [1883] 1884: 151–2; [1883] 1892: 120–31).[4] In this way we are led to a conception which counts, in the terms of Schopenhauer and Hartmann, as unequivocally 'optimistic' and with which, Lotze argues, the central doctrines of Christian theism are consistent ([1856–64] 1888: Bk. IX, Chs IV–V; [1883] 1892: 70–1 and Chs III–VIII).[5] That his metaphysics establishes the possibility of ethics and agrees with our extra-theoretical interests – our 'yearnings' – constitutes, Lotze maintains, a point in its favour (see Moore 1901).

Lotze's basic argument may be regarded as a novel application of the traditional objection to an atomistic metaphysics. If all existents necessarily take atomic form, exhausting the content of the world, then there must nevertheless be something – at the level of the world, a 'world-principle' – that determines this to be so. A non-aggregative, 'atomising' One must precede the atomic Many.

Lotze's major difference from the German idealists is that, while the architecture of his metaphysics is that of absolute idealism, his evaluation of the epistemic achievement of his system – the degree to which we can claim by its means to have *comprehended* reality – is tentative and closer to Kant. Though we can explain why certain metaphysical theses are forced on us – why they are at least consistent and are all that remain once the alternatives have been eliminated – we cannot regard them as establishing the Hegelian identity of Thought and Being: 'all our "thinking" by no means altogether comprehends, or in the least degree exhausts, what we could regard as the "actual constitution" and "inner Being" of Things' (Lotze [1883] 1884: 149). Because the principles to which we are ultimately led 'never admit of being "explained", "constructed", or "deduced"', they cannot be 'converted into a major premise from which to deduce the sum of metaphysical truth' (Lotze [1883] 1884: 159, 153–4).

Lotze affirms, therefore, that while the Many must be traced back to the One, the reverse route cannot be followed by finite human minds ([1883] 1892: 40–1). Whether or not this asymmetry is consistent with the final stability of Lotze's system, it is clear at least that Lotze, unlike Hartmann, offers a defence of idealism which begins where naturalism begins, that is, with nature mechanistically conceived and that, if Lotze succeeds, then a non-negligible portion of the content of German idealism will have been retrieved without reliance on its famously questionable methodological apparatus ('intellectual intuition', 'the Concept', 'determinate negation' and so on).

7. Anglo-American Idealism

Lotze did not induce further attempts at absolute idealist system-building in German philosophy, which instead returned to Kant, but the idealistic movement which took hold in the last quarter of the nineteenth century in Britain and America stands under Lotze's influence and in important respects counts as his successor.

The first full study in English of Hegel's philosophy, James Hutchison Stirling's *The Secret of Hegel*, appeared in 1865 and in the 1870s Benjamin Jowett, influential at Oxford as a teacher and translator of Plato, urged that an interest be taken in German idealism. William Wallace and Edward Caird pursued this path and, along with Thomas Hill Green, who made clear the ethical and political fruitfulness of idealist ideas, completed the first, delayed wave of Anglophone assimilation of classical German philosophy, which had existed previously only on the edges of cultural life.

In 1893 Francis Herbert Bradley published *Appearance and Reality*, arguably the most deeply elaborated of the Anglophone absolute idealist systems. In Book I of the work Bradley unfolds a series of arguments claiming to show that any conception which involves the attribution of relational structure – of any sort, including that of a thing with qualities – reveals itself on analysis to be incoherent, for the reason that all attempts to explain how relations and their terms 'stand to' one another generate contradictions, absurdities or an infinite regress (Bradley [1893] 1897: 32; and see chs II–III). In light of this negative result, naturalism falls to the ground immediately: natural phenomena, being relational, cannot have absolute reality. Giving application to his thesis that the mode in which a relation is 'together' with its terms resists comprehension, Bradley underlines the metaphysical limits of natural scientific explanation:

The principles taken up are not merely in themselves not rational, but, being limited, they remain external to the facts to be explained. The diversities therefore will only *fall*, or rather must be *brought*, under the principle. They do not come out of it, nor of themselves do they bring themselves under it. The explanation therefore in the end does but conjoin aliens inexplicably. The obvious instance is the mechanical interpretation of the world. (563; see also 353–4)

Intelligibility is not restored, Bradley argues, by declaring that certain ultimate complexes – for example, the inherence of a quality in a thing – are simply 'given to us as facts' (563), since these putative facts amount to mere conjunctions of elements and

> no such *bare* conjunction is or possibly can be given. For the background is present and the background and the conjunction are, I submit, alike integral aspects of the fact. The background therefore must be taken as a condition of the conjunction's existence and the intellect must assert the conjunction subject in this way to a condition. The conjunction is hence not bare but dependent and it is really a connection mediated by something falling outside it. (564)

The role of 'background' – the 'something' presupposed by, but 'falling outside', the allegedly given fact – is played ultimately by 'the Absolute', which enjoys unity without relationality.

Whereas Lotze had begun with the manifold of interacting natural objects, Bradley proceeds at a higher level of generality: Bradley's argument for holism pertains to the absolutely basic structure of (discursive, predicative) thought and the stronger conclusion which Bradley reaches allows Lotze's holism to be converted into a monism, the content of which is explained in Book II of *Appearance and Reality*. What keeps Bradley's monism on the side of idealism – that is, distinct from Spinozism – is his claim that the only thing which exhibits the undifferentiated unified reality which, he has argued, must characterise the One, is 'experience' or 'sentience in its widest meaning' (555): the Absolute is 'an all-inclusive and supra-relational experience' (556).

Bradley evinces less concern than Lotze to accommodate the naturalistic wisdom of modernity. The rationale for Bradley's attitude becomes clear when it is recalled that his position requires him to oppose, or at any rate to step far beyond, the naïve position of ordinary consciousness. For Bradley it is 'out of the question' that metaphysics should 'approve itself to common sense' (547) and equally, he holds, it would be a mistake to think that metaphysics could be informed by – or could inform – the results of natural science: metaphysics rightfully challenges the naturalistic presumption inspired by science, namely, the claim that science possesses absolute truth, but thereafter it disengages from all questions concerning the content and proper form of empirical explanation, the aim of which is essentially different from – more limited than – that of metaphysics (283–6). Metaphysics does not, therefore, urge the reintroduction of ends into natural science, even though its own conception of the order of nature is that of an order of degrees of perfection (496–9).

Like Lotze and many late idealists, Bradley may be regarded as having articulated in greatly clarified terms certain lines of argument which were present but obscurely formulated in German idealist writing, and many of the same issues as had occupied Fichte, Schelling and Hegel were reworked in Anglo-American idealism.

The confidence of the British and American idealist hegemony at the turn of the century can hardly be exaggerated. Taking itself to have survived the challenge of Darwinism (see, for example, Royce 1892: Lecture IX) and equipped with a large bank of metaphysical argumentation, the view arose that idealism had established itself in perpetuity and with complete security. The Anglophone philosophical journals – *Mind* and the *Philosophical Review* in Britain and the *Journal of Speculative Philosophy* in the US – were altogether dominated in the last decade of the nineteenth century and first decade of the twentieth by discussion of topics in idealist philosophy, directed to the question not of whether idealism is correct but of precisely which form of idealism is correct.[6] When, on occasion, a confrontation is staged between the idealist and the naturalist, the naturalistic challenge seems to be entertained only so that idealism should have the opportunity of flexing its muscles. By way of illustration, consider the following, from the opening of a paper called 'The present meaning of idealism' delivered by Ernest Albee to the American Philosophical Association in 1909. Albee asks: 'What, then, may we all fairly take for granted in discussing the present situation in philosophy, no matter how divergent our final conclusions may seem, or may in fact be?' Albee answers: 'In the first place, it seems fair to assume that, for the technical student of philosophy, materialism [used interchangeably at this period with naturalism] proper is a thing of the past.' What defines and suffices for idealism, Albee says, is 'the teleological standpoint, that of inner meaning or significance, which is the standpoint of philosophy itself' (Albee 1909: 308; for further discussion, see Gardner 2007: 21–3). This makes it clear that idealism continued to conceive itself right up until the end in the terms supplied by classical German philosophy, that is, as practically and axiologically motivated and as giving metaphysical expression to what must at all costs be preserved – against modernity's naturalistic tendency – from our theological and humanistic heritage.

8. Scientifically Orientated Neo-Kantianism

Having followed the absolute idealist tradition to its nineteenth-century conclusion – its self-proclaimed victory over naturalism – attention should now be given to a late development in the idealist tradition more receptive to naturalistic insights.

Neo-Kantianism as such was emphatically not a species of naturalism, but it constituted a broad church and one of the most important tendencies within it – represented by Hermann Cohen, Paul Natorp and Ernst Cassirer at Marburg and by Alois Riehl – exhibited an orientation towards scientific knowledge which had much in common with the outlook of naturalism and which could plausibly be claimed, for reasons noted earlier, to mirror Kant's own intentions for transcendental philosophy.

Riehl shows how it is possible to go far in the direction of positivism while yet remaining within a doctrinal context of Kantian derivation. Riehl's chief work, *The Principles of the Critical Philosophy* ([1887] 1894), argued that philosophy aims at a 'general theory of the world' – which is also the common goal of the sciences as a whole – and that 'its method consists in the generalization of the generalizations of the sciences' (14). The relevant theory can be derived only from the growth of scientific knowledge: a 'theory of the world' in the sense of metaphysics 'is nothing more than a universal anthropomorphism' (14–15). Nor can philosophy concern itself with the strife between optimism and pessimism, which is merely a question of 'temperament and mood' (15).

What establishes Riehl as a Kantian is his denial that the conditions of knowledge are objects of psychological enquiry or of a nature that would permit a Darwinian grounding in substitution for transcendental proof (77–84). Riehl insists, however, that this does not render the principles which ground knowledge merely subjective: they should be 'thought as existing on the side both of the object and of the subject' (80). Transcendental philosophy is thus allied by Riehl to realism.

Riehl's late nineteenth-century Kantian repudiation of metaphysics belonged to a tradition – going back to Jakob Friedrich Fries,[7] a contemporary and vocal critic of Fichte, Schelling and Hegel – which aimed to affirm the epistemic supremacy of modern science while holding fast to Kant's insight concerning the inadequacies of classical empiricism and also without commitment to materialism. In this last regard Friedrich Albert Lange played a crucial role. Lange's influential *History of Materialism* ([1866: expanded 2nd edn 1873–5] 1950) offered a clear and powerful message, supported by critical examination of the history of materialist doctrines. Scientific materialism is led by a genuine insight concerning the empirical character of genuine knowledge, but it surrenders to the temptation to enter a metaphysical claim regarding the essence of reality which it itself cannot warrant, for the teaching of scientific enquiry – also, on Lange's naturalistic construal, that of Kant – is that all our knowledge is conditioned at base by the physiology of the human senses, creating an epistemic circle out of which we cannot hope to step.

From the neo-Kantians' standpoint, the later nineteenth-century absolute idealists, by detaching themselves from the Kantian starting point of a concern with the conditions of possible experience, saved themselves the task of overcoming subjectivism only at the cost of regressing to dogmatic pre-Critical metaphysics. Instead, it was urged, we must start with the fact of experience and since experience is necessarily conceptualised and the highest (most systematic and rational) conceptualisation of experience lies in science, this means taking our bearings from the Fact of Science. Theoretical philosophy is thus in the first instance reflection on the conditions of scientific cognition and metaphysics merely the correlate of epistemology.

A standard part of this position was a further demotion of teleology. The concept of purpose, Riehl declares, is – pace Kant – 'not a logical principle for the unification of thought, but rather a practical principle, a principle of the will', which does not belong to theoretical philosophy ([1887] 1894: 314, 342, 346).[8] Lotze's teleological metaphysics, which interprets the connection of things according to a supersensible plan, gives according to Riehl the appearance of all-inclusive knowledge and appeals to our aesthetic sense, but is in truth merely an artefact of thought based on a personification of reason (89, 345). Relevantly similar views of teleology appear in Fries, who consigns it to the spheres of faith and aesthetic feeling (Fries [1822] 1982: 166–7, 172–3, 188–93) and in Lange, who regards teleological thinking as explanatorily idle and symptomatic of a primitive mentality (Lange [1866] 1950: Bk. II, Sect. 2, Ch. IV, 69–71).

Even further along the neo-Kantian spectrum than Riehl stands Hans Vaihinger, whose *Philosophy of 'As If'* – published in 1911, though the main part of the work was composed in 1877 – proposed a radical merger of Kantianism with naturalism. Thought, according to Vaihinger, rests on biological bedrock – it evolves as a means of negotiating physiologically grounded impulses and sensational contents. Intellectual constructions are analysed by Vaihinger, however, along the lines of Kant's notion of 'regulative' ideas: concepts in general, including those of metaphysics, natural science, teleology, ethics and religion, are one and all 'fictions', of various distinguishable types, each with their own degree and species of internal justification. Jointly they compose an '"As if" world', which lacks reality in the ordinary sense ([1911] 1949: xlvi–xlvii). On this account, thought is an 'organic function', as naturalists maintain, yet it manufactures for itself a kind of Kantian autonomy. Signalling recognition of his proximity to Schopenhauer and Nietzsche, Vaihinger allowed that his 'positivist idealism' might be classified as 'anti-rationalism or even irrationalism' (xlvii, xlvi), since it repudiates the orthodox Kantian assumption of a fixed eternal human reason without natural origin. Though not a typical neo-Kantian, Vaihinger is indicative of how thin neo-Kantianism in its more scientistic form had allowed the division between idealism and naturalism to become.

Neo-Kantians rejected the naturalisation of value as much as that of cognition. One question which therefore arose, and which Fries and others did address squarely, is that of how judgements which aspire to validity but do not satisfy the conditions of natural scientific knowledge, such as those of morality and religion, are to be regarded. The answer is that, by and large, the scientifically orientated neo-Kantians applied Kant's strategy of epistemological dualism, that is, of partitioning robust cognition from belief which has a merely subjective, albeit non-arbitrary, warrant. The particular forms of epistemological dualism vary, but the approach is exemplified in Fries's appeal to *Ahnung*, indefinite intuitive awareness, as a discrete basis for morality and religious belief (Fries [1822] 1982: esp. Dialogues VIII–X) and in Lange's conception of the 'Standpoint of the Ideal' (which Lange finds expressed in the works of Friedrich Schiller) as compensating for the limits imposed on cognition by natural science (Lange 1950: Bk. 2, Sect. 4, Ch. 4).

The net contribution of neo-Kantianism – above all the Marburg school – to the maturation of naturalism was substantial (see Friedman and Nordmann 2006). The naturalistic spirit had received in the latter half of the nineteenth century formidable encouragement. The fact that scientific practice could yield increasingly impressive results, in seeming independence from any metaphysical grounding, appeared to testify to the gratuitousness of other modes of knowledge-seeking; Darwin's success in reaching a conclusion with undeniable importance for the traditional philosophical question of the nature of man further underlined the self-sufficiency and unboundedness of scientific enquiry; empirical psychology, in particular the experimental psychology of Wilhelm Wundt, put down institutional roots in German universities and invaded the citadel of subjectivity which classical German philosophy had taken to provide a secure ground for idealism. The practical trappings of naturalism, which in the previous century had stood in the foreground, allowing campaigners like d'Holbach to represent their outlook as genuinely humanistic, now seemed inessential to the naturalistic world-view and were, to an increasing degree, left aside: the self-sufficiency on purely theoretical grounds which can be claimed for scientific knowledge transmits itself, it came to be supposed, to the philosophical standpoint which identifies with natural science.

Though neo-Kantianism insisted on qualifying this claim to self-sufficiency, its quarrel with naïve naturalism was, in the larger scheme of things, a relatively minor matter. In positive terms, what neo-Kantianism helped to add to the self-certainty of science was an improved self-understanding. Science is independent of any particular set of axioms (contra Kant, who had mistakenly supposed it to be committed to Euclidean geometry and Newtonian physics), just as it is from materialism. Nor does it involve the phenomenalist reductionism or neutral monism of Mach. It is defined by *methodological* commitments and so exists as a task, not a set of doctrines. This task presupposes, furthermore, constructive conceptual input, in a sense that the inductivist conception of science elaborated earlier in the century by Mill failed to appreciate. These lessons were absorbed thoroughly by twentieth-century philosophy of science.

9. Nietzsche

Earlier we noted the challenge, posed by Schopenhauer, to discover a means of avoiding pessimism that is not philosophically retrograde. This can hardly be said to have been met by late nineteenth-century absolute idealism, the conservative tendency of which has been noted, nor indeed by scientifically orientated neo-Kantianism, which consigns the issue of 'life-orientations' to the domain of faith or some other second-class epistemic category.

Another feature of the full-bloodedly idealistic positions represented by Hartmann, Lotze and the Anglophone idealists meriting comment is their elimination of any properly transcendental component, which is to say that they do not regard the necessity a priori of our having to think such and such as itself – independently of any ontological claim – possessing final philosophical authority, as sufficient for any epistemic purpose or as normatively self-standing.

One nineteenth-century thinker with deep investments in both of the traditions we are concerned with, who does take Schopenhauer's challenge seriously and who reinstates the transcendental dimension of Kant's philosophy in at least the practical domain, is Friedrich Nietzsche. Nietzsche's absorption of Kantian idealism – originally from Schopenhauer, but later through direct reading of Kant (see Hill 2003) – shows itself markedly in his earlier writings, where the notion recurs repeatedly that the arrow of cognition necessarily fails to hit its target and that the objects of experience are mere illusion, but it also survives in the 'perspectivist' doctrine of his mature writings, which (whatever its exact content as a theory of truth, a matter of dispute) has at its core the idea that the subject's conditioning of its objects is not accidental but essential to the process of cognition.

The naturalistic dimension of Nietzsche's thought, to which much recent commentary has been devoted (for example, Geuss 1997; and Leiter 2002), reveals itself first in the writings of his so-called 'positivist' phase from 1878 to 1881, where it is claimed that science (in place of art, the previous occupant of this role) furnishes a model meriting emulation in all contexts, on account of the virtues which it fosters and the ethos in the face of reality which it exemplifies; and it then appears in a different form, as an integral component in the great critiques of morality of the late 1880s, *Beyond Good and Evil* and *On the Genealogy of Morals*, above all in the latter's proto-psychoanalytic exposure of the concealed motivational roots and affective dimensions of moral belief.

The mix of idealistic and naturalistic elements in Nietzsche's writings poses an interpretative problem,[9] to which various solutions have been proposed, one of which is to classify Nietzsche as a naturalised Kantian on the pattern of Lange and Hermann von Helmholtz. On that account, Nietzsche's position is that the facilitating conditions of cognition which Kant deems 'transcendental' are identical with and owe their special status to physiological structures which are open to empirical investigation. In support of this interpretation, it may be pointed out that Nietzsche does in fact entertain quasi-mechanistic explanations of even the most basic logical and metaphysical concepts. But this also shows what is puzzling about the naturalistic interpretation. Nietzsche saw clearly that naturalising Kantian conditions of cognition opens a wide door to the very scepticism which transcendental philosophy was designed to afford protection against; it leads not to realism but to its destruction. This leaves it obscure what position Nietzsche could have intended to occupy by arguing that the concepts of identity and being, for example, are mere side-effects of physiological processes – an epistemologically nihilistic thesis that, if it does not refute itself, undermines the sorts of positive claims that Nietzsche himself apparently wishes to make regarding, among other things, morality and human psychology.

Other candidate solutions to the problem of Nietzsche's combination of aggressive and deflationary naturalism with an idealistic epistemology have been proposed and the scale of the problem can always be reduced, either by devaluing Nietzsche's attachment to science or by arguing that the idealistic elements represent residues of his philosophical prematurity, or merely signal an attitude of fallibilist caution towards empirical truth, or belong only to Nietzsche's rhetoric. But the question arises eventually whether the endeavour to assign Nietzsche a consistent position at the ground level of epistemology and metaphysics is well conceived.[10] The alternative, which allows a different view of Nietzsche to emerge, is to accept that Nietzsche's engagement with the themes of idealism and naturalism, along with his experiments in radical scepticism, have a far-reaching non-traditional orientation.

What is beyond dispute is that Nietzsche's philosophical project has ultimately a practical end, the nature of which is hard to state without tending to the nebulous, but which pertains to the conditions of individual and collective cultural flourishing. Also clear is that Nietzsche does not regard modern science, whatever its limitations, as in any sense epistemically arbitrary, whereas the notion that an idealistic system of even Kant's relatively modest sort could either possess genuine truth or further the critically appraised ends of human beings is not on the cards for Nietzsche. If it is then observed that Nietzsche's reflections return repeatedly to the theme of a fundamental conflict between 'truth' and the conditions of life and that he affirms (explicitly in the Third Essay of the Genealogy) that in this respect modernity has, through its commitment to science, reached a point of acute contradiction, then we are drawn to the view that there lies at the heart of Nietzsche's philosophy a perception of the impossibility – if not universally, then at least for us now, in our actual philosophical habitat – of reconciling idealism and naturalism, to both of which we are nonetheless wedded: what is incontrovertibly correct in naturalism is its alignment of (modern) truth with modern science, while what we should not and cannot do (if we understand ourselves correctly, that is, contra Schopenhauer) is deny authority to our will to life and to the demand for value which it incorporates. This last constraint has, therefore, transcendental status: it corresponds, in a demoralised form, to what Kant called the primacy of practical reason and Fichte adopted as a foundational metaphilosophical principle and it provides Nietzsche with the justification he requires for rejecting the staple naturalistic reduction of value to states of happiness.

This interpretation promises to make sense of additional aspects of Nietzsche's philosophical outlook, including his high valuation of the aesthetic and the interest which he displays in developing metaphysical doctrines (eternal recurrence, will to power) for which it is hard to suppose he wishes to claim literal truth. The intended vector of Nietzsche's thought, on this account, falls between Hume's naturalism and idealism: Nietzsche does not suppose, with Hume, that practical consciousness, guided by Nature's providential hand, is self-stabilising and insulated from theoretical reason; but equally he rejects the Kantian-Fichtean grounding of the practical in pure Reason. What is left is a difficult balancing act, in which practical consciousness has to forge a new kind of relation with theoretical reason, which has no precedent since the tragic age of the Greeks. Hence the special value of the aesthetic, which includes for Nietzsche the aesthetic force of philosophical quasi-fictions such as eternal recurrence and will to power.

This view of the present philosophical situation as having arrived at an impasse, of inherited intellectual resources as exhausted and calling for drastic action – to be taken in a spirit oscillating between crisis, despair and fierce hope for future transformation – is witnessed elsewhere in nineteenth-century philosophy and stands in sharp contrast to the self-assured standpoints of thinkers such as Lotze and Bradley. Kierkegaard, Max Stirner and Marx in so far as he is construed as attempting to 'leave philosophy' (Brudney 1998) – all, like Nietzsche, situated by choice or necessity outside university life – exemplify a will to break radically with existing modes of philosophy. Nietzsche has, therefore, no monopoly on deep dissatisfaction with modernity, nor on the notion that philosophy must begin to play a new kind of game in which *praxis* takes precedence over *theoria* and in which, consequently, the traditional questions which give rise to doctrines like idealism and naturalism are either relegated or abandoned altogether. What distinguishes Nietzsche, in terms of his systematic place in nineteenth-century philosophy and the specific narrative we are following, is his understanding of the modern problem as reflecting the collision of the naturalistic contraction of theoretical truth in modernity with the non-naturalistic standpoint of practical reason and thus as traceable back to the original Kantian duality of Nature and Freedom.

10. *Lebensphilosophie*

In so far as a single conception of Nietzsche's significance prevailed in the closing years of the nineteenth and early decades of the twentieth century, it consisted in an identification of the central message of Nietzsche's philosophy with an assertion of the ultimacy of the concept of Life. Nietzsche was taken to have demonstrated the fruitfulness of taking the conception of man as a living being as foundational for the traditional philosophical purpose of making visible the true nature of things and directing human action accordingly. In this *Lebensphilosophie*, Life was understood not in mechanistic or biologically reduced terms, but as comprehending the full range of distinctively human capacities displayed in man's freely developing cultural and historical being, just as the environment in which man is embedded was conceived non-materialistically and corresponded more closely to what Husserl would later call the *Lebenswelt*. Applying this conception, Wilhelm Dilthey offered a philosophical foundation for the human sciences circumventing empiricism and metaphysics, designed to secure the autonomy of the *Geisteswissenschaften* (see Dilthey [1883] 1989; and Chapter 8 in this volume). In the early twentieth century, a similar approach returns in the *philosophische Anthropologie* of Max Scheler, Helmuth Plessner and Arnold Gehlen.

The outlook of *Lebensphilosophie* is of major importance for tracking the history of the relations of idealism and naturalism and it manifests itself in thinkers whose ideas were influenced not at all or very little by Nietzsche, including Henri Bergson and John Dewey. In the latter's case, Hegel takes the place of Nietzsche as a source of influence and it is not hard to understand how the *Phenomenology of Spirit* might be read as providing a justification for taking the totality of consciousness in its social, cultural and historical setting as marking the outermost circumference of philosophical reflection.

It is difficult for us, given our acquaintance with austere forms of naturalism and sharp awareness of the need for naturalism to stay lean if it is to merit the name, to avoid classifying the approach of *Lebensphilosophie* as covertly idealistic, but it is important to appreciate that the appeal of its strategy for those persuaded by it lay in its transcendence at a stroke of the irksome and fruitless dichotomy of idealism and naturalism: if 'Life' is conceptually primary, then the categories on which idealism and naturalism are fixated may be regarded as conceptually derivative latecomers, fit only to describe parts abstracted from a prior whole. A rigorous account of what it means to treat metaphysical categories in such terms – taken to the extreme conclusion that knowledge of reality is the prerogative of sheer intuition, counterposed to discursivity – is given in Bergson, whose most influential work, *Creative Evolution*, was not published until 1907, but whose thought can be regarded as a late chapter in the nineteenth-century development.

The positing of Life as a primitive conceptual unity would serve, therefore, the same unifying purpose as the systems of classical German philosophy, but this result would be achieved without taking a step out of the concrete natural and historical world into metaphysics or transcendental subjectivity. The critical question which arises – from the perspective of those disposed to think along more traditional Kantian lines – is whether *Lebensphilosophie*, by simply asserting the unity of Nature and Freedom, rather than labouring to construct or demonstrate it, has not availed itself of a pseudo-concept which merely conceals their antinomy.

11. Conclusion

The application of loosely defined terms to whole centuries of philosophical activity carries obvious dangers, but there can be little doubt that idealism and naturalism provide categories with genuine historical purchase which are no less essential for an understanding of nineteenth-century thought than the concept of the historical turn. It is true that nineteenth-century philosophers did not one and all line themselves up under one of the two headings like opposing football teams and that, for some, the important issues lay elsewhere. But a substantial number, including some of the century's greatest philosophers, did conceive themselves as belonging to one of the two traditions or programmes and a shared set of reference points – drawn from classical German philosophy and constructed around the original Kantian template of Nature *versus* Freedom, though also reaching back to figures and debates in the earlier modern period – gave each of the two tendencies a definite and coherent identity. Idealists and naturalists conceived themselves moreover – increasingly so over the course of the century, as the German idealist-romantic union of Nature and Freedom receded further into historical memory – as standing in a relation of opposition and the fact that the two traditions existed in close proximity while standing in logical conflict bound each to justify itself by engaging in critique of the other. It also raised the question of whether the opposition could be *aufgehoben* or in any sense mediated and the philosophers we have looked at show what different views of this matter could be taken.

Arguments between idealism and naturalism converged characteristically on the subject of teleology, the question of its scope and reality, attitudes to which served as a reliable indicator of idealistic or naturalistic orientation. This is not hard to understand, in so far as application of the concept of teleology beyond the purely human sphere provides an entry point to the broader idealist thought that reality is mind-like and not in its essence alien or indifferent to human existence.

Kant's account of the topic, shared by the German idealists, allows the tendency for arguments between idealists and naturalists to gravitate towards teleology to be explained in a more systematic way. Teleological judgement is connected conceptually by Kant with the non-naturalistic concepts of, first, wholes which determine their parts and, second, what Kant calls the 'unconditioned' or 'supersensible'. To judge that a natural object exhibits a purpose is to represent it as (as if) caused by a concept – a type of cause which must be rational, hence non-natural – and so to represent its parts as determined by (the concept of) its whole; in so far as human reason conceives and seeks to cognise nature as a whole prior to its parts, it anticipates and refers itself implicitly to 'intellectual intuition', the trans-human mode of cognition necessary and sufficient for knowledge of things in themselves and unconditioned totality. To vindicate teleology at the level of general metaphysics would be, therefore, to subordinate Nature to a supersensible reality standing in relation to it as an unconditioned One to its conditioned Many. If, at the same time, the empirical manifold, the basic fact that there exists a plurality of natural phenomena, can be taken simply as given – if it as such presents no philosophical *explanandum* – then this central nineteenth-century argument against naturalism fails and teleological judgement, if it has any validity at all outside the context of human action, may be confined to the sphere of natural organisms and subordinated to the conditions of mechanistic explanation.

This construal of the options contrasts with our present philosophical outlook – wherever one stands – on several fronts.

In terms of the Anglophone or analytic mainstream, as remarked at the outset, not merely has the default switched from idealism to naturalism but the very notion of idealism as a deep, continuous tradition going back to Plato, which incorporates an ontological thesis concerning the grounds and underlying nature of the phenomenal world, has evaporated; to the extent that there is any unitary conception of an alternative to naturalism, it is neither identified with idealism nor thought to involve a commitment to a teleological metaphysics. The issues which now occupy those testing the limits of naturalism, such as mental content and the reducibility of normativity, although continuous with nineteenth-century debates about the analysis of cognition and psychologism, had no elevated place in nineteenth-century arguments about idealism and naturalism, which were of broader scope and in which a loud echo of the earlier modern conflict of science with religion can still be heard. This reflects the fact – which belongs, as observed previously, to the legacy of the nineteenth century – that naturalism, while refining itself as a set of finely differentiated and technically elaborated positions in theoretical philosophy, has ceased to advertise itself as a practical or cultural programme.

From the standpoint of the central currents of twentieth-century European philosophy, the gap is less marked, in so far as traditions such as phenomenology, hermeneutics and post-structuralism have retained connections with Kant and German idealism, repudiated naturalism and conceived the task of philosophy in terms which, if not always humanistic, at any rate preclude its contraction to questions of theoretical reason. In the case of phenomenology, in which transcendental concerns remain very much alive and the critique of naturalism has been developed further, the continuity with nineteenth-century concerns is clear. With regard to other Continental movements, particularly in the latter half of the twentieth century, the acute sense of the antinomy of Freedom and Nature, crucial for nineteenth-century developments, does not play a determining role, making it harder to appreciate the motivation of teleological idealism. Underlying this divergence is the fact that idealism and naturalism and the problem of their dichotomy belong to the project of the Enlightenment and earlier modern philosophy and inevitably lose significance in contexts where the philosophical agenda has taken a counter-Enlightenment turn.

These differences help to account for the strangeness of many of the figures populating the landscape of nineteenth-century philosophy, study of which throws into relief, whether or not it prompts us to reconsider, our present orientations.

Notes

1. Maurice Mandelbaum, in his outstanding study of the nineteenth century (1971), identifies 'positivism' as one of its two great tendencies. Positivism and naturalism are terms by no means always employed as equivalents, but in the present context we need not choose between them, since both must be understood broadly in order to serve the relevant historical purpose and Mandelbaum's definition of positivism (1971: 11) coincides with naturalism as I here understand it.
2. Translations from this (and other untranslated German texts) are the author's own.
3. For more detailed discussion, see Gardner 2010.

4. On Lotze's reasoning, see Moore 1901: ch. 2; Thomas 1921: ch. 12.
5. Note, however, Lotze's admission that the problem of evil is insoluble ([1883] 1892: 145).
6. It should be pointed out that, for reasons of space and because it does not interact in distinctive ways with naturalism, I have not discussed the important 'personalistic' strand of late idealism represented in Germany by Immanuel Hermann Fichte and Christian Hermann Weiße and in Britain and the US respectively by Andrew Seth (a.k.a. A. S. Pringle-Pattison) and George Holmes Howison. Such ('pluralistic') idealism countered Hegel with claims for the reality of both divine and individual human personality. Lotze too differentiates himself from the German idealists on this point. This theme is of particular importance for understanding Anglo-American idealist developments after Bradley. Personalism or 'spiritualism' – with its roots in Maine de Biran and Victor Cousin and a strong relation to Catholicism – comprised also the dominant force in later nineteenth-century French philosophy. The principal figures include Charles Renouvier, Félix Ravaisson, Jules Lachelier and Émile Boutroux. Renouvier, Lachelier and Boutroux may also be classified – alongside Léon Brunschvicg – as French neo-Kantians. On Maine de Biran and Ravaisson, see inter alia Mark Sinclair's discussion in Chapter 10 of this volume.
7. See Franks 2007, an illuminating account of the post-Kantian development in its relation to the challenge of naturalism; Fries is discussed at 253–6.
8. For Riehl's full account see Riehl [1887] 1894: Part II, Ch. 5, §§3–10.
9. To give a concrete idea of the difficulty, compare the following from Nietzsche's Nachlaß: (1) 'When I think of my philosophical genealogy, I feel connected to the anti-teleological, i.e. Spinozistic movement of our age . . . [and] to the mechanistic movement (all moral and aesthetic questions traced back to physiological ones, all physiological ones to chemical ones, all chemical ones to mechanical ones)' (1967–: VII (2): 264; from summer to autumn 1884). (2) '"Mechanical necessity" is not a fact: it is we who first interpreted it into events . . . We only invented *thinghood* on the model of the subject . . . If we no longer believe in the *effective* subject, then there also disappears belief in *effective* things, in reciprocity, cause and effect . . . The world of *effective atoms* disappears as well of course' (1967–: VIII (2): 47–8; from spring 1887).
10. Green 2002, concentrating on the tension of naturalistic and non-naturalistic elements in Nietzsche's epistemology, denies that Nietzsche had *one* considered epistemological position.

References

Albee, Ernest (1909), 'The present meaning of idealism', *Philosophical Review*, 18: 299–308.

Bradley, Francis Herbert (1897), *Appearance and Reality: A Metaphysical Essay*, 2nd edn with appendix, London: Swan Sonnenschein.

Brudney, Daniel (1998), *Marx's Attempt to Leave Philosophy*, Cambridge, MA: Harvard University Press.

Dilthey, Wilhelm [1883] (1989), *Introduction to the Human Sciences. Selected Works* vol. I, ed. Rudolf A. Makkreel and Frithjof Rodi, Princeton: Princeton University Press.

Feuerbach, Ludwig [1843] (1986), *Principles of the Philosophy of the Future*, trans. Manfred H. Vogel, Indianapolis: Hackett.

Fichte, Johann Gottlieb [1797] (1994): '[First] Introduction to the Wissenschaftslehre', in J. G. Fichte, *Introductions to the Wissenschaftslehre and Other Writings (1797–1800)*, trans. and ed. Daniel Breazeale, Indianapolis: Hackett, pp. 7–35.

Franks, Paul (2007), 'Serpentine naturalism and protean nihilism: Transcendental philosophy in anthropological post-Kantianism, German idealism and neo-Kantianism', in Brian Leiter and Michael Rosen (eds), *The Oxford Handbook of Continental Philosophy*, Oxford: Oxford University Press, pp. 243–86.

Friedman, Michael and Alfred Nordmann (eds) (2006), *The Kantian Legacy in Nineteenth-Century Science*, Cambridge, MA: MIT Press.

Fries, Jakob Friedrich [1822] (1982), *Dialogues on Morality and Religion*, trans. David Walford, ed. D. Z. Phillips, Oxford: Blackwell.

Gardner, Sebastian (2007), 'The limits of naturalism and the metaphysics of German idealism', in Espen Hammer (ed.), *German Idealism: Contemporary Perspectives*, London: Routledge, pp. 19–49.

Gardner, Sebastian (2010), 'Eduard von Hartmann's *Philosophy of the Unconscious*', in Angus Nicholls and Martin Liebscher (eds), *Thinking the Unconscious: Nineteenth-Century German Thought*, Cambridge: Cambridge University Press, pp. 173–99.

Geuss, Raymond (1997), 'Nietzsche and morality', *European Journal of Philosophy*, 5: 1–20.

Green, Michael Steven (2002), *Nietzsche and the Transcendental Tradition*, Urbana, IL: University of Illinois Press.

Gregory, Frederick (1977), *Scientific Materialism in Nineteenth-Century Germany*, Dordrecht: Reidel.

Hartmann, Eduard von [1868] (1931), *Philosophy of the Unconscious: Speculative Results According to the Inductive Method of Physical Science*, 3 vols, trans. William Chatterton Coupland, London: Kegan Paul.

Hill, R. Kevin (2003), *Nietzsche's Critiques: The Kantian Foundations of His Thought*, Oxford: Oxford University Press.

Kant, Immanuel [1790] (2000), *Critique of the Power of Judgement*, ed. Paul Guyer, trans. Paul Guyer and Eric Matthews, Cambridge: Cambridge University Press.

Lange, Frederick Albert [1873–5] (1950), *The History of Materialism, and Criticism of its Present Importance*, expanded 2nd edn, trans. Ernest Chester Thomas, London: Routledge and Kegan Paul.

Leiter, Brian (2002), *Nietzsche on Morality*, London: Routledge.

Lotze, Rudolph Hermann [1883] (1884), *Outlines of Metaphysics: Dictated Portions of the Lectures*, Boston: Ginn, Heath & Co.

Lotze, Rudolph Hermann [1856–64] (1888), *Microcosmus: An Essay Concerning Man and His Relation to the World*, trans. Elizabeth Hamilton and E. E. Constance Jones, New York: Scribner & Welford.

Lotze, Rudolph Hermann [1883] (1892), *Outlines of a Philosophy of Religion*, London: Sonnenschein.

Mandelbaum, Maurice (1971), *History, Man, and Reason: A Study in Nineteenth-Century Thought*, Baltimore: Johns Hopkins University Press.

Martin, Wayne (1997), *Idealism and Objectivity: Understanding Fichte's Jena Project*, Stanford, CA: Stanford University Press.

Marx, Karl, and Frederick Engels [1845–6] (1970), *The German Ideology*, ed. Christopher John Arthur, London: Lawrence & Wishart.

Moore, Vida F. (1901), *The Ethical Aspect of Lotze's Metaphysics*, New York: Macmillan.

Nietzsche, Friedrich (1967–), *Werke: Kritische Gesamtausgabe*, ed. Giorgio Colli and Mazzino Montinari, 9 divisions, 40 vols, Berlin: de Gruyter.

Riehl, Alois [1887] (1894), *The Principles of the Critical Philosophy: Introduction to the Theory of Science and Metaphysics*, trans. Arthur Fairbanks, London: K. Paul, Trench, Trübner & Co.

Royce, Josiah (1892), *The Spirit of Modern Philosophy: An Essay in the Form of Lectures*, Boston: Houghton Mifflin.

Schopenhauer, Arthur [1818/1844] (1966), *The World as Will and Representation*, 2 vols, trans. E. F. J. Payne, New York: Dover.

Schopenhauer, Arthur [1836] (1992), *On the Will in Nature: A Discussion of the Corroborations from the Empirical Sciences that the Author's Philosophy has Received since its First Appearance*, trans. E. F. J. Payne, ed. David E. Cartwright, New York: Berg.

Thomas, Evan Edward (1921), *Lotze's Theory of Reality*, London: Longmans, Green & Co.

Vaihinger, Hans [1911] (1949), *The Philosophy of 'As If': A System of the Theoretical, Practical and Religious Fictions of Mankind*, trans. C. K. Ogden, London: Routledge and Kegan Paul.

6

Darwinism and Philosophy in the Nineteenth Century: The 'Whole of Metaphysics'?

Gregory Moore

1. Introduction

More than twenty years before the publication of *The Origin of Species*, Charles Darwin was already certain that his embryonic hypothesis would have far-reaching consequences and not just in biology. 'My theory', he wrote in 1837, 'would give zest to recent and fossil comparative anatomy; it would lead to the study of instinct, heredity and mind-heredity, [the] whole [of] metaphysics' (Darwin 1887: 1: 370). By emphasising mutability and struggle instead of stability and harmony, by banishing the last intellectually respectable vestiges of supernaturalism, by asserting a genealogical continuity between humanity and the rest of the animal kingdom that shone light on the provenance of our proudest endowments – reason, morality, language – Darwin would surely turn the world upside down. Small wonder, then, that Josiah Royce, at the close of the nineteenth century, could conclude: 'With the one exception of Newton's *Principia*, no single book of empirical science has ever been of more importance to philosophy than this work of Darwin's' (Royce 1892: 286).

But what kind of influence did Darwin have on philosophy, exactly? The answer to this question, or at least part of the answer, was provided by John Dewey in a 1909 lecture celebrating the fiftieth anniversary of the appearance of *The Origin of Species*. Dewey, who was born in that auspicious year, 1859, argues that Darwinism 'introduced a mode of thinking that in the end was bound to transform the logic of knowledge and hence the treatment of morals, politics and religion'. It challenges us to throw off our stale intellectual habits and prejudices, to recognise grand, all-encompassing systems – the 'wholesale type of philosophy'– as futile. Philosophy must therefore become narrower in its focus, more honest in its aims and procedures; it must forswear 'inquiry after absolute origins and absolute finalities in order to explore specific values and the specific conditions that generate them'. But, as Dewey himself conceded, this novel practice had yet to be established. While there were many 'sincere and vital efforts' to revise our conceptions in accordance with the demands of the here and now – and Dewey had in mind his own instrumentalism, rooted in the pragmatic tradition – a 'recrudescence of absolutistic philosophies' was also discernible (Dewey 1910: 2, 16, 13, 18). These 'absolutistic philosophies', however, had never gone away. If some philosophers not only embraced Darwinism as a personal conviction but also weighed the problems thrown up by a consistently naturalistic understanding of the world, there were plenty of others who, though they readily adopted a pseudo-Darwinian vocabulary of evolutionary change, were either unable or unwilling to face up to the new reality, instead remaining loyal to obsolete patterns of thought. As we shall see from the following survey of contemporary philosophical discussions of nature, epistemology and ethics, Darwin's impact on the discipline before 1900 was more modest and superficial than either he or Dewey anticipated, failing to touch, in Darwin's youthful words, the 'whole of metaphysics'.

2. God and Cosmic Evolution

One of the enduring myths surrounding the so-called 'Darwinian Revolution' is that the author of *The Origin of Species* took an axe to the rotting timbers of the theological universe, fatally weakened since Copernicus first put the earth and the sun out of joint. Yet the old verities were not suddenly swept away to begin an era of dizzying contingency. Admittedly, the boldest thinkers of the time grasped the implications of what Daniel C. Dennett has called Darwin's 'dangerous idea' (Dennett 1995). Marx, who once offered to dedicate the English translation of *Das Kapital* to Darwin, recognised that the latter's achievement had been not only to abolish teleology and metaphysics but also (rather less plausibly) to deliver 'a basis in natural science for the class struggle in history' (Adoratsky 1934: 125). And Nietzsche spoke of the 'terrible consequence of Darwinism, which incidentally I hold to be true' (Nietzsche 1999: 7: 461).

At the other extreme was the founding father of British idealism, James Hutchison Stirling, who had nothing but sneering contempt for the philosophical cogency of what he alone dubbed 'Darwinianism'. As a devout Christian and an equally devout Hegelian, he recoiled from a restless, turbulent planet ruled by 'Mr Darwin's sinuosities of accident' and took solace in 'the eternal presence of all-pervading purpose' (Stirling 1894: 301).[1] Many thinkers, even if they were not overtly or conventionally religious, shared Stirling's palpable anxiety. John Stuart Mill, for example, worried that the 'principle of "the survival of the fittest"' would, if proven, vitiate the Argument from Design and thus the only 'scientific' case for the existence of God – an outcome he thought unlikely, though, since 'in the present state of our knowledge' there was 'a large balance of probability in favour of creation by intelligence' (Mill 1874: 172, 174). Others accepted the fact of evolution – of that much Darwin had persuaded them – but refused to accept a vision of life as unceasing struggle (Bowler 1983). Beyond the blood and butchery, they reassured themselves, there was an underlying order and meaning in nature. Evolution led to moral, social and intellectual improvement, a future 'golden age', in the words of one Berlin professor (Gizycki 1876: 93); it was no longer merely a means of accounting for species change, but also the basis of a modern theodicy. Even the zoologist Ernst Haeckel, Darwin's paladin in Germany, moved ever closer towards a pantheistic natural religion that found expression in a best-selling and much-translated 1899 work of speculative philosophy entitled *Die Welträtsel* (The Riddle of the Universe). Haeckel now insisted that evolution was a cosmic event, a manifestation of the creative, vital energy with which every atom was imbued. His 'monism', his affirmation of the unity of mind and matter, turned out to be little more than romantic nature-worship.

Perhaps the most influential example of this desire to soft-pedal the theory of evolution is also, not coincidentally, the very figure celebrated by his peers as the pre-eminent 'philosopher of the doctrine of Development' (Alexander Bain, quoted in Richards 1987: 244): Herbert Spencer. Though scarcely regarded today as a serious thinker, if he is remembered at all, Spencer was, in Darwin's estimation, 'by far the greatest philosopher in England; perhaps equal to any that have lived' (Darwin 1887: 2: 301) and his books sold tens of thousands of copies. Yet his commercial success owed less to the validity of his conclusions than to the felt need that his writings met. His major work, the multi-volume *Synthetic Philosophy*, which appeared from 1862 to 1893, was an ambitious attempt not only to unify the increasingly specialised domains of human knowledge – biology, psychology, sociology and ethics – on the basis of his own variety of evolutionism but also to bring the theory of evolution into harmony with more traditional beliefs. Spencer's bid to broker peace between science and religion in his 1862 work *First Principles* is a Victorian fudge. Both, he is confident, are easy allies, finding common cause in their recognition that there is an 'Ultimate Reality', an inscrutable and incomprehensible power that works through myriad agencies in shaping the universe. Like the divine, the biologist, despite finding an exhaustive catalogue of the substances complicit in the production of life, must stop short, for the essence of vitality 'cannot be conceived in physico-chemical terms' (Spencer 1898: 120). As an agnostic, a category of faith invented by his friend Thomas Henry Huxley, Spencer hastened to reject as fruitless investigations into this noumenal realm, of whose being we are intuitively convinced, but of whose nature we must remain ignorant; it was instead 'our highest wisdom and our highest duty to regard that through which all things exist as the Unknowable' – a pallid substitute for God and the proper sphere to which nebulous religious sentiments were consigned (Spencer 1862: 113). But for all its supposed mysteriousness, Spencer knew plenty about the Unknowable: it was infinite, impersonal, unfathomable, unconditional and indestructible and by the time he was finished many of his readers felt perfectly at home with it.

As he never tired of reminding a forgetful public, Spencer was an evolutionist before Darwin. It was Spencer, not Darwin, who popularised the term 'evolution' (which does not occur in the earliest editions of *The Origin of Species*) and who coined the fatal phrase 'survival of the fittest'. But in truth Spencer's concept of Evolution with a capital 'E' – adumbrated in his first major work, *Social Statics* of 1851 and elaborated throughout the 1850s (for example in the essays 'The Development Hypothesis' of 1852 and 'Progress: Its Law and Cause' of 1857) – bears little resemblance to the one with which Darwin would later operate. Spencer declared that biological evolution was just one instance of a developmental process unfolding on a cosmic scale, which he derived from the laws of the indestructibility of matter and the conservation of energy. Evolutionary transformation consisted in the redistribution of matter and the dissipation of motion, leading to the progress of all phenomena, whether plant, animal, human society or the solar system, from simple states to conditions of structural complexity through the determination and combination of their constituent parts. Or, in Spencer's oft-repeated formula: 'Evolution is a change from an indefinite, incoherent homogeneity to a definite, coherent hetero-geneity, through continuous differentiations and integrations' (Spencer 1862: 216). Some were impressed by Spencer's effort to explain the entire universe by this unitary evolu-tionary principle. 'The fluctuations of the Exchange', gushed one admirer, 'are thus subject to the same law as the passage of a comet; while the victories of Alexander and the works of Shakespeare are reducible to the same factors as the Falls of Niagara and the spots on the sun' (d'Alviella 1885: 41). Others, like the mathematician Thomas P. Kirkman, were struck only by the vagueness of Spencer's proposition: 'Evolution', he mocked, 'is a change from a nohowish, untalkaboutable, all-alikeness, to a somehowish and in-general-talk-aboutable not-all-alikeness, by continuous something-elseifications and sticktogethera-tions' (quoted in Spencer 1900: 519).

Spencer held that the emergence of life was an inevitable corollary of the tendency for matter to organise itself, as was the increasing diversity and sophistication of biological forms evident in the gulf that separates amoebae from human beings. Organic modification takes place through an adaptive mechanism which Spencer calls the principle of equilibriation: each organism exists in a delicate balance which it struggles to maintain between itself and its environment. Because the latter is in flux, however, internal systems of adjustments by which life preserves itself have also to be continuously rearranged, producing shifting equilibria until either the organism fails to adapt to its new circumstances or eventually succumbs to the processes of dissolution. Successful adaptations, though, are transmitted to offspring over many generations through the Lamarckian device of the inheritance of functionally acquired characters. When the *Origin of Species* was published and its terminology quickly gained currency, Spencer simply refined and updated his deductions: he granted that he was wrong on the details, on the mechanism by which evolution occurs, but saw in Darwin's work a vindication of his leading idea: 'to have the theory of organic evolution justified was of course to get further support for that theory of evolution at large with which . . . all my conceptions were bound up' (Spencer 1904: 2: 50). But if Darwin's views had very little effect upon the general structure of Spencer's philosophy, they had a notable effect upon its public reception. Spencer was indignant that he should be regarded as a mere mouthpiece of Darwin; yet his enormous popularity was due, at least in part, to the widespread presumption that his metaphysics had a sound scientific basis: the Darwinian theory of natural selection.

John Fiske was one of Spencer's most indefatigable champions in America; indeed, he was so besotted with the British philosopher that he read aloud from the *First Principles* when courting the woman who nevertheless agreed to marry him. Like his master, Fiske, whose heterodoxy barred his appointment to a permanent post at Harvard, was concerned to mitigate the repercussions of the evolutionary world-view, effecting a reconciliation between Darwinism and religion that was thoroughly in accord with American optimism. In his major work, *Outlines of Cosmic Philosophy* of 1874, and elsewhere, Fiske framed an evolutionary philosophy (called 'Cosmism') based on a notion of God as immanent in the world and 'disclosed in every throb of its mighty rhythmical life' (Fiske 1885: xxviii). Fiske's God was infinite power, stripped of anthropomorphic attributes, and, though he could be known only by his manifestations in nature, this deity was, for Fiske, a fitting object of reverence. The doctrine of evolution:

> brings before us with vividness the conception of an ever present God – not an absentee God who once manufactured a cosmic machine capable of running itself . . . The doctrine of evolution destroys the conception of the world as a machine. It makes God our constant refuge and support and Nature his true revelation; and when all its religious implications shall have been set forth, it will be seen to be the most potent ally that Christianity has ever had in elevating mankind. (Fiske 1891: 599)

Fiske thought that the perfection of humanity was the climax of this divinely orchestrated process and that we could look forward to the day when strife and sorrow would give way to peace and love, when the spirit of Christ would reign supreme.

Fiske's evolutionary theism has something in common with the cosmology advanced by the logician and mathematician Charles Sanders Peirce. Although best known today for his theory of sign relations and espousal of the pragmatic maxim, Peirce also worked out an idiosyncratic metaphysics rooted in an idea of evolution that, as he frankly disclosed, owed less to Darwin than it did to Schelling. In fact, Peirce was deeply ambivalent towards Darwinism. Peirce's admiration for Darwin was limited to the naturalist's methodology and meticulous observations and did not always stretch to the substance of his claims, 'which in themselves would barely command scientific respect' (Peirce 1931–55: 1: 33). Like many of his contemporaries, Peirce had misgivings, never quieted, about the adequacy of natural selection as an explanatory model, which in his view 'extends politico-economical views of progress to the entire realm of animal and vegetable life' and ought to carry the motto 'the Devil take the hindmost' (6: 293). Yet Peirce praised Darwin for having introduced into natural history similar mathematical innovations to those pioneered by James Clerk Maxwell in physics. 'The Darwinian controversy is, in large part, a question of logic', he wrote in 1877. 'Mr Darwin proposed to apply the statistical method to biology. The same thing has been done in a widely different branch of science, the theory of gases' (5: 364). Peirce was sure that this probabilistic understanding of the laws of nature, along with Darwin's emphasis on random variation, signalled the end of the determinist and mechanist biases of classical science.

The real legacy of Darwinism, in Peirce's eyes, was the room it left to chance and creativity in the world. This, then, would be the point of departure for his own cosmology, which he duly described as 'only Darwinism analyzed, generalized and brought into the realm of Ontology' (Peirce 1982–: 4: 552). For Peirce, the universe moves not from homogeneity to heterogeneity, as with Spencer, but from a primordial chaos to greater order, uniformity and 'concrete reasonableness', to the growth of what he called 'habit' and what we customarily label the 'laws of nature'. These laws, then, are the results of evolution, just like geological formations and biological species. Indeed, all things, from molecules to metaphysicians, manifest a tendency 'to take habits', whereby they come into being as discrete, self-identical entities. Since habit is the 'one sole fundamental' canon that governs the mind, though, 'it follows that physical evolution works towards ends in the same way that mental action works towards ends'. In fact, matter is simply 'mind whose habits have become fixed so as to lose the powers of forming them and losing them' (Peirce 1931–55: 6: 101).

Although the universe may display statistical regularity and predictability to a greater or lesser extent, it does not by any means run like clockwork. There lingers – particularly in the human realms of imagination and thought – an irreducible element of pure chance: the fallibilism of scientific measurement demonstrates that nature is a dynamic and dicey realm exhibiting considerable spontaneity. These departures from law:

> are perpetually acting to increase the variety of the world and are checked by a sort of natural selection and otherwise (for the writer does not think the selective principle sufficient), so that the general result may be called 'organized heterogeneity', or better rationalized variety. (Peirce 1931–55: 6: 101)

Of course, the road to rationality passes not only through the cosmos at large but also through the mind of man, inasmuch as intellectual inquiry is slowly improving its fit with the ever-sharper contours of nature. For Peirce, the emergent harmony between the reasonableness of things and that of human inquiry is evidence of God's effective and providential presence: he was unable to entertain a universe devoid of ulterior meaning. (Peirce's progressivism is of a subtler kind than that of Spencer, say; it does not impose a preordained structure on the final goal. Progress is possible, but it need not proceed inevitably in a single direction, because life has the freedom to create its own future.)

There are three modes by which Peircean evolution takes place: random variation (or 'tychasm', in Peirce's terms, exemplified by Darwinism), mechanical necessity ('anancasm', of which Hegelianism is an instance) or creative love ('agapasm'). Darwinism as such could not by itself explain change; rather, God's love must a play a greater role:

> [A] genuine evolutionary philosophy, that is, one that makes the principle of growth a primordial element of the universe, is so far from being antagonistic to the idea of a personal creator that it is really inseparable from that idea . . . But a pseudo-evolutionism which enthrones mechanical law above the principle of growth is at once scientifically unsatisfactory, as giving no possible hint of how the universe has come about and hostile to all hopes of personal relations to God. (Peirce 1931–55: 6: 157)

According to Peirce, the motor of the evolutionary process is not struggle, greed or competition, but rather nurturing love (*agape*), in which an entity is prepared to sacrifice its own perfection for the sake of the wellbeing of its neighbour. This doctrine had both a social significance for Peirce, who apparently had the intention of arguing against the vulgar social Darwinism of the late nineteenth century, and a cosmic significance, which Peirce derived partly from the Gospel of St John (a text that, Peirce once remarked, is 'the formula of an evolutionary philosophy' (6: 289)) and partly from the Swedenborgian writings of Henry James, Sr.

For all its many eccentricities, however, Peirce's evolutionary philosophy was indubitably of its time: like the systems of Spencer and Fiske, it was a metaphysical creed that dressed older Christian and Romantic ideas in more fashionable, Darwinian clothes.

3. Mind and Evolutionary Epistemology

3.1 Chauncey Wright

Chauncey Wright, philosopher of science and friend of Peirce, was a rare beast among nineteenth-century evolutionists. Not only was he a champion of the efficacy of natural selection, he insisted on the 'metaphysical neutrality' of science, which ought, in good Baconian fashion, to concentrate on advancing knowledge by means of careful empirical observations and experiments. He saw no warrant for applying Darwin's theory beyond the biological phenomena it was originally intended to describe and strenuously opposed those – like Spencer and other exponents of what he termed 'German Darwinism' – who indulged in unprovable speculation about the evolution of culture and the universe. To introduce design, destiny and deity into the evolutionary process was to make flagrant misuse of a scientific concept.

For a thinker given to short articles and reviews, Wright's most sustained and substantive work is his 1873 essay 'Evolution of Self-Consciousness'. Written at the instigation of Darwin himself, Wright's 'psychozoölogy' undertakes to solve a problem raised by a reviewer of the *Origin of Species*: explaining the gap between animal instinct and human intelligence. Wright argued that evolution was opportunistic. It need not imply 'continuity in the *kinds* of powers and functions in living beings, that is, by suggesting transition by insensible steps from one *kind* to another, as well as in the *degrees* of their importance and exercise at different stages of development'. On the contrary, Wright explained,

> new uses of old powers arise discontinuously both in the bodily and mental natures of the animal and in its individual developments, as well as in the development of its race, although, at their rise, these uses are small and of the smallest importance to life. (Wright 1878: 199–200)

Human self-consciousness was not a supernatural endowment, but had evolved quite naturally and accidentally out of faculties such as memory and imagination already present in other species. Where these are able to form representative images of the world and, based on some instinctive mnemonic function, act in accordance with 'enthymematic reasoning', by which the images or 'internal signs' are merely harbingers of events without recognition of the relation between the sign and the thing signified, human beings, through the acquisition of novel habits and dispositions, have learned by stages to treat the sign itself as the object of reflective attention and to recognise its semantic capacity, its relations to past, present and future significations. The difference between animals and their human kin is that the former merely have thoughts, whereas the latter are able to think about those thoughts and communicate them via a series of 'external signs' (language).

Wright was scarcely alone in seeking an evolutionary account of the mind. In his 1855 *Principles of Psychology*, Spencer had already tried to trace the emergence of consciousness from the incremental growth of nerve fibres, reflex arcs and ganglia prompted by waves of outward stimuli. In Germany, Wilhelm Wundt, the founding father of experimental psychology and, less memorably, the author of a systematic philosophy, was the first to meet the challenge of explaining animal behaviour and human mind with an evolutionary theory of instinct as early as 1863 in his *Vorlesungen über die Menschen- und Thierseele* (Lectures on the Soul of Men and Animals). Under the influence of Hegel, Fichte and Fechner, Wundt was prepared to discover the glimmerings of consciousness even among infusoria and to pursue its development into the transcendent brilliance of human reason. Although he invoked the principle of natural selection to 'illuminate puzzles of psychic development', he remained wedded to the idealistic assumption that mind guided all natural processes and never shed his belief that individual intention and habit were the principal moulding tools of evolution (Wundt 1863: 355). Finally, Haeckel's conviction that psychology was merely a branch of physiology – indeed, of cytology – rested on the claim, supposedly confirmed by 'every scientific man', that each living cell has a 'soul' that consists of 'a sum of sensations, perceptions and volitions' (the so-called 'cell-soul'); that, consequently, the thinking, feeling and willing of complex organisms is the aggregate of the psychic functions of their constituent cells. Human consciousness has evolved from the 'souls' of lower creatures and, ultimately, from the simple cell-soul of protozoa ('there is present in the egg-cell', Haeckel conjectured, 'a hereditary cell-soul, out of which man, like every other animal, is developed') (Haeckel 1894: 15).

3.2 William James

Like that of Wright, a fellow member of the Cambridge-based Metaphysical Club, the thought of William James, both as a psychologist and later as a philosopher, was irreversibly affected by his early encounter with Darwin's views. (And, like his older associate, he never declined an opportunity to attack Spencer.) In 1865 James witnessed at first hand the scientific battles fought over Darwinism, having joined an expedition to the Amazon led by Louis Agassiz, one of Darwin's most prominent critics, the purpose of which was to collect evidence consistent with the Harvard botanist's competing hypothesis of divine creation. Already persuaded by the explanatory fecundity of *The Origin of Species*, James disagreed with Agassiz's theory on methodological grounds, holding that it had no material implications and was hence unverifiable. It made no difference whether it was true or not and, for this reason, it had no influence on the way we interpret the world around us.

This insight – that the worth of a belief depends on the concrete difference that it makes – is one of the central planks of what would become pragmatism.

When is a belief true? From the outset, James thought that it was mistaken to assume, as Spencer did, that a belief is true or justified only if it corresponds with reality. The human mind, he argued, 'is not simply a mirror floating with no foot-hold anywhere', passively reflecting an external order of things; rather, the mind is creative and 'co-efficient of the truth'. Our postulates and suppositions,

> so far as they are bases for human action – action which to a great extent transforms the world – help to *make* the truth which they declare. In other words, there belongs to mind, from its birth upward, a spontaneity, a vote. It is in the game. (James 1975–88: 5: 21)

But how do we acquire our ideas about the world? James's answer, in the final chapter of his pioneering *Principles of Psychology* of 1890, is a Kantian one, albeit with a Darwinian twist. Beyond the instinctive and pre-rational responses to colour, taste, sound, pleasure and pain with which the mind comes equipped, we have at our disposal a number of innate ideas – 'intuitively necessary truths', ranging from logical relations to metaphysical axioms, that do not appear to derive from sense impressions. These, too, are the result of our brain structure: fortuitous variations that have passed through the winnowing fan of natural selection. Minds that possessed them were preferred over those that did not; but it need not follow that these ideas coincided with a reality *extra mentem meam* – here James parts company with his many contemporaries (among them Spencer, Helmholtz and Wundt) who presented a form of biologised Kantianism. Now, *all* traits are selected because they have adaptive value. The reason human beings came to possess the idea of causation, for example, is not because causation positively exists and would exist whether we were around to believe in it or not. We have no way of knowing whether this is so, nor should we care: we believe in causation because experience shows that it pays to believe in causation. Both instinct and a repertoire of innate ideas therefore constitute our evolutionary legacy. But Darwinian, too, is the generation of new ideas, the learning of new facts, in addition to those supposedly knowable a priori, through this inherited cognitive framework; hypotheses, guesses and cognitions erupt both in our quotidian and scientific interaction with the world; those that withstand the brunt of the actual live for another day. As James put it later in *Pragmatism* of 1907:

> The whole notion of truth, which naturally and without reflexion we assume to mean the simple duplication by the mind of a ready-made and given reality, proves hard to understand clearly . . . [A]ll our thoughts are *instrumental* and mental modes of *adaptation* to reality, rather than revelations or gnostic answers to some divinely instituted world-enigma. (James 1975–88: 1: 93–4)

So James's epistemology rests on Darwinian foundations. But this Darwinian epistemology implies a peculiar sort of metaphysics, a vision of the universe as provisional and in the making – an 'open universe'. The world, too, for James, was in a sense evolving, continually changing, growing, developing. Nothing was absolutely fixed and certain; there was a place for novelty and chance, without which the world would be little more than a machine, freedom an illusion and life bereft of meaning. It is chance that gives us the opportunity to exert choice and control over the direction of human affairs.

3.3 Ernst Mach

Like James, Ernst Mach also devised an evolutionary theory of knowledge. 'We are prepared', he wrote in his essay 'On Transformation and Adaptation in Scientific Thought', 'to regard ourselves and every one of our ideas as a product and a subject of universal evolution' (Mach 1895: 235). According to the scheme sketched out in his 1905 work *Knowledge and Error*, the multifaceted human undertaking that is science represents the culmination of countless adaptive interactions with the environment stretching back over the course of the history of life on earth and, for that very reason, exists on a continuum with earlier, simpler organic activity. From instinctive responses to an organism's immediate circumstances evolved ever more sophisticated mental capacities – chief among them imagination and memory – that brought into view a wider field of spatial-temporal relations than those present to the senses. Finally, the individual human being's memory was augmented by the retention and transmission of knowledge through culture. 'Indeed, the formation of scientific hypotheses', Mach averred, 'is merely a further degree of development of instinctive and primitive thought and all the transitions between them can be demonstrated'. But if science is a result of the evolutionary process, it is also an engine driving that same process, having 'taken over the task of replacing tentative and unconscious adaptation by a faster variety that is fully conscious and methodical' (Mach [1905] 1976: 171, 361). Its end, though, is the same as all adaptive strategies: survival and nothing else. As Mach put it in his celebrated *Analysis of the Sensations*: 'The biological task of science is to provide the fully developed human with as perfect a means of orientating himself as possible. No other scientific ideal can be realized and any other must be meaningless' (Mach [1886] 1959: 36–7).

How do ideas arise and how does scientific change come about? Mach suggests that ideas are brought forth in a thoroughly Darwinian manner: by random variation. Ideation, then, is not intentional, but relies instead on accident and luck, on flashes of inspiration. Selection is subsequently brought to bear when scientists choose those theories, out of the pool of available variations, which best fit the data and other pre-existing ideas. In other words, reason, both 'syllogism and induction', cannot by itself engender knowledge; it can 'merely make sure that there is no contradiction between our various insights and show clearly how these are connected and lead our attention to different sides of some particular insight, teaching us to recognize it in different forms' (Mach [1905] 1976: 231). The true source of knowledge, in other words, is as mysterious as the source of those mutations that furnish the raw material of evolution had recently been before the rediscovery of Mendel's work on genetics.

It was in psychology and epistemology that a Darwinian or at least quasi-Darwinian stance produced the most philosophically promising results. The different paths laid out here – Wright's and James's focus on the pedigree of cognitive mechanisms in animals and humans, for example, or Mach's description of the rise of concepts and hypotheses using models borrowed from biology – were continued in the twin programme of evolutionary epistemology set out in the latter half of the twentieth century: in the work of Konrad Lorenz and Donald T. Campbell in the former case and in that of Karl Popper and Stephen Toulmin in the latter case (see Lorenz 1977; Popper 1972; Toulmin 1972).

4. Ethics and Evolution

If Darwinism should prevail, wondered the historian Goldwin Smith gloomily, 'What will become of the brotherhood of man and of the very idea of humanity?' To which the

Reverend Minot J. Savage replied: 'As if "the brotherhood of man" were not one of the products of evolution!' (Savage 1890: 5). His response is typical of the many thinkers who addressed themselves to what seemed the most urgent task of all in the post-Darwinian age: rethinking the philosophical basis of morality. There was a belief that it would now be possible not only to give a satisfactory explanation of the genesis and development of moral sentiments, customs and judgements – one that was truly scientific – but also to provide a sanction for morality independent of the dogmas of religion (and, often enough, at least in Britain, corrective of the competing tenets of utilitarianism). Humanity might be just one species of animal amongst others, caught up in the same perpetual struggle for existence in an indifferent universe, but evolution need not entail, in Haeckel's words, 'a subversion of all accepted moral law and a destructive emancipation of Egoism' (quoted in Williams 1893: 27).

Darwin's own narrative of the growth of morality is outlined in *The Descent of Man* of 1871. Although he is certain that a moral sense originated through the natural selection of those tribes in whom the social instinct was strongest, he recognises that this primitive ethic was transformed into a 'higher morality' by the effects of habit, rational reflection and religious instruction. Not 'the survival of the fittest' but 'as ye would that men should do to you, do ye to them likewise' has come to be regarded as the true maxim of human conduct. Nor is moral improvement at an end. 'Looking to future generations', Darwin prophesies,

> there is no cause to fear that the social instincts will grow weaker and we may expect that virtuous habits will grow stronger, becoming perhaps fixed by inheritance. In this case the struggle between our higher and lower impulses will be less severe and virtue will be triumphant. (Darwin [1871] 1877: 1: 124–5)

As so often it was Spencer who, in his *Data of Ethics* of 1879, led the way. Indeed, Spencer admitted that he had conceived his entire 'Doctrine of Evolution' first and foremost as a means of finding, 'for the principles of right and wrong in conduct at large, a scientific basis' (Spencer 1879: v). This quest rests on the assumption that nature, especially human nature, is intrinsically moral. What he terms 'morality' is nothing but a particular instance of the incessant adaptation of internal relations to external relations which characterises the universal process of Evolution: the adjustment of acts to particular ends. This alignment becomes more complex and elaborate as organisms evolve. The ultimate end of all conduct is the preservation of the individual organism and the species to which it belongs. Actions are thus 'good' or 'bad' according as to whether they are relatively more or less adapted to this end. Organisms are led to perform these acts because 'there exists a primordial connexion between pleasure-giving acts and continuance or increase of life and, by implication, between pain-giving acts and decrease or loss of life' (Spencer 1879: iii, 82). Self-preservation is therefore necessarily bound up with the striving for pleasure, for those organisms in whom life-sustaining activity generally and consistently produced misery would perish in the struggle for existence. But the organism strives not only for the increase of its own pleasure but also for the greatest possible aggregate happiness; self-sacrifice for the good of the species is no less primordial than self-preservation. Once again, the organism is led to acts of renunciation because these acts are innately pleasurable and when pleasure is associated with repetitive actions it introduces principles of reinforcement and habit that justify increasingly complex social behaviours.

Moral evolution thus involves the greater refinement of these primitive altruistic impulses and ultimately leads to the reconciliation of egoism and altruism: acts through which the individual seeks its own pleasure in fact maximise the collective happiness and all altruistic acts also benefit the individual members of society. This development necessarily runs parallel to biological evolution and culminates in what Spencer calls the 'ideally moral man'. The members of this future race will subsist in a state of perfect equilibrium, of complete internal adaptation to both their physical and social environment; the 'moral man is one whose functions . . . are all discharged in degrees duly adjusted to the conditions of existence' (Spencer 1879: 76). These beings will have achieved the greatest general good, equal freedom and eternal peace, upheld by harmonious cooperation of all members of a society. Here, the feeling of moral obligation, present in lower stages of evolution, is lost; moral actions become, under the guidance of evolved 'moral sentiments', self-evident and natural, so that organic and moral behaviour are one and the same thing.

Following in Spencer's footsteps was Leslie Stephen with his 1882 treatise *The Science of Ethics*. Stephen's book is 'an attempt to lay down an ethical doctrine in harmony with the doctrine of evolution so widely accepted by modern men of science' and thereby to remedy what he saw as the shortcomings of Spencer's programme (Stephen [1882] 1907: vi). Stephen argued that it was imperative to look beyond the individual to the community in which we may discover the ethical process at work. This process works through the 'race' and the race forms a 'social tissue' through which moral qualities are passed on. This tissue is composed of individuals, just as the anatomical tissue which physiologists study is composed of cells. The reproductive organ in society is the family and the family is also the seat of morality because it inculcates in children those qualities that give life to the race. Since the law of natural selection compels humanity to become efficient in all walks of life, including that of conduct, moral qualities evolve to preserve the individual, the community and the race; the social tissue is constantly modified by evolution so that its various components may be better adapted to promote the health of the social organism. Morality is generated by social pressure and keeps the social tissue alive: if it grows faint, the tissue perishes and the race is threatened with extinction. In other words, a moral rule states a condition of 'social welfare' – the conceptual innovation of which Stephen was proudest – and this social welfare is the final motive for good conduct and a vital principle in the survival of the race.

Stephen was not alone in offering variations on Spencer. Some, like F. C. S. Schiller in *Riddles of the Sphinx* of 1891 or J. T. Bixby in *The Ethics of Evolution* of 1900, for all their criticisms of Spencer, merely offered a more explicitly theistic version of the *Data of Ethics*, according to which the 'ultimate aim of the world-process . . . is a harmonious society of perfect individuals, a kingdom of Heaven of perfected spirits, in which all friction will have disappeared from their interaction with God and with one another' (Schiller 1891: 432). Jean-Marie Guyau, in his 1885 *Esquisse d'une morale sans obligation ni sanction*, argues that a propensity to expansion, to growth beyond the limits of the single organism, is the physiological basis of altruism. Morality is not, therefore, a repressive external authority, as (allegedly) with Kant, but a natural, internal power for good that translates itself into action by means of the accumulation and explosive release of an individual's vital forces. One of the ways in which this current discharges itself is in generation: when two cells unite to form an individual there begins 'a new moral phase for the world'. Paul Rée lacked Spencer's and Stephen's roseate optimism, although he was, as his erstwhile friend Nietzsche later grumbled, persistently influenced by the 'English' mode of historical explanation. In his 1877 book *Der Ursprung der moralischen Empfindungen* (The Origin of Moral Sensations), Rée explained the eventual victory of altruism over egoism by pointing to the role played by habit in reinforcing ethical conduct. The human animal has not, during the millennia of social evolution, become less selfish; it has merely become more domesticated, learning to restrain its bestial urges. This process is explicable in terms of the same Lamarckian physiology on which Spencer's theory also relies. Self-control – imposed as a moral demand by state and society – requires the exertion of certain nerves and muscles; the more frequently these are exercised in order to suppress a particular passion, the greater the individual's success in achieving this end because the flow of 'nervous fluid' to those parts increases. These internal adaptations to the reigning moral circumstances are heritable. For Rée, then, morality not only emerges out of our evolutionary history, it can also have a retroactive effect on present and future biological evolution.

Another approach was taken by Bartholomäus von Carneri, an Austrian philosopher and liberal politician, in his *Sittlichkeit und Darwinismus* (and later in *Grundlegung der Ethik*), a typically Teutonic stew of Darwinism and Hegelianism, seasoned with a generous dash of Goethe and a pinch of Haeckel. Carneri understands evolution as the inevitable march of nature from insentience to self-reflexivity through the human spirit, as the distillation of matter into mind, a movement propelled by the dialectical rhythm of the struggle for existence. He begins by distinguishing between ethics and morality; where the latter is prescriptive, particular and time-bound, varying across history and cultures, the former is descriptive, universal and bodied forth by the course of evolution itself. When the triadic progression from instinct to consciousness to self-consciousness is completed and we have raised ourselves from our individual perspective and recognised our complex interrelationship with the world, the ideas of the Good and of Truth and Beauty are revealed to us. To do good means to act in accordance with a beneficent nature, as well as to work towards the fulfilment of the evolutionary process, the terminus of which is the perfection of humanity and the attainment of absolute good. To do good means to act without coercion, not out of momentary caprice, but out of knowledge and conviction. There is no oughtness; the moral man simply is as he does. He is free, since freedom lies in the absence of mental discord. And this overcoming of conflict is the direction of evolution: in time, the more clearly the laws of *Geist* are perceived, the struggle for existence becomes less painful yet more rapid, as the cruder, more bloody battles waged in the animal kingdom, in which brute strength and egoistical utility prevail, are sublated; then 'humanity will fully earn its name only when it knows no other struggle than *work*, no other shield than *right*, no other weapon than *intelligence*, no other banner than *civilisation*' (Carneri 1871: 362).

Lastly, in his 1889 *Moral Order and Progress*, the Oxford philosopher Samuel Alexander set out to show how morality is, inescapably, subject to the same laws of evolutionary progress that hold sway over the rest of the physical and cultural world. Evolution is essential to morality, which is dynamical, shifting, becoming ever more refined: for every ideal is merely provisional, a station in the passage to a higher value. (Although Alexander allows for the possibility of degeneration, this is merely a temporary setback on an otherwise upward trajectory.) An ideal, Alexander claims, is akin to a 'species' and the mechanism of species change, of moral evolution, is analogous to that operative in nature. Ideals must adapt, for there are always new conditions or situations for morality to resolve (or, to use Alexander's Spencerian term, 'equilibrate') and they are hence apt to vary, leading to a struggle between the emergent varieties, in which the good ideal, the most suitable and effective in a given socio-historical context, carries the day and evil is rejected. This is not some example of crass social Darwinism: Alexander is at pains to stress that the clash is between objects of the mind or will rather than persons and, although his mentor was A. C. Bradley, his ethics is rather reminiscent of James's pragmatic epistemology. He believes his analysis is able to account, among other things, for: the birth of moral distinctions; the multiplicity of different moral ideals at different stages of development in different parts of the globe at any one time; and the creeping but no less inexorable movement of morality towards comprehending all humanity in a universal system of duties. In fact, as with so many other ethical thinkers of the age, Alexander supposes that, in the future, the sense of obligation attached to virtuous conduct will be dispelled by the very highest conception of morality. This consummate morality is a 'spontaneous outflow of the sentiments': a man does good not because he is compelled to do so, but because he is entranced by the 'spell of affection' he has for his community willingly to render service to an order of life higher than himself, 'a continuously progressive society of free individuals' (Alexander 1889: 408, 412–13).

5. Critics of Evolutionary Ethics

There were many, and not merely among the religious orthodox, who found the project of an evolutionary ethics – especially Spencer's version of it – both superficial and arbitrary. Perhaps the most famous and the most devastating criticism came from G. E. Moore in his *Principia Ethica* of 1903. To describe the course of evolution, he remarks there, is to say something about how the world is and how it came to be as it is; but that tells us nothing about how the world ought to be. To think otherwise, to try to elicit from such facts a criterion for moral judgement and behaviour, is to commit the 'naturalistic fallacy'. Spencer's evolutionary ethics is built on the assumption that 'to be more evolved' is synonymous with 'better', but there is no logical connection between those terms. Therefore, Moore decided, 'Evolution has very little indeed to say to Ethics' (Moore 1903: 58).

There were others who worried that Spencer's programme failed to do justice to the normative character of morality; rules of conduct did not automatically follow from the premise that the moral sense was an ancestral legacy. That point was made by Henry Sidgwick in his 1876 essay 'The Theory of Evolution in its Application to Practice' (Sidgwick 1876). T. H. Green, in his posthumous *Prolegomena to Ethics*, concluded that anyone who undertook to 'reconstruct our ethical systems in conformity with the doctrines of evolution and descent' would, after 'having reduced the speculative part of them to a natural science' be compelled, were he consistent, 'to abolish the practical or preceptive part altogether' (Green 1883: 7). Certainly the most thorough critique of evolutionary ethics along these lines was mounted by the idealist William Ritchie Sorley, a disciple of Green and Bradley, in *On the Ethics of Naturalism*. Sorley argued that evolutionary theory was unable either to set up a comprehensive ideal for life or to yield any principle for distinguishing between good and evil, right and wrong. Spencer's attempt to show how moral conduct has arisen out of 'purely physical or reflex action' is misguided; he and his ilk ignore the element of self-consciousness in moral behaviour, for it is through self-consciousness that mere facts are translated into ends of action. And the ultimate end of all human action, of our conscious willing, is self-realisation; only when we can conceive of something as necessary for completing our idea of self, both individual and social, does it become a motive. 'Evolution', he opined,

> is thus not the foundation of morality, but the manifestation of the principle on which it depends. Morality cannot be explained by means of its own development, without reference to the self-consciousness which makes that development possible. However

valuable may be the information we get from experience as to the gradual evolution of conduct, its nature and end can only be explained by a principle that transcends experience. (Sorley 1885: 283, 291–2)

But not all detractors of nineteenth-century evolutionary ethics levelled their criticism against the method or logic of the enterprise. Nietzsche, perhaps the most radical, believed that values could be derived from the evolutionary process (at least as emanations of what he termed 'ascending' and 'descending' life) and their genealogical history laid bare, but he questioned those values which his contemporaries claimed to find there. T. H. Huxley, too, disputed the moral character of evolution: in the gladiatorial struggle for existence he witnessed self-assertion rather than self-restraint, only the enormous waste and pain suffered by those creatures thrust aside as unfit for their surroundings. Though morality is natural – and not God-given – it is not present in nature. Ethical progress 'depends, not on imitating the cosmic process, still less in running away from it, but in combating it' (Huxley 1894: 83). Nietzsche agreed with Huxley that nature was not moral, but contended that that was all the more reason to imitate it.

Throughout his career Nietzsche demonstrates a clear sense of the significance of evolution for human affairs. In *On the Uses and Disadvantages of History for Life*, he describes as 'true but deadly' the 'doctrines of sovereign becoming, of the fluidity of all concepts, types and species, of the lack of any cardinal distinction between man and animal' and suggests that, should these teachings find a wider audience, the fabric of society would disintegrate as moral and legal statutes lost their binding force (Nietzsche [1873–6] 1997: 112). But as his earlier diatribe against David Friedrich Strauss shows, he was already acutely aware that the lethal repercussions of evolutionism were being ignored by the very men who were its most vociferous champions. Strauss strove to reconcile the moral teachings of Christianity with the new evolutionary world-view instead of daring to draft a 'genuine Darwinian ethic, seriously and consistently carried through'. Having passed up the opportunity to derive 'a moral code for life out of the *bellum omnium contra omnes* and the privileges of the strong', Strauss perversely praises Darwin as one of the 'greatest benefactors of mankind' for having established a non-transcendental groundwork for ethical comportment (Nietzsche [1873–6] 1997: 29–30). But Strauss, Nietzsche would soon discover, was not the only thinker to shrink from making the clean break with traditional systems of morality which the theory of evolution would seem to demand.

Although Nietzsche quarrelled with Darwin on more than one occasion, casting doubt on natural selection and dismissing its author as an intellectual mediocrity, it was Spencer whom he more frequently (and more justifiably) charged with pusillanimity in the face of a nature red in tooth and claw. Nietzsche's own conception of evolution is more anti-Spencerian than it is anti-Darwinian. Indeed, in some respects Nietzsche simply turns Spencer's system on its head. Whereas Spencer posits a graduation from egoism to altruism, Nietzsche argues the opposite: organic change tends towards progressive individuation. Both moral and biological evolution lie in the refinement of egoism, which, in phylogenetic terms, represents 'something recent and still unusual' (Nietzsche 1999: 9: 513). Altruism, in contrast, as a rudimentary form of egoism, the egoism of what he calls the 'herd', must eventually become extinct. Like Spencer, Nietzsche sees evolution as delivering enhanced complexity and heterogeneity, but he suspects that the path which Spencer has marked out leads only to an evolutionary cul-de-sac of physiological uniformity. Spencer is reading the wrong values into the process.

What is a value? Values, according to Nietzsche, are the goals of an organism's drives. As dispositions to act in certain ways, they determine how we – indeed, all creatures – relate to the world around us. But the values of an individual and those of the group to which it belongs (humans, after all, are gregarious animals) must inevitably come into conflict. Both individual and herd, as vessels of the will to power, the very essence of life, want the same thing. They want to assert themselves and subdue others in the great struggle of existence (rather than the struggle *for* existence: strife is for Nietzsche, as it was for Schopenhauer, an ontological feature of the universe). Exploitation, Nietzsche says, is the 'fundamental organic function' (Nietzsche [1886] 1998: §259). The herd asserts itself and its values at the expense of the individual: entirely healthy, predatory and creative instincts must be suppressed in the interests of the collective. Instead, a range of behaviours and attitudes that promote social cohesion is favoured, bred into the members of the herd and labelled 'virtuous', such as selflessness, humility, gentleness, sympathy, abstinence and obedience. These values are injurious to the individual: they stunt and warp his growth. Nietzschean evolution, however, by no means predictable or regular, results in the 'sovereign individual', the antithesis of Spencer's 'ideally moral man'. Where the 'ideally moral man' is the embodiment of herd consciousness, Nietzsche's human being of the future can master the diverse perspectives and impulses that constitute his existence; he has emancipated himself from the alienating experience of serving ends that are not his own and, in the name of self-realisation, is thus free to posit his own goals and values, values that do not traduce life, values that ennoble humanity and contribute to our flourishing, values that are like the evolutionary process itself: provisional, natural, amoral.

6. Conclusion

'The Darwinian theory', Wittgenstein declared in the *Tractatus Logico-Philosophicus*, 'has no more to do with philosophy than any other hypothesis of natural science' (Wittgenstein 1922: 4: 1122). He was wrong. With its epochal significance, Darwinism issued and continues to issue a challenge to philosophy. Few thinkers rose to that challenge in the nineteenth century, even if many rushed to accommodate themselves to the changed intellectual climate. By invoking the concept of evolution they sought either to reframe the old, theistic picture of the world or to solve traditional philosophical questions. The extent to which they succeeded in that endeavour is perhaps indicated by Herbert Spencer, who, having devoted his life to this very task of placing political, social and moral problems in the new evolutionary perspective, finally confessed: 'The Doctrine of Evolution has not furnished guidance to the extent I had hoped. Most of the conclusions, drawn empirically, are such as right feelings, enlightened by cultural intelligence, have already sufficed to establish' (Spencer 1893: 2: v).

Note

1. Another philosophical critic of Darwin was the widely read Eduard von Hartmann, whose 1869 metaphysical system, *Die Philosophie des Unbewussten*, aimed to square Hegel with Schopenhauer (see Hartmann 1875). On Hartmann, see also the discussion by Gunther Gödde in Chapter 11 of this volume.

References

Adoratsky, V. (ed.) (1934), *Selected Correspondence of Karl Marx and Friedrich Engels*, New York: International Publishers.

Alexander, Samuel (1889), *Moral Order and Progress*, London: Trübner.

Bixby, James Thompson (1900), *The Ethics of Evolution*, Boston: Small, Maynard and Co.

Bowler, Peter J. (1983), *The Eclipse of Darwinism: Anti-Darwinian Evolutionary Theories in the Decades around 1900*, Baltimore: Johns Hopkins University Press.

Carneri, Bartholomäus von (1871), *Sittlichkeit und Darwinismus*, Vienna: Braumüller.

Carneri, Bartholomäus von ([1871] 1881), *Grundlegung der Ethik*, Vienna: Braumüller.

D'Alviella, Goblet (1885), *The Contemporary Evolution of Religious Thought in England, America and India*, London: Williams and Norgate.

Darwin, Charles [1871] (1877), *The Descent of Man*, 2nd edn, 2 vols, London: John Murray.

Darwin, Francis (ed.) (1887), *The Life and Letters of Charles Darwin*, 2 vols, New York: Murray.

Dennett, Daniel C. (1995), *Darwin's Dangerous Idea: Evolution and the Meanings of Life*, New York: Simon and Schuster.

Dewey, John (1910), *The Influence of Darwin on Philosophy and Other Essays*, New York: Holt.

Fiske, John (1885), *The Idea of God as Affected by Modern Knowledge*, Boston: Houghton Mifflin.

Fiske, John (1891), 'Doctrine of Evolution', *Popular Science Monthly*, 39: 577–99.

Gizycki, Georg von (1876), *Die philosophischen Consequenzen der Lamarck-Darwin'schen Entwick-lungstheorie*, Leipzig: Winter.

Green, Thomas Hill (1883), *Prolegomena to Ethics*, Oxford: Clarendon Press.

Guyau, Jean-Marie (1885), *Esquisse d'une morale sans obligation ni sanction*, Paris: Alcan.

Haeckel, Ernst (1894), *Monism as Connecting Religion and Science*, London: Black.

Hartmann, Eduard von (1875), *Wahrheit und Irrthum im Darwinismus*, Berlin: Duncker.

Huxley, Thomas Henry (1894), *Evolution and Ethics, and other Essays*, London: Macmillan.

James, William (1975–88), *The Works of William James*, 19 vols, Cambridge, MA: Harvard University Press.

Lorenz, Konrad (1977), *Behind the Mirror*, London: Methuen.

Mach, Ernst (1895), *Popular Scientific Lectures*, Chicago: Open Court.

Mach, Ernst [1886] (1959), *The Analysis of Sensations*, New York: Dover.

Mach, Ernst [1905] (1976), *Knowledge and Error*, Dordrecht: Reidel.

Mill, John Stuart (1874), *Three Essays on Religion*, London: Longmans.

Moore, George Edward (1903), *Principia Ethica*, Cambridge: Cambridge University Press.

Nietzsche, Friedrich [1873–6] (1997), *Untimely Meditations*, Cambridge: Cambridge University Press.

Nietzsche, Friedrich [1886] (1998), *Beyond Good and Evil*, trans. Marion Faber, Oxford: Oxford University Press.

Nietzsche, Friedrich (1999), *Werke: Kritische Studienausgabe*, ed. Giorgio Colli and Mazzino Montinari, 15 vols, Munich: DTV.

Peirce, Charles Sanders (1931–55), *Collected Papers*, 8 vols, Cambridge, MA: Harvard University Press.

Peirce, Charles Sanders (1982–), *Writings of Charles S. Peirce*, 30 vols, Bloomington: Indiana University Press.

Popper, Karl (1972), *Objective Knowledge: An Evolutionary Approach*, Oxford: Clarendon Press.

Rée, Paul (1877), *Der Ursprung der moralischen Empfindungen*, Chemnitz: Schmeitzer.

Richards, Robert John (1987), *Darwin and the Emergence of Evolutionary Theories of Mind and Behaviour*, Chicago: University of Chicago Press.

Royce, Josiah (1892), *The Spirit of Modern Philosophy*, Boston: Houghton Mifflin.

Savage, Minot Judson (1890), *The Morals of Evolution*, Boston: Ellis.

Schiller, Ferdinand Canning Scott (1891), *Riddles of the Sphinx*, London: Sonnenschein.

Sidgwick, Henry (1876), 'The Theory of Evolution in its Application to Practice', *Mind*, 1: 52–67.

Sorley, William Ritchie (1885), *On the Ethics of Naturalism*, Edinburgh: Blackwood.

Spencer, Herbert (1862), *First Principles*, London: Williams and Norgate.

Spencer, Herbert (1879), *Data of Ethics*, London: Williams and Norgate.

Spencer, Herbert (1893), *Principles of Ethics*, 2 vols, London: Williams and Norgate.

Spencer, Herbert (1898), *Principles of Biology*, 2nd edn, London: Williams and Norgate.

Spencer, Herbert (1900), *First Principles*, New York: Appleton.

Spencer, Herbert (1904), *Autobiography*, 2 vols, London: Williams and Norgate.

Stephen, Leslie [1882] (1907), *The Science of Ethics*, 2nd edn, London: Smith and Elder.

Stirling, James Hutchison (1894), *Darwinianism: Workmen and Work*, Edinburgh: T. and T. Clark.

Toulmin, Stephen (1972), *Human Understanding: The Collective Use and Evolution of Concepts*, Princeton: Princeton University Press.

Williams, Charles Mallory (1893), *A Review of the Systems of Ethics Founded on the Theory of Evolution*, London: Macmillan.

Wittgenstein, Ludwig (1922), *Tractatus Logico-Philosophicus*, London: Kegan Paul.

Wright, Chauncey (1878), *Philosophical Discussions*, New York: Holt.

Wundt, Wilhelm (1863), *Vorlesungen über die Menschen- und Thierseele*, Leipzig: Voss.

7
Faith and Knowledge

George Pattison

1. Introduction: Why Faith and Knowledge?

In the first decade of the twenty-first century, religion once more became a prominent topic of public discourse and the language of religion, and of atheism, became the *lingua franca* in which key issues of the day were formulated. Whatever might be thought of the general level on which it has been taken up in our contemporary debates, this resurgence of religion facilitates the leap of historical imagination required to take us back to the intellectual climate of the nineteenth century, especially its first half. Then, as now, religion offered a crucial focus for debating fundamental issues of human identity as these were reflected in questions of political order, ethical value, the meaning of cultural life and the scope and competence of reason itself. Although this last offered the most abstract form in which the question of religion was then posed, it condensed everything that was at stake in all those other areas where questions of religion were debated. In this way, the philosophy of religion came into the very centre of intellectual life and seemed to offer the ground on which the decisive battles of the day had to be fought. In 1841 the matter was put in these terms by Friedrich Engels, commenting somewhat sarcastically on Schelling's much-heralded lectures on the philosophy of revelation – lectures that were expected to refute the fundamental basis of Hegelianism:

> Ask anybody in Berlin today on what field the battle for dominion over German public opinion in politics and religion, that is, over Germany itself, is being fought, and if he has any idea of the power of the mind over the world he will reply that the battlefield is the University, in public Lecture-hall number 6, where Schelling is giving his lectures on the philosophy of revelation. (Engels [1841] 1975: 2: 181)

Both the importance and the novelty of the question of faith and knowledge had been similarly noted several years previously by the Hegelian historian of philosophy, Johann Eduard Erdmann. In the introduction to his lectures on *Faith and Knowledge* which were published in 1837, Erdmann stated that the question of faith and knowledge was essentially a modern question, unknown to antiquity and to the early Church since these lacked the modern idea of faith. Although adumbrated in scholasticism, this question came into its own only in the era – he means the Reformation – that saw a rebirth of both religion and science. Since then the question has featured prominently in the works of those whom Erdmann calls the 'heroes' of modern philosophy: Descartes, Spinoza, Leibniz, Wolff, Jacobi, Kant, Fichte, Schelling and Hegel. In modern theology, too, a similar reformulation of the question has occurred. Gone are discussions of the *lumen supernaturale* (supernatural illumination) versus the *lumen naturale* (natural illumination), to be replaced by debates on the relationship between natural and positive religion or between religion and knowledge. In the last couple of decades, Erdmann notes, this relationship itself has been the focus of many particular studies and

> [E]very trade catalogue brings us new writings about philosophy and religion, faith and knowledge, faith and reason, reason and revelation, philosophy and Christianity, not to mention the daily appearance of works on rationalism and supernaturalism that come out in such manifold forms that one can almost be sure that whenever two 'isms' are compared with one another one will encounter these two much-discussed subjects. (Erdmann 1837: 3)[1]

Despite this intense interest, within ten years of Erdmann's lectures being published Karl Marx was satisfied that, the critique of heaven being accomplished, it was time to move on to the critique of earth and leave behind the airy vacuities of philosophy of religion (Marx [1844] 1975: 244–5).

Not accidentally, Erdmann formulates the question to which his lectures are dedicated as that of faith and knowledge (*Glauben* and *Wissen*). Underlying this choice of words is a specific intellectual inheritance that Erdmann traces back to Kant's assertion that in conducting a critique of the ideas of pure reason, including especially such metaphysical ideas as God, freedom and immorality, he 'found it necessary to deny knowledge, in order to make room for faith' (Erdmann 1837: 218; see Kant [1781/1787] 1933). But if Kant was the starting point for the new phase of this discussion, it was Hegel whom both religious and anti-religious participants regarded as having established the paradigm that enabled the issues to be articulated in a decisive way. We shall return to Erdmann, who offers one of the more accessible versions of Hegelian philosophy of religion. But first we must turn back to Hegel and see how he gave a new shape to an old question.

2. Hegel and his Reception

In July 1802 the *Kritisches Journal der Philosophie*, a journal largely by Hegel and Schelling, published an article by Hegel entitled 'Faith and Knowledge'. It begins with the striking statement that:

> The culture of recent times has raised itself above the old opposition between reason and faith, between philosophy and positive religion to such a degree that this opposing of faith and knowledge has gained a quite other meaning and has now been relocated into philosophy itself. (Hegel [1802] 1970: 287)

Hegel sees this as a product of the impasse to which the Enlightenment critique of religion had led. For the struggle against religion carried out by the Enlightenment was mostly directed only against the external forms of religion, not its ideal. A striking example of this is the prominence given in that period to the debate about miracles.

Christian apologetics had laid especially heavy weight on miracles as evidence for Christ's divinity, but as the view spread that the laws of nature were uniform and without exception the possibility of miracles inevitably became a hotly contested topic. In Hegel's view this whole debate left the true essence of religion untouched, however, because it did not stop to consider the ideal or essence of religion. This failure meant that philosophy found itself once more having to confess itself incompetent in relation to knowledge of God. This (Hegel says) is precisely what we see happening in three very different ways in Kant, Jacobi and Fichte. When Kant argues that what is supersensuous cannot be known by reason, or Jacobi insists that God is knowable only through feeling or intimations (*Ahnung*), or Fichte speaks of God as inconceivable, they all assume that the world of finite things has no intrinsic connection to what is infinite. God is represented as somehow 'beyond' human capacities of knowing and therefore not a proper object of reason. This means that these philosophies can only ever deliver knowledge of humanity, not of God. Hegel therefore likens their efforts to a certain kind of portraiture,

> that would attain its ideal by putting a longing into the eyes of an ordinary face or [placing] a sorrowful smile on its lips, but which was utterly forbidden to portray the gods elevated above all longing and sorrow. Thus philosophy finds itself having to portray, not the idea of the human but an abstract version of empirical humanity burdened with limitations and with the arrow of an absolute contradiction immovably lodged within it. It is immaterial whether it analyses this abstraction or lets it express itself in the touching manner of a beautiful soul, whilst adorning itself with the superficial colouring of something supersensuous by invoking faith to suggest something 'higher'. (Hegel [1802] 1970: 299)

It is immaterial, because truth can only be established when this dualism is abolished and, as Hegel says, the attitude of those who assume the utter separation of finite and infinite is like that of a person who, looking at a painting, looks only at the feet and doesn't raise their eyes to look at the picture as a whole. The whole, the *idea* in Hegel's pregnant sense, is precisely composed of the finite *and* the infinite so that the finite itself cannot be known for what it is without being seen in relation to the infinite. But if this idea of the whole is the proper object of reason – and if reasoning means knowing the idea – then the true absolute is itself a matter not of faith but of knowledge. Our relation to it is not that of 'reasonable belief' (which would still suggest that it is somehow external to human experience) but *knowledge*.

However, the transition from the dualism of Kant, Jacobi and Fichte to a genuinely philosophical knowledge of the absolute is not simple or instantaneous. The point to which they bring us is not merely a kind of cognitive hesitancy, but 'the abyss of nothingness into which all Being sinks down'. As such, it elicits 'the infinite pain . . . on which the religion of the modern world rests: the feeling that "God himself is dead"' (Hegel [1802] 1970: 432) – although, Hegel adds, this feeling will be experienced only as 'a moment of the highest idea' and not as something final.

'Faith and Knowledge' is, of course, an early work and Hegel has not yet fully articulated his most distinctive terms and arguments. Nevertheless, it anticipates several themes that will become characteristic of his later treatments of religion. First, if we once assume an ontological separation between the finite and the infinite, between human beings and God, then we will never be able to reconcile the two. Second, it is therefore only on the basis of the actual experience of unity that genuine knowledge of God can be developed. Third, it follows that the history of religion and the history of philosophy will, to a considerable extent, coincide with regard to the question of God. In other words, the knowledge that philosophy is able to have of God presupposes a certain experience of God, whilst, conversely, there is no simple experience of God that is not at the same time a *thinking* experience of God possessed of a certain determinate thought content. What philosophy is to do, then, is simply to articulate and to develop in a systematic way the thought that is already implicit in the lived God-relationship. As regards content, faith and philosophy are therefore one and the same thing – only this one content is given under different forms. In faith it is given in the form that Hegel will call 'representation' (*Vorstellung* – also translated sometimes as 'picture-thinking'), whilst philosophy thinks this same content as 'concept' (*Begriff*).

Hegel generally seems to suggest that this latter is the truer and more adequate form of the idea. This has led to the long-running divide in the reception of his work: whether it is essentially theological, that is, preserves the essential content of Christian experience and teaching, or whether it is fundamentally a philosophical transformation of Christian faith which eliminates what is most distinctive of and proper to that faith – what, with reference to the Hegelian theologian Philip Marheineke, Kierkegaard calls a 'volatilisation' of Christian concepts. Why? Because it seems that the basic premise of the whole Hegelian undertaking is the elimination of a God who might transcend the capacities of human experience and knowledge, a God who would be 'Other' and intrinsically greater than anything the heart of man might conceive – that is, precisely the God Hegel saw mooted in various forms in Kant, Jacobi and Fichte. Instead, for Hegel, knowledge of God must be based on the relationship with God found in humanity itself and especially in what was most distinctive of humanity: reason. By making the God-relationship given in faith the object of 'scientific' enquiry and exposition, that is, by interpreting it as the self-explication of reason, Hegel could thus seem to prepare the way for those so-called Left Hegelians who enthusiastically transformed the theological legacy into the intoxicating new wine of a radical and thorough-going humanism.

Both some opponents of this Left Hegelianism (including Kierkegaard) and the Left Hegelians themselves could see the issue in these terms, but this was not the only way of reading Hegel. If subsequent history of ideas has tended to give privileged place to the passage of Hegelianism through the Hegelian Left and on to its 'progressive' transformation in Marx, a truer picture would need also to take account of the Hegelian theologians who sought to emphasise the positive opportunities that Hegelian method offered to theology and to a philosophy of religion essentially sympathetic to Christianity. In returning now to J. E. Erdmann and to his lectures on *Faith and Knowledge*, I shall take a small step towards rectifying this omission from the history of ideas of what, in their time, was an important group of thinkers. Erdmann was not the sole representative of this tendency. Perhaps the best-known in his time was Philip Marheineke, a colleague of both Hegel and Schleiermacher at Berlin. Karl Rosenkranz, Karl Daub, Christian Hermann Weisse and Julius Schaller were other figures of some significance. In connection with Kierkegaard, the Danish Hegelians Johan Ludvig Heiberg and Hans Lassen Martensen have also received some attention in recent literature (see, for example, Horn 2007; Stewart 2003, 2007; Thompson 2008). Although Heiberg was not essentially interested in theological questions, Martensen is an important representative of Hegelian-influenced 'speculative theology'.

The more exact definition of this speculative theology, its history and an evaluation of its significance is singularly lacking in the current history of ideas. These thinkers do pose some central issues for Christian theology and for the philosophy of religion. In addition to questions as to the possibility and scope of a 'knowledge' or even a 'science' (in the specific nineteenth-century sense of *Wissenschaft*) of God, they highlighted an issue that has ever since been a strong undercurrent in many theological and philosophical versions of idealism, namely, the issue as to the personality of God. I will not extensively address this particular issue, but it is important to note that, whether or not Hegel's own system allows for an adequate concept of personality, the Hegelian theologians unanimously demanded that a Christian Hegelianism would need also to be a personalism.

3. Erdmann on Faith and Knowledge

Erdmann is largely forgotten today, but he was a not insignificant figure in his own time. His *History of Philosophy* was translated into English in 1890 and passed through several English editions. Via its re-edition in the Muirhead Library of Philosophy it may be assumed to have played an important role in disseminating a certain version of Hegelianism in the English-speaking world. Erdmann is also interesting in relation to the particular question of faith and knowledge because, although he was undoubtedly 'Hegelian' in several of his key assumptions and intellectual ambitions, he was by no means narrowly or crudely so. Thus, although he regarded a fully speculative approach as going beyond Schleiermacher, Erdmann retained a considerable veneration for the 'father of modern theology' and was always willing to acknowledge the debt that the study of religion owed to him. In contrast to what caricatures of Hegelianism sometimes suggest, Erdmann made clear that he intended to be careful in doing justice to his sources and several times draws attention to the fact that particular individual thinkers can never be totally identified with particular ideological positions, since, in the actuality of individual life and historical development, ideas never or rarely appear unmixed or unqualified by what went before or came after. However, a more particular reason why Erdmann is of interest is that his *Faith and Knowledge* played a key role in the developing relation to Hegel and Hegelianism of the young Kierkegaard. Kierkegaard's reading of Erdmann is evidenced by extensive notes, including several pages of discussion. From these we see that some decisive features of Kierkegaard's later attack on speculation were formed concretely in the course of studying Erdmann. It would be wrong to ignore the role of other Hegelian sources both in this early *Auseinandersetzung* and in Kierkegaard's later attacks, but Erdmann's role is undeniably important.

Erdmann was struck by how much the question of faith and knowledge dominated the contemporary intellectual landscape. But, he asks, where does this question properly belong – in philosophy or theology? He answers: neither. This is a particular case of a general rule: the definition of the boundaries between intellectual disciplines cannot be decided from within one or other of those disciplines alone. As such, the question can properly belong only to the 'introduction' to a given science – in this case to what Erdmann calls *Religionswissenschaft überhaupt*. If we translate this as 'the science of religion in general' we must understand it as referring not to the late nineteenth century positivist idea of a 'science of religions' but to any disciplined and scholarly engagement with religion, including both philosophy and theology. Thus the sub-title of 'Faith and Knowledge' reads: 'Introduction to Dogmatics and to the Philosophy of Religion'. When this placing of the relationship between faith and knowledge is ignored, the consequences are dire. Once 'faith and knowledge' becomes a topic within philosophy, then it has the tendency – as, Erdmann believes, recent decades have shown – to turn philosophy as a whole into philosophy of religion. All other questions become incorporated into just this one and the equally important relation of philosophy to, for example, natural science or psychology is neglected.

But how is one to begin and how is the subject to be approached? Here Erdmann explicitly aligns himself with Hegel. But, he insists, Hegelian method is not a question of applying an abstract triadic schema of thesis-antithesis-synthesis to the data of religion but of approaching religion with the simple, single postulate that we do so *thinkingly*. Thought is distinctive of humanity and it is universally human, 'the true attribute of being human' (Erdmann 1837: 15). What the philosopher must do is think 'the matter at hand' (Erdmann uses the formulation associated with Husserl: *Die Sache selbst*) as it shows itself in its actual development. To follow science, Erdmann tells his students, is to board a ship bound for an unknown destination. Not in the 'introduction' but only at the end can one know where one has landed. However, as the contents page of the published version of the lectures invites us to do, we might note that Erdmann's procedure from here on is (1) to set out some basic issues around the idea of faith itself before proceeding to examine a sequence of dialectically unfolding forms of faith comprising (2) reflective faith, (3) doubt and (4) mysticism. Then, in the second part of the book, he turns to knowledge, looking in turn at (5) empirical, (6) critical and (7) speculative forms of knowledge. In this last the antithesis of faith and knowledge is resolved into a unity that reflects not only the interests of religion but also those of knowledge. The distinction between the two main parts, faith and knowledge, is that in the former Erdmann claims to be studying the actual forms of the religious life, in the latter the development of knowledge about that life, that is, theology.

But what, in this case, is the matter at hand? What is religion? Erdmann acknowledges that for himself and his auditors Christianity is the main form in which religion is known and that whether they are believers, doubters or unbelievers they will be familiar with the central teachings of Christianity. He proposes that the central idea of religion is the relationship between God and human beings, a relationship that Christian teaching figures as love and philosophy as identity – but, in each case, it is a matter of the 'unity of God and the human being' (Erdmann 1837: 23). He immediately adds, however, the religious believer also knows this to be a unity 'subsequent to a separation': it is the result of an atonement or reconciliation.

In the immediate forms of the religious life this sense of unity appears as a subjective attitude (*Gemüthszustand*) of unconditional certainty, as in Paul's declaration that he is certain that nothing can separate him from the love of God in Christ Jesus (Rom. 8:38–9). Such 'naïve' faith has an almost child-like quality. Whilst all religious people may have intimations of it at some moments, it is rarely found without qualification in any individual. Nevertheless, it is characteristic of the faith of the Church as a whole: it is faith, absolutely and as such, in its subjective aspect. But faith has a no less fundamental objective aspect which is found in doctrine. In the immediate life of faith, doctrine will be delivered in the form of *facts*, as the narration of what has happened and is to be believed as such. Such teaching does not involve suppressing the subjective side. Both say the same thing in different ways. The subjective believer says: I am blind; the objective faith of the Church teaches him: You are blind. This unity is expressed also in how the Creed, the faith of the Church, is, from another side, the *Credo*, what *I* (or any individual believer) believe. Here 'what' is believed is not distinguished from the act of believing – we can scarcely imagine Christ responding to the sick man who appeals to him with the words 'I believe!', by asking 'What do you believe?' (Erdmann 1837: 43).

Yet just as the subjective believer is aware that his union with God is a unity regained after sin, that is, the result of his being reconciled, so too the question as to 'what' is believed implies the possibility of doubt, which invites us to move from purely immediate or naïve faith to reflective faith. 'Reflective faith' is the focus of the second section of Erdmann's lectures. As such it generally presupposes the realisation of a possible distinction between subjective and objective forms of faith, the *fides qua creditur* (the faith that believes) and the *fides quae creditur* (the faith that is believed). This reflection is only 'higher' than naïve faith if it in turn progresses on to higher forms. Before this can happen, however, reflective faith must pass through a sequence of forms in which now the objective, now the subjective, side is one-sidedly emphasised.

The first one-sided form is what Erdmann calls 'dogmatism' or, as he somewhat apologetically calls it, dogmaticism. The point of this distinction is that religion is naturally dogmatic: the Church tells the believer what to believe, it can do no other; this, in its own way, is entirely in order. When this teaching is spontaneously accepted by the subjective believer, there is no problem. However, dogmaticism goes a step further and insists on the submission of the subject, often self-consciously opposing itself to reason. Faith is *what* is to be believed and no longer faith as such: it is 'holding something to be true but without having grounds for doing so' (Erdmann 1837: 56). Somewhat characteristic of the Protestant Scholasticism of the seventeenth and eighteenth centuries, this tendency is exacerbated in what he calls 'Dogmatic Superstition' where the teaching is not only set over against the subject for his acceptance or rejection but is also declared to be in total opposition to anything the subject could understand. This is the religion of those Erdmann calls 'head-hangers' and false Pietists, a religion in which God is declared incomprehensible (he cites Tertullian and Jacobi as examples) – a statement, he says, that tells us nothing about God but much about the minds of those who would believe it.

At this point we are faced with the slightly peculiar situation that although dogmaticism insists on the opposition between supernatural truth and the 'I' (comprising also the rationality to which the 'I' spontaneously subscribes), the fact that dogmatic assertions are formulated with a view to their antithesis to the 'I' means that, actually, the 'I' is making the running. This unacknowledged role of the 'I' comes to the fore in religious doubt. But this is also the moment in which the 'I' becomes capable of awakening to philosophy. Yet if the 'I' is not content with questioning the validity of its objects, but comes to reject anything that disrupts its sense of self-identity and makes itself the sole arbiter of truth, then this 'I' has become nihilistic, whether this appears as indifference to religious truth, tolerance of all truths, irony, or the reduction of morality to the requirement to be true solely to oneself. This is something that Erdmann sees widely attested in contemporary culture, especially amongst the educated. Nevertheless, even nihilism still allows for a certain relation to the object, although this is done away with in thorough-going unbelief, the most vivid (and alarming) example of which is the culmination of the French Enlightenment in the Terror and the annihilation of everything holy (Erdmann 1837: 93).

Once all relations between the 'I' and its objects have been broken in this way, there seems to be nothing to prevent a constant and merely random oscillation between the polarities of superstition and unbelief. Yet this oscillation itself can be understood as testifying to an inner contradiction in the self, an unrest, an impulse that, Erdmann suggests, is an essentially religious impulse towards unity. This impulse finds expression in mysticism (Erdmann seems chiefly to have in mind those forms of mysticism associated with Protestant Pietism). But the mystic's claim to unity with God is not organic. On the one hand, mysticism seems to resemble naïve faith in its immediate sense of the presence of God; on the other hand, mysticism seems to resemble speculative knowledge. But these are only analogies and the insufficiency of the mystical approach is seen in the tendency of mystical groups to separate themselves from the world: the self becomes one with God only by surrendering much of its own identity. A sense of this loss therefore drives the 'I' to seek a more organic unity with its object, a unity founded in what is truly universal in the 'I', its 'genuine substance or inner essence' (Erdmann 1837: 135). Once the 'I' discovers this, it is no longer merely an arbitrary 'I', since it has identified itself with the standpoint of reason, from which thinking and the pursuit of knowledge are the natural outcomes. With this transition (which he links historically with German Pietism rather than the French Enlightenment) Erdmann advances to the second part of the lecture series, devoted to knowledge.

What is the relationship between these two parts? Is everything in Part I superseded and therefore worthless? Not at all, Erdmann says. The relationship is akin to that between the Aristotelian *dynamis* and *energeia*. The former has the possibility of the latter *an sich* (in itself): when the bud becomes the flower it becomes what *an sich* it already was (Erdmann 1837: 146). The forms of faith examined in the first part 'were already reason, already forms of thought but not [experienced] *as* reason or *as* thought'. Popular prejudice might lead us to think that reasons and thoughts are merely subjective but, Erdmann says, being reasonable means seeing the reason of things and the relation of reason to the world is precisely that of knowing: knowledge is cognition based on reason. Thus, whereas the first part of the lecture series dealt with living forms of religious existence, the second deals with theologies. To an extent, as Erdmann acknowledges, this means repeating the same journey made in the first part, as we follow reason through the various one-sided and limited developments that precede its achievement of a definitive and infinitely satisfying form.

In three main sections – 'Empirical Knowledge', 'Critical Knowledge' and 'Speculative Knowledge' – Erdmann expounds and shows the internal logic of the main forms of post-Reformation theology, each with its further sub-divisions. Thus 'Empirical Knowledge' is first manifested as the 'practical Christianity' of early Pietism which, as he emphasises, was not just about the cultivation of religious emotions but was also directed toward moral conduct (thereby demonstrating its intrinsic rationality). This is the subjective pole – immediately followed by a swing to the objective pole that Erdmann calls 'experimental', focused on vindicating the factual basis of faith. This occurs either in attempts to prove the miracles as attestations of the Christ or to extract a core of 'essential' beliefs from the whole range of biblical and doctrinal sources. A further form of this 'empirical' moment in theology is the turn to history and to historical testimony as the basis of faith. In Catholicism this is seen in the role given to tradition, in Protestantism in the rise of the historical-exegetical school of biblical study – but these still do not give what is needed, namely, an understanding of the inner grounds for the truth of the witness. The interests of reason therefore drive it to seek these grounds not just in external testimony but in itself and with the recognition of this desire Erdmann makes the transition to the next section, 'Critical Knowledge'.

The first form of this critical knowledge is what Erdmann calls natural theology or naturalism. The second of these terms is the better guide to his meaning, since this is not 'natural theology' in the sense of Catholic or Anglican natural theologies from the Middle Ages or seventeenth century. Rather, it is the limitation of theology to what is universally and objectively demonstrable which leads to the specific Enlightenment period theology known as naturalism, a 'theology' that excluded anything supernatural. However, Erdmann sees its insistence on nature as theologically self-defeating, since to regard human beings in terms of nature is to see them in light of what they have in common with animals – but religion is precisely that in which human beings distinguish themselves from animals, from nature. Similarly, the requirement of universality found in the idea of a natural religion is inherently limiting, since the Christian concept of God is not identical with all the 'gods' of the various religions. The God who is love is not the fetish-worshipper's god. This kind of theology therefore leads to what Erdmann calls the theology of 'healthy common-sense', but this 'healthy common-sense' thinks and speaks only in abstract generalities. It is limited to the level that Hegel called that of the 'understanding' (*Verstand*) and, in religion, it leads to Unitarianism and the denial of the Incarnation.

Erdmann now arrives at what, for him, is a major watershed in the whole history of relations between faith and knowledge, namely, Kant's critical philosophy. Kant's decisive contribution was to turn reason back from external facts and empty generalities to its own inner laws. However, as Kant himself developed this self-examination of pure reason, it was unable to deliver any positive outcome. Whilst philosophy uncovered the transcendental forms of all possible knowledge, it could establish no knowledge of transcendent entities themselves, that is, of entities transcending human reason. This outcome could, however, be developed in a number of different directions. Negatively, it could issue in a theology of not-knowing, which in turn could take either a frankly nihilistic or a supernaturalistic form, in which the metaphysical space that Kant had excluded from knowledge was filled by dogmatic claims. Erdmann sees this as disingenuous, however, since dogmas are themselves essentially theoretical and it was precisely the possibility of theoretical knowledge of transcendent realities that Kant had sought to eliminate – whether this took dogmatic or philosophical forms. But supernaturalism contradicts not only the Kantian premises to which it appeals but also the Bible, where faith is both often used interchangeably with knowing and conceived of as a spiritual possession of truth. Both faith and knowledge in the Bible are only ever 'in part', but knowledge that is 'in part' is nevertheless knowledge. The not-knowing in which the Kantian critique culminates cannot satisfy the impulse (*Trieb*) or instinct of reason, to know the truth as not only subjective but also objective. Coinciding with the religious impulse, reason too seeks and will only be satisfied with the unity of subject and object.

This marks the transition to Speculative Knowledge (the third and final section of the treatment of 'Knowledge'). The first form of this is also a fruit of the Kantian revolution in philosophy, this time in its practical aspect. For where Kant had denied the possibility of a theoretical knowledge of God, he opened the way to a new approach to religious truth, as a matter 'not of knowing but of willing' (Erdmann 1837: 237). Now it was not a matter of God's existence, conceived as the existence of some external or alien being, since 'Not Being but only an Ought is to be attributed to God' (242). Yet this contains a paradox. If God is not, but ought to be, then that 'ought' itself is a requirement that God *should* be, that God's kingdom might come on earth as in heaven. The tension between these contradictory requirements generates what Erdmann sees as an infinite process, variously reflected in the theologies of Fichte and Schleiermacher. However, it finds its more satisfactory expression in dialectical reason:

> If the actual unification of Non-being and Being is Becoming (*Werden*), then truth is to be apprehended neither as Non-being nor as Being but as Becoming. Reason will thus reflect both requirements if it knows truth as becoming. Now something is known in its becoming when one knows the law or rule governing its becoming. But the law or rule of becoming is what we call its determination (*Bestimmung*) or concept (*Begriff*). This is the being of the object that is at one and the same time an Ought and an Ought that at one and the same time is a Being. Truth must therefore be known by knowing the concept. (255)

That speculative knowing – knowing in accordance with the concept – thus knows God as 'becoming' does justice to the religious conviction that God is a living God and not a 'dead something' (*todtes Daseyn*) (257). But this is not to be understood in terms of temporal succession but as an eternal, timeless becoming or process (Erdmann uses the Latinate term to emphasise the distinction of divine from merely historical becoming). The concept, whether of God or more generally, is neither a priori nor a posteriori: rather, it is simply thinking the genesis of the object as it reveals itself. Although it requires the activity of the thinking mind, it is not a matter of inventing 'merely' conceptual forms under which to catalogue real phenomena but it 'produces' only that which is itself coming into being. Conceptual thinking of this kind is therefore essentially maieutic and thinking about God is essentially 'letting His own thinking hold sway in us' (262). For what we think in thinking about God is itself an unqualifiedly thinking Being, a Being in whom thinking, willing and Being coincide absolutely. Speculative knowledge of God is thus also knowledge of God as subject or personality (263). Such knowledge can itself take two forms, speculative dogmatics (when it is determined by the specific content of Christian teaching) or philosophy of religion. This latter opens the way to a history of religion in which the world's religions are understood not (as Schleiermacher understood them) merely as a system of types of religion but as a progressive sequence of stages leading back to speculative knowledge of God itself as the highest point of religious development.

I have offered this summary of Erdmann's lectures largely without comment. From a contemporary standpoint, many of their shortcomings are by now long familiar tropes of debate amongst philosophers of religion – not least because we are heirs both of the Left Hegelian and Kierkegaardian critiques of Hegelianism. Yet even this somewhat sketchy summary allows us to see that, in at least some of its representatives, Hegelian theology and philosophy of religion was driven by and expressed a genuine religious interest as well as a concern to work out the development and implications of religious ideas in the detail of the concrete historical forms of religious life and theology. The inevitable selectiveness of such an approach to thinking about God marks it out for criticism (the Catholic world makes only an intermittent and marginal appearance in Erdmann's history, for example). Yet its historical grounding is nevertheless a challenge that has remained normative for most versions of philosophy of religion in the continental approach and that is similarly (if also differently) found in Erdmann's Left Hegelian and radical Christian critics. Only in relation to the actual, lived forms of religious life and consciousness can the truth (or otherwise) of religion be decided. The neglect of this challenge is, moreover, a feature of much contemporary atheism which renders the latter singularly ineffective in its account of how and why religion actually comes to exercise the power it does in human hearts and minds.

4. Hegelianism Rejected: Strauss, Feuerbach and Kierkegaard

Erdmann's lectures were, as he insisted, merely 'introductory' and could not guarantee the conclusion to a journey of which they merely offered the first stage. But his kind of Hegelianism nevertheless gave the impression of marking a point of arrival. Even if Hegel is misconstrued when he is seen as declaring an 'end of history', there seems to be a certain and inevitable finality implicit in the claim that we now have an absolute, speculative knowledge of God and of what is essential to human beings' God-relationship. Yet even by 1837 the so-called Hegelian synthesis of Christianity and philosophy was starting to unravel. Erdmann himself took note of one of the first critical voices from within Hegelianism itself, David Friedrich Strauss.

Strauss's *Life of Jesus Critically Examined*, published in 1835, was one of the few books of modern theology that can, without hyperbole, be called epochal. The subsequent development of Left Hegelianism would reach radical applications and conclusions with which Strauss could not go along. Biblical criticism too would move far beyond what Strauss achieved in this work. Nonetheless the work was experienced by its contemporaries as throwing wide open the whole issue of historical Christianity and its relation to knowledge.

Strauss's 'mythical' approach to the New Testament was, in its way, founded on naturalist principles, in that he allowed no exceptions to the universal laws of nature. Yet naturalist hermeneutics still largely understood the biblical texts as a kind of reportage – that is, that reports of miracles were indeed accounts of events that had happened, albeit highly erroneous and misleading accounts. Strauss, however, argued that once we have detected a mythical element in a given narrative we have no reason to suppose that there was any historical basis to it – or, even if there is, it has no decisive significance for the interpretation of the passage. For the meaning of the passage hinges precisely on the specific meaning of its mythical element which, in the specific context of the Gospels, is primarily determined by the belief that Jesus is the Messiah, *ergo* all the attributes associated with the Messiah must be ascribed to him. But speculative theology allows us to go a step further and add that the messianic idea itself is merely a mythical form of a more fundamental ideal truth, namely, the idea of the unity of the divine and human (the central element in Erdmann's definitions of faith and speculative knowledge). What is important in the Gospels is thus not a string of merely historical or factual occurrences but the speculative idea of divine-human unity. Thus, Strauss claims that whatever is lost to Christianity by a mythical approach to the Bible is returned with interest in his speculative Christology. The individual historical facts of Christ's life are stripped of the importance they previously enjoyed. But this is compensated for by the greater clarity with which the idea of divine-human unity can now be presented. Christ's physical presence on earth disappears or is absorbed into the ongoing spiritual life of the Christian community:

> The God-man, who during his life stood before his contemporaries as an individual distinct from themselves and perceptible by the senses, is by death taken out of their sight; he enters into their imagination and memory: the unity of the divine and human in him becomes a part of the general consciousness; and the church must repeat spiritually, in the souls of its members, those events of his life which he experienced externally. (Strauss [1835] 1972: 778)

Or, as he puts it still more succinctly: 'This is the key to the whole of Christology, that, as subject of the predicate which the church assigns to Christ, we place, instead of an individual, an idea' (780) – and this 'idea', he adds, finds its reality in the race, that is, in the common life of humanity as a whole. Where Christ *qua* individual healed 'some sick people in Galilee' we are now able to realise the Christ-idea:

> in the miracles of intellectual and moral life belonging to the history of the world – in the increasing, the almost incredible dominion of man over nature – in the irresistible force of ideas, to which no unintelligent matter, whatever its magnitude, can oppose any enduring resistance. (Strauss 1972: 781)

Yet although Strauss's approach thus issues in a celebration of the material applications of contemporary science, it is still couched in essentially idealistic terms. This laid it open to criticism both from more theologically conservative positions (including more conservative Hegelians, as well as supernaturalists) and from more consistently materialist developments of Hegelianism. An example of the response of the more conservative (or, we might say, the more theological) Hegelians is provided by Erdmann himself. Dealing with how religion necessarily represents its doctrines as fact, he objects to Strauss's separation of the ideal truth of doctrine from its factual representation. For religion, the fact is not merely the form of the idea, but that whereby the idea is the idea. Thus (as arguably for Hegel himself) the historical appearance of the 'idea' of divine-human unity is inseparable from its appearance in one single historical individual (Jesus Christ) who cannot therefore be construed merely as a transient 'form' for a trans-historical 'idea'.

The idealism inherent in Hegelianism is the subject of particular attention and particular criticism in the work of Ludwig Feuerbach, perhaps especially his 1843 *Principles of the Philosophy of the Future*. As he had argued at length in *The Essence of Christianity*, published in 1841, the distinctive contribution of modern philosophy (that is, Hegelianism) was 'the transformation and dissolution of theology into anthropology' (Feuerbach [1843] 1986: 5). The religious form of this achievement is found in the history of Protestantism, whilst 'speculative philosophy is the rational or theoretical elaboration and dissolution of God . . . [its] essence . . . is nothing but the rationalized, realized, presented essence of God. Speculative philosophy is the true consistent and rational theology' (5–6). However, although the transformation of theology into anthropology is a considerable achievement, both the theology and the anthropology of speculative philosophy are essentially idealistic. God is understood solely as a 'thinking being' who 'thinks only himself' in such a way that 'this unity of thought and the objects of thought is . . . the secret of speculative thought' (15) (which seems a reasonable summary of, for instance, Erdmann's version of speculative thought, where this unity of thinking subject and thinking object was both the theological premise and the theological conclusion of *Faith and Knowledge*). Moreover, since God is also understood as 'a purely immaterial being' and since 'only what is valid in and through God has being' this 'means nothing else than to determine matter as a thing of nothingness, as a non-being' (21). Even in Hegel 'the essence of God is actually nothing other than the absence of thought, or thought abstracted from the ego, that is from the one who thinks' (36). But real existence is not just something that is thought. What has real existence has existence not only in thought but also in the world, not only for the 'I' who thinks but also for others. 'A being that only thinks, and thinks abstractly, has no conception at all of being, of existence, or of reality' (40). Similarly, 'Thought that "overleaps its otherness" . . . [that is, reality] . . . is thought that oversteps its natural boundaries' and is comparable to suicide in that it negates bodily existence, surrendering itself to 'fantastic and transcendental practice' in which 'the difference between imagination and perception' is lost (46).

Against this, Feuerbach declares that the new philosophy must begin with what is real, which, for him, means what exists sensuously: 'Things must not be thought of otherwise than as they appear in reality,' he warns (Feuerbach [1848] 1986: 62). Or, more enthusiastically, the modern thinker must take to heart what Feuerbach calls categorical imperatives:

Desire not to be a philosopher, as distinct from a man; be nothing else than a thinking man. Do not think as a thinker, that is, with a faculty torn from the totality of the real human being and isolated for itself; think as a living and real being, as one exposed to the vivifying and refreshing waves of the world's oceans. Think in existence, in the world as a member of it, not in the vacuum of abstraction as a solitary monad, as an absolute monarch, as an indifferent, superworldly God; then you can be sure that your ideas are unities of being and thought. (67)

Feuerbach's 'world' is the human world: the real world of concretely existing human beings, encountering each other as an I and a Thou, of which he writes that 'man with man – the unity of I and thou – is God' (71). His materialist humanism thus 'takes the place of religion and has the essence of religion within itself. In truth, it is itself religion' (73).

Feuerbach's materialism would, famously, be criticised in turn by Marx as lacking historical specificity and, as has already been noted, Marx had from the early 1840s regarded the critique of religion – which remained such an abiding focus of Feuerbach's thinking – as essentially finished. It might also be questioned whether the seemingly naïve account of material existence to which Feuerbach so consistently appeals does justice to how human beings actually experience their own existence in the world. To pursue the question as to how 'existence' itself might be interpreted, we turn to Kierkegaard: it would be specifically from Kierkegaard – although without his religious presuppositions – and not from Feuerbach that twentieth-century philosophies of existence took their defining concept of existence.

Like Feuerbach, Kierkegaard developed the concept of existence with one eye on what he saw as the confusion of thinking and being in Hegelian or speculative thought. It was previously noted that Kierkegaard read Erdmann's lectures in the year they were published, making extensive notes and comments on them. These notes constitute one of the defining documents of his relation to Hegelianism. Even as a student he was developing the take on Hegelianism that would find fuller expression in such works as the *Concluding Unscientific Postscript* of 1846. He disputes some of Erdmann's (Hegelianism's) fundamental assumptions, such as the view that the human 'I' is constituted as the subjective pole of a subject–object relation that is properly describable as universal and reasonable. The analysis of human self-consciousness cannot yield a definitive account of reason, since we cannot presuppose that reason is limited to whatever human self-consciousness knows of it. (This is a point that would reappear in the *Postscript* when Kierkegaard cites Hamlet's comment to Horatio that 'there's more in heaven and earth than is dreamt of in your philosophy' (Shakespeare, *Hamlet*, I, v, 166).)

Furthermore, Erdmann does not adequately take account of Christianity's historical aspect. In this connection Kierkegaard accuses Erdmann of caricaturing the various historical positions that he takes as exemplifying the abstract positions he has deduced from the inner development of the idea. Nor can the individual abstract himself from the testimony of the Church's sacred texts and traditions, since there is always a quite specific interest in play in his relation to them, namely, the interest of faith itself. Moreover, Kierkegaard does not accept that post-Kant we have to choose between supernaturalism and agnosticism, since, as he says, supernaturalism is not just a matter of dogma but of the 'total transformation of consciousness' or a 'new consciousness' that is the basis for believing the dogma (Kierkegaard 2001: 167). Kierkegaard simply rejects the basic assumption, which is both Erdmann's and Hegel's, that what the believer experiences as union with God in faith and love is the same as what the philosopher experiences as identity.

The refusal to understand human existence in terms of a rationally constituted subject–object, or to allow the limits of reason to determine either what might be known (or, at least, believed) of God or even of the self's own possibilities on the far side of its rebirth into a new consciousness are all key features of Kierkegaard's later mature critique of Hegelianism. Somewhat like Feuerbach, he sees the Hegelian subject–object as a case of thinking thinking itself and, in so doing, cutting itself off from the larger reality of existence. As did Feuerbach, Kierkegaard depicts the philosopher who presumes to occupy such a standpoint of pure thought as a 'fantastic' being – and such a fantastic being 'that the most extravagant fancy has scarcely invented anything so fabulous' (Kierkegaard [1846] 1992: 117). Such a thinker has forgotten that he exists and, in identifying himself with humanity (that is, what is universally human), abolishes humanity ([1846] 1992: 124). Whilst, as a matter of fact, Hegelianism does not realise its own claim to operate without empirical observation (which it 'smuggles' into the system by a philosophical sleight of hand), its posture of having achieved a position of pure thought (conceived as identical with pure Being) and of absolute knowledge is simply ridiculous. An important part of Kierkegaard's strategy is to expose such claims to a sustained campaign of mockery which, whilst scarcely constituting a philosophical argument, makes for enjoyable reading and effectively undermines the whole tenor of Hegelianism's self-representation.

A crucial element in Kierkegaard's distinctive concept of existence is the relationship between subjectivity and time. The speculative thinker contemplates the world *sub specie aeternitatis* and forgets that he himself is living in time. Whilst existence may indeed constitute a system from God's eternal standpoint, that is not a standpoint any human being could ever actually occupy (Kierkegaard [1846] 1992: 118–25). To exist in time is to exist in a state of unfinishedness; as long as we are alive we are capable of only a partial view of life and of ourselves. Of course, we all know that we must die, but we cannot anticipate that death just by thinking about it and no knowledge of death would absolve us from the unthinkable confrontation with our own end (165–7). The existing person is always under way, always seeking to realise his or her possibilities, passionately seeking to give shape and coherence to existence through acts of choice and decision so that, as Kierkegaard repeatedly says, 'subjectivity is truth' – whereas 'for an existing person, objective truth is like the eternity of abstraction' (313). What is eternally true about me, who I really am, is therefore something I can only ever relate to uncertainly, although, at the same time, 'objective uncertainty, held fast in the most passionate act of inward appropriation is truth, the highest truth there is for an existing person' (41). Existence involves separating reality from the idea, therefore it is always in motion, necessarily temporal and open, and yet for the existing person precisely this 'unfinished business' is a matter of 'the highest interest' – as opposed to the supposed 'disinterested' stance of speculative thought (314).

By such manoeuvres Kierkegaard marks out the profound differences he believes there to be between his own position and that of speculative thought. Yet there is a point at which he does seem in essential agreement with at least the theological representatives of speculative thought. Although Kierkegaard denies that the union of the divine and human is essentially definable in terms of reason (and therefore cannot be understood by means of the self-interpretation of human consciousness), he does believe that, nevertheless, the divine and the human *can be* and in faith *are* united. Human beings were made in the image and likeness of God and that likeness is restored in the 'new consciousness', the 'rebirth' that is Christian faith. However, this new consciousness cannot be developed out of human consciousness as we know it, but becomes possible only on the basis of the Incarnation, the descent of God into human form, taking the 'likeness' of human flesh. But the Incarnation is a paradox and an offence to reason, since it involves identifying God with just this singular individual human being (and, moreover, a human being marked out by poverty, suffering, misunderstanding and a scandalous death). Indeed it is not just a paradox but the 'absolute paradox' (Kierkegaard [1844] 1985: 37–48). As such no human being could ever imagine it nor can a human being believe it, except by the regenerating action of God himself.

5. Conclusion

In these last points there is nothing especially unconventional from the point of view of Protestant theology (except for the humour, freshness and vivacity of Kierkegaard's presentation). Yet Kierkegaard's point is precisely to block the kind of move he saw being made by those contemporary Protestant theologians who associated themselves with speculative philosophy, and to render impossible any fusion of horizons between reason and faith, faith and knowledge. Kierkegaard himself never used the expression 'leap of faith', yet the overall thrust of his account of faith is that it is indeed possible only by leaping away from the standpoint of immanent reason towards a God who is knowable only as absolute paradox. From the point of view of an account of faith and knowledge such as that of Erdmann, Kierkegaard might seem to be reverting to the position of dogmatic superstition (that is, to be a 'head-hanger'), whilst from a Feuerbachian position he might seem to take all too little account of the immediate and enlivening possibilities of finding oneself in and through working for the material improvement of humanity. Yet the Kierkegaardian analysis of existence, in all its anguish and absurdity, was not simply a reactionary retreat from the 'breakthrough' supposedly achieved in Hegelian philosophy. Precisely this analysis, once reinterpreted in the philosophy of existence, would then be reappropriated by theology itself. Its resonances can be detected in several of the existentialist theologies of the mid-twentieth century (for example, Paul Tillich, Rudolf Bultmann and Karl Rahner) but also in the 'post-metaphysical' theologies of more recent years (Mark C. Taylor, Don Cupitt, John D. Caputo and others).

The point of these comments is not to initiate a historical argument for the 'superiority' of the Kierkegaardian separation of faith and knowledge over the way of Hegelian synthesis. Rather, it is simply to flag the unresolved status of the question. Since the Hegelian position seems to rest on the assumption that the question has been resolved, this might seem to require an outright rejection of Hegelianism. If the very possibility of a resolution is denied outright, however, then it is hard to see how the question could ever arise. If it is in the interests of faith to avoid being confused with one or other form of knowledge, the question as to the more exact relationship between faith and knowledge is one that it is in the interests of both faith and knowledge to address. It is perhaps striking in this connection that precisely this way of putting the question was reflected in the title Jacques Derrida chose for his contribution to a conference on religion, namely, 'Faith and Knowledge' – a lecture that addresses contemporary issues of religious pluralism and the relationship between religion and politics in a perspective significantly shaped by both Kant and Hegel (Derrida 1998).

However, perhaps the most striking contemporary presence of the basic terms of the faith and knowledge debates of the first half of the nineteenth century is in our own debates about the respective places of theology and religious studies in higher education, especially in contexts where religious studies is conceived as a 'science of religions' (*Religionswissenschaft*). This is scarcely surprising, since the nineteenth-century debate itself reflected the new institutional challenges posed by the founding of the University of Berlin and the consequent propagation of a new ideal of 'science' as a model for all university work, including the humanities (see Howard 2006). If some contemporary theologians have attempted to revivify the medieval notion of theology as Queen of the Sciences (for example, Milbank 2000; D'Costa 2005), this has by no means dampened the eagerness of some to banish theology from the academy, on the grounds that faith-based positions are incompatible with academic ('scientific' in the nineteenth-century sense) objectivity and rigour (Gill 1994). Such causes célèbres as the withdrawal of Hans Küng's license as a teacher of Catholic theology at Tübingen University or the dismissal of Gerd Lüdemann from Göttingen University also reflect these tensions. Today, both theology and the study of religions are also having to respond to the new technological environment of university life (Pattison 2005: 194–217), which may seem to have moved the parameters of the debate beyond recognition, but which can also be seen as bringing to a head what was already implicit in the Berlin reforms (Heidegger [1938] 2002). Abstract as it may seem, the question of faith and knowledge is once more focusing on central issues about the nature of university study and teaching, both reflecting and affecting the complex and ever-shifting self-understanding of scholarly life.

Our way of putting the question may have changed, but the question retains its urgency and its force. If, somewhere in the sound and fury of contemporary debates, a final and satisfying resolution has been found, it is clearly still far from finding universal acceptance, and until that has happened we have every reason to revisit the debates of the 1830s and 1840s. If our ways cannot quite be their ways, their ways may nevertheless help form and articulate ours – and, as with all historical study, help us both to resist claiming credit for re-inventing the wheel and to avoid falling into positions whose limitations have long since been exposed.

Note

1. All translations from German texts are the author's own.

References

D'Costa, Gavin (2005), *Theology in the Public Square: Church, Academy and Nation*, Oxford: Blackwell.

Derrida, Jacques (1998), 'Faith and knowledge', in Jacques Derrida and Gianni Vattimo (ed.), *Religion*, Cambridge: Polity Press, pp. 1–78.

Engels, Frederick [1841] (1975), 'Schelling on Hegel', in Karl Marx and Frederick Engels, *Collected Works* vol. 2, Moscow: Progress Publishers, pp. 181–8.

Erdmann, Johann Eduard (1837), *Glauben und Wissen*, Berlin: Duncker and Humblot.

Feuerbach, Ludwig [1843] (1986), *Principles of the Philosophy of the Future*, trans. Manfred H. Vogel, Indianapolis: Hackett.

Gill, Sam (1994), 'The academic study of religion', *Journal of the American Academy of Religion*, LXII (4): 965–76.

Hegel, Georg Wilhelm Friedrich [1802] (1970), 'Glauben und Wissen', in *Werke in zwanzig Bänden* vol. 2, ed. Eva Moldenhauer and Karl Markus Michel, Frankfurt: Suhrkamp, pp. 287–433.

Heidegger, Martin [1938] (2002), 'The age of the world picture', in Heidegger, *Off the Beaten Track*, ed. and trans. Julian Young and Kenneth Haynes, Cambridge: Cambridge University Press, pp. 57–72.

Horn, Robert Leslie (2007), *Positivity and Dialectic: A Study of the Theological Method of Hans Lassen Martensen*, Copenhagen: Reitzel.

Howard, Thomas Albert (2006), *Protestant Theology and the Making of the Modern German University*, Oxford: Oxford University Press.

Kant, Immanuel [1781/1787] (1933), *Critique of Pure Reason*, trans. Norman Kemp Smith, London: Macmillan.

Kierkegaard, Søren [1844] (1985), *Philosophical Fragments*, trans. Howard V. and Edna H. Hong, Princeton: Princeton University Press.

Kierkegaard, Søren [1846] (1992), *Concluding Unscientific Postscript*, trans. Howard V. and Edna H. Hong, Princeton: Princeton University Press.

Kierkegaard, Søren (2001), *Søren Kierkegaard Skrifter*, ed. N.-J. Cappelørn et al., vol. 19, Notesbøgerne 1–15, Copenhagen: Gad.

Marx, Karl (1975), *Early Writings*, ed. Lucio Colletti, Harmondsworth: Penguin.

Milbank, John (2000), 'The conflict of the faculties: Theology and the economy of the sciences', in Mark Thiessen Nation and Samuel Wells (eds), *Faith and Fortitude: In Conversation with the Theological Ethics of Stanley Hauerwas*, Edinburgh: T. & T. Clark, pp. 39–58.

Pattison, George (2005), *Thinking about God in an Age of Technology*, Oxford: Oxford University Press.

Stewart, Jon (2003), *Kierkegaard's Relations to Hegel Reconsidered*, Cambridge: Cambridge University Press.

Stewart, Jon (ed.) (2007), *Kierkegaard and His German Contemporaries. Tome II: Theology*, Aldershot: Ashgate.

Strauss, David Friedrich (1972), *The Life of Jesus Critically Examined*, trans. from 4th edn of 1840 by Marian Evans (George Eliot) (1846), Philadelphia: Fortress Press.

Thompson, Curtis L. (2008), *Following the Cultured Public's Chosen One: Why Martensen Mattered to Kierkegaard*, Copenhagen: Museum Tusculanum Press.

8

Philosophising History: Distinguishing History as a Discipline

James Connelly

1. Introduction

This chapter focuses on key themes, problems and concepts in the thinking of historians and philosophers about the nature and status of historical thought, practice and self understanding in the nineteenth century. It covers the concept of history in relation to Hegel and German idealism, the British idealists, the development of historicism and the issues surrounding the *Methodenstreit*. This story is also that of the other disciplines, such as psychology, sociology, economics and theology, with which history stands in relation.

Until the twentieth century, the term 'philosophy of history' usually denoted not an epistemological inquiry but systematic claims concerning the direction and meaning of the historical process as a whole. It does not follow that no epistemology was going on, for it was. But it went on under different names and frequently as part of a wider debate about the nature and methods of other disciplines. There are thus two important distinctions to note. The first is between philosophy of history as an epistemological inquiry or as the search for laws and patterns in history; this distinction was later characterised as that between analytical and speculative philosophy of history. The second distinction (not unrelated to the first) is between history as past events and history as historiography, as the study of the past. These distinctions are frequently – perhaps even typically – blurred. We should not expect to find 'pure' philosophy of history in any sense, but rather a hybrid and loosely related set of inquiries.[1]

An underlying concern in historical thought is (and always has been) the nature of the object studied and the implications for historical method of construing it in one way rather than another. Following a discussion of how this is conceived in Hegel and the idealist tradition, in historicism, and in the positivist and empiricist responses to these, the attempt to reconsider history as a discipline and to undertake serious inquiry into the differentiae of inquiry in the historical and related sciences in the work of Wilhelm Windelband, Heinrich Rickert, Wilhelm Dilthey and Max Weber will be considered. These debates primarily concern whether historical and natural processes are or should be the same or different. Central to this is the cluster of concepts around *Verstehen*, or understanding, and *Erklärung*, or explanation.

Parallel to these debates in Germany, other debates were being conducted in Britain within the prevailing idealist school of the latter part of the nineteenth century. These debates were not merely internal to British idealism but also represent an engagement with another nineteenth-century worry – biblical criticism and the historicity of Jesus. The latter debate led to philosophical questions concerning historians' sources, the nature of historical evidence and the validity and worth of eye-witness or contemporary testimony. These debates, issuing from David Strauss ([1835] 1846) and Ferdinand Christian Baur ([1853–63] 1878), led directly to works such as Francis Herbert Bradley's *The Presuppositions of Critical History* of 1874 (1935) (hereafter *Presuppositions*), which, in a secular fashion, took over the debate that they initiated and asked what the historian necessarily presupposes in thinking about the past. Bradley does not present himself as contributing to that debate so much as offering an account of historical knowledge as such. In contrast to his fellow idealist, Bernard Bosanquet, Bradley took history seriously as a form of knowledge. Bosanquet was rather more sceptical. This indicates that the British idealists never constituted a monolithic school on this (or indeed any other) philosophical matter.

2. Hegel, the Philosophy of History and Historicism

For Hegel, history is a rational process. Hence his famous dictum that 'what is actual is rational and what is rational is actual' (Hegel [1821] 1942: 10), by which he neither meant to defend the status quo, by asserting that whatever is is perfect, nor to deny it, by requiring it to abide by the standard of abstract reason. His point was that we have to look for the rationality in the historical process and that to achieve historical understanding we have to adopt methods appropriate to it as a rational object. In this sense Hegel was an idealist; and in this sense Marx is in many ways, despite his huge indebtedness to Hegel, his antithesis. Both regarded the historical process as a dialectical process, but for Hegel this is a rational process of mind or spirit, while for Marx it is a material process driven by economics. For Hegel historical facts are understood as expressions of thought rather than as the outcome of material causes (for discussion see Norman and Sayers 1980). Marx's thought belongs to a later period than Hegel's, both temporally and in the sense that he sought to combine Hegel's dialectic with the claim (more akin to that of the positivists) that laws of historical development could be discovered and harnessed for political action.

In the cases of Hegel or Benedetto Croce, although they utter distinctive first-order claims about the historical process (writing, for example, of *History as the Story of Liberty* – the title of a 1941 book by Croce), they do not claim that this is a necessary law-driven process. On the contrary, that would be self-contradictory and obviously so in the case of freedom. What they are asserting is that one unique set of circumstances changes into another through a dialectical process in which a shape of life transcends itself whilst both negating its previous stage of development and simultaneously preserving its truth. In their language, each form is an instance of a universal but not an instance of an *abstract* universal in the way in which a particular explained by a scientific law is indifferently an example and could be replaced by any other example. It is a *concrete* universal in which the universal and particular are fused into a unique individual.[2]

For Hegel, history is 'the development of Spirit in time'. What is 'spirit'? It 'may be defined as that which has its centre in itself'; whereas 'matter has its essence outside itself, Spirit is self-contained existence' (Hegel [1837] 1991: 17). Spirit is both immanent and transcendent; it is both universal and particular; it is both individual and collective:

> It is the concrete spirit of a people which we have distinctly to recognise and since it is Spirit it can only be comprehended spiritually, that is, by thought. It is this alone which takes the lead in all the deeds and tendencies of that people and which is occupied in realising itself, in satisfying its ideal and becoming self-conscious, for its great business is

self-production. But for spirit, the highest attainment is self-knowledge; an advance not only to the intuition, but to the thought – the clear conception of itself. This it must and is also destined to accomplish; but the accomplishment is at the same time its dissolution and the rise of another spirit, another world-historical people, another epoch of Universal History. ([1837] 1991: 71)

Although at first glance it might appear that Hegel conceives of the historical process as a form of necessary development according to fixed stages, this is not so. For Hegel, there is a crucial distinction between the world of mind or spirit and the world of nature. The natural world is spirit estranged from itself; it is spirit's other. Hence its processes are not spiritual processes; they are not processes of mind. History, as dealing with spirit, is a process that proceeds dialectically, not according to necessary or even probabilistic scientific laws. It is a realm of unfolding human self-understanding and this understanding in turn leads to historical development. This is not so for nature. For Hegel, understanding is a historical activity and includes not only whence something came but also whither it is going; in this sense it is proleptic, anticipating although not determining future states of itself. Hegel's approach to history has a distinctive flavour in which he marries the idea that the historian rethinks the thoughts of historical agents, a view of the historical subject as a collective agent instantiated in individuals as concrete universals, and the claim that, although there is no predictable course of history, the historical process is the dialectical working out of the principle of liberty. Progress is not automatic or predictable but there *is* progress and considered in retrospect it has a determinate shape. Considered in prospect it also has a shape whose achievement depends on will:

Since the substance of the individual, the World-Spirit itself, has had the patience to pass through these shapes over the long passage of time and to take upon itself the enormous labour of world-history, in which it embodied in each shape as much of its entire content as that shape was capable of holding, and since it could not have attained consciousness of itself by any lesser effort, the individual certainly cannot by the nature of the case comprehend his own substance more easily. Yet, at the same time, he does have less trouble, since all this has already been implicitly accomplished. (Hegel [1807] 1977: 17)

Also central to Hegel's thought is that the philosopher can no more transcend his own time than he can leap over Rhodes; thus 'philosophy is its own time apprehended in thoughts' (Hegel [1821] 1942: 11). The consequence of this line of thought is the belief that each era or epoch, although constantly unfolding into its successor, is constructed so that all parts are interrelated and to fully understand any part one must understand the whole. This, it might be said, is the historicising of the Absolute: absolute knowing is a process in time; it is the 'development of Spirit in time' (Hegel [1837] 1991: 65).

This is historicism. The term was not used at the time but by later commentators such as Friedrich Meinecke in characterising nineteenth-century thought (see Meinecke [1936] 1972). Although there have been different (not always congruent) senses of the term 'historicism' employed over the past century or so, Meinecke's characterisation attracts general agreement. For him, the essence of historicism lay in replacing generalising views of human forces in history with a process of individualising observation. This was not necessarily to the exclusion of attempts to find general laws and types in human life. Historicism did not deny the existence of a permanent foundation of basic human qualities, although it was certainly sceptical of the stability of human nature and argued that it constantly took on new and individual forms. Thus individuality is revealed in a process of development. The key point is that historicism denies the claims of positivism and asserts the individuality and uniqueness of each historical set of circumstances. To understand historically, therefore, is to understand an agent as acting within a determinate background context (see Burns and Rayment-Pickard 2000: 57–8). For Georg Iggers, historicism involved a philosophy of value, a theory of knowledge and a conception of politics and central to these was the rejection of natural law. In ethics this meant denial of universal norms; history consisted of individuals, each unique in character.

> Individual persons as well as collective bodies – states, churches, epochs – possessed the characteristics of individuality. Values did not exist in the abstract but only within concrete historical contexts. Each individual was to be judged in terms of its own laws of development and the unique values it represented. (Iggers 1967: 383)

Historicism was closely related to the *Verstehen* approach to social reality: historical individuals and institutions could never be reduced to abstract concepts but could only be understood from within in terms of their unique character. Looking to make generalisations in history or to find general laws of social development was a violation of the reality and variety of history.

Whatever its merits, the term 'historicism' rapidly acquired negative connotations, because it was thought to be an endorsement of relativism and hence a threat to fundamental ethical, intellectual and religious values. And because it was intimately connected to the questions of whether historical knowledge is subjective or objective and of whether it can be scientific and of whether social science is possible, historicism is a crucial part of what came to be known at the end of the nineteenth century as the *Methodenstreit* or war of methods. At that time the discussion spread far beyond its origin in German academia and embraced, for example, Croce in Italy, who took historicism further, firmly rejecting the claims of social science. For Croce, social science, whatever its pretensions to universality, could at most provide contingent historical knowledge of a society at a given time.

Before leaving Hegel and historicism, the role of Leopold von Ranke should be considered. The image of Ranke in the English-speaking world is largely that of someone devoted to 'the facts' and to knowing the past 'as it really was'. He has a reputation as an unphilosophical empiricist. He was rightly seen as dedicated to the sources and to scrupulous attention to the documentary evidence. On that basis his attitude was embraced by American historians who wanted to constitute history as a (natural) science and by English historians and writers on history who applauded him for his empiricism and anti-philosophical stance. These were seriously wrong assessments, for Ranke was no positivist. He was on the contrary a philosophical idealist and far more Hegelian than Comtean. It is a rich irony that his popular image is the opposite. Much hinges on the interpretation of a key phrase of his which repeatedly appears in his writings: the idea that the historian should capture the past *wie es eigentlich gewesen*. This is typically translated as 'as it really was' or 'as it actually was', whereas at the time of his using the phrase it was ambiguous in that it could also mean 'essentially' – and that was the sense in which Ranke used it. Thus he was seeking to find the essence of past events, to present them as they were and to avoid judging them. In Germany, at the same time as he was being embraced by the empiricists in the Anglo-Saxon world, Ranke was being attacked by positivists such as Karl Lamprecht for his idealism and defended by those who, like Meinecke, wished to defend the tradition of philosophical idealism. In Peter Novick's words, 'All German historians saw Ranke as the antithesis of a non-philosophical empiricism, while American historians venerated him for being precisely what he was not' (Novick 1988: 28).

Ranke should be considered as belonging in the company of those for whom *die Wissenschaft* primarily means scholarship or learning and for whom *eine Wissenschaft* primarily means a discipline. As Fritz Ringer remarks,

> In English it is possible to argue about whether sociology or history is 'a science'. In German, history is *eine Wissenschaft* by definition and to ask whether sociology is *eine Wissenschaft* is to wonder about its status as a distinct and clearly circumscribed discipline, not about its more or less 'scientific' methods. (Ringer 1969: 102–3)

As a term, *Wissenschaft* implied more than knowledge – it was also self-fulfilment, not merely practical knowledge but knowledge of ultimate meanings. In that sense, *Wissenschaft* was closely allied with philosophical idealism, as was the term *Geisteswissenschaft* (science of mind or spirit), which covers disciplines such as history, philosophy, theology and literature. It is accordingly not surprising that German historians reacted vehemently to the positivistic suggestion that the methods of the *Naturwissenschaften* (natural sciences) should be applied to their discipline (Novick 1988: 24).

3. Historical Empiricism and Positivism

A strong reaction to this Hegelian or idealistic lineage emerged in the forms of empiricism and positivism. Here it is claimed that historical events (particulars) can be subsumed as instances of general laws (universals). This form of explanation is typical of the natural sciences, where the occurrence of an event is explained not by focusing on its individuality but by considering it as an example of the operation of a general law of nature. Empiricism consists in a denial of central idealist claims; positivism consists in asserting that the forms of explanation typical of the natural sciences should be employed in *all* sciences. Some claim not only that particular events can be explained in this way but also that general laws of historical development can be discovered. What positivism signifies for Auguste Comte and for those who argue similarly, such as John Stuart Mill and Henry Thomas Buckle, is the belief that there is only one method appropriate in all disciplines and that the appropriate method is that of natural science. Historical and natural processes are taken as both subject to natural laws and the study of history, no less than that of the natural world, is conducted nomologically, by seeking underlying explanatory laws. Hence Comte claimed to have discovered laws of historical development:

> [T]he first characteristic of the Positive Philosophy is that it regards all phenomena as subjected to invariable natural laws. Our business is . . . to pursue an accurate discovery of these laws, with a view to reducing them to the smallest possible number. (Comte [1830] 1896: 31)

Comte characterised history as passing through several determinate stages, in which religious thought is superseded by metaphysical thought, which is in turn replaced by positive science. Thus positivism is both the correct account of thought and itself the necessary outcome of earlier phases. Buckle sharply rebukes history for its absence of settled scientific method:

[F]or all the higher purposes of human thought history is still miserably deficient and presents that confused and anarchical appearance natural to a subject of which the laws are unknown and even the foundation unsettled. (Burger 1977: 168)

Buckle's rebuke had the unintended effect of provoking Johann Gustav Droysen to respond and thereby usher in the search for a critique of historical reason (which it was Dilthey's explicit ambition to produce, along the lines of Kant's *Critique of Pure Reason*).

4. The Response to Positivism: Understanding and Explanation

The earliest post-Hegelian responses came with Droysen responding to Mill and Buckle. Thomas Burger claims that, with this, the age of methodological innocence came to an end for historians (Burger 1977: 168). Before that time there had been no well-worked out positivist method on offer as an alternative to the humanistic methods of Hegel and others. Now the situation was different, for Buckle's indictment

> was derived from a relatively well-developed and systematic theory of science within whose framework historical accounts appeared as devoid of any serious significance. Its logical conclusion was the demand to replace history by sociology. Traditional historians had little by the way of a worked-out theory of history to put forward against the positivists' charge. The closing of this gap and the provision of a secure methodological 'foundation' thus became the central preoccupation of the theorists of history in the last part of the nineteenth century. (Burger 1977: 168)

In responding to positivism, Droysen in 1858 referred to things which demand not to be explained but *understood* and hence drew the now standard distinction between explanation (*erklären*) and understanding (*verstehen*). In a reminder that historical method has wider connections, however, other factors were involved. Droysen's attack on positivism went beyond the historicist complaint that it introduces an inappropriate teleology into history, based on laws that violate the unique nature of historical individuality. His hostility centred

> not on its [positivism's] cognizable progressivism per se, but rather on what he regards as the political consequences of the particular kind of progressivism it espouses. By rooting the logic of historical development in inexorable laws rather than in human will, positivism for Droysen obscures the genuine normative significance of historical study and thereby threatens the moderate liberal practice which is its proper political expression. Knowledge of putative historical laws satisfies men's intelligence but, by masking history's ethical imperatives, starves their will. The result is an historical disorientation that reduces men from autonomous actors consciously exerting their wills in history in pursuit of the liberal millennium, to an undifferentiated mass of passive automatons eager to accept despotic political direction from above. (Maclean 1982: 349)[3]

As background to this debate, it is worth recalling the *verum-factum* principle enunciated by Giambattista Vico, in his *New Science* of 1744:

> in the night of thick darkness enveloping the earliest antiquity . . . there shines the eternal and never-failing light of a truth beyond all question: that the world of civil

society has certainly been made by man and that its principles are therefore to be found within the modifications of our own human mind. Whoever reflects on this cannot but marvel that the philosophers should have bent all their energies to the study of the world of nature, which, since God made it, He alone knows; and that they should have neglected the study of the world of nations or civil world, which, since men had made it, men could hope to know. (Vico [1744] 1948: 85, §331)

For Vico, we can know only what we have made; we make history, therefore we can know it. And, further, this claim implies a distinct way of viewing historical knowledge, a way developed by neo-Kantians such as Dilthey, Rickert, Windelband and Weber and later by neo-Hegelians such as Croce.

Wilhelm Dilthey popularised the distinction between the *Geisteswissenschaften* and the *Naturwissenschaften*. He did not, however, regard either the distinction or its terms as absolute. He argues that the range of concepts of human studies is

identical with that of understanding and understanding consistently has the objectification of life as its subject-matter . . . Mind can only understand what it has created. Nature, the subject-matter of the physical sciences, embraces the reality which has arisen independently of the activity of mind. Everything on which man has actively impressed his stamp forms the subject-matter of the human studies . . . Every fact is man-made and, therefore, historical; it is understood and, therefore, contains common features; it is known because understood. (Dilthey [1883] 1976: 192)

This shows Dilthey's acceptance of Vico's *verum-factum* principle, although Dilthey allows that knowledge of nature is possible by arguing that it is not that we *cannot* have natural scientific knowledge: it is merely that knowledge of nature and knowledge of history are *different*: 'we explain nature but we understand mental life' ([1883] 1976: 69).

The distinction between the human sciences and the natural sciences needs to be considered carefully. Although it is tempting to suggest, following Hegel's distinction between mind and nature, that the sciences map directly onto that distinction, the distinction can never be merely twofold. Although we should study the human world through the methods appropriate to mind, does that mean that any and every attempt to generalise and make law-like explanations is illegitimate? Conversely, although the natural history of the world presumably cannot be understood as mind, natural processes and their unique history cannot easily be subsumed under a simple set of laws. They are unique, with a unique history. The reason for this observation is that one characteristic of the historical is frequently taken to be that it is in search of the unique, the unrepeatable, that this is a characteristic of the activities of mind where repetition is never sheer repetition but always repetition with a difference. But this can be a feature of the natural as well as of the human world. Conversely, it is often thought that the world of mind can never be captured through general laws, but at some level this might not be true. There are emergent patterns in human activity; are we to be forbidden to look for law-like generalisations?

For Dilthey, *verstehen* is appropriate to the human studies and *erklären* to the natural sciences because of the difference in their respective subject-matters. The difference in method is the consequence of this difference in subject-matter. Dilthey rejected the positivist claim that all sciences can and should follow the methods of natural science. On the contrary, he suggested that the human world could only be made intelligible through understanding (*verstehen*). When studying nature we do not consider its inner side. We do not consider feelings, intentions, consciousness, volitions or desires to be involved in the study of nature. In the study of the human world we do consider these things. Through what Dilthey calls the re-experiencing or *Nacherleben* of an actor's behaviour, we understand the inner reason for that behaviour. This is *verstehen*. This can be construed in different ways: one would be psychologically, which in turn could be regarded as a way to discern regularities in human behaviour through the assumption that what holds for the person seeking to understand holds also for the understood. However, it is generally accepted that, in the words of one eminent commentator, 'Dilthey was not committed to a purely psychological approach, he did not advocate understanding at the expense of other cognitive approaches and he did not accept complete historical relativity' (Rickman 1979: 164). Further, understanding is not a method, but rather 'one ingredient of a method and, as an achievement, it may be the result of using a method'.

5. Patrolling the Boundaries: Rickert and Windelband

In *The Limits of Concept Formation in Natural Science* of 1902, Heinrich Rickert ignores the ontological question of what nature or culture or spirit are in themselves and focuses instead on the issue of values. The very existence of culture or spirit, he says, depends on human values, whereas nature is independent of human values. By linking this together with Windelband's distinction between the nomothetic and the idiographic, he gives us a different account of how the sciences might be subdivided. Rickert combines the positions of Dilthey and Windelband in arguing that there are two sorts of division possible between the various sciences. One is a formal distinction between the methods of concept formation, represented by the extremes of generalisation and individualisation, which does not correspond to the distinction between natural and social science. The other is a substantive division between the subject-matters of the sciences where the division lies between natural and socio-cultural objects. So the difference between nature and history lies not in the object but in our approach to the object. 'Empirical reality becomes nature when we conceive it with reference to the general. It becomes history when we conceive it with reference to the distinctive and the individual' (Rickert [1902] 1986: 54).

The two kinds of objects originate differently: natural objects come about by themselves; cultural objects are brought about specifically because of their value to mankind, therefore relevance to value can serve as the distinguishing methodological feature of the cultural sciences. Putting formal and substantive distinctions together, we can display the result as in Table 8.1.

Table 8.1 *Formal and substantive distinctions*

		Nomothetic	Idiographic
FORMAL			
	Natural (unrelated to values)	*Physics*	*Cosmology*
MATERIAL	**Socio-cultural** (related to mind and values)	*Social Science*	*History*

This typology is as much indebted to Wilhelm Windelband as it is to Rickert. In 1894 Windelband delivered a rectorial address in Strasbourg on 'History and Natural Science'. Like Rickert, he wanted to get away from the idea that the difference between the sciences was grounded simply in the nature/mind dichotomy:

At present, a certain classification of the disciplines which attempt to establish knowledge of reality is regularly employed. They are distinguished into natural sciences and sciences of the mind. Stated in this particular form, I regard the dichotomy as unfortunate. Nature and mind is a substantive dichotomy . . . this dichotomy, which has become fixed in our general modes of thinking and speaking, can no longer be acknowledged as so certain and self-evident that it may serve – just as it stands and without any inquiry into its grounds – as the foundation for a classification of the sciences. (Windelband [1894] 1980: 173)

For Windelband, the difference between different types of science lies not so much in their respective subject-matters as in what type of interest we have in the subject-matter. In particular, we can have an interest in deriving and elucidating laws and generalisation or, on the contrary, in the unique and the individual. This leads to two types of approach: the nomothetic and the idiographic. The nomothetic approach is concerned to establish general laws and general phenomena and the idiographic approach is concerned with unique and unrepeatable configurations of events (Gestalten). Windelband then pointed out that, despite our conventional reservation of the idiographic approach for history and our reservation of the nomothetic approach for natural science, we could, in fact, apply either to the other.

This methodological dichotomy classifies only modes of investigation, not the contents of knowledge itself. It is possible – and it is in fact the case – that the same subjects can be the object of both a nomothetic and an idiographic investigation. (Windelband [1894] 1980: 175)[4]

In seeking to understand the notion of verstehen in any of its senses, it is also important to maintain a distinction between understanding actions through the inner motives of individuals and the idea that its purpose is to understand the 'meaning' of action rather than the motives of acting individuals. In reflecting on the foregoing debates, Max Weber sought to establish the foundations of empirical social science. He took there to be an essential difference between meaningful human conduct and nature because the subject-matter of a socio-cultural investigation (human action and its artefacts) is already understood by the actor him- or herself: the contents of any culture are defined or identified as such by the natives who participate in it. As to how we should know human conduct, his answer was through verstehen. For Weber, verstehen was part of an empirical social scientific approach to the understanding of action, but not the whole. And, even in that part where it was appropriate for the understanding of action, he argued that it should not be construed as a matter of rethinking inner motives or feelings. This is both because that approach can take a psychologistic direction and because it is plagued with the problem (unless strict transhistorical psychological laws are postulated) of being beyond the scope of verification: how can we know that our process of re-thinking coincides with the original thinking or experience we seek to understand? To avoid this, Weber proposed that verstehen be concerned with the social meaning of actions. This is why he once memorably remarked that 'one need not have been Caesar in order to understand Caesar' (Weber [1921] 1947: 90). Caesar is understood through the *meaning* of his actions, not his inner mental states. And this was why Weber was sharply critical of Georg Simmel and Dilthey in so far as they employed a psychological approach to *verstehen*.

For Weber, the task of sociology is to achieve an interpretive understanding of social action, that is, of human behaviour to which the acting individual attaches a subjective meaning. In this sense, to identify socio-cultural phenomena is to identify its meaning as this meaning is understood by the actors or natives. Weber refers here to subjective meaning by which he means both the meaning of a situation as understood by the agent and the relevance of that meaning in respect of that agent's intentions; and he is also talking about social or objective meaning, that is, shared social constructs. Meaning in this latter sense is something which is not private to an individual. The meaning of an act should not be identified with the intention with which it is performed – action should be understood from within, but action takes place within a framework of shared meanings. This framework does not dictate individual actions, but individual actions are only intelligible within that framework. It is therefore important to be clear that the meaning assigned to an action might be prior to the determination of what the action was intended to do or why it was performed here and now in this given situation. Actions have a socially shared and understood meaning and we need to identify and recover this meaning in order to locate what is being done. As Weber remarks:

> we owe to Simmel the elucidation of the most extensive range of cases which fall under the concept of 'understanding' – 'understanding', that is, in contrast to 'discursive knowledge' of reality which is not given in 'inner' experience. He has clearly distin- guished the objective 'understanding' of the meaning of an expression from the subjective 'interpretation' of the motive of a (speaking or acting) person. In the first case, speech is the object of 'understanding', in the second case, the speaker (or agent). (Weber [1903–6] 1975: 152)

However, instead of following the *verstehen* debate into modern sociology and the phenomenology of Alfred Schutz, let us at this point revert to the idealist tradition, this time in Britain, and consider the British idealists' attitude to history.[5]

The British idealists are often taken to be followers of Hegel, who domesticated his thought to make it presentable for the English-speaking world. In so far as Hegel had a historicist approach to philosophy, a teleological view of world history and an organic theory of the state, it is often assumed that they followed this also. The truth is much more interesting. Their relation to Hegel and the German idealists was much more subtle, much more critical and much more oblique. The influences on the thought of Bradley and Bosanquet, for example, were as likely to be Lotze (whom Bosanquet translated) or Kant or Fichte. Also, it should always be remembered that they were arguing against a native background of empiricism, positivism and utilitarianism, as exemplified by the thought of Mill, Comte, Spencer, Henry Longueville Mansel, William Hamilton and others now largely forgotten, but the lines of whose thought can still be traced by the careful reader in the shape and concerns of the British idealists' writing.

However, it is certainly the case that the philosophy of history did not feature greatly in the work of the first wave of British idealists in the last quarter of the nineteenth century. Although the volume *Essays in Philosophical Criticism* (Seth and Haldane 1883), largely a posthumous *Festschrift* for Thomas Hill Green who died in 1882, contained two essays on history, neither can be said to constitute a major contribution to debates in the philosophy of history. The first, by William Ritchie Sorley, on 'The Historical Method' (Sorley 1883), is largely devoted to considering the merits of the 'historical method', conceived as the study of the aetiology and development of the various sciences. It is thus not a discussion of either the methods or the principles of history as a form of inquiry and was written without mention of F. H. Bradley, whose groundbreaking contribution to the subject we will consider shortly. The paper by David George Ritchie, on 'The Rationality of History' (Ritchie 1883), is Hegelian in spirit, taking the term 'philosophy of history' to refer to a teleology of world history. It is epistemological in so far as it addresses the question of how we can know the 'plot of history'. But it does not address (although it occasionally alludes to) the central epistemological questions concerning historical knowledge per se identified above. Like Sorley's piece, it also is innocent of reference to Bradley.

Given these dispiriting facts, why should we be concerned with the attitude of the British idealists to history? For three reasons: (1) because Bradley produced a vitally important positive contribution to the debate; (2) because the very lack of consideration of historical knowledge as a form of inquiry narrowed their angle of vision and thereby stultified (in some cases) the idealists' own attempt to construct their philosophical system; (3) because the generation of idealists who emerged in the first part of the twentieth century – in particular Oakeshott and Collingwood – were instrumental in the development of modern philosophy of history. Modern philosophy of history is thus rooted in a resurgence of idealistic thought as applied fruitfully to the question of historical knowledge. Given this movement of thought, it is clearly important to investigate the trials and tribulations of the philosophy of history in the thought of the idealists on its path towards its emergence as the foundation of later work in the subject. We will examine the positive contribution of Bradley, who sought to establish the presuppositions of historical inquiry, and the more negative contribution of Bosanquet, who found himself unable to rely on history as a form of knowledge and experience.[6]

6. Bradley and *The Presuppositions of Critical History*

For Hegel, history was not the whole, but part of the whole, the whole being absolute knowledge. For the British idealists, similarly, history was not typically dealt with in and for itself – Bradley's essay is a rare exception. Rather, it was taken as part of an examination of what we might call (in Bradley's phrase, converted into the title of a book by Michael Oakeshott) 'modes of experience' or (in R. G. Collingwood's terms) 'forms of experience' (see Oakeshott 1933; Collingwood 1924). As in Hegel, the forms or modes are taken to be rival ways (overlapping for Collingwood, non-overlapping for Oakeshott) of understanding or experiencing the world. The task of the philosopher is to examine these modes and place them in the 'map of knowledge'. Hegel did this in the *Phenomenology of Spirit* and in the *Encyclopaedia of the Philosophical Sciences* (as distinct from the speculative history of some of his other works). Bradley and Bosanquet – whom I have chosen as my representatives of the British idealists – are doing much the same in their own way.

Following Green, the most important and influential of the British idealists was Bradley, who was a Fellow of Merton College from 1870 until his death in 1924. Bradley's major works were *Ethical Studies* ([1876] 1927), *The Principles of Logic* ([1883] 1922) and *Appearance and Reality* ([1893] 1930). Generally speaking, as we have seen, the British idealists were not over-concerned with the philosophy of history (in either sense of the term). The major exceptions in the twentieth century are Collingwood and Oakeshott.

The latter's *Experience and Its Modes* contains a chapter on 'Historical experience' of which Collingwood in *The Idea of History* claims that it

> not only represents the high-water mark of English thought upon history, but shows a complete transcendence of the positivism in which that thought has been involved, and from which it has tried in vain to free itself, for at least half a century. (Collingwood [1946] 1993: 158–9)

For Collingwood, then, the way to a proper conception of historical knowledge is through idealism, but this path was not properly taken until the mid-1930s and it was certainly not taken by the great British idealists such as Green and Bosanquet. However, it was embarked upon by Bradley (see Walsh 1984; Rubinoff 1996).

Collingwood claims that Bradley's metaphysics was a profoundly historical one. Although Collingwood considered Bradley's *Presuppositions* infected by 'positivism', this was remedied in later works. First, the *Principles of Logic* constructed 'a logic orientated . . . towards the epistemology of history' and *Appearance and Reality* presented 'a metaphysic in which reality was conceived from a radically historical point of view' (Collingwood [1946] 1993: 140). The precise meaning and validity of this claim need not concern us here. What is indisputably the case is that Bradley wrote a very important essay on the philosophy of history, which was, according to Collingwood, so important that it should be regarded as nothing less than a Copernican revolution in the philosophy of history.[7] Collingwood regarded the *Presuppositions* as a work of major significance, not simply for what it accomplished in itself but for what it promised:

> in it the Copernican revolution in the theory of historical knowledge has been in principle accomplished . . . Bradley has seen that the historian brings with him to the study of his authorities a criterion of his own by reference to which his authorities are judged. (Collingwood [1946] 1993: 240)

What was Bradley seeking to do in the *Presuppositions*? His work here followed on directly from the thunderous debates in the nineteenth century on the historicity of Jesus, the value of the Bible as a historical source, the debates about miracle and so on – debates which in Germany were associated with Baur and Strauss. In response Bradley sought to ask by what criterion the historian should judge claims made about the past, in particular claims contemporary with the events they purport to describe or report. Although written in a rather obscure manner (especially the preface) Bradley's essay seeks to answer the question as to the possibility of historical knowledge. Bradley argues that history requires judgement, both in the testimony of witnesses and in the evaluation of that testimony by the historian, and judgement in turn rests on certain presuppositions. 'History is necessarily based upon prejudication; and experience testifies that, as a matter of fact, there is no single history which is not so based, which does not derive its individual character from the particular standpoint of the author' (Bradley [1874] 1935: 15).

Each judgement rests on an inference and 'an inference, it will be admitted, is justified solely on the assumption of the essential uniformity of nature and the course of events' ([1874] 1935: 16). This is a necessary presupposition: 'the universality of law and what loosely may be termed causal connection is the condition which makes history possible' (17). This, however, is a very general presupposition and hence Bradley goes on to assert that, on the basis of historical testimony, we cannot accept 'the existence of any causes or effects except on the conviction that there is now for us something analogous to them' (19). The critical historian is the judge – there can be no other: 'the historian, as he is, is the real criterion; the ideal criterion . . . is the historian as he ought to be. And the historian who is true to the present *is* the historian as he ought to be' (2).

So one of the particular presuppositions of historical knowledge is the uniformity of nature and this rules out, for example, the possibility of the historian taking seriously reports of the miraculous. In other words, the historian in the present is constrained in believing the testimony of eye witnesses by the presupposition that whatever they saw, or thought they saw or interpreted in what they thought they saw, cannot be contrary to natural law. Here are Bradley's own words:

> [W]hat then . . . is the presupposition of criticism? . . . the ground of criticism is that which is the justification of inference; and an inference, it will be admitted, is justified solely on the assumption of the essential uniformity of nature and the course of events . . . the universality of law . . . is the condition which makes history possible and which, though not for her to prove, she must nonetheless presuppose as a principle and demonstrate as a result worked out in the whole field of her activity. To this extent the characteristics of history are the characteristics of (natural) science, for both carry into the particulars an anticipation which the particulars have already realized in implication: and the reason of this is that for both the fact can exist so far only as already possessed of attributes conferred on it by virtue of the principle and can oppose the principle by no means but its own self-annihilation. 'Science', we may be told in answer, 'is founded on experiment and not on a presupposition.' 'The fact of the existence of scientific experiment proves', we must return, 'the existence of an absolute presupposition, which it can be said to found, only because upon that itself is already founded.' We base our action on that which our action itself supports and testifies to. (21–2)

Surely Bradley is right to consider the role that our conception of what is possible or impossible in the natural world plays in historical inquiry. Granted, it is a merely negative criterion, a criterion 'not of what did happen but of what could happen' (239), but it is nonetheless *a* criterion, even if it can hardly be the sole one. Further, there is nothing in Bradley's argument which precludes the addition of other criteria: all he is arguing, it might be said, is that critical history requires at least this one.

In *The Idea of History*, Collingwood gave an appreciative but critical account of Bradley's essay. In discussing the role of the critical historian, Collingwood remarks that:

> On the positive side of the account, Bradley is absolutely right in holding that historical knowledge is no mere passive acceptance of testimony, but a critical interpretation of it; that this criticism implies a criterion; and that the criterion is something the historian brings with him to the work of interpretation. (Collingwood [1946] 1993: 138)

But he then convicts Bradley of still being in the grip of an empiricist philosophy from which he was later to break free:

> Where he goes wrong . . . is in his conception of the relation between the historian's criterion and that to which he applies it. His view is that the historian brings to his work a ready-made body of experience by which he judges the statements contained in his authorities. Because this . . . is conceived as ready-made, it cannot be modified by the

historian's own work as an historian: it has to be there, complete, before he begins his historical work. Consequently this experience is regarded not as consisting of historical knowledge but as knowledge of some other kind and Bradley in fact conceives it as scientific knowledge, knowledge of the laws of nature. This is where the positivism of his age begins to infect his thought. He regards the historian's scientific knowledge as giving him the means of distinguishing between what can and cannot happen; and this scientific knowledge he conceives in the positivistic manner, as based on induction from observed facts on the principle that the future will resemble the past and the unknown the known. The inductive logic of John Stuart Mill is the shadow which broods over all this part of Bradley's essay. But there is an inner inconsistency in this logic itself. On the one side, it claims that scientific thought reveals to us laws of nature to which there cannot be exceptions; on the other, it holds that this revelation is based on induction from experience and therefore cannot ever give us universal knowledge that is more than probable. ([1946] 1993: 138–9)

Whatever the truth of Collingwood's claim that Bradley, at the time of writing the *Presuppositions*, was still infected by the positivism of the age, it is plain for us and for Collingwood too that the *Presuppositions* was an opening salvo in the development of analytic philosophy of history in the twentieth century (for recent discussions, see *Bradley Studies* 3 (1)).

The other British idealists wrote little on the philosophy of history – but there is one exception: Robert Flint, who was not a full-blooded idealist but was sympathetic in many ways to the idealist project. Flint was the author of a book on Vico (Flint 1884) and of two works on the history of the philosophy of history (Flint 1874, 1893). His dissemination of Vico's thought was important in energising interest in the epistemology of historical thought in the early twentieth century. Vico became popular in Edwardian Oxford and Croce's book *The Philosophy of Giambattista Vico* was translated into English in 1913 by Collingwood, who mentioned Flint's books on the history of the philosophy of history, while denying that Flint had any positive doctrines of his own (Collingwood [1946] 1993: 142; see also O'Sullivan 2009).

Other idealists were less interested in historical thought and on occasion positively hostile. A case in point would seem to be Bernard Bosanquet. With the phrase 'The doubtful story of successive events', Bosanquet is often taken to have damned historical knowledge to oblivion (Bosanquet 1912: 78–9). However, although he wrote these words, it is less clear what their import is and whether he intended to damn history as a form of knowledge as such. In fact, Bosanquet's animosity to history derived not from a desire to condemn but from a desire to draw more from history than the historiography of his time would allow. He was not, in other words, rejecting history outright but, as I will explain, he needed a better account of historical experience to flesh out his account of the concrete universal.

It is worth remembering that 'Green, Bradley and Bosanquet wrote in an intellectual environment saturated with evolutionary and historical perspectives and historians themselves had begun the process of establishing their subject as a professional university activity' (Parker 1988: 213). The *Literae Humaniores* degree at Oxford included a considerable amount of history as an integral part. Fellows of Oxford colleges in the latter part of the nineteenth century were multi-disciplinary and those whom we now remember as primarily philosophers taught a lot of history and not necessarily ancient history. Green, for example, gave lecture courses on the English Civil War and Bosanquet taught history throughout the first ten years of his academic life and often returned to historical themes in his writings. This does not mean that they paid any great attention to the claims of history as a form of knowledge, however, or, indeed, that they necessarily regarded history as a reliable form of knowledge at all. Looking back to this time, Collingwood wrote that Bosanquet was typical of his idealist colleagues in his lack of interest in history as a form of knowledge:

[T]he 19th century idealists in England were not, in general, historically minded: there are traces of the historical point of view in Bradley and Green and Caird – but they are not very strong and in Bosanquet they vanish entirely and the relics of that school in Oxford are quite out of touch with history. (Collingwood 1931)

Despite this judgement, history was not something the idealists could lightly discount, for 'the holistic presumptions of idealist philosophers made a consideration of the relationship between past and present almost essential and their idealism made an examination of the relationships between ideas and the social world important' (Parker 1988: 214). And Bosanquet's social and political thought is strongly historical in tone and presupposition. He might have been less enthusiastic about history than some of his idealist contemporaries, but 'nevertheless, his social theory constitutes a strong incitement to understand everything in terms of the context to which it is inextricably related' (Boucher 1984: 194). However, Bosanquet failed to integrate historical knowledge and history in his account of the concrete universal.

The notion of the concrete universal is central to the thought of the British idealists and it is integral to all of Bosanquet's writing, whether on logic, metaphysics, ethics, or social or political philosophy. The concrete universal is both a logical and a metaphysical doctrine. It is logical in that it consists in a rejection of the idea of a particular being a mere instance of an abstract universal. A *concrete* universal is one in which an individual both exemplifies and contributes to the universal, hence it is a universal which is not merely transcendent and indifferent to its particulars but both immanent and transcendent. This is a metaphysical view in its claim that the world (and our experience of the world) is structured on this principle. It is also a social, political and ethical doctrine in the sense that our being is construed as inherently social, both our absolute responsibility and also as contributory to a whole greater than ourselves, a whole which is not a mere aggregate of individual actions but both their ground and result. This is an organic whole in which each part functions only as part of the whole and the whole is more than the sum of its parts. This leads to a strongly communitarian tendency in idealist thought but one in which individual responsibility is a necessary moment in the life of the concrete universal. Bosanquet developed his theory of the concrete universal most fully in his Gifford Lectures delivered in 1911 and 1912 and published as The Principle of Individuality and Value and the Value and Destiny of the Individual (Bosanquet 1912, 1913; for a recent account of the concrete universal, see Stern 2007).

For later idealists such as Collingwood, the concrete universal was a *historical* universal. Bosanquet was rather less confident in history as a foundation and he looked elsewhere in developing his account of the concrete universal. The irony for Bosanquet, as I shall show, is that he implicitly relied on historical experience in his account of the social whole and the formation of institutions and individual souls but provided no satisfactory account of how historical knowledge was possible. For him, it appears, the historical process was doomed to be an unknowable thing in itself because he could see no satisfactory account of how we could come to know it. Lived historical experience was a necessary presupposition of his doctrine of the concrete universal, while knowledge of that experience was impossible. It seems that he wanted more from history than historians could provide and that he relapsed into a scepticism which he could not overcome.

Much of Bosanquet's work was indebted to Bradley and often consisted in responding to the positions that Bradley had developed. But one piece that he did not respond to or develop was the *Presuppositions*. Despite this, when he referred to work in historiography or the philosophy of history it was usually Bradley that he cited. For example, he wrote that the *Presuppositions* 'gives the best account known to me of the process by which all parts of a whole can be criticised and adjusted on the basis of each other' (Bosanquet 1885: 332).[8] Despite this, he thought it inadequate and this seems to be because he failed to grasp its full significance.

Picking up the threads of Bradley's discussion, let us note that Bradley did not doubt the existence of history apart from the historian, nor that it is possible for the historian to know it:

> contrariwise we must take it for granted that there is no such thing as history which is merely 'subjective', or, in other words, that whatever is 'created' by the historian is not in a proper sense history at all. For that history as a whole has been so 'made', that in it we have nothing but a series of projections of present consciousness in the form of a story of past events, from time to time gathered up or abolished in a larger and more inclusive projection – this has, so far as I know, been upheld by no sober-minded man, nor could be. (Bradley [1874] 1935: 8)

Bosanquet, it seems, constantly reverts to something near to the scepticism which Bradley denies. For Bradley, however, critical history is able to progress beyond this doubt: 'It is when history becomes aware of its presupposition that it first becomes truly critical and protects itself . . . from the caprices of fiction' (Bradley [1874] 1935: 21).

Bradley is not claiming that historical knowledge is certain and indubitable. On the contrary, he asserts, it is inferential and incomplete. Relying on the uniformity of law and the principle of analogy, however, the historian can generate criteria governing what it is reasonable to accept as evidence for events in history. This, taken together with the overall web of historical inference and reconstruction, enables the historian to construct an account which is more than 'a story of past events'. Our puzzle is this: although Bosanquet thought highly of the *Presuppositions*, he implicitly denied its worth in his critical comments on history as a form of experience. What is the source of his scepticism?

To answer this, let us return to the context of his utterance of the phrase 'the doubtful story of successive events'. The remark was made in the course of Bosanquet developing his view of the concrete universal in his *The Principle of Individuality and Value* of 1912. It was in part a response to comments made by the Cambridge philosopher James Ward. The whole issue turns on Bosanquet's understanding of what history (as process) is conceived to be and therefore on whether or not it can be understood or intelligibly captured by the historian. There is no doubt that, given the way Bosanquet characterises history, it is unintelligible to the historian and that his conclusion follows. But is he committed to this view of history? Or is he implicitly committed to a different view integral to his theory of the concrete universal and to his account of self-realisation?

For Collingwood, Bosanquet 'treated history with open contempt as a false form of thought'. In his *Logic* (1911), Bosanquet pays great attention to the methods of scientific research and says nothing of history. History is ignored because 'he assumed as correct the positivistic view of its subject-matter as consisting of isolated facts separated from one another in time and he saw that if this was their nature historical knowledge was impossible'; and he describes history as 'a hybrid form of experience, incapable of any considerable degree of "being or trueness," in which reality is misconceived by being treated as contingent' (Collingwood [1946] 1993: 143). Here Collingwood is right to suggest that Bosanquet is working out the logical implication of a certain conception of historical method, but it is the method rejected and superseded by Bradley. Bosanquet was too unfamiliar with the work of critical historians to realise that Bradley had already made the Copernican revolution in historical studies.

Bosanquet begins by stating that for Ward 'the actual is wholly historical . . . it alone is concrete experience . . . it is contingent, admitting contingency into the heart of things as against the necessity of thought-connections' (Bosanquet 1912: 78–80). This, for Bosanquet, is 'little better than natural realism' because

> we are to accept as richer than thought a reality consisting in the fragmentary diorama of finite life-processes unrolling themselves in time, seen from the outside, not strictly knowable because a tissue of mere conjunctions; and yet not given, because a mere construction on the basis of the present; and contingent through and through.

This is why he concluded that 'history is a hybrid form of experience, incapable of any considerable degree of "being or trueness"' and that the 'doubtful story of successive events' could not 'amalgamate with the complete interpretation of the social mind, of art, or of religion'. Bosanquet is attempting to develop a conception of the concrete universal and Ward's conception of history is antithetical to that:

> [T]he reason for taking this hybrid form of experience for the type of reality lies in ignoring the concrete universal. This is the defect which leads us to suppose that concreteness and contingency are inseparable and makes us confound the apparent contingency of details within a cosmos, whose main members are necessary to the whole, with the contingency at the heart of a spatio-temporal world of incident, which has never been recreated by experience of the fullest type. (Bosanquet 1912: 79)

For Bosanquet, life at its best cannot be contingent and freedom is 'the logic of individuality and as remote as possible from contingency'; and, finally, 'Social morality, Art, Philosophy and Religion take us far beyond the spatio-temporal externality of history' (Bosanquet 1912: 80).

The enemy here is contingency and this is linked with Bosanquet's claim that we cannot enter into the inward aspect of things in history (Bosanquet 1912: 74–7). History is an inferior form of experience because it cannot be a true concrete universal, unlike art and religion. Bosanquet's strictures on history are, then, directed negatively against Ward's enthusiasm for contingency as a mark of the concrete. Bosanquet characterises history naturalistically and he takes the view that no satisfactory explanation or understanding of what is important in human experience can be gained in this way. Bosanquet is interested in the richness of human experience and given that Ward and Bradley have provided no account of how mind can understand mind in history, of how the historian can provide a full picture of the historical process, Bosanquet is left with the view that the reconstructive work of the historian is a poor thing, which necessarily fails to do justice to the concrete experience of historical individuals. His is a critique born of frustration, a scepticism derived from what he saw as the absence of an account showing how a fuller knowledge of history was possible. Bradley, his one acknowledged authority, provided only the sketch of such an account. Equally Bosanquet was aware that the 'scissors-and-paste' methods advocated by others were inadequate. In the absence of a richer conception of history he relapsed into scepticism about the claims and value of history as a form of experience.

Bosanquet wants something more than history: he wants the concrete universal because 'it is impossible for life at its best to be contingent' (1912: 79). But is he concerned with historiography as a form of experience or with history as the lived experience of people in time? It is perfectly possible that lived experience is beyond our capacity to grasp it historically, but Bosanquet does not give us enough to convince us and equally it might be that history, as a form of inquiry, is both a valid form of knowledge and also a valuable form of experience. What exactly is Bosanquet denying? It is easy to allow that history and historical experience are not ultimately satisfactory – but that does not show that historical knowledge is impossible; and, against the Absolute, finite historical experience of either type will be found wanting, but that does not mean that it is non-existent.

Despite the above, a positive account can be drawn from Bosanquet's thought on historical knowledge. In a paper on 'Atomism in history' he asks what the narrative historian can offer and suggests that

> [H]e brings to your notice in an orderly way a number of documents and achievements of intense human interest, the connection and interpretation of which must always be in some degree doubtful, but in each of which, as a whole, the spirit of humanity speaks to your spirit. (Bosanquet 1917: 22)

In discussing 'Time and the Absolute' he indicates that we can transcend some of the difficulties attendant upon history conceived as the contingent succession of spatio-temporal events:

> The more that history and science bring before us a unified past, the more closely do we weld it to the content on which we base our construction of the future and the less do we actually live in a world of temporal succession. (Bosanquet 1927: 116)

This points to a view in which history can provide self-knowledge, a key part of any doctrine of self-realisation. For this to be possible,

> [I]t would not be that the absolute had come into being after time, but that in the temporal succession it had more or less completely manifested itself and something as to a deeper reality might be inferred from this manifestation. But for this we require, not the annihilation of temporal experience, but the power of seeing through it. (119)

We can rescue history for Bosanquet if (within his philosophy) it is possible to conceive of a way in which we can transcend temporality. On this Bradley had provided a clue:

> [T]he facts which exist for critical history are events and recorded events . . . although the work of the mind, they now at any rate are no mere feelings, nor generally the private contents of this or that man's consciousness, but are fixed and made outward, permanent and accessible to the minds of all men. Failing to be thus they have failed to be for history and history can never be for them. (Bradley [1874] 1935: 13)

This leads us to the notion of re-enactment, which is *verstehen* in its English and Italian form, primarily associated with the writings of Croce and Collingwood. In re-enactment we see through temporality by fastening on the outward expressions of thought which are in principle accessible to all. Inwardness is achieved because it can be reached through the outward expression of thought. Towards the end of his life Bosanquet engaged with the work of the Italian idealists who had developed a philosophy which radically historicised all acts of knowing (Bosanquet 1920; Harris 1960a, 1960b). Bosanquet did not accept the full implications of Croce's and Giovanni Gentile's philosophies. But he moved some way towards a more historical view, one in which the answer to his riddle is to recover the sense that the world of history is a world of mind – a world in principle accessible to the mind of the historian. In such a world the inwardness of the spiritual world is captured and made the principle of the possibility of historical knowledge. And, as shown above, this view was already implicit in Bosanquet's own thought, but never developed (and indeed, over-looked) by him. In re-enactment, as adumbrated by Bradley and developed by Croce, Gentile and Collingwood, time is transcended in history because

> [T]he historian, in discovering the thoughts of a past agent, re-thinks that thought for himself. It is known, therefore, not as a past thought . . . but as a present thought living now in the historian's mind. Thus, by being historically known, it . . . triumphs over time and survives in the present. (Collingwood 1937: 143)

This is Collingwood's summary of Gentile's view, which he concludes by conjuring and exorcising Bosanquet's ghost and remarking that 'so conceived, history is no longer a "story of successive events": it is the actual possession by the historian, here and now, of the thought whose history he studies'. This approach provides what Bosanquet was looking for when he stated that we require 'not the annihilation of temporal experience, but *the power of seeing through it*' (Bosanquet 1927: 119). Finally, on Bosanquet's behalf, we can bring history and the concrete universal into harmony and thereby rescue history from the charge that it is a 'hybrid form of experience'.

Michael Foster suggests that Bosanquet's account of the concrete universal should be construed in an historical fashion. He defines the concrete universal as 'the universal which determines its own particularisation' (Foster 1931: 1). He then argues that Bosanquet's characterisation of the concrete universal and his insistence that it cannot be historical derive in part, from the limitations of his Logic, which he regarded as 'derived almost exclusively from reflection upon the comparative sciences . . . and its conclusions then applied uncritically to the whole of knowledge'. However, below these sciences – the sciences of life – are the sciences of matter, working with the conception of causal law, and above them are 'the sciences of spirit (the historical sciences) which work with the notion of the individual'. It was the illegitimate extension of what was appropriate to the middle sphere to the sciences of spirit which led to Bosanquet's confusion (Foster 1931: 13–14).

If, having 'transcended time in history', we can now similarly transcend biological metaphor in logic, we can achieve a conception of the concrete universal unimpeded by a residual naturalism. We can, according to Foster, see that the concrete universal that Bosanquet is striving for is historical:

> [T]he conception which supplies the deficiencies of the 'individual system' is the historical individual – not primarily the individual person, but such individuals as 'the Athenian [empire], 'the Roman Catholic Church', 'the Renaissance'. These do

indeed penetrate the very being of their constituent particulars and obliterate for the first time the hard and fast distinction within them of essential from accidental qualities; and they determine not merely the spatial boundaries and temporal limits within which their members shall exist, but the precise time and place of their existence. They are the objects par excellence of intellectual intuition; they are the true concrete universals, because they are concrete qua universal and universal qua concrete; they do not, like all other universals, leave a residuum of 'the accidental' unpenetrated and therefore inaccessible to thought. (19)

What prevented Bosanquet from taking this final step? According to Foster it was his failure to comprehend the nature of the historical universal. Yet he was driven to seek a more adequate realisation of the concrete universal than the 'individual system' which had satisfied him in his *Logic*. He saw that what was required was something 'individual' and that the individual person was inadequate as a solution. He was 'precluded from recognising the true historical individual' and 'condemned therefore in his later work to conduct a fruitless search for adequate examples of the concrete universal, which can none of them in reality supply more than a plausible analogy' (Foster 1931: 20). For example, Bosanquet claimed that 'the best way to think of a finite individual is to bear in mind the nature of a work of art, or of the moral temper as analysed by Aristotle, or of an organic being' (Bosanquet 1912: 120–1). For Foster, the use of these analogies prevented Bosanquet from grasping the relation of thought, history and the concrete universal, with the result that

> [H]e is driven finally to the paradoxical conclusion that that concrete universal, which was shown to be the culmination of the proper development of thought, is yet realised never as thought, but as Art, Religion or Love. If we once claim any degree of concreteness for the universal, there is no stopping along that path short of the historical individual. (Foster 1931: 19–20)

Despite himself, this is what Bosanquet is committed to by the logic of his own arguments. If he had continued to develop his thinking on history in line with his thinking on the concrete universal, then plausibly Foster is right that Bosanquet would not have stopped short of the historical individual (see Connelly 2000).

7. Conclusion

This survey has tracked some of the key concepts and themes typical of debates over the nature of historical method and knowledge in the nineteenth century and has placed them in the historical context of developments in the disciplines not only of history but also of sociology and the social sciences in general. The key themes in the debate can also be located in debates concerning the status of psychology, the ethical and social import of evolutionary thought and Darwinism in particular, theology, biblical criticism and textual interpretation (hermeneutics). Space precludes following these fascinating paths here. But the foregoing shows how active these debates were in intellectual circles in the nineteenth century.

Notes

1. Whether analytic and speculative philosophy of history can be entirely separated is a matter of contention. See: Burns and Rayment-Pickard 2000; and Connelly 2004a and 2004b. For good

general accounts of the topics under discussion in this chapter, see: Burns and Rayment-Pickard 2000; Antoni 1959; Burrow 2009; Hughes 1979; Parker 2000; and Iggers 1983.

2. In the hands of some late nineteenth-century British idealists, the role of the historical individual is downplayed, as a consequence of the view that history is an inferior mode of knowing by comparison with philosophy, which alone can understand and generate the concrete universal: see below.

3. This view has an exact counterpart in Walter Benjamin's objections that a certain type of Marxist conception of laws of inevitable progress in history leads to passivity in (and ultimately defeat for) the working class. See Connelly 2004b.

4. For criticism of Rickert and Windelband, accusing them of disastrously confusing the formal methods and the material content of scholarly disciplines, see Muller 1967.

5. On Weber and his thought in relation to history, see Whimster 1980.

6. I do not mean to imply that the work of Collingwood and Oakeshott is an undisputed foundation of later work in the subject, merely that it provided the subject with much-needed impetus and rigour.

7. On this essay and Collingwood's commentary on it, see Burns 2006. On some of the debates surrounding idealism and sociology in this period, see Collini 1978.

8. For his other references to the *Presuppositions* see Bosanquet 1912: 331; 1917: 22.

References

Antoni, Carlo (1959), *From History to Sociology: The Transition in German Historical Thinking*, London: Merlin Press.

Baur, Ferdinand Christian [1853–63] (1878), *The Church History of the First Three Centuries*, trans. Allan Menzies, London: Williams and Norgate.

Bosanquet, Bernard (1885), *Knowledge and Reality*, London: Swan Sonnenschein.

Bosanquet, Bernard (1911), *Logic: or the Morphology of Knowledge*, 2nd edn, Oxford: Clarendon Press.

Bosanquet, Bernard (1912), *The Principle of Individuality and Value*, London: Macmillan.

Bosanquet, Bernard (1913), *The Value and Destiny of the Individual*, London: Macmillan

Bosanquet, Bernard (1917), 'Atomism in history', in Bernard Bosanquet, *Social and International Ideals*, London: Macmillan, pp. 20–40.

Bosanquet, Bernard (1920), *The Meeting of Extremes in Contemporary Philosophy*, London: Macmillan.

Bosanquet, Bernard (1927), *Science and Philosophy*, London: Allen and Unwin.

Boucher, David (1984), 'The creation of the past: British idealism and Michael Oakeshott's philosophy of history', *History and Theory*, 23: 193–214.

Bradley, Francis Herbert [1883] (1922), *The Principles of Logic*, 2nd edn, Oxford: Clarendon Press.

Bradley, Francis Herbert [1876] (1927), *Ethical Studies*, 2nd edn, Oxford: Clarendon Press.

Bradley, Francis Herbert [1893] (1930), *Appearance and Reality*, 9th impression, corrected, Oxford: Clarendon Press.

Bradley, Francis Herbert [1874] (1935), *The Presuppositions of Critical History*, in Francis Herbert Bradley, *Collected Essays*, Oxford: Clarendon Press, pp. 1–70.

Burger, Thomas (1977), 'Droysen's defense of historiography: A note', *History and Theory*, 16: 168–73.

Burns, Robert M., and Hugh Rayment-Pickard (eds) (2000), *Philosophies of History from Enlightenment to Post-modernity*, Oxford: Blackwell.

Burns, Robert M. (2006), 'Collingwood, Bradley and historical knowledge', *History and Theory*, 45 (2): 178–203.

Burrow, John (2009), *A History of Histories*, Harmondsworth: Penguin.

Collini, Stefan (1978), 'Sociology and idealism in Britain 1880–1920', *Archives Européenes de Sociologie*, 19: 3–50.

Collingwood, Robin George (1924), *Speculum Mentis*, Oxford: Clarendon Press.

Collingwood, Robin George (1931), Letter to Guido de Ruggiero of 9 January 1931, Bodleian Library.

Collingwood, Robin George (1937), Review of *Philosophy and History: Essays Presented to Ernst Cassirer*, *English Historical Review* 52: 141–6.

Collingwood, Robin George ([1946] 1993) *The Idea of History*, revised edn, ed. Jan van der Dussen, Oxford: Clarendon Press.

Comte, Auguste [1830] (1896), *Course of Positive Philosophy*, trans. Harriet Martineau, London: Bell.

Connelly, James (2000), 'Doubtful story or heartbeat of the Absolute? Bosanquet, Bradley and history', *Bradley Studies*, 6 (1): 46–62.

Connelly, James (2004a), 'A time for progress?', *History and Theory*, 43: 410–22.

Connelly, James (2004b), 'Facing the past: Benjamin's antitheses', *The European Legacy*, 9 (3): 317–29.

Croce, Benedetto (1941), *History as the Story of Liberty*, trans. Sylvia S. Sprigge, London: Allen and Unwin.

Dilthey, Wilhelm ([1883] 1976), *Introduction to the Human Sciences*, in Wilhelm Dilthey, *Selected Writings*, ed. H. P. Rickman, Cambridge: Cambridge University Press.

Flint, Robert (1874), *The Philosophy of History in Europe*, vol. 1: *The Philosophy of History in France and Germany*, Edinburgh and London: Blackwood & Sons.

Flint, Robert (1884), *Vico*, Edinburgh and London: Blackwood & Sons.

Flint, Robert (1893), *History of the Philosophy of History: Historical Philosophy in France, French Belgium, and Switzerland*, Edinburgh and London: Blackwood & Sons.

Foster, Michael B. (1931), 'The concrete universal: Cook Wilson and Bosanquet', *Mind*, 40 (157): 1–22.

Harris, Henry S. (1960a), *The Social Philosophy of Giovanni Gentile*, Urbana, IL: University of Illinois Press.

Harris, Henry S. (1960b), 'Introduction', in Giovanni Gentile, *Genesis and Structure of Society*, Urbana, IL: University of Illinois Press, pp. 1–52.

Hegel, Georg Wilhelm Friedrich ([1821] 1942), *Philosophy of Right*, trans. T. M. Knox, Oxford: Clarendon Press.

Hegel, Georg Wilhelm Friedrich [1807] (1977), *Phenomenology of Spirit*, trans. A.V. Miller, Oxford: Clarendon Press.

Hegel, Georg Wilhelm Friedrich [1837] (1991), *The Philosophy of History*, trans. J. Sibree, Buffalo, NY: Prometheus.

Hughes, Henry Stuart (1979), *Consciousness and Society: The Reorientation of European Social Thought 1890–1930*, Brighton: Harvester.

Iggers, Georg G. (1967), 'The decline of the classical national tradition of German historiography', *History and Theory*, 6 (3): 382–412.

Iggers, Georg G. (1983), *The German Conception of History: The National Tradition of Historical Thought from Herder to the Present*, Middletown, CT: Wesleyan University Press.

Maclean, Micheal J. (1982), 'Johann Gustav Droysen and the development of historical hermeneutics', *History and Theory*, 21 (3): 347–65.

Meinecke, Friedrich [1936] (1972), *Historism: The Rise of a New Historical Outlook*, trans. J. E. Anderson, London: Routledge and Kegan Paul.

Muller, Gert (1967), 'History as a rigorous discipline', *History and Theory*, 6 (3): 299–312.

Norman, Richard, and Sean Sayers (1980), *Hegel, Marx and Dialectic: A Debate*, Brighton: Harvester Press.

Novick, Peter (1988), *That Noble Dream: The 'Objectivity Question' and the American Historical Profession*, Cambridge: Cambridge University Press.

O'Sullivan, L. (2009), 'Robert Flint: Theologian, philosopher of history and historian of philosophy', *Intellectual History Review*, vol. 19, no. 1, pp. 45–63.

Oakeshott, Michael J. (1933), *Experience and Its Modes*, Cambridge: Cambridge University Press.

Parker, Christopher (1988), 'Bernard Bosanquet, historical knowledge and the history of ideas', *Philosophy of the Social Sciences*, 18: 213–30.

Parker, Christopher (2000) *The English Idea of History from Coleridge to Collingwood*, Aldershot: Ashgate.

Rickert, Heinrich [1902] (1986), *The Limits of Concept Formation in Natural Science*, ed. and trans. Guy Oakes, Cambridge: Cambridge University Press.

Rickman, Hans Peter (1979), *Wilhelm Dilthey: Pioneer of the Human Studies*, London: Elek.

Ringer, Fritz K. (1969), *The Decline of the German Mandarins: The German Academic Community 1890–1933*, Cambridge, MA: Harvard University Press.

Ritchie, David George (1883), 'The Rationality of History', in Andrew Seth and R. B. Haldane (eds), *Essays in Philosophical Criticism*, London: Longmans, Green and Co., pp. 126–49.

Rubinoff, Lionel (1996), 'The autonomy of history: Collingwood's critique of F. H. Bradley's Copernican revolution in historical knowledge', in James Bradley (ed.), *Philosophy after Bradley*, Bristol: Thoemmes Press, pp. 127–46.

Seth, Andrew, and R. B. Haldane (eds) (1883), *Essays in Philosophical Criticism*, London: Longmans, Green and Co.

Sorley, William Ritchie (1883), 'The Historical Method', in Andrew Seth and R. B. Haldane (eds), *Essays in Philosophical Criticism*, London: Longmans, Green and Co., pp. 102–25.

Stern, Robert (2007), 'Hegel, British idealism and the curious case of the concrete universal', *British Journal for the History of Philosophy*, 15: 115–53.

Strauss, David Friedrich (1846), *The Life of Jesus Critically Examined*, trans. Marian Evans (George Eliot) from 4th edn of 1840, London: Chapman.

Vico, Giambattista [1744] (1948), *The New Science*, trans. Thomas Bergin and Max Fisch, Ithaca, NY: Cornell University Press.

Walsh, W. H. (1984), 'Bradley and critical history', in Anthony Manser and Guy Stock (eds), *The Philosophy of F. H. Bradley*, Oxford: Clarendon Press, pp. 33–52.

Weber, Max ([1921] 1947), *The Theory of Social and Economic Organization*, trans. A. M. Henderson and Talcott Parsons, New York: Free Press.

Weber, Max [1903–6] (1975), *Roscher and Knies: The Logical Problems of Historical Economics*, trans. Guy Oakes, New York: Free Press.

Whimster, Sam (1980), 'The profession of history in the work of Max Weber: Its origins and limitations', *British Journal of Sociology*, 31: 352–76.

Windelband, Wilhelm [1894] (1980), 'Rectorial address', *History and Theory*, 19: 169–85.

9

Genealogy as Immanent Critique: Working from the Inside

Robert Guay

– only as persons of *this* conscience do we still feel ourselves related to the German rectitude and piety of millennia, even if as its most questionable and final descendants, we immoralists, we godless ones of today, indeed even in a certain sense as its heirs, as the executors of its innermost will . . .

(Nietzsche, *Daybreak*)

1. Introduction

Of the distinctive terminology of nineteenth-century thought, perhaps no word has been more widely adopted than 'genealogy'.[1] 'Genealogy', of course, had a long history before Nietzsche put it in the title of a book, but the original sense of pedigree or family tree is not the one that has become so prominent in contemporary academic discourse.[2] Nietzsche initiated a new sense of 'genealogy' which, oddly, has become popular despite a lack of clarity about what it is.[3] My aim here is to clarify this sense of genealogy by situating it in the context of nineteenth-century narrative argument and identifying its general features. I contend that the famous Nietzschean genealogy is actually the least distinctive narrative form. Its features are to be found, usually together, in others' argumentation. This is by no means to disparage Nietzsche, but the contemporary prominence of genealogy comes not from Nietzsche offering the most extreme or radical account, but from his offering the one that most neatly represents the critical, historical, consciousness of the nineteenth century.[4]

Genealogy, as with other prominent philosophical-historical accounts, involves narratives that, by relating the functioning of a process, explain some feature of the present. The presence of the past is thus implicit in such accounts: with certain phenomena, understanding them requires seeing not only their immediate condition but also their extension backward through time. There are, I contend, four features that both distinguish genealogy as such and establish its common ground with other prominent accounts. First, genealogy involves what I call *historical agency*. The events narrated in a genealogy are considered as, if only in an inchoate or unconscious way, actions. Genealogy thus explains human events by appeal to terms familiar from the domain of human agency: purposes, reasons and above all freedom. Second, genealogy involves a form of *cosmopolitanism*. There are many forms of cosmopolitanism and that of genealogy is not a typical one, such as one in which ethnic or national differences are ethically insignificant. The cosmopolitanism of genealogy, rather, is that human identity is collective and in particular historical: being oneself involves relations to a broader community. Indeed, genealogy typically characterises identity, in its increasingly particularised form in the modern world, as coordinate with membership in increasingly broad groups, such that some identities are only possible as the legacy of enormous historical projects. Third, genealogy is typically *critical*. Genealogy, that is, takes normative (or, for that matter, social) authority to be problematic and responds to this by showing that certain claims to authority are in some way defective. As Nietzsche characterised it, genealogy is a 'no-saying' enterprise, whose purpose is to exhibit the failure of ideals (Nietzsche 1967–77: 6: 350).[5] Fourth, genealogy is *historical-hermeneutic*. Genealogy does not merely provide accounts of a sequence of events or of the changing circumstances of stable entities. Genealogy provides accounts of things that are themselves historical: because they are so fluid or indefinable, they can only be accounted for within the temporal scope of the narrative.

Together these features render genealogy into what might be called 'immanent critique'.[6] By this I mean that it offers a kind of critique that does not involve the adoption of a privileged position with respect to the object of critique. One might conceive of a typical critique in terms of a superior standpoint: the critic or the criticism has some kind of epistemic privilege or better reasons or more information and is thus well-placed to pass judgement on something. In an immanent critique, by contrast, no such privileged standpoint is available, either because there are reasons to doubt any such claim of privilege or because the legitimacy of one's standpoint is itself part of what the critique addresses. Immanent critique thus proceeds by taking up the very position or standpoint to be criticised and identifying 'internal' flaws: ones that count as such from within the standpoint under consideration. In accordance with the basic features of genealogy, particular claims are inseparable from the more general commitments that shape an outlook. Advancing these commitments turns out to be self-undermining in a way that produces a transformative result. This provides the critical conclusion: the transformation is explicable as an immanent failure of the old position. The critical conclusion is thus always at least potentially vindicating: the result is a claim of relative superiority, if only that almost anything would be better than the old position.

Here my procedure will be to examine genealogy as a general approach by considering the main exemplars of philosophical-historical argumentation of the nineteenth century, along with some precursors and heirs. Unfortunately I have to neglect some worthy possibilities, but I hope to cover a full range of variations on genealogy. I shall not be concerned with presenting the content of the particular stories that these philosophers tell: the particular *personae*, events and dynamics are less important for present purposes than the ways in which their narratives function as arguments. Indeed, one thing I hope to show is that, apart from the distraction of differences on particular substantive issues, there is a commonality in the way these philosophers regard the relationship between historical self-understanding and normative critique.

2. Nietzsche's Example: Genealogy

I will not try here to present an uncontroversial view of Nietzsche's genealogy: since there is no such thing, the attempt would be in vain. In this section, my aim is instead to bring out some main features of Nietzsche's approach, in order to show how genealogy operates as immanent critique. I hope that showing how these features function together does illuminate Nietzsche's philosophical position in general: the elements of my reading should be mutually reinforcing. But resolving interpretative issues is less important for present purposes than locating, in Nietzsche's work, a critical, historical, cosmopolitan account of normative and in particular, ethical authority.

One might think that there is a relatively clear path for ascertaining in what Nietzschean genealogy consists.[7] One should simply turn to Nietzsche himself for a statement of method, or at least a definition of the term 'genealogy', or failing that to identify the key elements or commonalities among the paradigm cases. But apart from referring to the title of his own 1887 work, On the Genealogy of Morals (Zur Genealogie der Moral), Nietzsche hardly ever uses the word 'genealogy', let alone identifies a method that is supposed to be distinct from historical method in general. Even locating the titular 'genealogy of morals' is a challenge. The promise of a single, complete account of morals is undercut by the preposition that begins the title, 'on' or possibly 'to' (zu) and by the three narratives with a chronologically and otherwise indeterminate relationship to one another which comprise the book.

We can nevertheless identify enough of Nietzsche's genealogical account to be able to isolate its main features. In the Preface to On the Genealogy of Morals, Nietzsche declares that his true concern in offering genealogical hypotheses has been to provide a 'critique of moral values' (Nietzsche [1887] 1967–77: 5: 253, P6). He suggests that we lack self-knowledge in part because 'our moral prejudices' (5: 248, P2) have gone unexamined: what we are is so thoroughly bound up with moral values that narratives of self-understanding must take the form of critique. Three sets of narratives that manage to be both polemical and ambiguous then follow: they offer unflattering reports of successes that have turned out to be destructive. In the first Treatise, the main subject is the invention of the good/evil dichotomy. Nietzsche claims that the spontaneous self-affirmation of nobles was replaced by the 'slave revolt in morality' (5: 270, I.10), wherein the weak exacted 'imaginary revenge' (5: 271, I.10) against the nobles by inverting their value system. The weak refer to the noble and powerful as 'evil' and themselves, by contrast, as 'good', and meekness and humility comprise this new form of goodness. Nietzsche later refers to slave morality – or simply 'morality' – as undoubtedly victorious, but at the same time as a form of 'anti-nature' that succeeds at the cost of health. The second Treatise primarily concerns what Nietzsche calls 'the fundamental moral concept' (5: 297, II.4), namely, guilt. According to Nietzsche, the notion of guilt has its origin in the non-moral notions of debt and indebtedness. The creditor–debtor relationship was the forum in which human beings first measured themselves against one another and, when creditors suffered losses, they made the debtors suffer as compensation. This gave rise to pre-moral notions of guilt and duty which, when 'turned backwards' (5: 331, II.21) into the 'bad conscience', made a final discharge of the creditor–debtor relationship impossible. This, claims Nietzsche, has produced memory, the inwardisation of humankind and also 'the self-crucifixion and self-violation of the human' (5: 333, II.23). The third and final Treatise explains how the priest, in teaching the sufferers that they are to blame for their suffering, 'changes the direction of ressentiment' (5: 375, III.15) and invents 'the ascetic ideal'. The ascetic ideal functions as an expedient that comforts the sick by providing an explanation for suffering, but at the same time exacerbates their sickness. Nietzsche suggests in concluding the narrative that 'all will to truth' (5: 410, III.27) has put itself forward as a candidate to replace the ascetic ideal but turns out to be the ideal's especially pure form.

Even this skeletal account of Nietzsche's approach in one text evinces the four main features of genealogy. Historical agency makes its appearance above all in the form of the ascetic ideal. Nietzsche characterises human history as the working out of an ideal in particular manifestations: Christian morality and the will to truth, for example, thereby take on causal roles. By way of the specific appeal to asceticism, moreover, Nietzsche insists that we cannot understand our historical condition except as something we have done to ourselves. Nietzsche's account involves appeals to a common agency that extends across millennia: 'We moderns, we are the heirs of the conscience-vivisection and animal-self-cruelty of millennia: this is our longest practice, our artistry perhaps, or in any case our refinement, our discriminating palate' (5: 335, II.24; cf. 5: 410, III.27). This very feature also shows the *cosmopolitanism* of Nietzsche's account. Nietzsche characterises human history as one slowly developing action – indeed, as a kind of meta-action, that of furnishing a meaningful end for the will through an intensifying asceticism. The result of this project is that a common human identity outweighs all the particular forms that contributed to it. The *critical* element of genealogy is obvious: in addition to the declared intention to offer a critique of moral values, there is the conclusion that modernity represents a self-enervating will to nothingness.

The *historical-hermeneutic* aspect of genealogy comes out more strongly in Nietzsche's statements on 'historical methodology' than in the above summary: for example, in his famous claim that 'only that which has no history is definable' (5: 317, II.13). Nietzsche connects this methodological claim both to the features of the narrative and to the other features of genealogy, however. The context of the claim about history is a claim about the primacy of the 'fundamental concept' of *activity* over 'the mechanistic senselessness of all happening' (5: 315, II.12). Undefinability, that is, comes from understanding events as actions; this is what also generates the availability of critique. Nietzsche declares this to be the most important proposition of historical method:

> The cause of the origin of a thing and its final utility, actual employment and place in a system of purposes lie worlds apart; that something existing, having somehow come-into-being, is always again and again appropriated by a power superior to it and interpreted from new viewpoints, reorganised and redirected toward a new use; that everything that happens in the organic is an *overcoming*, a *becoming master* and on the other hand that all overcoming and becoming master is a new-interpreting, a preparation in which the prior 'meaning' and 'purpose' must necessarily be obscured or entirely obliterated. (5: 313f., II.12)

This continual reappropriation of purposes is what allows Nietzsche to claim that our modern commitments to institutions have a meaning fundamentally different from the one that they are supposed to have. And history as self-subverting activity not only brings light to failures in human agency; it also connects the opacity of the 'continuous sign-chain of new interpretations' (5: 314, II.12) with the cosmopolitan nature of the 'actual problem of the human' (5: 291, II.1). A genealogical approach is necessary, Nietzsche suggests, because we lack privileged access to our own meanings and must therefore locate them in the history of the human more generally.

These features of genealogy suffice to distinguish it from a Humean account, or what Nietzsche referred to as that of the 'English psychologists'.[8] Such an account is primarily explanatory. It attempts to identify the basic psychological features of human nature, along with the principles of association or causal regularities that are sufficient to explain the emergence of familiar ethical dispositions. The aim is to show that and how complex systems of value could develop out of simple elements of our psychology. This kind of account shares with Nietzsche's enterprise the view that morality itself has a causal explanation and thus requires an account of historical change in order to understand it. Even the meaning of this narrow commonality would be in dispute, however. For Nietzsche, as we have seen, purposive activity plays a distinctive explanatory role. Such activity in a Humean account, by contrast, is indistinguishable from other events determined by antecedent causes. The meaning of historical change is different, too. For Hume, this can only mean that the 'original constitution' of human nature manifests itself in different ways, depending on causal history: everything, furthermore, is either definable in empirical terms or meaningless. But for Nietzsche's genealogy there are no stable entities that endure through history as the subject of change. Historical change, rather, is so pervasive that the basic elements of the narrative are fluid and indeterminate – 'punishment' is Nietzsche's most famous example (5: 316, II.13). This makes Nietzsche's form of cosmopolitanism different, too. Rather than being rooted in a common human nature, Nietzsche's version only enters at the end of his story, as a shared ascetic patrimony. The principal aim of genealogy, moreover, is critical rather than explanatory.

Critique is indeed the very point of Nietzsche's genealogical enterprise. The Humean approach can provide a causal history of moral belief and thereby perhaps an account of its meaning, but genealogy aims to assess moral beliefs. And such a critique cannot presume epistemic superiority – 'the value of truth must be experimentally called into question' (5: 401, III.24), writes Nietzsche – because such a presumption is potentially implicated in the outlook under scrutiny. So genealogy functions as 'immanent critique': it provides a critical assessment without appealing to the independent authority of its critical stance. Genealogy criticises moral values – or, more generally, 'ideals' – by taking them as not merely furnishing a measure or standard but also functioning to structure the conduct and understanding of life. And because ideals are purposive in this way, they can be assessed, on their own terms, by their success or failure.

The dynamic of this is complex, at least on Nietzsche's account, since living in light of an ideal transforms not just one's life but also the ideal and oneself. As Nietzsche sees the process, having ideals affects the life that one leads, sometimes in line with the ideals and sometimes perversely. In either case, the resulting transformation of life also changes the self: a new human type is cultivated or 'bred', as Nietzsche would have it. This transformation of the self alters the meaning of ideals, which in turn changes the way in which lives are led and so on. Genealogy's critical point is that this whole process has conclusively failed: morality represents a purposiveness that cannot possibly be redeemed. There are three different ways in which Nietzsche makes the case for the failed teleology of morality. One, it turns out to have achieved defective purposes: it reduces humanity to 'the botched, diminished, atrophied and poisoned' (5: 277, I.11). Two, morality generates purposes that are opposite from what had been intended: here Nietzsche's main example is the 'priestly medication' of the interpretation of suffering 'that makes people sicker' (5: 391, III.21). Three, and most importantly, the purposiveness of morality has come to a dead end, in which all other purposes have been co-opted or measured 'only according to the meaning of its interpretation' (5: 396, III.23) and yet the possibility of any further purposiveness has been foreclosed. In the concluding section of On the Genealogy of Morals, the ascetic ideal has moved from the 'faute de mieux par excellence' to 'will to nothingness' (5: 412f., III.28). Nietzsche's argument qualifies as immanent critique because of his claim that it is precisely from adopting a moral standpoint that we are led to conclude that it has failed: in Nietzsche's simplest formulation, it is the Christian cultivation of responsibility and 'will to truth' that finally turns against itself. What is more, Nietzsche insists that there is no alternative to the 'One Goal' (5: 396, III.23) of the ascetic ideal, so we cannot help but draw the conclusion against the moral standpoint.

There remains more to be said about Nietzsche's genealogical enterprise and the way it functions as immanent critique. The range of possibilities for immanent critique is better exhibited, however, in others' critical narrative forms. After a consideration of these I shall return to Nietzsche.

3. The Prehistory of Genealogy

One element of the understanding of genealogy would have to be the reflexive one: a genealogy of genealogy. Such a project would be limitless in its complexity. Places of honour could be given to Greek tragic irony, the Judeo-Christian hope for messianic intervention in temporal history, the self-image of the 'Renaissance', Vico, the higher criticism, teleology in biology and chemistry, Darwin and much more. Here, however, I wish to merely point out two significant contributions to the flurry of productivity following the Enlightenment's invention of the term 'philosophy of history' (this is attributed to Voltaire in Lemon 2003: 7). Rousseau and Kant offered philosophies of history that, together, laid much of the groundwork for the development of genealogy.

In the opening words of *The Social Contract*, Rousseau introduces most of the basic preconditions of genealogy: 'Man is born free and everywhere he is in chains' (Rousseau [1762] 1966: 41). Here there is the cosmopolitanism of the human condition, the consideration of human beings as freely active, the perverse operation of that activity to self-enslavement and the iron necessity of historical processes. In the philosophy of history, with Rousseau's famous claim that we have become corrupt and sick precisely by our own freedom and 'perfectibility' (Rousseau [1755] 1992: 184), even deeper affinities with genealogy can be found.

In Rousseau's critique of the Enlightenment, modern forms of social organisation, in seeking to legitimate themselves, have mistaken what unjust institutions have made of 'men' for human nature itself. As a result, putatively rational institutions only serve to legitimate and intensify existing forms of domination. Our social order has thereby reached a dead end, in which we have reached the 'extreme state of corruption' (Rousseau [1755] 1992: 252) and old processes of legitimation no longer function at all. This pattern of argument, despite all of Rousseau's differences from Nietzsche (on which see Ansell-Pearson 1996), represents a crucial formative step towards genealogy: ironic historical agency. Rousseau's argument is not that Enlightenment efforts to vindicate a modern social order have failed because of implementation problems, or because the institutions were somehow too good for the world. Rousseau's argument was that precisely because such institutions succeeded, in proportion to their immense effectiveness, they generated human misery and thus their own delegitimation. Rousseau takes the Enlightenment narrative of progress and provides a counter-narrative in which all the same events occur but every single change has been for the worse. To put this point in its simplest form, 'The majority of our ills are our own doing' (Rousseau [1755] 1992: 179). An appropriate critical narrative will therefore tell the story of how we, by our own agency, continuously made things worse and made things especially bad when we were most successful.

Rousseau's other main contribution to the development of genealogy was that he was the first to theorise the speculative enterprise of cosmopolitan self-knowledge in which Nietzsche also engaged. Just as Nietzsche opened his Preface to *On the Genealogy of Morals*, Rousseau begins the Preface to the Second Discourse, *On the Origin of Inequality*, by invoking missing self-knowledge: 'the most useful and least advanced of all the fields of human knowledge seems to me to be that of man' (Rousseau [1755] 1992: 157). In his Introduction, Rousseau further emphasises the cosmopolitan import of his account. He writes, 'O man, from whatever land you come, whatever your opinions, listen. Here is your history that I have thought to read, not in the books of your compatriots, who are liars, but in nature, which never lies' (169). What is most distinctive about Rousseau's account is how he conceives of his method, however. This conception of method emerges in two passages:

> Let us begin therefore by setting aside all the facts, because they do not touch upon the question. One must not take the investigations that can be carried out on this subject for historical truths, but only for hypothetical and conditional reasonings, more appropriate for clearing up the nature of things than for showing their true origin . . . (169)

> Because it is no easy enterprise to separate what is original from what is artificial in the present *nature of man* and to know well a state that does not exist, that perhaps did not exist and probably *never will exist* and about which it is nevertheless necessary to have *correct notions* in order to *judge our present state*. (158)

In Rousseau's historical enterprise, the factual is not merely absent, say because of epistemic difficulties with respect to the past. The factual is irrelevant. Because Rousseau's aim is to identify 'the nature of things' rather than the 'true origin', 'hypothetical and conditional reasonings' are appropriate. And this is so in spite of Rousseau's concession in the second passage that there never was nor ever will be a state of nature. Rousseau is not indifferent to the realism of the story and the causal effectiveness of its elements: at the very least, arriving at the 'correct notions' is critical. But whereas empirical evidence can only support causal inferences, one can from speculation 'draw the nature of things' (221). In this way, Rousseau moves historical narrative away from contingent happenings toward the normative analysis of the internal character of human agency. As in genealogy, narrative elements function to show something about who we are and what we are doing.

Kant builds on Rousseau's contributions, in particular Rousseau's story of cosmopolitan freedom. What Rousseau formulates in terms of the incommensurable value of human liberty, Kant explains, most famously, in terms of a universal legislative capacity. Rational beings are thus 'ends-in-themselves' (Kant [1785] 1994: 51) and a source of unconditional worth. In conceiving of persons in this way, Kant decisively marks a shift in cosmopolitanism, from imagining that there is some significant quality that all human beings possess in common, to granting everyone the same normative status. Kant's insistence, that is, that all should be entitled to 'rational esteem for individual value' (Kant [1784] 1999: 21) contributed to genealogy's interest in the sustainability of ideal commitments.

Kant is worth mentioning in this context because of two additional contributions. The most important is critique. Of course, there was a notion of critique before Kant and Rousseau was certainly, in some sense, critical of his culture. But Kant makes clear that critique is not simply an epistemological notion but also a historical-cultural one. In declaring an 'age of critique' (Kant [1781/1787] 1956: A xii), he placed critique within the historical dynamic, so that critical adequacy became part of the explanation of events. And just as important was Kant's specific conception of critique in terms of self-scrutiny and real possibility. Critique proceeds immanently: a 'critique of pure reason' is reason's critique of itself. In particular, critique proceeds by identifying possibility conditions. For example,

Kant claims that the pure concepts of the understanding are necessary for the possibility of experience. His argument does not concern logical possibility: experience without such concepts is not self-contradictory. His argument, rather, is that judgement involving the pure concepts constitutes the possibility of experience and that the concepts are therefore objectively valid. By thus connecting legitimacy with real possibility, Kant makes way for the critical practice of the nineteenth century: that supposed value commitments are somehow unsustainable or unliveable in practice and must therefore be rejected.

The other main contribution of Kant's to the development of genealogy was his invocation of the question of hope. In the *Critique of Pure Reason*, Kant offered 'What may I hope?' (Kant [1781/1787] 1956: B832) as one of three questions that express the complete interest of reason. Indeed, this is the most important of the questions, since it promises a unified resolution of the other two. What is important about this is not Kant's specific answer, in terms of the 'development of humanity's original capacities' (Kant [1784] 1999: 3), nor even the appeal to hope in general (although this reappears, for example, in Adorno [1951] 2006: 121; see also Bernstein 2001: 338ff.). What is important about the appeal to hope is that it signifies that we make sense of ourselves in narrative terms. Kant posed a question that would eventually be answered in his philosophy of history. By locating our deepest interest in hope and insisting that it would sustain philosophical scrutiny, Kant suggested that we should see ourselves in terms of a narrative that extends indefinitely into the future, so that our commitments and even what we are transcend the present moment.

With Rousseau's and Kant's contributions, then, most of the theoretical underpinning of genealogy is already present at the end of the eighteenth century. History is a field of purposive, if ironically self-subverting agency; cosmopolitan commitment to the distinctive standing of persons is in place; and the immanent critique of our own human powers has ascended to cultural supremacy. But the distinctively historical form of genealogy is still lacking. Even though he thinks it has been completely effaced, Rousseau still makes appeal to a Humean 'original constitution', if only as a benchmark. Rousseau thinks that there is an independently specifiable content to what sort of creatures we naturally are and that this content, even if irretrievably lost, can help us make sense of ourselves now. Kant more fully abandons the normative significance of nature, except insofar as its cunning leads us to develop our moral capacities. But for him reason, even if merely formal, is fully determinate: through a consideration of the form of legislative capacities, one can derive the content of the moral law and the human vocation. Original constitution is thus replaced by the 'original capacities' of humanity. History, then, can reveal or conceal what already in some sense is, but shows no discontinuities in its underlying actors. To arrive at genealogy, then, what so far remains stable must still be historicised: being must be considered as 'absolutely mediated' (Hegel [1807] 1988a: 29) through human activity and reason and nature thereby reunited with transformed content. This is Hegel's task.

4. Hegel: Phenomenology on the *Via Dolorosa*

Hegel offers his Jena Phenomenology as, at first encounter, an account of adequately 'scientific' cognition: 'The goal is Spirit's insight into what knowing is' (Hegel [1807] 1988a: 23). The initial presentation of this topic is indeed what one might expect. Hegel sets forth ways of conceiving of the relationship between consciousness and the world, with a view to assessing whether the objects of consciousness might count as knowledge. Even the initial formulation, however, suggests that Hegel's account will depart from the familiar framework: the goal is *Spirit's* insight. The story that Hegel tells turns out not to be one of increasing accuracy in specifying the relationship between two stable things but one of each side being transformed in a developmental process until Spirit's 'certainty of being all reality is raised to truth' (288). In the 'science of the experience that consciousness goes through' (28), meeting the demands of knowing turns out to require reconceptualisations in the self-understanding of the subject of experience and thus turns out to require both self-transformations of the subject and objective experience in the world.

Hegel characterises the path that consciousness follows as the 'way of *despair*' (61). The achievement of every new perspective, or 'shape of consciousness', that is, comes at the cost of increasingly deeper, more self-alienating, more conclusive failures. The process does not involve a stable subject who succeeds in making incremental progress toward the realisation of some theoretical insight. Instead, movement comes from adopting forms of self-understanding that turn out to collapse completely. The relevant failures generate 'despair' and not just abdication: they must be personal in two ways. One is that they provoke a loss of identity. Since some form of self-understanding is always at stake in the relationship to the world, failure on the path to science always appears as the loss of any familiar way of going forward. The other way in which the relevant failures are personal is that they are self-provoked. In a phrase that could have come from Nietzsche, Hegel writes, 'consciousness suffers this violence . . . from its own hands' (63). The dissatisfaction that leads to collapse is generated internally.

Hegel's claims about 'absolute mediation' and reason 'knowing itself to be all reality' are indeed his way of setting out his conclusion that there is nothing outside our own conceptual activity that sets authoritative standards for us. As he characterises his phenomenological approach, 'Consciousness gives its standard to itself and the investigation will thereby be a comparison of itself with itself' (64). Hegel in this way offers a form of immanent critique.[9] The dialectic does not proceed by measuring the stages against some external standard; it proceeds by each shape of consciousness being occupied, as it were, and contradictions arising amid the attempts to carry it out, until the contradictions come to seem unresolvable from within the current standpoint. As Hegel puts this, 'reason is purposive activity' (16). Failures emerge from trying to live out normative self-understandings; as a matter of practice, they generate scepticism about themselves and undermine their own authority. In this way Hegel is the heir of Kant: real possibility takes on a negative form, as the impossibility of avoiding contradiction within the dialectical movement.

The dynamic by which consciousness generates its own scepticism involves the determinacy of conceptual content. Any form of self-understanding will be, as such, conceptually mediated. But the specific mediations that constitute self-understanding only gain determinate content in the context of lived experience. Within lived experience, however, the more determinate meanings turn out to be self-subverting and require replacement. There is a particularly clear explanation of this point in the *Philosophy of History*. Hegel writes, 'The logical nature and moreover the dialectical nature of the concept in general is that it is self-determining: it posits determinations in itself, then negates them and thereby gains in this negation an affirmative, richer and more concrete determination' (Hegel [1840] 1988b: 67; cf. Hegel [1807] 1988a: 39). In Hegel's picture, this dynamic is completely general: even Spirit's recognition of itself in its freedom requires making its own content available through a long, historical process of failed self-definition.

That the dynamic proceeds in this way conveys a hermeneutic import. Since, on Hegel's picture, content emerges out of negating activity and there is nothing extra-conceptual that can function as a ground, all meanings are unstable, at the very least until scepticism 'completes itself' (Hegel [1807] 1988a: 61). Meanings depend on their historical location, relative both to past determination and to the future negations that they will resist. The very shape that Spirit can take depends on historical externalisations of content in this way. As a result, meaning is never available ready-to-hand. It must be traced out across temporal contexts with degrees of complexity that depend on how closely it is involved with Spirit's self-understanding.

Hegel moves beyond the Enlightenment form of philosophy of history by historicising all the way down. He recounts a story in which there are discontinuities in the *dramatis personae* (or *persona*) and in the processes of change; interpreting these elements thus becomes a matter of locating the context of self-activity rather than re-identifying stable objects. With Hegel, then, all the elements of genealogy are already together: historical agency, cosmopolitanism, critique and historical hermeneutics. What might make Hegel seem far removed from genealogy is that he thinks not only that this process has a point of completion, as does Marx, but also that his time has reached this end point. But the substantive details of the narrative do not have much of an effect at the level of genealogical practice. Immanent critique is always potentially, in a qualified way, vindicatory. That Hegel deemed the historical process to be largely successful does not change this approach. For Hegel, too, absolutely everything needs to be submitted to justificatory scrutiny, even the demand for justificatory scrutiny itself. And nothing, it turns out, could possibly count as an answer that lies outside what I have been calling historical agency.

The main difference in approach lies in Hegel's attempt to circumvent what might be called the 'starting point problem' in immanent critique. Since immanent critique proceeds by showing that flaws are internal to the standpoint under criticism, its critical reach only extends as far as the standpoint within which it works. It can show, that is, that particular positions fail and lead to comparatively better results; but it cannot show that an entirely different trajectory, with an entirely different starting point, might not have led to an even more satisfactory position. Hegel addresses this potential shortcoming with a category theory, or 'logic', the burden of which is to show that his narrative is perfectly general: no other starting point could be available. No one else has thought to make such a claim as a matter of logic; but, as we shall see with Marx, the strategy of denying that there is any alternative starting point worthy of consideration has endured.

5. Marx: Materialist Dialectics

By illuminating the pervasive effects of economic institutions and the distinctive character of capitalism, Marx has become the most influential genealogist outside philosophy. At the same time, however, Marx is the most eccentric, in ways that often pass unrecognised. Marx, uniquely among genealogists, claims to offers the genuine causal account of actual historical events and indeed depends on the accuracy of his account for his argument to succeed. With Marx, any gap between real possibility and justification is closed off: the only issue to be addressed is the sustainability of institutionalised practices and any question of justification is deferred until some social practice is realised that does not generate its own contradiction. Marx's version of immanentism, his view of thought as operating internal to its context, accordingly leads him away from taking evaluative questions seriously until the causal structure of human practices is resolved.

In the *German Ideology*, written in 1845–6, Marx introduces his historical approach with an account of 'science' that was to endure throughout his career: 'Where speculation ends, where real life starts, there consequently begins positive science, the exhibition of practical activity, of the practical process of development of men' (Marx and Engels 1976a: 37, modified). Science, which for Hegel was distinguished by the absolute reach of critical scrutiny, is for Marx distinguished by its deferral. 'Communists', furthermore, 'do not preach morality at all' (247). Justificatory and evaluative claims reflect material conditions, so those matters, insofar as they are relevant, must wait for a post-revolutionary consciousness. Accordingly Marx, by appeal to the material, the real, the empirically verifiable, resolved to exhibit the actual historical process and the contradictions that it generates. In the *German Ideology*, Marx thus identifies 'real individuals, their activity and the material conditions of their lives' as his 'premises' (31): his narrative is meant simply to be a chronicle, once the correct ontology and the genuine causal factors are identified.

The conception of history that Marx then offers involves the basic elements needed to explain productive activity, the formation of social relations and the creation of new needs. With these basic elements in place, the historical process takes on its own dynamic. New generations continually transform their material inheritance to increase productive capacity; this necessitates a change in social institutions to accommodate the new economic relations; this in turn changes the goods that a society requires for itself, which in turn changes the organisation of production and so on. Above all, this process is characterised by greater and greater 'division of labour'. As productive tasks become more and more narrowly circumscribed, economic activity takes on its own logic, separate from the purposes of any and all participants: 'This consolidation of what we ourselves produce into a material power above us, growing out of our control, thwarting our expectations, bringing to naught our calculations, is one of the chief factors in our historical development up till now' (47f.). This consolidation, as a chief causal factor, at the same time generates the critical conclusion.

The division of labour is effective not only at increasing material power but also at consolidating it apart from human agency. This is what, on Marx's account, generates the contradictions that bring about revolution. Human productive activity alienates its own causal efficacy from itself more and more until it can do so no further; a dynamic internal to the process compels it finally to break down once its self-alienating character is complete. Marx thus is not primarily concerned to offer theoretical claims about reality or an account of the reasons that we might currently have to revolt. Marx is, rather, arguing that we can anticipate the resolution of a general practical problem: social contradictions will bring about their own demise. Although no evaluative standpoint is presently available, we shall be able to gain some purchase on the defects of current institutions after their conclusive failure. We can thus see how, although Marx's account is causal, it differs from a Humean one. In appealing to the 'actual relations springing from an existing class struggle' (498), Marx invokes the distinctive character of human activity, even when that activity is ironically subverted. For Marx, as with Hegel, the causal process is one of agency that finds itself in self-externalisation; the developmental account belongs to the *Geisteswissenschaften* rather than the *Naturwissenschaften*. And, as with genealogical accounts in general, the aim is critical: to show that current social conditions are indefensible.

The similarities with Hegel at the level of historical approach are noted, in a different respect, in Marx's 1872 Preface to *Capital*. There Marx, although insisting that Hegel's approach 'must be turned right side up again', nevertheless gives him credit for working out the dialectical method in a full and comprehensive manner (Marx 2000: 458). Indeed, in defending his own dialectical approach against a mixed review, Marx argues that it is inherently 'critical and revolutionary':

[Dialectic] includes in its comprehension and affirmative recognition of the existing state of things at the same time also the recognition of the negation of the state, of its inevitable breaking up . . . it regards every historically developed social form as in fluid movement and therefore takes into account its transient nature not less than its momentary existence . . . it lets nothing impose upon it and is in its essence critical and revolutionary.

The reason to adopt a dialectical approach is, of course, that doing so serves the revolutionary ends of critique. Marx's explanation for how it does so, however, appeals to historical-hermeneutic grounds. One cannot employ the appropriate social categories, take note of the shifts in categories, account for the dynamics of change, or recognise the 'fluid movement' of all social forms without a dialectical approach.

We can now see that Marx's way of identifying his differences with Hegel, that Hegel offers a 'mystical' rather than 'rational' form of dialectic that needs to be inverted, is unfair. They share an approach to history that criticises institutions on the basis of a dialectical logic that exhibits their real possibility. Hegel's famous formulation of this point, that the rational is the *wirklich* (Hegel [1821] 1995: 24), the actual or effective, could just as well apply to Marx's analysis of the contradictions of capitalism.[10] Of course, the details of the narratives differ completely, but it is not fair to claim that, for Hegel, 'the real world is only the external, phenomenal form of "the Idea"' (Marx 2000: 457) – as if Hegel were not, like Marx, criticising the picture in which the ideal and the material were 'self-standingly' independent of one another (Marx and Engels 1976a: 35, modified). Marx radicalises, amongst other things, the philosophical tradition of hyperbolic assertion of a break with the past.

In any case, there are significant divergences from Hegel and the others. Although Marx could fairly be called a genealogist of capitalism, his is the most eccentric account. Almost uniquely, he stakes out an anti-speculative account. Whereas Rousseau, Kant, Hegel and Nietzsche want to identify causally significant features of the world to support their normative claims, Marx wants to identify particular causal interactions in the world. Unlike the others, he attempts to explain historically identifiable events – indeed, the historical process as a whole. There are then three main implications of this anti-speculative approach. One, already mentioned, is that Marx claims to have no evaluative purchase on the world; under present conditions, such judgements must be ideological. Two, Marx insists that historical narrative must follow 'order in time' rather than 'order in the idea' (Marx and Engels 1986: 44). Narrative elements must follow a chronological sequence rather than 'their logical sequence and their serial relation in the understanding' (Marx and Engels 1976b: 62). Three, Marx has a different response to the 'starting point problem' that Hegel addressed by his logic. For Marx, worrying about whether the actual historical process neglects some better, alternative possibility for human existence is simply a waste of time. Marx writes, 'The premises from which we begin are not arbitrary ones, not dogmas, but real premises from which abstraction can only be made in the imagination' (Marx and Engels 1976a: 31). A better possibility is purely imaginary and thus does not merit serious consideration. Marx promises that *the real* will eventually provide hermeneutic closure to the real possibilities of human social life.

6. Mill: The Commitments of Modernity

John Stuart Mill is not especially known for his philosophy of history. However, in *The Subjection of Women*, published in 1869, he offers an account of the distinctive character of modernity as a necessary supplement to his better-known account of the moral development of the individual. His specific end in that work is critical: to show that the legal principle of the subordination of women is wrong and needs to be replaced. Mill makes his case by explaining the emergence of a distinctively modern outlook and arguing that it calls for equality as a condition of human development. In making his case, he offers something close to a genealogy of gender difference, but ultimately retreats to perfectionist commitments and an empiricist mode of explanation.

Mill's famous notion of 'experiments in living' implies a great deal of plasticity in human nature (Mill [1859] 1998: 89). One can and indeed should shape oneself into many different forms, as a response to the basic open-endedness of human existence. This process of individual self-development, furthermore, functions best when it proceeds without external constraint. In *The Subjection of Women*, Mill offers an account of the historical character of the normative commitments involved in this picture of the self. Although his argument focuses on the legal status of women, he draws his critical conclusion from a more general claim about the character of modernity. Modernity represents both the 'fruit of a thousand years of experience' (Mill [1869] 1988: 18) and that by which old customs are 'undermined and loosened' (2). And it offers, above all else, this distinctive conviction: 'human beings are no longer born to their place in life . . . but are free to employ their faculties and such favorable chances as offer, to achieve the lot which may appear to them the most desirable' (17). This is deployed in order to criticise laws and institutions, but Mill is fully aware that this is not merely a legal doctrine. He offers it more fundamentally as a social doctrine and one concerning the formation of the self.

In defending this social and personal ideal, he argues against the belief that it must be conditioned by natural, morally significant differences between the sexes. This is where his argument takes the shape of a genealogy of gender difference:

> Women have always hitherto been kept, as far as regards spontaneous development, in so unnatural a state, that their nature cannot but have been greatly disguised and disfigured . . . I shall presently show, that even the least contestable of the differences which may now exist, are such as may very well have been produced merely by circumstances, without any difference of natural capacity. (61)

He claims to provide a genetic narrative of entrenched gender differences to show that they could be contingent or arbitrary. From this speculative narrative, together with an analysis of our present epistemic condition with regard to gender differences, he concludes that they are in fact arbitrary and contingent rather than revelatory of natural capacity and thus should ideally play no role in our practical deliberation. Here, then, we see most of the basic features of genealogy.

Historical agency is present, as gender difference is the product of social institutions ruled by 'the law of superior strength' (7). The critical aspect is certainly present. Indeed, it even appears in its continental form, involving the causality of reason and the necessity of contradiction: customs and social forms that 'have owed their existence to other causes than their soundness' (4) are 'discordant with the future and must necessarily disappear' (17). And Mill's outlook is cosmopolitan: he aims to show that present social conditions do not represent the human condition in general.

Mill's departure from the genealogical framework comes with respect to the historical-hermeneutic. Mill seems to view the self as fluid or variable in its manifestations, but not in a way that requires historical interpretation. The variability, instead, simply provokes an epistemic problem, of recognising the underlying nature that has been 'distorted and disfigured' (61). The correct approach is thus the regrettably speculative one of identifying the causal influences that have disfigured nature.

> I have said that it cannot now be known how much of the existing mental differences between men and women is natural and how much artificial . . . but doubt does not forbid conjecture and where certainty is unattainable, there may yet be the means of arriving at some degree of probability . . . I shall attempt to approach it by tracing the mental consequences of external influences. (72f.)

History, for Mill, is not the field of possibility for self-relating agency, but that of evidence for an unchanging nature that should ultimately regulate our thoughts and ends, if only we had access to it.

Mill views his contemporary circumstances as the contingent outcome of a historical process whose preconditions are now forgotten and thus decides to engage with the sphere of social meaning with a view to changing it. But he retreats from a genealogical approach to a more Humean approach to the explanation of change. This departure from the continental approach is, of course, unsurprising on Mill's part and not necessarily a flaw, but it does seem to stem from a pair of ambivalences. One, the plasticity of the human that Mill invokes in his defence of liberty either manifests an underlying nature or is somehow more deeply indeterminate. Two, Mill embraces both a Humean causal view of human mentality and an Aristotelian view of nature's purposes providing the measure of social progress and individual perfection. The rest of the genealogical tradition takes more care to address the plasticity in human nature and the relation between efficient and final causes. Without having resolved these tensions in his position, Mill does little to justify his starting commitments or the value of liberal culture.

7. Nietzsche's Distinctiveness

Although it was Nietzsche who appropriated the term 'genealogy', his philosophical approach to history was not especially distinctive. If we bracket off the substantive details of his narrative and focus on the basic features of their accounts – admittedly, a big qualification – then Hegel, Marx and Mill share a broadly similar historical outlook. They each offer a historicised view of human freedom in a narrative that connects legitimacy with social practices and historical actuality. Nietzsche, without a category theory, materialism or Mill's mixture of commitments, arguably offers the least distinctive form of genealogy. There is one significant respect in which Nietzsche's approach is distinctive, however: he forestalls and inverts his narrative's vindicatory element. That vindicatory element, as with the others, is present; but it appears with such thoroughgoing irony that there is little hope of it ever being redeemed.

There are more and less innocuous-seeming versions of this feature of Nietzsche's approach. The more innocuous-seeming version appears in *The Antichrist*, written in 1888. In that work, the single overarching objection to Christianity concerns historical understanding. Nietzsche characterises healthy cultures as having undertaken centuries of learning from experience and having then incorporated that learning in customs and habits until it becomes unconsciously authoritative. 'There', writes Nietzsche, 'the yields of reason from long ages of experiment and uncertainty should be laid out for the most distant uses and the greatest, richest, most complete harvest possible be brought home' (Nietzsche 1967–77: 6: 245, §58). But Christianity's typical feature, according to Nietzsche, is that it seeks out such historical wisdom and destroys it in the name of a new era and a beyond. This is his greatest complaint:

> The entire labour of the ancient world *in vain*: I have no words to express my feelings over something so monstrous. – And considering that its labour was preparatory, that it was just the foundation laid with granite self-consciousness for a labour of millennia, the entire *meaning* of the ancient world in vain! (6: 247, §59)

Christianity has been productive: by destroying tradition, or whole ways of life, it opened up the possibility of a modern historical sense. But it did so at the cost of destroying healthy relationships with the past – indeed, with any past. And this problem is irremediable.

No triumph is possible here; the loss is permanent. The only response is to recuperate some of the historical experience by reinterpreting our historical self-understanding. But no conclusive measure of success could be even potentially available and learning proceeds by way of painful failures. Above all, no triumph is possible because genealogy itself belongs to the Christian sense of the historical. Nietzsche writes, discussing the *Book of Manu*: 'A law book never recounts the use, the reasons, the casuistry in the prehistory of a law: then it would forfeit its imperative tone . . . The problem is precisely here' (6: 241, §57). Genealogy is this problem: in looking to the past with an eye to the open-ended future, it represents knowledge as 'a form of asceticism' (6: 243, §57) that undermines the higher values. Turning this against the Christian sense of history combats 'decadence' (6: 172, §6), but it also represents a decadence that has always been going on. Even the very hope to get beyond the Christian inheritance is part of the Christian inheritance, suggests Nietzsche. And yet there is no alternative.

The less innocuous-seeming form of this distinctive feature of Nietzsche's approach appears in his claim that there is no alternative to the ascetic ideal. In the concluding sections of *On the Genealogy of Morals*, Nietzsche identifies the ascetic ideal with the 'One Goal' of human history and then asks, 'Why is the counterpart *lacking*? Where is the other "One Goal"?' (Nietzsche 1967–77: 5: 396, III.23) Nietzsche considers the modern scientific conscience as a possible alternative, but then immediately argues, 'it is not the contrary of the ascetic ideal, but rather its most recent and distinguished form'. So Nietzsche offers no helpful suggestion in concluding his genealogy, in part because of the unavailability of any good suggestion, but in part also because the very project of trying to overcome the ascetic ideal is an exacerbation of the ascetic ideal. Nietzsche's genealogy, unlike those of the others, promises no ultimate vindication, no constructive result, no future culmination; indeed, it subverts the very idea of vindication by suggesting that it would be another ascetic gesture. Seeking justification is both part of who we are in our projects of getting beyond the present and also hopelessly entangled with the ascetic ideal. Nietzsche does concede that the modern person 'at least turned out relatively well, at least is still capable of living, at least still says "Yes" to life' (5: 277, I.11). And he very unhelpfully suggests, 'the ascetic ideal has at present only one kind of enemy who truly *harms* it: the comedian of this ideal' (5: 409, III.27). But in general, Nietzsche's genealogy points to irony: any success in vanquishing the ascetic ideal leads deeper into its inescapability.

8. The Post-history of Genealogy

Many of the contemporary invocations of 'genealogy' are perhaps arbitrary: they make a body of work seem better theorised by the name alone. Many contemporary invocations are connected to Nietzsche's practice, but in a much looser sense than the one that I have suggested here. For example, Bernard Williams writes that: 'A genealogy is a narrative that tries to explain a cultural phenomenon by describing a way in which it came about, or could have come about, or might be imagined to have come about' (Williams 2002: 20). Nietzsche arguably fits here – if we do not press too hard on 'explain' or the counterfactual options – but so does Hume, state of nature theory and myth, according to Williams.[11] Beyond such an appropriation of 'genealogy', however, there remain others with a more direct lineage to Nietzsche and the nineteenth-century historical forms. The popularity of these appropriations is owed to Adorno's formulation of 'immanent critique' and Foucault's practice of genealogy. Here I cannot begin to offer accounts of their approaches, or even their divergences. Instead I merely wish to suggest how these approaches are continuous with the past in ways that lead into the present. In particular, these approaches can be seen as taking up versions of what Hegel called 'absolute mediation' that lead away from the distinctively philosophical to more wide-ranging accounts of self, desire and society.

When Hegel referred to 'absolute mediation' he was referring to mediation by conceptual activity. So, for example, our experience of the world is not directly received from 'outside'. Rather, it is mediated by the conceptual repertoire that we have available and employ to structure our experience. 'Absolute' mediation suggests that *everything* is mediated and that everything is *fully* mediated: there is no element that even provisionally escapes the human production of determinations. That which does the mediating changes from Marx to Nietzsche and beyond, but the basic point endures. There is no moment of anything outside of our social or cultural conditions within the entire human world; the merely artificial does not come into contact with the purely natural; mediation is everywhere and must itself be illuminated if we are to understand even the most familiar phenomena. Adorno's version of this point is called, simply, 'infinite mediation' (Adorno 1967: 7) and entails that nothing is ever 'to be taken simply at face value'. Foucault expresses a similar point in terms of the 'rule of immanence' (Foucault [1976] 1978: 98) and his analytics of power: 'Where there is power, there is resistance and yet, or rather consequently, this resistance is never in a position of exteriority to power' (95). On Foucault's conception, nothing is outside of power because power produces, constitutes or conditions everything.

Contemporary genealogy, following Adorno and Foucault, has drawn two consequences from absolute mediation that owe more to Nietzsche than to anyone else in the genealogical tradition. The first is to find something sinister in it. For Hegel the explicit recognition of absolute mediation was a mark of success; even for Marx it suggested that, as the product of human activity, everything was liable to be changed. But for Adorno and Foucault it suggests that there is no possibility of human self-liberation: nothing that we could try to accomplish could possibly count as a departure from our subjection. Adorno writes, for example, 'Of course, even the immanent method is eventually overtaken by this. It is dragged into the abyss by its object' (Adorno 1967: 34). Foucault is slightly more sanguine about the possibility of genuine resistance. In an early essay, genealogy effects this by introducing 'discontinuity into our very being' (Foucault [1971] 1977: 154). Later, the genealogical enterprise is meant to help to 'counter the grips of power with the claims of bodies, pleasure and knowledges, in their multiplicity and their possibility of resistance' (Foucault [1976] 1978: 157). Even here, however, the relationship to power seems permanently ambiguous and thus at best there is a 'perpetual danger of relapse' (Foucault [1971] 1977: 160).

The second consequence of absolute mediation is that *everything* has become the subject of genealogy. Given absolute mediation, no longer are only Nietzsche's 'highest values' the subject of genealogy. Chains of determination lead back everywhere: from the self and social institutions and desires into all the constituting activities that have shaped what we are. With absolute mediation, then, every element of the human world becomes a subject for genealogy. And thus genealogy is no longer a distinctively philosophical enterprise. Instead it looks critically everywhere, to interpret everything that shapes the human.[12]

Notes

1. Any list of examples must be radically incomplete. For some examples within philosophy, see: Agamben 2000; Nichols 2002; and Williams 2002. For examples from other disciplines, see: Benn Michaels 1992; Der Derian 1987; Liu 2002; Miller 1998; Saldivar 1991; and Turner 2000. See also David Owen's (2005) valuable review essay. I discuss Foucault's important appropriation of genealogy below; most of these examples (and many besides) refer to Foucault.
2. For an early usage, see Herodotus (1920: 448), where he writes of 'genealogizing oneself'. Nietzsche's book is of course *On the Genealogy of Morals*; he had not used the word 'genealogy' in any previously published work. On the difference between genealogy as pedigree and genealogy in Nietzsche's sense, see Geuss 1994.
3. This perhaps explains why, despite its popularity, the new sense of genealogy is absent from dictionaries, except for this bland attempt from Merriam-Webster: 'an account of the origin and historical development of something' (2003: 520).
4. I discuss some additional reasons below. The popularity of 'genealogy' no doubt also benefits from it being a common term (unlike, say, 'historical materialism') that nevertheless does not suffer from competition with common meaning, since, outside the Church of Jesus Christ of Latter-Day Saints and the US Senate, no one cares about family pedigree anymore.
5. Translations from French and German texts are the author's own. Emphasis is original unless otherwise noted. In references to Nietzsche's *Genealogy*, page number is followed by essay number (in Roman numerals) then section number (for example, III.25), or, in references to the Preface, 'P' followed by section number, for instance, P4). In references to other works of Nietzsche's, page number is followed by paragraph number (§) when applicable.
6. 'Immanent' and 'critique' had currency long beforehand – see Benhabib 1986. But to the best of my knowledge the phrase 'immanent critique' stems from Adorno 1967 and Adorno [1966] 1973. Here, however, I am more interested in a general idea of immanent critique, not specifically in Adorno's notion of it. In particular, immanent critique as I characterise it does not represent a distinctive 'method', as it does in Adorno (1967: 31) or Jay (1986: 266).
7. On some textual difficulties in identifying Nietzsche's view of genealogy see Guay (2005: 355).
8. On the identification of Hume, somewhat oddly, as an English psychologist, see Clark and Swensen (1998: 129). For an attempt to read genealogy as a Humean enterprise, see Leiter 2002.
9. Stern (2002: 41) refers to Hegel as carrying out 'immanent critique'. Pinkard (1996: 6) offers the similar idea of an 'internal test'.
10. By claiming that the rational is the *wirklich* and the *wirklich* rational, Hegel shows his willingness to attribute rationality to the movements prior to the ultimate resolution of contradiction. Marx, despite occasional encomia for the bourgeoisie, is less sanguine about resolutions that generate new contradictions.
11. Williams explicitly refers to state of nature theories and Hume as presenting genealogies. Myth implicitly qualifies as genealogy, I believe, in Williams (2002: 161).
12. I thank my research assistants during the writing of this paper, Joshua Wretzel and Jack Marsh; Amy Wendling, for her discussion of Marx; Sean Johnston, for his discussions of Mill and Foucault; Anna Gebbie and my students at Binghamton for their discussions of everything. My benefactors are, as usual, not responsible for my errors and in this case especially so.

References

Adorno, Theodor W. (1967), 'Cultural Criticism and Society', in Theodor W. Adorno, *Prisms*, trans. Shierry Weber Nicholson and Samuel Weber, Cambridge, MA: MIT Press.

Adorno, Theodor W. [1966] (1973), *Negative Dialectics*, trans. E. B. Ashton, New York: Continuum.

Adorno, Theodor W. [1951] (2006), *Minima Moralia*, trans. E. F. N. Jephcott, New York: Verso.

Agamben, Giorgio (2000), 'Absolute immanence', in Giorgio Agamben and Daniel Heller-Roazen (eds), *Potentialities: Collected Essays in Philosophy*, Stanford: Stanford University Press, pp. 220–41.

Ansell Pearson, Keith (1996), *Nietzsche contra Rousseau*, New York: Cambridge University Press.

Benhabib, Seyla (1986), *Critique, Norm, and Utopia*, New York: Columbia University Press.

Benn Michaels, Walter (1992), 'Race into culture: A critical genealogy of cultural identity', *Critical Inquiry* 18 (4): 655–85.

Bernstein, Jay (2001), *Adorno: Disenchantment and Ethics*, New York: Cambridge University Press.

Clark, Maudemarie and Alan J. Swensen (eds) (1998), *Friedrich Nietzsche: On the Genealogy of Morality*, Indianapolis: Hackett.

Der Derian, James (1987), *On Diplomacy: A Genealogy of Western Estrangement*, Cambridge, MA: Blackwell.

Foucault, Michel [1971] (1977), 'Nietzsche, genealogy, history', in Michel Foucault, *Language, Counter-Memory, Practice*, ed. Donald F. Bouchard, Ithaca, NY: Cornell University Press, pp. 139–64.

Foucault, Michel [1976] (1978), *The History of Sexuality. Volume I: An Introduction*, trans. Robert Hurley, New York: Vintage.

Geuss, Raymond (1994), 'Nietzsche's genealogy', *European Journal of Philosophy* 2 (3): 274–92.

Guay, Robert (2005), 'The philosophical function of genealogy', in Keith Ansell Pearson (ed.), *A Companion to Nietzsche*, Malden, MA: Blackwell, pp. 353–71.

Hegel, Georg Wilhelm Friedrich [1807] (1988a), *Phänomenologie des Geistes*, Hamburg: Meiner.

Hegel, Georg Wilhelm Friedrich [1840] (1988b), *Introduction to the Philosophy of History*, trans. Leo Rauch, Indianapolis: Hackett.

Hegel, Georg Wilhelm Friedrich [1821] (1995), *Grundlinien der Philosophie des Rechts*, Frankfurt: Suhrkamp.

Herodotus (1920), *The Histories* vol. 1, ed. A. D. Godley, Cambridge, MA: Harvard University Press.

Jay, Martin (1986), *Marxism and Totality*, Berkeley: University of California Press.

Kant, Immanuel [1781/1787] (1956), *Kritik der reinen Vernunft*, Hamburg: Meiner.

Kant, Immanuel [1785] (1994), *Grundlegung zur Metaphysik der Sitten*, Hamburg: Meiner.

Kant, Immanuel [1784] (1999), *Was ist Aufklärung?: Ausgewählte kleine Schriften*, Hamburg: Meiner.

Leiter, Brian (2002), *Nietzsche on Morality*, New York: Routledge.

Lemon, Michael C. (2003), *Philosophy of History: A Guide for Students*, New York: Routledge.

Liu, Xin (2002), *The Otherness of Self: A Genealogy of Self in Contemporary China*, Ann Arbor: University of Michigan Press.

Marx, Karl (2000), *Selected Writings*, 2nd edn, ed. David McLellan, New York: Oxford University Press.

Marx, Karl and Frederick Engels (1976a), *Collected Works* vol. 5, Moscow: Progress Publishers and New York: International Publishers.

Marx, Karl and Frederick Engels (1976b), *Collected Works* vol. 6, Moscow: Progress Publishers and New York: International Publishers.

Marx, Karl and Frederick Engels (1986), *Collected Works* vol. 28, Moscow: Progress Publishers and New York: International Publishers.

Merriam-Webster's Collegiate Dictionary (2003), 11th edn, Springfield, MA: Merriam-Webster.

Mill, John Stuart [1869] (1988), *The Subjection of Women*, Indianapolis: Hackett.

Mill, John Stuart (1998), *On Liberty and Other Essays*, New York: Oxford University Press.

Miller, William Ian (1998), *The Anatomy of Disgust*, Cambridge, MA: Harvard University Press.

Nichols, Shaun (2002), 'On the genealogy of norms: A case for the role of emotion in cultural evolution', *Philosophy of Science* 69 (2): 234–55.

Nietzsche, Friedrich (1967–77), *Kritische Studienausgabe*, 15 vols, ed. Giorgio Colli and Mazzino Montinari, New York: de Gruyter.

Owen, David (2005), 'On genealogy and political theory', *Political Theory* 33 (1): 110–20.

Pinkard, Terry (1996), *Hegel's Phenomenology: The Sociality of Reason*, Cambridge: Cambridge University Press.

Rousseau, Jean-Jacques [1762] (1966), *Du contrat social*, Paris: Flammarion.

Rousseau, Jean-Jacques [1755] (1992), *Discours sur l'origine et les fondements de l'inégalité parmis les hommes*, Paris: Flammarion.

Saldivar, José David (1991), *The Dialectics of Our America: Genealogy, Cultural Critique, and Literary History*, Durham, NC: Duke University Press.

Stern, Robert (2002), *Hegel and the Phenomenology of Spirit*, New York: Routledge.

Turner, William B. (2000), *A Genealogy of Queer Theory*, Philadelphia: Temple University Press.

Williams, Bernard (2002), *Truth and Truthfulness: An Essay in Genealogy*, Princeton: Princeton University Press.

10

Embodiment: Conceptions of the Lived Body from Maine de Biran to Bergson

Mark Sinclair

1. Introduction

In contemporary philosophy the phenomenological movement has offered a compelling challenge to the mind–body dualism that was instituted by Descartes amongst others in the seventeenth century. This challenge, perhaps most notably in the work of the French phenomenologist Maurice Merleau-Ponty, does not consist in the reduction of one of the opposed terms to the other in the manner of a thoroughgoing or 'eliminative' materialism but rather rests on a broader critique of both terms. The self, it is argued, is not originally an isolated thinking subject, certain of its own thoughts and separable from the body, whilst the body is originally not an object *partes extra partes*, divisible like any other (see Merleau-Ponty [1945] 1962). Of course, I can seek the certainty of the *cogito* just as I can objectify my body in the manner of the physiologist studying it from the outside. But prior to this, experience shows us that the self or subject is the body and that the body as a lived body, a cognitive corporeality, a capacity for intelligent action, is the subject or self. We exist as embodied beings in a manner that both escapes and precedes the objectifying approach to the body in the modern sciences.

These arguments are fundamental to contemporary philosophy and the present essay aims to situate them historically by elucidating how they first emerge in the French philosophy of the nineteenth century. The essay focuses on three thinkers who are often characterised as the principal representatives of the French 'spiritualist' tradition in this period: Pierre Maine de Biran, Félix Ravaisson and Henri Bergson. The term 'spiritualism', like any '-ism', is vague but, in a broad philosophical sense, one applicable to the work of Descartes, it can be taken to denominate philosophical doctrines asserting the primacy of an intellectual principle – mind or spirit – in relation to matter. In a narrower sense that relates more particularly to nineteenth-century French philosophy, 'spiritualism' denominates doctrines holding that an intellectual principle is not only primary but also the ontologically grounding principle of matter. (See the entry on spiritualism in Lalande 1993.)

To demonstrate the enduring significance of the nineteenth-century French spiritualist tradition for reflection on embodiment, the essay advances in three stages. In Section II I show how, early in the century, Maine de Biran articulates an idea of *le corps propre* – 'one's own body' – within his philosophical psychology of the will, an idea which Merleau-Ponty will make famous.[1] In Section 3, I show how Ravaisson, by means of philosophical reflection on the nature of habit, offers a viable response to the problems and limitations of his predecessor's approach. In Section 4, I argue that Bergson's conception of the body, for all that it offers an interesting challenge to Cartesian conceptions of embodiment, in fact retreats from the originality of the insights of both Biran and Ravaisson. I thus contend that Ravaisson's thinking, insofar as it responds to the problems of Biran's approach, represents the summit of nineteenth-century philosophical reflection on embodiment.

2. *Le corps propre* in Maine de Biran

Maine de Biran published little in his lifetime. He was known by his contemporaries more as a politician than as a philosopher, but he left a body of work which proved extremely influential (see Copleston [1975] 1999: 21–2, for a brief but reliable summary of Biran's political life). Ravaisson borrowed much from his thinking and Bergson later claimed that 'from the beginning of the century, France had a great metaphysician, the greatest that she had produced since Descartes and Malebranche: Maine de Biran' (Bergson [1915] 1972: 1157).[2] Biran's reluctance to publish seems to be because of a constant dissatisfaction with his attempts to present his ideas in a complete and definitive form. He more than once began work on a new synthesis of his ideas before completing the last one, so that it has been claimed that 'Maine de Biran is the man of a single book and this book he never wrote' (Gouhier 1947: 22).[3]

The first text he did publish, however, and the only one to have been translated into English (see Maine de Biran 1970), was his 1802 dissertation entitled *Influence of Habit on the Faculty of Thinking*. This was presented as the winning entry in a competition organised by the *Académie de sciences morales et politiques* in which candidates were to determine the effect that frequent repetition of the same operations produces on our intellectual faculties. Biran addresses this specific issue of habit from the perspective of a psychology of the will whose most immediate source was the work of Antoine Destutt de Tracy, a member of the jury assessing the entries to the competition and principal representative of the Ideological school in France. Ideology, in the most general terms, aimed to offer a form of descriptive psychological analysis independent of metaphysical speculations concerning the causes or ultimate nature of the soul. Its approach was influenced by the arguments of the eighteenth-century French philosopher Étienne Bonnot de Condillac, according to which higher psychological faculties can be explained on the basis of a primary capacity of receptivity. In the work of Pierre-Jean-George Cabanis, Ideology took the particular form of reductive physiological explanations of the operations of thought. Destutt de Tracy, however, had begun to underline the importance and irreducibility of our motor activity. Biran develops this idea of voluntary action or 'motility' as the basic principle of a philosophical psychology that will lead him to break from the Ideologists and, by 1807 at least, to an explicit discovery of the subjective body.[4]

In the introduction to the 1802 dissertation (see Maine de Biran 1987) Biran advances his psychology according to a distinction between 'active and passive impressions'. Each of the five senses, to varying degrees, admits of a distinction between passively receiving an impression and actively apprehending that now only partially passive impression. Whereas passive impressions occur 'in me without me', without any agency on the part of the subject, perception or active impressions, on the contrary, involve the voluntary movement of the sense organs. Active movements of the eye, for example, although they might pass unnoticed by us, allow us to perceive visual objects, just as active movement of hand and body allows us to trace the contours of things. Biran argues, however, that this voluntary movement constitutive of active impressions necessarily involves an awareness of oneself as a voluntary agent or 'acting self [*moi agissant*]', an awareness that is given through an 'impression of effort' which admits of degrees. Effort involves not only awareness that it is 'I who move, or who *wants* to move' (Maine de Biran 1987: 131),[5] but also, and at the same time, an experience of the resistance to the will offered by the body and, through the latter, by other objects. Effort is hence understood as the unity of will and resistance and although Biran describes it here as an 'impression' it is given to what he terms *le sens intime*, an intimate or inner sense that necessarily accompanies external perception.

For Biran, effort comprises the 'two terms of the necessary relation to ground the first simple judgment of personality: *I am*' (134). This is the keystone of his thinking: perception and, at the same time, my sense of self is originally given through my voluntary relation to the resistance of my body and the things of the world and thus consciousness is originally as much a matter of an 'I will' as it is of an 'I think'. This is not to say that Biran opposes a practical conception of self-awareness to a theoretical one, as we might be tempted to think. It is simply the case that the *volo* and *cogito* are here co-extensive: there is an identity of the thinking and motor principle in man (see Maine de Biran 1995: 94–6; Henry 1965: 75). Biran is not, of course, the first philosopher of the tradition to argue that consciousness is grounded in the will. In this connection it should be noted that in his 1805 *Mémoire sur la décomposition de la pensée* (Dissertation Concerning the Decomposition of Thought), his second prize-winning entry to an Académie competition, he cites the German idealist philosophers Fichte and Schelling (Maine de Biran 1988: 108–10).[6] Yet Biran cites them critically, for they have not understood that free, voluntary activity can be the origin of consciousness only insofar as it meets a resistant term. In pure activity without resistance, he argues, as much as in pure passivity, consciousness would be absent. Consciousness is thus conceived as an irreducible relation or duality; but this is not the 'union' of two separable substances, since the will can exist only in an active relation to a resistant term.

Already in 1802, this emphasis on the relational nature of consciousness has important consequences for the status of the body. The latter cannot be considered as something secondary and accidental, given that it is one of two necessary terms for the advent of consciousness. The Cartesian claim that the existence of the body, as opposed to that of the mind, can be subject to sceptical doubt is contrary to the basic structure of experience. The reality of the body, as Biran will later state, 'is just as certain as that of our own existence from which it is inseparable' (Maine de Biran 2001: 142). The best way to comprehend how the idea of consciousness as a voluntary relation is developed in Biran's later work and leads to a conception of *le corps propre*, however, is to examine his critique of David Hume's sceptical arguments concerning our experience of causality or force.

This critique first appears in Biran's 1807 *De l'aperception immédiate* (On Immediate Apperception), the winning entry to a competition organised by the Berlin Academy. Hume had argued that in the external world we experience a mere succession of events and not causal relations between them. Biran accepts this, but he refuses the further claim that we have no experience of force or causal power internally, in our own actions. In Section VII of the *Enquiry Concerning Human Understanding* Hume focuses on the relation of volitions to the physical movements following from them. Biran takes up three points of the argument in order to unveil and attack the presuppositions that underlie it.[7]

First, Hume sets up the problem by arguing that the fact that the 'motion follows the command of the will is a matter of common experience, like other natural events' (Hume, [1748] 1975: 67). He therefore considers inner experience, that is, the relation of the will to the body, on the model of outer experience and the relations between objects. This is tantamount to a reification and objectification of the human being. Our volitions, even if they are recognised not to be spatial objects, are considered by Hume as things in the particular region of the world that we call 'mind' or 'soul' and as related to the body in the manner that other external objects are related to it. Such an approach, for Biran, is a 'naturalistic' prejudice that deforms the entirety of Hume's analysis.[8] Biran argues that the difference between inner and outer, spatial, experience is more radical than has heretofore been understood and that conscious experience must be considered from a genuinely first-person perspective. The 'primitive fact [*fait primitif*]' of consciousness is the relational unity of will and resistance, but this 'fact' is not proper to the world of objects and it is known not by means of perception, by 'common experience' in Hume's terms, but rather by a *sens intime* now understood as an 'immediate apperception' rather than as an 'impression' of effort.

Second, concerning the 'influence of volitions over the organs of the body' Hume writes that 'this influence . . . can never be foreseen from any apparent energy or power in the cause, which connects it with the effect, and renders the one an infallible consequence of the other' (Hume [1748] 1975: 65). The argument, in separating volition from movement according to a traditional, Cartesian distinction of soul and body, is that we have no experience of a causal relation or necessary connexion underlying the temporal succession of the two terms. Yet, for Biran, 'the relation of *causality* is completely different to that of *succession*' (Maine de Biran 1995: 117). The presupposition that causality, if it exists, must be a matter of succession is another motivation for the scepticism Hume professes. The causal force or power in our action is not prior to the effect but is rather present in it: 'the internal energy of the cause is directly *felt* in the effect or the movement produced' (119). This is to say that the volitions preceding action of which Hume writes are mere ideas or wishes and it is therefore no surprise that we find no energy or causal power within them. Genuine volition, force and power are given nowhere but in the act itself. Concerning the status of the body in its relation to the will, we learn here that the 'relation' is neither the simple relation of two separable entities nor a temporal relation of succession. It becomes difficult, it might be thought (and I shall return to this point), to conceive of the unity of will and resistance as a relation at all.

Third, Hume argues in Cartesian fashion that 'we are so far from being immediately conscious' of how the mind affects the body 'that it must forever escape our most diligent enquiry' (Hume [1748] 1975: 65). We know neither why only some of our bodily organs can be directed by the 'soul', nor how the soul affects the parts that it can direct, particularly when we consider what 'we learn from anatomy', namely, 'that the immediate object of power in voluntary motion is not the member itself which is moved, but certain muscles and nerves and animal spirits and, perhaps, something still more minute and unknown' (66). We might think that we feel an immediate power to move our limbs, but in reality our will does not have to act on the limb as a whole, but rather on a host of physiological intermediaries, and we have no knowledge of this in our experience. Biran responds first by attacking the claim that we have to know *how* the will moves the body in order for us to know *that* it moves the body. The claim is spurious insofar as there is nothing to distinguish it from the more evidently erroneous claim that we can see only if we know the physiological processes according to which we see, and it presupposes the possibility of taking simultaneously a first-person and a third-person perspective on our experience:

> [J]ust as, in order to have an immediate direct perception, both of the luminous fluid of the eye in itself, and of its effect on the fibres of the retina, we would have to have two eyes seeing at once inside and outside of themselves, so too, in order to know the efficacious means of the will or the muscles at the same time as we feel this efficacy we would have to be *ourselves* and other than *ourselves*. (Maine de Biran 1995: 121)

It is, however, precisely such a third-person and anatomical perspective on the body that Biran seeks to displace within philosophical reflection on the nature of voluntary action. Hume's argument, for Biran, makes obvious the necessity of a certain distinction:

> [T]he knowledge acquired by the representation of things or images outside of us is not at all the same as that which is bound to the facts of *le sens intime* . . . What relation is there, for example, between the images that the anatomist or philosopher make of the position of the different organs, or of their play in a phenomenon such as that of muscular contraction, and the feeling that the individual has of these contractions produced, or of the power that effects them in a freely determined effort? Is there any relation between the *secondary* objective knowledge that the individual acquires successively from the external parts of his body in studying them with his hands and eyes and the *internal* knowledge of the parts obeying the same will, acquired in the first deployment of *effort*, a knowledge without which the *self* does not begin to exist for itself?

Biran couches in interrogative form a revolutionary insight: a distinction between a primary and a secondary knowledge and thus between a primary and secondary existence of the body. The secondary knowledge of the body I gain by objectifying it by means of the senses of touch and sight, in the manner of the physiologist studying it from the outside. In contrast, the primary knowledge of the body, the body experienced as *le corps propre*, belongs to *le sens intime* or immediate apperception.[9]

Biran develops these remarks in the most deliberate manner in his *Essai sur les fondements de la psychologie* (Essay on the Foundations of Psychology). He began this in 1811 and appears to have intended it to be a masterwork developing his earlier dissertations, but again, even after reworking it in 1822, he left it unpublished. In the section 'Origin of the Knowledge that we have of our own Body', he recognises the radical nature of his own thinking in proposing 'a completely new point of view according to which I consider the primary knowledge of *le corps propre*' (Maine de Biran 2001: 141). To understand the primitive fact of consciousness, he argues, we must recognise that there are 'two sorts of *outsides*, or two objects, two elementary terms, the one relative to internal immediate apperception, the other relative to intuition or external perception'. The body not only possesses its own kind of resistance or inertia, distinct from that of worldly objects, but it also possesses its own kind of spatiality that is irreducible to the spatiality of other things. This internal spatiality is 'a sort of vague extension without limits or figures . . . a mode of purely internal space that is . . . the inherent form of the proper object of internal apperception'. In my actions, I do not usually have a precise knowledge of the locations of my members, but rather have a vague, pre-thematic understanding of their position and possibilities. Psychologists in the twentieth century will come to talk of this bodily awareness in terms of a 'body schema' or 'body image' but, for Biran, it can in no way 'be represented in the form of an image', nor does it have an explicit distinction of parts. This vague, non-imagistic understanding of space is not a derivative and less precise mode of external spatial representation. On the contrary, it is primary and only on its basis can I isolate the particular form and position of what I already understand to be my body when I view it objectively via external perception.[10]

In this way Biran offers at least the framework of an original phenomenology of bodily awareness and bodily being, which seeks to demonstrate the inadequacy of traditional conceptions of embodiment. As he writes:

> When philosophy has raised the question: 'How does a motor and sensitive being first of all learn to know its own body', it has in mind only an objective and external mode of

knowledge; it has taken a secondary phenomenon to be a primary fact . . . In posing the origin of the representative knowledge of the body as a problem, one considers the problem of existence to be resolved, or else one does not believe that there is a problem at all. (Maine de Biran 2001: 287–8)

It is therefore no exaggeration to claim, following Michel Henry, that 'Maine de Biran is the first philosopher to have understood . . . the derivative and secondary character of any objective conception of the body' (Henry 1965: 182). It is in recognising this derivative character and in remembering that anatomy always presupposes a corpse that we can overturn Hume's appeal to objective anatomical studies in order to advance his scepticism. In, say, moving an arm, the will does not have to act on objective parts of the body such as nerves or even 'animal sprits', but can rather immediately move the arm insofar as it belongs to the pre-objective primary and lived body.[11]

Biran argues, then, that the primary fact of consciousness consists in the relation of the will to a resistant term and this resistant term is *le corps propre* as the object of immediate apperception. Notwithstanding the originality of this conception of the body, Biran always maintains his conception of consciousness as a relation and always maintains concomitantly that 'the self [*le moi*] is distinguished' from the body 'without ever being able to separate itself from it' (Maine de Biran 2001: 142). Certainly, Biran's descriptions of this relation, as we have seen, challenge ordinary conceptions of the nature of a relation. Yet we go beyond at least the letter of the texts if we claim, as does Michel Henry, that what is described as a relation 'is ultimately not a relation' and that, for Biran, 'there is an identity of the being of the body and the ego' (Henry 1965: 166). Such a claim is certainly one way to deal with the difficulty and, perhaps, the equivocations of Biran's thinking. Yet from the perspective of the twentieth-century phenomenological philosophy to which Henry's reading is indebted, we might also wonder whether Biran has sufficiently uprooted the Cartesian paradigm. It might be asked whether Biran, espousing a conception of consciousness as a relation to the lived body as a resistant term, offers an all too intellectualist and spectatorial conception of action which is unable to apprehend that the body *is* the self and the intentional subject of action.

In Biran's defence against this charge of intellectualism, it must be noted that he recognises, already in 1802, that some actions are more voluntary and thus conscious than others, that there is a 'multitude of degrees' between passive impressions and fully conscious action.[12] Yet this defence brings us to another more telling problem in Biran's thinking, a problem that, as commentators such as Henry and Merleau-Ponty have noted, limits the originality of his conception of *le corps propre* (Moore 1970: 105ff.; Henry 1965: ch. 5). Biran never renounces the supposition that he adopts from Condillac and the Ideologists and which he first presents in the 1802 dissertation, of impressions occurring without any measure of consciousness or voluntary activity. Although he claims that activity is always a matter of degree and although he seeks to demonstrate that 'passive impressions' are not, in fact, wholly passive since they are accompanied by a form of vital, unconscious and non-voluntary activity, he always radically distinguishes non-voluntary from voluntary activity. As he writes in the *Essai*:

> [I]t is not impossible to trace, so to speak, in human organisation, the terminating circle of the light of consciousness, or the line of demarcation that separates the proper and individual sense of effort or of will and this other sense, a general and common organ, that can be called a vital sense. (Maine de Biran 2001: 140)

Biran acknowledges here and elsewhere the difficulty of isolating such a line of demarcation within our own experience, but he claims that prior to voluntary perception and apperception, there is a vital sense and physiological 'system' wholly independent of the will and consciousness. Biran cites approvingly the dictum of Herman Boerhaave: *homo simplex in vitalite, duplex in humanitate* (133). Man is simple, for Biran, as a biological being governed by a vital principle, but dual in his humanity insofar as the latter comprises, in addition, the will as the principle of perception and apperception. The consequences of such claims, though perhaps confusing, are evident. What Biran describes as the 'primitive fact' of consciousness turns out, in fact, not to be the most primary or primitive truth of existence as such. It now emerges that before being *le corps propre* the body is a physiological object independent of consciousness. Biran's thinking thus always operates on two levels. His phenomenology of *le corps propre* as distinct from the body objectified in experience is always counter-posed to a physiological account of the body considered as both ontologically and chronologically prior to our actual experience. What is secondary in our actual experience is held ultimately to be primary and, from the position of philosophical reflection in the first person, Biran thus posits the primacy of the body apprehended in third-person terms. It should be noted that in maintaining this position, which he inherits from the Ideologists, Biran does not attain a thoroughgoing or consistent spiritualist philosophy asserting the primacy of an intellectual principle. It is therefore not simply because of his reluctance to offer his work to the public that Biran can be characterised as a '*philosophe de bonnes intentions*' (Merleau-Ponty 1997: 66), a philosopher whose intentions and insights are never adequately or consistently realised.[13]

In Section 3, however, I aim to show how Félix Ravaisson offers a viable response not only to this problem in Biran's work but also to the problematic issue of the 'relation' of will to the body. If, as Jacques Derrida has remarked, Ravaisson 'derives his axioms' from Biran's thinking (Derrida 2005: 155), he nevertheless develops these axioms in a manner which brings nineteenth-century thought into the closest proximity to contemporary phenomenological conceptions of the body.

3. Ravaisson and the Habituated Body

In 1834, at the age of 21, Ravaisson was the remarkably young winner of another competition organised by the *Académie des Sciences morales et politiques*, this time concerning the meaning and historical reception of Aristotle's *Metaphysics*. Four years later, in 1838 and after having gained first place in the *agrégation* – the state examination – in philosophy, he was awarded a doctorate on the basis of a principal thesis entitled *De l'habitude*, recently translated as *Of Habit* (Ravaisson 2008). In this essay and thus in returning to the question that had animated Biran's dissertation of 1802, Ravaisson presents an original conception of embodiment together with a philosophy of nature that develops his predecessor's insights. It seems unlikely, however, that Ravaisson had actually read any of the later Biran's explicit discussions of *le corps propre* given the limited number of his texts available at the time.[14]

It was remarked above that Biran had responded in 1802 to the question posed by the *Académie* about the influence or effects of habit on the 'faculties of thinking'. For Ravaisson, in contrast, the explicit task of philosophical reflection on habit is to 'aspire, beyond noting its apparent law, to learn its how and its why, to illuminate its genesis and finally to understand its cause' (Ravaisson 2008: 20). Ravaisson's philosophical ambitions in reflecting on habit, then, are further reaching than those of the younger Maine de Biran.

Ravaisson's account of the force or cause constituting motor habits constitutes the kernel of his text and leads to his particular conception of embodiment.

Ravaisson offers this account in attempting to show the inadequacy of both intellectualist and physiological – or 'idealist' and 'realist' – accounts of motor habit. On the one hand, the hypothesis that habitual action is guided by a succession of judgments or acts of will that occurs unbeknownst to ourselves neither explains nor corresponds to our experience, given that habitual acts appear to occur independently of conscious thought and the will.[15] On the other hand, Ravaisson refuses any solely physiological explanations of motor habit. Here it should be noted that the Swiss naturalist Charles Bonnet, whose work Biran had cited in the introduction to his 1802 text as a pivotal influence, had offered neurological hypotheses concerning acquired habitual dispositions as consisting in the changed state of the molecular state of nerve fibres (Bonnet 1760; Whitaker and Turgeon 2007). Ravaisson certainly admits that 'the increasing ease of the movements could perhaps by explained hypothetically by some change (which anatomy has not yet discovered) in the physical constitution of the organs' (Ravaisson 2008: 53). Thus he does not deny the possibility of organic changes accompanying motor habits. Although Bonnet's ideas were largely speculative, contemporary neurobiology has offered more concrete accounts of such changes (see: Hawkins and Kandel 1984; Squire and Kandel 1999). Yet habit properly so called consists not simply in a developed capacity to carry out an action, or in an increasing ease in carrying out that action, but rather in an active tendency or inclination to carry it out. It is this tendency, Ravaisson argues, that cannot be accounted for physiologically: 'no organic modification can explain the *tendency*, the inclination whose progress coincides with the decline of . . . effort' (Ravaisson 2008: 53). The claim is that habitual tendencies or inclinations are no mere third-person or mechanical phenomenon but are rather intrinsically related to the freedom of the will and to intelligence. Habitual movements do not, he argues, become the 'mechanical effect of an external impulse but rather the effect of an inclination that follows from the will' (Ravaisson 2008: 55). Even if a habitual action leaves the 'sphere of will and reflection, it does not leave that of intelligence' (Ravaisson 2008: 55), given that it still inclines toward a goal. In other words, habitual tendencies present themselves as a spontaneous force that is 'at once active and passive, equally opposed to mechanical Fatality and to reflective Freedom' (55).

Materialist explanations of habit, Ravaisson argues, do not take into account the specific nature of habitual tendencies. Yet there is another problem that such explanations face. Unless they adopt a form of 'eliminative' materialism, the problem of how the mind affects the body at all remains unaddressed. Yet the ontological presuppositions of this traditional mind–body problem are brought into question by Ravaisson's reflection on habit. Consideration of the specific nature of motor tendencies leads us to think beyond the conception of a mechanical, material body that stands *partes extra partes* opposed to a sphere of thought and freedom. For if movements are originally determined by a theoretically posited goal as an idea in the mind, then in their continuity or repetition

> [t]he *idea* becomes being, the very being of the movement and of the tendency that it determines. Habit becomes more and more a *substantial idea*. The obscure intelligence that through habit comes to replace reflection, this immediate intelligence where subject and object are confounded, is a *real* intuition, in which the real and the ideal, being and thought, are fused together. (Ravaisson 2008: 55)

This conception of a fusion of the ideal and the real is certainly influenced by Schelling's philosophy of nature and *Identitätsphilosophie*, for, even though *Of Habit* does not contain a direct reference to the German thinker, Ravaisson had previously translated some of his work.[16] Yet Ravaisson thinks this fusion according to an original conception of bodily being. In the acquisition of motive habits, ideal goals come to constitute the very nature, 'the very being', of the organs of the body. The progress of motive habits consists in a descent of thought and will into bodily being. The habituated body *is* not simply an extended, mechanical thing, since ideas and then habitual inclinations 'become more and more the form, the way of being, even the very being of these organs' (Ravaisson 2008: 55). What the body is, or, better, the *manner in which* the body exists comes to be transformed through the duration or repetition of a change.

It is in this way, then, that Ravaisson might seem to develop – without naming it as such – Biran's conception of *le corps propre* as distinct from the objective body. The habits incorporated in the body cannot be located in it from the outside in the way that a physiologist can isolate a tear in a muscle or a calcium growth in a joint. Thus the habituated body must be conceived as irreducible to the body objectified and viewed from the outside. Ravaisson's thinking, however, offers a particular response to the problem of the 'relation' of will to the lived body that we encountered in Biran's work. This relation is to be thought according to a conception of being and, in fact, according to an 'ontological difference'. There is a difference between being and beings, between that which exists and its existence, but this difference is not the difference between two separable entities and neither can it be accounted for as the successive relation of a cause and an effect.[17] For Ravaisson, the habituated body, rather than being caused to move by its tendencies, *is* those tendencies that animate it. But the verb 'being' here must be understood, precisely, in a verbal and active sense as an inclination that will tend to realise itself in action. This means that although the conscious self, as Biran had argued, might be able to distinguish itself from the lived body in voluntary action, that voluntary action will always contain habitual aspects. In these habitual aspects the self, in the more profound guise of habitual tendencies, does not distinguish itself from the body but rather 'relates' to it as being 'relates' to beings. With Ravaisson's thinking, then, it becomes more legitimate to argue, following Michel Henry, that there is an 'identity' of 'the being of the body and the ego'. But identity here must be understood as the identity in difference of being in beings, whilst the ego has to be understood first of all in terms of the unthematic and pre-conscious tendencies that animate the body.

Ravaisson's ontological approach, then, provides a means of conceiving what Biran had discussed as the relation of will to body. Yet *Of Habit* also presents a response to the second problem noted above in Biran's work, that concerning 'passive impressions'. Although Ravaisson also considers the consciousness in perception and action to be a matter of degree, the continuum he describes is not subtended by a primary stratum of sensations and affections independent of the will. For Ravaisson, nothing like pure passivity is given in experience because activity and passivity always work together as 'proportionately and inversely related' (Ravaisson 2008: 43). The more an experience is passive, the less it is active and vice versa. Just as there is no pure activity of movement or perception that would exist without a measure of passivity, there is no such thing as a purely passive impression: 'in every sensation . . . motility and perception have a role' (Ravaisson 2008: 43). It takes a very peculiar frame of mind to attempt to apprehend something like a pure sensation. Far from coming first, what is alleged to be mere passive sensation, it can be argued, is rather 'the last effect of consciousness' (Merleau-Ponty [1945] 1962: 37). Concomitantly, Ravaisson never adopts Biran's claim that a 'vital sense' and physiological system exist prior to and independently of the will and consciousness. He finds, again, a continuum in the place of his predecessor's dualism: although there is a difference between habit and instinct, between habit and the natural and vital operations of the body, the progress or development of habits – which we might take to be natural instincts if we did not know that we once acquired them – shows us that the 'difference is merely one of degree' and 'can always be lessened and reduced' (Ravaisson 2008: 43). If habit is a second nature, then this second nature cannot be clearly demarcated from our primary nature and is in fact grounded in the latter. On Ravaisson's account, the principle of biological life is intrinsically 'related' to consciousness, but this is not to say, in the manner of the eighteenth-century 'animism' traditionally ascribed to Georg Ernst Stahl, that all physiological functions are controlled by consciousness. Rather it is to say that there can be no absolute lines of demarcation between the will, habitual inclinations and natural, vital tendencies.[18]

I have contended that Ravaisson offers a viable response to both of the key problems with Biran's conception of embodiment. To be sure, it might be argued that Ravaisson's thinking is still the less developed and the less radical insofar as he does not clearly distinguish the lived, primary body from the secondary or objective body. Ravaisson's concern to synthesise eighteenth-century animist and vitalist philosophies by arguing that the force of habit is continuous with, on the one hand, a vital, non-mechanical principle of biological life and, on the other hand, the principle of conscious will leads him to integrate the embodied self into a general philosophy of nature instead of immediately distinguishing it from other things. Yet recognition of the distinction between the primary and secondary body is at least implicit in his thinking. This is particularly so when he acknowledges that the sciences may be able to discover material changes having occurred in the body as a result of the acquisition of habits. To use the fact of such changes to explain the habituated body in third-person, material and ultimately mechanical terms is to approach the body and human experience from the outside. In contrast the metaphysical force or principle of habit as constituting the veritable being and the original existence of the body can be known, as he claims, only through a mode of subjective experience or reflection – after Biran we might say 'apperception', but Ravaisson in *Of Habit* does not. In this 'the same being at once acts and see[s] the act', a being in which 'the author, the drama, the actor, the spectator are all one' (Ravaisson 2008: 39). Ravaisson offers, then, a solution to the two key problems of Biran's thinking, but the fact that a distinction between a primary and secondary body is only implied in *Of Habit* suggests that in 1838 he had not actually read his predecessor's explicit remarks concerning *le corps propre*.

4. Bergson's Dualism

Ravaisson's ideas were influential in the nineteenth century in France, particularly as a result of his becoming in 1863 the chairman of the committee charged with adjudicating and determining the programme of the *agrégation*. Generations of candidates to the examination, as Henri Bergson would later remark, learnt by heart the final pages of his 1867 *Rapport sur la philosophie en France au XIXème siècle* (Report on Philosophy in France in the nineteenth century), which outlined a spiritualist philosophy that would overcome the more materialist philosophies of the age. In Bergson's *Matter and Memory* of 1896, however, a text in which we find its author's most developed conception of embodiment, Bergson seems, at least at first glance, to be little influenced by Ravaisson's work.

This book affirms the reality of spirit, the reality of matter, and tries to determine the relation of the one to the other with a precise example, that of memory. It is therefore clearly dualistic. But, on the other hand, it envisages body and mind in such a manner that it hopes to attenuate, if not to suppress, the theoretical difficulties that the dualism has always caused. (Bergson [1896] 1991: 9)[19]

In opposition to the continuist ontological monism that Ravaisson proposes, Bergson professes to be a philosophical dualist and he will indeed discover 'differences of nature' between the mind and the body where his predecessor had found only differences of degree.

The dualism articulated in *Matter and Memory*, for all that, differs markedly from traditional Cartesian dualisms of mind and body. In the opening pages of the text's first chapter, Bergson presents a biological account of the 'role' of the body within what can be described as a realist and pragmatist theory of perception. The body, in opposition to things governed by constant physical laws, is conceived as a centre of action in the world, which, as a function of its capacity to introduce a delay in its reaction to stimuli and affections, can bring forth events that are unforeseeable, unpredictable and, that is to say, undetermined. Moreover, this body is not the producer or container of internal representations of the external world. In claiming that representational theories of perception are contradictory and mythical, Bergson urges us to recognise that the body is a centre of action which responds to the movements it receives from things with other movements (see Bergson [1896] 1991: 17–30; also Lawlor 2003: 11f.). Perception, on this account, is not a theoretical or intellectual inspection of representations of things but is instead conceived as a bodily response to the things themselves: 'the objects which surround my body reflect its possible action upon them' (Bergson [1896] 1991: 21).

The upshot of these arguments is that it is originally the body in itself, and not simply the body as the instrument of memory and mind, which acts and perceives the world. The limitations of this quite particular conception of the body become evident, however, when Bergson presents his distinction of two forms of memory in the second chapter of the text. On this account, the past 'survives under two distinct forms: first, in motor mechanisms; secondly, in independent recollections' and these two forms are at least 'theoretically independent' of each other (Bergson [1896] 1991: 78). The past can either be recollected as individual events that occurred at a particular moment in time and are therefore unrepeatable, or it can be taken up and repeated by means of the habitual actions of the body. In the process of learning a poem by heart, to use Bergson's celebrated example, it is possible to recollect any particular reading of the poem, whereas the result of the process is not a recollection in this sense at all; it is rather an acquired aptitude or motor habit. Bergson delineates, in fact, three essential moments or aspects of habit.[20] The acquisition of a habit requires not only the repetition of an act but also, in the beginning, an intellectual act of analysis or decomposition. I originally separate the words and syllables, so as to be able to learn them, before they are recomposed as a whole once I have developed the habit to pronounce them without hesitation, that is, once I have learnt the poem by heart. Yet the learning or acquisition of the habit through decomposition and repetition consists in the development of a motor mechanism, which is described as follows.

These movements, as they recur, contrive a mechanism for themselves, grow into a habit and determine in us attitudes which automatically follow our perception of things. This . . . is the main office of our nervous system. The afferent nerves bring to the brain a disturbance, which, after having intelligently chosen its path, transmits itself to motor mechanisms created by repetition. Thus is ensured the appropriate reaction, the correspondence to environment – adaptation, in a word – which is the general aim of life. (Bergson [1896] 1991: 84)

Although habits require a principle of intellect and freedom in their acquisition, it is argued that once acquired they can simply be explained in third-person and mechanistic terms.

Whilst Ravaisson challenges the philosophical dualism underlying the classically modern determination of habit as a 'mechanical' principle of action, Bergson reverts to it. This means that the idea of the living or biological body presented in the first chapter of *Matter and Memory* is not conceived as a personalised, 'lived', body, as a fulcrum of intelligent agency with its own relation to time and history. Ultimately, the body as Bergson conceives it has no relation to time beyond the present at all. The idea of a 'survival' of the past in the neurological changes of which habit consists is a 'verbal artifice' – as Merleau-Ponty argues when reading *Matter and Memory* in a lecture course given in 1948/49 (Merleau-Ponty 1997: 87). This artifice serves only to bind, after the fact and when Bergson addresses dualism as a problem in the final sections of his text, the two terms that he initially separates as different in nature: habit and memory, the body and the mind. Certainly, Bergson seems to be well aware of the problem insofar as he repeatedly wonders whether it is legitimate to describe habit as a form of memory at all. Yet if an acquired habit is purely a question of material and mechanical changes, one wonders why we could not also say that the past persists in things independent of the body; that other things – such as the piece of paper I have folded – have their own memory.[21] The fact that the changes in the body were originally occasioned as a result of effort and conscious decision in no way distinguishes, of course, my body from the folded piece of paper.[22]

The body-subject is still very much a body-object in Bergson's text, then, precisely because he accepts wholeheartedly objectifying and scientific explanations of the habituated body. On this basis we can understand the argument of Merleau-Ponty concerning the status of the body in *Matter and Memory*: 'The body never manages to be a subject – although Bergson tends to accord this status to it – for if the body was subject, the subject would be the body and this is what Bergson wants to avoid at all costs' (Merleau-Ponty 1997: 87). As we have seen, Bergson tends to accord the status of subject to the body insofar as it is originally the body, he argues, that acts and perceives the world. Yet, in the end, Bergson wants to avoid any assertion of the body as a genuine subject because of his basic dualist position. His biological, pragmatist and realist conception of the living body is accompanied by an idealism of the mind or spirit, according to which memory constitutes the very essence of the self and its character and thus of 'subjectivity'.

To be sure, in the third chapter of *Matter and Memory* Bergson will attempt to show how the body and mind work together in experience by arguing that the difference between the 'two forms of memory', although a difference in kind or nature, is merely a functional difference.

> Since they are not two separated things, since the first is only, as we have said, the pointed end, ever moving, inserted by the second in the shifting plane of experience, it is natural that the two functions should lend each other a mutual support. So, on the one hand, memory offers to the sensori-motor mechanism all the recollections capable of guiding them in their task and of giving to the motor reaction the direction suggested by the lessons of experience . . . But, on the other hand, the sensori-motor apparatus furnish to ineffective, that is unconscious, memories, the means of taking on body, of materialising themselves, in short of becoming present. (Bergson [1896] 1991: 152)

In perception not only does memory guide the motor mechanisms or 'motor schema' of recognition but also these mechanisms, from the opposite perspective, allow for memory to be incorporated into experience. This incorporation is held to occur, in a manner clearly influenced by Ravaisson's thinking, according to a continuous scale that descends from the absolute, ultimately unconscious singularity of pure memory to the increasing generality of the memory image and then to concrete perception.

This argument concerning the functional unity of matter and memory in experience leads to Bergson's infamously difficult attempt, in the final sections of the text, to posit a monistic principle underlying and uniting the two principles that he has separated.[23] This principle is a conception of time as *duration*. Because the briefest slice of perceptual experience that we might designate with the word 'now' is always and already a stretch of time and thus always and already implies a temporal synthesis, there is, in the end, no such thing as pure perception. Bergson argues, in fact, that there is a temporal principle of synthesis uniting both perception and memory. It is not possible to discuss here the viability and full significance of this attempt to attenuate, in Bergson's own words, the 'theoretical difficulties' that dualism in general has caused. Suffice it here to say that this response to the problem of dualism in no way distinguishes the human body from other worldly objects occupying a minimal slice of duration. Once again, and although the first chapter of *Matter and Memory* might seem to accord a subjective status to the body as a living body, the specific ontological status of the lived body remains undisclosed.

5. Conclusion

As has become clear, the history of conceptions of embodiment in the nineteenth-century French 'spiritualist' tradition amounts to something quite different from a linear or progressive development. Ravaisson does not explicitly discuss Biran's idea of *le corps propre* and Bergson, towards the end of the century, seems unconcerned with either of his predecessors' conceptions of the body. However, I hope to have clarified a point that twentieth-century thinkers such as Michel Henry and Merleau-Ponty seem not to have acknowledged: Ravaisson offers compelling responses to the two fundamental problems of his predecessor's conception of the body. Thus his work can be understood to represent the pinnacle of nineteenth-century reflection on embodiment and the problem of mind–body dualism.

To reinforce this claim, I want to conclude by addressing an outstanding issue that was initially raised concerning Biran, namely, the problem of intellectualism. It might be asked: is there not an underlying intellectualism and idealism that unites the conceptions of embodiment offered by Biran, Ravaisson and Bergson? For do not all three thinkers conceive the acquisition of bodily, motor habits as necessarily guided in the first instance by reflective thought? It is on this point that Merleau-Ponty explicitly criticises Bergson's account of the acquisition of habit (see Merleau-Ponty [1942] 1963: 65 and [1945] 1962: 142; see also Marin 2004). The progress of habit does not – or at least does not necessarily – consist of acts learnt by intellectual decomposition and analysis coming by means of repetition to occur without any operation of the understanding. For 'it is the body which "catches" and "comprehends" movement: the acquisition of a habit is indeed the grasping of a significance, but it is the motor grasping of a motor significance' (Merleau-Ponty [1945] 1962: 143). The organist accustoming herself to an unfamiliar instrument, for example, does not necessarily proceed by means of intellectual analysis, by means of the intellectual decomposition and re-composition that Bergson describes. Rather she adjusts her body and lets her body adjust itself to the new arrangement of stops and pedals. The acquisition of habit is thus a 'rearrangement and renewal of the corporeal schema' (Merleau-Ponty 1962:

143) which can occur without the mediation of reflective thought. There is certainly intelligence in the acquisition of habit, but this is neither necessarily nor primarily the intelligence of a reflective consciousness.

If it is supposed, as we have seen Ravaisson and Bergson explicitly affirm, that the progress of habit begins from ideas in the mind, then we risk failing to recognise the primary and cognitive corporeality that Merleau-Ponty attempts to reveal. Ravaisson may appear to offer the sort of intellectualist account in question here when he describes the acquisition of habit as the incorporation of ideas. Yet it is precisely because he offers something other than the mechanistic physiology involved in Bergson's thinking that the essay of 1838 does not preclude the idea that habits can be acquired prior to the intervention of reflective thought. Ravaisson does not state that the acquisition of habit must proceed from reflective thought, just as Merleau-Ponty does not state that it cannot do so. Crucially, Ravaisson will argue that voluntary action and effort is always preceded by an 'effortless antecedent tendency' (Ravaisson 2008: 37).[24] The progress of habit can be pictured as descending a continuous scale underlying the opposition of mind and matter, but this descent shows us that prior to the advent of explicit consciousness, and all the way from the most elementary instinctive movements, an intelligent but not yet reflective tendency or desire was at work. Hence the intelligent but not reflective or explicitly conscious desire that is manifest in habit is not only post-reflective, as it might seem to be on the basis of certain passages of Ravaisson's text, but also pre-reflective. The idea of a pre-reflective consciousness, then, is not foreign to Ravaisson's thought, even if it will be developed much more deliberately according to ideas of an 'operative intentionality' or 'cognitive corporeality' within the twentieth-century phenomenological movement.[25]

Notes

1. Merleau-Ponty's appropriation of Biran's idea of *le corps propre* is seldom acknowledged, but see Engel 2008.
2. All translations are the author's own unless otherwise stated.
3. See Moore 1970: 188–90, Appendix 1, on the extent and fate of Biran's manuscripts.
4. On the Ideological school and its influence on Maine de Biran see Copleston [1975] 1999: 19–21; Truman 1904.
5. I refer directly only to the most recent French edition of the text, not to the incomplete English translation.
6. Biran cites Fichte and Schelling from the French translations in Dégérando 1804.
7. This critique of Hume deserves increased attention and I develop here F. C. T. Moore's brief presentation of it: Moore 1970: 85–6.
8. Biran responds to Hume's claim concerning action as a 'matter' of experience thus: 'That this is a fact is enough for us: but is it a fact of experience of the same nature as the other operations of an external nature? I deny the equivalence. It is precisely this that seems to me to be the source of the illusions that give such heart to the sceptics' (Maine de Biran 1995: 119).
9. On the basis of responding to these three points of Hume's argument, Biran argues that when Hume concludes that 'our idea of power is not copied from any sentiment or consciousness of power within ourselves, when we give rise to animal motion, or apply our limbs to their proper use and office' (Maine de Biran 1995: 67) he is simply denying an evident fact. Ultimately, such a denial cannot be met with an argument, as Biran will write in the *Essai sur les fondements de la psychologie*: 'What should we say to someone who denies a visible or tangible fact? Perhaps nothing. We should only make him see or touch what he denies and if he persists in saying that his senses lead him into error, all discussion will end there' (Maine de Biran 2001: 165). Descartes, it should be noted, had at least recognised that we do have the feeling of such causal power, even

though he claims that we are unable to understand how the mind can affect the body. Hume's refusal to acknowledge this feeling means, from Biran's perspective, that his scepticism is simply extravagant and that the philosophical presuppositions that underlie it are insufficiently empirical, insufficiently attentive to the modality of our own experience.

10. In his 1823 *Considérations sur les principes d'une division des faits psychologiques et physiologiques* (Considerations on the Principles of a Division of Psychological and Physiolological Facts), Biran discusses the theses of the German physiologist Johann Christian Reil concerning 'coenaesthesis', understood as a form of internal sensory awareness of the body that is proper to living beings. Yet according to Biran's concern for a correct division between the physiological and the psychological, what Reil characterises as coenaesthesis is to be distinguished from voluntary awareness and thus from awareness of *le corps propre*. Biran's conception of the spatiality of the lived body, in other words, is not simply a doctrine of coenaesthesis even though it is related to the latter. See, on this point, Maine de Biran 1990: 129–35.

11. Moore highlights the importance of Biran's distinction between the experience of bodily movement and the 'symbolic' interpretation of that movement by the physiologist. But – without reference either to Biran's explicit discussions of *le corps propre* or their interpretation by Michel Henry in 1965 – Moore makes remarkably little of this distinction, considering it 'lamentably obscure' (Moore 1970: 94–8).

12. If intellectualism is defined as a position according to which 'consciousness does not admit of degree' (Merleau-Ponty [1945] 1962: 121–2), then Biran is not an intellectualist.

13. After the *Essai* Biran will resort to the hypothesis of a non-phenomenal substantial self in response to difficulties about the continued existence of the soul when it is not actively willing. This allows us to understand Merleau-Ponty's further claim concerning the final form of Biran's thinking: that he 'poses once again, and in terms that are just as difficult, the traditional problem of the soul and body; he re-establishes the absolute soul in the face of the absolute body: we find ourselves back at the starting point' (Merleau-Ponty 1997: 78).

14. *Of Habit* is unhelpful in relation to what exactly Ravaisson had read, since in it he refers only to Biran's 1802 dissertation by name and otherwise uses '*passim*' to refer to the basic themes of Biran's thinking as a whole. The only readily available works by Biran in 1838 were the 1802 habit dissertation, the 1817 *Examen des leçons de philosophie de M. Laromiguière*, the 1819 *Exposition de la doctrine de Leibniz*, and the 1821/22 *Nouvelles considérations sur les rapports du physique et du moral chez l'homme* (New Considerations on the Relations of the Physical and Psychological in Man) edited by Victor Cousin, the most prominent French philosopher of the time, in 1834. In none of these texts is there an explicit discussion of *le corps propre*. It is nevertheless not impossible that Ravaisson read Biran's work on this question within the manuscripts that Cousin, to whom Ravaisson in the mid-1830s was close, had in his possession and published in four volumes in 1841. On this point see Blondel 1999.

15. Biran had already offered this critique of intellectualist conceptions of habit in a footnote added to the section of his text entitled 'The Influence of Habit on Perception' (a footnote not contained in the English translation); see Maine de Biran 1987: 179. This footnote also suggests Biran was not wholly convinced by the neurological explanation of habit articulated by Charles Bonnet (see below).

16. On Ravaisson's relation to Schelling see the Editors' Introduction to Ravaisson 2008: 1–21.

17. For Martin Heidegger's reflections on the idea of an 'ontological difference' see, for example, Heidegger 1999: §266, 327–8.

18. Ravaisson disagrees with this traditional reading of Stahl's animism and claims that 'the letter and the spirit' (Ravaisson 2008: 122, n. 53) of his doctrine is rather that there is a graduated principle of consciousness which in its different modalities underlies all bodily functions. In arguing, therefore, that the principle of habit is continuous with the principle of biological life and that of conscious will, Ravaisson claims to present a position close to that of Stahl.

19. These are the first lines of the 1911 preface to the text's seventh edition, a preface originally written for its first English translation.

20. See Bergson ([1896] 1991: 80) on the learning of a poem: 'Like a habit it is acquired by the repetition of the same effort. Like a habit, it demands first a decomposition and then a

re-composition of the whole action. Lastly, like every habitual bodily exercise, it is stored up in a mechanism.'

21. Our treatment of habit sheds light on Merleau-Ponty's argument that Bergson makes of subjectivity a simple function of representation: he conserves the dichotomy of movement 'in the third person and the subject' (Merleau-Ponty 1997: 87). It also allows us to see the limitations of claims (see Mullarkey 1994: 346) that *Matter and Memory* offers us a veritable 'phenomenology of the body' and that the 'Bergsonian body is a true body-subject with its own desires'.

22. If habit is a form of memory, if the body has a relation to time beyond the present, a principle of the acquisition of habit, then a power synthesising the past, present and future must be rooted within the body itself. Ravaisson offers a hint of such a temporal conception of active and intelligent habitual dispositions when he writes that 'habit remains for a change which either is no longer or is not yet; it remains for a possible change' (Ravaisson 2008: 25) and that habit comes to 'anticipate [*prévient*]' (51), but not simply in the sense of a mechanical precedence, the conscious activity of the will. So it is no surprise that when Gilles Deleuze in *Difference and Repetition* (Deleuze 1994: 70–2) presents habituation as a 'first synthesis of time' there is no direct reference to Bergson's own conception of habit. The lack of reference to Ravaisson is more surprising.

23. As Vladimir Jankélévitch – perhaps the greatest of Bergson commentators – notes, the pages of *Matter and Memory* in which Bergson aims to overcome the dualism that the text has previously established are 'among the most obscure and embarrassing of his entire work' (Jankélévitch [1930] 1999: 116).

24. This is, in fact, Ravaisson's response to a problem with which Biran often and already in 1802 grapples: resistance and will both presuppose each other, a fact which presents a vicious circle when attempting to account for how voluntary perception arises on the basis of sensation. As a way out of this circle, Biran argued that sensation already possesses a form of 'instinct', which, although non-voluntary, encounters resistance and that it is out of this instinctive effort that the will arises. This hypothesis is problematic, as Dominique Janicaud notes, in that it 'undermines the specificity of effort' within Biran's analysis (Janicaud [1969] 1997: 26). In contrast, Ravaisson argues that there is neither will nor resistance in pre-reflective desire, but that the will arises when this effortless tendency meets resistance. On the problem in Biran's texts, see Moore 1970: 90–4.

25. Merleau-Ponty does not discuss *Of Habit* in any of his published texts or lectures, not even in his course on Maine de Biran and Bergson – both authors were on the programme of the *agrégation* in philosophy – in 1948–9. Janicaud (1997: 11) relates that Merleau-Ponty had claimed at his thesis defence that Ravaisson was of interest only as a precursor of Bergson. But Ravaisson's importance was recorded soon afterwards by another French philosopher concerned with habit and the body, Paul Ricoeur. He writes in his *Freedom and Nature: The Voluntary and Involuntary* that the 'intuitions of that great philosopher are the source of many of the reflections in this book' (Ricoeur [1950] 1966: 286).

References

Bergson, Henri [1915] (1972), *Mélanges*, Paris: Presses Universitaires de France.
Bergson, Henri [1896] (1991), *Matter and Memory*, trans. N. M. Paul and W. S. Palmer, New York: Zone.
Blondel, E. (1999), 'Ravaisson lecteur de Maine de Biran', in Jean-Michel Le Lannou (ed.), *Ravaisson*, Paris: Kimé, pp. 15–32.
Bonnet, Charles (1760), *Essai analytique sur les facultés de l'âme*, Copenhagen: Philibert.
Copleston, Frederick [1975] (1999), *A History of Philosophy, Vol. 9: Nineteenth and Twentieth Century French Philosophy*, London: Continuum.
Dégérando, Joseph Marie (1804), *Histoire comparée des systèmes de philosophie*, Paris.
Deleuze, Gilles (1994), *Difference and Repetition*, trans. Paul Patton, London: Athlone.
Derrida, Jacques (2005), *On Touching – Jean-Luc Nancy*, trans. Christine Irizarry, Stanford, CA: Stanford University Press.

Engel, Pascal (2008), 'Psychology and metaphysics from Maine de Biran to Bergson', in Sara Heinämaa and Martina Reuters (eds), *Psychology and Philosophy: Inquiries into the Soul from Late Scholasticism to Contemporary Thought*, Amsterdam: Springer, pp. 235–46.

Gouhier, Henri (1947), *Les conversions de Maine de Biran*, Paris: Vrin.

Hawkins, Robert D., and Eric R. Kandel (1984), 'Steps toward a cell-biological alphabet for elementary forms of learning', in Gary Lynch et al. (eds), *Neurobiology of Learning and Memory*, New York: Guilford Press, pp. 65–77.

Heidegger, Martin (1999), *Contributions to Philosophy*, trans. Parvis Emad and Kenneth Maly, Bloomington: Indiana University Press.

Henry, Michel (1965), *Philosophie et phenomenology du corps: Essai sur l'ontologie biranienne*, Paris: Presses Universitaires de France.

Hume, David [1748] (1975), *Enquiries Concerning Human Understanding*, ed. L. A. Selby-Bigge and P. H. Nidditch, Oxford: Oxford University Press.

Janicaud, Dominique (1997), *Ravaisson et la métaphysique: Une généalogie du spiritualisme français*, Paris: Vrin.

Jankélévitch, Vladimir [1930] (1999), *Henri Bergson*, Paris: Presses Universitaires de France.

Lalande, André (1993), *Vocabulaire technique et critique de la philosophie*, 3rd edn, Paris: Quadrige.

Lawlor, Leonard (2003), *The Challenge of Bergsonism*, London: Continuum.

Maine de Biran, Pierre (1970), *The Influence of Habit on the Faculty of Thinking*, trans. Margaret D. Boehm, Westport, CT: Greenwood Press.

Maine de Biran, Pierre (1987), *Oeuvres* vol. II, *Influence de l'habitude sur la faculté de penser*, ed. François Azouvi, Paris: Vrin.

Maine de Biran, Pierre (1988), *Oeuvres* vol. III, *Mémoire sur la décomposition de la pensée*, ed. François Azouvi, Paris: Vrin.

Maine de Biran, Pierre (1990), *Oeuvres* vol. IX, *Nouvelles considérations sur les rapports du physique et du moral de l'homme*, ed. Bernard Baertschi, Paris: Vrin.

Maine de Biran, Pierre (1995), *Oeuvres* vol. IV, *De l'aperception immédiate*, ed. Ives Radrizzani, Paris: Vrin.

Maine de Biran, Pierre (2001), *Oeuvres* vol. VII, *Essai sur les fondements de la psychologie*, ed. F. C. T. Moore, Paris: Vrin.

Marin, C. (2004), 'L'être et l'habitude dans la philosophie française contemporaine', *Alter* 12: 149–72.

Merleau-Ponty, Maurice [1945] (1962), *Phenomenology of Perception*, trans. Colin Smith, London: Routledge.

Merleau-Ponty, Maurice [1942] (1963), *The Structure of Behaviour*, trans. A. L. Fisher, Boston: Beacon Press.

Merleau-Ponty, Maurice (1997), *L'union de l'âme et du corps chez Malebranche, Biran et Bergson*, Paris: Vrin.

Moore, F. C. T. (1970), *The Psychology of Maine de Biran*, Cambridge: Cambridge University Press.

Mullarkey, John (1994), 'Duplicity of the flesh: Bergson and current philosophy of the body', *Philosophy Today* 38 (3): 339–55.

Ravaisson, Félix (2008), *Of Habit*, ed. Clare Carlisle and Mark Sinclair, London: Continuum.

Ricoeur, Paul [1950] (1966), *Freedom and Nature: The Voluntary and Involuntary*, Evanston, IL: Northwestern University Press.

Squire, Larry R., and Eric R. Kandel (1999), *Memory: From Mind to Molecules*, New York: Scientific American Library.

Truman, Nathan (1904), *Maine de Biran's Psychology of the Will*, London: Macmillan.

Whitaker, Harry A. and Yves Turgeon (2007), 'Charles Bonnet's neurophilosophy', in Harry Whitaker et al. (eds), *Brain, Mind and Medicine: Essays in 18th-Century Neuroscience*, New York: Springer, pp. 191–200.

11

The Unconscious in the German Philosophy and Psychology of the Nineteenth Century

Günter Gödde
Translated from the German by Ciaran Cronin

1. Introduction

The adjective 'unconscious' designates a quality that can be found in psychical processes such as imagining, remembering, thinking, feeling, desiring, wishing and acting. The processes which exhibit this quality differ from those with the quality 'conscious' in that the former are not present in the current field of consciousness but nevertheless remain psychologically effective, indeed, often far more so than the processes which have the quality of being conscious. The substantive, the 'unconscious', expresses the fact that psychological phenomena are not confined in principle to conscious experiences but are profoundly shaped by unconscious forces. In psychoanalysis, this concept also designates a region of mental life (in contrast to the preconscious and the conscious) or a system with specific functions and regularities (primary process, pleasure principle).

For many years Sigmund Freud was acclaimed as the discoverer of the unconscious, without acknowledgement that his doctrine is rooted in a philosophical tradition which can be described as the 'philosophy of the unconscious'. Freud studied a range of clinical conceptions concerning the effects of unconscious psychological processes (those of Jean-Martin Charcot, Hippolyte Bernheim, Pierre Janet and Josef Breuer) before presenting a first systematic exposition of his discoveries concerning the unconscious dynamics of 'defence', 'repression' and 'resistance' in *Studies in Hysteria* of 1895, which he co-authored with Breuer (Freud and Breuer [1895] 2004). In *The Interpretation of Dreams* of 1900 he went on to introduce the concept of the unconscious as a central concept in psychoanalysis and later modified it in 'The Ego and the Id' of 1923.

A paradigm shift in the dominant view of the history of the idea of the unconscious was precipitated only by Henry Ellenberger's 1970 book *The Discovery of the Unconscious* (Ellenberger [1970] 1985). Ellenberger's achievement consisted in resituating Freud's notion of the unconscious 'within its historical context, in identifying precursors and offering a wide-ranging, well-documented description of the intellectual space within which psychoanalysis arose' (Schröter 2006: 218). Following Ellenberger, a whole series of important works have appeared which forge links between psychoanalysis and the philosophical tradition of the unconscious. Two postdoctoral theses merit special mention in this connection, namely, Odo Marquard's *Transzendentaler Idealismus, Romantische Naturphilosophie, Psychoanalyse* (1987) and Reinhard Gasser's *Nietzsche und Freud* (1997). Also highly recommended are the survey article by Mai Wegener (2005a) and the volumes edited by Michael Buchholz and Günter Gödde (2005a) and by Angus Nicholls and Martin Liebscher (2010). In my own book, *Traditionslinien des 'Unbewußten': Schopenhauer, Nietzsche, Freud* (Gödde [1999] 2009), I distinguish three lines of development in the philosophy of the unconscious in the opening three chapters, before going on to establish connections to Freud and post-Freudian psychoanalysis, including the most recent developments.

2. The Origins of the Conception of the Unconscious in the Enlightenment

The opposed conceptions of consciousness and the unconscious originated in the eighteenth-century Enlightenment era. Descartes, who subordinated all mental processes to consciousness in his *Discours de la méthode* of 1637, is regarded as the founder of the philosophy of consciousness. To body or material substance he ascribed just the two properties of spatial extension and movement (*res extensa*). 'It is nature that acts' in the operations of these machines 'according to the dispositions of their organs – just as we see that a clock composed exclusively of wheels and springs can count the hours and measure the time more accurately than we can with all our carefulness' (Descartes [1637] 1998: 33). Thus it was only consistent that he made thought the defining criterion of the mind and described the latter as *res cogitans*. Descartes is the source of the statement '*Anima semper cogitans*' ('the mind is always thinking'). The mind is always in a thinking and hence a conscious state. This rational model of the mind left no room for an unconscious activity of feeling, imagining and thinking. It is hardly surprising that Descartes's mind–body dualism led to mechanistic and 'soulless' anthropologies such as La Mettrie's famous *L'homme machine* (Machine Man) of 1747.

Only as a result of this separation of mind from body did the problem arise of how to classify mental processes which exist without our being immediately aware of them. Leibniz, who developed his famous doctrine of the '*petites perceptions*' in his *New Essays on Human Understanding* of 1704 and 1765, became Descartes's most prominent opponent. Leibniz's doctrine in the *Monadology* of 1720 (Leibniz 1965) can be regarded as his starting point. With this doctrine he postulates that the whole of the universe is animate and that there is a hierarchy of simple monads extending from animal souls and human psychological monads up to God as the absolute monad. For Leibniz the basic mental capacities of the monads are the 'small inconspicuous perceptions' which are located at the margins of consciousness, as it were, or do not enter consciousness at all. At any moment there are a countless number of such 'inconspicuous perceptions' of which we are unaware because they are 'either too minute and too numerous, or else too unvarying . . . But when they are combined with others they do nevertheless have their effect and make themselves felt, at least confusedly, within the whole' (Leibniz [1704/1765] 1996: 53). Every cognition, however unclear and obscure it may be, has a multiplicity of effects on perception, thought, taste and habits and constitutes a component of every clear conscious perception. This can be illustrated, for instance, by the roaring of the sea and the murmuring of crowds. Inconspicuous perceptions can also leave residues of past mental states in memory or can find expression in diffuse states of indecision and doubt or can spur the will to counteract mental irritations. With his doctrine of the '*petites perceptions*', Leibniz paved the way for a tradition which can be described as that of the *cognitive* unconscious (see Pongratz 1984: 188–96).

Johann Friedrich Herbart's philosophy and psychology is situated within this tradition. In express opposition to idealist philosophy and psychology, Herbart pursued the project of grounding a psychology on 'realist metaphysics'. Although he remained beholden to metaphysics, he founded an 'explanatory psychology' which tried to comprehend the regularities of mental life with the methods of natural science. His psychology of representation and association has a mechanistic and dynamic character and is devoted to investigating the facts which are given in consciousness. However, it already points in a rudimentary way towards a theory of the unconscious.

Herbart employs 'representation' (or 'idea': Vorstellung) as a central concept to define the contents of experience which are given in consciousness. Representations are understood as particular elements of mental life which can have varying destinies. This raises in particular the question of the regularities exhibited by the processes through which representations become associations and undergo change. For Herbart, representations are in constant motion. They can attract and repel each other, sink below the 'threshold of consciousness' or re-enter consciousness. Only because they 'resist' each other – that is, become caught up in a relation of pressure and counterpressure – do they become forces in the dynamic sense with specific, and in principle measurable, magnitudes. Herbart distinguishes in connection with Leibniz and Kant between clear representations – that is, those which are located above the threshold of consciousness – and obscure representations whose 'level of clarity' is partially reduced ('inhibited') or diminishes to nothing ('obscured'). He explicitly states that weaker representations can be 'suppressed' (verdrängt) below the threshold of consciousness by stronger representations (see Herbart [1816/34] 2008: 9–14).

The concept of the threshold of consciousness, which at first sight seems to be meant only as a spatial metaphor, is for Herbart a mathematically measurable factor within his realistic psychology. In this connection he distinguishes between a 'static' threshold, in which a representation, even though it is no longer in consciousness, can nevertheless re-enter consciousness without encountering major resistance, as it were, and a 'mechanical' threshold, in which a representation is completely suppressed from consciousness for a certain time, but nevertheless strives with all its force to return to consciousness, or at least to exercise an indirect influence on consciousness (14). In this way Herbart developed a doctrine of the 'statics and mechanics of representations' which studies changes in degrees of clarity and intensity as representations unfold.

The representations which are suppressed below the mechanical threshold raise the more far-reaching question of the psychological reality of what is hidden but nevertheless continues to exercise psychical effects. This question is often addressed by Herbart and his successors. Since the clear representations are only islands in the ocean of obscure representations, they regarded it as worthwhile to explain the dynamics of the obscure representations and their reproducibility (Herbart [1824] 1886: 340–1; Lindner [1873] 1889: 81). However, they thought that the connection between what is perceptible and what is imperceptible could only be inferred.

Among Herbart's successors, Gustav Theodor Fechner more than anyone else took up Herbart's constructions and gave them an empirical grounding within the framework of his psychophysics (see Heidelberger 2004; Wegener 2005b). This extremely creative research-er operated at the intersection of Romantic philosophy of nature and exact science. Whereas Herbart's attention remained focused on the more-or-less conscious representa-tions, Fechner turned to the 'unconscious sensations' which lie beyond the 'psychophysical threshold'. According to Fechner, as long as stimuli remain below the psychophysical threshold, the corresponding sensations are unconscious, yet nevertheless effective. Thus the concept of the psychophysical threshold already acquires central importance, as Fechner writes in his major work Elemente der Psychophysik, because it provides a secure foundation for the concept of the unconscious as such. Psychology cannot abstract from unconscious sensations and ideas [*Vorstellungen*] . . . Sensations, ideas, have, of course, *ceased actually to exist* in the state of unconsciousness, insofar as we consider them apart from their substructure. Nevertheless, something persists within us, i.e. the psychophysical activity of which they are a function and which makes possible the re-appearance of sensation. (Fechner [1868] 1966; quoted from Brentano [1874] 1995: 104n.)

In this context we should also mention the theory of '*unconscious inferences*' which has a long prehistory in philosophy. Hermann von Helmholtz placed it at the centre of his theory of perception. Wilhelm Wundt, too, defended this theory in his *Beiträgen zur Theorie der Sinneswahrnehmung* (Contributions to the Theory of Perception) of 1862, although he later abandoned it.

From the assumption of unconscious cognitive states, in the sense of unconscious ideas, perceptions, thoughts, inferences and the like, it was then but a short step to anthropological and psychological concepts dealing with unconscious strivings, drives, intentions, actions, as well as with unconscious memories, motives, feelings, emotions, conflicts and so forth. The basic assumption that unconscious psychical processes exist and are capable of exercising profound effects played a key role in this theoretical development. From here one can forge a link to contemporary cognitive psychology (see Mertens 2005).

3. From the 'Vital Power' to the Vital Unconscious in Romanticism

Whereas the tradition of the cognitive unconscious developed *within* the Enlightenment, a second tradition evolved out of a reaction *against* the Enlightenment. Underlying this second tradition was the fear that the Enlightenment would ossify into a shallow rationalism unless more attention was paid to the emotional, the natural, the corporeal, the imaginative and the irrational. This alternative tradition had its origins in the *Sturm und Drang* or pre-Romantic era. Amongst its first representatives were J. G. Hamann, Herder and the younger Goethe.

Two quotations can serve to illustrate Goethe's statements concerning the unconscious: 'Man cannot persist long in a conscious state, he must throw himself back into the Unconscious, for his roots live there' (quoted from Eysenck 1995: 108). Here the unconscious features as a refuge, as a place of inner peace and of self-recollection. Another passage deals, as so often with Goethe, with the creative forces of the unconscious:

no great thought which bears fruit and has results, is in the power of any one . . . Man must consider them as an unexpected gift from above . . . They are akin to the demonic, which overwhelms him and does what it pleases and to which he unconsciously resigns himself, whilst he believes he is acting from his own impulse. (Goethe [1848] 2005: 309–10; translation amended)

This second tradition of thinking about the unconscious had its heyday in the Romantic philosophy of nature and in Romantic medicine. The concept of 'vital power' or 'life force' (*Lebenskraft*) can be regarded as an essential precursor of the Romantic idea of the unconscious (see Goldmann 2005). Within two decades of its introduction by Friedrich Casimir Medicus (1774), the concept of vital power became a central *topos* of the medical anthropology of the era. As the German physician Christoph Wilhelm Hufeland writes in his posthumously published autobiography, at the time he and a whole range of other doctors were striving 'to bring the whole of medicine under a single principle of life or of the vital power and thereby to establish unity in the various parts of the same' (Hufeland 1937: 83). Vital power was understood – in contrast to Descartes and to all attempts to explain the internal, for the most part unconscious, movements of life in mechanistic terms – as a *third substance* in addition to the thinking mind and matter. It was regarded as the 'source of all of the movements' in the organic domain – for example, metabolic processes, digestion, secretion, blood formation, pulse and circulation – which take place without the influence of the mind. Hufeland explicitly stated that 'vital power' exists 'without the power of thought [*Denkkraft*] (mind)'. The thinking mind is connected with the vital power only by the fact that

> it [the thinking mind] can influence, guide, direct and determine it [that is, the vital power], though only in accordance with certain laws and limits, for there exist organs whose vital power is not subject to its influence. Thus mind is not vital power itself, but should be viewed as one of the most powerful and most direct stimuli acting upon it. (Hufeland 1795: 36–7)

For Hufeland, the vital power is

> one of the most general, the most incomprehensible and the most powerful of all the powers of nature. It fills and gives motion to everything; and, in all probability, is the grand source from which all the other powers of the physical, or at least the organized, world proceed. It is that which produces, supports and renews everything . . . In short, it is this which, purified and exalted by a more perfect organization, kindles up the powers of thought and of the soul; and which gives to rational beings, together with life, the sensation and enjoyment of it. (Hufeland [1797] 2003: 35)

The concept of the unconscious itself first appears in 1800 in Schelling's *System of Transcendental Idealism* (Schelling 1978). In the Schelling school, the concept of the unconscious was employed primarily in connection with the dark side of nature and of the mind – mental illnesses, madness, dreams, genius and parapsychological phenomena.

In his work *Psyche* of 1846, the late Romantic Carl Gustav Carus developed a first psychology of the unconscious. He distinguished three regions of mental life: the 'absolute' unconscious, understood as a delimited domain which is intimately related to the body, constituted for him the central region; he viewed the 'relative' unconscious as the region of what has temporarily become unconscious but can at any time return to consciousness; and consciousness for him was synonymous with feeling, cognition and action.

Carus remained beholden to the notion of the vital power, but he subordinated it to his postulated unity of the 'psyche'. Amongst the essential characteristics of the unconscious he counted 'tirelessness': in the unconscious there is no pausing, interrupting, or stopping. A second feature can be termed 'immediacy': what takes place in the unconscious has no need of 'tedious study, [needs] no practice to achieve dexterity': 'all is done and achieved easily and immediately as required by the nature of a particular being' (Carus [1846] 1989: 57). A further feature is the 'inexhaustible health' of the unconscious (70). Carus speaks of the 'healing power of nature'. One can speak in connection with Carus of an essential polarity between the conscious and the unconscious, but one that contrasts sharply with the stark dualism to be encountered in Schopenhauer, Nietzsche and Freud – although it should be noted that, in his definition of the unconscious, Carus anticipated some of the features of the Freudian unconscious. Since the term 'the unconscious' was henceforth accorded central importance in psychological life, one can speak of a replacement or appropriation of the vital power by the unconscious (see Goldmann 2005). This second line of tradition can be termed that of the *Romantic-vital* unconscious.

4. The Turn Towards the Primacy of the 'Unconscious Will' in the Post-idealist Period

A third tradition is represented by Schopenhauer with his major work *The World As Will and Representation* (Schopenhauer [1818/1844] 1966), by Eduard von Hartmann with his *Philosophy of the Unconscious* (Hartmann [1868] 2001) and by Nietzsche with his *Thus Spoke Zarathustra* ([1883–5] 1961) and other works. These works lead to the breakthrough of the idea of human beings' dangerous instinctual nature (*Triebnatur*) and thus also of that of 'evil', which was largely tabooed in Romanticism. The – philosophical – problem which these works shared concerned the dialectics of the power/powerlessness relation between the ego (in the sense of reason, intellect, consciousness) and the unconscious (in the sense of instinctual nature, will, id).

Schelling, amongst others, had already paved the way for greater attention to be devoted to the compulsive and irrational sides of human nature. In his work on freedom of 1809 (Schelling 2006), he developed a fundamentally new conception of nature – as compulsion, drive, desire and addiction – and he called this irrational power 'will', in stark contradiction to the traditional understanding of the will as a rational faculty. Schelling's successors, Schopenhauer and Nietzsche, took his redefinition of the will as their starting point. They no longer accepted the enchanted conception of nature of Romanticism, but treated it instead as a dangerous instinctual nature. Thus at the beginning of the nineteenth century there was, in Odo Marquard's words, a new 'turn towards reality'. Nature lost 'the attributes of harmony, egohood and purposiveness, its rational-historical and intact, organic character; it is stripped of its aesthetic properties. This process can be called the "disenchantment of Romantic nature"' (Marquard 1987: 199). Egoism, aggression and the striving for power – and thus also the long-tabooed 'evil' – were henceforth numbered among the natural human drives.

Schopenhauer's philosophical system turned the traditional hierarchy of mind and instinctual nature completely on its head (see Gödde 2005; Baum et al. 2005): human beings are the slaves of their egoistic cravings, of the 'will to live', against which their intellect can offer little by way of resistance. The will, which is depicted as blind and devoid of cognition and intention, is, for Schopenhauer, always the primary and fundamental reality. By comparison, for him, the intellect is in every respect 'secondary, subordinate and conditioned'. To demonstrate this is all the more necessary for Schopenhauer because all philosophers before him

> place the true or real inner nature or kernel of man in the knowing consciousness. Accordingly, they have conceived and explained the I, or in the case of many of them . . . [the] soul, as primarily and essentially *knowing* and only in consequence of this, secondarily and derivatively, as *willing*. This extremely old, universal and fundamental error . . . must first of all be set aside. (Schopenhauer [1844] 1966: 2: 198)

The world of the will 'is not essentially united with consciousness', but is related to consciousness 'as something illuminated to light, as the string to the sounding-board' (199). In another passage, from his manuscript remains, he writes:

> Everything original, all genuine *being* is unconscious; that which has passed through consciousness has become *representation* and its expression is the communication of a representation. All genuine qualities in the character or mind of man are therefore unconscious and only as such do they make a deep impression. All awareness of the manner of acting is at any rate half affectation, i.e. deception. (Schopenhauer 1988–90: 3: 480)

At the psychical level the main expressions of the unconscious will are the somatic emotions, feelings and passions. The will's symbol is the 'heart', whereas only the cognitive and rational are ascribed to the 'head':

> Accordingly, we say: he has a bad heart; his heart is in this business; it comes from his heart; it cut him to the heart; it breaks his heart; his heart bleeds; the heart leaps for joy; who can read a man's heart? . . . Quite especially, however, love affairs are called affairs of the heart, *affaires du coeur*, because the sexual impulse is the focus of the will and the selection with reference thereto constitutes the principal concern of the natural, human willing . . . (Schopenhauer [1844] 1966: 2: 237)

In an astonishingly radical move, Schopenhauer proceeded in his metaphysics of sexual love to anticipate Freud's notion that sexual desire is the strongest and most active of all of the natural human being's drives and passions. 'This, however, is the piquant element and jest of the world, that the principal concern of all men is pursued secretly and ostensibly ignored as much as possible' (513). From the perspective of the history of philosophy, Schopenhauer made a turn both from the mind to the body and the drives and from the rational to the irrational. That his metaphysics of the compulsive-irrational will contains a new kind of psychology of the unconscious is largely a function of his doctrine of the primacy of the will and of the subordinate status of the intellect. He expressed the underlying point in the formula: 'What opposes the heart is not admitted by the head' (218).

In his *Philosophy of the Unconscious*, Eduard von Hartmann appealed to Schopenhauer's conception of the unconscious 'will' but also to Hegel's 'idea' and he tried to reconcile the two opposed currents in his philosophical system. The twofold nature of the unconscious as powerful will and as purposive cognition (*zweckrationale Erkenntnis*) finds expression in the following descriptions:

1. The unconscious does not become ill.
2. The unconscious does not succumb to fatigue.
3. All conscious representation assumes the form of sensuousness; unconscious thinking is exclusively non-sensuous.
4. The unconscious does not vacillate and doubt, it does not need time to reflect but grasps the result instantaneously.
5. The unconscious does not err.
6. The unconscious acquires its value through memory.
7. In the unconscious, will and representation are inextricably bound up with one another – nothing can be willed which is not represented and nothing represented which is not willed (see Hartmann [1868] 2001: 2: 47–8).

The characterisation of the unconscious as a tireless source of energy, as a workshop of desires and as the adversary of the conscious coheres for the most part with Carus's earlier conception and with Freud's later conception.

From an epistemological point of view, unconscious willing and unconscious representing lie outside experience and hence can be discovered only indirectly. The will can be inferred from its motives, from its accompanying and ensuing feelings, from its effects and from the conscious representation which constitutes the goal or the content of the will. Representing falls under the generic concept of *representation* only as an 'essential ideal anticipation of a performance of the will to be realised'. Since willing and representing are inextricably bound up with one another in the unconscious, reverse inferences can be made from either side:

> Where unconscious representation can be discovered, one must also infer back to a will whose content it is and which represents its tendency towards realisation; where an unconscious will can be discovered, one must also infer back to an unconscious representation which lends this willing determinateness, direction, aim and content. (Hartmann 1901: 79–80)

With his hypothesis that psychology is primarily concerned with unconscious psychological activity, Hartmann occupies a middle ground between the materialists and the idealists, although this did not prevent his opponents from attacking him vigorously from both sides. Hartmann agreed with the materialists that conscious processes are physiologically determined. However, he rejected the view that all psychological and mental phenomena can be explained in terms of the dispositions of physical molecules. This objection suggests that Hartmann understood the unconscious in anti-materialistic and anti-mechanistic terms. In fact, he conceived of the unconscious in terms of a 'a teleological activity alongside and above the molecular processes of the unconscious' (116). All processes in the human organism, as well as those in animal and plant organisms, are marked by purposiveness. This shows that Hartmann was opposed not only to physiological materialism but also to Darwin's anti-teleological principle of selection. Hartmann was a staunch anti-Darwinist and a founder of neo-vitalism (on this, see also Chapter 6 in this volume).

Against the idealists, who postulated the supremacy of the intellect and consciousness over the body, Hartmann argued that consciousness is purely passive and unproductive. This objection to idealism reveals that Hartmann, with his proof of unconscious psychological activity, rejected the ideas of God's absolute consciousness and of the immortality of the soul and that, like Schopenhauer before him, he attempted to dethrone consciousness. For Hartmann, consciousness is 'merely an intermittent epiphenomenon' in the stream of the unconscious and arises only at intersections where the unhindered activity of the unconscious is blocked and reflected back upon itself (81).

When Hartmann describes his philosophy as 'inductive metaphysics' he is trying to reconcile the inductive procedure of the natural sciences with the deductive procedure of metaphysics by, on the one hand, explaining conscious phenomena in terms of the physiological and psychical unconscious and, on the other, tracing them back deductively to a psychical activity in the form of unconscious willing and representing. As laudable as Hartmann's approach was, it proved to be problematic to draw inferences from the inductively ascertained material to an 'absolute' unconscious and to proceed to make deductions which could be productive for theory-guided induction. An empirically grounded psychology, such as that realised by Freud, remained beyond Hartmann's purview.

It is a well-known fact that the young Nietzsche was a passionate follower of Scho-penhauer. After his 'Schopenhauerean conversion' at the age of twenty-one, his philo-sophical thought was inspired for the most part by the metaphysical idea of the will to life. Schopenhauer's idea of redemption through art offered Nietzsche an escape from this pessimistic outlook. Through Richard Wagner's musical drama, he sought to gain access to and a foothold in a deeper – 'Dionysiac' – stratum of life. If Nietzsche's early work remains influenced by Romantic notions of the unconscious as more original, higher and more authentic by comparison with consciousness, in his second – pro-enlightenment – developmental phase he distances himself increasingly from Schopenhauer, Wagner and the Romantic philosophy of nature. He ultimately rejects the metaphysics of the will to life as still Romantic – in the sense of being not sufficiently enlightened and scientific. During this period he takes his orientation from the idea of science, which is supposed to take the place of the old metaphysics, and he looks for connections to the then highly topical findings of physiology and of Darwinian evolutionary theory.

Nietzsche views the drives, accordingly, as the decisive forces of life which set the whole psychophysical organism in motion and force their way out from inside in order to discharge their physiological energy. In this way he arrives at the conception of a drive-unconscious. Thus in *Daybreak* he writes:

> However far a man may go in self-knowledge, nothing however can be more incomplete than his image of the totality of *drives* which constitute his being. He can scarcely name even the cruder ones: their number and strength, their ebb and flood, their play and counterplay among one another and above all the laws of their nutriment remain wholly unknown to him. (Nietzsche [1881] 1997: 74)

The underlying activity of the drives is explained on the following hypothesis:

> there come into play motives in part unknown to us, in part known very ill, which we can *never* take account of *beforehand*. *Probably* a struggle takes place between these as well, a battling to and fro, a rising and falling of the scales – and this would be the actual 'conflict of motives': – something quite invisible to us of which we would be quite unconscious . . . the struggle itself is hidden from me and likewise the victory as victory; for, though I certainly learned what I finally *do*, I do not learn which motive has therewith actually proved victorious. *But we are accustomed to exclude* all these unconscious processes from the accounting and to reflect on the preparation for an act only to the extent that it is conscious. (79–80)

In this context Nietzsche poses a radical challenge to the pre-eminence of consciousness in mental life: 'One thinks that it constitutes the *kernel* of man; what is abiding, eternal, ultimate, most original in him! One takes consciousness to be a given determinate magnitude! . . . Sees it as the "unity of the organism"!' But this is a 'ridiculous over-estimation and misapprehension of consciousness' (Nietzsche [1887] 2001: 37). Nietzsche regards the view of consciousness as 'the highest achievable form, as the supreme kind of being' (1968: 286) as an egregious error. The genuine dynamics of life play out below the level of consciousness. More important than 'all our beautiful moods and heights of consciousness' are the 'animal functions'. 'What one used to call "body" and "flesh" is of such unspeakably greater importance' (355).

From the realisation that 'the superficiality of psychological observation has laid the most dangerous traps for human judgement and conclusions and continues to lay them anew' ([1878] 1996: 41) Nietzsche derives the motivation to develop a new kind of '*unmasking psychology*' in the field of tensions between instinct and reason, the rational and the irrational, appearance and reality, falsehood and truth. Since psychoanalysis grew out of a similar dialectic of veiling and unveiling, masking and unmasking, hiding and revealing, deceiving and disenchanting, one can speak of a shared basic structure in the psychologies of Nietzsche and Freud. To this common basic structure belong:

1. the guiding anthropological conception of a drive-related unconscious,
2. a model of motivation in terms of the psychology of drives,
3. the idea of self-delusion,
4. the closely related conflict-defence model (*Konflikt-Abwehr-Modell*),
5. the illness-triggering dynamics of the suppression of emotions,
6. 'internalisation' as the origin of exaggerated guilt feelings and
7. the assumption that 'ascetic ideals' have pathogenic effects (see Gödde 2010: 528–9).

Given the wealth and variety of his unmasking psychology, Nietzsche is rightly regarded as an influential precursor of the later psychologies of the unconscious (see Gödde 2002). In his later work he again falls back upon Schopenhauer's conception of the will, but lends it a new interpretation: the restlessly longing will to life which craves redemption is replaced by a dynamic, expansive and life-affirming will to power. For Nietzsche, Schopenhauer's basic misconception consisted in viewing desire as the 'essence' of the will, thereby 'lowering the value of the will to the point of making a real mistake' and regarding ceasing to will as 'something higher, indeed the higher as such' (Nietzsche 1968: 52, translation amended). Nietzsche, on the contrary, sees in the will to power a tendency of all living beings to go beyond mere self-preservation and the preservation of the species and to extend their own sphere of power in every direction. For him the will to power is not an ultimate metaphysical unity but can be conceived only as 'organization and cooperation' or as 'a pattern of domination' (303) designed to coordinate and integrate the multiplicity of one's drives and, once unity has been achieved, to defend it both within oneself and towards the outside.

Summing up, one can speak with reference to Schopenhauer's and Nietzsche's philosophy of the tradition of a *compulsive-irrational* unconscious.

5. The Unconscious in Freud

In the nineteenth century the unconscious underwent a major transfer from the philosophical disciplines of metaphysics, aesthetics and ethics to psychology, medicine (above all neurology and psychiatry) and psychotherapy. The most influential contributor to this development was Sigmund Freud (see Gödde 2010).

When the 'discovery of the unconscious' is attributed to Freud, what first springs to mind is his clinical experiences and findings in the treatment of neuroses and the interpretation of dreams. His guiding assumption was that, when conflicts arise within the psyche, especially embarrassing ideas which are marked by aversion are repressed without losing their efficacy. Freud identified the deeper reason for the repression in a more or less systematic dishonesty towards oneself. He recognised that revealing repressions, and thus the means by which truth is discovered, has liberating and healing effects. As he later remarked, it was primarily through 'the study of pathogenic repressions' (*Verdrängungen*) that psychoanalysis was compelled 'to take the concept of the "unconscious" seriously' (Freud [1925] 1954–73f: 20: 31).

Parallel to his clinical theory, from 1895 onwards Freud envisaged a farther-reaching general theory – the so-called metapsychology – intended to ground the scientific character of his new direction in psychology. In developing this project, he proceeded at first in the manner of a neurological psychologist. He found himself faced with the question of 'how the theory of mental functioning takes shape if quantitative considerations, a sort of economics of nerve-force, are introduced into it' (Freud 1985: 129). Following a period of serious self-doubt, he informed his Berlin friend Wilhelm Fliess, clearly in an ecstatic frame of mind, that:

> In one energetic night . . . the barriers suddenly lifted, the blinders fell away and one's gaze encompassed everything from details on neurosis to the conditions of consciousness. Everything seemed to fit everything else, the gear-wheels meshed, one got the impression that the thing was now actually a machine, that it would soon be running on its own steam. The three systems of neurons, the free and the bound states of quantity, the primary and secondary processes . . . the two biological rules of attention and defence, the quality signs, real[ity] signs and thought signs . . . the sexual conditions of repression, ultimately the conditions of consciousness in its perceptual function – it all passed muster and it still does today! Of course, I can hardly contain my delight . . . (149)

The result of these theoretical efforts was the *Entwurf einer Psychologie* (the 'Project for a Scientific Psychology', as it was titled in English) of 1895, a manuscript published only after Freud's death, which reveals his materialistic orientation at the time. One can draw a line here from Descartes, through the mechanistic materialism of the nineteenth century, up to the group of physiologists around Hermann von Helmholtz, to which Freud's teacher Ernst Brücke also belonged. The thinkers within this tradition consistently sought a material support for psychological processes and thus adopted an opposing programme to the Romantic philosophy of nature and its central principle of vital power, which they rejected as deductive and speculative.

Although Freud distanced himself from his neurologically oriented apparatus model of the psyche soon after writing the *Entwurf*, in *The Interpretation of Dreams* he continued to speak of a 'psychical apparatus', of psychological instead of physiological energies, of a psychological instead of a physiological principle of constancy and of a psychological instead of an anatomical topography. The concepts, analogies and metaphors employed in *The Interpretation of Dreams* were henceforth to be understood in purely psychological terms, even though they were still beholden to the general conceptions of the materialist tradition.

The central question for the constitution of psychoanalysis was whether an unconscious psychological domain exists alongside the conscious at all. Answering this question called for a critical engagement with the then-dominant philosophy of consciousness. Among those who, towards the end of the nineteenth century, identified psychical with conscious phenomena were, in particular, the two dominant schools of philosophy in Austria, namely, those of Johann Friedrich Herbart and Franz Brentano.

Herbartianism represented the mainstream psychology in Austria at the time. Comparisons between Herbart's and Freud's basic conceptions of the 'psychological mechanism', the 'machine' or 'apparatus' constructed in the manner of a physical structure, have revealed profound similarities (see Dorer 1932; Hemecker 1991). Yet even if one can already speak of a repression-resistance theorem in Herbart, this must be seen within the framework of a rationalist and metaphysical philosophy of a traditional kind. Freud did not merely adopt these abstractions but filled them with life in the context of his clinical theory and practice, in the process subjecting them to crucial transformations (see Gödde 2010: 272–5).

Freud also kept his distance from the epistemology of his former philosophy teacher Brentano, the founder of a second major direction in psychology in Austria. In his work of 1874 *Psychology from an Empirical Standpoint*, Brentano took an uncompromising stance against the hypothesis of an unconscious and claimed that, in addition to the consciousness of facts, there is a second consciousness directed to one's own person which is accessible to 'inner perception'. Indeed, the judgements of inner perception possess that 'immediate infallible evidence' which no other cognition possesses (Brentano [1874] 1995: 126). Such an optimistic assessment stood in stark contrast with Freud's clinical results in the treatment of neuroses and self-analysis.

Freud instead began to take his orientation from philosophers who defended the hypothesis of the unconscious. In his letters to Fliess we find explicit references to the philosopher Wilhelm Jerusalem who taught in Vienna, to Hippolyte Taine, to 'old Fechner' and above all to Theodor Lipps, a philosophy professor who taught in Munich. In the letter of 31 August 1898, Freud writes:

> I found the substance of my insights stated quite clearly in Lipps . . . Consciousness is only a sense organ; all psychic content is only a representation; all psychic processes are unconscious. The correspondence [of our ideas] is close in details as well; perhaps the bifurcation from which my own ideas can branch off will come later. (Freud 1985: 325)

Lipps had already taken a firm stance in favour of the hypothesis of the unconscious in his 1883 work *Die Grundtatsachen des Seelenlebens* (The Basic Facts of Mental Life; Lipps 1883). At the Third International Congress of Psychology in Munich, he delivered a programmatic lecture on 'Der Begriff des Unbewußten in der Psychologie' (The Concept of the Unconscious in Psychology) in which he defended the thesis that the question of the unconscious in psychology 'is less *a* psychological question than *the* question of psychology' (Lipps 1897: 146). For Freud, he became the chief witness in defence of the scientific character of the basic assumption of the unconscious in psychology.

In Chapter VII of *The Interpretation of Dreams*, Freud introduced a topographical model which distinguished between the systems of the 'conscious', of the 'preconscious' and of the 'unconscious' in the strict sense. The idea of the unconscious was at first informed by the theory of repression. One can speak of a repression-unconscious associated exclusively with the psychological domain; the somatic – in the sense of the later theory of drives – remained excluded for the present. What was decisive for the distinction between the (merely) preconscious and the unconscious (proper) in the first topography was the hypothesis that there is a threshold between the two where a 'censorship' resists wishes as they try to force their way out of the unconscious. The unconscious proper, as a region of repressed wishes, passions and fantasies, exhibits certain features and functions which do not appear in the preconscious domain: the processes of condensation and displacement, the characteristics of indestructibility and non-contradictoriness, regulation in accordance with the pleasure principle and the mode of operation of the primary process. These features stem in part from the tradition of the Romantic-vital unconscious, in part from the models of the modern natural sciences. Freud describes the unconscious proper as the 'dynamic' unconscious.

Thus Freud's original conception of the unconscious emerged at the intersection of two philosophical traditions: on the one hand, a tradition which assigned the unconscious to the psychological domain and accorded it primacy in mental life and, on the other, the materialist tradition which sought to integrate the unconscious into an apparatus model of the psyche. Since Freud's attention in this early phase was focused on the effectiveness and the knowability of the psychical unconscious, he was influenced by the tradition of the cognitive unconscious, although his conception of the dynamic unconscious envisaged more deep-lying motivational substrates than his predecessors. On a merely cognitive conception, according to Freud, illumination and enlightenment would end at the level of the preconscious and would remain too much beholden to the rational model of consciousness.

In his work between 1900 and 1915, Freud made a turn to a foundation based on the theory of drives. With the help of two drive theories – the dualism of the sexual and ego drives and later the additional dualism of narcissistic and object libido – he tried to place his conception of the unconscious on a new foundation. In the 1915 essay 'The Unconscious', he relativised the previous equation of the unconscious with the repressed; he now states that the repressed is not coextensive with the unconscious but is merely a part of the latter. From this perspective there is also an original unconscious, which Freud compared with an 'aboriginal population of the mind' (Freud [1915] 1954–73a: 14: 195). He spoke in this context of 'inherited mental formations' which formed the core of the unconscious; to this later accrues 'what is discarded during childhood development as unserviceable'. With this step from a point of view centred on repression to a genetic one geared to drives, the previous orientation to a pure psychology was changed in favour of a biologically grounded developmental theory.

In Freud's later work, psychosexuality, the life instincts and Eros are no longer the sole centre. The dynamics of the unconscious which spring from the instinctual nature of human beings seemed to Freud to be even more shaped by irrational forces which are hostile to life than he had assumed until then. With the dualism of Eros and Thanatos (or the death drive) in 'Beyond the Pleasure Principle' of 1920, Freud developed a third theory of drives. He assigned Eros the task of connecting the natural with the psychical: in relations between the sexes, in the family, in the formation of groups and masses and, above all, in the highest forms of cultural activity. The death drive, by contrast, counteracted the progressive tendencies of tension, change and advancement.

In the 1923 essay 'The Ego and the Id', Freud presented a new structural model. He divided the psychological apparatus into the three agencies of the 'id', the 'ego' and the 'super-ego' and stressed that 'we land in endless obscurities and difficulties if we keep to our habitual forms of expression and try, for instance, to derive neuroses from a conflict between the conscious and the unconscious' ([1923] 1954–73d: 19: 17). Among the difficulties discussed here are, most importantly, the problem of localising the forces of repression; the problem of moral values, conscience and ideals; that of internalisation, narcissism and the self; that of anxiety and that of aggression and the instincts of self-preservation (see Sandler et al. 1997: 141–52).

Freud postulates the 'id' as the original location both of the libidinous and of the aggressive and destructive drives. As a dark, inaccessible and scarcely controllable part of our personality, the id has 'no organization, produces no collective will, but only the striving to bring about the satisfaction of the instinctual needs subject to the observance of the pleasure principle' (Freud [1933] 1954–73g: 22: 65). In this context, Freud's affinity with the idea of the compulsive-irrational will, as prefigured in Schopenhauer's and

Nietzsche's philosophy of life, becomes increasingly apparent. If Freud had already declared that Schopenhauer's 'unconscious "Will" is equivalent to the mental instincts [*Trieben*] of psycho-analysis' (Freud [1917] 1954–73b: 17: 143–4), the Frankfurt School social theorist Max Horkheimer re-emphasised this when he wrote that:

> The unconscious in Schopenhauer is in fact 'the main reality: the will'; the will, which human beings in fact generally did not know how to describe. However, both are identical insofar as one can also interpret Schopenhauer's philosophy . . . in psychological terms and, conversely, one can also interpret the concept of the unconscious in Freud in a philosophical sense. (Horkheimer [1972] 1987: 454–6; see also Schmidt 1988: 393–5)

The characterisation of Schopenhauer's will agrees literally with the Freudian id and a corresponding comparison can be drawn between Freud's ego and Schopenhauer's intellect (see Zentner 1995: 87–8).

According to Freud, the ego must not be identified with consciousness, because the ego cannot become conscious of the acts of repression and resistance which originate in it, for otherwise the success of the repression would be jeopardised. Instead of speaking of a conflict between the conscious and the unconscious, therefore, one must speak of a conflict between 'the coherent ego and the repressed which is split off from it'. Consistently thought through, this leads to the conclusion that: 'A part of the ego, too, and Heaven knows how important a part, may be *Ucs.*, undoubtedly is *Ucs*' (Freud [1923] 1954–73d: 19: 9). With this Freud paved the way for an ego-psychological research programme in psychoanalysis in which the ego was liberated from its previous odium of rationality and superficiality by comparison with the profundity of the unconscious.

The key innovation made in 'The Ego and the Id' resides in the fact that the superego is introduced as a so-called 'step' or 'differentiation' (*Stufe*) within the ego and thus as a third agency. Although the concepts 'ego ideal', 'ideal ego' and 'super-ego' had already cropped up in earlier works, from now on Freud uses the term 'superego' as a *terminus technicus* and distinguishes between its functions as ideal and as prohibition. (Subsequently he divided the superego into the three functions of self-observation, ideal formation and conscience.)

In the context of the structural model, the importance of the substantive concept of the unconscious gradually declined in favour of the concept of the id. The word 'unconscious' was now used in the adjectival form to designate a psychical quality of the three agencies. The essential point was that the former region of the unconscious psychological processes was augmented by particular ego and superego components. Following the introduction of the structural theory, Freud understood psychoanalysis as 'a psychology of the id (and of its effects upon the ego)' ([1924] 1954–73e: 19: 209). In the subsequent development marked by 'Inhibitions, Symptoms and Anxiety' of 1926, through the 1933 lecture 'The Dissection of the Psychical Personality' and up to 'An Outline of Psycho-analysis' of 1940, he continued to refine his structural theory, but without making any further essential changes.

A fundamental difficulty was and remains the conceptual ambiguity of the unconscious. A prominent representative of the orientation which leans towards the Enlightenment pole was Alfred Adler, the founder of individual psychology, with his major 1912 work *The Neurotic Character* (Adler 2002). Adler attached much less importance than Freud to the opposition between the spheres of the rational-conscious and the irrational-unconscious. His sought to demythologise the understanding of the unconscious as a dark, fateful power in the life of the mind. Carl Gustav Jung, the founder of analytical psychology, took the opposite route. In his 1954 work *The Archetypes and the Collective Unconscious* (Jung 1980), he introduced the idea of a 'collective' unconscious which is determined by 'archetypes', that is, primordial images or templates (*Urbilder*) of structural possibilities of the mind. In psychoanalysis, authors such as Sándor Ferenczi, Georg Groddeck, Michael Balint, Donald W. Winnicott and Heinz Kohut also belong to the tradition of Romantic thought.

6. The Unconscious in Post-Freudian Psychoanalysis

During the 1960s and 1970s, Freud's successors undertook a critical re-examination of psychoanalytical metapsychology and of the associated concepts derived from the mechanistic tradition. The American psychoanalyst Roy Schafer (1976: 104) objected that the talk of psychical systems, structures or agencies, of primary and secondary processes, of drives and energies, depict these as 'purposive, meaning-creating, choice-making, action-oriented entities', 'as if they were minds within the mind, or homunculi'.

The three agencies have experienced shifting careers in psychoanalysis. In the late 1920s, there began a trend away from the psychology of the id to the psychology of the ego (Anna Freud, Heinz Hartmann, Ernst Kris, Rudolph Loewenstein), which remained dominant for decades. In so-called object relations theories, from the 1950s and 1960s onwards the primary emphasis shifted from the drives and the ego to the influence of internalised object relations (Melanie Klein, W. R. D. Fairbairn, D. W. Winnicott, Wilfred Bion). Then John Bowlby and later Joseph D. Lichtenberg underlined the independence of the needs for attachment, contact, security, exploration and coping from the sexual and aggressive drives. In the 1970s, the emerging self psychology and the psychology of narcissism (Heinz Kohut and Otto Kernberg) appeared on the scene as a further challenge to the dominant ego psychology. Whereas psychoanalysis at the time still operated within an individual-centred frame of reference in which the id-, ego-, superego-, self- and object-related perspectives could be distinguished, family therapy developed interaction-related and systemic perspectives which shifted the focus from the childhood self to parental influence and the family system as a whole and which took the reciprocity of relationships as its main concern. In recent years, an 'intersubjective turn' in psychoanalysis has been postulated (Altmeyer and Thomä 2006). The primary determining factor in this paradigm shift was the impressive findings of early childhood research concerning the intersubjective exchanges between mother and child (following Daniel Stern), after a large number of interpersonal approaches (drawing on Harry Stack Sullivan) and, above all, Stephen Mitchell's relational psychoanalysis had already pointed in this direction (see Buchholz 2005).

Freud already provided a few, sparse, conceptual points of orientation for an intersubjective perspective. Thus, he wrote in the introduction to 'Group Psychology and the Analysis of the Ego' of 1921 that: 'In the individual's psychic life, other people ordinarily must be considered as either models, objects, helpers or opponents. Thus, from the beginning, individual psychology is simultaneously social psychology' (Freud [1921] 1954–73c: 18: 71). Freud elaborates on this in 'The Ego and the Id' when he writes that 'the ego is a precipitate of abandoned object-cathexes' and contains within itself 'the history of those object-choices' (19: 29). The psychical processes which play a role here were dealt with under the headings of identification, introjection and internalisation, among others. In addition to the focus on the 'internal' as opposed to the 'external', in both his topographical and his structural models, Freud worked with the metaphors of the 'depth' of the unconscious in contrast to the 'surface' of the conscious. The intersubjective turn, by comparison, involves a displacement in both directions, both upwards from below and outwards from within, although not in the sense of a mere antithesis, but rather in that of a new synthesis of the psychical and the social, of self and other: 'The self needs the object – reflection in the other, recognition by the other, resistance from the other and so forth – if it is to develop something like an identity'. Accordingly, as regards the dialogue with the other, the self 'must not break it off or let it be imposed from without; the self possesses a dialogical internal structure into which the other is admitted and in which it already occupies a "virtual" place' (Altmeyer 2005: 655, 657). The individual self evolves in an interactive intermediate space which has been conceived as a 'psychic matrix' (Hans Loewald), as a 'relational matrix' (Stephen Mitchell), as 'mutual recognition' (Jessica Benjamin) or as an 'analytic third' (Thomas Ogden) (see Altmeyer and Thomä 2006).

If the division into the systems of the unconscious, the preconscious and the conscious can be described as the first topography and the distinction between the agencies of the id, the ego and the superego as the second topography, then the present-day discourse can be thought of as offering a third topography of the internal, the external and the intermediate, or, alternatively, of self, other and interaction. To this effect, the concepts which have been understood until now in intrapsychic terms must be reconceptualised and elaborated from intersubjective perspectives. For the present it is difficult to predict whether the intersubjectivists' hope for an integration of psychoanalysis under a unifying paradigm will be fulfilled; but they have certainly contributed to a reassessment and re-examination of the assumptions underlying Freud's structural model.

7. Concluding Remarks

Although the polarity between consciousness and the unconscious was prefigured by the dialectic of Enlightenment and Romanticism in the seventeenth and eighteenth centuries, it exercised its full effects only in nineteenth-century philosophy, psychology and medicine. Several currents played a role in this upsurge of the unconscious, in particular the cognitive psychologies of Herbart, Fechner and Lipps, the Romantic tradition of the Schelling school and the late Romantic Carus, the philosophy of the compulsive-irrational will in Schopenhauer, Eduard von Hartmann and Nietzsche and, not to be forgotten, the medical-psychological research of Charcot, Bernheim and Pierre Janet. The idea of the unconscious acquired central importance in Freud and Jung and subsequently in psycho-analysis and depth psychology in general up to the present day, although here an unmistakable multiplicity of perspectives was already apparent from an early date (see Buchholz and Gödde 2005a; 2005b).

The fact that Freud consistently upheld the demarcation of psychoanalysis from the philosophy of the unconscious was presumably primarily a consequence of his positivistic theory of science, which seems to be marked by unresolved contradictions. The notion of a purely clinical theory of psychoanalysis which is free from any residue of metaphysics appears to be illusory. There is no science without philosophical presuppositions and background assumptions. The philosophical tradition of the unconscious was integrated from the beginning into Freud's metapsychology as an important component and lives on in it in a latent fashion.

Today there is a broad agreement that unconscious processes also exhibit a logic and an intentionality. Even the more recent cognitive psychology and findings in neuroscience assume that cognitive processes occur for the most part unconsciously. Unconscious perception, unconscious thought and unconscious influences on mental processes are among the accepted topics of research in modern psychology. Bringing the unconscious into consciousness – not just in the sense of rational clarification, but as the integration of undeveloped and fragmented personality components – remains a general principle of analytic and depth-psychological therapies.

References

Adler, Alfred (2002), *The Neurotic Character: Fundamentals of a Comparative Individual Psychology and Psychotherapy*, *The Collected Clinical Works of Alfred Adler* vol. 1, San Francisco: Alfred Adler Institute of San Francisco.

Altmeyer, Martin (2005), 'Das Unbewusste als das virtuelle Andere', in Michael B. Buchholz and Günter Gödde (eds), *Macht und Dynamik des Unbewussten: Auseinandersetzungen in Philosophie, Medizin und Psychoanalyse*, Gießen: Psychosozial, pp. 650–9.

Altmeyer, Martin, and Helmut Thomä (eds) (2006), *Die vernetzte Seele: Die intersubjektive Wende in der Psychoanalyse*, Stuttgart: Klett-Cotta.

Baum, G. et al. (eds) (2005), *Die Entdeckung des Unbewussten: Die Bedeutung Schopenhauers für das moderne Bild des Menschen*, Würzburg: Königshausen & Neumann.

Brentano, Franz [1874] (1995), *Psychology from an Empirical Standpoint*, ed. Oskar Kraus, trans. Linda McAlister, Antos Rancurello and D. B. Terrell, London: Routledge.

Buchholz, Michael B. (2005), 'Stephen Mitchell und die Perspektive der Intersubjektivität', in Michael B. Buchholz and Günter Gödde (eds), *Macht und Dynamik des Unbewussten: Auseinandersetzungen in Philosophie, Medizin und Psychoanalyse*, Gießen: Psychosozial, pp. 627–49.

Buchholz, Michael B., and Günter Gödde (eds) (2005a), *Macht und Dynamik des Unbewussten: Auseinandersetzungen in Philosophie, Medizin und Psychoanalyse*, Gießen: Psychosozial.

Buchholz, Michael B., and Günter Gödde (eds) (2005b), *Das Unbewusste in aktuellen Diskursen: Anschlüsse*, Gießen: Psychosozial.

Carus, Carl Gustav [1846] (1989), *Psyche: On the Development of the Soul*, trans. Renata Welch, Dallas: Spring Publications.

Descartes, René [1637] (1998), *Discourse on the Method and Meditations on First Philosophy*, 4th edn, trans. Donald A. Cress, Indianapolis: Hackett.

Dorer, Maria (1932), *Historische Grundlagen der Psychoanalyse*, Leipzig: Meiner.

Ellenberger, H. F. [1970] (1985), *The Discovery of the Unconscious: The History and Evolution of Dynamic Psychiatry*, New York: Basic Books.

Eysenck, Hans J. (1995), *Genius: The Natural History of Creativity*, Cambridge: Cambridge University Press.

Fechner, Gustav Theodor [1868] (1966), *Elements of Psychophysics*, trans. Helmut E. Adler, New York: Holt, Rinehart and Winston.

Freud, Sigmund [1915] (1954–73a), 'The Unconscious', *The Standard Edition of the Complete Psychological Works of Sigmund Freud*, ed. and trans. James Strachey, London: Hogarth Press, vol. 14, pp. 159–215.

Freud, Sigmund [1917] (1954–73b), 'A Difficulty in the Path of Psycho-analysis', *The Standard Edition of the Complete Psychological Works of Sigmund Freud*, ed. and trans. James Strachey, London: Hogarth Press, vol. 17, pp. 135–44.

Freud, Sigmund [1921] (1954–73c), 'Group Psychology and the Analysis of the Ego', in Sigmund Freud, *The Standard Edition of the Complete Psychological Works of Sigmund Freud*, ed. and trans. James Strachey, London: Hogarth Press, vol. 18, pp. 65–144.

Freud, Sigmund [1923] (1954–73d), 'The Ego and the Id', *The Standard Edition of the Complete Psychological Works of Sigmund Freud*, ed. and trans. James Strachey, London: Hogarth Press, vol. 19, pp. 19–28.

Freud, Sigmund [1924] (1954–73e), 'A Short Account of Psycho-analysis', *The Standard Edition of the Complete Psychological Works of Sigmund Freud*, ed. and trans. James Strachey, London: Hogarth Press, vol. 19, pp. 189–209.

Freud, Sigmund [1925] (1954–73f), 'An Autobiographical Study', *The Standard Edition of the Complete Psychological Works of Sigmund Freud*, ed. and trans. James Strachey, London: Hogarth Press, vol. 20, pp. 7–70.

Freud, Sigmund [1933] (1954–73g), *New Introductory Lectures on Psycho-Analysis*, in Sigmund Freud, *The Standard Edition of the Complete Psychological Works of Sigmund Freud*, ed. and trans. James Strachey, London: Hogarth Press, vol. 22, pp. 5–182.

Freud, Sigmund (1985), *The Complete Letters of Sigmund Freud to William Fliess, 1887–1904*, trans. and ed. Jeffrey Moussaieff Masson, Cambridge, MA: Harvard University Press.

Freud, Sigmund, and Josef Breuer [1895] (2004), *Studies in Hysteria*, trans. Nicola Lockhurst, Harmondsworth: Penguin.

Gasser, Reinhard (1997), *Nietzsche und Freud*, Berlin: de Gruyter.

Gödde, Günter (2002), 'Nietzsches Perspektivierung des Unbewussten', *Nietzsche-Studien* 21: 154–94.

Gödde, Günter (2005), 'Schopenhauers Entdeckung der Psychologie des Unbewussten', *Schopenhauer-Jahrbuch* 86: 15–36.

Gödde, Günter [1999] (2009), *Traditionslinien des 'Unbewußten': Schopenhauer, Nietzsche, Freud*, 2nd edn, Gießen: Psychosozial.

Gödde, Günter (2010), 'Freud and nineteenth century philosophical sources on the unconscious', in Angus Nicholls and Martin Liebscher (eds), *Thinking the Unconscious: Nineteenth-Century German Thought*, Cambridge: Cambridge University Press, pp. 261–86.

Goethe, Johann Wolfgang von [1848] (2005), *Conversations of Goethe with Eckermann and Soret*, trans. John Oxenford, reprint from 1875 edn, Whitefish, MT: Kessinger Publishing.

Goldmann, S. (2005), 'Von der "Lebenskraft" zum Unbewussten – Stationen eines Konzeptwandels der Anthropologie', in Michael B. Buchholz and Günter Gödde (eds), *Macht und Dynamik des Unbewussten. Auseinandersetzungen in Philosophie, Medizin und Psychoanalyse*, Gießen: Psychosozial, pp. 125–52.

Hartmann, Eduard von (1901), *Die moderne Psychologie*, Leipzig: Haacke.

Hartmann, Eduard von [1868] (2001), *Philosophy of the Unconscious: Speculative Results According to the Inductive Method of Physical Science*, 3 vols, trans. William Chatterton Coupland, reprint of 1931 edn, London and New York: Routledge.

Heidelberger, Michael (2004), *Nature from Within: Gustav Theodor Fechner's Psychophysical Worldview*, trans. Cynthia Klohr, Pittsburgh: University of Pittsburgh Press.

Hemecker, Wilhelm (1991), *Vor Freud: Philosophiegeschichtliche Voraussetzungen der Psychoanalyse*, Munich: Philosophia Verlag.

Herbart, Johann Friedrich [1824] (1886), *Psychologie als Wissenschaft neugegründet auf Erfahrung, Metaphysik und Mathematik. Erster synthetischer Theil*, in *Sämmtliche Werke* vol. 5, Hamburg and Leipzig: Voss, pp. 191–514.

Herbart, Johann Friedrich [1816/1834] (2008), *A Textbook in Psychology*, trans. Margaret K. Smith, Whitefish, MT: Kessinger Publishing.

Horkheimer, Max [1972] (1987), 'Das Schlimme erwarten und doch das Gute tun' (conversation with Gerhard Rein), in *Gesammelte Schriften* vol. 7, Frankfurt: Fischer, pp. 442–65.

Hufeland, Christoph Wilhelm (1795), *Ideen über Pathogenie und Einfluß der Lebenskraft auf Entstehung und Form der Krankheiten als Einleitung zu pathologischen Vorlesungen*, Vienna.

Hufeland, Christoph Wilhelm (1937), *Leibarzt und Volkserzieher, Selbstbiographie*, ed. Walter von Brunn, Stuttgart: Schramm.

Hufeland, Christoph Wilhelm [1797] (2003), *Art of Prolonging Life*, Whitefish, MT: Kessinger Publishing.

Jung, Carl G. [1954] (1980), *The Archetypes and The Collective Unconscious*, trans. R. F. C. Hull, Princeton: Princeton University Press.

Leibniz, Gottfried Wilhelm (1965), *Monadology and Other Philosophical Essays*, trans. Paul Schrecker and Anne Martin Schrecker, New York: Macmillan.

Leibniz, Gottfried Wilhelm [1704/1765] (1996), *New Essays on Human Understanding*, trans. and ed. Peter Remnant and Jonathan Bennett, Cambridge: Cambridge University Press.

Lindner, Gustav Adolf [1873] (1889), *Manual of Empirical Psychology as an Inductive Science*, trans. C. De Garmo, Boston: Heath.

Lipps, Theodor (1883), *Die Grundtatsachen des Seelenlebens*, Bonn: Cohen und Sohn.

Lipps, Theodor (1897), 'Der Begriff des Unbewußten in der Psychologie', *International Psychological Congress* 3: 146–64.

Marquard, Odo (1987), *Transzendentaler Idealismus, Romantische Naturphilosophie, Psychoanalyse*, Köln: Dinter.

Medicus, Friedrich Casimir (1774), *Von der Lebenskraft*, Mannheim.

Mertens, Wolfgang (2005), 'Das Unbewusste in der Kognitionspsychologie – wird damit Freuds Unbewusstes hinfällig?', in Michael B. Buchholz and Günter Gödde (eds), *Das Unbewusste in aktuellen Diskursen: Anschlüsse*, Gießen: Psychosozial, pp. 264–309.

Nicholls, Angus, and Martin Liebscher (eds) (2010), *Thinking the Unconscious: Nineteenth-Century German Thought*, Cambridge: Cambridge University Press.

Nietzsche, Friedrich [1883–5] (1961), *Thus Spoke Zarathustra*, trans. R. J. Hollingdale, Harmondsworth: Penguin.

Nietzsche, Friedrich (1968), *The Will to Power*, trans. Walter Kaufmann and R. J. Hollingdale, New York: Vintage.

Nietzsche, Friedrich [1878] (1996), *Human, All Too Human*, trans. Marion Faber and Stephen Lehmann, Lincoln, NE: University of Nebraska Press.

Nietzsche, Friedrich [1881] (1997), *Daybreak: Thoughts on the Prejudices of Morality*, trans. R. J. Hollingdale, ed. Maudemarie Clark and Brian Leiter, Cambridge: Cambridge University Press.

Nietzsche, Friedrich [1887] (2001), *The Gay Science*, ed. Bernard Williams, trans. Josefine Nauckhoff and Adrian Del Caro, Cambridge: Cambridge University Press.

Pongratz, Ludwig (1984), *Problemgeschichte der Psychologie*, 2nd rev. edn, Munich: Francke.

Sandler, Joseph, et al. (1997), *Freud's Models of the Mind: An Introduction*, Madison, CT: International Universities Press.

Schafer, Roy (1976), *A New Language for Psychoanalysis*, New Haven, CT: Yale University Press.

Schelling, Friedrich Wilhelm Joseph von (1978), *System of Transcendental Idealism*, trans. Peter L. Heath, Charlottesville, VA: University Press of Virginia.

Schelling, Friedrich Wilhelm Joseph von [1809] (2006), *Philosophical Investigations into the Essence of Human Freedom*, trans. Jeff Love and Johannes Schmidt, Albany, NY: SUNY Press.

Schmidt, Alfred (1988), 'Schwierigkeiten einer philosophischen Freud-Rezeption', *Psyche* 42: 392–405.

Schopenhauer, Arthur [1818/1844] (1966), *The World as Will and Representation*, 2 vols, trans. E. F. J. Payne, New York: Dover.

Schopenhauer, Arthur (1988–90), *Manuscript Remains in Four Volumes. Volume 3: Berlin Manuscripts*, trans. E. F. J. Payne, ed. Arthur Hübscher, Oxford and New York: Berg.

Schröter, Michael (2006), 'Autobiographische Schriften [von Freud]', in Hans-Martin Lohmann and Joachim Pfeiffer (eds), *Freud-Handbuch. Leben – Werk – Wirkung*, Stuttgart: Metzler, pp. 215–19.

Wegener, M. (2005a), 'Unbewusst/das Unbewusste', in Karlheinz Barck et al., *Ästhetische Grundbegriffe. Historisches Wörterbuch in sieben Bänden* vol. 6, Stuttgart and Weimar: Metzler, pp. 202–40.

Wegener, M. (2005b), 'Das psychophysische Unbewusste – Gustav Theodor Fechner und der Mond', in Michael B. Buchholz and Günter Gödde (eds), *Macht und Dynamik des Unbewussten: Auseinandersetzungen in Philosophie, Medizin und Psychoanalyse*, Gießen: Psychosozial, pp. 240–61.

Wundt, W. (1862), *Beiträge zur Theorie der Sinneswahrnehmung*, Leipzig.

Zentner, Marcel (1995), *Die Flucht ins Vergessen: Die Anfänge der Psychoanalyse Freuds bei Schopenhauer*, Darmstadt: Wissenschaftliche Buchgesellschaft.

12

Individuality, Radical Politics and the Metaphor of the Machine

Alex Zakaras

1. Introduction

The concept of individuality expresses an ideal of personal emancipation and self-realisation. For many philosophers of the late eighteenth and nineteenth centuries, individuality was the highest end, the *telos*, not only of human life but also of social and political organisation. Its attainment, however, often seemed a distant goal: virtually all of the philosophers who defended individuality believed that it was endangered, if not entirely stifled, in their own societies. Individuality was, for them, a way of imagining a modern world worth living in. It gave ethical content to their imagined utopias; it also served as the normative foundation of their social and political criticism.

What sort of emancipation did individuality promise? What were its social and political implications? And what would it emancipate us from, exactly? These are the questions I set out to address in this chapter. The impressions I sketch here are designed to be not so much representative as illustrative and to reveal some, at least, of individuality's varied moral, social and political significance. Three philosophers – Wilhelm von Humboldt, Pierre Leroux and John Stuart Mill – are central to the essay. Two others – Friedrich Schleiermacher and Ralph Waldo Emerson – appear more peripherally. Each of them treated individuality as a centrepiece of his ethical and political theory; none of them used it in precisely the same way. Together, their writings form a rudimentary conceptual map that connects individuality to many of the reformist moral and political ideas – liberal, democratic and socialist – of the period.

Individuality is often defined with reference to the contrasting term 'individualism'. The French *individualisme* was first used by conservatives in the 1820s. Steven Lukes locates its origins in the work of Joseph de Maistre, the reactionary Catholic critic of the French Revolution. He used the term to describe a condition of epistemic anarchy, in which the infallibility of Church teachings had given way to an 'infinite fragmentation of all doctrines' (see his 'Extrait d'une conversation': Maistre [1820] 1884–93: 14: 286). Maistre believed that such fragmentation gave rise to civil anarchy, since church doctrine formed the very foundation of human association. For him, *individualisme* described the anti-nomian and anti-social legacy of both Reformation and Enlightenment rationalism (culminating as it did in the French Revolution).

But it was another group of French critics of the Revolution, the utopian socialists who identified with the teachings of Claude Henri de St Simon, who began to use the term 'individualism' more regularly (Lukes 1973: 6). For St Simon, individualism was an ideology that sanctified private egoism and celebrated individual conscience above shared moral standards. It was a stubborn refusal to countenance 'any attempt at organization from a centre of direction for the moral interests of mankind' (Moulin 1955: 185). For St Simon too, individualism was part of the ideology of the eighteenth-century philosophers which had precipitated the Revolution and its ensuing horrors. Individualism would need to be overcome before humanity could enter the final, 'organic' period of its progress toward perfection. While Maistre looked to the Catholic Church and the absolutist state as sources of social cohesion, St Simon worked to subject modern society to the authority of an entirely new religious hierarchy and to a caste of modern technocrats. The pejorative connotations of the French term remained for many nineteenth-century English writers, including John Stuart Mill, who used it in his *Chapters on Socialism* to describe a state of 'competition, each one for himself and against all the rest' (Mill [1879] 1963–91: 5: 715). It was in America that the term was transformed into a liberal ideal.[1]

The concept of individuality has different, Romantic origins, which can be traced to Germany in the closing decade of the eighteenth century (and before that, to the writings of Goethe and Johann Gottfried Herder). Early Romantic writers, including Novalis, Schleiermacher and Wilhelm von Humboldt,[2] celebrated what Georg Simmel has called an 'individualism of uniqueness' (Simmel 1971: 224). Theirs was an ideal of individual self-realisation and self-expression. It is best illustrated in the figure of the artist, so ubiquitous in early Romantic thought, who boldly rejects the strictures of bourgeois respectability and asserts his subjectivity and freedom; who remains fiercely faithful to his own idiosyncratic creative vision; whose highest aim is the fullest possible development and expression of his particular talents and capacities; whose life has itself become a work of art.

Unlike individualism, individuality was, in the writings of its inventors, an ideal to which to aspire. It was an aesthetic ideal, to be sure: the life that attained to some measure of individuality was, as Mill would put it in *On Liberty*, 'a noble and beautiful object of contemplation' (Mill 1963–91: 18: 269). But it was also an ethical ideal: the Romantics believed that self-realisation and expression were matters of personal obligation. As Charles Taylor argues, describing the rise of expressivism in the eighteenth century,

> The differences [between individuals] define the unique form that each of us is called on to realize. The differences take on moral import; so that the question could arise for the first time whether a given form of life was an authentic expression of certain individuals or people. This is the new dimension added by a theory of *self*-realization. (Taylor 1975: 17)

As in Aristotelian ethics, the perfection and realisation of one's own humanity became an ethical, not strictly an aesthetic, matter. But in the Romantic age, self-realisation comes unhinged from its Aristotelian *telos:* each individual now has his or her own way, in Taylor's words, of 'being human' (Taylor 1975: 15). There was no shared, objective ideal of human excellence to give form to human lives.

By the 1830s, French socialists not only recognised a distinction between individualism and individuality but also treated them as antitheses. The Saint-Simonian Alexandre de Saint-Cheron, for instance, warns against 'confounding individuality with individualism, with that mean egoism, lonely and disunited, which chokes all dignity . . . while the sentiment of individuality is the holy exaltation of man, conscious of the life in himself and all others, in God and nature' (Saint-Cheron 1831: 600). Indeed, as Sacvan Bercovitch has argued, the ideal of individuality became a 'rallying point against liberal ideology' which animated critics of the left and right alike (Bercovitch 1993: 315). It was, of course, also appropriated by a number of prominent liberal philosophers, including Humboldt and Mill.

Though it is first of all an ideal of personal self-realisation, individuality was never a strictly private concept. For the poets and philosophers who celebrated it, it was invariably bound up with an ideal of the good society and the just polity. Indeed, for virtually every thinker who espoused it, the ideal of individuality is best understood as part of a complex of ethical, social and political ideas: it describes an aspiration to individual self-development which presupposes, on the one hand, certain enabling relations between individuals and, on the other, a certain buttressing framework of political institutions. This complex relationship helps to explain why many nineteenth-century philosophers used individuality as the normative basis of their social and political criticism. They condemned existing regimes for stifling human individuality; in its name, they proposed radical political reforms.

At the same time, the idea of individuality casts light on some fears that troubled many social and political critics of the period. Individuality was, in their eyes, an ideal under threat of extinction. Each of the philosophers I consider could imagine a modern world, not so far removed from their own, in which individuality was entirely suppressed. All of them used mechanical metaphors to describe these darker modern possibilities. Barred from individuality, individuals, and sometimes also communities and states, would become like machines. The machine functions, for many writers of the time, as individuality's antithesis: the machine has no distinctive character; its movements are calculated to serve ends that are not its own; it is incapable of growth or development; and efficiency is the sole measure of its worth. If individuality casts some light on the utopian imagination of the time, the metaphor of the machine gives us glimpses of the imagined dystopias that lurked in the background.

2. Beginnings: Humboldt and Schleiermacher

The end of man, or that which is prescribed by the eternal or immutable dictates of reason and not suggested by vague and transient desires, is the highest and most harmonious development of his powers to a complete and consistent whole. (J. S. Mill, On Liberty)

These lines of Humboldt's, quoted by John Stuart Mill, account for a great deal of the scholarly interest in Humboldt in the English-speaking world.[3] They are drawn from Humboldt's most important work of political theory, The Limits of State Action, penned in 1791–2 when he was twenty-four years old. The book appeared in print only in the 1850s after his death (although excerpts from the book were published by Friedrich Schiller in the 1790s). By the 1850s the intellectual climate was receptive to the ideas expressed there, not only in Humboldt's native Prussia but also in France and England (see Sweet 1973: 469–70).

Humboldt was one of the earliest champions of the idea of individuality (Eigentümlichkeit). For him it balanced two competing aspirations: diversity and variety, on the one hand, and harmony or coherence, on the other. As J. W. Burrow puts it, Humboldt wanted to achieve 'unity in diversity', to retain 'coherence without sacrificing variety, richness, diversity' (1969: xxiv). What can this mean? First, Humboldt believed that the human individual possessed a very broad variety of intellectual, aesthetic and emotional capacities or potentials. Like Herder before him, Humboldt's study of history led him to believe in the malleability and variety of human character and personality. There were many different goods – sensual as well as rational – and many forms of human mastery and excellence to which individuals might aspire, and these could be known both through the study of history and, more importantly, through the accumulation of varied personal experience.

Humboldt therefore lists 'variety of situations' as one of the essential preconditions of individuality: the greater the variety of our personal experience, the more different capacities we can tap and develop. 'Even the most free and self-reliant of men is hindered in his development, when set in a monotonous situation' (Humboldt [1851] 1969: 10). Monotony can be avoided in several ways. In less developed societies, he suggests that the sheer variety of physical struggles and the diversity of the untamed natural world were enough to stimulate a varied and active human character (14). In more developed societies, where the natural world has been mastered and reduced to a less recalcitrant uniformity, variety comes from association with diverse people, but also through receptive engagement with the subtler 'intellectual and moral variety' of modern life (14–15). In modern life, more than in earlier stages of human history, diverse experiences must be deliberately and openly courted.

Diversity alone is not enough, however, to constitute individuality. Individuals must then labour to bring this diversity into coherent expression, much as the painter subsumes the myriad elements of a landscape under a single, coherent vision or idea. Out of experiential variety, individuals must fashion a coherent self and life. Humboldt divides human nature into 'form' and 'substance' or 'idea' and 'sensuous perception'. Individuality requires that sense experience be expressed as idea and 'the richer and more various the substance that is combined, the more sublime is the resulting form' (12). Such combination and expression allow the individual to avoid the serial 'one-sidedness' of one who is buffeted by successive and various experiences but fails to refine them cumulatively into a unified character (11). The idea of Bildung, so important to Humboldt and other German writers of his generation, describes this process of deliberate self-formation through exposure to difference.

Just as every work of art was unique, both in its constituent details and in the quality of its idea or vision, so too would every well-developed individual be without precedent in the world. The fully developed individual, the person who had attained to individuality, would thus himself contribute to the diversity of the world and also help create the conditions of variety within which others could flourish. The ideal human community, for Humboldt, is an association of independent individuals, each of whom might inspire the others to grow and learn. The 'true art of social intercourse consists in a ceaseless endeavour to grasp the innermost individuality of another, to avail oneself of it and, with deepest respect for it as the individuality of another, to act upon it' (27–8). Each individuality is at once an end in itself and a catalyst for the strivings of others.

Humboldt's use of a mechanical metaphor helps brings his idea of individuality into clearer focus. He bridled against the political forces that reduced the human individual to a functional part in some larger, efficient whole; this reduction spelled the death of individuality. Like other young Romantics of the period, Humboldt reaches time and again for organic metaphors – 'flowering', 'blossoming' – when describing individual self-development.

What, exactly, threatened to make machines out of men? For Humboldt, it was above all the paternalist state. He vehemently rejected the theory of enlightened absolutism that had prevailed in Prussia since the seventeenth century. According to this theory, as Frederick Beiser summarises it, 'the purpose of the state is to ensure the happiness, morality and piety of its subjects through wise legislation and administration' (Beiser 1996: xxiii). Citizens were not themselves thought competent judges of their own interests. Such states were a moral and aesthetic travesty, in Humboldt's view, because they imposed cultural and intellectual uniformity, crowded out voluntary association and reduced their subjects to dependents who 'look for instruction, guidance and assistance from without' rather than relying on their own energies and initiative (Humboldt [1851] 1969: 19). The growth of paternal state bureaucracy crushed the individuality both of the bureaucrats themselves and of the subjects who came to rely habitually on the state's initiative and largesse.

Such bureaucracies transformed not just individual character but the whole tenor of social or communal life. In *The Limits of State Action*, Humboldt contrasts two visions of human community. The community organised and governed by the paternalist state, he says, 'resembles an agglomerated mass of living but lifeless instruments of action and enjoyment' (31). Though Humboldt is here criticising the Prussian monarchy, these lines anticipate later Romantic criticisms of mass, commercial society; their target is, in any case, recognisably modern: bureaucratised government presiding over a passive mass of pleasure-seeking subjects. 'Under such a system', he continues, 'we have not so much the individual members of a nation living united in the bonds of a civil compact; but isolated subjects living in a relation to the State' (18). To this dystopian image, Humboldt juxtaposes a contrasting ideal of a civil society constituted by voluntary association – a 'multitude of active and enjoying energies' taking responsibility for their own lives and their collective affairs, affiliating on their own terms (31). This latter form of community induces self-reliance and active character.

Humboldt thought that such community could thrive only under certain political conditions. He defended what we would now call the 'minimal state': a government dedicated strictly to preserving the security of its subjects, nothing more. He condemned all government initiatives to advance the 'positive welfare' of its subjects, including poor laws, 'the encouragement of agriculture, industry and commerce', 'all regulations relative to finance and currency, imports and exports', all provision of national education and even 'all measures employed to remedy or prevent natural devastations' (17). All such measures, says Humboldt, are bound to have 'harmful consequences', to produce passive, dependent individuals. They are also bound to weaken human sympathy: where government provides for the poor and vulnerable, private subjects are less likely to help each other voluntarily and even to *feel* for the suffering of others. Voluntary community, grounded either in shared responsibility or mutual sympathy, would atrophy.

To specify the limits of state action, Humboldt defends a version of the 'one very simple principle' that Mill would later articulate in *On Liberty*: 'any State interference in private affairs, where there is no immediate reference to violence done to individual rights, should be absolutely condemned' (1969: 16). Government is necessary, Humboldt thought, because human beings are naturally inclined both to take more than their share and to encroach on the rights of others. Left to redress these harms on their own, people only initiate a cycle of revenge and counter-revenge that has no foreseeable end. The state, however, can impose a 'species of revenge which does not admit of any further revenge' (Humboldt 1969: 16); herein lies its necessity and genius. Anything it does beyond this, however (and beyond defence against foreign aggressors), is illegitimate: kings should be leaders in war and merely judges in times of peace (39).

Like Mill's, Humboldt's justification of his principle is consequentialist: government interference in private affairs has harmful effects. But Humboldt's defence of limited government is more clearly perfectionist than Mill's: the purpose of politics, in Humboldt's view, is to encourage human flourishing and the state should be designed with this end in view. But since the form of human flourishing he admires cannot be *created* by any power external to the individual, since state action is inherently homogenising, the scope and powers of government must be severely limited. The best it can do is help create the two conditions – freedom and variety – in which individuality is likely to flourish. It creates freedom by protecting individuals from harm so that they can live, speak, worship and associate freely, without interference from would-be assailants, either public or private. It promotes variety by constraining its actions to these minimal guarantees, so as not to create uniformity among its subjects.

As many commentators have observed, the young Humboldt held strikingly optimistic conceptions of both human nature and civil society. Freed from the suffocating intrusions of the paternalist state, individuals could be expected to pursue virtue and self-development.

> There can be no one, surely, so degraded as to prefer, for himself personally, comfort and enjoyment to greatness; and he who draws conclusions for such a preference in the case of others may justly be suspected of misunderstanding human nature and of wishing to make men into machines. (18)

Strip away their restraints and men would strive for perfection, would make their lives works of art. To deny this was to treat men like machines, governed by a single, simple (in this case hedonic) goal. Humboldt gives no sign of the profound anxiety, felt by later theorists of individuality, that human beings may not ultimately *want* greatness or uniqueness or perpetual exposure to new and unfamiliar experience; that they may be perfectly satisfied with a complacent, hedonistic conformity. Humboldt has no concern that both heteronomy and uniformity might themselves be objects of individual desire, or that (mass) civil society, unaided by the coercive agency of the state, might itself give rise to a rigid uniformity of belief, desire and character.

One particular manifestation of Humboldt's optimism is worth emphasising here, because it contrasts to the attitudes of many other Romantics, including Leroux and Schleiermacher, to whom I turn next. Humboldt held the view, very radical for his time, that the Church and state should be entirely separated. The state should make no attempt to promote religion of any kind. He adamantly rejected the conservative view that morality itself depended on religion:

> The citizen who is wholly left to himself in matters of religion will mingle religious feelings with his inner life, or not, according to his own individual character; but, in either case, his system of ideas will be more consistent and his sensations more profound; his nature will be more coherent and he will distinguish more clearly between morality and submission to the laws. (69)

Strip away state-sanctioned religious uniformity and we are left with a rich variety of moral vocabularies, secular and religious, from which individuals can draw freely in fashioning their own characters. The main current of European Romanticism would soon run directly against this view: Romantics would turn to the state and especially to religion as a way of elevating the human person from a condition of degradation from which individuals could or would not escape without help.

If Humboldt was an optimist about human nature, he considered himself a sober realist in politics. Though he approved of the French Revolution for its bold assertion of individual rights and liberties, he doubted that modern French citizens could attain the virtue required to sustain republican institutions (Beiser 1992: 118). He was deeply sceptical, moreover, of democracy: 'properly speaking', he wrote to Schiller in 1792, 'free constitutions do not seem to me so important and salutary. A moderate monarchy on the whole puts far less straitening fetters on the education of the individual' (Aris 1965: 157).

He also thought that political reform must come gradually and should be initiated by political elites themselves. Humbolt, therefore, ends *The Limits of State Action* not with a rousing call to action, but rather with a plea for patience. Political reforms too hastily pursued, he says, before the people are 'ripe' for them, can only undermine their own goals (Humboldt [1851] 1969: 141–4). In this sense, although he bristled at Burke's assessment of the French Revolution, Humboldt held decidedly Burkean attitudes about the likely consequences of abrupt social and political change.

Frederick Beiser has argued that the young Romantics defined themselves in self-conscious opposition to both absolutist and liberal political ideas. Against the absolutists, they asserted the personal and political freedom of the individual; against the liberals, who seemed to them to celebrate hedonism and egoism, they asserted an ideal of community that often hearkened back to an imagined, rural medieval idyll (Beiser 1992: 223). If their political ideals were forward looking, inspired by the ambitions of the French Revolutionaries, their social and communal ideals were nostalgic. There is much less of this nostalgia in Humboldt than in other young Romantics of his generation. Unlike other young Romantics, such as Novalis and Schleiermacher, Humboldt did not perceive liberal civil society itself as a danger to individuality, nor indeed as a threat to community. As I have emphasised, Humboldt shared the Romantics' acute sense of the importance of close community, bound together by sympathy and love, and this allowed him to share also an idealised vision of rural, pre-modern life ('Their participation in that beneficent toil and the common enjoyment of its fruits, entwine each family with bonds of love, from which even the ox, the partner of their work, is not wholly excluded' (Humboldt [1861] 1969: 22)). But unlike his Romantic contemporaries, Humboldt believed that this vision was fully consistent with liberal politics, which would provide a minimal framework of protections within which (voluntary) communities would flourish.

To sharpen the contrast between Humboldt and other contemporary Romantics, it is worth comparing him to Schleiermacher, whose *Monologues* of 1800 offer a more paradigmatic statement of the early Romantic ethical and political perspective. Like Humboldt, Schleiermacher treats individuality (*Eigentümlichkeit*) as the highest human goal. Like Humboldt, he understands individuality to mean the full development of the individual's unique capacities and the reflective unification of varied personal experience into a single harmonious character. 'It has become clear to me', he writes, 'that every person presents humanity in his own unique way, by his own mixture of its elements, so that humanity reveals itself in every possible manner and so that everything diverse realized itself in the fullness of infinitude' (Schleiermacher [1800] 1996: 174–5). Like Humboldt, Schleiermacher placed the aspiration to individuality higher even than the will to conform to the dictates of reason, which imposed uniform obligations on everyone alike. And like Humboldt, Schleiermacher was a vehement critic of political absolutism, which he thought stifled individual self-development.

But Schleiermacher saw more dangers to individuality than Humboldt did. In his *Monologues*, he finds humanity – European civilisation in particular – squandering its talents on what he calls its 'profane task': the mastery of nature and the provision of material goods for human welfare. The cultivation of individual character is everywhere subordinated to this collective enterprise:

the ingenious machine of the community conducts the slightest movement of each individual along a chain of a thousand links to achieve a single goal, as if they were all members of a whole and everything they did were its work. (187)

The modern economy and with it the division of labour threaten to reduce humans to machine parts, to destroy their spontaneity, creativity and spiritual depth. 'From such a world', he laments, 'you can hope for nothing for your strivings, nothing for your inner development' (188).

Schleiermacher saw Humboldt's ideal of the liberal state as an accomplice in this degradation of the human person. Here again, the mechanical metaphor returns: Schleiermacher dismisses the notion that the state should be 'a merely necessary evil, a mechanism to prevent and control crime' (192).[4] Instead, he describes the state as humanity's 'most splendid work of art', through which individual citizens can realise their own higher aspirations. 'Where is the power', he asks, surveying the barren landscape of European politics, 'that this highest form of existence gives to a person, the consciousness that everyone should have of being part of its reason, fantasy and strength?' (191). He is talking about the state here and presenting a view of its relationship to individuality at odds with Humboldt's. In Schleiermacher's ideal, the free citizen participates lovingly in the collective creation and perpetuation of a republican state and this activity motivates and expresses his individuality. Citizens become artists, each of whom contributes something distinctive to a shared political design.

Schleiermacher's several uses of the machine metaphor reveal the depth of his differences with Humboldt. For Schleiermacher, as we have seen, the modern economy could itself be described as an ungodly machine that used and disciplined human beings to suit its own ends. What was needed, in its place, was a spiritual community of free and equal people, dedicated to the realisation of individuality. But Schleiermacher goes further in condemning mechanical descriptions of the state itself and insisting it be regarded as a work of art or an organic entity. One can see the beginning, here, of a shift in the locus of moral concern within the Romantic tradition, from the individual to the state and, eventually, the nation. This was a move Humboldt resisted: he was content to describe the state as 'a complex and intricate machine' designed to serve human ends (Humboldt [1851] 1969: 63). 'The State is not in itself an end', he reminds us, 'but is only a means towards human development'.

3. Pierre Leroux: Between Individualism and Socialism

By the 1830s, the Romantic ideal of individuality was being used, in France too, to underwrite a politics substantially more collectivist than Humboldt's. It was used by leftist philosophers such as Leroux to distance themselves from the authoritarian statism of St Simon and to articulate a form of socialism that was more hospitable to individual freedom and more consistent with the ideals of the revolution. For Leroux and other socialists (and communists) after him, individuality became an animating goal of political and economic reform; Leroux would have agreed with Edouard Bernstein who at the end of the nineteenth century wrote that 'the aim of all socialist measures . . . is the development and the protection of the free personality' (Bernstein [1899] 1993: 147).

Pierre Leroux was arguably the first democratic socialist. He was widely admired in his day as one of the leading French philosophers and political theorists and earned high praise from such motley figures as Heinrich Heine, Alexander Herzen and Guiseppe Mazzini (Bakunin 1976a: 14–17). He rose to prominence first as a literary critic; along with Jean Reynaud, he edited the *Encyclopédie Nouvelle;* he edited a number of influential journals and also wrote a number of philosophical treatises – including *Of Equality* of 1838 and *Of Humanity* of 1840. He was a pacifist and held himself aloof from reformist politics for much of his life, though he was involved as a deputy in the Assemblies of the Second Republic. He rejected calls to violent revolution and preached gradual reform through the peaceful propagation of socialist and democratic ideas (Bakunin 1976b: 473).

Leroux's criticisms of his society (in this case, France in the 1830s and 1840s, under the July Monarchy) are more varied than Humboldt's and his outrage more palpable. Yet like Humboldt, who was infuriated by newly aggressive state censorship in Prussia in the late 1780s, Leroux was first moved to outrage by political repression. In a brilliant 1834 entry in the *Revue Encyclopédique* (titled 'Of Individualism and Socialism'), Leroux draws attention to the violent repression of the silk workers in Lyon, which he likens to a civil war. Workers, he says, are being brutalised simply for associating to protect their livelihoods (Leroux [1834] 1948: 225). Leroux was especially appalled by the government's apparent motives in the conflict. 'In the Sixteenth Century', he writes, 'when we assassinated each other in our civil wars, it was in the name of God, crucifix in hand; it was about the holiest matters, matters which, while they held our conviction and faith, so rightly dominated our nature' (224).[5] Now, he says, we are killing each other over strictly material interests. In the striking paragraphs that open the essay, Leroux is almost nostalgic for the days of religious violence, when there remained at least some measure of nobility, 'which took for its maxim the neglect of lucre', which shed human blood only for spiritual ends (225). Now that the Catholic, clerical hierarchy has been replaced by class hierarchy, now that the priest has given way to the bourgeois, people are killed simply over disruptions in business (226).

The principles that Leroux finds ascendant in France of the 1830s are materialism and individualism. Individualism, for him as for St Simon, was the ideology of the English political economists – the ideology that licenses the unyielding pursuit of personal, material gain. It was the ideology that 'makes men, amongst themselves, ravenous wolves and reduces society to atoms, letting everything arrange itself at random' (231). It was corrosive of all moral bonds among humans, it was the negation of all moral and social order. He compares France in his day to pagan Rome – a society founded on individualism and slavery – which was overtaken at last by the Christian ideal of communal life and property (227). Such passages contain strong traces of the St Simonian doctrine of the transitional or critical age, ushered in by the rupture of an existing moral and social order. St Simon had taught that history moved through such critical stages on the way to more settled and progressively more perfect periods of social cohesion.

Leroux was no St Simonian, however. He flirted with St Simonian doctrine briefly, for a few years in the early 1830s. By 1834, he was sharply critical of its authoritarian political tendencies. Leroux was one of the first writers to use the term 'socialism' (if not the very first) and in his early writings he uses it to criticise the St Simonian social and political ideal.[6] Socialism, Leroux argues, has emerged as a leading response to the individualism of the age, but it is no less misguided (231). St Simon and his followers had argued that society should be reorganised hierarchically under the supervision of a caste of scientists and captains of industry, who would preside over a planned economy, as well as a new theocratic elite who would raise the masses from their moral and spiritual torpor. Leroux denounced such ideas as regressive betrayals of the egalitarian spirit of the Revolution.

Leroux traces an intellectual trajectory from Pope Gregory VII and the Spanish Inquisition through Robespierre to the St Simonian creed itself, which he describes as the latest atavistic manifestation of the Catholic impulse to dominate and control (232). The Revolution had brought temporary chaos, but it was not, as St Simon and other conservative critics had held, a strictly negative assault on the clerical and aristocratic order. Rather, it expressed the positive commitments – liberty, equality and fraternity – upon which a new, democratic order would soon be founded. Leroux saw himself as one of the prophets of this new order, which would ultimately be dedicated to the ideal of individuality.

To better understand this ideal of individuality, it is worth clarifying *why* exactly Leroux found both individualism and its antithesis, socialism, so objectionable. Leroux associated individualism with unfettered egoism. He thought it inconsistent with the ideal of human equality, which required that we each recognise our own beholdenness to the human species itself. In perhaps his most ambitious work, *Of Humanity,* he would argue that egoism was self-contradictory, for it involved neglecting the interests of humanity as expressed in the lives of other human beings. Since individuals were themselves manifestations of this common humanity and since they depended on human community and society for their flourishing, egoism was a form of self-destruction. Self-interest rightly understood should lead us to embrace human solidarity and charity for our fellows (Leroux [1840] 1985: 147, 154).

Equality and solidarity are values Leroux often champions for their own sake. At the same time, he maintains that the very goal of egalitarian societies is to realise the ideal of individuality. And he objects to individualism precisely because it inhibits this goal. First, in transforming humans into 'wolves' and unrepentant materialists, it obscures the higher forms of flourishing to which they might attain. Second, in virtually ensuring the desperate poverty of the proletariat, it prevents the working classes from attaining the material preconditions of individuality. 'It is his dignity, his humanity, his liberty, his independence, that the proletarian demands, when he aspires to possess material goods' (Leroux [1834] 1948: 229). Though Leroux decries materialism, he warns also against the naïve, monastic view that material goods are of no consequence whatever.

There is, finally, a third kind of harm that Leroux associates with individualism and with the broader liberal ideology that justifies it. Liberal individualism defends the separation of Church and state and with it the privatisation of religious belief. It encourages the anarchic proliferation of religious sects. Leroux, like St Simon and other critics of the Revolution, including Joseph de Maistre, rejected this tendency. Leroux held that the privatisation of religion leads to a form of human alienation or incompleteness. Civic perfection and spiritual perfection are consigned to two different areas of life, are artificially separated one from the other, so that civic man must hold his religious beliefs at a distance and religious man must confine himself to the private domain.

If individuality was threatened by individualism, so too was it threatened by 'socialism'. Socialism was objectionable to Leroux mainly because, in subjecting adult human beings to yet another authoritarian hierarchy, it infantilised them and stunted their development as free beings. Leroux's rejection of state paternalism recalls Humboldt's: anyone attached to the ideals of freedom and individuality should, he writes, reject 'this new papacy, crushing, absorbing, which would transform humanity into a machine, in which the true living beings, individuals, would be but useful matter instead of arbiters of their own destiny' (Leroux [1834] 1948: 233). The metaphor of the machine returns here; Leroux uses it deliberately in place of the organic metaphors favoured by many conservatives.

Individuality, for Leroux as for Humboldt, meant individual self-development, meant the full realisation of each individual's distinctive talents and capacities. Among these were physical, intellectual and emotional capacities which should be brought into mutual harmony (Bakunin 1976a: 163). Such harmonious self-development required the freedom to direct one's own life:

We must organize for the free development of man's individuality and not against this development; in such a way that everyone seeks, according to his affinities, the beings with whom he should form alliances and the different objects that his personality feels a need for – and not in such a manner that everyone thinks, loves, works, according to a guidance that is imposed and impressed upon him as if he were a slave or a machine. (Leroux 1846: 109)

Like Humboldt, Leroux believed that individuality could flourish only in a free society in which individuals enjoyed basic rights and liberties. The draft constitution that he proposed to the National Assembly in 1848 articulates rights to free expression, association and conscience (among the 'nine general rights of the man and the citizen') (Leroux 1848: 26–9). Unlike Humboldt, however, Leroux envisioned a very active role for the state in creating economic opportunities for the working class. He was sharply critical of the 'policeman' state of the individualists, who in the name of private property abandoned the poor to abject poverty and economic slavery (Leroux [1834] 1948: 232). He never outlined systematic prescriptions for economic reform, though he favoured the socialisation of the means of industrial production, as well as a system of regulations designed to safeguard the health and salary of workers and guarantee them a pension (Evans 1948: 80–4; Bakunin 1976a: 99).

Leroux was also a democrat – in fact, he was more deeply committed to democracy than to individual rights. Democracy was, in his view, the only form of government suited to develop human individuality. In making each individual a legislator, in giving each individual the power to shape society itself, democratic politics demanded that individuals develop their own voice and capacity for judgement (Leroux 1846: 125). Democracy refused to subject the ordinary citizen's judgement and personality to the authority of some higher power. Like Mill after him, however, Leroux worried that democratic politics might subject individuals to an invasive tyranny of the majority and he was adamant that the individual could never surrender to the state control of 'his thoughts, his loves, his friendships, the direction of his work or its fruits, in brief the multitude of acts which together constitute his personality' (1846: 102).

A striking feature of Leroux's political ideal was a national religion, the content of which would be determined democratically. Though all citizens must retain absolute freedom of conscience and with it the right to dissent vocally against the state religion and the right to try to change it through democratic suasion, he believed that the state should nonetheless establish a single religion, prevent the emergence of rival sects and educate children in its doctrines. He imagined that its basic tenets would be the equality and solidarity of all humans, as well as a commitment to their individuality. Jack Bakunin writes, of this religion, 'human freedom would be furthered by the dogmas of this new religion, which would be designed to keep an ideal of autonomous individual self-realisation in the minds and hearts of its adherents' (Bakunin 1976a: 162). Official positions within the church would be open to all and Church decisions taken through egalitarian, democratic procedures.

It is important to notice why Leroux thought this religion necessary to the flourishing of human individuality. The alienation or incompleteness that afflicted liberal societies would strip individuals of the motivation to strive for their own development and perfection (Leroux 1846: 88). Society and culture were sources from which individuals must draw, and draw freely, in developing themselves. And if the source should fail to encourage self-development in the first place, should fail also to provide a moral and ethical foundation upon which individual personality should be layered, it would yield only egoists, materialists or immoralists (109–11). Here the contrast with Humboldt could hardly be sharper. Leroux's views on religion are much closer to Schleiermacher's, who, like other young German Romantics, had called for the creation of a new church, founded on an ideal of human brotherhood, which would help cultivate the spirit and inspire pursuits of perfection. Neither man, however, held a merely instrumental view of religion: Leroux believed that the democratic religion would at last realise the true, egalitarian moral teachings of God, which had been straining to make themselves manifest (with progressively great success) throughout human history.

Leroux believed that people needed help in achieving individuality. Unlike Humboldt, who believed that government should simply clear a space for individual freedom and let individuals do the rest, Leroux maintained that the state would be instrumental in the cultivation not only of individuality itself but also of the communities in which it could flourish. The state would first redistribute wealth massively and empower workers to manage their own economic affairs. It would oversee the founding of a new, democratic religion, which would itself inculcate the values of democratic culture. Without the government's agency, individuals would be at the mercy of brutal economic forces and an egoistic, philistine culture. Individuality's enemies had multiplied and they would not be subdued without the agency of the state.

4. John Stuart Mill's Synthesis

Mill was deeply influenced both by Humboldt's libertarianism and by French socialism. Since his philosophy is more familiar to Anglophone readers than either Humboldt's or Leroux's, it needs less exegesis here. I focus mainly on how his treatment of individuality compares (and contrasts) with the others'.

Mill absorbed the idea of individuality largely from Humboldt and did not stray far from Humboldt's use of the term, except in shearing it of some of its metaphysical accompaniments. Individuality, for Mill in On Liberty, means the development of the individual's own distinctive talents and capacities – including, notably, not just his rational and moral faculties, but also his 'desires and impulses' (Mill 1963–91: 18: 267).[7] Like Humboldt, Mill emphasised the importance of inner harmony or balance: 'strong impulses', he says, 'are only perilous when not properly balanced; when one set of aims and inclinations is developed into strength, while others, which ought to co-exist with them, remain weak and inactive'. And like Humboldt, he thought that our diverse capacities could be realised only through varied personal experience and self-conscious experiments in living.

Perhaps even more than Humboldt, Mill emphasised the educative effects of choice itself; that is, the *act* of choosing. 'The human faculties of perception, judgment, discriminative feeling, mental activity and even moral preference', he argues, 'are exercised only in making a choice' (18: 266–7). Mill argued that beliefs and desires that were simply absorbed from others unreflectively, or dictated by them, tended to compromise our very humanity: 'one whose desires and impulses are not his', Mill writes, 'has no character, no more than a steam-engine has character' (18: 268). For Mill, as for Humboldt, this notion of owning one's own mental states is ambiguous. On the one hand, we own our attitudes by choosing them; on the other, we own them insofar as they accord with our authentic, individual 'nature' – a nature that becomes apparent to us only through lived experiments, but that is itself unchosen. The cultivation of individuality is part self-creation and part self-discovery.

Andrew Valls has argued that Humboldt's ideal of individuality was more indeterminate than Mill's. 'There is no pursuit whatever', writes Humboldt, 'that may not be ennobling and give to human nature some worthy and determinate form. The manner of its performance is the only thing to be considered' (Humboldt [1851] 1969: 23). Mill disagreed; for him, individuality required the development of 'higher' human faculties, including the moral, aesthetic and intellectual faculties. Not all ways of life, not all kinds of human activity – no matter the style in which they are conducted – would conduce to such development. Humboldt would not, I think, have demurred from Mill's account of the higher faculties; rather, he was more optimistic than Mill that such faculties could be realised across a very broad range of human activities. Consider, for instance, his description of the peasant life:

> It seems as if all peasants and craftsmen might be elevated into artists; that is, men who love their labour for its own sake, improve it by their own plastic genius and inventive skill and thereby cultivate their intellect, ennoble their character and exalt and refine their pleasures. (Humboldt [1851] 1969: 22)

Where did Mill locate the principal threats to individuality? Like both Humboldt and Leroux, Mill thought that it was threatened by the paternal state.[8] In his 1861 *Considerations on Representative Government*, Mill invites his readers to imagine a perfectly virtuous, benign and omniscient despot who acts always in the best interest of his subjects. On what grounds, he asks, could anyone conceivably object to such a despot's rule? The answer, he argues, lies in this regime's effect on individual character: even the most benevolent despotism renders its subjects passive and dependent, strips them of a sense of responsibility for their own lives and for their common affairs. It crushes their individuality. 'Nor is it only in their intelligence that they suffer', says Mill. 'Their moral capacities are equally stunted' and their sentiments 'narrowed' (Mill [1861] 1963–91: 19: 73). He reproduces Humboldt's argument here that the human capacity for sympathy atrophies when people no longer feel responsible for one another, when they rely on the state as a caregiver.

Like Leroux, he argued that participatory democracy would give citizens the incentive to assume responsibility for their collective affairs and might hence encourage not only mutual sympathy but also active characters – that is to say, characters who strove to improve themselves and their circumstances. Indeed, democracy was his response not only to paternal government but also to paternal capitalists and factory bosses, whose pacifying effects on the worker's mind and character were no less objectionable. Mill argued that participatory democratic politics, both in the public sphere and in the management of worker-owned, private cooperatives, could lend some 'largeness' to the ideas and sentiments of modern citizens (19: 81). Such largeness had been stamped out not only by infantilising subjection to factory bosses but also by the repetitive drudgery of modern industrial labour. Self-government could educate citizens and contribute to the development of the higher faculties, which were indispensable to the pursuit of individuality.

Democracy was not enough, however, to protect and encourage the cultivation of individuality. Mill mistrusted democratic governments almost as much as any other; he worried that paternal despotism would simply be re-created in democratic form. He worried that democratic governments, supported as they were by a majority of the population, would impose their will on dissenters more efficiently than any other. He famously designed the harm principle to constrain the power of democratic majorities and preserve space for individual autonomy and eccentricity. Individuality became, in this way, one of the ethical centrepieces of his liberal political philosophy. Unlike Humboldt, however, whose justification of limited government rests exclusively on the value of individuality, Mill gave it a utilitarian justification: limited government would maximise human happiness. The pursuit of individuality was, granted, an integral *part* of happiness – for many people, anyway. But Mill's political theory is less unambiguously perfectionist than Humboldt's: he would not have said, as Humboldt did, that the purpose of government is to realise a certain ideal of human character.

Mill differed most from Humboldt in his insistence that civil society, not government, posed the most serious threat to individuality. Mill believed that the yoke of conformity, enforced for the most part not by the state but by 'society', most threatened to render humans uniform and machine-like. He describes this pressure to conform throughout *On Liberty*:

> The mind itself is bowed to the yoke: even in what people do for pleasure, conformity is the first thing thought of; they live in crowds; they exercise choice only among things commonly done: peculiarity of taste, eccentricity of conduct, are shunned equally with crimes: until by dint of not following their own nature they have no nature to follow: their human capacities are withered and starved. (18: 268)

Mill was responding here to a mass, proto-democratic culture that Humboldt never knew. In describing the origins of this culture, he admitted to a much darker view of human nature than either Humboldt or Leroux would have accepted. Mill doubted that many people wanted either individuality or freedom. Many of us, Mill thought, want little more than the reassuring embrace of the group and aspire to nothing more than 'collective mediocrity' (18: 272). What is more, because the aspiration to individuality is easily understood as an implicit condemnation of the group, we take a certain pleasure in stamping it out; we then sanctify our intolerance, and the pleasure we derive from it, as a form of communal virtue. Mill worried that moderns were *making themselves* into machines and then sanctimoniously intimidating anyone who refused to fit the mould (see Zakaras 2007).

The metaphor of the machine had special significance for Mill. It recurs throughout Chapter 3 of *On Liberty*, and also surfaces in a crucial passage of his *Autobiography*:

> I conceive that the description so often given of a Benthamite, as a mere reasoning machine, though extremely inapplicable to most of those who have been designated by that title, was during two or three years of my life not altogether untrue of me. (Mill [1873] 1963–91: 1: 172)

He means that his intellect was, at this early stage in his life, a creation of his father's, designed to pursue certain goals which had as yet no firm grounding in John's own emotions. His philosophical zeal 'had not its root in genuine benevolence, or sympathy with mankind' (1: 172). Mill believed that this deficit was responsible for his ensuing crisis and depression. And throughout his adult writings, Mill would locate human authenticity in the emotions: if the personae we fashion through experiments in living are to be expressions of *ourselves*, not just false roles, they must reflect and develop our passions. This helps explain why emotional development was such an important piece, for him, of individuality. It helps also explain Mill's enthusiasm for a 'religion of humanity', to which I turn shortly.

The libertarian currents of Mill's philosophy are somewhat weakened by two other currents, both of which run closer to Leroux (and to Auguste Comte, whom Mill admired) than to Humboldt. The first is Mill's (liberal) socialism. Like Leroux, Mill believed that in the absence of certain economic preconditions, individuality would remain the exclusive privilege of the few and that such conditions entailed a substantial, structural overhaul of the modern economy. The deep divide between capitalist and worker would have to be overcome by reorganising industrial production around a system of worker-owned (rather than state-run) cooperatives, which would emancipate workers from dependence on their capitalist bosses and help ensure a fairer distribution of the fruits of modern productivity (see Ten 1998; Baum 2007). Also like Leroux, Mill was concerned about the moral effects of competition in the absence of a strong, egalitarian public spirit, without which 'man never thinks of any collective interest, of any objects to be pursued jointly with others, but only in competition with them and in some measure at their expense' (Mill [1861] 1963–91: 19: 82). He acknowledged the familiar socialist concern that competition might promote a form of 'individualism' that would erode human sympathy (5: 249).

Second, Mill turned not only to democracy but also to religion for the cultivation of moral feeling. This religion, which Mill called a 'religion of humanity', would above all help cultivate a feeling of deep sympathy with all humankind, 'a desire to be in unity with our fellow creatures' (10: 276). Like Leroux, Mill imagined that such a religion would socialise children and help motivate utilitarian moral behaviour – it would serve as the 'ultimate sanction for the happiness morality' (10: 280). The relationship between individuality and the ideal of universal sympathy cultivated by the religion of humanity is under-theorised in Mill's work. Daniel Brudney (2008) has suggested that these form two separate ideals of human perfection in Mill's philosophy and are, if not logically incompatible, very difficult to reconcile practically.

Mill did not think so. He hoped that the pursuit of individuality would be balanced and directed by sympathy for others. If we took pleasure in the happiness of others, and if this pleasure was more edified and durable than sensual pleasure, then the sort of life and personality we would want to cultivate and express would be devoted, in part, to moral ends – to the wellbeing of others. Sympathy would give shape to our individualities. In another sense, too, Mill thought the religion of humanity could complement individuality. In 'Theism', he writes,

> To me it seems that human life, small and confined as it is, and as, considered merely in the present, it is likely to remain even when the progress of material and moral improvement may have freed it from the greater part of its present calamities, stands greatly in need of any wider range and greater height of aspiration for itself and its destination, which the exercise of imagination can yield to it without running counter to the evidence of fact. (Mill [1874] 1963–91: 10: 475)

Mill thought that religion could inspire the pursuit of excellence itself and that the very idea of the divine, understood as a projection of human perfection, could draw us out of our collective mediocrity. Here Mill and Leroux agreed: unlike Humboldt, neither trusted that human beings would strive for transcendence or beauty or moral perfection without collectively organised social inducements; both thought that religion could serve this purpose.

One final point of similarity between Mill and both Humboldt and Leroux is worth mentioning. Classical antiquity figured prominently in each of their accounts of individuality: when they reached for an example of a time when individualities flourished, they reached invariably for ancient Greece or Rome. In an early essay titled 'On Genius' (1832), Mill worried that his own age could not possibly measure up to Greek antiquity, especially in the quality of its individuals. Humboldt and Leroux shared his belief that classical individuals had been more complete and in some ways more brilliant than their modern counterparts. None of them, however, used such comparisons as ways of condemning modernity. Individuality was not, for any of them, part of a nostalgic vision of either politics or society; rather, it justified social and political reforms that each author understood to be progressive.

5. The Idea of Individuality and its Tensions

The idea of individuality is part of the broader notion of self-development. Like other ideals of self-development, it suggests that human lives are best lived in pursuit of a higher self, a self as yet unattained. It is distinctive, though, in celebrating the uniqueness of each individual, in prioritising openness or receptivity to new and diverse experiences and in encouraging us to fashion (and refashion) ourselves out of the raw material of such experience, to create ourselves expressively. Individuality urges one, as George Kateb puts it, 'to become the architect of one's soul' rather than passively accepting the imprint of society or circumstance (Kateb 1992: 90). There was, of course, over the course of the nineteenth century, much disagreement about the precise content and scope of the ideal. I will conclude by drawing attention to two areas of dispute in particular, both of which concern individuality's relationship to the egalitarian moral and political ideals that animated much political radicalism of the age.

Humboldt, Leroux and Mill believed that individuality was an ideal to which everyone could in principle aspire. It was not restricted to the genteel class, nor even to the middle classes (as Humboldt's description of the farmer illustrates), nor strictly to men. In this assertion of inclusiveness, all these thinkers were rejecting the common view, decried by the American William Ellery Channing in his 1838 oration 'Self-Culture', 'that the mass of the people need no other culture than is necessary to fit them for their various trades' (Channing 1838: 21).[9] The ideal of individuality rested, for these three thinkers, on the view that all human persons had something valuable and distinctive to bring into the world. This inclusive, egalitarian conception of individuality resonated throughout nineteenth-century political thought, not least in Marx's writings.

Inclusive individuality also found powerful expression in the works of several American Transcendentalists, notably Ralph Waldo Emerson, Henry David Thoreau and Walt Whitman. For them, individuality was part of the promise of constitutional democracy, which destroyed both the cultural boundaries and the material inequalities that confined individuals to certain classes or social stations. Democracy was an invitation to cease being merely a serf or a proletarian or a petty bourgeois and to be simply oneself. 'No law can be sacred to me', writes Emerson in 'Self-Reliance', 'but that of my nature. . . . The only right is what is after my constitution, the only wrong what is against it' (Emerson [1841] 1983: 262). In these lines (and many others like them), the celebration of individual idiosyncrasy and the radical rejection of authority reach a higher pitch than even Mill could tolerate. Still, Emerson's self-reliance, in its celebration of uniqueness, receptivity and expressive self-creation, is a recognisable iteration of the ideal of individuality.

The very inclusiveness that individuality attained through its association with democracy gave rise, however, to new anxieties. What if most people want no part of such a demanding ideal? What if they not only prefer conformity and mediocrity for themselves but also demand it of others? Mill's concerns about mass conformity arose partly out of his reading of Alexis de Tocqueville, who famously criticised the tremendous homogenising power that the American majority exercised over the minds of all citizens. 'I know of no country where there is in general less independence of mind and true freedom of discussion than in America' (Tocqueville [1835] 2004: 293). Such observations led Tocqueville to conclude that democracies, where power resided in the mass, would contain fewer brilliant and distinctive individuals than aristocratic societies. Though they ultimately rejected this conclusion, the American Transcendentalists, too, were urgently aware of the dangers of mass conformity, which they denounced as the most important remaining obstacle to individuality. Thus mass conformity, rather than political oppression at the hands of either absolutist or socialist government, became the focal antipode of individuality.

Other philosophers rejected the more inclusive conception of individuality outright. Friedrich Nietzsche, who was greatly influenced by Emerson, also inveighs against the conformity of modern individuals and also espouses an ideal of self-creation that has its origins in Romantic individuality. Unlike Emerson, he concluded that most people were either incapable or constitutionally averse to the creative self-fashioning and honest self-scrutiny that individuality required. Whereas Emerson always held out hope that the conformist could be awakened, if only momentarily, to the allure of a higher self, Nietzsche suggests that a deep and insuperable divide separates the overman from the 'last man' – a phrase he used to describe the passive, weak-willed, comfort-seeker who eschews truth for pleasing illusion. For Nietzsche, as for Schopenhauer before him, self-creation was the domain of the gifted few. Traces of such pessimism – momentary lapses of faith – can be found in the works of Emerson and Mill both; in Nietzsche it is unequivocal.

A second tension also emerged between individuality and egalitarianism. For some defenders of individuality, morality itself came to seem like yet another impediment to individual self-creation. Such aesthetic amoralism can be found in Max Stirner's 1844 work *The Ego and Its Own*, which urges its readers to reject not only social norms and customs but also moral restraints that fetter the free play of the individual will. Traces of it can also be found in Emerson, whose essays sometimes elevate self-reliance above the imperatives of any moral code: 'If I am the Devil's child', he writes whimsically, 'I will live then from the Devil' ('Self-Reliance' (1841), in Emerson 1983: 262). And of course this amoralism finds fullest expression in Nietzsche, who treats moral egalitarianism as an atavism of the slave morality, which draws its strength from the majority's resentment of individual distinction. In these later iterations of individuality – certainly in Stirner and Nietzsche – the moral and the aesthetic come unhinged from one another in ways that Humboldt and the Romantics of his generation would have found appalling (although their own elevation of self-reliance above reason itself surely foreshadowed these later developments).

There remained, finally, an enduring tension between the ideal of individuality and the practice of politics. Whereas Schleiermacher could understand political participation as an act of creative self-expression, later writers tended to be more sceptical. For Emerson, for instance, most forms of political participation threatened to subsume the individual into partisan rancour or party ideology, both of which were simply manifestations of conformity. Emerson's politics, like those of Thoreau, Marx and Stirner, had a strong anarchist streak: 'we shall one day learn to supersede politics by education' ('Culture' (1860), in Emerson 1983: 1020). All of these thinkers sometimes entertained the fantasy of a society regulated only by the voluntary commitments of well-formed individuals. At other times, they – Mill,

Emerson and Thoreau especially – worked hard to reconcile the demands of individuality with the claims of politics and in so doing articulated a distinctive conception of democratic citizenship.[10]

Notes

1. Yehoshua Arieli writes: 'Although individualism as a historical and sociological concept was elaborated in Europe, its value-content changed completely with its transplantation to America. The term, which in the Old World was almost synonymous with selfishness, social anarchy and individual laissez-faire, connoted in America self-determination, moral freedom, the rule of liberty and the dignity of man' (Arieli 1964: 193).
2. Humboldt is often described as a liberal rather than a Romantic. But these distinctions are highly artificial: his early writings express many of the themes and concerns that are usually thought to define the Romantic point of view. See Beiser 1992: 111–14.
3. Discussing *On Liberty* in his autobiography, Mill describes Humboldt as 'the only author who has preceded me . . . of whom I thought it appropriate to say anything' (Mill [1873] 1963–91: 1: 227).
4. Schleiermacher's German word is *Maschinenwerk*, which could be translated as 'machine shop'.
5. All translations from this text are the author's own.
6. Leroux is usually credited with the invention of the term 'socialism'. It was 'a neologism necessary', he wrote, 'to set against individualism' (see Evans 1948: 223–4). Later in his life, Leroux began to accept the term as a description of his own philosophy. 'When I invented the term *socialism*', he writes, 'to oppose it to the term *individualism*, I did not expect that twenty years later this term would be used to describe, in a general sense, the democratic religion. I wanted to capture, with this word, the doctrine or the diverse doctrines which, under one pretext or another, sacrificed the individual to society and, in the name of fraternity or under the pretext of equality, destroyed liberty. To see in my work a criticism of socialism, in the new meaning given to this word, would be to misunderstand me' (Leroux 1850: 161 n).
7. In this sense, Mill followed Humboldt's emphasis on the balance of reason and sensuality or sensual passion. On sensuality in Humboldt, see Sweet 1973: 477–9.
8. Mill was aware of Leroux and had by 1833 both met Leroux and read parts at least of the *Revue Encyclopédique*, according to a letter that Mill wrote to Thomas Carlyle on 25 November 1833. See Mill 1963–91: 12: 194.
9. The full passage reads: 'I do not look on a human being as a machine, made to be kept in action by a foreign force, to accomplish an unvarying succession of motions, to do a fixed amount of work and then to fall to pieces at death, but as a being of free spiritual powers . . . [but] I am aware, that this view is far from being universal. The common notion has been, that the mass of the people need no other culture than is necessary to fit them for their various trades' (Channing 1838: 21).
10. On this conception of citizenship in Emerson and Mill, see Zakaras 2009.

References

Arieli, Yehoshua (1964), *Individualism and Nationalism in American Ideology*, Cambridge, MA: Harvard University Press.
Aris, Reinhold (1965), *History of Political Thought in Germany from 1789 to 1815*, New York: Russel & Russel.
Bakunin, Jack (1976a), *Pierre Leroux and the Birth of Democratic Socialism, 1797–1848*, New York: Revisionist Press.
Bakunin, Jack (1976b), 'Pierre Leroux on democracy, socialism and the Enlightenment', *Journal of the History of Ideas* 37 (3): 455–74.
Baum, Bruce (2007), 'J. S. Mill and Liberal Socialism', in Nadia Urbinati and Alex Zakaras (eds), *J. S. Mill's Political Thought: A Bicentennial Reassessment*, Cambridge: Cambridge University Press, pp. 98–123.

Beiser, Frederick (1992), *Enlightenment, Revolution, and Romanticism: The Genesis of Modern German Political Thought, 1790–1800*, Cambridge, MA: Harvard University Press.

Beiser, Frederick (1996), 'Introduction', in Frederick Beiser (ed.), *The Early Political Writings of the German Romantics*, Cambridge: Cambridge University Press.

Bercovitch, Sacvan (1993), *Rites of Assent: Transformations in the Symbolic Construction of America*, New York: Routledge.

Bernstein, Eduard [1899] (1993), *The Preconditions of Socialism*, ed. and trans. Henry Tudor, Cambridge: Cambridge University Press.

Brudney, Daniel (2008), 'Grand ideals: Mill's two perfectionisms', *History of Political Thought* 29 (3): 485–515.

Burrow, John W. (1969), 'Editor's introduction', in Wilhelm von Humboldt, *The Limits of State Action*, Cambridge: Cambridge University Press, pp. xvii–lviii.

Channing, William Ellery (1838), *Self-Culture*, Boston: James Monroe & Co.

Emerson, Ralph Waldo (1983), *Emerson: Essays & Lectures*, New York: Library of America.

Evans, David Owen (1948), *Le socialisme romantique: Pierre Leroux et ses contemporains*, Paris: Rivière.

Humboldt, Wilhelm von [1791–2/1851] (1969), *The Limits of State Action*, trans. John W. Burrow, Cambridge: Cambridge University Press.

Kateb, George (1992), *The Inner Ocean: Individualism and Democratic Culture*, Ithaca: Cornell University Press.

Leroux, Pierre (1846), *D'une religion nationale, ou du culte*, Paris: Boussac.

Leroux, Pierre (1848), *Projet d'une constitution democratique et sociale*, Paris: Sandre.

Leroux, Pierre (1850), *Oeuvres de Pierre Leroux: 1825–1850*, Paris: Imprimerie du Gerdès.

Leroux, Pierre [1834] (1948), 'De l'individualisme et du socialisme', in David Owen Evans, *Le socialisme romantique: Pierre Leroux et ses contemporains*, Paris: Rivière, pp. 223–38.

Leroux, Pierre [1840] (1985), *De l'humanité*, Paris: Fayard.

Lukes, Steven (1973), *Individualism*, Oxford: Blackwell.

Maistre, Joseph de (1884–93), *Oeuvres Complètes* vol. 14, Lyon: Vitte.

Mill, John Stuart (1963–91), *The Collected Works of John Stuart Mill*, 33 vols, Toronto: University of Toronto Press.

Moulin, Léo (1955), 'On the evolution of the meaning of the word "individualism"', *International Social Science Bulletin* 7 (1): 181–5.

Saint-Cheron, Alexandre de (1831), 'Philosophie du Droit', *Revue Encyclopédique* LII: 593–606.

Schleiermacher, Friedrich Daniel Ernst [1800] (1996), *Monologues* II and III, in Frederick Beiser (ed.), *The Early Political Writings of the German Romantics*, Cambridge: Cambridge University Press, pp. 169–97.

Simmel, Georg (1971), 'Freedom and the individual', in Georg Simmel, *On Individuality and Social Forms*, ed. Donald N. Levine, Chicago: University of Chicago Press, pp. 217–26.

Sweet, Paul (1973), 'Young Wilhelm von Humboldt's writings (1789–93) reconsidered', *Journal of the History of Ideas* 34 (3): 469–82.

Taylor, Charles (1975), *Hegel*, New York: Cambridge University Press.

Ten, C.L. (1998), 'Democracy, socialism and the working class', in John Skorupski (ed.), *The Cambridge Companion to Mill*, Cambridge: Cambridge University Press, pp. 372–95.

Tocqueville, Alexis de [1835] (2004), *Democracy in America*, vol. 1, trans. Arthur Goldhammer, New York: Library of America.

Valls, Andrew (1999), 'Self-development and the liberal state: The cases of John Stuart Mill and Wilhelm von Humboldt', *The Review of Politics* 61 (2): 251–74.

Zakaras, Alex (2007), 'J. S. Mill, individuality and participatory democracy', in Nadia Urbinati and Alex Zakaras (eds), *J. S. Mill's Political Thought: A Bicentennial Reassessment*, Cambridge: Cambridge University Press, pp. 200–20.

Zakaras, Alex (2009), *Individuality and Mass Democracy: Mill, Emerson, and the Burdens of Citizenship*, New York: Oxford University Press.

13

The Rise of the Social

William Outhwaite

1. Introduction

This chapter will examine social philosophy in the nineteenth century in terms of three interrelated processes: the consolidation of a conception of society or the social; the reformulation of issues of poverty and inequality in the form of 'the social question' and related attempts at social regulation; and the emergence of the social sciences 'between literature and science' (see Lepenies [1985] 1988). Although the term 'rise' may seem to suggest an inevitable or desirable process, we shall see that the status of the social sciences and the relation between the social and the political were no less contentious at the end than at the beginning of the nineteenth century, and they remain so in the twenty-first.

How was the social conceptualised at the beginning of the nineteenth century? By 1790, there was already, in many parts of Europe, a concern with issues of poverty and inequality and a developed concept of society in the modern sense of an encompassing structure (Baker 1994; Sewell 2005: 324–8). Herder described Hume to Kant in 1767 as 'in the most literal sense a philosopher of human society' (see Masaryk 1994: 139). This sense of 'society' can be distinguished from earlier usage, where it tends to refer either to a small-scale association such as a secret society or the Society of Friends, or to the fact of association with one's 'fellows'. In contrast, the modern conception was of what Norbert Elias [1939] (1991) called a 'society of individuals', not just in the crude sense of economic individualism (though this was a substantial part of the story) but one where the relations between individuals and society were being reconfigured in thought and practice. For Elias, the emergent conception and practice of personal privacy in early modern Europe 'causes the individual to feel that "inside" himself he is something that exists quite alone, without relation to other people and that only becomes related "afterwards" to others "outside"' (Elias 1991: 28). What Elias called the 'I–We relation' is reconfigured; the (problematic) idea of an opposition between individual and society becomes a topic. It becomes increasingly possible to find people saying that their society is credulous about gods, monarchs, etc., but that they and their friends are not. As Charles Taylor wrote in a classic article on the 'Modern Social Imaginary', 'we start with individuals' (Taylor 2002: 96). He contrasts this conception with an earlier one of natural hierarchies and their harmony or disharmony. '[T]he inevitable flip side of the new understanding of the individual is a new understanding of sociality: the society of mutual benefit, whose functional differentiations are ultimately contingent and whose members are fundamentally equal' (2002: 99).

But, as Taylor readily conceded, this conception took time to bed down and replace earlier ideas of essential hierarchical difference. For example, he says, 'it is really only in our own time that the older images of hierarchical complementarity between men and women are being comprehensively challenged' (2002: 98). The secular understanding of society is another example: organised religion, far from having been seen off by the *philosophes*, continues to pervade the social conceptions of many citizens and politicians in the twenty-first century. In the nineteenth century, ideas of natural theology, which are hard to place on a continuum between credulity and secularism, played a notoriously important part. The concept of society itself remained suspect in the nineteenth century, as noted below, in politically backward parts of Europe (including Germany) and Russian serfdom, like US slavery, was not abolished until 1861.

The two themes of a society of individuals and of equality came together, before the nineteenth century began, in Rousseau's 1755 *Discourse on the Origins of Inequality*. And just before the end of the eighteenth century, Nicolas de Condorcet drew a distinction between domestic and international inequality in a way which has recently preoccupied Amartya Sen and many others. 'Our hopes for the future condition of the human race can be subsumed under three important heads: the abolition of inequality between nations, the progress of equality within each nation and the true perfection of mankind' (Condorcet [1793] 1796: 251).[1]

We also see, well before the beginning of the nineteenth century, the emergence of a distinction between political phenomena and underlying social processes. Charles-Louis Montesquieu (despite his obsession with climate which tends to embarrass modern readers in their centrally heated and/or air-conditioned rooms)[2] had already in 1748 clearly expressed the basic idea that political and legal arrangements depend on broader social processes.[3] In a more polemical vein, Thomas Paine in 1792 contrasted the necessity of society with the undesirable contingency of government. 'Government', he wrote,

> is no farther necessary than to supply the few cases to which society and civilisation are not conveniently competent; and instances are not wanting to show, that everything which government can usefully add thereto, has been performed by the common consent of society, without government [he cited the case of North America]. (Paine [1792] 1995: 215)[4]

However, what we do not find until well into the nineteenth century is the fixation on the proletariat rather than merely the poor, the masses, the *peuple* or the *Pöbel*.[5] The shift in value associations marked by the German term is unmistakable: what had been mostly a positive term in France became in Germany a negative expression of class fear. Towards the end of the century, Nietzsche extended the term *Pöbel* to the upper classes as well: 'Pöbel oben, Pöbel unten' ([1883–5] 2009: 215). '*Gesellschaft*', too, was a problematic concept for many on the political Right in what we now call Germany, where their counterparts in Britain and France had long learned to live with *society* and *société*. Blüntschli's influential dictionary of 1857–70 described *Gesellschaft* as a concept of the third estate (Adorno 1973b: 17) and Treitschke polemicised against it in 1859 (see Wagner 2001).

The German-French divide was symbolically bridged at mid-century by a German aristocratic conservative, Lorenz von Stein, writing about French socialists and communists in terms of the concept of society, and by German radicals like Marx and Engels, driven west by German reaction. At the beginning of the century, the French Revolution shaped the political imaginary of Europe and much of the world for another two centuries with its imagery of liberty and barricades. At mid-century, the 1848 revolutions pointed, depending on your political preferences, towards a 'proper' proletarian revolution, to a reinforced conservative desire for order, or to the third way, as we would now say, of the securitisation of social order through social policy. The last of these was combined with the first in reformist and gradualist socialism which was intended, in theory at least, to lead more gently to the same goal as that of the revolutionaries. Alternatively, as in Bismarckian Germany, conservatism was allied with social policy: the development of the welfare state went along with a ban on the socialist party, the Sozialdemokratische Partei Deutschlands.

Philosophy, Hegel pronounced in 1821 in his *Elements of the Philosophy of Right*, is its time apprehended in thought and this simplification will suffice for the purposes of this chapter. In the nineteenth century, the conceptualisation of the social as an object of knowledge went hand in hand with a political concern for what was coming to be called the social question and with a more academic concern for something like a social science. Some philosophers turned into militants or were rebadged as sociologists or – like Marx – both. The philosopher Leszek Kolakowski's opening line in his massive account of Marxism, 'Karl Marx was a German philosopher' (Kolakowski 1978: 1), can be read either as a truism or as an error, as it was by the British Marxist sociologist Tom Bottomore (1984). Yet Marx would probably have been even more annoyed at his posthumous designation as a sociologist and as part of a now entrenched holy trinity, along with Max Weber and Emile Durkheim from the following generation. As Herbert Schnädelbach writes,

> [I]t was more or less immediately after Hegel that sociology emerged as an independent discipline which from the beginning reserved the theme of 'society' for itself alone. Social scientists of all tendencies at that time placed no value on being regarded as philosophers; rather, philosophers presented themselves as sociologists . . . (Schnädelbach [1982] 1984: x)

Auguste Comte is a good example. He was clearly a philosopher, but he invented the term sociology in 1831 and can therefore hardly be deprived of the label sociologist, although some would prefer to assign him, along with Marx, to a category of proto-sociologists.[6] What came to be called sociology claimed a kind of special right to talk about the social, sweeping up elements of the philosophy of history,[7] ethics and related fields. At the end of the nineteenth century, Georg Simmel wrote about both and his 1900 work the *Philosophy of Money* could as easily have been called the Sociology of Money. (One of his earlier essays on the topic calls it a psychology of money; see Simmel [1889] 1997.)

In this context, the following brief remarks on the philosophy of history may be worth making. The term 'philosophie de l'histoire' was used by Voltaire in a pseudonymous text of 1765, but, as Bertrand Binoche (1994) stresses, it was in an idiosyncratic sense. Binoche focuses on Condorcet's 1793 *Tableau historique des progrès de l'esprit humain*, Dugald Stewart's natural history in his introduction to Adam Smith's *Theory of Moral Sentiments,* and Kant's discussion of historical theodicy in his 1798 *Streit der Fakultäten* (The Conflict of the Faculties). Binoche suggests that these three *genres* define the project of the philosophy of history at the end of the eighteenth century (Binoche 1994: 11). This comparative approach, in addition to its other merits, brings out the inter-relations between these and other writers. Comte, for example, learning of J. S. Mill's Scottish connection, wrote in 1843 of his enthusiasm for the Scottish enlightenment and his disinclination to look more closely at German contemporaries. This judgement contrasts with that of Victor Cousin, who had met Hegel in 1817 (and was later freed from prison in Berlin partly through his intervention). Cousin admired the German tradition and thought Adam Ferguson's *Essay on the History of Civil Society* to be feeble and moralising (Binoche 1994: 80–1).

2. Kant, Hegel and the Social

The transition from Kant to Hegel, so fundamental for modern philosophy as a whole, is also central to conceptions of the social. Kant's massive influence on objective idealist and neo-Kantian philosophy continues right through the nineteenth century and up to the present. Habermas's philosophy, for example, is essentially strung on a set of tightropes between Kant and Hegel and he makes a more general and plausible claim for the continuing influence of themes which preoccupied the Young Hegelians, who remain, as he often puts it, our contemporaries. Gillian Rose, in a hunt of McCarthyite intensity (though of course infinitely greater intelligence) for neo-Kantians, upheld the claims of *Hegel Contra Sociology* (Rose 1981), although in a way which demonstrated Hegel's importance as a social thinker in a broader sense. For Rose, 'The very idea of a scientific sociology, whether non-Marxist or Marxist, is only possible as a form of neo-Kantianism' (Rose 1981: 1–2). This is of course an exaggeration, but the importance of neo-Kantian thought for social theory, including Marxism, at the end of the nineteenth century and well into the twentieth is not in doubt.

Hegel's place in European *social* theory has still not been fully recognised, however, partly no doubt because so much twentieth-century philosophy was either analytic or Marxist or (occasionally) both.[8] The Hegelian critique of Kant was in part a sociological one (Wagner 2008: 183–5). As Frederick Copleston wrote,

> When at Berlin Hegel lectured on political theory and described the State in highfalutin terms, he was concerned with making his hearers socially and politically conscious and with overcoming what he regarded as an unfortunate one-sided emphasis on the inwardness of morality . . . (1962: 29)[9]

More fundamentally, although the idealism which was dominant throughout the century, in successive waves in different parts of Europe and North America, might be thought to be inimical to social theory, in fact this is far from the case. As Randall Collins suggests, there is both an intellectual and a practical reason for this. 'The [dialectical] method of showing the one-sidedness of concepts and their dependence on others, when applied to the ideals of morality and politics, leads to the recognition that such ideas are always social' (Collins 1998: 660). In practice, 'Hegel opened up the social sciences as disciplines and made dialectical philosophy available as an instrument of social criticism' (Collins 1998: 660). According to Collins's sociology of philosophy, which stresses competition within networks, Hegel was impelled towards this historical and social focus because Fichte and Schelling had already appropriated other areas of philosophy.

> Located at the center of action in a crowded and highly competitive space, he got virtually the last attention slot available . . . He found the slot by focussing on history, both of the intellectual community itself and of its links to the surrounding social world in general. (657)

Whatever one thinks of this slightly reductive account (see Baehr 2002: 43–55), Hegel remains at the centre of action in any account of nineteenth-century philosophy and social theory. Even if Marx and Engels had not existed, he would no doubt have been recognised in the following century as a major figure. In the event, as Paul Vogel wrote, 'with Lorenz von Stein and the Marxists . . . Hegel's concept of society . . . shook the world. A single movement of thought leads from Hegel via Stein to Lassalle' (Vogel 1925: 122). What was so revolutionary about Hegel's conception of the social? One can point to the notion of dialectical contradiction, as orthodox Marxism does, or to the role of labour, which is of course crucial also for less orthodox Marxists such as the young Habermas. Most funda- mental, though, is Hegel's historicisation both of philosophy and of what we would now call social and political structures and what Hegel terms civil society and the state. As Manfred Riedel writes, commenting on paragraphs 259 and 340 of the *Philosophy of Right*, this is no longer the traditional concept of the state, the static and ahistorical model of classical politics and modern natural law, but a radically historical conception (Riedel 1970: 24). And this is of course what Marx stressed as Hegel's principal contribution.

Against this background, the oppositions between 'young' and 'old' Hegelians and conflicts of Hegel-interpretation pale into insignificance. Even the famous contrast in which Marx set himself to Hegel with the metaphor of putting him back the right way up appears more like a continuum between a Hegel who was solidly rooted, despite his flowery language, in the contradictions of his own times and a Marx who was offering a clearer alternative to those contradictions. It is, however, useful to note how Hegel's model of society was developed through the conception of class and in particular the proletariat in Stein and Marx and Engels, through the Marxist emphasis on the primacy of society – and hence its contradictions – over the state and into the idea that there was one further step before anything like Hegelian reconciliation could be expected.

The Marxist use of Hegel has of course been historically the most important, but there has also been a conservative development of his thought, particularly in Germany and to some extent in Britain. In between these was a liberal perspective which probably owes more to Wilhelm von Humboldt (and others elsewhere in Europe) than to Hegel, but which Hegel might himself in the end have found most congenial and which predominated in the social theory of the end of the nineteenth and the early twentieth century. Liberal thought was strongly influenced by the belated publication of Wilhelm von Humboldt's book *The Limits of State Action*, written in 1791–2 (on which see Alex Zakaras's chapter in this volume), as well as by J. S. Mill's *On Liberty* and the work of Alexis de Tocqueville. Tocqueville, although he might not have sought the title, must be acknowledged, as he increasingly is, as an important political philosopher and incipient sociologist. In the Introduction to his *Democracy in America*, published in 1835, he also explicitly invokes the notion of political science: 'Il faut une science politique nouvelle à un monde tout nouveau' ('there must be a new political science for a completely new world') (Tocqueville [1835] 1888: 9). Via the neo-Kantian philosopher Charles Renouvier, this liberal tradition fed into the sociology of Emile Durkheim which dominated French social thought in the early twentieth century (see Logue 1983: 1993).

Finally, it is useful to set Hegel in counterpoint to Comte, as Marcuse ([1941] 1955) did. Comtean positivism was highly influential in France and, in a more muted form, in Britain, via the mediation of J. S. Mill.[10] Again, Durkheim assured the survival of essential elements of Comtean positivism and of the idea of a sharp break between social science and common sense, which persisted in the later twentieth century in the work of Louis Althusser and Pierre Bourdieu.

3. The Beginning of the Nineteenth Century: One Revolution or Two?

The beginning of the nineteenth century in Europe was fundamentally shaped by the French Revolution. Reactions to it fell into three broad classes. First, it could be seen as a successful, if flawed, attempt to create a rational polity which embodied the universal values of liberty, equality, fraternity and human rights. Fichte risked his youthful reputation with a bold attempt in 1793 to 'correct the Judgement of the Public on the French Revolution' and Dugald Stewart in Edinburgh was criticised for his praise of Condorcet (Collini, Winch and Burrow 1983: 32–3). In France itself, the Universal Declaration of Human Rights includes a social theory as well as legal prescriptions. As Georges Gusdorf wrote in his massive history of the human sciences, 'La Déclaration manifeste solennelle-ment les premiers principes métaphysiques de la science sociale' ('the Declaration solemnly expresses the first metaphysical principles of social science' (Gusdorf 1978: 207)). The *idéologues*, as we shall see, fought an uphill battle to preserve some of these principles of the Revolution (and, by extension, of the Enlightenment) against opposition from Napoleon and more conservative forces. In a more muted way, liberals like Tocqueville argued that one had to learn to live with the consequences of the Revolution and to try to mitigate its disadvantages. The United States, having come to this 'democratic' state without a cataclysmic revolution of the French kind, could show the way forward.

The conservative reaction was the second main line of response to the Revolution, marked in 1790 by Edmund Burke's very influential *Reflections on the Revolution in France* and, in a less nuanced way, by more explicitly conservative thinkers in France and Germany, notably Joseph de Maistre and Louis de Bonald. Karl Mannheim's classic study of *Conservatism* ([1925] 1986) remains a fundamental analysis of how responses to the Revolution shaped European conservative politics. The US sociologist Robert Nisbet (1966) brilliantly made the case for the conservative origins of sociology and although this claim cannot be sustained, as Anthony Giddens (1972) and others have pointed out, it remains the case that many of what Nisbet called the 'unit-ideas' of the emergent 'discipline' of sociology – such as those of community and the sacred – are shared with the conservative tradition. And as Mannheim stressed in his better-known *Ideology and Utopia* ([1929] 1960), the conservative critique of liberal rationalist politics – namely, the critique that it neglects more fundamental social forces – is shared by socialist and, in particular, by Marxist critics of liberalism.

This, then, was the third line of response to the Revolution: that it needs to be completed by a social revolution which really would deliver social justice and equality, rather than just a looser Tocquevillean equality of condition. Lorenz von Stein posed the issue in neutral terms:

> The basic tenet of the new Constitution of 1793 was absolute personal equality. Public law, the right to vote, public representation and legislation were established according to this principle. The state did not want to recognize, still less create, any differences. This state form, according to the law which determines the relationship between state and society, is based on the assumption that society too is not differentiated. But did social equality really exist side by side with political equality? (Stein [1850] 1964: 145)

In this third line of response, some of the more radical strands of Revolutionary thought, notably that of Gracchus Babeuf, which themselves echoed the most radical wing of the Enlightenment, were picked up in the 1830s by Marx and others.

The Revolution, then, was a fundamental caesura in social thought no less than in practical politics.[11] In France, the Revolution's after-effects under Napoleon produced a lengthy latency period until the 1820s. Napoleon's critique of the *idéologues* (to which we owe the modern, originally Marxist, use of the term ideology) succeeded in marginalising what was in fact a quite innovative approach to knowledge, which continued the themes of the pre-Revolutionary Enlightenment and which eventually came to fruition in positivism. The *idéologues* popularised the term *science sociale*, taking up Condorcet's theme of social mathematics, and they linked moral and political science to political economy and to what they called the science of legislation. Gusdorf, who gave them a prominent place in his history of the human sciences, called them 'a lost generation' (Gusdorf 1978: 549). Fredric Jameson elegantly summarises accounts of this thirty-year gap, before arguing that it is in fact substantially filled by Charles Fourier (Jameson 2005: 238–9). There were of course other continuities across this gap. The idéologues represented one line, but there were also longer-term continuities between thinkers such as Montesquieu and Tocqueville, widely separated by history but sharing many concerns and habits of thought.

The French Revolution was a massive fact.[12] The second revolution at the beginning of the nineteenth century was more conceptual and conjectural. Its most explicit advocate is perhaps Michel Foucault, in *Les mots et les choses*. As he wrote in the forward to the English translation of this work,

> Within a few years (around 1800), the tradition of general grammar was replaced by an essentially historical philology; natural classifications were ordered according to the analyses of comparative anatomy; and a political economy was founded whose main themes were labour and production. (Foucault [1966] 1970: xii)

These are of course the three foci of Foucault's book, but as he claims in the main text, they are symptomatic of a much broader shift.

> Whereas in Classical thought [that is, the thought of the seventeenth and eighteenth centuries] the sequence of chronologies merely scanned the prior and more fundamental space of a table which presented all the possibilities in advance, from now on, the contemporaneous and simultaneously observable resemblances in space will be simply the fixed forms of a succession which proceeds from analogy to analogy. ([1966] 1970: 218)

> European culture is inventing for itself a depth in which what matters is no longer identities, distinctive characters, permanent tables with all their possible paths and routes, but great hidden forces developed on the basis of their primitive and inaccessible nucleus, origin, causality and history. (251)

This is in essence the same historicising shift which Hegel performed in philosophy.

As Robert Wokler points out in a sympathetic discussion of Foucault's argument, this picture needs to be filled out with a discussion of the emergent *institutions* that were concerned with developing the human sciences in the period of the Revolution and with developing the concept of social science itself (Wokler 1987: 326–7). The term 'science sociale' seems to have been first used in a classic pre-Revolutionary text, the Abbé Sieyès's *Qu'est-ce que le tiers état?* (What Is the Third Estate?) and the term was subsequently used by Condorcet and others.

It appears from these early, almost casual, invocations of *la science sociale* . . . that the term was at first ill-defined . . . More important, however, is the fact that each author assimilated his conception of a social science with other human sciences, including . . . *la morale* and *la politique*, whose integration it was the task of *la science sociale* to achieve. (Wokler 1987: 329)

The next section addresses this issue of the emergence of what we now call the social and political sciences.

4. The Social and the Political

What emerged in the nineteenth century was the notion, in both Marxist and non-Marxist social theory, that states were secondary to broader social processes. Collini, Winch and Burrow make this point negatively in relation to the philosophy of history and they would undoubtedly say the same of much sociology: 'the category of the political is deprived of all significant autonomy by incorporation in some larger story of the unfolding and mutation of social and economic forms' (1983: 7).[13] William Sewell Jr. characterises the social in a related sense: 'The social . . . is best understood as, first, an articulated, evolving, web of semiotic practices . . . that, second, builds up and transforms a range of physical frameworks' (Sewell 2005: 369).

Putting the same issue in historical terms, Peter Wagner (2001) has traced the rise and fall of the concept of society and has shown how sociology can be seen as offering a certain set of answers to questions of political philosophy, rather than transcending or relativising them, as it had once claimed to do. In other words, the social and the political are more like two sides of the same coin than two separate, if intersecting, spheres. As Pierre Manent wrote in 1982 of Tocqueville,

> To distinguish between democracy as a social state and democracy as a political institution is not to apply to democracy a general 'sociological' distinction. Nor does the heavier weight attached to the social state derive from a causal primacy attributed in general to the social over the political instance. Nor, finally, are the social and the political two 'aspects' of democracy, distinguished arbitrarily in the face of the massive opacity of the fact, or two 'conceptual levels' deliberately constructed for expository convenience by the observer of democracy. It is democracy as *the thing itself* which is given in this *real* duality. (Manent [1982] 1993: 48)

At the same time, however, there was a clear tension between the social and the political in much early use of the term social science or sociology. Both positivists and Marxists tended to present themselves as undercutting or transcending what was conventionally seen as political. Even someone such as Saint-Simon, who was closely attuned to political issues (including the issue of what we now call European integration), saw himself as undercutting the political.[14]

This theme of undercutting the political is evident in one of Marx's earliest and richest texts, his essay 'On the Jewish Question' of 1844 (see Marx 1975). This includes a critique of the political illusion (which was later taken up by Régis Debray and others). The political illusion parallels and mimics the religious illusion, both expressions of distorted social relations. The diremption (*Entzweiung*) of heaven and earth, god and human, state and civil society expresses in a transfigured or distorted form that between exploiters and exploited.[15]

There is, however, a further aspect of both positivist and Marxist thought in the nineteenth century which demands attention: the idea that something like a social science would also supersede philosophy. In Comte's religion of humanity, philosopher kings were to be replaced by sociologists, while Marx and Engels anticipated a realisation of philosophy which would also be its *Aufhebung* (Labica 1976). Adorno wrote one of many epitaphs of this conception: 'Philosophy lives on because the moment to realize it was missed' (Adorno [1966] 1973a: 3). While this deeply ambiguous remark seems to let Marx off the hook, Stefan Collini is more thoroughly negative about positivism and, by implication, Marxism as well.

> [I]f the positivist project of much of nineteenth-century social science now seems to have been a deeply flawed one . . . this must shift our attention to the philosophical anthropology, the metaphysical sympathies and the scale of values which actually animated these theories. And this points to the final irony of the matter, for it means that in writing the history of those nineteenth-century attempts to supersede philosophy by social science we cannot help engaging in philosophical criticism of them. (Collini 1980: 231)

I shall suggest in the conclusion that there is a little more to be said in defence of the social, but first we should look at the third main theme of this chapter, that of the 'social' question – a theme that is far from exhausted, even if the terms of it have changed from the early nineteenth to the early twenty-first century. We may argue about whether we have a Marxist or Lukácsian proletariat, or a Fanonist third world one, or a post-Marxist global *Lumpenproletariat* – but the poor are always with us.

5. The 'Social' Question

There was a substantial convergence of analysis among nineteenth-century thinkers concerned with poverty and related issues. However much their prognoses and prescriptions may have differed, Hegel (and even Fichte [1806] 1847: 236–9), Lorenz von Stein, Marx and Engels and Tocqueville all characterise the situation of the growing working classes in very similar terms. At the most descriptive level, Tocqueville and Engels converged on Manchester (Tocqueville in 1833 and 1835, Engels in 1842) and said much the same about it.

> From this foul drain the greatest stream of human industry flows out to fertilise the whole world. From this filthy sewer pure gold flows. Here humanity attains its most complete development and its most brutish; here civilisation works its miracles and civilised man is turned back almost into a savage. (Tocqueville [1835] 1958: 107–8)

This is Tocqueville, but even the antithesis in the last phrase sounds like Engels; the difference lies only in the prognosis. For Engels, 'It is too late for a peaceful solution' (Engels [1844] 1987: 292). For Tocqueville, in contrast,

> England seems to me in a critical state in that certain events, which it is possible to predict, can from one moment to another throw her into a state of violent revolution. But if things follow their natural course, I do not think that this revolution will come . . . (Tocqueville [1835] 1958: 73)

Somewhat later, Tocqueville, Stein, Marx and Engels converged again on the 1848 revolutions. For Marx and Engels, of course, they embodied the spectre of communism haunting Europe in *The Communist Manifesto*. For Tocqueville, speaking in 1835 just before the revolutions, 'we are at this moment sleeping on a volcano . . . the earth is quaking once again in Europe' ([1835] 1958: 12–13).

As for Stein, as Kaethe Mengelberg notes, 'Stein never identifies himself with any class position; he takes rather a detached point of view' (see Stein 1964: 29). Stein's social reformist approach won out in most of Western Europe. In Britain, the term 'social science' essentially meant a cluster of social reformist concerns with the working classes and the poor, prefiguring what in disciplinary terms we would now call social policy. This 'social science' had links to eighteenth-century Scottish moral philosophy, to philosophical radicalism and, more antagonistically, to utilitarianism and political economy and to Comtean positivism (Yeo 1996: x, 34–5, 110–12). But its principal concerns were more practical. Thus, social reformist concerns invoked and even colonised the term 'social science'. The Statistical Societies of Manchester, London and a number of other British and US cities were founded in the 1830s, the Social Science Association in 1857, followed in 1862 by the Association Internationale pour le Progrès des Sciences Sociales and in 1865 by the American Association for the Promotion of Social Science. The Verein für Sozialpolitik, best known today for Max Weber's later involvement in it, was founded in Germany in 1872. The semantic associations between the social question, socialism and social science persisted into the late twentieth century (for example, into the attack made on social science in the UK by the Thatcher government, which led to the renaming in 1983 of the Social Science Research Council as the Economic and Social Research Council).

6. The Later Nineteenth Century

If philosophy took a significant turn toward the social in the middle of the nineteenth century, a second impetus, which both preceded it and continued well into the twentieth century, was what came retrospectively to be called historicism.[16] Schnädelbach writes of a 'historicist Enlightenment' and stresses that the critique of Enlightenment was only one of the three strands that he identifies in historicism.

> The first sense of 'historicism' (historicism1) is positivism in relation to the human sciences: the value-free accumulation of material and facts without distinction between what is and what is not important, which nevertheless makes a claim to scientific objectivity . . .

> In another use, 'historicism' refers to what can be regarded as the theoretical justification of historicism1: historicism in the sense of historical *relativism* (historicism2) . . .

> [Historicism3] . . . is the view that all cultural phenomena are to be regarded, to be understood and explained as historical. (Schnädelbach [1982] 1984: 37–8)

I shall focus here on the epistemological and methodological issues raised in relation to the human sciences as a whole, notably by the German historian Droysen and by Dilthey and by the 'historical schools' of law and economics. Droysen launched in the 1850s an anti-positivist programme, based around the idea of 'understanding' (*Verstehen*), the implications of which went well beyond history and shaped the anti-naturalist or 'methodological dualist' approach to the social sciences, especially, but not only, in Germany, for the following century and a half up to the present. The notion of under-standing historical materials had been developed in early nineteenth-century classical philology and theological hermeneutics (notably by Schleiermacher), but it acquired its polemical point in the reaction against Kantian rationalism, Hegelian speculative philo-sophy of history and scientific and historiographical positivism. For Droysen, as later for Dilthey, we are to understand historical expressions from the inside, as psychic expressions located in a broader intellectual context. Dilthey later took Hegel's concept of objective spirit but removed it from its developmental sequence in the Hegelian architectonic. The emphasis was now more on the diversity of human personality and culture, against a background of an underlying unity of human nature which underwrites the process of understanding. In the classic phrase, you don't need to *be* Caesar to understand him, but you do need to be a human being (and not, as we might now add, just a smart system observing regularities and applying algorithms to them as in predictive texting).

These principles were extended from the study of history and culture to the social sciences (although this development lies largely outside the time-frame of this volume). Throughout the nineteenth century, however, there were complementary developments in law and economics which stressed the importance of understanding legal and economic principles and structures in a broader social and historical context. Friedrich Carl von Savigny, who had argued in 1814 against the over-hasty codification of German law, co-founded in 1815 a journal, the *Zeitschrift für geschichtliche Rechtswissenschaft* (Journal for the Historical Science of Law), representing the historical approach to law inaugurated by Gustav von Hugo. Savigny's *History of Roman Law in the Middle Ages* (1815–31) was one of the emblematic texts of the historical school of law.[17]

As for the historical school of economics, this is conventionally divided into three phases. The first is represented by Wilhelm Roscher, Karl Knies and Bruno Hildebrand.[18] The second phase is dominated by Gustav von Schmoller, whose response to Carl Menger initiated the controversy known as the *Methodenstreit*. The third phase is dominated by Werner Sombart and Max Weber. Roscher explicitly announced his intention to do 'something akin to what the method of Savigny and Eichhorn has achieved for jurispru-dence' (Roscher 1843: 2). And Knies gives a clear statement of the basic principles:

> The economic life of a people is so closely interwoven with other areas of its life that any particular observation can only be made if one keeps in view its relation with the whole . . . political economy is therefore enjoined to take its place with the moral and political sciences. Only then does it effect a proper connection with real life . . . (Knies 1883: 436–7)[19]

The 'historical schools' of law and economics formed the basis of much twentieth-century social science, not least that of Max Weber (who, however, increasingly distanced himself from them).[20]

Philosophical theories of the social, then, were very substantially shaped by issues in historiography and the philosophy of history. The early part of the century was heavily influenced by the speculative philosophy of history of Hegel and the Young Hegelians – what Karl Popper (1945) misleadingly called historicism. For Marx, the end of history, or of pre-history as an antagonistic process of class conflict, was also the end or *Aufhebung* of philosophy as an intellectual reflection on and of human history and its conflicts. The later part of the century was dominated, at least in Germany, by historicism properly so called, a more scientific and, as Hans-Georg Gadamer was later to complain, even scientistic or objectivistic methodology. But in the early twentieth century social theory cut itself off from philosophy of history and from historicism (Antoni 1959), as it had from natural law (Löwith [1941] 1965; Chernilo forthcoming). The leading midwife of this process was Max Weber, who emerged from the Historical Schools of law and economics and came to call himself a sociologist in the last decade of his life.

Yet this separation left a good deal of unfinished business, in the form of neo-Kantian methodologies, an unclear relation to law – which has opened up again in the late twentieth century with the rise of universalistic and globalised notions of human rights – and a continuing tension between unitary and dualistic conceptions of science and between scientific and more speculative approaches to the social world.

7. Conclusion

Historians of ideas from Stuart Hughes (1958) to John Burrow (2000) have pointed to the pessimistic tone of much of the thought of the later nineteenth century compared to that of the period before 1848. Georg Lukács ([1937] 1962) echoes Marx's account according to which there was a degeneration of political economy after the 1848 revolutions, as the bourgeoisie went on the defensive against the working class and its economic thinkers. Lukács also argues against a similar shift that he saw in literature away from grand historical themes and towards 'bourgeois interiority'. Burrow, while critical of Lukács for exaggerating this, points to the reaction against 'the tedium of contemporary life' which was particularly strong in France in the 1850s and 1860s (Burrow 2000: 28).[21] Something like a retreat to a more cautious or realistic position can also be found in the philosophical scene of the period, with the rejection of Hegelian idealism in Germany in favour of a more relativistic historicism in history and in what came to be called the social sciences, and a greater engagement with natural science. In France, the latter was sustained throughout the century by the strength of positivism. In Germany, the philosophy of life, which had its origins in Dilthey's work in the 1880s and onwards, took an increasingly irrationalist turn in the late nineteenth century, forming a lethal mix with anti-Semitism (which, as well as having been called 'the socialism of fools', in a remark often attributed to Bebel, should also be seen as the sociology of fools; Stoetzler 2009). In a less dramatic turn, as we saw in the previous section, German historicism, as well as British caution, curbed the enthusiasm earlier in the century for holistic evolutionary sociology, which was also much more muted in the form in which Durkheim, following Comte, introduced it in France. By 1890, the golden age of classical social theory, represented by Ferdinand Tönnies, Georg Simmel, Durkheim and eventually Max Weber, was well established.

Notes

1. In his 1782 acceptance speech to the Paris Academy of Sciences, Condorcet was similarly optimistic about the emergent social sciences: 'Those sciences, created almost in our own days, the object of which is man himself, the direct goal of which is the happiness of man, will enjoy a progress no less sure than that of the physical sciences . . .' (Condorcet, cited in Hankins 1985: 183).
2. As Melvin Richter (1976) pointed out, however, climate does not in fact play such a large part in Montesquieu's explanations and he sees its influence as diminishing over historical time.
3. As well as The Spirit of the Laws, see Montesquieu's 'Essay on the Causes That May Affect Men's Minds and Characters' ([1736] 1976) and Richter's introduction to it (Richter 1976). David

Carrithers writes: 'Hindsight suggests that Montesquieu was the single most important figure in the Enlightenment for the science of society. No other theorist inspired so much "sociological" investigation and speculation, sometimes to corroborate and sometimes to rebut the diverse materials and contentions within *L'esprit des lois*' (Carrithers 1995: 264, n. 39).

4. This is a familiar theme, echoed for example by the Russian Ivan Aksakov: 'Society . . . is that medium in which is shaped the conscious mental activity of a people . . . society alone can save the people and stop the diseased overgrowth of the state' (cited in Hare 1951: 150). In the conservative version of Louis de Bonald (1796), nature creates necessary relations between members of society and laws based on human opinions can only cause damage.

5. As John Burrow notes, 'The French idea of the people – though one finds it also in Carlyle – was not quite the German *Volk*, the nation as autonomous creator and poet, though it could come very close to it. It was more like the Marxist proletariat, seen as the essence of humanity itself, though more sentimentally conceived' (Burrow 2000: 12).

6. See, for example, Ritzer and Stepnisky 2010. Robert Brown writes: 'Comte did not, and could not correctly, claim to be practising empirical sociology, for that discipline remained to be invented. He believed that the task of the sociologist of the future would be to discover social laws that . . . would take account of two facts: the cumulative effect on people's behaviour of social factors over time and the way in which social institutions and customs are always parts of a social system and operate as an "ensemble" of interrelated factors . . .' (Brown 1994: 160).

7. Masaryk runs these together: 'After Kant and Hume philosophy . . . became more collectivistic, especially sociological philosophy (in Germany, philosophy of history)' (Masaryk 1994: 225; see Flint 1893 for a discussion of Comte and others in these terms; also Barth 1897; Schnädelbach [1982] 1984: ch. 2). As Collini, Winch and Burrow write of Britain: 'devotees of the science of politics in the second half of the nineteenth century increasingly had to come to terms with the cultural hegemony of "the philosophy of history" and "the science of society"' (Collini, Winch and Burrow 1983: 11). Later they write more impatiently of 'the nineteenth-century tendency to reduce politics to a residual appendage of "civilisation" (more usually "society") and to tell it, essentially, to keep out of the way' (193).

8. Marcuse ([1941] 1955) remains an excellent overview of the development of social thought and philosophy, focusing on the conceptual opposition between Hegel and Comtean positivism and giving substantial attention to Lorenz von Stein.

9. Axel Honneth has, however, argued that Kant's philosophy of history is closer to Hegel's than is often realised and takes a more 'sociologically realistic' form (Honneth 2007: 26–7; see also Kleingeld 1999).

10. As well as Mill's work, notably Book VI of his *System of Logic*, works such as Buckle's *History of Civilisation in England* (1857–61) were extremely influential. Buckle's positivism attracted the hostility of the German historicist Droysen, who wrote in 1852 that 'crass positivism is unfortunately finding great support even in the development of the German sciences' (Spieler 1970: 20 n; cf. Outhwaite [1975] 1986).

11. It also, as Koselleck (2008) notes, shaped attitudes to the Enlightenment – a term which had recently come into use.

12. Randall Collins, however, downplays the Revolution's intellectual influence on the idealist philosophical community in favour of more internal processes. He writes that: 'The effects of the Revolution on the content of philosophy were not so much ideological as structural. It coincided with quite different activity in various nations because the material means of intellectual organization were different in these places' (Collins 1998: 661–2). More generally, the 'long' nineteenth century is strung between two world-historical revolutions, the French and the Russian. The latter, of course, failed in 1905 and succeeded only in 1917, but is prefigured in much of the political activity in the late nineteenth century.

13. Stefan Collini writes, for example, of Herbert Spencer that 'His was one of the most extreme of those nineteenth-century theories which claimed to detect a progressive trend in social development which would lead to the ultimate disappearance of the traditional problems of politics' (Collini 1980: 209). In more recent social and political theory, however, there has been a

reaffirmation of the importance of political processes in the creation or 'institution' of societies, marked in one way by the work of Hannah Arendt.

14. Comte, however, stresses the interdependence of society and government: 'Although it may be useful and, in certain cases, even necessary to consider the idea of society, abstracted from that of *government*, it is universally recognized that these ideas are in fact inseparable' (Comte [1826] 1974: 227).

15. Anthony Polan (1984), in his very suggestive book on Lenin, traces this anti-political theme into twentieth-century Marxism.

16. See also James Connelly's discussion of historicism in Chapter 8 of this volume.

17. For a brilliant discussion of later neo-Kantian theories of law and their implications for twentieth-century philosophy and social theory, see Rose 1984. Britain had the equivalent of a historical school of law in the work of Henry Maine and others.

18. Roscher and Knies are best known now for Max Weber's critiques of 1903–6 (Weber 1975). Roscher also published a short book on democracy.

19. This is a new edition of a book published under a marginally different title in 1833. See Jun Kobayashi (2001: 56), where these passages are translated. I am indebted to Pearson and Kobayashi respectively for these quotations and their translations.

20. See, for example, Eucken 1940; Koslowski 2005. For a more sceptical account of the 'historical school', see Pearson 1999. Pearson, arguing that the 'German historical school' was neither German nor historical nor a school, shows at least that these terms have to be taken with a grain of salt. Hirschman (1982) is a brilliant discussion of the interrelations between theories of the economy from the seventeenth century to the twentieth.

21. There were also, he suggests, three principal areas of anxiety for the middle classes: the rise of democracy, the growth of cities and the urban proletariat and the decline of religion (Burrow 2000: xi).

References

Adorno, Theodor [1966] (1973a), *Negative Dialectics*, trans. E. B. Ashton, London: Routledge.

Adorno, Theodor (1973b), 'Society', in The Frankfurt Institute for Social Research, *Aspects of Sociology*, trans. John Viertel, London: Heinemann, pp. 16–36.

Antoni, Carlo (1959), *From History to Sociology: The Transition in German Historical Thinking*, London: Merlin Press.

Baehr, Peter (2002), *Founders, Classics, Canons: Modern Disputes over the Origins and Appraisal of Sociology's Heritage*, London: Transaction.

Baker, Keith Michael (1994), 'Enlightenment and the institution of society: Notes for a conceptual history', in Wilhelm Melching and Wyger Velema (eds), *Main Trends in Cultural History*, Amsterdam: Rodopi, pp. 95–121.

Barth, Paul (1897), *Die Philosophie der Geschichte als Soziologie*, Leipzig: Reisland.

Binoche, Bertrand (1994), *Les trois sources des philosophies de l'histoire (1764–1798)*, Paris: Presses Universitaires de France.

Bonald, Louis de (1796), *Théorie de l'éducation sociale*, Paris.

Bottomore, Tom (1984), *Sociology and Socialism*, Basingstoke: Macmillan.

Brown, Robert (1994), 'Comte and Positivism', in C. L. Ten (ed.), *The Nineteenth Century*, Routledge History of Philosophy, vol. 7, London: Routledge, pp. 148–76.

Burrow, John (2000), *The Crisis of Reason. European Thought, 1848–1914*, New Haven and London: Yale University Press.

Carrithers, David (1995), 'The Enlightenment science of society', in Christopher Fox, Roy Porter and Robert Wokler (eds), *Inventing Human Science. Eighteenth-Century Domains*, Berkeley: University of California Press, pp. 232–70.

Chernilo, Daniel (forthcoming), *The Normative Foundations of Modern Social Theory: The Case of Natural Law*, Cambridge: Cambridge University Press.

Collini, Stefan (1980), 'Political theory and the "science of society" in Victorian Britain', The Historical Journal 23 (1): 203–31.

Collini, Stefan, Donald Winch and John Burrow (1983), That Noble Science of Politics: A Study in Nineteenth-Century Intellectual History, Cambridge: Cambridge University Press.

Collins, Randall (1998), The Sociology of Philosophies: A Global Theory of Intellectual Change, London: Belknap Press.

Comte, Auguste [1826] (1974), 'Considérations sur le pouvoir spirituel', Le Producteur 13: 20–1; reprinted as an appendix to Comte's Système de politique positive; and translated as 'Considerations on the spiritual power', in Auguste Comte, The Crisis of Industrial Civilisation: The Early Essays of Auguste Comte, ed. Ronald Fletcher, London: Heinemann, pp. 214–45.

Condorcet, Marquis de [1793] (1796), Outline of an Historical View of the Progress of the Human Mind, Philadelphia: Lang and Ustick.

Copleston, Frederick (1962), A History of Philosophy, vol. 7, part 1: Fichte to Hegel, New York: Doubleday.

Elias, Norbert [1939] (1991), The Society of Individuals, ed. Michael Schroter, trans. Edmund Jephcott, Oxford: Blackwell.

Engels, Friedrich [1844] (1987), The Condition of the English Working Class, Harmondsworth: Penguin.

Eucken, Walter (1940), 'Wissenschaft im Stile Schmollers', Weltwirtschaftliches Archiv 52 (2): 468–506.

Fichte, Johann Gottlieb [1806] (1847), The Characteristics of the Present Age, London: John Chapman.

Flint, Robert (1893), History of the Philosophy of History: Historical Philosophy in France, French Belgium, and Switzerland, Edinburgh and London: Blackwood & Sons.

Foucault, Michel [1966] (1970), The Order of Things: An Archaeology of the Human Sciences, trans. Alan Sheridan, London: Tavistock.

Giddens, Anthony (1972), 'Four myths in the history of social thought', Economy and Society 1 (4): 357–85.

Gusdorf, Georges (1978), Les sciences humaines et la pensée occidentale: La conscience révolutionnaire; Les idéologues, Paris: Payot.

Hankins, Thomas (1985), Science and the Enlightenment, Cambridge: Cambridge University Press.

Hare, Richard (1951), Pioneers of Russian Social Thought, London: Oxford University Press.

Hirschman, Albert (1982), 'Rival interpretations of market society: Civilizing, destructive, or feeble?', Journal of Economic Literature XX: 1463–84.

Honneth, Axel (2007), 'Die Unhintergehbarkeit des Fortschritts. Kants Bestimmung des Verhältnisses von Moral und Geschichte', in Axel Honneth, Pathologien der Vernunft. Geschichte und Gegenwart der Kritischen Theorie, Frankfurt: Suhrkamp, pp. 9–27.

Hughes, Henry Stuart (1958), Consciousness and Society: The Reorientation of European Social Thought, 1890–1930, New York: Knopf.

Jameson, Fredric (2005), 'Fourier, or, Ontology and Utopia', in Fredric Jameson, Archaeologies of the Future, London: Verso, pp. 237–53.

Kleingeld, Pauline (1999), 'Kant, history and the idea of moral development', History of Philosophy Quarterly, 16 (1): 59–80.

Knies, Karl (1883), Politische Oekonomie vom geschichtlichen Standpunkt, Braunschweig: Schwetschke.

Kobayashi, Jun (2001), 'Karl Knies' conception of political economy', in Yuichi Shionoya (ed.), The German Historical School, London: Routledge, pp. 54–71.

Kolakowski, Leszek (1978), Main Currents of Marxism, Vol. 1: The Founders, Oxford: Oxford University Press.

Koselleck, Reinhart (2008), 'The status of the Enlightenment in German history', in Hans Joas and Klaus Wiegandt (eds), The Cultural Values of Europe, Liverpool: Liverpool University Press, pp. 253–64.

Koslowski, Peter (ed.) (2005), The Discovery of Historicity in German Idealism and Historism, Berlin: Springer.

Labica, Georges (1976), Marxism and the Status of Philosophy, Sussex: Harvester.

Lepenies, Wolf [1985] (1988), *Between Literature and Science: The Rise of Sociology*, Cambridge: Cambridge University Press.

Logue, William (1983), *From Philosophy to Sociology: The Evolution of French Liberalism*, Dekalb: Northern Illinois University Press.

Logue, William (1993), *Charles Renouvier, Philosopher of Liberty*, Baton Rouge and London: Louisiana State University Press.

Löwith, Karl [1941] (1965), *From Hegel to Nietzsche*, London: Constable.

Lukács, Georg [1937] (1962), *The Historical Novel*, London: Merlin.

Manent, Pierre [1982] (1993), *Tocqueville et la nature de la démocratie*, Paris: Fayard.

Mannheim, Karl [1929] (1960), *Ideology and Utopia*, London: Routledge and Kegan Paul.

Mannheim, Karl [1925] (1986), *Conservatism*, London: Routledge.

Marcuse, Herbert [1941] (1955), *Reason and Revolution: Hegel and the Rise of Social Theory*, London: Routledge and Kegan Paul.

Marx, Karl (1975), 'On the Jewish Question', in *Karl Marx: Early Writings*, ed. Lucio Colletti, Harmondsworth: Penguin, pp. 243–59.

Masaryk, Thomas (1994), *Constructive Sociological Theory*, ed. Alan Woolfolk and Jonathan B. Imber, London: Transaction.

Montesquieu, Charles-Louis de [1736] (1976), 'Essay on the causes that may affect men's minds and characters', *Political Theory* 4 (2): 139–62.

Nietzsche, Friedrich Wilhelm ([1883–5] 2009), *Also Sprach Zarathustra*, Munich: GRIN Verlag.

Nisbet, Robert (1966), *The Sociological Tradition*, New York: Basic Books.

Outhwaite, William [1975] (1986), *Understanding Social Life: The Method Called* Verstehen, Lewes: Jean Stroud.

Paine, Thomas (1976), *Common Sense*, Harmondsworth: Penguin.

Paine, Thomas [1792] (1995), *The Rights of Man*, in Thomas Paine, *The Rights of Man, Common Sense and Other Writings*, ed. Mark Philp, New York: Oxford University Press.

Pearson, Heath (1999), 'Was there really a German historical school of economics?', *History of Political Economy*, 31 (3): 547–62.

Polan, Anthony (1984), *Lenin and the End of Politics*, Berkeley: University of California Press.

Popper, Karl (1945), *The Open Society and its Enemies*, London: Routledge.

Richter, Melvin (1976), 'Introduction to Montesquieu's essay on the causes that may affect men's minds and characters', *Political Theory* 4 (2): 132–8.

Riedel, Manfred (1970), *Bürgerliche Gesellschaft und Staat: Grundproblem und Struktur der Hegelschen Rechtsphilosophie*, Berlin: Luchterhand.

Ritzer, George and Jeff Stepnisky (eds) (2010), *The New Companion to Classical Social Theorists*, Oxford: Blackwell.

Roscher, Wilhelm (1843), *Grundriss zu Vorlesungen über die Staatswirtschaft nach geschichtlicher Methode*, Göttingen: Dieterischen Buchhandlung.

Rose, Gillian (1981), *Hegel Contra Sociology*, London: Athlone.

Rose, Gillian (1984), *Dialectic of Nihilism: Post-Structuralism and Law*, Oxford: Blackwell.

Schnädelbach, Herbert [1982] (1984), *Philosophy in Germany 1831–1933*, Cambridge: Cambridge University Press.

Sewell, William H, Jr. (2005), *Logics of History: Social Theory and Social Transformation*, Chicago: Chicago University Press.

Simmel, Georg [1889] (1997), 'On the psychology of money', in Georg Simmel, *Simmel on Culture*, eds David Frisby and Mike Featherstone, London: Sage, pp. 233–42.

Spieler, Karl-Heinz (1970), *Droysen*, Berlin: Duncker.

Stein, Lorenz von [1850] (1964), *The History of the Social Movement in France, 1789–1850*, ed. Kaethe Mengelberg, New York: Bedminster Press.

Stoetzler, Marcel (2009), *The State, the Nation, and the Jews*, Lincoln: University of Nebraska Press.

Taylor, Charles (2002), 'Modern social imaginaries', *Public Culture*, 14 (1): 91–124.

Tocqueville, Alexis de [1835] (1888), *De la démocratie en Amérique*, Paris: Calmann Lévy.

Tocqueville, Alexis de [1835] (1958), *Journeys to England and Ireland*, trans. George Lawrence and K. P. Mayer, ed. J. P. Mayer, London: Faber and Faber.

Vogel, Paul (1925), *Hegels Gesellschaftsbegriff und seine geschichtliche Fortbildung durch Lorenz Stein, Marx, Engels und Lassalle, Kant-Studien*, Ergänzungsheft Nr. 59, Berlin: Heise.

Wagner, Peter (2001), *A History and Theory of the Social Sciences*, London: Sage.

Wagner, Peter (2008), *Modernity as Experience and Interpretation*, Cambridge: Polity.

Weber, Max (1975), *Roscher and Knies: The Logical Problems of Historical Economics*, trans. Guy Oakes, New York: Free Press.

Wokler, Robert (1987), 'Saint-Simon and the passage from political to social science', in Anthony Pagden (ed.), *The Languages of Political Theory in Early-Modern Europe*, Cambridge: Cambridge University Press, pp. 325–38.

Yeo, Eileen (1996), *The Contest for Social Science: Relations and Representations of Gender and Class*, London: Rivers Oram.

14

Theory and Practice of Revolution in the Nineteenth Century

Paul Blackledge

1. Introduction

The word 'revolution' was first used in an unmistakably modern sense in the eighteenth century to describe the American and French Revolutions. And although it had begun to gravitate towards something like this modern meaning in England in the wake of her seventeenth-century revolutions (Williams 1976; Hill 1991; Hobsbawm 1962: 74–5), John Dunn is right that 'in a few short months, in the year of 1789, the people of France set their stamp ineffaceably on a political idea which has loomed over the history of the world ever since' (Dunn 2008: 17). In fact, as Krishan Kumar points out, the French Revolution inspired 'practically every important statement about revolution in the subsequent century and a half' (Kumar 1971: 2).

Maximilien Robespierre's name is pivotal to this contested legacy. His linkage of virtue and terror through revolutionary government proved not only to be a fundamental point of reference for all subsequent analyses of the Revolution itself but it also provided the backdrop to all ensuing debates on the nature of revolution more broadly. The most important contribution to these debates was made by Karl Marx, who, alongside Frederick Engels, engaged with this issue from a position that was deeply influenced not only by his reading of Hegel but also by engagements with other critics of capitalism. To make sense of the meaning of the word revolution in the nineteenth century, therefore, necessarily means engaging with the ideas of Marx, through the lens of his relationships both to Jacobinism and classical German philosophy and to other socialist and anarchist intellectuals.

2. The Jacobin Legacy

In his classic critique of Marxism, *The Preconditions of Socialism* of 1899, Eduard Bernstein insisted that Marx had failed to transcend the Jacobin perspective, that is, the perspective of the followers of Robespierre who supported his programme of revolutionary Terror. Bernstein claimed that Hegelian philosophy was 'a reflex of the great French Revolution' and that insofar as Marxism failed to disentangle itself from this framework it too remained politically tied to the far-left tendencies which carried forth the Jacobin tradition into the nineteenth century (Bernstein [1899] 1993: 36–46). For Bernstein these tendencies were represented classically by two revolutionary communists: François-Noël 'Gracchus' Babeuf who was guillotined after a failed insurrection in 1796 and Louis-Auguste Blanqui who attempted many similar insurrections throughout the nineteenth century and consequently spent most of his adult life in prison.

Bernstein did not believe that Marx and Engels were uncritical of Babeuf and Blanqui. Rather, he thought that their attempt to synthesise the 'destructive' politics of these early socialists with more modern and more 'constructive' tendencies was a failure that bequeathed an unstable compromise to their followers. Concretely, Bernstein argued that whereas Babeuf and Blanqui had followed the Jacobins in demanding the violent over-throw of the old order, modern socialism – Bernstein was writing specifically about the German Social Democratic Party (SPD) at the turn of the twentieth century – emerged in a radically different context. Once the political rights of voting, association and a free press had been established, the old methods of 'political expropriation' were no longer relevant. Emancipation was now to come through 'economic organisation'. Bernstein claimed that Marx, in trying 'to combine the essentials of both [of these] streams' in his political theory, bequeathed to his followers an incoherent compromise from which Bernstein intended to extricate them (Bernstein [1899] 1993: 40–1).

Bernstein's claim that there is a direct lineage from Robespierre to Marx has often been repeated (Birchall 1997: 126, 155). Indeed, even Mikhail Bakunin, who challenged Marx from a diametrically opposed perspective, agreed with Bernstein that the faults with Marxism could be traced back to its Jacobin heritage. Admittedly, Bakunin claimed that the lineage from Robespierre to Marx passed not through Babeuf and Blanqui but via a more reformist route, arguing that 'in respect to politics [Marx] is a direct disciple of Louis Blanc' (Bakunin [1873] 1990: 142). Nonetheless, he would have agreed with Bernstein that the faults with Marxism traced back to his inheritance from Robespierre, for – Bakunin claimed – Marx, like Robespierre and Blanc, believed that radical reforms could come through the state.

A problem with both Bernstein's and Bakunin's claims is that while Marx obviously admired Robespierre's 'historical greatness and revolutionary energy', he explicitly rejected Jacobinism 'as a model or source of inspiration for socialist revolutionary praxis' (Löwy 1989: 119). From his earliest writings, Marx drew on Hegel's analysis of Jacobinism to criticise the one-sidedly political character of Robespierre's practice (Marx [1844] 1975c: 413). Moreover, as Michael Löwy suggests, Babeuf was the only actor from the Great French Revolution whom Marx saw as a 'really important . . . precursor' (Löwy 1989: 119). To untangle Marxism from Jacobinism thus requires first making sense of Babeuf's relationship with Robespierre.

One aspect of the difference between these two revolutionaries is uncontentious. Whereas Robespierre followed Rousseau in believing that the 'general will' could be represented in a modern society, Babeuf began to move towards a class analysis of the Revolution which, by placing conflicts between the rich and the poor at the centre of the struggle for 'common happiness', pointed beyond Rousseau's politics (Birchall 1997: 147). This is not to suggest that Robespierre was an uncritical follower of Rousseau. He was well aware that, although Rousseau had suggested that tyrannies could be overthrown by revolutionary movements, he had had no developed theory of revolution (O'Hagan 1999: 56). Robespierre thus recognised that his own revolutionary politics was 'as new as the revolution which brought it into being' (Robespierre [1793] 2007: 98).

Andrew Levine highlights one aspect of this difference between Robespierre and Rousseau. He points out that in the Social Contract of 1762 Rousseau had suggested that a 'suspension of sovereignty' was permissible only in exceptional circumstances when the republic was threatened from 'without'. However, in contrast to this model, divisions within the French community between revolutionaries and counter-revolutionaries were rooted in conflicting class interests and these divisions meant that 'what threatened the

French Revolution in the autumn of 1793 was, in very large measure, internally generated' (Levine 1987: 54–5). Levine claims that Robespierre responded to this problem by extending the idea of the suspension of sovereignty in a way that revealed both his own inability to articulate the 'general will' and perhaps also a more general problem of articulating any kind of general will in a class-divided society. The Jacobins discovered 'that in revolutionary times the general will cannot be exercised if, indeed, it makes sense to speak of a general will at all' (Levine 1987: 56).

The Terror was therefore evidence that far from articulating the 'general will', the Jacobins represented the interests of a particular social group. In fact, George Rudé argues that they represented the so-called *sans-culottes* of urban 'small shopkeepers and craftsmen (both masters and journeymen), servants and day-labourers' (Rudé 1988: 94–5). Because Robespierre de facto recognised the limited nature of his social base, even if he was unable to provide an adequate theoretical account of this, he came to believe that the common good would have to be imposed on society as a correction against 'the shortcomings and defects of individual men' (Israel 2001: 717). So, despite his fervent advocacy of democracy, he held to a more-or-less implicit belief not only that 'democracy had to be directed from above' but also that 'no reliance could be placed on the spontaneous revolutionary ardour of the people' (Soboul [1965] 1977: 107).

In contrast to this perspective, Babeuf pointed towards a very different form of revolutionary organisation. Unfortunately, this difference was obscured by Filippo Buonarroti, who had been a member of Babeuf's Conspiracy of Equals in the 1790s and subsequently authored the first serious analysis of this group's politics: *Conspiration pour l'égalité dite de Babeuf* of 1828. In this book, Buonarroti underplayed the divergences between Babouvism and Jacobinism by both glossing over Babeuf's criticisms of the Jacobins and overstating the conspiratorial and clandestine nature of the Conspiracy of Equals (Birchall 1997: 90). He thus distorted Babeuf's belief that his 'organisation was an instrument of the people, not something [like the Jacobins] that substituted itself for it' (Birchall 1997: 158). Ian Birchall argues that it was this democratic characteristic of Babouvism which allowed Marx to trace a lineage through it from earlier to more modern forms of socialism in a way that bypassed Jacobinism (Birchall 1997: 96; cf. Marx and Engels [1844] 1975: 119). More generally, Marx's delineation between bourgeois and proletarian revolutions was formulated in part to explain the historical specificity of modern socialism and thus to differentiate it from Jacobinism (Marx [1852] 1973b).

According to Marx, bourgeois revolutions emerged out of developing contradictions between emergent capitalist relations of production and existing pre-capitalist states and where they were successful resulted in the removal of fetters to further capitalist development. Although these revolutions were generally marked by a progressive break with pre-capitalist hierarchies, because they were characterised by the transference of power from one ruling class to another, they involved at best a contradictory relationship between their leadership and the mass of the population. For instance, bourgeois revolutions 'from above' such as Bismarck's unification of Germany involved no mass action at all, whereas England's, America's and France's bourgeois revolutions 'from below' were won through the involvement of the lower classes but ended similarly with the exclusion of the poor from power. Proletarian revolutions, by contrast, because they are made for and by the working class – 'the emancipation of the working classes must be conquered by the working classes themselves' (Marx [1864] 1974a: 82) – were necessarily qualitatively more democratic in both their execution and outcome. Their triumph required the workers to be organised as a political force and, because the workers exploit no social group below them, once the bourgeois counter-revolution was suppressed the workers' state would itself 'wither away' (Callinicos 1989; Draper 1978: 28–32; Hobsbawm 1986: 26; Lukács [1923] 1971: 282).

Despite this divergence, Marx did recognise a degree of continuity between bourgeois and proletarian revolutions, for it was at the radical extremes of the more democratic examples of the former that the germ of the latter emerged. For instance, socialism was not only hinted at in the French constitution of 1793, especially in excluded clauses that had been suggested for this constitution by Robespierre (Rudé 1975: 108–9), but was more properly prefigured in the writings and actions of Babeuf in the 1790s and also of Gerrard Winstanley a century and a half earlier in England. Following their lead, Marx argued that the aim of German socialists should be to make their 'bourgeois' revolution 'permanent': that is, to fight within it for the realisation of its most democratic, that is, socialist, implications (Marx [1850] 1973a: 330). So while Marx expected proletarian revolutions, at least sometimes, to grow out of bourgeois revolutions, his differentiation between these two types of revolution points to fundamental problems with Bernstein's claim that there was an unbroken trajectory from Robespierre to Marx via Babeuf and Blanqui: Marx's revolutionary strategy was based upon a total reorganisation of society based upon the prior emergence of new social forces, not a one-sidedly political change of leadership within the state.

Nevertheless, it is true that Blanqui was deeply influenced by the Jacobins and his model of revolution as the act of a small elite of revolutionaries did build upon their substitutionalist politics. For instance, in the oath of membership to his organisation he suggested that the malicious consequences of existing inegalitarian social structures included the ideological contamination of the people which left them unable to liberate themselves. From this premise, he surmised that the revolution should be led by a 'revolutionary power' (Blanqui [1830] 1983: 34). Hal Draper comments that Blanqui believed that socialism could only be inaugurated through the 'revolutionary dictatorship' of a small conspiratorial band, who would take power in the name of the workers before leading them forward to socialism through a benign educational tyranny (Draper 1986: 37–8).

Discussing the arguments put forward by the Blanquists in the wake of the Paris Commune of 1871, Engels argued that they were 'socialists only in sentiment', because their model of socialism was not underpinned by anything like an adequate account of either the class struggle or of the historical basis for socialism itself. He thus dismissed Blanqui's proposal that the revolution be a 'coup de main by a small revolutionary minority' and claimed that Blanquist politics was an 'obsolete' model of revolution as 'dictatorship' (Engels [1874] 1989a: 13).

This argument is interesting not only for the light it sheds on Marx and Engels's relationship to Blanquism and through it to Jacobinism but also for its illumination of their criticisms of both anarchist and reformist tendencies within the European socialist movement. At the centre of all of these debates was Marx's deployment of the concept of the 'dictatorship of the proletariat'. This concept is often confused with Blanqui's concept of 'revolutionary dictatorship' and many commentators have assumed the truth of the unfounded myth that Marx borrowed his concept from Blanqui. In fact the phrase 'dictatorship of the proletariat' 'cannot be found anywhere in Blanqui either as a term or as an idea' (Draper 1986: 35).

It is important to register the distinction between Marx's concept of 'dictatorship of the proletariat' and Blanqui's idea of 'revolutionary dictatorship' because it provides a basis from which to explain Engels's justification both of the criticisms of Blanqui noted above and his argument against Bakunin's anarchism, made for instance in his essay *On Authority* written just a year earlier, that 'a revolution is certainly the most authoritarian thing there is; it is the act whereby one part of the population imposes its will upon the other part by means of rifles, bayonets and cannon' (Engels [1873] 1988: 425). If this claim appears to suggest that Engels favoured a Blanquist model of revolution, this interpretation of his ideas is reinforced by his later critique of the SPD's Erfurt Programme. In this essay he insisted that 'our party and the working class can only come to power under the form of a democratic republic. This is even the specific form of the dictatorship of the proletariat' (Engels [1891] 1990c: 227). To make sense of these seemingly contradictory statements – in favour of the dictatorship of the proletariat and yet against the (Blanquist) idea of a revolutionary dictatorship – it is necessary to examine Marx and Engels's relationship to other forms of anti-capitalism.

3. Marxism, Hegelianism and the Historical Model of Human Nature

In his important study of Marx's relationship to anarchism, Paul Thomas argues that although Marx and his anarchist counterparts desired the overthrow of the state it would be a misconception to claim that the differences between them were of a merely tactical kind (Thomas 1980: 13). On the contrary, because the anarchists did not have a historical conception of human nature as Marx did, they did not understand, as he did, the overthrow of the state to mean that 'socialised man . . . man freely associated with his fellows, could control the totality of his social existence and become master of his own environment and activity' (Thomas 1980: 106). The historical conception of human nature was not merely the basis from which Marx criticised anarchism. It was also first formulated, in no small part, as a response to Max Stirner's extreme egoistic anarchism.

Stirner developed this perspective against what he saw as the limitations of Feuerbach's materialism. Both Feuerbach and Stirner were prominent members of Berlin's radical Young Hegelian circle in the 1830s and 1840s. This milieu was characterised in part by its interrogation of what Engels later described as tensions between Hegel's (conservative) system and his (revolutionary) dialectical method (Engels [1886] 1990a: 363). Indeed, many of Hegel's followers believed that he had resisted the revolutionary implications of his analysis of the contradictory character of bourgeois society. This is apparent in Hegel's analysis of the Jacobins. Like Kant (Kersting 1992: 360; Kant [1798] 1991: 182, 188), Hegel welcomed the ideals of the French Revolution, but he rejected the revolutionary means by which they were realised, and he detested Robespierre.

This is not to say that Hegel simply counterposed 1789 to 1793. Rather, he believed that although the Terror was the inevitable excess which accompanied the progressive realisation of the freedoms of civil society, the idea that the Jacobins pointed beyond the limits of the Revolution towards a freer society was unfounded. This was because, for Hegel, Robespierre's Terror was the culmination of the abstract political will's attempt to impose its vision on society from the top down without transforming the nation's 'dispositions and religion' (Hegel [1837] 1956: 446, 449, 450). More specifically, because Hegel believed that personal freedoms were realised in civil society, he saw this type of social organisation as the historical limit on human progress. So, although he recognised that the modern contradiction identified by Rousseau between *homme* and *citoyen* had its roots in civil society, he believed that this contradiction was a necessary manifestation of personal freedom. Against the chaotic implications of this perspective, he argued that the universal class of state bureaucrats would subordinate the fragmenting interests of civil society to the broader interests of the community as a whole (Hunt 1974: 53–4; Taylor

1975: 437). So while he rejected Jacobinism, he at least believed that Robespierre had been part of an excessive but necessary evil through which progress had been realised. Nevertheless, he dismissed the idea that the proletarian 'rabble' (Hegel [1821] 1952: 150), who had taken up the struggle against the bourgeoisie in the wake of the Revolution, could forge an ethical alternative able to overcome the contradictions of bourgeois society.

After Hegel's death, one issue faced by the Young Hegelians was, as Marx suggested in 1843, that the state bureaucracy, far from operating in the universal interest of the community, seemed to be alienated from the people's will and in fact to have its own particular interests (Marx [1843] 1975a). The Young Hegelians explored this problem, and the tensions between the conservative and revolutionary aspects of Hegel's thought generally, through a debate on the issue of religion. Because this debate was effectively about the nature of authority, its political implications were apparent from the outset. This was nowhere truer than in the work of Feuerbach, who challenged Hegel's claim that human history was a product of the Absolute, arguing instead that the idea of God was a property of human consciousness. Feuerbach also rejected the egoistic freedom of civil society. He argued that 'man is conscious of himself not only as an individual, but also as a member of the human species' and that 'God is really the perfected idea of the species viewed as an individual' (McLellan 1969: 92). This concept of species-being both challenged the liberal naturalisation of the egoism of civil society and informed a turn towards socialism amongst a layer of the Young Hegelians.

The concept of species-being also influenced the young Marx. But from a very early stage he was aware that the naturalistic morality which Feuerbach extrapolated from it was inadequate to the needs of modern politics (McLellan 1969: 113). Interestingly, it was partly to the same weakness with Feuerbach's moralism that Stirner addressed The Ego and His Own (1844) (McLellan 1969: 131; Hook [1950] 1962: 174). And it was through answering Stirner's criticisms of Feuerbach that Marx moved beyond the limitations of the latter's perspective.

Stirner argued that all political systems – conservative, liberal, socialist or whatever – led in practice to authoritarian suppression of the individual ego. Even revolutions, by claiming to be in the common interest, involved the suppression of individual egoism. Consequently, Stirner conceived 'self-liberation' to be possible through an act of rebellion rather than revolution (Martin [1963] 2005: xiii; see also Thomas 1980: 130). Drawing on Hobbes, but in a way that prefigured Nietzsche (Hook [1950] 1962: 165), Stirner insisted that

> because each thing *cares for itself* and at the same time comes into constant collision with other things, the *combat* of self-assertion is unavoidable . . . The victor becomes the *lord*, the vanquished one the *subject* . . . But both remain *enemies*. (Stirner [1844] 2005: 9)

Nevertheless, in contrast not only to Hobbes but also to his liberal critics, Stirner did not extend this argument into a justification of some form of political state. Quite the reverse, he suggested that 'political liberty' amounts to nothing less than the 'individual's *subjugation* in the state' (Stirner [1844] 2005: 106, 196, 255). In a comment on the French Revolution which he believed to have general salience, he suggested that this upheaval was not directed against 'the *establishment*, but against the *establishment in question*, against a particular establishment. It did away with *this* ruler, not with *the* ruler'. That the French Revolution ended in reaction should therefore come as no surprise: for it is in the nature of revolutions that one authority is merely exchanged for another (110). The embrace of the post-revolutionary state by 'political liberalism' revealed its authoritarian implications, implications that were also inherent in socialism and communism (ideologies that Stirner subsumed under the heading 'social liberalism'), for these too would merely repeat the transference of power from one authority to another (122, 130). Even the 'humane liberalism' of the best of the Young Hegelians was suspect, because it too saw the egoism of others as a weakness while denying it in itself.

In contrast to Hegel's socio-historical understanding of the conception of freedom, Stirner argued that 'freedom can only be the whole of freedom, a piece of freedom is not freedom' (160). From this perspective, he concluded that all moral approaches, including Feuerbach's, were the enemies of freedom because they preached self-sacrifice in the name of some metaphysical notion – god, man, the state, class, nation and so on. If 'the road to ruin is paved with good intentions', the correct egoistic response was not revolution in the name of some 'good' but a more simple rebellion of the ego against authority (54, 75). Moreover, communism was not so much a radical alternative to the status quo as its latest moralistic variant (18, 164, 258).

The vast bulk of the almost universally unread sections of Marx and Engels's *The German Ideology* ([1845–6] 1976) is a critique of Stirner's book. Against Stirner's claim that socialists had embraced a static model of human essence which provided them with a moral basis for criticising existing society, Marx outlined a Hegelian historicised transformation of his earlier Feuerbachian materialism. On this basis he insisted that people made and remade themselves through history. As he argued in *Capital*, by working purposefully together on nature to meet our needs, people not only change the world around them, they also change themselves (Marx [1867] 1976: 283). In the modern world this process underpinned the emergence of both egoistic and more social forms of individualism. Morality, as it was understood by Stirner, was an essential authoritarian characteristic only of communities made up of the former. By assuming the universality of egoism, Stirner was unable to comprehend the concept of workers' solidarity. By contrast, Marx argued, solidarity had become a real need for workers, such that it was wrong to contrast individual and social emancipation. So, whereas Feuerbach's abstract humanism tended to dissolve the individual into the species, whilst Stirner saw only the conflict between these two elements, Marx countered both of these models. He did so by claiming that socialism would be a working-class-based movement whose goal was an 'association, in which the free development of each is the condition for the free development of all' (Marx and Engels [1848] 1973: 87; see also Thomas 1980: 154). From this perspective there would be no need to impose the idea of community on the working class from without. This is why, Marx claimed, 'communists do not preach morality' (Marx and Engels [1845–6] 1976: 247).

Embedded in this argument is a general historical model of human nature. This model built upon Hegel's attempt to point towards an ethically (that is, socially and materially) grounded theory of social transformation. But Marx did so while simultaneously rejecting Hegel's dismissal of the proletariat as a 'rabble'. Marx claimed that while the division of labour separated and fragmented its members, the 'new fangled' working class (Marx [1856] 1980: 656) could be characterised also by a rebellion against this fragmentation, which was manifest as a growing desire for community. He first drew these conclusions in the 1840s on the basis of his engagement both in the Silesian weavers' revolt and in socialist circles in Paris (Perkins 1993: 33). Generalising from these experiences, Marx commented that in struggling against the power of capital workers begin to create modes of existence which offer a virtuous alternative to egoism. This is an alternative both to the egoism of capitalist society generally and, more specifically, to the enforced egoism of working-class life within that society.

When communist workmen gather together, their immediate aim is instruction, propaganda, etc. But at the same time, they acquire a new need – the need for society – and what appears as a means had become an end. This practical development can be most strikingly observed in the gatherings of French socialist workers. Smoking, eating and drinking, etc., are no longer means of creating links between people. Company, association, conversation, which in turn has society as its goal, is enough for them. The brotherhood of man is not a hollow phrase, it is a reality, and the nobility of man shines forth upon us from their work-worn figures. (Marx [1844] 1975b: 365)

This class analysis differentiated Marx's model of liberation from both Robespierre's abstract conception of the 'general will' and the moralistic approach embraced by Feuerbach's 'true socialist' followers. Because Marx's politics were based upon a socio-historical analysis of the emergence of a new social class it escaped the abstract character of Robespierre's practice. From this perspective Marx also criticised the 'true socialists' for aiming to liberate not real men and women but rather some disembodied 'Man' (Marx and Engels [1845–6] 1976: 468). He insisted that because 'true socialism' abstracted the human essence from its real manifestation in history it acted as a barrier to the real diffusion of socialist consciousness, which could only arise through the recognition of the class-divided nature of society (469). The true socialists forget

that the 'inward nature' of men, as well as their 'consciousness' of it, i.e., their 'reason', has at all times been an historical product and that even when . . . the society of men was based 'upon external compulsion', their 'inward nature' corresponded to this 'external compulsion'. (Marx and Engels [1845–6] 1976: 468)

This historical model of human nature is central not only to Marx's theory of history but also to his theory of revolution. In *The German Ideology* he suggested two reasons why socialism could only come through revolution. First, in common with revolutionaries such as Robespierre and Blanqui, he argued that the ruling class could not be overthrown by any other means. Second, and much more profoundly, he differentiated his conception of revolution from those of these earlier revolutionaries by insisting that 'the class over-throwing it can only in a revolution succeed in ridding itself of all the muck of ages and become fitted to found society anew' (Marx and Engels [1845–6] 1976: 53). Revolutionary activity was therefore not merely system-changing, it was also individually transformative: it was the necessary means through which workers could come to realise in consciousness the power of their situation at the centre of the new socialised mode of production. Moreover, Marx suggested that workers, in tending to rebel against the process of their dehumanisation, begin to act as potential agents for not only their own liberation but also the universal liberation of humanity, because they exploit no groups below them (Marx and Engels [1844] 1975: 36–7).

This model of revolutionary practice is of the first importance to an understanding of Marx's theory of revolution, because it is the basis on which he and Engels criticised Blanqui's Jacobinism. While Marx agreed with Blanqui, and for that matter Robert Owen, that capitalism had made workers unfit to rule, he departed from their respective solutions to this problem – Blanqui's revolutionary elitism and Owen's philanthropic elitism (Owen [1817] 1991: 188). Instead Marx insisted that workers could *become* fit to rule through the revolutionary process itself: 'the coincidence of the changing of circumstances and of human activity or self-changing can be conceived and rationally understood only as *revolutionary practice*' (Marx [1845] 1975d: 422). Indeed it was the collective struggles in the revolutionary process that did away with the need for Blanqui's elitist model of 'revolutionary dictatorship'.

Marx also rejected Blanqui's political voluntarism. He believed that while individuals would play pivotal roles within them, revolutionary situations developed, fundamentally, out of objective historical circumstances over which individuals had little control (Marx [1852] 1973b: 145). He was adamant that capitalism was subject to systemic contradictions which could not be reformed away and that these were a specific instance of a pattern of structural crises recurring throughout history. Consequently, whereas Alexis de Tocqueville famously pointed to a political explanation of the genesis of the French Revolution as a specific instance of a more general pattern, Marx attempted to analyse the underlying causes of the political shifts themselves. According to Tocqueville's classic formulation, revolutions tend to occur when bad regimes move to reform themselves:

> [I]t oftener happens that when a people which has put up with an oppressive rule over a long period without protest suddenly finds the government relaxing its pressure, it takes up arms against it, and experience teaches us that, generally speaking, the most perilous moment for a bad government is one when it seeks to mend its ways. (Tocqueville [1856] 1966: 196)

While Marx had read Tocqueville's study of the French Revolution (Marx 1981: 939), I am unaware of any substantive comments he made on it. Nonetheless, we can probably assume that while he would have accepted the limited power of Tocqueville's suggestion, he was himself interested in uncovering not only the political dynamics of revolutions but also the seismic shifts that underpinned their emergence. As Rudé has argued, for all Tocqueville's 'brilliance', he leaves unanswered the general problem of why Louis XVI's ministers and why other reforming governments before and since 'have to stop short' their reforms. More specifically, Tocqueville does not explain the actual circumstances of the outbreak and the process through which a revolt of the elites was transformed into a revolution from below (Rudé 1988: 15). For Marx, by contrast, revolutions emerged at specific historical junctures: when the mode of production entered a structural crisis.

> At a certain stage of development, the material productive forces of society come into conflict with the existing relations of production . . . From forms of development of the productive forces these relations turn into their fetters. Then begins an era of social revolution. (Marx [1859] 1970: 20)

Under capitalism, Marx argued, the contradiction between forces and relations of production is expressed through the tendency of the rate of profit to decline. Because it is rooted in the capital accumulation process, this tendency cannot ultimately be resolved without a revolutionary transformation of social relations. Moreover, capitalism is also characterised by the growth in size and strength of the working class, such that when workers join together to resist the consequences of crisis they begin to offer a potential political alternative to capitalism (Marx [1867] 1976: 929; Marx and Engels [1848] 1973: 68; see also Callinicos 1995: 151–65).

This process is obscured so long as it is viewed from the point of view of the atomised individual within capitalist society and it becomes fully apparent only when examined from the point of view of the totality of the capitalist system (Marx [1867] 1976: 732).

Moreover, it is from the standpoint of workers' struggles that the nature of the social totality itself becomes clear (Lukács [1923] 1971: 28, 129). This perspective provides the point of contact between Marx's scientific, explanatory account of the dynamics of the capitalist mode of production and his normative critique of capitalism. Far from being mutually exclusive, these two aspects of his social theory are two sides of the same coin: capitalism as a system for the exploitation of wage labour becomes apparent from the point of view of class struggles over the length of the working day. These struggles simultaneously point beyond what Alasdair MacIntyre suggests is the structure of incommensurable moral preferences which characterises modern, bourgeois, moral theory (MacIntyre 1985: 8). It is therefore from the perspective of workers' struggles that we can begin to make sense of Marx's condemnation of morality. He dismisses those moral attitudes that pretend to offer some mechanism through which a universal good can be promoted in a world in which social divisions undermine such a project. But he does this from the point of view of a class-based morality which, through the emergence of a need for solidarity, not only points beyond liberal naturalisations of egoism, but also, he believes, has become universal in the modern context. Marxism therefore presupposes and reaffirms the sort of social practice – collective working-class struggles – which simultaneously reveal and point beyond the facts of exploitation (Blackledge 2008).

It is because Marx's perspective is rooted in a historical materialist analysis of the emergence of a new social class with novel needs and capacities (that is, a new nature), that he points beyond the one-sidedly political character of both Jacobinism and Blanquism, while nonetheless remaining a revolutionary. It is this dual character of Marx's revolutionary theory that underpins Engels's criticisms of Bakunin's anarchism, Blanquism and statist reformism noted above. Despite appearing to be opposites, both Blanquism and state socialism are united as examples of what Hal Draper called 'socialism from above', to which Engels opposed Marx's 'socialism from below' (Draper 1992). Moreover, whilst anarchism and Marxism are both rooted in movements from below, Marx differs from Bakunin in recognising, on the one hand, the historical novelty and social specificity of the modern socialist movement and, on the other hand, the need for a revolution which not only 'smashes' the old state machine but also simultaneously builds new forms of workers' power (see Blackledge 2010b).

4. Marxism, Anarchism and Social Democracy

This historicised conception of human nature also underpinned Marx's criticisms of Pierre-Joseph Proudhon's anarchism. Proudhon's anarchism was of a very different stripe to Stirner's. Whereas Stirner dismissed Proudhon as a moralist (Stirner [1844] 2005: 47), Proudhon could not have accepted Stirner's claim that 'labouring does not make you a man, because it is something formal and is . . . accidental' (130). For Proudhon, labouring and the morality attendant upon it were at the centre of his critique of capitalism; and, according to Thomas, he believed that while 'power corrupts, labour ennobles' (Thomas 1980: 148). Indeed, against Lockean attempts to derive the rights of private property from a basic labour theory of value, he insisted not only that the transformation from 'possession into property' necessarily involved something 'besides labour' but also that even in a situation of wage labour the labourer retains 'a natural right of property in the thing which he has produced' (Proudhon [1840] 1994: 85, 88).

Proudhon's famous claim that 'property is theft' (Proudhon 1994: 13) therefore rested on the distinction he drew between possession and property. Whereas he believed that the act of labouring entitled the labourer to the possession of the product of his labour (and for

Proudhon it most certainly was *his* rather than *her* labour), he believed that such possessions did not underpin entitlements either to the ownership of the means of production (primarily land) or to the appropriation of the product of the labour of others (McNally 1993: 140). It was these latter forms of property which he believed were artificial and immoral. Consequently, as Peter Marshall has argued, Proudhon 'did not attack private property as such', since he believed that freedom was threatened both by communist plans to collectivise and by the way that large property owners ate into the property of the petty bourgeoisie (Marshall 2008: 239). And although his critique of property might appear to be a rehash of the attacks on individual rights associated with Robespierre's rule, nothing could be further from his thoughts (Proudhon 1994: 13). The error of the revolutionaries of the 1790s, from Proudhon's point of view, was that their attack on the *ancien régime* had been hamstrung by an inability to think beyond the old monarchical system. Rather than overthrowing the property system, they generalised it downwards: 'the people finally legalised property. God forgive them, for they knew not what they did' (30). Because Proudhon saw in the bourgeoisie's defence of property not the ideological reflection of class interest but an intellectual error, he aimed to correct it through a 'revolution' that was primarily 'a movement of the mind' (27; see also Proudhon [1851] 1989: 8). In fact, when a decade later he published a monograph on the concept of revolution, he dedicated it to the 'bourgeoisie', because he believed that its members were, not only in 1789 but also in the 1840s and 1850s, 'the boldest and most skilful revolutionaries' ([1851] 1989: 7).

Proudhon insisted that 'revolution was necessary' because the aims of 1789 had yet to be realised (45). Far from being a 'natural order', France had become a 'fractitious order' with 'parasite interests, abnormal morals, monstrous ambitions, [and] prejudices at variance with common sense'. Interestingly, despite his claim that he alone represented 'the revolutionary point of view' (Proudhon [1851] 1989: 125), like Stirner he explained the injustices of the status quo in a way that tended to naturalise particular modern capitalist social relations. As David McNally has argued, Proudhon's critique of modern capitalism involved an actual accommodation with bourgeois ideology in a number of important ways. First, he defined justice by 'equal market exchange'; second, he used commodity exchange as 'the model for the social contract'; third, he depicted exploitation not as a product of commodity production but as its violation through monopoly; fourth, he aimed to foster equal exchange of commodities by opening a 'People's Bank' which would use paper money to overturn 'the royalty of gold'; fifth, he equated socialism with the 'abolition of monopoly and the realisation of free trade'; and, sixth, he argued within the workers' movement against strikes and political struggles against the state and in their place for 'mutualism and equal exchange' (McNally 1993: 141–3). This 'absolute pure morality' emerged, or so Marx argued, out of Proudhon's critique of the classical political economists 'from the standpoint of political economy' (Marx and Engels [1844] 1975: 31).

The political consequences of this perspective are apparent in Proudhon's critique of socialism. The dominant voice of socialism in France at the time was that of the reformist state-socialist Louis Blanc. According to Proudhon, Blanc was heir both to Robespierre's statism and, through him, to the dictatorial methods of 'the scoundrel' Rousseau (Proudhon [1851] 1989: 188, 152–3). What these figures shared was a common focus on reform through the state. This approach, Proudhon believed, confused legitimate with illegitimate forms of authority: the state transferred patriarchal authority from the family, which was its proper abode, to an unnatural situation (171). Practically, this meant that whereas anarchists focused upon demands for jobs and a 'living wage', socialists followed the Jacobins in their focus on politics (166). This was just as true of revolutionary socialists such as Blanqui (and before him Babeuf) as it was of Blanc's reformism: Proudhon claimed that both were counter-revolutionary because they failed to see that power and liberty were absolutely 'incompatible' (Thomas 1980: 180, 212). Against these socialists, the key issue of the day was not which kind of government but rather 'Government or No-Government', or absolutism *versus* anarchy, and the aim of the revolution was 'to do away with . . . the state' (Proudhon [1851] 1989: 153; see also 105, 128, 286).

In place of the state, Proudhon envisioned a social contract which was the opposite of Rousseau's statism because it was to be freely entered into by independent producers (113–27; see also 130, 206). While Proudhon accepted the need for workers' trade unions as a buffer against the power of capital, at a deeper level he insisted that these organisations were antithetical to his idea of anarchy. Commenting on Blanc's advocacy of the needs principle – 'from each according to his ability, to each according to his need' – Proudhon responded that such a principle could operate only through a 'binding' union that would infringe individual liberty. Given this situation, he asked, who is to decide what my needs and capacities are? Noting the tyrannical consequences of this perspective, he suggested that the only beneficiaries of such an agreement would be 'weak or lazy workers' (84–5, 96). More generally, while he agreed that unions were important to workers, the role of workers in the coming revolution was not to fight for their 'petty union interests', but rather to deny 'the rule of capitalists, money lenders and governments, which the first revolution left undisturbed' (99).

The second half of this sentence allows us to make sense of how Proudhonists and Marxists were able to work together within the International Working Men's Association or First International (1864–72). However, the first half of the sentence and Proudhon's anti-political perspectives more generally point to the tensions embedded in this relationship from the start. From Marx's standpoint, Proudhon's mutualism – the idea that capitalism could be transformed 'by means of producer cooperatives financed by a "people's bank"' – was the most extreme muddle, which reflected his inability to look beneath capitalism's surface appearance as a system of equal exchange to the underlying appropriation of value from workers. 'We may well', wrote Marx, 'feel astonished at the cleverness of Proudhon who would abolish capitalist property – by enforcing the eternal laws of property which are themselves based on commodity production!' (Marx [1867] 1976: 734)

Within the International, debate became focused on the issue of working-class demands made on the state. On one side, the Proudhonists opposed this approach, while Marx, supported by English trade unionists, stressed the necessity of fighting for reforms. According to Collins and Abramsky, whereas Marx believed that 'trade union struggle represented a necessary phase through which the workers must pass on the road to full emancipation', 'for the French they were a barbaric expedient, necessary perhaps, as a last resort in particular circumstances, but contributing nothing of value to the movement' (Collins and Abramsky 1964: 101, 117; see also Gilbert 1981: 90). Thus, whilst Proudhon's mutualism meant that his followers tended to reject both strikes and 'political' struggles, Marx insisted that when workers won reforms and then acted to enforce these laws they did not 'fortify governmental power. On the contrary, they transform that power, now used against them, into their own agency' (Marx quoted in Fernbach 1974: 17).

Marx was generally successful in his struggles against the Proudhonists. But from 1867–8 onwards the torch of anarchism was taken up within the International by Bakunin. He described his version of anarchism as 'Proudhonism greatly developed and pushed to its furthest conclusion' (Guerin [1965] 1970: 4). Concretely, this meant that Bakunin agreed with Proudhon's general argument that natural social harmony was possible only through the eradication of government and the state. But he went further than Proudhon in a collectivist direction (12). If anarcho-syndicalism or libertarian-communism was the logical culmination of this intellectual movement, Bakunin himself was keen to stress his 'detestation' of communism's top-down, state-led approach, which he compared unfavourably to the bottom-up democratic processes that gave rise to collectivism (22). Nevertheless, in the first instance the gap between Marx and Bakunin was less than it had been between Marx and Proudhon and at the 1869 conference of the International Bakunin supported Marx's motion in favour of 'public ownership of land and industry' against the Proudhonists (Collins and Abramsky 1964: 228; see also Thomas 1980: 268).

This convergence was soon overshadowed by renewed debates on the question of reformist political demands. On this issue, Bakunin's position 'was of a piece with Proudhon's' (Thomas 1980: 294). Draper comments on their differing approaches to this issue. He suggests that whereas both Marx and Bakunin aimed at 'abolishing' the state, this for Marx – unlike Bakunin – did not mean an end to authority but rather its 'democratisation'. This, in turn, Marx thought would be possible only after 'a sufficient period of socialist reconstruction of society' (Draper 1990: 174; Blackledge 2010a).

Rather ironically, given the animosity of the debate between them and their followers, both Marx and Bakunin embraced the Paris Commune of 1871 as an example of real living socialism. Nevertheless, Bakunin insisted that whereas 'the communists [that is, Marxists] believe it necessary to organize the workers' forces in order to seize the political power of the State', 'the revolutionary socialists organize for the purpose of destroying – or, to put it more politely – liquidating the State'. Concretely, Bakunin proclaimed his support for the Commune not only because it was made by 'the spontaneous and continued action of the masses' but also because it was the 'negation of the state' (Bakunin [1872] 1973: 263, 264, 268). Marx had already written, in a document published under the auspices of the International, that 'the working class cannot simply lay hold of the ready-made state machinery and wield it for its own purposes'. Nevertheless, Marx insisted that although the Commune was the 'direct antithesis to the Empire', it was still 'a working-class government' (Marx [1871] 1974c: 206, 208, 212). This last point is important, because despite Bakunin's attempt to paint Marx's model of the dictatorship of the proletariat in Jacobin, Blanquist or Lassallean colours, Marx did not mean by this term the dictatorship of an elite. Rather, for him it meant more simply the rule of the working class (Draper 1987: 29). Thus, two decades later Engels could write that

> of late, the Social-Democratic philistine has once more been filled with wholesome terror at the words: Dictatorship of the Proletariat. Well and good, gentlemen, do you want to know what this dictatorship looks like? Look at the Paris Commune. That was the Dictatorship of the Proletariat. (Engels [1891] 1990b: 191)

The difference between Marx and Bakunin was, however, about more than mere semantics. Bakunin argued that Marx's approach was mistaken because 'every state power, every government, by its nature and by its position stands outside the people and above them and must invariably try to subject them to rules and objectives which are alien to them' (Bakunin [1873] 1990: 136). Therefore, whereas Marx predicated his political practice on a historical model of human nature which underpinned his differentiation between more and less democratic states, between better and worse laws and indeed between workers' and capitalist states, Bakunin believed that the desire for freedom was a universal human characteristic and declared himself the enemy 'of every government and every state power'. This informed his refusal of reformist political demands (Bakunin [1869] 1992: 109). It is not clear, however, how this position cohered with his embrace of the Paris Commune as an example of his model of revolution. For, as Peter Kropotkin argued a few years later from a perspective very close to Bakunin's, the Commune's key failing was its embrace of a representative structure which meant that it reproduced the typical vices of parliamentary governments. The weaknesses of the Commune were due not to the men who led it but to the 'system' it embraced (Kropotkin [1880] 2002a: 237–42). Kropotkin went on to reject the Blanquist idea of a 'revolutionary government' as the dream of 'budding Robespierres' and like Bakunin he conflated Marx's conception of revolutionary leadership with Blanqui's elitism. Consequently, like Bakunin's claim that Marx was a Jacobin, Kropotkin's critique of Marxism tended to miss its mark (Kropotkin [1880] 2002a: 242–50; [1887] 2002b: 61; see also Bakunin [1873] 1990: 182).

To this conceptual problem was added a more substantive issue. Bakunin's approach immunised his followers against the malign appeal of reformism. But by rejecting a whole series of 'political' struggles for reform he found that he had little to say to those workers in the advanced capitalist states who were engaged not only in struggles to extend the laws that protected them but also to defend existing laws from the encroachment of individual capitalists. More generally, by tarring all states with the same brush, Bakunin was unable to formulate an adequate model of the revolutionary transformation to socialism. So, although he had no trouble conceiving of a violent struggle between classes, he avoided the problem of how workers might win victory without violently replacing the old order with one of their own. As Marx pointed out in his notes on *Statism and Anarchy*, it was precisely the need for violent revolution which implied that the working class must be organised as an armed force, that is, as a form of state (Marx [1874–5] 1974b: 517).

The trouble with Marx's approach, by contrast, was that, in focusing on the necessity for socialist revolutionaries to engage in struggles for reform, he left himself open to misrepresentation as a reformist (Fernbach 1974: 17). To counter this problem, he wrote his 'Critique of the Gotha Programme'. This programme was agreed to by the German Social Democratic Party (SPD) under the influence of the followers of the state-socialist Ferdinand Lassalle (see Draper 1990: 41–71, 241–69) at the Gotha unity congress in 1875. The programme was an odd amalgam which brought together some ultra-radical verbiage with a series of practically moderate political demands. Both aspects of this 'synthesis' were evident in the programme's central demand for a 'free state'.

Marx famously subjected a draft of the programme to a brutal interrogation. Beyond pointing to the authoritarian implications of the aim of fighting for such a goal, he insisted that in the transitional period from capitalism to communism the state could only exist as 'the revolutionary dictatorship of the proletariat'. He suggested that in avoiding this issue the SPD had opened itself up to a possible evolution towards liberalism (Marx [1875] 1974d, 355). Contrary to Bakunin's attempt to paint him as a statist, Marx was careful to differentiate between the dictatorship of the proletariat and the modern capitalist state. Indeed, he criticised the statism of the draft programme, claiming that beneath its 'democratic clang' could be discerned 'the Lassallean sect's servile belief in the state' (357).

Engels similarly criticised the draft programme, commenting that 'all the palaver about the state ought to be dropped, especially after the commune, which has ceased to be a state in the true sense of the term' (Engels [1875] 1989b: 71). Nevertheless, Marx and Engels did not carry out their threatened break with the SPD after the programme was ratified. In a context in which both the bourgeois press and the workers read into the Gotha Programme their views (Engels [1875] 1991: 97–8), they wagered that, despite the shortcomings of the party's programme, the general superiority of the perspectives of the Party's Marxist tendency would lead to its eventual hegemony within the organisation. In the medium term this was precisely the turn taken by events, a process which culminated with the revision of the party's programme at the Erfurt congress of 1891 (Schorske [1955] 1983: 3). While Engels welcomed the Erfurt Programme as an improvement on that of Gotha, however, he once again criticised the failure to address the question of state power scientifically: 'The political demands of the draft have one great fault. It lacks precisely what should have been said' (Engels [1891] 1990c: 225). Noting that reformism was 'gaining ground in large sections of the Social-Democratic press', Engels argued that it was incumbent upon the framers of the programme to spell out clearly to the German workers that the transition to socialism could only come 'by force', insisting that if the SPD did not make this clear then, in the long run, the party would go 'astray' (226–7).

5. Conclusion

Despite Engels's prescient warnings, reformist tendencies grew in strength across the European socialist movement towards the end of the nineteenth century. Partly as a reaction to this tendency, a syndicalist current emerged within the workers' movement which combined a rejection of reformism with a focus on independent working-class action. Syndicalism was rooted in a renewal of class struggle from below and drew on Proudhon's and Bakunin's rejections of bourgeois politics, alongside Marx's conception of socialism as working-class self-emancipation (Darlington 2008: 74–5). Expressed in the writings of intellectuals such as Georges Sorel, the syndicalists had 'nothing but contempt for 'politics' in the form of compromise and opportunism which characterised parliamentary affairs' (Portis 1980: 44–5; Sorel [1908] 1999). A parallel reaction against the growing reformism of the Second International developed within the Marxist movement itself. Associated with the writings of Lenin, Trotsky and Rosa Luxemburg, Lenin in *The State and Revolution* ([1917] 1968) traced the intellectual basis of reformism in the Marxist movement to a wilful misrepresentation of Marx's critique of the state within the Second International (1889–1914).

The trajectory taken by Antonio Gramsci highlights both the differences and similarities between this renewed Marxism and anarcho-syndicalism in the early twentieth century. In response to the accusation that he and the L'Ordine Nuovo group around him in Turin in 1919 and 1920 had acted in a syndicalist fashion, he replied that, yes, like the syndicalists and against the mechanical interpretation of Marxism which had been dominant with the Second International, his grouping had attempted to root their socialism in the real spontaneous movement of workers from below instead of offering an 'abstract' model of leadership. However, the weakness with this approach, and for Gramsci the weakness with syndicalism more generally, was that L'Ordine Nuovo did not articulate a strategy for replacing the capitalist state with a workers' state, a lacuna which informed their failure to build an all-Italian revolutionary socialist party (Gramsci 1971: 197–8; Williams 1975: 145–68).

Over the next few years Gramsci sought to overcome these weaknesses while building on the strengths of the L'Ordine Nuovo period. Like the anarcho-syndicalists, he rooted his practice in the day-to-day struggles of ordinary workers, but unlike them he extended this approach into a strategy that included fighting for 'immediate' reforms within capitalism as part of the broader struggle against capitalism (Gramsci 1978: 369). In so doing he moved towards a Leninist position which had little in common with caricatures of Lenin as a latter-day Jacobin, but which did cohere with Marx's broader historical analysis of the emergence of new class relations and thus of new forms of class struggle. It was these historically novel class relations which pointed towards a revolutionary political project that aimed to escape the abstract character of Jacobinism.

This strategy was both 'political' and 'statist' in the limited senses criticised by Bakunin and Proudhon, because it was based upon the distinctions Marx made between proletarian and bourgeois revolutions and between bourgeois and workers' states, including the claim that the latter would wither away in a post-revolutionary context. The strategy was, however, anti-statist and thus anti-political in the sense in which Marx and Engels had described the Commune as the antithesis of the capitalist state. Unfortunately, the anti-statist character of Marxism was subsequently and wilfully obscured by Stalin who reinterpreted the success of his counter-revolution as the victorious culmination of the Russian Revolution itself (Blackledge 2006: 126–30). While academic discussions of Marxism in the twentieth century tended to be distorted by the Stalinist lens through which Marx's ideas were interpreted, the divisions between Marx, Proudhon and Bakunin were rehearsed on the libertarian left throughout this period. These debates relate, on the one hand, to the coherence of Marx's claim that his model of the 'dictatorship of the proletariat' is distinct from Blanqui's Jacobin-influenced model of 'revolutionary dictatorship' and to whether Marx's vision of the 'withering away' of such a state is a utopia and, on the other hand, to whether anarchist models of revolution can adequately confront not only capitalist society but also the system of capitalist states. These divisions, in turn, relate to the coherence of Marx's historical model of human nature and, what is the corollary of this, his distinction between bourgeois and proletarian revolutions and thus to the coherence of the distinction between his politics and Jacobinism.

It is perhaps ironic that although the libertarian left welcomed the collapse of Russian state communism, this event, in a context overdetermined by defeats suffered by the workers' movement over the last three decades of the twentieth century, ensured that the voices of the left became even more marginalised within the academy in the 1990s. Nevertheless, since the emergence of a global anti-capitalist movement at Seattle in 1999, revolutionary voices have once again found a hearing. If these voices include, most prominently, thinkers such as Alain Badiou and Slavoj Žižek, perhaps the pre-eminent amongst them are Michael Hardt and Tony Negri, who in *Empire* (2000) and *Multitude* (2004) attempted to synthesise Marxist with post-modernist themes to reach recognisably anarchistic conclusions. Each of these thinkers has been criticised from a more classical Marxist perspective by Alex Callinicos (2006). Whatever one thinks of the relative merits of these arguments, it is undoubtedly true that their power has helped to push the concept of revolution back into the academic mainstream over the last decade, opening the door to a welcome revival of engagements with this issue both as a philosophical problem and as a political necessity.[1]

Note

1. For an instance of this re-engagement, see Foran *et al.*, eds, 2008.

References

Bakunin, Mikhail [1872] (1973), 'The Paris Commune and the Idea of the State', in Sam Dolgoff (ed.), *Bakunin on Anarchy*, trans. Ida Pilat Isca, London: Allen and Unwin, pp. 259–73.
Bakunin, Mikhail [1873] (1990), *Statism and Anarchy*, ed. and trans. Marshall Shatz, Cambridge: Cambridge University Press.

Bakunin, Mikhail [1869] (1992), 'The Policy of the International' in Robert Cutler (ed.), *The Basic Bakunin*, New York: Prometheus, pp. 97–110.

Bernstein, Eduard [1899] (1993), *The Preconditions of Socialism*, ed. and trans. Henry Tudor, Cambridge: Cambridge University Press.

Birchall, Ian (1997), *The Spectre of Babeuf*, London: Macmillan.

Blackledge, Paul (2006), 'The New Left's renewal of Marxism', *International Socialism* 2 (112): 125–53.

Blackledge, Paul (2008), 'Marxism and ethics', *International Socialism* 2 (120): 125–50.

Blackledge, Paul (2010a), 'Marxism, nihilism and the problem of ethical politics today', *Socialism and Democracy* 24 (2): 101–23.

Blackledge, Paul (2010b), 'Marxism and anarchism', *International Socialism* 125: 53–80.

Blanqui, Louis-Auguste [1830] (1983), 'Oath of membership into the Société des Saisons', in Paul Corcoran (ed. and trans.), *Before Marx: Socialism and Communism in France, 1830–48*, London: Macmillan, pp. 34–5.

Callinicos, Alex (1989), 'Bourgeois revolutions and historical materialism', *International Socialism* 2 (43): 113–71.

Callinicos, Alex (1995), *Theories and Narratives*, Cambridge: Polity.

Callinicos, Alex (2006), *Resources of Critique*, Cambridge: Polity.

Collins, Henry, and Chimon Abramsky (1964), *Karl Marx and the British Labour Movement*, London: Macmillan.

Darlington, Ralph (2008), *Syndicalism and the Transition to Communism*, Aldershot: Ashgate.

Draper, Hal (1978), *Karl Marx's Theory of Revolution*, vol. 2, New York: Monthly Review.

Draper, Hal (1986), *Karl Marx's Theory of Revolution*, vol. 3, New York: Monthly Review.

Draper, Hal (1987), *The Dictatorship of the Proletariat: From Marx to Lenin*, New York: Monthly Review.

Draper, Hal (1990), *Karl Marx's Theory of Revolution*, vol. 4, New York: Monthly Review.

Draper, Hal (1992), *Socialism from Below*, New Jersey: Humanities Review.

Dunn, John (2008), 'Understanding revolution', in John Foran et al. (eds), *Revolution in the Making of the Modern World*, London: Routledge, pp. 17–26.

Engels, Frederick [1873] (1988), 'On authority', in Karl Marx and Frederick Engels, *Collected Works*, vol. 23, Moscow: Progress Publishers and New York: International Publishers, pp. 422–5.

Engels, Frederick [1874] (1989a), 'Programme of the Blanquist Commune Refugees', in Karl Marx and Frederick Engels, *Collected Works*, vol. 24, Moscow: Progress Publishers and New York: International Publishers, pp. 12–18.

Engels, Frederick [1875] (1989b), 'Letter to August Bebel 18th–28th March 1875', in Karl Marx and Frederick Engels, *Collected Works*, vol. 24, Moscow: Progress Publishers and New York: International Publishers, pp. 67–73.

Engels, Frederick [1886] (1990a), 'Ludwig Feuerbach and the end of classical German philosophy', in Karl Marx and Frederick Engels, *Collected Works*, vol. 26, Moscow: Progress Publishers and New York: International Publishers, pp. 357–98.

Engels, Frederick [1891] (1990b), 'Introduction to K. Marx's *The Civil War in France*', in Karl Marx and Frederick Engels, *Collected Works*, vol. 27, Moscow: Progress Publishers and New York: International Publishers, pp. 179–91.

Engels, Frederick [1891] (1990c), 'A critique of the Draft Programme of 1891', in Karl Marx and Frederick Engels, *Collected Works*, vol. 27, Moscow: Progress Publishers and New York: International Publishers, pp. 219–32.

Engels, Frederick [1875] (1991), 'Letter to August Bebel 12th October 1875', in Karl Marx and Frederick Engels, *Collected Works*, vol. 45, Moscow: Progress Publishers and New York: International Publishers, pp. 97–8.

Fernbach, David (1974), 'Introduction' to Karl Marx, *The First International and After*, Harmondsworth: Penguin, pp. 9–72.

Foran, John et al. (eds) (2008), *Revolution in the Making of the Modern World*, London: Routledge.

Gilbert, Alan (1981), *Marx's Politics*, Oxford: Martin Robertson.

Gramsci, Antonio (1971), *Selections from the Prison Notebooks*, ed. and trans. Quinton Hoare and Geoffrey Nowell Smith, London: Lawrence and Wishart.

Gramsci, Antonio (1978), *Selections from Political Writings 1921–1926*, ed. and trans. Quinton Hoare, London: Lawrence and Wishart.

Guerin, Daniel [1965] (1970), *Anarchism*, trans. Mary Klopper, New York: Monthly Review.

Hardt, Michael, and Antonio Negri (2000), *Empire*, Cambridge, MA: Harvard University Press.

Hardt, Michael, and Antonio Negri (2004), *Multitude*, New York: Penguin.

Hegel, G. W. F. [1821] (1952), *Philosophy of Right*, trans. T. M. Knox, Oxford: Oxford University Press.

Hegel, G. W. F. [1837] (1956), *The Philosophy of History*, trans. J. Sibree, New York: Dover.

Hill, Christopher (1991), 'The word "revolution"', in Christopher Hill, *A Nation of Change and Novelty*, London: Routledge, pp. 82–101.

Hobsbawm, Eric (1962), *The Age of Revolution*, London: Weidenfeld & Nicolson.

Hobsbawm, Eric (1986), 'Revolution', in Roy Porter and Mikulá Teich (eds), *Revolution in History*, Cambridge: Cambridge University Press, pp. 5–46.

Hook, Sidney [1950] (1962), *From Hegel to Marx*, Ann Arbor: University of Michigan Press.

Hunt, Richard (1974), *The Political Ideas of Marx and Engels* vol. 1, London: Macmillan.

Israel, Jonathan I. (2001), *Radical Enlightenment: Philosophy and the Making of Modernity 1650–1750*, Oxford: Oxford University Press.

Kant, Immanuel [1798] (1991), 'The contest of faculties', in Immanuel Kant, *Kant: Political Writings*, ed. Hans Reiss and trans. H. B. Nisbet, Cambridge: Cambridge University Press, pp. 176–90.

Kersting, Wolfgang (1992), 'Politics, freedom and order: Kant's political philosophy', in Paul Guyer (ed.), *The Cambridge Companion to Kant*, Cambridge: Cambridge University Press, pp. 342–66.

Kropotkin, Peter [1880] (2002a), 'Revolutionary government', in Peter Kropotkin, *Anarchism*, ed. and trans. Roger Baldwin, New York: Dover, pp. 237–50.

Kropotkin, Peter [1887] (2002b), 'Anarchist Communism', in Peter Kropotkin, *Anarchism*, ed. and trans. Roger Baldwin, New York: Dover, pp. 46–78.

Kumar, Krishan (1971), 'Introduction', in Krishan Kumar (ed.), *Revolution: The Theory and Practice of a European Idea*, London: Weidenfeld and Nicolson.

Lenin, Vladimir [1917] (1968), *The State and Revolution*, in Vladimir Lenin, *Selected Works*, Moscow: Progress Publishers, pp. 263–348.

Levine, Andrew (1987), *The End of the State*, London: Verso.

Löwy, Michael (1989), 'The poetry of the past: Marx and the French Revolution', *New Left Review* 177: 111–24.

Lukács, Georg [1923] (1971), *History and Class Consciousness*, trans. Rodney Livingstone, London: Merlin Press.

MacIntyre, Alasdair (1985), *After Virtue*, London: Duckworth.

McLellan, David (1969), *The Young Hegelians and Karl Marx*, London: Macmillan.

McNally, David (1993), *Against the Market*, London: Verso.

Marshall, Peter (2008), *Demanding the Impossible: A History of Anarchism*, London: Harper.

Martin, James [1963] (2005), 'Editor's introduction' to Max Stirner, *The Ego and His Own*, New York: Dover, pp. vii–xvi.

Marx, Karl [1859] (1970), *A Contribution to the Critique of Political Economy*, London: Lawrence and Wishart.

Marx, Karl [1850] (1973a), 'Address of the Central Committee to the Communist League (March 1850)', in Karl Marx, *The Revolutions of 1848*, ed. David Fernbach, Harmondsworth: Penguin, pp. 319–30.

Marx, Karl [1852] (1973b), 'The Eighteenth Brumaire of Louis Bonaparte', in Karl Marx, *Surveys from Exile*, ed. David Fernbach, Harmondsworth: Penguin, pp. 143–249.

Marx, Karl [1864] (1974a), 'Provisional Rules of the International', in Karl Marx, *The First International and After*, ed. David Fernbach, Harmondsworth: Penguin, pp. 82–4.

Marx, Karl [1874–5] (1974b), 'Conspectus of Bakunin's *Statism and Anarchy*', in Karl Marx, *The First International and After*, ed. David Fernbach, Harmondsworth: Penguin, pp. 333–8.

Marx, Karl [1871] (1974c), 'The Civil War in France', in Karl Marx, *The First International and After*, ed. David Fernbach, Harmondsworth: Penguin, pp. 187–268.

Marx, Karl [1843] (1974d), 'Critique of the Gotha Programme', in Karl Marx, *The First International and After*, ed. David Fernbach, Harmondsworth: Penguin, pp. 339–59.

Marx, Karl [1843] (1975a), 'Contribution to a critique of Hegel's Philosophy of Right', in *Karl Marx: Early Writings*, ed. Lucio Colletti, Harmondsworth: Penguin, pp. 243–58.

Marx, Karl [1844] (1975b), 'Economic and philosophical manuscripts', in Karl Marx, *Early Writings*, ed. Lucio Colletti, Harmondsworth: Penguin, pp. 279–400.

Marx, Karl [1844] (1975c), 'Critical notes on the article "The King of Prussia and Social Reform. By a Prussian"', in Karl Marx, *Early Writings*, ed. Lucio Colletti, Harmondsworth: Penguin, pp. 401–20.

Marx, Karl [1845] (1975d), 'Theses on Feuerbach', in Karl Marx, *Early Writings*, ed. Lucio Colletti, Harmondsworth: Penguin, pp. 421–3.

Marx, Karl [1867] (1976), *Capital*, vol. 1, trans. Ben Fowkes, Harmondsworth: Penguin.

Marx, Karl [1856] (1980), 'Speech at the anniversary of The People's Paper', in Karl Marx and Frederick Engels, *Collected Works*, vol. 14, Moscow: Progress Publishers and New York: International Publishers, pp. 655–6.

Marx, Karl (1981), *Capital*, vol. 3, trans. David Fernbach, Harmondsworth: Penguin.

Marx, Karl, and Frederick Engels [1848] (1973), 'Manifesto of the Communist Party', in Karl Marx, *The Revolutions of 1848*, ed. David Fernbach, Harmondsworth: Penguin.

Marx, Karl, and Frederick Engels [1844] (1975), 'The Holy Family', in Karl Marx and Frederick Engels, *Collected Works*, vol. 4, Moscow: Progress Publishers and New York: International Publishers, pp. 5–211.

Marx, Karl, and Frederick Engels [1845–6] (1976), *The German Ideology*, in Karl Marx and Frederick Engels, *Collected Works*, vol. 5, Moscow: Progress Publishers and New York: International Publishers, pp. 20–539.

O'Hagan, Timothy (1999), *Rousseau*, London: Routledge.

Owen, Robert [1817] (1991), 'Letter published in the London Newspaper of August 19th 1817', in Robert Owen, *A New View of Society and Other Writings*, Harmondsworth: Penguin, pp. 186–90.

Perkins, Stephen (1993), *Marxism and the Proletariat*, London: Pluto.

Portis, Larry (1980), *Georges Sorel*, London: Pluto.

Proudhon, Pierre-Joseph [1840] (1994), *What Is Property?*, ed. and trans. Donald Kelley and Bonnie Smith, Cambridge: Cambridge University Press.

Proudhon, Pierre-Joseph [1851] (1989), *General Idea of the Revolution in the Nineteenth Century*, trans. John Beverley Robinson, London: Pluto.

Robespierre, Maximilien [1793] (2007), 'On the principles of revolutionary government', in Maximilien Robespierre, *Virtue and Terror*, trans. John Howe, London: Verso, pp. 98–107.

Rudé, George (1975), *Robespierre*, London: Collins.

Rudé, George (1988), *The French Revolution*, London: Phoenix.

Schorske, Carl [1955] (1983), *German Social Democracy 1905–1917*, London: Harvard University Press.

Soboul, Albert [1965] (1977), *A Short History of the French Revolution 1789–1799*, trans. Geoffrey Symcox, Berkeley: University of California Press.

Sorel, Georges [1908] (1999), *Reflections on Violence*, trans. Thomas Hulme, rev. Jeremy Jennings, Cambridge: Cambridge University Press.

Stirner, Max [1844] (2005), *The Ego and His Own*, trans. Steven Byington, New York: Dover.

Taylor, Charles (1975), *Hegel*, Cambridge: Cambridge University Press.

Thomas, Paul (1980), *Karl Marx and the Anarchists*, London: Routledge & Kegan Paul.

Tocqueville, Alexis de [1856] (1966), *The Ancien Régime and the French Revolution*, trans. Stuart Gilbert, London: Fontana.

Williams, Gwyn (1975), *Proletarian Order*, London: Pluto.

Williams, Raymond (1976), 'Revolution', in Raymond Williams, *Keywords*, London: Fontana, pp. 226–30.

15

Nihilism in the Nineteenth Century: From Absolute Subjectivity to Superhumanity

Michael Gillespie

1. The Varieties of Nihilism

The term 'nihilism' has been used to denote a philosophical concept or position, a psychological or sociological state or mood, a doctrine or agenda for political action and a cultural condition or movement. Moreover, the connotations of the term within each of these areas are multiple, complicated and contested. It is thus not easy to define the term or to determine the nature of the phenomenon that the term describes. This difficulty is exacerbated by the fact that the term has been principally used as a pejorative by opponents to characterise a condition, doctrine, or movement that they fear, disagree with or detest.

The term itself presents peculiar difficulties. In all of its modern variations 'nihilism' derives from the Latin *nihil*, 'nothing'. Nihilism is thus literally 'nothingism' and nihilists are 'nothingists'. Typically, 'ism' terms such as nationalism refer to something substantive. 'Nihilism', by contrast, is a pure negation. It thus has no specific content. This has led some to conclude that, in contrast to all other 'isms', nihilism is not directed to any specific end (Thielicke 1961: 27). Even if this claim is exaggerated, the lack of a clear referent has allowed the term to be used in multiple and conflicting ways.

The term is generally thought to describe a phenomenon that began in the second half of the nineteenth century and which was during that time given its guiding definition by Ivan Turgenev and by Nietzsche. It is generally thought, too, that the phenomenon became acute in the first half of the twentieth century, driving and informing not merely German thought during the inter-war years but also German and French existentialism in the period after World War II. At the same time, the two leading theorists of nihilism, Friedrich Nietzsche and Martin Heidegger, argue that the explicit nihilism of the nineteenth century and after is only the revelation of an implicit nihilism that has characterised European civilisation since its Greek beginnings. Similarly, the leading French writer on the subject, Albert Camus, used Sisyphus and Caligula as his examples of nihilists. Nietzsche and Keiji Nishitani, a leading Japanese theorist of nihilism, were not even convinced that nihilism was a merely Western phenomenon and they thought that it had explicit affinities to Buddhism (Nishitani 1990). Moreover, the basic character of nihilism is in dispute. While nihilism is generally considered atheistic, many scholars have argued that it has a Christian or proto-Christian origin, connecting it to Plotinus's notion of the One, Dun Scotus's notion of the univocity of being, or Ockham's notion of divine omnipotence (Zamir 2000; Cunningham 2002; Gillespie 1995). Others see nihilism as the result of a shift from other-worldly to this-worldly concerns which began with medieval realism and nominalism

(Manschreck 1976). From this perspective, Christianity is neither the victim of nor the antidote to nihilism but its driving cause – so that again nihilism would significantly predate the nineteenth century.

Even those who associate nihilism with the decline in belief in the Christian God and the rise of atheism and materialism do not agree about the nature or origin of the phenomenon (Thielicke 1961; Rosen 1969). Many believe that it was humanism that turned the West away from orthodox Christianity. Others attribute the origins of modern atheism to Galileo, Bacon, Descartes, Hobbes and Spinoza or to the critique of religion by Enlightenment thinkers such as Voltaire. Still others focus on Hume's scepticism or Kant's transcendental idealism. From this point of view nihilism is the result of a frustrated foundationalism. Others lay greater weight on the deification of man that pushes God and religion to the side. Still others, such as Max Weber, see nihilism as a symptom of the disenchantment of the world produced by late capitalism or, like Heidegger or Jacques Ellul, of the homelessness produced by the ceaseless operation of global technology. Others see nihilism as a profound world-weariness and/or hatred of the present that leads to the radical rejection of all existing modes and orders. Existence from this point of view is meaningless and absurd and the only appropriate human response is murder and/or suicide.

Given the variety of conceptions of nihilism, it is difficult to determine how to make sense of the term. To come to terms with nihilism we need to examine its genealogy, that is, to trace the development of the concept in specific contexts and determine how the meaning and use of the term have changed. In this way it may be possible to obtain some idea not of the specific meaning of nihilism but of a constellation or range of meanings of nihilism and the relationships between them.

2. The Critique of Post-Kantian Idealism as Nihilism

The term nihilism was apparently first used by F. L. Goetzius in his *De nonismo et nihilismo in theologia* of 1733, but this work was little known and probably did not influence the later development of the term. The concept of nihilism, as it has come down to us, was first used by the critics of German idealism, who attacked the thought of radical Kantians and particularly of Fichte as nihilism. They did so because they believed that such radical egoism was a form of atheism.

Jacob Hermann Obereit, a theosophist, used the term in 1792, complaining that the inaccessibility of the thing-in-itself which was proclaimed by the Kantians put a bare nothing in the place of God (Timm 1971: 80–1). Daniel Jenisch, a Lutheran theologian, similarly characterised transcendental idealism as nihilism in his *On the Ground and Value of the Discoveries of Herr Professor Kant in Metaphysics, Morals, and Aesthetics* (Pöggeler 1970: 180, 186–9). His title notwithstanding, he applies the term not to Kant or even to Fichte but to the radical Kantians who denied the existence of the thing-in-itself.[1]

While Obereit and Jenisch were the first to use the term, it was Jacobi who first popularised the term in his open letter to Fichte in 1799: 'Truly, my dear Fichte, it should not grieve me, if you, or whoever it might be, want to call *chimerism* what I oppose to idealism, which I reproach as *nihilism*' (Jacobi [1799] 1959: 2: 268–71).[2] Raised as a Pietist, Jacobi became a critic of the Enlightenment and the French Revolution, arguing that we must ultimately rely on feeling and belief.[3] In the 1780s he had been the principal antagonist in the Pantheism Controversy, when he characterised the Spinozism of thinkers such as Lessing and Mendelssohn as atheism.

Jacobi's letter to Fichte was written during the similar Atheism Controversy at the

University of Jena, a controversy which eventually cost Fichte his professorship. Jacobi used his letter to distance himself from Fichte, whom he had begun to suspect of defending an inverted Spinozism and whom he knew to be a supporter of the French Revolution. Jacobi was convinced that Fichte recognised no truths beyond those of consciousness or reason and thus fell into an absolute subjectivism which attributed everything to man and left no room for God – indeed, which made God into a product of the human imagination. This, for Jacobi, was the 'most horrible of horrors' (Jacobi 1959: 3: 29). Jacobi was convinced that

> [M]an has this choice and this alone: nothing or God. Choosing nothing he makes himself God; that means he makes God an apparition, for it is impossible, if there is no God, for man and all that is around him to be more than an apparition. I repeat: God is and is outside me, a living essence that subsists for itself, or I am God. There is no third possibility. (3: 49)

There are several possible explanations for how Jacobi and other critics of German idealism came to this German use of the term 'nihilism'. First, it may have been adopted from the French term *rienniste*, which was used to describe the extreme Jacobins. In discussing new French coinages, Louis-Sébastien Mercier defined a *Rienniste*, a nihilist or a nothingist, as 'one who believes in nothing, who interests himself in nothing. A beautiful result of the bad philosophy which brought itself into the world in the great *Dictionnaire encyclopédique!*' (Mercier 1801: 2: 143). While there is no evidence that the German term was borrowed from the French, the connection of a philosophical/theological and a revolutionary element within the concept over the course of its development is unmistakable.

A second possibility is that the theological connotations of the term reflect a connection to an earlier analogous term. The term *nichilianist(a)e* – nothingist(s) – was used in the second half of the twelfth century by Gauthier of St-Victor to describe a heretical strain of Christianity which argued that the divine logos is eternal and thus cannot become man. According to this heresy, Christ was merely accidental rather than necessary and thus was 'nothing' real. While there is no direct evidence that any of the early Germans who used the term knew of Gauthier's work, the term *Nihilianimus* did appear in Heinrich Matthais August Cramer's *Dictionary* (1775–86), and we know that Jacobi used this work. A third possibility is that Jacobi settled on this term by adapting the term 'annihilation' which was used by two other critics of Fichte in the Atheism Controversy (Süss 1951; Pöggeler 1970).

The term was adopted by Jacobi's student Friedrich Köppen in 1803 to critique the thought of Schelling. In 1803 Kajetan von Weiller suggested that Schelling's thought would be better called absolute nihilism than absolute idealism (Weiller 1803: 1: 195). What Jacobi and his followers found so 'nihilistic' in the thought of Fichte and Schelling was their attempt to resolve the diremption in Kant's thought between the phenomenal and noumenal without reference to God. Fichte, in their view, sought to derive everything from the activity of an absolute I that posits itself as an empirical I and the rest of the world as the not-I. This seemed to Jacobi to remove any possibility of transcendence and to attribute to man the freedom and power to create all existence, thus turning man into God and rendering God superfluous. Fichte's thought was thus essentially atheistic. Schelling avoided such an absolute subjectivism, but only by a return to a pantheistic – and thus, in their view, atheistic – philosophy of nature akin to that of Spinoza. Nihilism, then, for Jacobi, is not merely atheistic in denying the existence or importance of God; it is also hubristic in attributing to man superhuman or, indeed, divine powers.

3. Romantic Nihilism

In this early period the term 'nihilism' was also used to describe and critique the Jena Romantics, Friedrich Schlegel, August Wilhelm Schlegel, Novalis, Ludwig Tieck et al. – almost all of whom were students of Fichte. In 1804 Jean Paul (Richter), a follower of Jacobi, called them 'aesthetic nihilists' because they attempted to portray Fichte's absolute I as an actual human possibility that would allow finite human beings to challenge or replace God. The thought of the Jena Romantics, in Jean Paul's view, was an expression of 'the lawless, capricious spirit of the present age, which would egoistically annihilate the world and the universe in order to clear a space merely for free *play* in the void' (Richter 1973: 15). Jean Paul had already captured this wild spirit and its consequences in the 'Speech of the Dead Christ from the Celestial Sphere that There Is No God' in his novel *Siebenkäs* of 1796–7, but he adopted Jacobi's formulation to encapsulate and dramatise his critique (Richter 1959: 2: 268–71).

While Jean Paul's description was pejorative and critical, it was not unjustified terminologically. As Dieter Arendt has argued, the Jena Romantics' conception of poetry and poetic creation grew out of a fascination with the 'nothingness' of the world, which was reflected in their emphasis on the night and night wisdom (Arendt 1970: 9–62). The world as these Romantics saw it was quite different from the rational cosmos of the Enlightenment. In works such as Ernst August Friedrich Klingemann's *The Night Watches of Bonaventura* of 1804 and Novalis's *Hymns to the Night* of 1800, this darker element takes centre stage. As in William Blake's 1794 poem 'Tyger' and Samuel Taylor Coleridge's 1798 'Rime of the Ancient Mariner', the world appears to be a dark and chaotic place where very little makes sense to human reason. This view of the world leads to reflection on the dark, mysteriously hidden side of the human soul. Within Jena Romanticism this was sometimes connected with an interest in Eastern religion. Friedrich Schlegel, for example, saw nihilism as connected to mysticism, especially as it was practised in Indian Buddhism, where God is an endless nothing (a view shared by Schopenhauer, himself a Fichte student and reader of the Jena Romantics) (see Schlegel [1823] 1958–: 15/1: 95–7).

This notion of a hidden noumenal power or will that guides our feelings was not unique to the Jena Romantics. It was broadly shared by Romantics in Germany, Europe and the United States who saw themselves at odds with Enlightenment notions of rationality and order. From the Romantic perspective, rational laws and mores are merely forms of oppression that prevent individuals from discovering their own affective roots in the natural and spiritual world. The heroic man is thus not good and reasonable but bold and powerful, acting against prevailing rules, shattering all of the boundaries that are imposed upon him. The pre-eminent example of such a person in their minds was Napoleon, but artists such as Beethoven and Byron came to play a similar role for later Romantics. Such transgressive individuals who challenged authority and generally followed a meteoric path of ascent and descent were a favourite subject of Romantic fiction not merely in Germany but across Europe. Hölderlin's Hyperion, Brentano's Godwi, Tieck's William Lovell, Byron's Don Juan and Manfred, Shelley's Prometheus, Mary Shelley's Victor Frankenstein, Stendhal's Julien Sorel, Pushkin's Eugene Onegin and Lermontov's Pechorin are only the most famous examples of these titanic beings (Hildebrand 1984).

These bold individuals may not ascend to the level of God but they are great and independent powers who can and do challenge his hegemony. They typically suffer from *Weltschmerz*, from a sense of alienation, wanderlust, isolation and misanthropy. They feel themselves to be above all laws and look down with aristocratic disdain on lesser men, often violating the most fundamental prohibitions through seduction, incest and murder, thus irrevocably detaching themselves from the community. Surprisingly, while they are libertines and sensualists, rapists and murderers, they are not villains in the context of Romantic fiction. Indeed, their libertinism and criminality are often portrayed as paths to liberation. These characters are expressions of what Goethe called the demonic, which:

> comes forward in overpowering fashion among men . . . a monstrous power goes out from them, and they exercise an unbelievable power over all creatures, indeed even over the elements, and who can say how far their influence reaches? All of the unified powers of the community cannot resist them . . . they can be overcome by nothing except the universe itself with which they have entered into competition; such observations may have led to the strange but monstrous maxim: *Nemo contra deum nisi deus ipse* [None against God save God himself]. (Goethe, *Faust* [1832], ll. 11,934–7, 1950–60: 10: 177)

Goethe included Napoleon, Karl August, Byron, Frederick II of Prussia, Paganini and Peter the Great as demonic natures and he was clearly attracted to them. He also recognised the dangers they posed. However, while they may try to do evil, Goethe believed that, like Mephistopheles, they end up doing good – and thus that, like Faust, they can because of their striving be saved (*Dichtung und Wahrheit* [1811–25] 1950–60: 12: 299).

Goethe's attempt to constrain these demonic characters within a broader Christian perspective, however, was rejected by the Romantics themselves. Their hero was not Faust but Byron's Manfred, who, in the poetic drama of 1817, asserted his independence of Christianity:

> The Mind which is immortal makes itself/ Requital for its good or evil thoughts,–/ Is its own origin of ill and end–/ And its own place and time: its innate sense/ . . . [I] was my own destroyer and will be / My own hereafter. (Byron 2009: Act 3, Scene 4, lines 132–40)

Striving to become a god, the demonic hero of Romanticism becomes a beast or, more correctly, a beast god, represented most clearly by Frankenstein's monster. Jean Paul summarises what he sees as the essential nihilism of these characters: 'in an age when God has set like the sun, soon afterwards the world too passes into darkness. He who scorns the universe respects nothing more than himself and at night fears only his own creations' (Richter 1973: 15).

4. Hegel: Nihilism and Absolute Knowledge

Like Goethe, Hegel was concerned about the dangers of Romantic nihilism, but he recognised that the problem that gave rise to it was real and compelling. In his view, the diremption in Kantian idealism had disastrous consequences, undermining faith, severing subject from substance, making consciousness itself contradictory, and thus, contrary to Kant's intentions saving neither science nor religion nor morality. Hegel was also convinced that neither Fichte's absolute egoism nor Schelling's philosophy of nature offered a solution to this problem. In contrast to Jacobi, however, Hegel did not simply condemn or reject idealism. In his 1802 essay, *Faith and Knowledge*, Hegel argued rather that it was out of this abyss of nothing [*Abgrund des Nichts*] . . . the feeling: God is dead . . . [that] the highest totality, in its complete seriousness and out of its deepest ground, at once all-encompassing and in the most joyful freedom of its form, can and must arise. (Hegel [1802] 1970: 2: 432–3)

The nihilistic diremption at the heart of idealism had to be reconciled on idealist grounds without reliance on a transcendent God.

In Hegel's view, Kant in his antinomies had demonstrated that reason necessarily came into contradiction with itself when it attempted to grasp the infinite. This demonstration led Kant to conclude that humans could not understand the divine and thus that the understanding had to limit itself to an investigation of the finite world, to what Kant called the island of truth. Hegel tried to show that it was precisely the *necessity* of the contradiction that was the answer to the contradiction, since it pointed to a reason and necessity that transcended the contradiction itself. Hegel thus attempted to demonstrate that the principle of freedom or negation that had been conceived by Jacobi and Jean Paul as the source of nihilism did not lead to meaninglessness but to absolute knowledge and to a rational ethics and politics.

Hegel understood why Jacobi and Jean Paul characterised Fichte and the Jena Romantics as nihilists and in many respects he agreed with them. However, he believed that Jacobi's notion that knowledge could only be grounded in the affective experience of an unknowable God was an even more profound form of nihilism. This was because it eternally separated us from the truth and, as Hegel put it in his *Phenomenology of Spirit*, 'the true alone is absolute and the absolute alone is the truth' (Hegel [1807] 1970: 3: 70). Hegel was thus convinced that the path of Fichte and the Romantics pointed to a solution, a true 'nihilism' through which humans could come to participate in the absolute. This is possible because in Hegel's view the absolute is not an I or nature but absolute spirit, the unity not merely of being and knowing but of the individual, society and the divine. Hegel's thought is an attempt to demonstrate that all of these disparate moments are reconciled with one another in a speculative synthesis.

This demonstration rests upon a kind of nihilism, which Hegel refers to as absolute negativity, the 'motion from nothing to nothing and thereby back to itself . . . the nothing of a nothing, and this being the negation of a nothing, constitutes being. – Being only is the motion of nothing to nothing' (Hegel [1812–16] 1970: 6: 24–5). Hegel's solution to the problem of nihilism is thus the demonstration that nothing turned back on itself, as the negation of negation, is being. Concretely, for Hegel, this means that the 'power of the negative' – that is, the freedom of self-consciousness that liberates itself repeatedly from its content – is the driving force in world history. In contrast to Fichte, Schelling and the Romantics, Hegel thus argues that there is no nothingness, but only an active nothing that negates something, and that this negated something is again not nothing but something else. Negation for Hegel is thus always determinate and not absolute negation and brings about change and new forms of meaning, rather than absolute annihilation and meaninglessness.

The principal agents of the negative in history are those men whom Hegel calls 'world-historical individuals'. On the surface, these individuals seem to be the same titanic or demonic characters that had entranced the Romantics, men who live beyond the standards of good and evil and who, like Napoleon, repeatedly lay down new codes of laws and new ways of life. Hegel argues, however, that they are merely agents of spirit, successful because they will what everyone else already (unknowingly) wants. Each may believe he is a titan and that he works his will on others, but in fact he is himself directed by the 'cunning of reason' and, like Goethe's Mephistopheles, he unwittingly but inevitably serves the progressive movement of spirit. Moreover, at the end of history, when spirit has become completely self-conscious of itself as being all reality, such individuals are no longer needed. In the rational state that Hegel saw coming into being in his own time, the world-historical individuals are thus replaced by a universal class of bureaucrats who maintain the liberal order that is the final outcome of history.

Hegel thus recognised the problem of nothingness that leads to nihilism and he sought to provide a solution to it. This solution, however, rests on his notion of absolute negativity, that is, on the speculative unity that is the culmination of his thought. Hegel himself admitted that this unity was only a spiritual unity, that is, a unity in thought and not a unity in the objective realm of political and social life. Within civil society poverty, inequality and human misery were ineliminable.

But, already in Hegel's lifetime, his system was called into question. Few understood his speculative claim and many were unwilling to believe that nothing could be done to ameliorate human misery. The collapse of Hegelianism (and the speculative synthesis at its core) after 1840 and the failure of the Revolutions of 1848 to institutionalise the rational states that Hegel had predicted led to the recognition of the continuing importance of heroic human action to effect fundamental historical change. The demonic heroes of Romanticism, whom Hegel had sought to harness to the chariot of spirit, thus reappeared, although not as asocial or antisocial individuals but as the charismatic leaders of social movements aiming at revolutionary change. The Left Hegelians play an important role here. Unlike the Right Hegelians who interpreted Hegel's synthesis in a more Christian manner as the basis of the unity of throne and altar and who were drawn toward Romantic nationalism, the Left Hegelians rejected Hegel's synthesis as merely spiritual and they sought to bring about the actual transformation of social reality.

5. Left Hegelianism and Nihilism

The rejection of Hegel's speculative synthesis led to a re-evaluation of the nature of the Absolute and of the rationality of existing social and political institutions. In this context, a new form of nihilism arose. The attack on orthodox Christianity was at the centre of this effort. David Friedrich Strauss, who was influenced by Hegel, called into question Christ's divinity in his *Life of Jesus* of 1835; Bruno Bauer declared that Jesus was merely mythical; and Ludwig Feuerbach took the matter to its logical conclusion, declaring God to be only the outward expression of man's inward nature. His atheism had a wide and powerful influence on the young and especially on those who were active in the Revolutions of 1848.

We also see this nihilistic impulse in its extremity in the thought of Max Stirner (Johann Caspar Schmidt) who sought to free the individual not only from God but also from society and indeed from humanity as such. The nihilistic dimension of this project was particularly evident in Stirner's magnum opus, *The Ego and his Own* of 1844, in which he claimed that, 'I am not nothing in the sense of emptiness, but I am the creative nothing, the nothing out of which I myself as creator create everything' (Stirner [1844] 1907: 6). Here the connection to the earlier Fichtean and Romantic nihilists and to later nihilism is especially apparent. This is equally true of Stirner's moral stance, for he was willing to countenance incest, infanticide and murder (Stirner 1907: 58, 65, 124, 247, 424).

The impact of Left Hegelianism on politics and theology was particularly evident in the Young Germany movement of the 1830s which included Heinrich Heine, Georg Büchner and Karl Gutzkow, among others. Büchner, for example, explicitly abandons Hegel's speculative synthesis in *Danton's Death*: 'The nothing killed itself, creation is its wound and we are its drops of blood and the world is the grave into which they fall' (Büchner 1980: 55). Negation, for Büchner and his fellows, does not negate itself as Hegel suggested, producing a new and higher form of life; instead it is an open wound that leads only to our annihilation. Heine is less explicit in his rejection of Hegel, but he clearly believes that the death of God is not the well-spring of a higher form of life but the source of meaninglessness. However, he treats this fact ironically rather than tragically, in part because he views the world not absolutely but perspectively. He and other members of this group sided with the Left Hegelians and were unequivocal opponents of Romanticism and of the union of church and state, instead advocating more liberal social and political institutions. Many of these thinkers were ardent supporters of the Revolution of 1848 and thought of themselves as nihilists. However, they distinguished their nihilism from that of the Romantics, pursuing methodical and continuous reforms, rather than a single apocalyptic and revolutionary transformation.

The character of this new nihilism and its differences from Romantic nihilism are evident in Gutzkow's novella *The Nihilists* of 1853. The story is set in the period before and during the Revolution of 1848. It depicts two nihilists. The first is Konstantine Ulrichs, a charismatic and egoistical nihilist, reminiscent of Romanticism. He wants all or nothing, America or Russia, and wants above all to be admired. With the failure of the Revolution, he gives up his nihilism and marries into the ruling class. The second nihilist, Eberhart Ott, is quiet and practical, a dedicated reader of Feuerbach, someone who favours effective reform over radical revolution. In contrast to Konstantin, Eberhart does not wants to impose his subjective will upon events but to bring about reforms that are in the public good. The failure of the Revolution does not daunt him and he continues to work for whatever reforms can be achieved.

Gutzkow sees Romantic nihilism as radical egoism, the Mephistophelean spirit of criticism and negation. Like Hegel, he believes that this egoistic nihilism must be replaced by a practical nihilism that is concerned not with the individual but with society as a whole. Like the Left Hegelians, however, he is convinced that much still needs to be done to bring about a truly rational state. His hero Eberhart is a nihilist in the sense that he aims at the negation of the existing order. He does not think of himself as a world-historical individual but as a part of a new universal class, not of Hegelian bureaucrats but of Left Hegelian reformers. The novella ends with the Feuerbachian claim that while such negation may not yet have achieved its goals, the path it follows spirals continually upward. In this way the egoistic nihilism of Romanticism was replaced by a self-sacrificing, reformist nihilism. This new nihilism continued to play a role in Germany in the succeeding decades, particularly within the socialist movement, but it played an even more important role in Russia.

6. Russian Nihilism

Russian nihilism was part of the movement to reform the autocratic Czarist régime. Russian reformers drew heavily on Left Hegelian thinkers such as Feuerbach because they believed that a more atheistic stance was necessary to break the connection of throne and altar which they saw as essential to the Russian régime. The connection to German thought was longstanding. Czar Nicholas I's attempts to Prussianise Russian society under the rubric of 'autocracy, orthodoxy and nationality' led to the introduction of Schelling's Romantic idealism and his millenarianism. The movement from Romanticism to Right Hegelianism, then to Left Hegelianism and finally to anarchism/nihilism was typical of many Russian radicals and the enduring connection to a millenarian element helps to illuminate the apocalyptic hopes that they placed in human will. It was, however, just such an apotheosis of man that led the orthodox to characterise Russian Left Hegelians as nihilists, employing arguments similar to those of Jacobi and Jean Paul.

While they were initially enraged to be called nihilists, many radicals came to accept and deploy the term as a self-description (Kravchinskii 1883). Alexander Herzen, for example, asserted that

> Nihilism is logic without structure, it is science without dogmas, it is unconditional submission to experience and the resigned acceptance of all consequences, whatever they may be, if they follow from observation, or are required by reason. Nihilism does not transform something into nothing, but shows that nothing which has been taken for something is an optical illusion and that every truth, however it contradicts our fantastic ideas, is more wholesome than they are and is in any case what we are duty bound to accept. (Herzen [1868] 1973: 642)

These radicals were convinced that the elimination of repression would produce freedom, but were uncertain where this freedom would lead. Indeed, they thought a positive goal could only be formulated once the old order had been destroyed. Their purpose in the moment was sheer negation and they felt that anything that delayed progress 'is immoral, unjust, harmful, irrational' (Moser 1964: 37). Dmitri Pisarev proclaimed:

> Here is the ultimatum of our camp: what can be smashed should be smashed; what will stand the blow is good; what will fly into smithereens is rubbish; at any rate, hit out right and left – there will and can be no harm from it. (Yarmolinsky 1956: 120)

While Russian nihilists drew heavily on Feuerbach, they did not feel themselves bound by the notion of dialectical development that characterised German thought. History in their view was determined by the free actions of individuals. In this respect they were closer to Fichte, whom Bakunin declared 'the true hero of our times', than to the Left Hegelians (Mendel 1981: 56–83, 134–6, 145). The apocalyptical character of the power that they attributed to freedom was awe-inspiring. Nikolai Dobrolyubov, for example, thought that they would have to wait only a single night for the social transformation they expected (Volski 1969: 209–10).

The main organs of this movement were two journals, the populist *The Contemporary*, edited by Nikolai Chernyshevsky and Dobrolyubov, and the positivist the *Russian Word*, edited by Dmitry Pisarev. The former was dedicated to mobilising the peasantry; the latter aimed to create a managerial elite. Both believed in the decisive importance of the intelligentsia, whom they imagined would be organised like a Jesuitical order. Many of their members were drawn from the seminary and even their opponents recognised that they acted more like a religious order than a political party or social movement. Chernyshevsky was the son of an orthodox priest but was attracted to Hegel and the Left Hegelians in his student days, and especially to Feuerbach. Human beings, in his view, were complex chemical compounds, driven entirely by rational egoism. His theory of rational self-interest, however, was underpinned by the optimistic assumption that the interests of society and those of the individual naturally coincide.

It was Turgenev's portrayal of these men in *Fathers and Sons* of 1862 that first brought the term 'nihilism' into broader circulation. Turgenev modelled his nihilist hero, Eugene

Bazarov, on Chernyshevsky, Dobrolyubov and Pisarev. Bazarov is a doctor by training, a thorough positivist, unwilling to accept anything on faith. However, at his core he is a nihilist and a revolutionary (although because of the censorship this could not be explicitly stated). He has a very high opinion of himself, likening himself to a god, and is, as the author indicates, a bottomless pit of self-conceit. He has rejected all Romanticism and idealism and studies natural science not for its own sake but in order to understand men.

Bazarov wants to be useful and he believes that at the present time negation is the most useful of all. Everything, in his view, is corrupt and only absolute negation can bring substantive change. The important thing, he proclaims, is hate and negation. Unfortunately, he meets and falls in love with a beautiful, rich, young widow, Odnitsova, and thus finds it impossible to live up to his own principles. Heedless of his own safety and in contradiction with himself, he fails to cauterise a wound during the dissection of a cholera victim and dies. Bazarov believes he is a self-creating being, a Prometheus, but Turgenev adopts a more Romantic attitude, suggesting that Bazarov is only an expression of mother earth and in the end is reunited with her. While Turgenev had misgivings about nihilism, he considered Bazarov a 'hero for our times' – although he admitted that that said more about the times than the hero.

The nihilists themselves believed that Turgenev's book was an attack upon their movement. In response Chernyshevsky published his 1863 novel *What Is to Be Done?*, which presents a more attractive picture of the new men, most of whom bear a striking resemblance to Gutzkow's practical nihilists. They are all disciples of Feuerbach, self-sacrificing reformers, living and working together in a socialist commune. Their goal is the production of a socialist society in which everyone has enough to eat, lives comfortably and dies quickly at a great age.

There is one character in the novel, Rakhmetov, who is radically different from the others. He is a nihilist revolutionary who rivals Bazarov, a titanic being in Chernyshevsky's view. He steels himself for the rigours of revolutionary action, even sleeping on a bed of nails to prepare for torture. In describing him and his like Chernyshevsky remarks that

> there are few of them, but through them flourishes the life of all; without them life would become dead and putrid; there are few of them but they will help all people to breathe; without them people would suffocate . . . they are the salt of the earth. (Chernyshevsky [1863] 1986: 291)

The populist nihilists clearly hoped that a path of reform that engaged the peasantry could eventually bring about needed political reform, but when the peasantry showed no interest in such changes it became clear that any real reform within Russian itself could only be achieved through conspiratorial politics.

The best known of these conspiratorial nihilists were Bakunin and Sergei Nechaev. Bakunin was a Left Hegelian, an anarchist, an atheist and a revolutionary (on Bakunin, especially in respect of his relation to Marxism, see also Chapter 14). Bakunin's turn against religion was decisive. He wrote in 1871: 'If God is, man is a slave; now, man can and must be free; then God does not exist . . . [Therefore] it will be necessary to eliminate, first of all, this fiction of God, the eternal and absolute enslaver' (Bakunin [1871] 1895: 15, 25). And yet there was a revolutionary ardour in him that took the form of religiosity, even if it was more Satanic than angelic. He suggested to his fellow revolutionaries: 'Let us put our trust in the eternal spirit which destroys and annihilates only because it is the unsearchable and eternally creative source of all life – the passion for destruction is also a creative passion!' (Bakunin

[1942] 1973: 58). He had no doubt where this was leading and was entranced by his own apocalyptic visions: 'The star of revolution will rise high and independent above Moscow from a sea of blood and fire, and will turn into a lodestar to lead a liberated humanity', Bakunin wrote in his 'Appeal to the Slavs' of 1848 (quoted in Woodcock 1962: 154).

This vision of the nihilist revolutionary is even more fully embodied in Nechaev, who, along with Bakunin, composed the infamous *Catechism of a Revolutionary* of 1869, which authorised and promoted the use of what most nihilists themselves considered immoral techniques to organise a conspiratorial organisation. For Nechaev,

> The Revolutionary is a man set apart. He has no personal interests, no emotions, not attachments; he has no personal property, not even a name. Everything in him is absorbed by the one exclusive interest, the one thought, one single passion – the revolution. In his innermost being he has, not only in words but in deeds, broken every bond with the present-day society and with the whole civilized world including its laws, customs, conventions and morality. If he continues to live in it, he does so as the implacable enemy for the sole purpose of destroying it. (Prawdin 1961: 63)

The public trial of the Nechaevists, who, following Nechaev's lead, had murdered one of their own members, propagated nihilist doctrines to a broad audience, inspiring many who had previously been unaware of the movement. Not all intellectuals, however, sided with the nihilists. In fact, many saw nihilism as a social disease. Fyodor Dostoevsky has Raskolnikov dream of a plague that makes people go mad in *Crime and Punishment* of 1866. In his 1872 novel *Demons*, the nihilists appear to be filled with evil spirits and in Aleksey Pisemsky's *In the Whirlpool*, they are portrayed as men driven by uncontrollable passions (Moser 1964: 154).

Dostoevsky played an important role in shaping the larger European conception of nihilism. While he was originally attracted to the revolutionary movement, he became an ardent critic of it later in life. With a few exceptions, he portrays the nihilist revolutionaries as men who do not understand themselves, are taken in by foreign ideas, driven by dark motives, capricious, pathological, embittered and/or in search of revenge. They may claim they have ideals, but Dostoevsky reveals them at best to be confused and mistaken.

The nihilists in Dostoevsky's *Demons* reflect his views. Kirilov has decided that his own will is the ultimate reality and he intends to commit suicide as a way of rejecting God and proving his own divinity. Shigalyov is an anarchist socialist who is driven by a kind of hatred of everything Christ-like. Pyotr Verkhovensky is a duplicitous manipulator, who believes in little more than negation and is and willing, like Nechaev, to kill or abandon his fellows at a moment's notice. Nikolai Stavrogin is a charismatic sociopath, a paedophile who refuses to repent and who ultimately commits suicide.

The characterisation of the nihilists in *The Brothers Karamazov* of 1881 is equally grim. Even Ivan Karamazov, the most coherent of Dostoevsky's nihilists, is ambiguous. He takes the suffering of the innocent as a demonstration either that God does not exist or that he does exist and that no right-thinking person would want to live in the world he has created. Moreover, if God is dead, then in Ivan's view everything is permitted. This doctrine inspires his half-brother Smerdyakov to kill their father. In the end Ivan goes mad and Smerdyakov commits suicide.

Dostoevsky thus does not develop a univocal image of the nihilist. All are atheists of one kind or another and recognise no moral bounds, acting as if everything were permitted. Some have been influenced by earlier European thought; some are cynical Machiavellian manipulators; some are debauched sensualists; and their number includes seducers, paedophiles, parricides, murderers and thieves. Even the best of them self-destruct in one way or another, killing themselves or falling into madness. In Dostoevsky's view the denial of God produces a radical freedom, but it is only the freedom to err, to injure and to destroy. Far from being revolutionary heroes, these nihilists are sinners who construct their own inferno.

While Dostoevsky's portrayal of the Russian nihilists had a broad and lasting impact on the European imagination, it did not impede the nihilist movement in Russian itself. The members of conspiratorial groups modelled themselves on Bazarov and on Chernyshevsky's character Rakhmetov and they adopted the methods of Bakunin and Nechaev. Though they were small in number, they succeeded in assassinating the liberalising Czar Alexander II in 1881. The régime, however, did not collapse and in fact became more repressive, quickly eliminating the nihilist movement within Russia. Nihilist thought, however, helped to shape Russian Marxism and was important for the later development of Bolshevism. Vladimir Lenin, for example, was deeply influenced by Chernyshevsky, whose Rakhmetov became his great hero. And while Lenin and many others became Marxists, they employed a Bakuninist strategy. They also continued to believe that human will and freedom could overcome everything and bring about an apocalyptic transformation of society. Leon Trotsky perhaps best expressed the nihilists' belief in the superhuman, which they had inherited from their idealist and Romantic progenitors: through permanent revolution, he writes, man will be able

to raise himself to a new plane, to create a higher social biological type, stronger, wiser, subtler; his body will become more harmonized, his movements more rhythmic, his voice more musical. The forms of life will become dynamically dramatic. The average human type will rise to the heights of an Aristotle, a Goethe, or a Marx. And above this ridge new peaks will rise. (Trotsky [1924] 1957: 256)

7. Nietzsche's Conception of Nihilism

The idea of the superhuman also played an important role in the development of nihilism in Germany during the latter half of the nineteenth century, especially in the hands of Friedrich Nietzsche. Nietzsche is generally regarded as the philosopher most responsible for developing and propagating the concept of nihilism, but this is a misperception. He actually only began using the term in his notes in 1880 and in his published work in 1886, two years before slipping into madness (Kuhn 1992). It was one of a series of terms that he used to describe what he perceived as the spiritual and cultural crisis of European civilisation and he used it only briefly, replacing it with 'decadence'.

The notion that nihilism was central to his thought was the result of a deception perpetrated by his sister who constructed a work from his notes and pawned it off as his magnum opus, the *Will to Power*. This book presents nihilism as the focus of Nietzsche's thought. As a result, the early twentieth century came to think of Nietzsche as the archpriest of nihilism. Nietzsche struggled for his entire life to come to terms with the cultural crisis that he saw engulfing Europe. He was by no means convinced that the term 'nihilism', with all of its connotations and connections, was the appropriate way to describe this crisis. However, as a result of the impact of the *Will to Power*, the connection to nihilism became indelible and exercised an enormous influence on almost everyone who came after him.

Nihilism, as Nietzsche understood it, is connected to the death of God. God, as Nietzsche's Zarathustra argues, died out of pity for man, that is, because man was no longer powerful enough to sustain him. Extending Feuerbach's argument, Nietzsche thus suggests that God is a projection of human spirituality and that the death of God is a reflection of the degeneration of humanity. Man is no longer capable of creating or sustaining gods. Or, to use Nietzsche's later language, the highest values devalue themselves. The immediate consequences of the death of God in Nietzsche's view would be cataclysmic: the collapse of European morality, a monstrous logic of terror and wars the like of which the world had never seen.

The long-term consequences, however, are more ambiguous. Freed from the shackles of Christian morality, European humanity could become more than it has been or less, rising to glorious new, superhuman heights or sliding into the lowest of human possibilities, becoming what Nietzsche calls the last man. The advent of nihilism confronts humanity with a decision between these two possibilities. The contrast could not be starker – choosing the superhuman, or as Nietzsche also calls it the 'Dionysian', path means saying Yes to life in all of its terrifying chaos and complexity; choosing the path of the last man means choosing banality. It is within his formulation of these two possibilities that Nietzsche deploys the concept of nihilism.

Nietzsche's use of the term 'nihilism' almost certainly derives from his reading of Turgenev, but Dostoevsky, Chernyshevsky, Bakunin, Alexander Herzen and Peter Kropotkin also had an impact on his understanding of the phenomenon (Nietzsche 1967–: III (4): 26; V (2): 264; VI (2): 424; VIII (1): 2; see Kuhn 1992: 21; Janz 1978: 1: 677). Nihilism, for Nietzsche, thus initially meant Russian nihilism. However, Nietzsche was misled about the character of Russian nihilism by his reading of Prosper Mérimée and Paul Bourget who wrongly portrayed Russian nihilism as Schopenhauerian and thus a form of resignation and despair (Bourget 1885: 2: 225, 239; Mérimée 1927–33, 9: cviii–cix; 11: 548; see Kuhn 1984: 266, 269, 271).

In his development of the concept of nihilism in his late notes (and as it was presented in the *Will to Power*), Nietzsche distinguishes between incomplete and complete nihilism. He identifies incomplete nihilism with positivism, materialism and utilitarianism, all of which attempt to escape from nihilism without facing the consequences of the death of God. Complete nihilism confronts this problem and the devaluation of the highest values that it entails. Complete nihilism takes one of two forms. It is either passive nihilism, which in Buddhist or Schopenhauerian fashion leads to resignation, or it is active nihilism, which as in the case of Russian nihilism seeks to destroy the existing order. Both of these Nietzsche saw as fundamentally negative and standing in contrast to the affirmative and creative, 'Dionysian' nihilism that he himself favours.

The solution to the problem of nihilism in Nietzsche's view lies in nihilism itself. For some, the death of God and the collapse of all Christian values mean that they can simply follow their momentary passions. These are incomplete nihilists, the banal last men. They do not seek discipline and order of rank but a democracy of the passions in which each is satisfied in turn without repression or sublimation. The passive nihilist, by contrast, can no longer believe in God but still needs an absolute. He is driven to despair and resignation in the face of nothingness. The active nihilist is also distraught by the death of God, but he does not fall into despair, nor does he resign himself to the world as he finds it. Rather, he is thrown into a destructive rage and seeks to destroy the existing order, to have done with all moral commands. This active nihilist is free but is filled, like Turgenev's nihilist hero Bazarov, with hatred of the existing world. These active nihilists, however, are necessary in Nietzsche's view to wipe away all of the vestiges of Christianity and its morality of pity. He believes that their impulse to destruction will produce two hundred years of warfare, at the end of which a new group of harder, stronger, more disciplined, more nihilistic human beings will arise (Nietzsche 1967–: VI (3): 364; VII (2): 25, 261). Out of these hardened men will grow the superman, the Dionysian nihilist who will establish a thousand-year Dionysian empire (Kuhn 1992: 237).

The reception of Nietzsche's *Will to Power* convinced his readers that for him nihilism was a social or cultural malaise that was characterised by the death of God and the devaluation of the highest values. These led to a sense of the meaninglessness of life that undermined all goals, unity, truth, reason and purpose. In their reading of Nietzsche, to overcome nihilism it was necessary to create a new order based on the will to power that cultivates a super-humanity, whose members are stronger, more violent, less pitying than their human predecessors. While the effect of the *Will to Power* was blunted by the reception of Nietzsche's other works, there is little doubt that it exercised an inordinate and misleading influence on the conception of nihilism that developed after Nietzsche plunged into insanity.

8. Nihilism After Nietzsche

The end of the nineteenth century was a period of peace and stability, but under the influence of Nietzsche many intellectuals perceived it as an era of decadence and decline. In the literature of the period a sense of world-weariness is palpable and many identified this as the consequence of a creeping nihilism (Ascheim 1992: 52). Like Nietzsche, they looked for the antidote to the meaninglessness and purposelessness of their lives in a variety of sources, including an exploration of the primitive, the mythical, the wild, the unconscious and the irrational.

One manifestation of Nietzsche's impact was the elegant nihilism of the 1890s, exemplified in the works of Oscar Wilde and his circle, who were preoccupied with aestheticism, decadence, Hellenism and homoeroticism. But in others, many of whom were also inspired by Nietzsche, there was a growing fascination with nihilistic and primitive violence. This was evident in the literary works of Joseph Conrad and Jack London and the political tracts of Georges Sorel and F. T. Marinetti, amongst many others. The impact of this nihilistic notion of the positive value of destructive violence also fuelled actual political movements, such as the socialist God-building movement of Maxim Gorky and Anatoly Lunacharsky in Russia and the Young Bosnia movement which assassinated Archduke Franz Ferdinand of Austria.

The story of nihilism in the twentieth century is marked by the shattering impact of the two world wars and the holocaust on the Western psyche. Nihilism played an important role in the cultural pessimism of post-World War I Europe, the sense of meaninglessness and despair that characterised the literature of the lost generation, the apocalyptic spirituality of the interwar years, the rise of Fascism and Nazism and, later, many philosophical movements, including existentialism. The reception of Nietzsche's thought and his notion of nihilism had a decisive impact on this development at almost every point.

However, the concept of nihilism had its origins in the late eighteenth and early nineteenth century. As I have argued, it arose as part of the effort of European intellectuals such as Jacobi and Jean Paul to come to terms with the deep problems that they saw growing out of the new notion of human freedom which found its first articulations in radical Jacobinism and in the absolute egoism of Fichte and the Jena Romantics, and which was at the heart of the broader Romantic notion of the demonic hero. It was this Promethean notion of human freedom and power, which seemed to render God irrelevant, that intellectuals such as Jacobi characterised as nihilism. Hegel, too, recognised the dangers of such a radical egoism, but he was not willing to dismiss it as nihilism, since he believed that it was essential as a moment of the realisation of freedom within the rational state. Moreover, he was convinced that the negative element could be transformed into something positive within the speculative synthesis at the heart of his philosophy.

Hegel's Left Hegelian followers, however, rejected this synthesis, as they rejected his assertion that freedom could not actually be attained within the existing social and political order. In this way they revived the idea of radical freedom that had characterised Fichtean and Romantic nihilism, but they transformed it into a realist plan for collective reform. This Left Hegelian nihilism was further developed in Russia into first a movement of political reform, then a notion of radical critique and agitation and finally a conspiratorial organisation employing terror and assassination which aimed at the immediate and total transformation of society. While focusing as well on the superhuman possibilities of the human will, Nietzsche vastly expanded the meaning of nihilism, which in his thought became a name not for a doctrine or a political movement but for a cultural and psychological condition of meaninglessness, aimlessness, despair and destruction. It was this more extensive notion of nihilism that became definitive in the last decade of the nineteenth century and throughout the twentieth century. Since its beginnings, then, the term has been connected to atheism, the death of God, the collapse of absolute values, the assertion of human freedom – and the collapse of European civilisation.

Notes

1. The *Historisches Wörterbuch der Philosophie* entry on 'Nihilismus' claims that Friedrich Schlegel and Novalis used the term as early as 1787. This is clearly an error, since at the time they were both only fifteen. This may be a typo that should read 1797. The entry has a number of such errors and should not be relied on without confirmation.
2. All translations from non-English language texts are the author's own.
3. For a different account of Jacobi, see George di Giovanni's account in Chapter 1 of this volume.

References

Arendt, Dieter (1970), *Nihilismus: Die Anfänge von Jacobi bis Nietzsche*, Cologne: Hegner.
Ascheim, Steven (1992), *The Nietzsche Legacy in Germany: 1890–1999*, Berkeley: University of California Press.
Bakunin, Mikhail [1871] (1895), *God and the State*, trans. Benjamin Tucker, New York: Benjamin R. Tucker.
Bakunin, Mikhail [1942] (1973), *Selected Writings*, ed. Steven Cox and Olive Stevens, trans. Arthur Lehning, New York: Grove.
Bourget, Paul (1885), *Essais de psychologie contemporaine*, 2 vols, Paris: Lemerre.
Büchner, Georg (1980), *Werke und Briefe*, Munich: Hanser.
Byron, George Gordon (2009), *Manfred*, at <http://www.english.upenn.edu/Projects/knarf/Byron/manfred3.html> (accessed 9 March 2009).
Chernyshevsky, Nikolai [1863] (1986), *What Is to Be Done?*, trans. N. Dole and S. Skidelsky, Ann Arbor: Ardis.
Cramer, Johann Andreas (1775–86), completion of Jacob Benignus Bossuet, *Einleitung in die Geschichte der Welt und Religion*, Johann Conrad Altdorfer.
Cunningham, Conor (2002), *Genealogy of Nihilism*, London: Routledge.
Dostoevsky, Fyodor (1929), *The Brothers Karamazov*, trans. Constance Garnett, New York: Knopf.
Gillespie, Michael Allen (1995), *Nihilism before Nietzsche*, Chicago: University of Chicago Press.
Goethe, Johann Wolfgang (1950–60), *Werke*, 14 vols, Hamburg: Wenger.

Hegel, Georg Friedrich Wilhelm (1970), *Werke in zwanzig Bänden*, eds Eva Moldenhauer and Karl Marcus Michel, Frankfurt: Suhrkamp.

Herzen, Alexander [1868] (1973), *My Past and Thoughts: The Memoirs of Alexander Herzen*, trans. Constance Garnett, New York: Knopf.

Hildebrand, Bruno (1984), 'Literarische Aspekte des Nihilismus', *Nietzsche-Studien*, 13: 80–100.

Jacobi, Friedrich Heinrich (1959), *Werke*, 6 vols, Munich: Hanser.

Janz, Curt Paul (1978), *Nietzsche: Biographie*, 3 vols, Munich: Hanser.

Kravchinskii, Sergei M. (1883), *Underground Russia: Revolutionary Profiles and Sketches from Life*, New York: Scribner's Sons.

Kuhn, Elisabeth (1984), 'Nietzsches Quelle des Nihilismus-Begriffs', *Nietzsche-Studien*, 13: 253–78.

Kuhn, Elisabeth (1992), *Friedrich Nietzsches Philosophie des europäischen Nihilismus*, Berlin: de Gruyter.

Manschreck, Clyde (1976), 'Nihilism in the twentieth century: A view from here', *Church History*, 45 (1): 85–96.

Mendel, Arthur (1981), *Michael Bakunin: Roots of Apocalypse*, Santa Barbara, CA: Praeger.

Mercier, Louis-Sébastien (1801), *Néologie: ou Vocabulaire des mots nouveaux. À renouveler, ou pris dans des acceptions nouvelles*, 2 vols, Paris: Moussard.

Mérimée, Prosper (1927–33), *Oeuvres complètes*, ed. P. Trahard and H. Champion, 12 vols, Paris: Champion.

Moser, Charles (1964), *Antinihilism in the Russian Novel of the 1860s*, The Hague: Mouton.

Nietzsche, Friedrich (1967–), *Werke: Kritische Gesamtausgabe*, ed. Giorgio Colli and Mazzino Montinari, 9 divisions, 40 vols, Berlin: De Gruyter.

Nishitani, Keiji (1990), *The Self-Overcoming of Nihilism*, trans. Graham Parkes, Albany, NY: SUNY Press.

Pöggeler, Otto (1970), 'Hegel und die Anfänge der Nihilismus-Diskussion', *Man and World*, 3 (3): 163–99.

Prawdin, Michael (pseud. M. Charol) (1961), *The Unmentionable Nechaev: A Key to Bolshevism*, London: Allen & Unwin.

(Richter), Jean Paul (1959), *Werke*, 6 vols, Munich: Hanser.

(Richter), Jean Paul (1973), *Horn of Oberon: Jean Paul Richter's School of Aesthetics*, trans. M. Hale, Detroit: Wayne State University Press.

Rosen, Stanley (1969), *Nihilism: A Philosophical Essay*, New Haven: Yale University Press.

Schlegel, Friedrich [1823] (1958–), *Indische Untersuchungen*, in Friedrich Schlegel, *Kritische Friedrich Schlegel Ausgabe*, ed. Ernst Behler, Jean Jacques Anstett and Hans Eichner, 35 vols, Munich: Schöningh.

Stirner, Max [1844] (1907), *The Ego and His Own*, trans. Steven Byington, New York: Tucker.

Süss, Theobald (1951), 'Der Nihilismus bei F. H. Jacobi', *Theologische Literaturzeitung*, 76: 193–200.

Thielicke, Helmut (1961), *Nihilism: Its Origin and Nature – with a Christian Answer*, trans. John Doberstein, New York: Harper & Brothers.

Timm, Hermann (1971), 'Die Bedeutung der Spinozabrief Jacobis für die Entwicklung der idealistische Religionsphilosophie', in Kai Hammacher (ed.), *Friedrich Heinrich Jacobi: Philosoph und Literat der Goethezeit*, Frankfurt: Klostermann, pp. 35–81.

Trotsky, Leon [1924] (1957), *Literature and Revolution*, trans. R. Strunsky, New York: Russell & Russell.

Volski, N. K. (Nikolai Valentinov) (1969), *The Early Years of Lenin*, trans. Rolf Theen, Ann Arbor: University of Michigan Press.

Weiller, Kajetan von (1803), *Der Geist der allerneuesten Philosophie der Hh. Schelling, Hegel, und Kompagnie: Eine Uebersetzung aus der Schulsprache in die Sprache der Welt*, 2 vols, Munich: Lentner.

Woodcock, George (1962), *Anarchism: A History of Libertarian Ideas and Movements*, Cleveland: World.

Yarmolinsky, Avrahm (1956), *Road to Revolution: A Century of Russian Radicalism*, New York: Macmillan.

Zamir, Tzachi (2000), 'Upon one bank and shoal of time: Literature, nihilism and moral philosophy', *New Literary History* 31: 529–51.

16

Repetition and Recurrence: Putting Metaphysics in Motion

Clare Carlisle

1. Introduction

In *Difference and Repetition*, Gilles Deleuze writes that Kierkegaard and Nietzsche 'are among those who bring to philosophy new means of expression':

> They want to put metaphysics in motion, in action. They want to make it act and make it carry out immediate acts. It is not enough, therefore, for them to propose a new representation of movement; representation is already mediation. Rather, it is a question of producing within the work a movement capable of affecting the mind outside of all representation; it is a question of making movement itself a work . . . (Deleuze [1968] 1994: 8)

In identifying this common ground between Kierkegaard and Nietzsche, Deleuze focuses on their ideas of repetition and eternal recurrence and his remarks offer a point of departure for our discussion of these two themes. Neither repetition nor recurrence can be adequately expressed through concepts; both are movements that are 'produced' rather than represented within the writings of Kierkegaard and Nietzsche. For Deleuze, at least, this production responds to the consummation of idealism that is attained in Hegelian philosophy.

This is not to say that we should never speak of the 'concepts' or 'ideas' of repetition and recurrence and indeed it would be inconvenient to dispense with these designations altogether. But we must at the same time recognise that for both Kierkegaard and Nietzsche the content of their thought is inseparable from its communication: 'what' is inseparable from 'how'. Repetition, if it is possible, is something that *happens* within the individual – within the fictional individuals that populate Kierkegaard's texts, but also, the author hopes, within the individual reader of these texts. Repetition is therefore linked to Kierkegaard's themes of subjectivity, inwardness and lived truth. In Nietzsche's philosophy, the eternal recurrence or return of the same is not a proposition or a hypothesis but a doctrine, a teaching, a thought to be incorporated and it is linked essentially to the idea of transition.

Another key issue that unites the philosophies of Kierkegaard and Nietzsche is the importance of interpretation. In both cases, interpretation is not merely subsequent to and separate from the writer's presentation of certain claims but is rather essential to the work. This aspect of Kierkegaard's authorship is continuous with a religious tradition of scriptural exegesis, while in Nietzsche's thought the concept of interpretation, understood as a creative act, undermines belief in objective truths and meanings. Even in relation to the rest of

Kierkegaard's or Nietzsche's work, however, repetition and recurrence are especially enigmatic and as soon as we attempt to make sense of repetition and recurrence we find ourselves in an open domain of interpretation that may never yield certainty or satisfaction. We also find ourselves – particularly in Nietzsche's case – confronted with an extensive scholarly literature that includes many different ways of making sense of repetition and recurrence.

Repetition and eternal recurrence have so much and perhaps more in common with one another. In fact, the following interpretations of the themes will point to the conclusion that they both signify a concern for human freedom, in a way that attempts to challenge and even to break with the philosophical tradition from Plato to Hegel. Repetition and recurrence signal a rethinking of temporality and futurity that is decisive for twentieth-century and contemporary philosophy. However, none of this undermines the fact that they are distinct concepts and that they originate from very different philosophical perspectives. They do not represent a point of convergence for Kierkegaard and Nietzsche. This essay will attempt to clarify the differences between them, as well as situating both themes within the history of European thought.

2. Kierkegaard's Category of Repetition

Kierkegaard's first discussion of repetition (*Gentagelse*)[1] occurs in the final pages of his unpublished work *Johannes Climacus, or De omnibus dubitandum est* (Kierkegaard 1985b: 171–2). But the idea comes to occupy centre stage in *Repetition*, which was published under the pseudonym Constantin Constantius in October 1843, on the same day as *Fear and Trembling*. Both books had been written, in an astonishing burst of productivity, during Kierkegaard's second visit to Berlin in May 1843. At the end of that year the influential Danish Hegelian J. L. Heiberg published a review of *Repetition* which provoked Kierkegaard to write, in the name of his pseudonym and with characteristic sarcasm, a lengthy response that defended *Repetition* against Heiberg's misunderstandings – which were perhaps excusable, given the elusive nature of the text.[2] Kierkegaard decided not to publish his polemical 'Open Letter to Professor Heiberg', but it now stands as an indispensable supplement to *Repetition*, since it explains in greater detail points that are only hinted at in the book and clarifies the significance of repetition.[3]

Kierkegaard's next pseudonymous work, *The Concept of Anxiety*, contains a long footnote concerning repetition (Kierkegaard [1844] 1980a: 17–19), but in subsequent texts the term is hardly mentioned. This may seem surprising, given Constantin Constantius's claims that 'repetition is the new category that will be discovered' (Kierkegaard [1843] 1983: 148) and that 'the question of repetition . . . will play a very important role in modern philosophy' (131). However, if the question of repetition is the question of human freedom; if repetition signifies the movement of becoming that characterises existence and constitutes an existential, spiritual version of the Aristotelian concept of *kinesis* – then this remains essential to Kierkegaard's thinking throughout his authorship. Ideas expressed in the 1843 writings relating to *Repetition* anticipate the account of despair presented in *The Sickness Unto Death* of 1849, perhaps Kierkegaard's finest work and certainly a text in which philosophical, theological and psychological themes from earlier books are brought together in a penetrating analysis of the human condition. When in 1853 – two years before his death – Kierkegaard reflected on his 'productivity' as a whole, he remarked that 'repetition is the category about which it will revolve' (Kierkegaard 1983: 329).

Before we turn to *Repetition*, it will be helpful to consider certain passages from Kierkegaard's journals and papers that illuminate the indirect and enigmatic presentation of repetition in the published text. In his response to Heiberg, who was most interested in repetition in the natural world, Kierkegaard makes explicit what we might call the domain of his concept of repetition: this is 'the domain of the spirit', which cannot, as in Hegel's philosophy, be conflated with 'the world-historical process', but which rather denotes a distinct 'spiritual existence that belongs to individuals' (1983: 287). It is this domain – which is sometimes labelled simply 'inwardness' or 'the existing individual' – that Kierkegaard endeavours throughout his authorship to preserve and protect in the face of the totalising, all-encompassing force of the Hegelian system. What is at stake here is human freedom, 'all the tasks of freedom' (288) that constitute the substance of an individual's inner life. The words 'individual' and 'freedom', hardly mentioned in *Repetition* itself, and no doubt for this very reason, recur to excess in the letter to Heiberg:

> As soon as one considers individuals in their freedom . . . – then [the question arises of] what meaning repetition has in the domain of the spirit, for indeed, every individual, just in being an individual, is qualified as spirit and this spirit has a history . . . More particularly, the question concerns the relation of freedom to the phenomena of the spirit, in the context of which the individual lives, inasmuch as his history advances in continuity with his own past and with the little world surrounding him. Here the question becomes that of repetition within the boundaries of his life . . . The issue will arise at this point again and again, insofar as the same individual in his history makes a beginning many times, or the question will again be whether each individual is capable of it, or whether he is lost through his initial beginning, or whether what is lost through his initial beginning is not recoverable. Here the individual does not relate contemplatively to the repetition, for the phenomena in which it appears are phenomena of the spirit, but he relates to them in freedom. (288–9)

The question of 'whether there is repetition' is, Kierkegaard insists, 'the first issue of freedom'. This passage emphasises the link between freedom and the 'spiritual' being of the individual and a couple of Kierkegaard's journal entries discussing repetition accentuate its religious significance – which is certainly alluded to in *Repetition*, although not in an explicitly Christian context. In 1844 Kierkegaard wrote in his journal that '"Repetition" is and remains a religious category' (Kierkegaard 1967–78: 3: 3794). This suggests that *Repetition* is oriented towards Christianity; that it must be read, like all of Kierkegaard's texts, in the context of his concern to communicate to his contemporaries – whose spiritual authenticity he doubted and whose complacency he sought to unsettle – the nature of the task of becoming a Christian.

Although it is not easy to ascertain exactly what Kierkegaard means by repetition, we can go some way towards clarifying the concept – having acknowledged that it is not merely a concept – by considering how it is connected to other philosophical ideas. In *Repetition* the pseudonym Constantin Constantius contrasts his 'new category' to Platonic recollection, compares it to Aristotle's concept of *kinesis* and opposes it to Hegelian mediation. We shall now examine each of these connections in turn.

The opening paragraph of *Repetition* states that

> the question of repetition – whether or not it is possible, what importance it has – . . . will play a very important role in modern philosophy, for *repetition* is a crucial expression for what 'recollection' was for the Greeks. Just as they taught that all knowing is a recollecting, modern philosophy will teach that all life is a repetition. (1983: 131)

For Plato, recollection is a process through which the individual attains truth: with the help of a teacher and prompted by her own experience of the world, she recollects the eternal Ideas which her immortal soul has already encountered before her birth. In the passage just cited, Constantin Constantius links the contrast between recollection and repetition to the contrast between knowledge and life: if recollection seeks the truth as knowledge, repetition concerns a different kind of truth that belongs to life – a truth that is lived. This subjective, existential truth will not take the form of idea or a concept, for it signifies a way of living sincerely, authentically, faithfully; it is a question of *being true* to oneself, to another person or to God.

Constantin's remark that 'repetition and recollection are the same movement, except in opposite directions' gives more precise content to this conception of truth. Both recollection and repetition are movements between two modes of being: between the ideal and the actual. In the case of Platonic recollection (as interpreted by Kierkegaard), truth is reached by a movement from the individual's particular, situated, temporal existence to a realm of eternal, unchanging Ideas, or Forms, which are the only real objects of knowledge. In his doctoral dissertation *On the Concept of Irony* of 1841, Kierkegaard writes that 'Socrates ferried the individual from reality over to ideality' (1989: 255) and here 'reality' must signify temporal existence. The movement of repetition, on the other hand, is a transition in the opposite direction, from ideality to temporal existence – but in this case ideality signifies not a realm of eternal Forms, but the sphere of possibility.[4] For Kierkegaard, possibilities are not abstract ideas to be accessed through reason but vivid and dynamic projections of the self imbued with anxiety, hope, desire, expectancy and so on. They are what one might become: at each moment the future takes the form of various possibilities and as that future becomes the present particular possibilities are chosen, brought into being, actualised.

At the end of *Johannes Climacus, or De omnibus dubitandum est*, Kierkegaard writes that 'when ideality and reality touch each other, then repetition occurs' (Kierkegaard 1985b: 171) and a key theme of this text is an existential form of truth conceived in terms of fidelity to certain ideals: as one commentator puts it, Johannes Climacus

> is 'faithful' in the sense that his conduct displays his fidelity to a philosophical ideal of integrity or inner harmony – a harmony of thought and existence, or, in Kierkegaardian terms, of 'ideality' and 'actuality,' that is apparently no longer to be found among philosophers. (Howland 2006: 14)

The discussion of repetition in *Johannes Climacus* is too brief and too obscure for us to establish whether Kierkegaard had at this stage developed the temporal, dynamic understanding of the concept that is expressed in *Repetition*, but the thought that repetition constitutes a new form of truth can already be detected in the earlier text.

> If speculative philosophy is 'untrue' it is . . . because its practitioners act 'falsely' in that their deeds do not accord with their words. Conversely, it would seem that a philosophy is true only if one is true to *it*. To be a true philosopher is not merely to espouse philosophical doctrines, but to live a philosophical life. (Howland 2006: 15)

In *Repetition*, however, the concern is not only with the truth of a philosophy or a philosopher, but also, more broadly, with the subjective, 'lived' truth of any individual.

The invocation of repetition as a 'new category', a new form of truth to take the place of the idealising movement of recollection, undertakes a radical ontological reorientation.

According to the Platonic view, recollection moves from the sphere of becoming to the sphere of being, which is the locus of reality and truth. The movement of repetition, however, takes place within becoming; it is the movement *of* becoming – of becoming a self – and the being of what becomes, the truth of what becomes, is nothing other than this movement. For Kierkegaard, this being and this truth are essentially relational: in relating to herself, to another person or to God, the individual *is* this dynamic relation – but only insofar as the relation is actualised again and again, repeatedly brought into being.

This philosophical emphasis on becoming is linked to a theological understanding of the human condition as characterised by sin. Kierkegaard understands sin ontologically, as non-being and as untruth: as a failure to actualise the relation to God, a failure to *be true to* God, which is also the failure to become oneself insofar as the self is so fully dependent on God that it *is* its relation to God. This Lutheran anthropology is expressed most clearly in *The Sickness Unto Death*, where Kierkegaard emphasises that the self is continually 'in a process of becoming' ([1849] 1980b: 30). Thus, although in essence – or, as he puts it, 'kata dunamin' – the self *is* 'a relation which relates itself to itself and in relating itself to itself relates itself to another [that is, to God]' (13), from an existential point of view it 'has the task of becoming itself' (35), the task of actualising its constitutive relations.

According to Constantin Constantius, 'the Greek view of the concept of *kinesis* corresponds to the modern category "transition" and should be given close attention' (1983: 149).[5] Repetition is like *kinesis* – defined by Aristotle in the *Physics* as the transition from potentiality (*dunamis*) to actuality (*energeia*) – insofar as it involves the actualisation of a possibility, the bringing into existence of an idea.[6] In borrowing and adapting the ancient concept of *kinesis*, Kierkegaard transfers it from physics and metaphysics to the existential sphere, where, as repetition, it becomes central to his account of human freedom: when a person makes a choice, she actualises the chosen possibility at the expense of various alternative possibilities. (We can do no more than note here that Kierkegaard's interpretation of *kinesis* involves a highly questionable slide between the concepts of potentiality and possibility.) In *The Concept of Anxiety* the pseudonym Vigilius Haufniensis suggests that 'when Aristotle says that the transition from possibility to actuality is a κίνησις, this is not to be understood logically but with reference to historical freedom' (Kierkegaard [1844] 1980a: 82).

Constantin's claim that Leibniz is the only modern philosopher who had 'an intimation' of the significance of repetition supports this interpretation. In the early 1840s Kierkegaard read and took notes on Leibniz's works, especially the *Theodicy*, and was struck by the idea that God chose from all the possible worlds and in this choice created, or actualised, the best one. In 1843 Kierkegaard wrote in his journal that 'when I am going to act, my action has existed in my consciousness in conception and thought' (1967–78: 3: 3793), which suggests – together with the further discussion of possibility and actuality in the *Philosophical Fragments* of 1844 – that Kierkegaard's understanding of human agency draws on Leibniz's account of divine creation.

In *Repetition*, as in many of his other texts, Kierkegaard presents an indirect but polemical critique of the Hegelian philosophy and theology that was being promoted in Copenhagen by prominent intellectuals such as Heiberg and H. L. Martensen.[7] Constantin Constantius opposes repetition to the Hegelian movement of mediation – and it is in this opposition that the question of human freedom is at stake. The pseudonym writes that 'there is no explanation in our age as to how mediation takes place' (1983: 148) and emphasises the significance of *kinesis* 'in this connection'. This point is clarified in the letter to Heiberg, where freedom is understood in terms of 'movement' and 'transcendence':

Movement is a concept that logic simply cannot support. Mediation, therefore, must be understood in relation to immanence. Thus understood, mediation may not again be used at all in the sphere of freedom, where the subsequent always emerges – by virtue not of an immanence but of a transcendence . . . In the sphere of freedom, the word 'mediation' has again done damage, because, coming from logic, it helped to make the transcendence of movement illusory. In order to prevent this error or this dubious compromise between the logical and freedom, I have thought that 'repetition' could be used in the sphere of freedom. (1983: 308)

Here Constantin Constantius echoes an earlier Kierkegaardian pseudonym, *Either/Or*'s Judge William, who insists that the 'sphere of thought' and the 'sphere of freedom' – the sphere of logic and the sphere of existence – must be clearly distinguished in order to avoid confusion. To the sphere of thought belong mediation, reflection and logical necessity; this is the sphere of immanent movement, of the dialectic. The sphere of freedom is the sphere of power, of becoming, of transcendent movement. But the distinction between these two spheres is not a new version of Platonic or Kantian dualism: although Kierkegaard insists that they are separated by a rift, by a qualitative difference, he also describes a leap from one to the other, a 'qualitative transition' that cannot be mediated – that thus leaves the sphere of thought and *in doing so* institutes the sphere of freedom. On the one hand, then, there is a gap between the two spheres; on the other hand, the leap across this gap is itself an expression of the sphere of freedom and at the same time the difference between the two spheres. Returning to Constantin's response to Heiberg, we find that repetition is to be understood in terms of freedom and of the transition that constitutes it:

When movement is allowed in relation to repetition in the sphere of freedom, then the development becomes different from the logical development in that the *transition becomes*. In logic, transition is movement's silence, whereas in the sphere of freedom it becomes. Thus, in logic, when possibility, by means of the immanence of thought, has determined itself as actuality, one only disturbs the silent self-inclosure of the logical process by talking about movement and transition. In the sphere of freedom, however, possibility remains and actuality emerges as a transcendence. Therefore, when Aristotle long ago said that the transition from possibility to actuality is a *kinesis*, he was not speaking of logical possibility and actuality but of freedom's, and therefore he rightly posits movement. In all of Schelling's philosophy, movement likewise plays a major role, not only in the philosophy of nature, but also in the philosophy of spirit, in his whole conception of freedom. What gives him the greatest trouble is precisely this, to include movement. (1983: 309–10)

From an historical point of view, it is quite natural that Kierkegaard appeals to Aristotle and to Schelling in his critique of Hegelian thought. During the 1830s, debates between the Danish Hegelians and their opponents, notably Bishop Mynster, often focused on whether or not the principles of Aristotelian logic really were overcome by Hegel's dialectical logic. Mynster, for example, invoked Aristotle's principle of non-contradiction and law of the excluded middle in his attack on Martensen's attempt to relativise the differences between opposing theological positions – and both of these theologians used the phrase 'either/or' to denote the Aristotelian laws of logic.[8] *Either/Or* of 1843 represents Kierkegaard's contribution to this debate, for here 'either/or' becomes a kind of existential version of the law of the excluded middle, signifying that each individual is faced with a choice between mutually exclusive alternatives (for example, to marry or not to marry) – just as repetition would become an existential version of Aristotle's *kinesis*. In the case of Schelling, whose lectures Kierkegaard attended during his first visit to Berlin in 1841–2, it seems that the influence of the German philosopher helped to focus Kierkegaard's attention on the issue of movement and to make this central to his polemic against Hegelian thought.[9]

Repetition signifies freedom as the actualisation of a possibility. In this movement there is at once repetition and newness, insofar as something that *is* in one way *is* again in another way: a possibility, an essence, becomes an actuality, an existence. But there is another level of repetition: the repetition of repetition, of the *kinesis*, of the moment of freedom. A possibility must be actualised repeatedly if it is to persist in existence, for whatever is actualised is immediately past, immediately lost. This second repetition – or rather, repetition raised to the second power – is the restoration of freedom, of the self, and it is only through this renewal that there can be self-constancy through time. Kierkegaard finds in this repetition the possibility of subjective truth: the possibility of being true or faithful to oneself, to another person, to God. It is as if an individual, once she makes a decision, loses herself – loses her freedom – in the result, unless the moment of freedom recurs and the choice is taken again. This point is clarified in response to Heiberg:

> If it were the case that freedom in the individuality related to the surrounding world could become so immersed, so to speak, in the result that it cannot take itself back again (repeat itself), then everything is lost. (1983: 302)

The double nature of repetition can be illustrated by means of an example from *Philosophical Fragments*, where the pseudonym Johannes Climacus suggests that belief involves the actualisation of a possibility – indeed, that 'belief and coming into existence correspond to each other' (Kierkegaard [1844] 1985a: 86–7). Here he is discussing belief in the Incarnation and is arguing that the past is no more necessary than the future:

> The possibility from which emerged the possible that became the actual always accompanies that which came into existence and remains with the past, even though centuries lie between. As soon as one who comes later repeats that it has come into existence (which he does by believing it), he repeats its possibility. (Kierkegaard 1985a: 86–7)

Kierkegaard's purpose here is to argue that the individual's relationship to Christian doctrine is not a matter of knowledge, belonging to the 'sphere of thought', but a task within the 'sphere of freedom'. On this view, believing is an instance of repetition – but if an individual is to hold fast to her belief, to attain constancy as a believer, then this repetition must itself be repeated. How else could freedom endure, other than by repeating itself?

The philosophical contribution of *Repetition* consists not in a claim or a thesis, but in a question: 'is repetition possible?' Any assertions about repetition have to be understood in relation to this question, because the answer to it depends on how the question is asked and thus on who asks it. The book's three main characters – Constantin Constantius; a nameless young poet going through an engagement crisis; and the biblical character of Job, whose story the fiancé reads in his despair – personify different existential perspectives and exhibit different relationships to repetition. While Constantin exemplifies the perspective of a theorist, a disinterested observer, the young poet undergoes an existential transition when he finds himself in an ethical situation, facing a choice that concerns not only his own happiness but also that of his fiancée. Job, meanwhile, also finds himself in a crisis, but his situation unfolds before God and in relation to God. He loses his family, his home, his possessions; he questions God; he expresses his faith: 'the Lord gave, the Lord taketh away; blessed be the name of the Lord!' According to the existential schema presented more explicitly in some of Kierkegaard's other pseudonymous texts, Constantin belongs to the aesthetic sphere, the fiancé to the ethical sphere and Job to the religious sphere.

Kierkegaard's response to Heiberg clarifies some of the peculiar literary aspects of *Repetition*, for he here has his pseudonym explain his role within the text. As a reader familiar with Kierkegaard's pseudonymous works might guess, Constantin Constantius presents a reflection on repetition from a limited and self-effacing perspective: this involves a misunderstanding that works, indirectly, to push repetition out of the theoretical sphere. Because Constantin's own relation to repetition is confined to this theoretical sphere, he fails to attain repetition and eventually abandons his investigation into its possibility: 'I in despair have relinquished my theory of repetition, because my position also lies within immanence' (1983: 317–18). He claims that his own discussion of repetition 'is always either a jest or only relatively true, adequately illustrated by the fact that I who said it despair of (its) possibility' (305) and suggests that his own efforts to realise repetition are just a 'parody' and a 'pun' on the true repetition. His aim in writing *Repetition* was

> to depict and make visible psychologically and aesthetically; to let the concept come into being in the individuality and the situation, working itself forward through all sorts of misunderstandings . . . I myself play the stoic in order to . . . suggest *in abstracto* what cannot be realised *in abstracto* . . . (302–3)

Constantin confesses to misleading the reader by treating 'the most interior problem of the possibility of repetition' in an external way, by seeking repetition outside himself 'when in fact it must be found within the individual' (304). Nevertheless, we may allow ourselves to take many of his remarks seriously – while acknowledging that his theoretical account does not exhaust the significance of repetition – because these remarks clearly cohere with aspects of Kierkegaard's thought presented in earlier and later texts.

Although the notion of repetition as the actualisation of a possibility provides an account of freedom that is articulated in relation to certain figures within the history of philosophy – Plato, Aristotle, Leibniz, Schelling, Hegel – for Kierkegaard the question of freedom unfolds within the context of a theological problem. Christian theology posits two absolute limitations of human freedom: sin, a condition that is not itself chosen but which rather conditions the will itself and which constitutes a form of bondage from which the sinner is unable to release herself; and God's power, on which all beings are completely dependent. These two limitations go together, of course: integral to sin is the failure to acknowledge one's dependence on God and yet the very condition of sin intensifies the individual's lack of freedom.[10]

As we have seen, Kierkegaard understands sin as loss of the self and defines the self as spirit, that is to say as freedom. He also conceives sin philosophically as non-being and untruth, while faith, as the opposite of sin, is the transition from non-being to being, from untruth to truth. Kierkegaard emphasises that the condition of the possibility of faith has to be given to the individual who lacks it. To put the point in more conventional theological terms, faith, which signifies release from sin, is possible only through grace. Grace and sin, gift and loss, are reciprocal movements – what Kierkegaard calls a 'double movement' – and human existence oscillates between the two. Human freedom must therefore be thought in this oscillation between the double limitation of grace and sin. Only when the self is lost can it be given again; only once given can it be lost again. The influence of Martin Luther on Kierkegaard's category of repetition should not be underestimated, for we can trace this religious anthropology back to the German reformer:

> Progress is nothing other than constantly beginning . . . For we who are justified are always in movement, always being justified, for so it comes about that all righteousness in the present instant is sin with respect to what will be added at the next instant. (Luther 1883: 4: 350, 364)[11]

This is the Christian significance of repetition, which in Kierkegaard's 1843 texts is indicated only indirectly, by the stories of the poet and of figures from the Hebrew bible. When he falls in love the young fiancé of *Repetition* discovers his wish to be a poet, but this self he discovers is already lost because he cannot devote himself both to marriage and to his poetic vocation and he feels bound by the ethical commitment; he seeks 'to make [himself] into a suitable husband, to take away everything that is incommensurable in order to become commensurable' (1983: 214). His self and his freedom are finally and unexpectedly returned to him when his fiancée marries someone else. 'I am myself again', he writes to Constantin, 'Is there not, then, a repetition? Did I not get everything double? Did I not get myself again and precisely in such a way that I might have a double sense of its meaning?' (220–1). He also writes of 'the movement . . . in one's interior being, there where every moment one is staking one's life, each moment losing it and finding it again' (221). Job gives expression to the double movement of gift and loss by his words, 'The Lord gave and the Lord took away: blessed be the name of the Lord'.

Kierkegaard's interpretation of the story of Abraham and Isaac in *Fear and Trembling* also indicates a religious repetition. The birth of Isaac to Sarah, who was ageing and barren, was a gift from God; this gift seems to be taken back when God commands Abraham to sacrifice his son; the last-minute reprieve means that Abraham, 'contrary to expectation, got a son a second time' (1983: 9). In this instance, God gives, takes away and gives again. But there is also a corresponding subjective movement, which Kierkegaard's pseudonym Johannes de silentio describes as the 'double movement' of resignation and faith: in resignation Abraham gives up both his claim on Isaac and his claim to happiness and justice in return for obedience to God, and thus reconciles himself to God at the expense of his worldly life; in faith he opens himself to God's love, receiving *this* life itself as a blessing, a gift.

Kierkegaard emphasises the paradoxical quality of the movement of faith – for how can Abraham continue to experience his existence as a gift from God, as an expression of divine love, when God has commanded him to kill his beloved son?

> It takes a purely human courage to renounce the whole temporal realm in order to gain eternity . . . but it takes a paradoxical and humble courage to grasp the whole temporal realm now by virtue of the absurd and this is the courage of faith. By faith Abraham did not renounce Isaac, but by faith Abraham received Isaac. (1983: 49)

The double movement of resignation and faith is symbolised by Abraham's journey up to Mount Moriah, where the sacrifice is to take place, and then home again, with Isaac restored to him. But in fact the double movement is performed in every step in both directions, for Abraham walks *to* Mount Moriah in faith. Abraham exemplifies the way in which the double movement of religious faith must be repeated at every moment. Through repetition Abraham 'remained true to his love' (120) and it is this that the pseudonym Johannes de silentio marvels at and professes himself unable to understand.

In *Fear and Trembling* the question of whether repetition is possible receives a complicated answer, for according to Kierkegaard Abraham's faith, his remaining 'true to his love', is in a sense impossible and cannot be understood – and yet Abraham achieves the impossible. The point seems to be – and this highlights the Christian significance of the text – that humanly speaking faith is impossible. This takes us back to the transcendent aspect of repetition, according to which it is God's grace that provides the condition for faith and which needs to be given repeatedly if faith is to be sustained.

3. Nietzsche's Thought of Eternal Recurrence

Kierkegaard draws on Aristotle's concept of *kinesis* to articulate a new conception of truth in opposition to the idealism that characterises the philosophical tradition from Plato to Hegel. Likewise, Nietzsche takes from Greek thought the doctrine of eternal recurrence (*ewige Wiederkunft*) or eternal return (*ewige Wiederkehr*)[12] – which was discussed by the Stoics and perhaps also by Heraclitus – and resituates it in a specifically modern context: the confrontation with European nihilism. However, Nietzsche's challenge to the philosophical tradition is more radical than Kierkegaard's, whose Christian interpretation of human existence as grounded in the eternal being of God is still Platonic, despite his focus on the existential, subjective aspect of Christianity and thus on the movements of becoming that constitute the medium of the religious life. The idea that the world and everything within it recurs eternally presents an image of eternity very different from both the Platonic doctrine of unchanging Ideas and the Christian doctrine of an eternal life to come following bodily death. To these two forms of eternity – equally essential to Western thought and alike in transcending the transient world of human life – Nietzsche opposes an eternity *of* this world, precisely in its fleeting character: not as eternally enduring but as arising and passing away and arising again, again to pass away and to return and so on, endlessly. The doctrine of eternal recurrence provides, like Platonic metaphysics or Christian theology, a kind of context or a bigger picture within which the world and life within it can appear as meaningful – for Nietzsche seems to suggest that mere immersion in the matters of this life can never produce meaning – but rather than invoking a transcendent perspective, the eternal return never steps outside the world and recognises nothing beyond it. Indeed, the absolute inescapability of this world is one of the terrifying aspects of the thought.

In *Philosophy in the Tragic Age of the Greeks*, written in 1873 and based on his lectures at Basel University in the early 1870s, Nietzsche emphasises the importance of Heraclitus' belief 'in a periodically repeated end of the world and in an ever renewed rise of another world out of the all-destroying cosmic fire' (Nietzsche 1962: 60, §6).[13] He also emphasises the 'innocence' of this process: 'In this world only play, play as artists and children engage in it, exhibits coming-to-be and passing away, structuring and destroying, without any moral additive, in forever equal innocence' (62, §7). Nietzsche suggests that Heraclitus' doctrine of everlasting becoming and the impermanence of everything is 'a terrible, paralyzing thought' and that it 'takes astonishing strength to transform this reaction into its opposite, into sublimity and the feeling of blessed astonishment. Heraclitus achieved this'. On this point Nietzsche compares Heraclitus to Schopenhauer, citing several passages from

The World as Will and Representation and, while noting similarities between the two philosophers, he argues that 'the basic tone' of their reflections is very different: in contrast to Heraclitan affirmation, Schopenhauer regards continual becoming, in the form of 'will to life', as a 'menacing and gloomy drive, a thoroughly frightful and by no means blessed phenomenon' (56, §5). In a passage from *The World as Will and Representation* which Nietzsche does not mention, but with which he was no doubt familiar, Schopenhauer envisages a kind of person

> whose love of life was so great that he willingly and gladly accepted all the hardships to which it is exposed for the sake of its pleasures . . . (he) could calmly and deliberately desire that his life, as he had hitherto known it, should endure forever or repeat itself ever anew. (Schopenhauer [1818/1844] 1966: 1: 283–4)

However, in a later section he writes that, in view of the suffering inherent in existence, this person 'will much prefer absolute annihilation' (324).

In August 1881 the thought of the eternal return of the same apparently came to Nietzsche with renewed force, indeed as a sort of revelation, while he was out walking in Sils-Maria. Eighteen months later – after what he subsequently described as an elephantine 'pregnancy' – he published *Thus Spoke Zarathustra*, in 1883–5, a work whose 'fundamental conception' is 'the idea of the eternal recurrence, this highest formula of affirmation that is at all attainable' (Nietzsche 1967b: 295). This idea had in fact already been discussed in *The Gay Science* of 1882 and it appears again in Nietzsche's later works *Beyond Good and Evil* ([1886] 1966: 68, §56) and *Twilight of the Idols* ([1888] 1968b: 108–11, §§4 and 5). It also appears in the collection of notes from the 1880s that were published posthumously under the title *The Will to Power*. In his influential lecture courses on Nietzsche, delivered in Freiberg between 1936 and 1940, Martin Heidegger identifies the doctrine of eternal return – together with the will to power, since the two are for Heidegger inseparable – as Nietzsche's most essential thought.

The fact that in *Ecce Homo* (written in 1888, but first published posthumously in 1908) Nietzsche very definitely identifies the time of 'conception' of the eternal return as August 1881 suggests that from this point onwards the thought had a significance that exceeds the discussion of Heraclitus' and Schopenhauer's versions of recurrence in *Philosophy in the Tragic Age of the Greeks*. There was something more in the 'revelation' of the thought in the Swiss mountains than the ideas of affirmation and innocence and fear at the prospect of endless recurrence. Nietzsche's notebook from the autumn and winter of 1881 contains several passages on the eternal recurrence (in this notebook Nietzsche always uses the term *Wiederkunft*, recurrence, rather than *Wiederkehr*, return) and these indicate the various aspects of the new significance of the thought. Subsequent discussions through the rest of the 1880s seem merely to echo and at times to elucidate the ideas in this notebook, where Nietzsche describes eternal recurrence as 'the new *heavy weight*'; 'the weightiest knowledge, one which prompts the terrible reconsideration of all forms of life'; 'the *greatest* weight'; the 'most powerful thought' that 'has a *transforming* effect'. The fullest and clearest exposition of the doctrine is provided in the following passage:

> The world of forces does not suffer diminution: otherwise in infinite time it would have grown weak and perished. The world of forces suffers no cessation: otherwise this would have been reached and the clock of existence would have stopped. So the world of forces never reaches equilibrium; it never has a moment of rest; its force and its movement are

equally great for all time. Whatever state this world *can* attain, it must have attained it and not once but countless times. Take this moment: it has already been once and many times and it will return as it is with all its forces distributed as now: and so it stands with the moment that gave birth to it and with the moment that is its child. Man! Your whole life will be turned over like an hourglass time and again and time and again it will run out – one vast minute of time in between, until all the conditions that produced you, in the world's circular course, come together again. Then you will find again every pain and every pleasure and every friend and enemy and every hope and every error and every leaf of grass and every shade of sunlight, the whole nexus of all things . . . And in every ring of human existence altogether there is always an hour when – first for one, then for many, then for all – the most powerful thought surfaces, the thought of the eternal recurrence of all things: each time it is for humanity the hour of *midday*. (Ansell Pearson and Large 2006: 240)

Here Nietzsche presents eternal recurrence as a sort of scientific hypothesis, based on the idea of a 'world of forces', and then addresses directly to 'Man!' this thought, which will, as we have seen, have a transforming effect. This idea of transformation dominates another entry in the notebook:

'But if everything is necessary, how can I determine my actions?' This thought and belief are a heavy weight pressing down on you alongside every other weight and more than them. You say that food, location, air, company transform and condition you? Well, your opinions do so even more, since it is they that determine your choice of food, location, air, company. If you incorporate the thought of thoughts within yourself, it will transform you. The question in everything that you want to do: 'is it the case that I want to do it countless times?' is the *greatest* weight.

In the very first entry concerning the eternal return, which is dated August 1881 and takes the form of an 'outline', apparently for a book entitled 'The Recurrence of the Same', Nietzsche follows the introduction of the thought with the question, 'What shall we do with the *rest* of our lives – we who have spent the majority of our lives in the most profound ignorance?' (Ansell Pearson and Large 2006: 238). Following the thought of eternal recurrence, 'the question is whether *we* still want to live: and how!' (239)

These questions about how to live, which imply freedom, seem to be in conflict with the deterministic thesis that this life as a whole has already been lived thus innumerable times. Nietzsche's presentation of the eternal return is also marked by a contrast between the 'infinite importance' (Ansell-Pearson and Large 2006: 238) of our actions and our utter insignificance: 'The eternal hourglass of existence is turned upside down again and again and you with it, speck of dust!' (Nietzsche [1882] 1974: 273–4, §341). Another contrast is between the immense weight of a 'new burden' and a new-found lightness, symbolised by Zarathustra's liberation from the 'Spirit of Gravity' (Nietzsche [1883–5] 1961: 178–80, §2).[14]

These contradictions have prompted several commentators to prioritise one aspect of the thought – either its 'cosmological' face or its 'ethical' face – over the other and even in some cases to dismiss altogether the aspect of the thought deemed less acceptable. On this view, we must choose whether to regard the doctrine of eternal recurrence as *either* a theory about the nature of reality *or* a sort of thought-experiment that tests one's capacity to say yes to life.[15] This is problematic, however, since both aspects are undeniably present in notes written within quite a short period of time, when Nietzsche was first struck by the significance of eternal recurrence. In more than one of these notes Nietzsche deliberately accentuates its contradictory implications. He himself raises the question, 'But if everything is necessary, how can I determine my actions?' and in another passage he writes that 'My doctrine says: the task is to live your life in *such* a way that you have to *want* to live it again – you will *in any case!*' (241). This suggests that the contradiction between freedom and necessity is itself an important element of the doctrine of eternal return. Moreover, we should bear in mind that a 'doctrine' is not a set of propositions referring to objective facts but a way of teaching something that eludes our grasp. This applies to the doctrine of eternal return just as it applies to religious doctrines.

How the ethical and the cosmological or scientific faces of the eternal return belong together in their contradiction can be grasped in a preliminary way only in light of the historical character of Nietzsche's thinking and in light of his critique of the notion of bare, objective facts that precede interpretations. For Nietzsche, science itself is an interpretation of being and a way of looking at the world which has developed through history, which rests on faith in certain metaphysical ideas and which derives its force from a 'will to truth' rooted in the moral imperative 'I will not deceive' (Nietzsche 1974: 280–3, §344).[16] He argues that science is nihilistic – that is to say, it devalues this world – insofar as it denies perspective, the condition of all life. The scientist '*thereby affirms another world* than that of life, nature and history; and insofar as he affirms this other world, does this not mean that he has to deny its antithesis, this world, *our* world?' Science 'rests on a certain impoverishment of life' ([1887] 1967a: 154, III.25). In notes from 1887 Nietzsche writes that 'mechanical necessity is not a fact but an interpretation' (1968a: 297–300, §552).

If we take the risk of supposing that he is consistent on this point, then it appears unlikely that he would propose an eternally-valid scientific theory concerning the objective nature of the universe; rather, the very possibility of science would be a phenomenon within the world which, according to the doctrine, recurs eternally. And just as he attacks science, Nietzsche challenges the 'error' or 'superstition' of free will (Nietzsche 1974: 279–80, §345; see also 1966: 25–7, §19; 1968b: 53–4, §§7–8) and related metaphysical 'fictions' such as that of an agent distinct from his acts, a doer prior to his deeds. For Nietzsche, belief in free will is as nihilistic as belief in science. The contradiction between freedom and necessity is a specific historical event that finds expression in Platonic idealism, in Christian theology and in Kantian thought, which makes explicit the antinomy between the mechanistic world of knowledge, conceived scientifically in terms of causality, and the sphere of free action, of disembodied willing. (Today we might point to the contradiction inherent in the popular secularism that on the one hand teaches biological determinism and on the other insists on 'freedom of expression' and 'freedom of choice'.)

Of course, Nietzsche's doctrine of eternal return of the same is also an historical phenomenon, an interpretation of being that emerges from the nihilistic contradiction of European thought, makes it manifest and calls on us to *think it through*. According to Heidegger,

[T]he thinking of the thought of eternal recurrence, as a questioning that perpetually calls for decision, is the fulfilment of nihilism. Such thinking brings to an end the veiling and painting over of this event, in such a way that it becomes at the same time the transition to the new determination of the greatest burden. The doctrine of eternal return is therefore the 'critical point', the watershed of an epoch become weightless and searching for a new centre of gravity. It is the crisis proper. (Heidegger 1979–87: 2: 159)

Thinking the thought of eternal recurrence will be transformative insofar as it demands a new understanding of both freedom and necessity that challenges the idealism of western metaphysics. The first of Nietzsche's 1881 notes on the doctrine emphasises the importance of 'incorporation', which denotes precisely a non-idealistic form of thought, according to which the mind is a 'little intelligence', a mere part of the body, which is a 'great intelligence' (Nietzsche 1961: 61–3). One possibility that emerges from the thinking through, or incorporation, of the eternal return is *amor fati*, which unites the necessity of fatalism with the freedom of love.

The contradiction between the so-called ethical and cosmological aspects of eternal recurrence is at once a contradiction between freedom and necessity and between the 'what' and the 'how' of the thought – that is to say, the content of the thought and the way in which it is thought. As Heidegger argues, both of these contradictions are integral to the eternal return:

> In thinking the most burdensome thought *what* is thought cannot be detached from the *way in which* it is thought. The *what* is itself defined by the *how* and, reciprocally, the *how* by the *what*. . . The distinction between a 'theoretical' doctrinal content of the thought and its 'practical' effects is impossible from the very start. (Heidegger 1979–87: 2: 119–20)[17]

He also states that

> [T]he question of freedom, and hence of necessity too and of the relation between these two, is posed anew by the teaching of the eternal return of the same. For that reason we go astray when we reverse matters and try to cram the doctrine of return into some long-ossified schema of the question of freedom. (2: 138)

Heidegger, for whom Nietzsche is not, as the latter claims, the first anti-metaphysician, but rather 'the *last metaphysician* of the West' (3: 8) who failed to 'recognise the truth of the thought of return in terms of the history of metaphysics' (3: 164), adds that 'Nietzsche never pursued these interconnections' between freedom and necessity.

However, a recent interpretation develops Heidegger's analysis but contends that Nietzsche recognised that the eternal return bears within itself the contradiction between freedom and necessity:

> That is why Nietzsche says that this thought brings together 'the two most extreme ways of thinking – the mechanistic and the platonic' (see *The Will to Power*, §1061) . . . Nietzsche's task was precisely to bring out the essence of the world we live in, in order to demonstrate that it is, inescapably, nihilistic . . . We are halfway-houses between heaven and earth and, having arrived at the end of the Platonic age, these two sides of our being have come unstuck. One interpretation sees the world as pure necessity; the other tries to grasp our freedom. The task then is to bring these together and this task has already been approached in that it is here the same thought, the same teaching, which gives expression to both freedom and necessity. (Haase 2008: 129, 138, 144)

This 'task' is linked to another aspect of the doctrine that is indicated in one of the 1881 notes: 'Only those who consider their existence capable of eternal repetition will *remain*: with such ones, though, a state is possible which no utopian has yet reached!' (Ansell Pearson and Large 2006: 241). This is echoed in notes from 1884, where Nietzsche describes eternal recurrence as 'the great cultivating idea' (1968a: 544, §§1053, 1056). This is because it functions to discriminate between 'the weak' and 'the strong': between those who suffer nihilism passively and reactively and those who actively and affirmatively grasp the nature of the illness and thus make possible a convalescence. The weak will recoil at the doctrine, while the active are able to think it through and to be transformed in the process; 'this is how the thought of the *Eternal Return of the Same* is supposed to become a historical crisis for humankind' (Haase 2008: 144). It is important to add to this interpretation that until we ourselves have fully incorporated the teaching of eternal recurrence we do not know what such a transformation – sometimes described by Nietzsche as a transition to the *Übermensch* – would be like, or even how it could occur.

The 1881 notes also bring out the way in which the doctrine of eternal return emphasises this life rather than invoking a transcendent realm in relation to which the world could be given meaning. 'Let us impress the image of eternity on *our* life!', writes Nietzsche; 'This thought contains more than all the religions that have taught us to despise this life as something fleeting and to look towards an indeterminate *other* life' (Ansell Pearson and Large 2006: 240). The idea of eternal recurrence provides Nietzsche with a way to explore the meaning of the world and of life – understood historically – from the inside. The doctrine has an extraordinary quality of outsidelessness: the whole of nature and history, everything we can experience, know and imagine is within the circle of becoming and yet the thought of eternal return itself is inside this world, indeed inside this moment and a singular product of it. In *Thus Spoke Zarathustra* the image of the gateway named 'Moment' captures this – and it is here that Zarathustra teaches the eternal return:

> And if all things have been here before: what do you think of this moment . . . ? Must not this gateway, too, have been here – before? And are not all things bound together in such a way that this moment draws after it all future things? *Therefore* – draws itself too? . . . And this slow spider that creeps along in the moonlight and this moonlight itself and I and you in this gateway whispering together, whispering of eternal things – must we not all have been here before? (Nietzsche 1961: 178–80, §2)[18]

To be in the moment is to be inside life, inside time. It is significant that the dwarf or 'Spirit of Gravity' who has accompanied Zarathustra thus far, upon his shoulders, refuses to enter the gateway and then vanishes. Perhaps this stunted 'Spirit' (*Geist*) represents, in its nihilistic rejection of becoming, the rational mind, which Nietzsche calls the 'little intelligence'; perhaps at this point in the text the reader is being invited into the moment and thus presented with a choice between Zarathustra and the dwarf.

An important aspect of Nietzsche's commitment to immanence that is not mentioned in his 1881 notebook is the refusal of teleology. In *The Will to Power* Nietzsche writes that 'becoming is not merely an *apparent state* (and) does not aim at a *final state* . . . I seek a conception of the world that takes this fact into account';

> If the world could in any way become rigid, dead, dry, *nothing*, or if it could reach a state of equilibrium, or if it had any kind of goal (that were a once-and-for-all *telos*) then this state must have been reached. But it has not been reached. (1968a: 377–8, §708; 548–9, §1066)

Teleology is a form of transcendence because in positing a purpose for life as a whole it invokes a perspective outside life – perhaps a creative God who designs the world for a reason; perhaps an Aristotelian 'unmoved mover' or final cause. There are two ways of interpreting the immanence of the eternal return. One way sees this as an attempt to overcome nihilism by offering an alternative to metaphysical and Christian appeals to transcendence (see Löwith 1945: 278). The other way would see the denial of transcendence as itself nihilistic – as a negation of a negation, so to speak – so that the thought of eternal recurrence would be making this nihilism explicit and thus forcing human beings to a crisis-point where they are faced with the possibility of incorporating it actively. This brings us back to the idea that the doctrine has a selective, cultivating power.

One question that may arise here is why Nietzsche needs to invoke the doctrine of eternal return in order to insist on immanence. Why not just affirm the transience of all things and deny any notions of transcendence and purposiveness? Why 'impress the image of eternity' onto this life? It might be objected that this is just another denial of temporality and finitude, another instance of metaphysical thinking. Nietzsche offers some kind of response to this question in one of the 1881 notes, where he criticises the 'political delusion' of 'secularization', which focuses on the world and deliberately ignores the possibility of 'the beyond'. The goal of this secular world-view

> is the wellbeing of the *fleeting* individual, which is why its fruit is socialism, i.e. *fleeting* individuals who want to conquer their happiness through socialisation – they have no reason to *wait*, as do human beings with eternal souls and eternal becoming and future improvement. (Ansell Pearson and Large 2006: 240–1)

Nietzsche wants to provoke a transition to a new form of human life, to a new form of human being – the *Übermensch* – and he regards modern secularism as the culmination of passive nihilism that neglects the human being in favour of social 'progress'. In his later writing he discusses the 'future improvement' mentioned here in terms of processes of 'discipline and breeding' (*Zucht und Züchtung*), which is the title of the fourth book of *The Will to Power*.

> Breeding, as I understand it, is a means of storing up the tremendous forces of mankind so that the generations can build upon the work of their forefathers – not only outwardly, but inwardly, organically growing out of them and becoming something stronger. (1968a: 215, §398)

Nietzsche announces his intention to replace metaphysics and religion with 'the theory of eternal recurrence (this as a means of breeding and selection)' (255, §462). He shares with Kierkegaard the view that a spiritual illness – whether despair or nihilism – can be overcome only by going through it; only from the inside, as it were. It would not be possible to avoid or put an end to nihilism from the outside, by proposing some kind of alternative (see Heidegger 1979–87: 2: 179). Nietzsche illustrates this symbolically in Zarathustra's vision of a shepherd with a black snake in his mouth: when Zarathustra fails to pull out the snake, he tells the shepherd to bite off its head and spit it out, thus expelling it from the inside.

4. Kierkegaard and Nietzsche

Kierkegaard and Nietzsche were precisely a generation apart. Nietzsche's father was born in the same year as Kierkegaard, in 1813, and Nietzsche himself was born thirty-one years

later, exactly twelve months after the publication of *Repetition*. Both men came from
Lutheran backgrounds; both were drawn to Greek philosophy and wrote works on Socrates
while in their late twenties; both spent most of their adult lives writing furiously and were
enormously prolific; both produced philosophies that bear the mark of Hegel's legacy – a
preoccupation with history and with questions of movement and becoming. Both thinkers
seek, in different ways, to challenge idealism; both are concerned above all with questions
of spiritual health. If there had been just a few more years between them Nietzsche would
probably have read Kierkegaard's works and the affinities and differences between their
ideas would no doubt have been clarified by a Nietzschean polemic against the Danish
'poet of the religious'.

   One striking point of affinity between Kierkegaard's repetition and Nietzsche's recurrence is the production of a thoroughgoing movement that encompasses both the 'what'
and the 'how' of the task of philosophy. It is this that Deleuze describes so aptly as 'putting
metaphysics in motion' (Deleuze [1968] 1994: 8). Repetition is a concept of movement –
the transition from ideality to actuality – that Kierkegaard dramatises in several texts and
that he hopes as an author to bring into being within the reader. Just as repetition is an
actualising movement, so the literary technique of dramatisation signifies the bringing into
being, within a fictional world, of philosophical concepts and arguments. Finding herself
addressed and reminded that she is an existing individual, the ideal reader of these texts
makes her own movements of self-discovery and self-actualisation, although of course in
going through these motions she will realise her inability fully to accomplish them by
herself, without God. Nietzsche's eternal recurrence is a thought of movement that must be
thought through – that is to say, 'incorporated' – and this process is supposed to bring about a
transformation. For both philosophers, the inseparability of 'what' and 'how' in these
thoughts of transition indicates also the coming-together of being and becoming.

   However, Kierkegaard and Nietzsche seek to produce movement within different *milieux*.
This becomes clear when we compare their attitudes to the historicism that characterises
nineteenth-century thought. Kierkegaard is determined to resist Hegelian historicism and
constantly ridicules speculative philosophy's preoccupation with 'world history'. He con-
cedes that human beings are part of nature, of history and of society, but he also wants to keep
separate from these a 'sphere of freedom': the *milieu* of subjectivity or inwardness. The
movements within Kierkegaard's texts both represent this inner being indirectly and attempt
to touch it directly. His resistance to historicism comes not from a reactionary individualism
but from a conviction that faith, love and passion are the most important tasks of a human
life and that these cannot be accomplished by the progress of history:

> Whatever one generation learns from another, no generation learns the essentially
> human from a previous one. In this respect, each generation begins primitively, has no
> task other than what each previous generation had, nor does it advance further . . . For
> example, no generation has learned to love from another. (Kierkegaard 1983: 121)

It is this position that constitutes the heart of Kierkegaard's 'existentialism'.

   In contrast to Kierkegaard – whose commitment to an interiority somehow apart from
the body he would surely disparage – Nietzsche's movements take place on the stage of
European history. Nietzsche's thought is even more radically historicist than Hegel's,
because what the latter regards as the end of history is for Nietzsche the brink of a transition
to new forms of life. He understood his own life and philosophy in terms of the fate of
Europe: he described himself as 'a destiny' and as 'dynamite' (1967b: 326–7) because he

found himself unable to evade the task of bringing Europe to a point of crisis where the essence of nihilism comes into the open. It was this task, which involved the intense suffering of loneliness, poor physical health and eventual madness, that Nietzsche urged himself to love when he wrote of *amor fati*.

To be sure, the doctrine of eternal recurrence is supposed to lead to an overcoming of nihilism by making explicit the contradiction between freedom and necessity inherent in modern thought; and this is indebted to the Hegelian idea that contradiction leads not to an impasse, but to movement. However, the contradiction present in eternal recurrence is not resolved or reconciled in the kind of rational movement at work in the Hegelian dialectic. Rather, the crisis encountered in thinking the thought will be a crisis *of* reason, among other aspects of human life that have dominated hitherto. The 'transition' effected by the thought is foreseen by Nietzsche not as reconciliation but as decision. In a way, this echoes Kierkegaard's argument, against the principle of mediation, that contradiction ('either/or') compels a choice between alternative possibilities. But this Kierkegaardian moment of decision is individual and existential, while for Nietzsche it must be fateful and historical. The thought of eternal return calls into question the very meaning of decision and the very being of the individual.[19]

Both Kierkegaard and Nietzsche are transitional thinkers in relation to the history of European thought, although Nietzsche is more self-conscious about his own transitional status. Commentators wonder whether Nietzsche succeeds in going 'beyond metaphysics',[20] and the same question might meaningfully be asked of Kierkegaard, insofar as he insists that truth is inseparable from life and from becoming. But instead of focusing on an 'overcoming' or 'ending' of metaphysics, it perhaps makes more sense to assess the contributions of these two extraordinary thinkers in terms of how and to what extent they 'put metaphysics in motion'. We do not know where the movements of repetition and recurrence lead, for they exceed knowledge, calculation, expectation – and precisely because of this they shake the foundations of secular humanism. By making questionable the form and motion of time itself, Kierkegaard and Nietzsche call into being a radically open future that may transform the past, that may disrupt the boundary between the possible and the impossible. They are transitional thinkers in precisely this sense. Philosophers of the twentieth and twenty-first centuries who set themselves the task of thinking thoughts such as singularity, gift and event (*Ereignis*, *événement*) are following and continuing movements instituted by Kierkegaard and Nietzsche.

Notes

1. Some scholars have argued that the term *Gentagelse* as used by Kierkegaard should be translated as 'resumption' rather than as 'repetition', since the former better conveys the idea of 'taking again' or 'taking anew' that is implied by the Danish term. See Croxall 1956: 128–9; Fulford 1911: 8.
2. Heiberg's discussion of *Repetition* occurs in 'Det astronomiske Aar' (The Astrological Year), in his yearbook *Urania Aarbog for 1844*. For a translation of the relevant passages, see Kierkegaard 1983: 379–83.
3. See Kierkegaard 1983: 283–323, for an English translation of Kierkegaard's response to Heiberg.
4. On possibility in Kierkegaard's thought, see Carlisle 2006: 63–89; Walsh 1992: 11–15.
5. Note the following journal entries concerning *kinesis*: 'Hegel has never done justice to the category of transition. It would be significant to compare it with the Aristotelian teaching about *kinesis*' (Kierkegaard 1967–78: 2: 260); 'The category to which I intend to trace everything, and which is also the category lying dormant in Greek Sophistry if one views it world-historically, is motion (*kinesis*), which is perhaps one of the most difficult problems in philosophy. In modern

philosophy it has been given another expression – namely, transition and mediation' (Kierkegaard 1967–78: 5: 5601).

6. On Kierkegaard's debt to Aristotle, see Stack 1974; Løkke and Waaler 2010; Come 1991.
7. On *Repetition* as a response to Hegelian thought, see Stewart 2003: 292–304.
8. On these Danish debates of the 1830s, see Stewart 2003: 50–89; Carlisle 2005: 39–45.
9. An English translation of Kierkegaard's notes on Schelling's lectures of 1841–2 is in Kierkegaard 1989. On Kierkegaard's relation to Schelling, see Olesen 2007.
10. A journal entry from 1843 lists three forms of repetition, the second of which involves 'the problem of sin': 'Repetition comes again everywhere. (1) When I am going to act, my action has existed in my consciousness in conception and thought – otherwise I act thoughtlessly – that is, I do not act. (2) Inasmuch as I am going to act, I presuppose that I am in an original integral state. Now comes the problem of sin, which is the second repetition, for now I must return to myself again. (3) The real paradox by which I become the single individual, for if I remain in sin, understood as the universal, there is only repetition no. 2' (Kierkegaard 1967–78: 3: 3793).
11. On Kierkegaard's thought in light of Luther's influence, see Hampson 2001: 249–84.
12. On the translation of these two terms, see Ansell Pearson 2005: 19–20, note 1.
13. In references to works of Nietzsche's, page number is followed by paragraph number (§) when applicable. In references to Nietzsche's *Genealogy*, page number is followed by essay number (in Roman numerals) then section number (for example, III.25).
14. Eugen Fink has commented on this contradiction between futility and significance: 'All doing, all risk is senseless and futile since everything is already determined. But one could equally say this: all is still to be done, whatever we decide now, we will need to decide over and over again. Every moment has an importance that extends beyond any individual life . . . The importance of eternity rests on the moment' (Fink 2003: 78).
15. On the various interpretations of the eternal recurrence that follow this pattern, see Dudley 2002: 202–7.
16. For his critique of science, see Nietzsche [1887] 1967a: 145–61, III.23–7; Nietzsche 1968a: 324–31, §594–617.
17. Nietzsche criticises the distinction between theory and practice in 1968a: 227–9, §423; 251–2, §458.
18. On this section of *Thus Spoke Zarathustra*, see Heidegger 1979–87: 2: 43–4, 56–7.
19. Pierre Klossowski accentuates how the eternal recurrence brings into question the nature of selfhood and identity; see Klossowski 1995: 108–14. On the Nietzschean idea of decision, see Heidegger's lecture 'Nietzsche as the thinker of the consummation of metaphysics', in Heidegger 1979–87: 3: 3–9.
20. See, for example, Heidegger 1968: 88–110; Fink 2003: 6, 8, 80–1, 164–73.

References

Ansell Pearson, Keith (2005), 'The eternal return of the overhuman: The weightiest knowledge and the abyss of light', *Journal of Nietzsche Studies* 30: 1–21.

Ansell Pearson, Keith, and Duncan Large (eds) (2006), *The Nietzsche Reader*, Oxford: Blackwell.

Carlisle, Clare (2005), *Kierkegaard's Philosophy of Becoming: Movements and Positions*, Albany, NY: SUNY Press.

Carlisle, Clare (2006), *Kierkegaard: A Guide for the Perplexed*, London: Continuum.

Come, Arnold B. (1991), *Trendelenburg's Influence on Kierkegaard's Modal Categories*, Montreal: Inter Editions.

Croxall, T. H. (1956), *Kierkegaard Commentary*, London: Nisbet.

Deleuze, Gilles [1968] (1994), *Difference and Repetition*, trans. Paul Patton, London: Athlone.

Dudley, Will (2002), *Hegel, Nietzsche, and Philosophy: Thinking Freedom*, Cambridge: Cambridge University Press.

Fink, Eugen (2003), *Nietzsche's Philosophy*, trans. Goetz Richter, London: Continuum.

Fulford, Francis W. (1911), *Søren Aabye Kierkegaard: A Study*, Cambridge: Wallis.

Haase, Ullrich (2008), *Starting with Nietzsche*, London: Continuum.

Hampson, Daphne (2001), *Christian Contradictions*, Cambridge: Cambridge University Press.

Heidegger, Martin (1968), *What Is Called Thinking?*, trans. J. Glenn Gray, New York: Harper & Row.

Heidegger, Martin (1979–87), *Nietzsche*, 4 vols, trans. David Farrell Krell, San Francisco: Harper & Row.

Howland, Jakob (2006), *Kierkegaard and Socrates: A Study in Philosophy and Faith*, Cambridge: Cambridge University Press.

Kierkegaard, Søren (1967–78), *Søren Kierkegaard's Journals and Papers*, 6 vols, ed. and trans. Howard V. Hong and Edna H. Hong, Bloomington: Indiana University Press.

Kierkegaard, Søren [1844] (1980a), *The Concept of Anxiety*, trans. Reidar Thomte, Princeton: Princeton University Press.

Kierkegaard, Søren [1849] (1980b), *The Sickness unto Death*, trans. Howard V. Hong and Edna H. Hong, Princeton: Princeton University Press.

Kierkegaard, Søren [1843] (1983), *Fear and Trembling/Repetition*, trans. Howard V. Hong and Edna H. Hong, Princeton: Princeton University Press.

Kierkegaard, Søren [1844] (1985a), *Philosophical Fragments*, trans. Howard V. Hong and Edna H. Hong, Princeton: Princeton University Press.

Kierkegaard, Søren (1985b), *Johannes Climacus, or De omnibus dubitandum est*, trans. Howard V. Hong and Edna H. Hong, Princeton: Princeton University Press.

Kierkegaard, Søren [1841] (1989), *The Concept of Irony*, trans. Howard V. Hong and Edna H. Hong, Princeton: Princeton University Press.

Klossowski, Pierre (1995), 'Nietzsche's experience of the eternal return', in David B. Allison (ed.), *The New Nietzsche*, Cambridge, MA: MIT Press, pp. 107–20.

Løkke, Håvard, and Arild Waaler (2010), '*Physics* and *Metaphysics*: Change, modal categories and agency', in Jon Stewart (ed.), *Kierkegaard and the Greek World*, Aldershot: Ashgate, pp. 25–46.

Löwith, Karl (1945) 'Nietzsche's doctrine of eternal recurrence', *Journal of the History of Ideas* 6 (3): 273–84.

Luther, Martin (1883), *Martin Luthers Werke, Kritische Gesamtausgabe*, Weimar: Bohlau.

Nietzsche, Friedrich [1883–5] (1961), *Thus Spoke Zarathustra*, trans. R. J. Hollingdale, Harmondsworth: Penguin.

Nietzsche, Friedrich (1962), *Philosophy in the Tragic Age of the Greeks*, trans. Marianne Cowan, Chicago: Regnery.

Nietzsche, Friedrich [1886] (1966), *Beyond Good and Evil*, trans. Walter Kaufmann, New York: Random House.

Nietzsche, Friedrich [1887] (1967a), *On the Genealogy of Morals*, trans. Walter Kaufmann and R. J. Hollingdale, New York: Random House.

Nietzsche, Friedrich [1908] (1967b), *Ecce Homo*, trans. Walter Kaufmann, New York: Random House.

Nietzsche, Friedrich (1968a), *The Will to Power*, trans. Walter Kaufmann and R. J. Hollingdale, New York: Random House.

Nietzsche, Friedrich [1888] (1968b), *Twilight of the Idols*, trans. R. J. Hollingdale, Harmondsworth: Penguin.

Nietzsche, Friedrich [1882] (1974), *The Gay Science*, trans. Walter Kaufmann, New York: Random House.

Olesen, Tonny Aagaard (2007), 'Schelling: A historical introduction to Kierkegaard's Schelling', in Jon Stewart (ed.), *Kierkegaard and His German Contemporaries – Tome I: Philosophy*, Aldershot: Ashgate, pp. 229–76.

Schopenhauer, Arthur [1818/1844] (1966), *The World as Will and Representation*, 2 vols, trans. E. F. J. Payne, New York: Dover.

Stack, George (1974), 'Aristotle and Kierkegaard's existential ethics', *Journal of the History of Philosophy* 12 (1): 1–19.

Stewart, Jon (2003), *Kierkegaard's Relations to Hegel Reconsidered*, Cambridge: Cambridge University Press.

Walsh, Sylvia (1992), 'Kierkegaard: Poet of the religious', in George Pattison (ed.), *Kierkegaard on Art and Communication*, Basingstoke: Macmillan.

17

Nineteenth-Century Philosophy in the Twentieth Century and Beyond

Andrew Bowie

1. Methodological Reflections

Reflections on the relationships between one period of philosophy and another raise important methodological issues which first emerge in their modern form in the wake of Kant, Herder and other thinkers in the second half of the eighteenth century. This is the period in which the ramifications of the idea that philosophy is bound up with the historical circumstances of its production begin to be apparent. In the light of these ramifications, the apparently obvious aim of identifying anticipations or echoes of twentieth-century forms of philosophy in the nineteenth century is by no means as straightforward as it might at first seem.[1]

Is what is anticipated necessarily superior to what preceded it, or is it merely a response to a different historical situation? For it to be superior, philosophy would have to progress in something like the manner in which a science can be said to progress, namely by expanding its explanatory and predictive capacity and by enabling new technological solutions. This sort of progress already looks unlikely in a discipline notorious for its lack both of consensus and of uncontested direct application to real-world problems. Moreover, a key aspect of nineteenth-century philosophy, perhaps most apparent in the work of Nietzsche, is the idea that progress in *any* sphere can be questioned, on the basis that what is progress from one perspective may well not be progress from another. This latter approach makes philosophy more analogous to art than to the sciences, because on this view philosophical value does not necessarily lie in making the next move in a cumulative or progressively bigger story, but rather in illumination of some particular aspect of life and the world. The nature of this illumination, as Hans-Georg Gadamer suggests, changes in differing social and historical contexts, rather than being something that can be established in objective terms for all time. Marx famously wrestled with the fact that Greek art could still give pleasure, even though the means of production of Greek society had long been superseded and nineteenth-century science had taken over from mythology. Does the same apply to Plato's philosophy – or, for that matter, any philosophy from the past where the means of production and the state of reliable scientific knowledge are not as developed in the present? The very fact that there are analytical reinterpretations of 'Platonic' arguments which are intended to contribute to contemporary debates, as well as readings, like those of Heidegger and Gadamer, which interpret Plato via what has happened in philosophy since Plato, suggests that the assignment of philosophy to a status akin to science or art is itself a philosophical problem, any answer to which will itself depend on contested philosophical assumptions.

In twentieth-century academic philosophy in the Western world a split develops between 'European' and 'analytical' philosophy, investigation of which has become an issue in contemporary philosophy (see, for example, Glock 2008). The nature of the split tells us a great deal about the reception of nineteenth-century philosophy in the twentieth and twenty-first centuries. The split also echoes that between the idea that philosophy is more like art, in which progress is not a dominant criterion of evaluation, and the idea that philosophy is more like a science, because it is supposed to produce rigorously argued theories that account for the nature of reality. The issue is complicated by the fact that some 'European' forms of philosophy have effects on the production of art – Schopenhauer influenced Wagner, Mahler, Thomas Mann and many others, for example – and some analytical forms of philosophy play a role in the development of scientific theories – the Vienna Circle, for instance, had an impact on quantum mechanics. In these cases the boundary between philosophy and other disciplines and cultural practices ceases to be as definite as it is sometimes assumed to be. What these issues imply for the presence of nineteenth-century philosophy in the twentieth century and beyond is complex, as the following can suggest.

Is one looking for those ideas in nineteenth-century philosophy which have proved to be durable because they are repeated or echoed by later thinkers or movements? Given the massive divergences of approach to key philosophical issues which characterise twentieth-century philosophy, the danger here is that one will end up with a series of arbitrary echoes that do not add up to anything philosophically significant. One can always find ways in which an idea can be said to be echoed by another idea. A more radical alternative is to look for those aspects of nineteenth-century philosophy which are in some way superior to what happens in key areas of twentieth-century philosophy: if there are such aspects, they will necessarily put into question assumptions about philosophical progress. As we shall see, parts of twentieth-century analytical philosophy were dominated by empiricist assumptions and a now widely accepted argument against these assumptions was central to Hegel's philosophy. Does this mean that philosophy has had to 'go backwards'? Or is the use of Hegel really an advance that has only been made possible by the thorough working out of the contradictions in empiricism by analytical philosophers?

These questions involve an issue which has considerable effects on the nature of institutionalised philosophy in the Anglo-American world and which sheds important light on how nineteenth-century philosophy relates to twentieth- and twenty-first-century philosophy. This is the notional division between 'philosophy' and the 'history of ideas'. In the former one supposedly seeks to build theories in order to answer philosophical problems, in the latter one is supposedly looking at attempts to do this in the past which are interesting for historical reasons, but which no longer play a role in the debates of real philosophers. How, though, does one know whether one is doing the former or the latter, especially in the light of issues like that concerning Hegel and empiricism? What are the criteria for knowing that one is dealing with a real philosophical problem? The criteria presumably have themselves to be philosophically legitimated, but how does one avoid what Hans Albert terms the 'Münchhausen Trilemma', the danger of circularity, regress or dogmatism with respect to the adoption of such criteria – a danger already identified by Jacobi at the end of the eighteenth century? Often philosophers simply assume that they are already in touch with the true problem, even though they are actually merely joining a debate on an issue as it has been constituted by those who contingently happen to be their philosophical peers. Were there a universally agreed stock of such issues and how to formulate them (and were there objectively accredited peers), the problem might be soluble, but the history of philosophy is littered with approaches that have turned out to be dead-ends. The meta-philosophical difficulty remains: how does one prove that something is a real philosophical problem rather than part of the 'history of ideas'?

A key nineteenth-century idea, which appears in various versions in Hegel, Marx, Nietzsche and others, is that philosophical positions can only be fully understood by understanding their origins, philosophy being, in Hegel's phrase, 'its age written in thought'. Why, then, did people make a philosophy/history of ideas separation, who did so and how did they make the distinction? The term 'history of ideas' seems to stem from Arthur Lovejoy, who saw it in positive terms, as a discipline with its own justification, which was to trace the historical development of key concepts. However, the vital point here is that the term's actual employment in philosophy goes along, in ways which deeply influence the discipline, with the rejection of a historical approach to philosophy on the part of many (analytical) philosophers. This rejection is usually justified by the argument that the genesis of a philosophical issue is separate from the validity of the claims made about that issue. This rejection constitutes a crucial interpretative divide between key aspects of nineteenth- and twentieth-century philosophy.

The most frequent analytical response to genesis/validation issues tells us something important about aspects of that approach to philosophising in the present context. For the difference to be a logical necessity, the object of the philosophical problem has to be, in some senses at least, clearly definable. The so-called 'mind/body' and 'mind/world' problems can illustrate the difficulty here. Historically these emerge as a central concern with Descartes, when the issue of how to connect thinking substance and extended substance appears to be quite clear, insofar as thinking substance can be defined as that which constitutes the limit of epistemological doubt and extended substance is defined precisely by its contrast with the certainty of the 'I think'. The issue is then analysed on the assumption that the key problem is a scepticism-threatening dualism that makes mind's connection to the world incomprehensible. The genesis of this problem might seem to be separate from the issues to which it gives rise and so to belong to the 'history of ideas'.

However, it is far from clear either that this approach to these issues is self-justifying, or that it is the approach which has necessary philosophical priority. An equally valid question would be why, with sporadic exceptions, the 'mind/body' and 'mind/world' problems did not turn on the issue of self-consciousness until the seventeenth century in Europe, before becoming absolutely central in German idealism via Fichte's responses to Kant. Does this mean that the phenomenon of self-consciousness did not 'exist' until then (whatever that might mean), at least in the form of 'self-reflection' which it takes from Descartes to Kant, in German idealism, phenomenology and beyond? In the Cartesian version of the two substances, each term is dependent for its definition on the scope of the other term. The idea that what is being analysed has a clear sense is therefore open to question, because the object of analysis changes its status as it is redescribed via different contrasting terms at different periods.[2]

The last point is precisely why ideas from Hegel and others in the nineteenth century, which are regarded as part of the very substance of philosophy by Heidegger, Adorno and others in the twentieth, can be used to question whether there *are* clearly identifiable essential mind/body or mind/world problems which can be solved by a definitive explanatory theory. The basis of Hegel's *Phenomenology of Spirit* is the idea that we cannot understand 'mind' if we separate it from 'world'. That is why the book is about the ways in which mind 'appears' as forms of consciousness which develop via interactions with the world. Now this might seem just to take us back into the domain of 'real philosophy', on the grounds that Hegel is proposing an argument for a version of monism, which can be compared with other arguments about monism and either found wanting or found superior to those arguments. The alternative here would seem, then, either to be that one should pursue the true theory of monism, 'neutral', 'anomalous' or whatever, because that is the aim of philosophy, or that one should trace the history of differing versions of monism as responses to the idea that mind and world cannot be wholly separate. Both stances involve instructive problems.

The former stance is best seen from the vantage point of successful scientific theories. These will, in the main, definitively refute what preceded them, provided that they enable better prediction or account for the phenomena in ways which better cohere with other theories in the same area. A return to a previous theory will only be possible via the kind of alteration to the theory which effectively means that it is a different theory anyway. One can worry about whether successful theories 'correspond to reality', but it is not clear that this notion can be made intelligible at all, as many leading philosophers in both the analytical and European camps suspect. Moreover, the real-world test of theories tends to be whether it is rational to act in terms of them, by, for example, getting on a plane built according to proven aerodynamic principles, or taking a drug which kills a specific bacterium. None of this applies to philosophical theories of monism, which may predominate at some times and not at others.

This is not an argument against detailed philosophical theorising on an issue. The point is to see how such theorising is embedded in contexts which can affect the *content* of the theory. Here the very notion of 'philosophical analysis' comes into question, because it may not be possible strictly to separate the elements of what is being analysed. Once this is admitted, one has to ask fundamental questions about the relationship between argument and interpretation. Such questions are a major reason why aspects of nineteenth-century philosophy have enjoyed a revival in recent years.

On the other hand, the latter historically oriented stance is open to the threat of what Herbert Schnädelbach has termed '*morbus hermeneuticus*', in which 'the philologisation of philosophy turns *means* into *ends* and the *medium* into the *content* of philosophy'. Schnädelbach asserts that 'one should ask the historical hermeneuticists why one should *also* have the hermeneutic problems which *they* have with the philosopher X' (Schnädelbach 1987: 283–4).[3] By dint of making the issue of context the primary focus of philosophy, one can lose sight of why an issue matters beyond the context in question. One can, however, turn this argument around and ask why one should be bothering about 'problem X', the 'content' of philosophy, if, for example, it becomes apparent that putative solutions to it have no bearing on anything that matters in other contexts. The history of philosophy, as Nietzsche, Wittgenstein and Richard Rorty suggest, can sometimes be written not as the history of successful argument and counter-argument but rather as the waning of interest in issues that may dominate one period before coming to appear irrelevant in a subsequent period. The tension between the conflicting stances just outlined is itself a historical issue which seems unlikely to be definitively resolved. It is for this reason that certain approaches to history and philosophy, particularly those influenced by Hegel and Marx, can legitimately concentrate more on what contradictions between theories can tell us about the world that produces the contradictions than on striving to decide between the conflicting theories. The tension between the desire to resolve a philosophical issue and the sense that the issue may be a historical expression of perhaps irresolvable conflicts can be as 'philosophically' productive as either putatively resolving the issue or reducing it to its historical context.

2. Back to the Future

Any attempt to give a general account of twentieth-century Western philosophy faces a huge number of disparate positions, all of which have some roots in the nineteenth century. A taxonomy of the differences between the positions would become hopelessly complex, especially if one tried to detail the local differences within, say, phenomenology or the Vienna Circle. There is, however, a notional aspect of both European and analytical philosophy which would seem to connect the traditions, even as in other respects they begin to become distinct. This is criticism of 'metaphysics', usually in conjunction with a new evaluation of the effect of considerations of language on dealing with traditional philosophical problems. The problem is, though, that the very meaning of the term 'metaphysics' points to further fundamental philosophical divisions.

The most familiar analytical criticism of metaphysics during the 1920s consists in the attempt to demonstrate that metaphysical propositions are 'meaningless'. This requires the establishment of a criterion for meaning and leads to the notorious limitation of meaningful propositions to those of logic and observation statements. The objection to this project is that claims that these are the only meaningful statements do not themselves belong to the class of meaningful statements. As the early Wittgenstein realised (in a probably unconscious echo of a theme in Novalis),[4] this meant that philosophical propositions about what was meaningful, of which his own *Tractatus* was itself composed, were in some sense 'metaphysical', although they were at the same time 'nonsense'. Given the result of such a critique, it has to be asked why it was advanced with such emphasis by the Vienna Circle in particular. The answer has to do with their aim of establishing a 'scientific philosophy' and the crucial point is that the attempt to do so comes up against a defining issue in modern philosophy.

To see what is at stake here, it is important to remember that, while the Vienna Circle sought to get rid of metaphysics by prioritising a certain conception of reliable scientific method, Heidegger, in his work from the mid-1930s onwards, came to contend that metaphysics had itself *become* modern science, metaphysics being the subject's way of gaining mastery over being. Heidegger's stance involves a questioning of all the ways in which modern philosophy had sought to ground its relationship to being, from Descartes's *cogito* to Kant's transcendental subjectivity to Hegel's movement of absolute spirit, to the forces of production in Marx to Nietzsche's will to power. The attempt to overcome 'Western metaphysics' is a key aim of certain kinds of European philosophy at the latest from Marx onwards. The attempt at such overcoming can take a rather apocalyptic form, as it sometimes does in the work of Jacques Derrida, or can be more compatible with some analytical approaches, as it is in Jürgen Habermas's (1988) notion of 'post-metaphysical thinking', which seeks a way out of philosophy based on the attempt to ground subjectivity, as Heidegger thinks the metaphysical tradition to be. Both Derrida and Habermas see the critique of metaphysics as dependent on the primacy of intersubjective language before subjectivity and this suggests a possible bridge between the analytic and European traditions, especially in the light of how nineteenth-century concerns become part of debates about language in the ways we shall see in a moment. However, at this point a crucial difference between these traditions becomes clear.

The basis of one version of the analytical project in the strict sense (it is increasingly clear that there is no consensus on how to define analytical philosophy) is summed up in Michael Dummett's claim that 'words have meanings in themselves, independently of speakers' (Dummett 1986: 473) and was established by the nineteenth-century Czech logician Bernard Bolzano. The essential analytical goal is suggested by Bolzano's assertion that the 'objective representation designated by any *word* is, as long as this word is not ambiguous, single' (Bolzano 1963: 66). Bolzano's idea is to come up with a theory of meaning in which psychology plays no role and so to put the objective knowledge provided by the sciences on a firm philosophical footing. Doing this depends on finding a way of making clear what 'objective representations' are. This might seem straightforward, as the ability to make true assertions seems to depend on them, given that truths about things in the world cannot be wholly dependent on psychological states of speakers, if they depend on these at all. How, then, does one give an account of an 'objective representation', which equates to something like an account of a Fregean 'sense' or, more broadly, to the idea that there are such things as 'meanings' in Dummett's sense?

Making a representation objective can be seen in terms of formulating the correct rule for the use of a word, so rendering the word non-ambiguous. Alternatively, one can seek to identify a class of words whose meaning is given in a way which is free of the contingent associations attached to words by individual language users. In both cases the aim is to find a location from which the objectivity of meaning can be grounded. The problem with the first option was already apparent (in a non-linguistic form) to Kant and the consequences of the problem are part of what gave rise in the nineteenth century to the development of modern hermeneutics. In his account of judgement Kant realises that if one wishes, in order to make a judgement about it, to 'distinguish whether something belongs under the rule or not, this could only happen via a further rule' (Kant [1781/1787] 1968: A133/B172). This leads to a regress of rules for rules, which means that judgement cannot be made wholly objective by subjecting it to rules: there has to be a moment in judgement which involves some kind of non rule-governed interpretation.

A version of this point about rules and their application is developed by the later Wittgenstein, but it has too rarely been appreciated just how presciently Schleiermacher dealt with this issue. His prescience becomes apparent when he describes the task of his *Dialectic*:

> [I]nstead of setting up a science of knowledge in the hope that one can thereby put an end to disagreement it is now a question of setting up a doctrine of the art [*Kunstlehre*] of disagreement in the hope that one can thereby arrive at common bases for knowledge. (Schleiermacher 1942: 43)

For Schleiermacher 'art' is 'that for which there admittedly are rules, but the combinatory application of these rules cannot in turn be rule-bound', on pain of the regress of rules for rules suggested by Kant, which would render the activity impossible (Schleiermacher 1998: 229). Schleiermacher asks how children could ever begin to learn a language if understanding were essentially based on rules, because they would have no basis for learning the first rule. The contrast between science and art suggested in Schleiermacher's conception gets beyond the clichéd view of what 'art' signifies in Romantic philosophy, because 'art', with its sense of judgement that has to transcend rules, is essential to human communication. He therefore makes a connection between what is generally dealt with in terms of epistemology and the pragmatics of human communication in all spheres, at the same time as opening up ways in which aesthetics has to be seen as germane to more than the consideration of works of art or natural beauty.

The second option, that of identifying a special class of words, also has a connection to

Kant, via his distinction between analytic and synthetic judgements. The former involve a notional class of concepts whose predicate is 'contained' in the subject concept (although exactly what this means is much disputed), as in 'a bachelor is an unmarried man', whereas in synthetic judgements the predicate is not 'contained' in the subject and so depends on information from the world. The notion of analytic judgements presupposes that there are truths which are purely conceptual (although exactly what this means is still much disputed) and do not rely on empirical data, which was part of the reason why the Vienna Circle saw logical statements as being a reliable basis for a criterion of meaning. Famously, Quine put this idea into question in the 1950s, on the grounds that whether or not a statement is analytic depends on its relation to other statements in the wider 'web' of language. Changes in one part of the web result in changes in other parts, so that the idea of stable conceptual truths is highly questionable.[5] Schleiermacher makes precisely this point (although his example of an analytical proposition is probably not a good one) in his *Dialectic*:

> The difference between analytic and synthetic judgments is a fluid one, of which we take no account. The same judgment (ice melts) can be an analytic one if the coming into being and disappearance via certain conditions of temperature are already taken up into the concept of ice and a synthetic one, if they are not yet taken up . . . This difference therefore just expresses a different state of the formation of concepts. (Schleiermacher 1839: 563)

If all concepts gain determinacy by their relations to other concepts, then there can be no concepts that have a privileged logical status by dint of their possessing invariable meanings: all there can be is a 'state of the formation of concepts', not a definitive end to that formation. Samuel Wheeler, who associates this idea with Quine, Davidson and Derrida, has put this point in terms of there being no 'magic language': 'A magic language is a system of representation such that the senses and referents of that language's terms are determined by the intrinsic nature of those terms' (Wheeler 2000: 217). The basic point had already been adumbrated in the eighteenth century by Hamann, when he questioned the rationalist assumption of a 'general philosophical language' which would obviate all the kinds of meaning which can only be understood by full engagement with the culture in which a language occurs. Versions of the rationalist assumption reappeared in the now generally rejected notion, from the early days of analytical philosophy, of a logically purified language that would serve as the touchstone for whether utterances are meaningful.

There is ongoing debate about the status of analytic propositions and purely conceptual truths, but the reasons for the widespread questioning of these notions involve more than the specific arguments of Quine, being part of a more general sense that attempts at such grounding of purely conceptual meaning misrecognise what actually happens in human communication. What is at issue is thus one aspect of the suspicion of metaphysics as a way of thinking supposedly capable of transcending the contingencies of human existence. If these points are accepted, the idea of a strictly 'analytical' philosophy has to dissolve and a way would seem open to bridging any European/analytical divide. However, there are a number of important questions here. In relation to the role of nineteenth-century philosophy in twentieth-century analytical philosophy, the question arises of why the conception that I have exemplified by core ideas that informed Schleiermacher's dialectic and hermeneutics – which are developments of aspects of widely held ideas in German idealist and Romantic philosophy – gained no real purchase in the Anglo-American world until others came up with much the same ideas independently of these nineteenth-century sources. One simple answer is that too many of the relevant German texts remained untranslated. But there are obviously a whole range of other contingent historical factors in play here and, while one should not reduce the issue to these, it is remarkable how rarely philosophers reflect on the fact that the ways philosophy develops can depend on often quite arbitrary factors.

Significant new approaches were established in philosophy in the analytical tradition stemming from Frege, Russell and the early Wittgenstein. At the same time, it is clear that isolating problems and analysing them in great detail is an inappropriate method for dealing with many aspects of human life, because aspects of life are interconnected in ways which can be obscured by this method. It is this realisation which, for example, makes Wittgenstein think so differently about language in his later work. The inappropriateness of a strictly analytical approach is particularly obvious in questions involving ethical and aesthetic matters, where establishing boundaries between, for example, deontological and consequentialist ethical positions, or expressivist and non-expressivist theories of art, fails to see that it is often the contradictions between the positions which bring us closest to real ethical and aesthetic life, rather than the resolution of the conflict in favour of one or other of its sides.[6]

One of the few things that still seems to unify analytical philosophers is the idea that analytical philosophy brings a new standard of rigour and clarity into the practice of philosophy. The problem with this stance, which is obviously justified in some respects, is twofold. First, the rigour and clarity is often assumed to be of the same order as that to be found in theories in the natural sciences. The problem here is that the internal rigour in the presentation of philosophical positions is not necessarily matched by any gain in warrantable insight. Given that modern philosophy can be said to begin at the point when dogmatic founding certainties dissolve, internal consistency of argument is anything but a guarantee of a position's veridical nature. The case of Nietzsche offers a useful reminder here: his wilful self-contradiction and inconsistency (which can sometimes be a serious failing) can be a source of some of his most important insights. A glance at history also has to make one wonder just where the insistence upon rigour and clarity actually leads. For a long time the Vienna Circle defined the project of analytical philosophy as the philosophy of science, but this project has become a relatively insignificant aspect of analytical philosophy in recent years and not because definitive philosophical answers were given to the kind of questions of epistemology and semantics which concerned the Circle. It may be that the sciences work too well for most people to want to spend their time failing to explain in philosophical terms why this is the case. The desire to give science firm foundations in the 1920s and 1930s, a desire common to thinkers in the analytical camp and in phenomenology, is these days probably more significant as another example of why consideration of the history of philosophy should be inseparable from its content than as a durable philosophical issue.

Second, the assumption that clarity is the ultimate virtue in all philosophy easily leads to an ideological refusal to take seriously forms of philosophy which are not clearly expressed, but which may turn out to be more durable than forms which are. Russell initiated one strand of analytical philosophy with his rejection of Hegel and his move from holism to logical atomism and this helped to lead to the ignoring of Hegel for most of the twentieth century by those schooled in the analytical tradition (see Hylton 1992). If one does not regard Russell's move against holism merely as an internal issue based on philosophical argument alone, but rather as an expression of wider cultural changes, then the return of Hegel and German idealism in recent philosophy can be used to suggest how certain kinds of nineteenth-century perspective on philosophy now offer crucial cultural and political resources (see Hammer 2007).

3. The Return of German Idealism

Perhaps the most influential book in recent philosophy has been John McDowell's *Mind and World* of 1994. The book is an explicit espousal of a version of Hegelianism: McDowell commits himself to a kind of holism which, as his detractors argue and as he is happy to concede, means that he may no longer be doing analytical philosophy. But how would as subtle and forensic a thinker as McDowell, who was probably best known for work on Frege and proper names, arrive at the judgement that Hegel is the best source of therapy for some of the concerns of modern epistemology? Hegel, as he was understood in the Anglo-American tradition for much of the twentieth century, is the philosopher who inflated Mind into some kind of demiurge, rejected inconvenient facts in the name of the completion of a philosophical system and was an enemy of the 'open society' with quasi-totalitarian views on the relation between state and individual. How does one move from this Hegel to one whom McDowell actually uses to salvage aspects of empiricism? The initial answer has to do with the fact that Hegel's specific engagements with forms of philosophy like empiricism are formulated in terms which can still be used directly to address contemporary versions of such philosophy. The answer to the wider question of why Hegel has become a major focus of contemporary philosophy is, however, again not to be sought solely in the realm of philosophical argument.

Research into Hegel and nineteenth-century philosophy both in the US and Germany in the last thirty years (at the time of writing) has uncovered more and more of the 'constellations' of issues that Hegel, German idealist and Romantic philosophers were addressing. (The term 'constellation' is associated with Dieter Henrich's research into the contexts of German idealism, though it also has roots in Walter Benjamin and Adorno.) By establishing the richness of the contexts of Hegel's work, it becomes less possible to use his potentially unfortunate formulations (such as 'the real is the rational') to reduce his concerns to the caricature familiar in the Anglo-American philosophical world. For McDowell, Hegel sees through what Wilfrid Sellars terms the 'myth of the given', the idea that there is a source of self-authenticating epistemic certainty in 'sense data', which function as the foundation of knowledge in empiricism. This supposed source is a myth because nothing intelligible can be said about it which does not already involve notions that cannot be derived from sense data, understood as the brute causal impacts of the world on the human organism. The basic point is made by Hegel in his critique of the immediacy of 'sense certainty' in the *Phenomenology*. Anything we say about the apparently most immediate data, such as what is in front of me now, requires indexical and other forms of thought which take us beyond the supposed immediacy of the data.

McDowell's focus on this issue might seem rather narrow, but what he is questioning is the kind of scientistic naturalism that reduces issues of mind and world to causal explanatory theories and this has major consequences. Exclusively causal theories eliminate serious consideration of the 'space of reasons', the dimension of spontaneous judgement that allows us to take a stance on epistemic and moral issues, which cannot be explained in terms of natural causality. McDowell's aim is, he claims, nothing less than a reconciliation of reason and nature, by seeing how spontaneity and receptivity relate in our apprehension of the world.

As I have shown elsewhere (Bowie 1996), the problematic taken up by McDowell is a version of the one opened up by Jacobi in his 'On the Doctrine of Spinoza in Letters to Herr Moses Mendelssohn' of 1785, the ramifications of which echo right through the history of modern philosophy, appearing, for example, in Nietzsche's reflections on how the attempt to ground cognition leads to the 'abyss' (see Bowie 1997). Jacobi's concern with Spinoza prefigures contemporary objections to scientism, because Jacobi refuses to accept that restricting our account of reality to what science tells us is self-legitimating (a restriction that he sees as being implicit in Spinoza's monistic system of determination by negation). Rather, science depends on a prior non-scientific 'revelation' of the world as something meaningful. (This theme later forms the core of Heidegger's thinking about science and philosophy.) McDowell makes the same point as follows: 'When we ask the metaphysical question whether reality is what science can find out about, we cannot, without begging the question, restrict the materials for an answer to those that science can countenance' (McDowell 1998: 72).

McDowell's key concern in *Mind and World* is with a 'coherentism that threatens to disconnect thought from reality' (McDowell 1994: 24). Jacobi sees the coherentist problem of grounding cognition as follows:

> [I]f everything which is supposed to arise and be present in a manner which we can comprehend has to arise and be present in a conditioned manner; then we remain, as long as we comprehend, in a chain of *conditioned conditions* [this is the way he talks about Spinoza's closed system, in which cognition is based on defining things by their relation to other things that 'condition' them]. Where this chain ceases [that is, where we require the 'unconditioned'] we cease to comprehend and the context which we call *nature* itself also ceases. (Jacobi in Scholz 1916: 276)

German idealism revolves around attempts to explicate the 'unconditioned' which connects thought and reality, mind and nature, and so hopefully to resolve the dilemma Jacobi sees in any systematic philosophy which tries to ground human reason.

Hegel's solution is to give up the idea of an initial, 'immediate' founding 'unconditioned', of the kind that Fichte suggests is manifest in thought's capacity freely to reflect on its own nature. Instead, one is to arrive at 'absolute knowledge' by working through what is lacking in the conceptions of objectivity in Kant, Jacobi, Fichte and others. The aim is to show that there is ultimately no split between subject and object, because what appears to lie outside the conceptual realm, like Kant's thing-in-itself, is in fact within it, the thing-in-itself being a notion generated in the space of reasons by abstraction from everything we concretely know about a thing. In McDowell's version: 'the deliverances of receptivity [via which we grasp the objective world] already draw on capacities that belong to spontaneity [that is, the subject's thinking]' (McDowell 1994: 41), so that the very notion of objectivity already depends on subjectivity. There are numerous versions of this point in Early German Romantic philosophy. Friedrich Schlegel puts it thus:

> The *grasping* of what is given demands spontaneity, one's own exertion, own activity. The smaller is the quantity of spontaneity which the grasping of the appearance demands, the *more* the appearance appears. There are no absolute maxima on either side; without any spontaneity there is no receptivity: and if *all* receptivity stopped, then the appearance would cease to be appearance and become a concept, for pure spontaneity. (Schlegel 1988: 170)

The Hegelian solution has considerable strengths because, in line with Friedrich Schlegel and Schleiermacher, it sees the issue of cognition as always in some sense involving 'beginning in the middle'. As Hegel suggests, you can't learn to swim without being in the water, so building reliable cognition can only come about by overcoming unreliable cognition, the pure starting point which would ensure that everything is built on solid ground being part of the 'myth of the given'. The full Hegelian route, however, as Habermas puts it, lays claim to a philosophical account of the 'context of all contexts' (Habermas 1988: 219), which, in some much-disputed sense, supposedly obviates the contingency inherent in real knowledge acquisition. Contemporary pragmatist alternatives to wholesale Hegelianism draw on the aspects of Nietzsche in which knowledge is essentially just one form of social practice whose value depends on its contribution to one's aims rather than its true representation of the world. The main question in the present context, though, is why McDowell needs to offer his therapeutic version of Hegel at all so long after essentially the same moves took place in German idealism.

The problem is that one needs a convincing account both of the demise of Hegelianism, which meant that there had to be a revival of Hegel, and of what the demise and the revival mean. This is once again not something that can simply be described in terms of competing philosophical arguments. Habermas has contended that 'There is nothing for it: we are philosophically still contemporaries of the Young Hegelians' (Habermas 1988: 277), because their 'arguments reclaim the finitude of spirit against the self-related-totalising thinking of the [Hegelian] dialectic' (47). Suspicion of Hegelian claims to a total system is, then, part of the wider move against 'metaphysics' discussed above.

One of Hegel's most insightful twentieth-century critics, Habermas's mentor, Adorno, suggests the complexity of the mediation between the nineteenth and twentieth centuries here. He sees Hegel's system as a reflection of how the modern world becomes a systematic totality via the expansion of the commodity system, which renders everything potentially equivalent by turning all things into exchange values. Adorno's concern is closely related to Jacobi's fear that Spinoza's system led to 'nihilism', because in it things only had value by their relations to other things. Read in this way, Hegel ceases to be essentially the philosopher who overcomes traditional epistemological concerns about sceptical doubt and instead his thought becomes a symptomatic expression of modernity, and Adorno links this aspect of Hegel's thought to Weber's views of rationalisation and bureaucracy. Adorno uses this link not least to understand how the Holocaust was in part a function of what he terms 'identity thinking', which can take the form of the reduction of people (and things) to their function in a system. The idea is that identification based on systematic relations between things represses the awareness of the particularity of the things, to the point where people can cease to matter as suffering individuals and can be reduced to material to be processed.[7] The same kind of identification, as Adorno is fully aware, is what enables modern societies to function in often advantageous ways. It is precisely the fact that the same kind of rationalising processes produce effective transport, communication and health systems, as well as mass murder, that is the crux of Adorno's approach to philosophy. At the same time as adverting to the danger of which Hegel's systematic approach can be interpreted as an expression, then, Adorno also adopts and adapts key aspects of Hegel in most of his significant philosophical work.

Whereas McDowell aims for a Wittgensteinian 'quietism' that tries therapeutically to dissolve philosophical contradictions, Adorno reads philosophical contradictions, of the kind which Hegel seeks to reconcile in his account of the role of philosophy in modernity, as expressions of historical tensions. Adorno sometimes does this in a questionable manner, but his dialectical account of, for example, the free-will/determinism issue offers a model of philosophy which confronts the simple fact that this issue, like many of the central problems of modernity, seems constitutively to resist philosophical resolution (see Adorno 2001). Rather than seeking to transcend the contradiction, Adorno interprets it as one expression of the modern dilemma of how to relate to nature within us and outside us, a dilemma made urgent by the success of the sciences in transforming external nature. As he points out, the idea of the third antinomy is a product of the modern period, not a perennial concern of philosophy. Rather than resolve the Kantian antinomy, therefore, Adorno uses it to explore how the concept of freedom can be interpreted in different contexts and how it has differing historical effects in those contexts.

Despite their considerable differences, Adorno and McDowell share a sense that the ways of conceiving of nature in much twentieth-century philosophy are inadequate. This again turns out to involve a revival of a strand of late eighteenth- and early nineteenth-century thinking which was rejected both in the analytical tradition and in many parts of the European tradition, namely, the idea of *Naturphilosophie*, as it appears in Schelling in particular (see Bowie 1993). Because *Naturphilosophie* could easily become a hindrance to empirically warrantable science and contained much that is now beyond any kind of retrieval, the fact that it was at its best an expression of a key aspect of modernity was easily ignored. As the world faces an ecological crisis of unforeseeable proportions, a crucial challenge to the very legitimacy of philosophy lies in the lack of ways of thinking which respond to the fact that for most of the history of philosophy 'nature' was seen as an essentially limitless resource, whereas now it has become something finite and fragile.

Schelling already warned against regarding nature merely as an object for realising human purposes when he criticised Fichte for giving total primacy to practical reason:

> I am thoroughly aware of how small an area of consciousness nature must fall into, according to your conception of it. For you nature has no speculative significance, only a teleological one. But are you really of the opinion, for example, that light is only there so that rational beings can also see each other when they talk to each other and that air is there so that when they hear each other they can talk to each other? (Schelling in Schulz 1968: 140)

Schelling later became even more critical of Fichte:

> [I]n the last analysis what is the essence of [Fichte's] whole opinion of nature? It is this: that nature should be used . . . and that it is there for nothing more than to be used; his principle, according to which he looks at nature, is the economic-teleological principle. (Schelling 1856–61: 7: 17)

One would search in vain in most twentieth-century analytical philosophy for any sense that there might be a whole dimension of human responses to nature which was not addressed by such philosophy. A philosophical method which takes as its model the analytical procedures of the sciences is ill-suited to grasping the kind of radical questions posed by the cumulative effects of the sciences. Heidegger is often criticised for his observation that 'science does not think', but what he meant is clear: while each element of a successful science can legitimate itself in its own terms, how each of those elements in conjunction with all the others changes the very nature of the world we inhabit (and our relationships to ourselves and other people) is not itself a scientific question.

It is not that a revival of a substantive *Naturphilosophie* is now a realistic proposition, but rather that a new examination of how nature has been understood in modern philosophy seems inevitable. Adorno suggests what is needed here with his idea that nature necessarily has a history, because what 'nature' means for humankind changes radically as societies change. Rather than the contemporary view of nature in terms of the 'final physics', Adorno aims to find a way out of the objectifying assumption that there is nothing more to nature than will be explained by the final physics. His aim is not to produce a positive metaphysics of nature, but he realises that the need which leads to the attempt to produce such a metaphysics is not simply destroyed by philosophical arguments which demonstrate its impossibility. The kind of thing Adorno means is suggested when he claims, in reflections from lectures of 1961 on Kant's *Critique of Judgement*, that: 'There is no other determination of the beauty of nature . . . than as the appearance of something as speaking . . . as expression which is not made by human beings', that is, which is not a result of instrumental manipulation of nature for human purposes (Adorno 1961: 6851). This comes close to an indefensible attempt to 're-enchant' nature and Adorno is more careful in his reflections on natural beauty in his published work. However, the fact that his reflections are now echoed in many areas in relation to the ecological crisis is a sign that what they advert to is highly significant. The revival of interest in German idealism is closely connected to a growing suspicion that scientism is a sign of a wider malaise in the dominant goals of contemporary capitalist societies.

A related constellation is apparent in the growing interest in the hermeneutic questioning of the idea of science as the solution to the problems of modernity. Although the natural sciences are indispensable to human survival, as Gadamer contends,

> this does not mean that people would be able to solve the problems that face us, peaceful coexistence of peoples and the preservation of the balance of nature, with science as such. It is obvious that not mathematics but the linguistic nature of people is the basis of human civilisation. (Gadamer 1993: 342)

Despite Gadamer's apparent inability to see his proximity to Schleiermacher, Schleiermacher is one of the first to insist on this point: 'Language never begins to form itself through science, but via general communication/exchange [*Verkehr*]; science comes to this only later and only brings an expansion, not a new creation, in language' (Schleiermacher 1942: 511). What these echoes of nineteenth-century modes of philosophical reflection share is the sense that the role of philosophy is to mediate between conflicting ways of addressing the issues of modernity, rather than to adopt a stance which gives primacy to the natural sciences, seeks a theory that will definitively tell us how language connects to the world or wishes 'to discover what fundamental kinds of things there are and what properties and relations they have' (Williamson 2007: 19).

Rorty's contention that contemporary philosophy should take the form of 'cultural politics' brings into focus perhaps the other main constellation between the nineteenth century and developments in contemporary philosophy (see Rorty 2007). Strange as it may seem, Rorty wishes to establish an approach which uses both Hegel and Nietzsche and the reasons for this apparently impossible combination tell us much about how philosophy from the past is mediated by the present. Hegel and Nietzsche are routinely regarded as essentially opposed, the former offering a narrative of the progress of Reason in history, the latter regarding such a narrative as just another 'shadow of God' that is meant to hide the contingency of human existence. Recent readers of Hegel, notably

Terry Pinkard (1996) and Robert Pippin (1989, 1997, 2005), however, argue that Hegel's is a philosophy of socially developed norms, there being no extra-social, extra-mundane perspective from which norms can be legitimated. Rather than *Geist* ('mind'/ 'spirit') somehow driving the empirical world from the outside, *Geist* is just the immanent development of the 'sociality of reason', for which a practice can only be justified in terms of an account of why it has come to be the socially accepted norm. Seen in this light, Nietzsche's desire to get rid of forms of legitimation which claim any kind of transcendent authority is not necessarily so far from what Hegel seeks to do. For Rorty, the key element in Nietzsche is his questioning of the correspondence theory of truth and his related insistence on considering how philosophical convictions relate to practical dealings with the world, which are summarised in his questions about the value of truth.

The real division here is, then, between the ways in which philosophy regards the status of norms: are they, as they are for Hegel, the rationally justifiable result of understanding what informs the dominant social practices of a culture, or are they, as they are for Nietzsche (and those most influenced by him), the form which power takes in a particular historical situation? Are these positions necessarily opposed? Rorty's work can be seen as a negotiation between them.

An alternative which still dominates much work in the analytical tradition lies in the pursuit of some way of transcending such debates, by, for example, making the correspondence theory of truth work and so gaining a firm philosophical grasp on how language can truly represent the world. Part of the value of a historical perspective on such an enterprise is to remind us of the fate of previous enterprises of this nature and of the fact that alternatives to such enterprises have often been neglected. Perhaps the key hermeneutic reminder that nineteenth-century philosophy now offers us, then, is of the need to consider why the questions which dominate the analytical agenda should still form the focus of philosophy. This approach involves accepting the perennial tension between arguing towards resolutions of philosophical problems and the reminder that history can show us that such argument always involves more than we could be aware of when we are engaged in it. In retrospect, many positions, even in the more technical reaches of philosophy, such as Kant's antinomy between determinism and free will, or the aim for a logically purified language, can come to be seen as unresolved expressions of social and cultural tensions. Although we cannot say now what the current revival and development of nineteenth-century conceptions will mean for the future of philosophy, we can be aware of the limitations of perspective that resulted from the idea that those conceptions were no longer philosophically significant.

Notes

1. I shall not approach the nineteenth century in a purely chronological sense. Like those who argue that the twentieth century really begins in 1914, I think that the philosophical nineteenth century begins with Kant's 1781 *Critique of Pure Reason*, which sets the agenda for what is chronologically in the nineteenth century.
2. This issue relates to that discussed below, concerning the distinction between analytic and synthetic judgements, which is one form in which the doubts that I am considering made their way into analytical philosophy.
3. Translations from German language texts are the author's own.
4. 'The essence of identity can only be established in a pseudo-proposition [*Scheinsatz*]. We leave the identical in order to represent it' (Novalis 1978: 8).

5. It is worth remembering that Otto Neurath came to hold related views (see Bowie 2000). The caricature of nineteenth-century philosophy often presented in the analytical tradition should not be repeated for the twentieth century. As Friedman (1999) has shown, the Vienna Circle held very diverse, often incompatible, views.

6. See also Richard Bronk's (2009) *plaidoyer* for Romantic ideas as a way out of the patent inadequacies of the sort of economic theorising that seeks to analyse human agency as based on the rational optimisation of preferences, missing out the role of fantasy, projection and other kinds of motivation in real actor's lives.

7. See Bauman (1989), who explicates ideas that are sometimes only implicit in Adorno in relation to detailed historical research on the Holocaust.

References

Adorno, Theodor W. (1961), *Ästhetik Vorlesungen*, Berlin: Adorno-Archiv, Akademie der Künste.

Adorno, Theodor W. (2001), *Zur Lehre von der Geschichte und von der Freiheit*, Frankfurt: Suhrkamp.

Bauman, Zygmunt (1989), *Modernity and the Holocaust*, Cambridge: Polity.

Bolzano, Bernard (1963), *Grundlegung der Logik*, Hamburg: Meiner.

Bowie, Andrew (1993), *Schelling and Modern European Philosophy*, London: Routledge.

Bowie, Andrew (1996), 'John McDowell's *Mind and World*, and early romantic epistemology', *Revue internationale de philosophie* 197: 515–54.

Bowie, Andrew (1997), *From Romanticism to Critical Theory: The Philosophy of German Literary Theory*, London: Routledge.

Bowie, Andrew (2000), 'The Romantic Connection: Neurath, the Frankfurt School and Heidegger', *British Journal for the History of Philosophy* 8 (2): 275–98.

Bronk, Richard (2009), *The Romantic Economist*, Cambridge: Cambridge University Press.

Dummett, Michael (1986), ' "A nice derangement of epitaphs": Some comments on Davidson and Hacking', in Ernest LePore (ed.), *Truth and Interpretation: Perspectives on the Philosophy of Donald Davidson*, Oxford: Blackwell, pp. 459–76.

Friedman, Michael (1999), *Reconsidering Logical Positivism*, Cambridge: Cambridge University Press.

Gadamer, Hans-Georg (1993), *Ästhetik und Poetik I. Kunst als Aussage*, Tübingen: Mohr.

Glock, Hans-Johann (2008), *What Is Analytic Philosophy?*, Cambridge: Cambridge University Press.

Habermas, Jürgen (1988), *Nachmetaphysisches Denken*, Frankfurt: Suhrkamp.

Hammer, Espen (ed.) (2007), *German Idealism: Contemporary Perspectives*, London: Routledge.

Hylton, Peter (1992), *Russell, Idealism, and the Emergence of Analytic Philosophy*, Oxford: Clarendon Press.

Jacobi, Friedrich Henrich (1916), 'Über die Lehre des Spinoza, in Briefen an Herrn Moses Mendelssohn', in Heinrich Scholz (ed.), *Die Hauptschriften zum Pantheismusstreit zwischen Jacobi und Mendelssohn*, Berlin: Reuther und Reichard, pp. 45–282.

Kant, Immanuel [1781/1787] (1968), *Kritik der reinen Vernunft*, Frankfurt: Suhrkamp.

McDowell, John (1994), *Mind and World*, Cambridge, MA: Harvard University Press.

McDowell, John (1998), *Meaning, Value and Reality*, Cambridge, MA: Harvard University Press.

Novalis (Friedrich von Hardenberg) (1978), *Das philosophisch-theoretische Werk*, Novalis Schriften vol. 2, ed. Hans-Joachim Mähl, Munich: Hanser.

Pinkard, Terry (1996), *Hegel's Phenomenology: The Sociality of Reason*, Cambridge: Cambridge University Press.

Pippin, Robert (1989), *Hegel's Idealism: The Satisfactions of Self-Consciousness*, Cambridge: Cambridge University Press.

Pippin, Robert (1997), *Idealism as Modernism: Hegelian Variations*, Cambridge: Cambridge University Press.

Pippin, Robert (2005), *The Persistence of Subjectivity: On the Kantian Aftermath*, Cambridge: Cambridge University Press.

Rorty, Richard (2007), *Philosophy as Cultural Politics. Philosophical Papers Vol. 4*, Cambridge: Cambridge University Press.

Schelling, Friedrich Wilhelm Joseph von (1856–61), *Sämmtliche Werke,* ed. Karl Friedrich August Schelling, 14 vols, Stuttgart: Cotta.

Schlegel, Friedrich (1988) *Kritische Schriften und Fragmente* vol. 5, Paderborn: Schöningh.

Schleiermacher, Friedrich Daniel Ernst (1839), *Dialektik,* ed. L. Jonas, Berlin: Reimer.

Schleiermacher, Friedrich Daniel Ernst (1942), *Friedrich Schleiermachers Dialektik,* ed. Rudolf Odebrecht, Leipzig.

Schleiermacher, Friedrich Daniel Ernst (1998), *Hermeneutics and Criticism,* ed. and trans. Andrew Bowie, Cambridge: Cambridge University Press.

Schnädelbach, Herbert (1987), *Vernunft und Geschichte,* Frankfurt: Suhrkamp.

Scholz, Heinrich (ed.) (1916), *Die Hauptschriften zum Pantheismusstreit zwischen Jacobi und Mendelssohn,* Berlin: Reuther und Reichard.

Schulz, Walter (ed.) (1968), *Fichte-Schelling Briefwechsel,* Frankfurt: Suhrkamp.

Wheeler, Samuel C., III (2000), *Deconstruction as Analytic Philosophy,* Stanford, CA: Stanford University Press.

Williamson, Timothy (2007), *The Philosophy of Philosophy,* Oxford: Blackwell.

Notes on contributors

Paul Blackledge is Reader in Political Theory at Leeds Metropolitan University. He is the author of *Marxism and Ethics* (SUNY Press, 2011), *Reflections on the Marxist Theory of History* (Manchester University Press, 2006) and *Perry Anderson, Marxism and the New Left* (Merlin Press, 2004). He has co-edited *Virtue and Politics* (University of Notre Dame Press), *Alasdair MacIntyre's Engagement with Marxism* (Brill, 2008), *Revolutionary Aristotelianism* (Lucius & Lucius, 2008) and *Historical Materialism and Social Evolution* (Palgrave, 2002).

Andrew Bowie is Professor of Philosophy and German at Royal Holloway, University of London. He has published very widely on modern philosophy, music and literature, and is a jazz saxophonist. His books include *Aesthetics and Subjectivity: From Kant to Nietzsche* (Routledge, 1990; 2nd edn 2003); *Schelling and Modern European Philosophy* (Routledge, 1993); *From Romanticism to Critical Theory: The Philosophy of German Literary Theory* (Routledge, 1996); *Introduction to German Philosophy: From Kant to Habermas* (Polity, 2003); *Music, Philosophy, and Modernity* (Cambridge University Press, 2007); and *German Philosophy: A Very Short Introduction* (Oxford University Press, 2010). He has translated works by Schelling and Schleiermacher.

Clare Carlisle is Lecturer in Philosophy at the University of Liverpool. She is the author of *Kierkegaard's Philosophy of Becoming* (SUNY Press, 2005), *Kierkegaard: A Guide for the Perplexed* (Continuum, 2006) and *Kierkegaard's Fear and Trembling: A Reader's Guide* (Continuum, 2010).

James Connelly is Professor of Politics at the University of Hull. He is the author of *Metaphysics, Method and Politics: The Political Philosophy of R. G. Collingwood* (Imprint Academic, 2003). He has published extensively on the philosophy of Collingwood, the British idealists and the philosophy of history. He also writes and researches in environmental politics and applied ethics.

Sebastian Gardner is Professor of Philosophy at University College London. His research interests lie in Kant and post-Kantian philosophy, especially German idealism. His publications include the *Routledge Philosophy GuideBook to Kant and the* Critique of Pure Reason (Routledge, 1999) and *Irrationality and the Philosophy of Psychoanalysis* (Cambridge University Press, 1993).

Michael Allen Gillespie is Professor of Political Science and Philosophy at Duke University. He works in political philosophy, with particular emphasis on modern continental theory. He is the author of *Hegel, Heidegger and the Ground of History*

(University of Chicago Press, 1984), *Nihilism before Nietzsche* (University of Chicago Press, 1995) and *The Theological Origins of Modernity* (University of Chicago Press, 2008). He is also co-editor of *Nietzsche's New Seas: Explorations in Philosophy, Aesthetics, and Politics* (University of Chicago Press, 1988) and *Ratifying the Constitution* (University Press of Kansas, 1992).

George di Giovanni is Professor of Philosophy at McGill University, Montréal, specializing in late Enlightenment studies and German idealism. His previous publications include *Friedrich Heinrich Jacobi: The Main Philosophical Writings and the Novel* Allwill (McGill-Queen's University Press, 1994; pbk edn, 2009), *Freedom and Religion in Kant and His Immediate Successors: The Vocation of Humankind, 1774–1800* (Cambridge University Press, 2005) and *Between Kant and Hegel: Texts in the Development of Post-Kantian Idealism* (rev. edn, Hackett, 2000).

Günter Gödde is a practising psychotherapist, a lecturer at the Berliner Akademie für Psychotherapie and a scholar who works on the history and theory of psychoanalysis. He is the author of numerous publications on the history and theory of psychoanalysis, including *Traditionslinien des Unbewußten: Schopenhauer, Nietzsche, Freud* (2nd edn, Psychosozial, 2010) and *Mathilde Freud* (2nd edn, Aufbau, 2005). He is also co-editor of a three-volume history of the concept of the unconscious and related discourses, *Das Unbewusste vols I–III* (Psychosozial, 2005–6).

Robert Guay is Associate Professor of Philosophy at Binghamton University, State University of New York. He is currently working on contributions to *Key Concepts: Nietzsche* (Acumen, forthcoming) and on a book on Nietzsche's ethical thought.

Philippe Huneman is a philosopher of science at the Institut d'Histoire et de Philosophie des Sciences et des Techniques (CNRS/Université Paris I Sorbonne). Trained in mathematics and philosophy, he has published on Kantian metaphysics and modern biology. He is author of *Métaphysique et biologie: Kant et la constitution du concept d'organisme* (Kimé, 2008) and edited *Understanding Purpose: Essays on Kant and the Philosophy of Biology* (University of Rochester Press, 2007). He also works on philosophical issues in evolutionary biology.

Gregory Moore is Lecturer in the School of Modern Languages at the University of St Andrews. He is the author of *Nietzsche, Biology and Metaphor* (Cambridge University Press, 2002) and has translated works by Herder and Fichte.

Dalia T. Nassar is Assistant Professor of Philosophy at Villanova University. She has written articles on Romanticism and idealism, most recently 'Interpreting Novalis' *Fichte-Studien*', in *Deutsche Vierteljahrsschrift*, and 'From a philosophy of self to a philosophy of nature: Goethe and the development of Schelling's *Naturphilosophie*', in *Archiv für Geschichte der Philosophie*. She is presently completing a manuscript on the metaphysics of German Romantic philosophy.

Judith Norman is Professor of Philosophy at Trinity University in San Antonio, Texas. She has published numerous articles on Schelling, Nietzsche and early German Romanticism and co-edited *The New Schelling*, a collection of contemporary readings of Schelling

(Continuum, 2004). In addition, she has translated books by Nietzsche and Schelling and is currently co-translating Schopenhauer's *The World as Will and Representation* (Cambridge University Press, forthcoming).

William Outhwaite is Professor of Sociology at Newcastle University. His recent publications include *The Future of Society* (Blackwell, 2006), *European Society* (Polity, 2008), *Habermas* (2nd expanded edn, Polity, 2009) and (with Larry Ray) *Social Theory and Postcommunism* (Blackwell, 2005). He is currently working on social and political change in Europe since 1989, supported by a Leverhulme Major Research Fellowship.

George Pattison is Lady Margaret Professor of Divinity at the University of Oxford and a Canon of Christ Church Cathedral. He has written extensively on modern theology and philosophy of religion, with particular emphasis on nineteenth- and twentieth-century existentialism. His books include *Kierkegaard, Religion and the Nineteenth-Century Crisis of Culture* (Cambridge University Press, 2002), *The Philosophy of Kierkegaard* (Acumen, 2005), the *Routledge Philosophy Guidebook to the Later Heidegger* (Routledge, 2000), *Thinking about God in an Age of Technology* (Oxford University Press, 2005) and, most recently, *God and Being: An Enquiry* (Oxford University Press, 2001).

Mark Sinclair is Senior Lecturer in Philosophy at Manchester Metropolitan University. He has published *Heidegger, Aristotle and the Work of Art* (Palgrave, 2006) and, with Clare Carlisle, a critical edition of Félix Ravaisson's *Of Habit* (Continuum, 2009). He is currently working on a book-length study of the French spiritualist tradition, entitled *Before Bergson: Phenomenology and Ontology in Nineteenth-Century French Thought*.

Alison Stone is Reader in European Philosophy at Lancaster University. Her research interests lie in Early German Romanticism, German idealism including Hegel, the Frankfurt School and feminist philosophy. Her publications include *An Introduction to Feminist Philosophy* (Polity, 2007), *Luce Irigaray and the Philosophy of Sexual Difference* (Cambridge University Press, 2006) and *Petrified Intelligence: Nature in Hegel's Philosophy* (SUNY Press, 2004).

Alistair Welchman is Assistant Professor of Philosophy at University of Texas at San Antonio. He has published numerous articles on Kant, Schelling and Deleuze and co-edited *The New Schelling*, a collection of contemporary readings of Schelling (Continuum, 2004). In addition, he has co-translated Maimon's *Essay on Transcendental Philosophy* (Continuum, 2010) and is currently co-translating Schopenhauer's *The World as Will and Representation* (Cambridge University Press, forthcoming).

Alex Zakaras is Assistant Professor of Political Science at the University of Vermont. His first book was *Individuality and Mass Democracy: Mill, Emerson, and the Burdens of Citizenship* (Oxford University Press, 2009). He is co-editor of *J. S. Mill's Political Thought: A Bicentennial Reassessment* (Cambridge University Press, 2007).

Index

a priori, 70, 71, 72, 97
Abrams, M. H., *Natural Supernaturalism*, 50, 51, 52, 53
Abramsky, Chimon, 270
Absolute, the, 6, 26, 34–6, 92, 100, 130
  and difference or indifference, 37–9, 41–2
  Fichte's, 30, 33–4
  in German idealism and Romanticism, 29–46
  Hegel and, 29, 30, 39–42, 264
  Kant on, 34–5
  knowing the, 30, 31–4, 42–5, 147
  relation with the world, 35–42
  in Schelling, 29, 30, 36–9, 64
  time and, 162
  use of term, 29, 45
absolutism, 224, 226, 229, 270
abstraction, and explanation, 16–17
adaptation, 72, 114, 118, 119, 120, 197–8
Adler, Alfred, *The Neurotic Character*, 217
Adorno, Theodor, 175, 183, 250, 316, 322, 324–6
aestheticism, 25, 291
aesthetics, 105, 224, 239, 281, 319
  and language, 321
Agassiz, Louis, 117
agnosticism, 113, 140
Albee, Ernest, 101
Albert, Hans, 315
Alexander II, Czar, 289
Alexander, Samuel, *Moral Order and Progress*, 122–3
alienation, 51, 52, 62, 65, 178–9, 232–4, 281–2
Althusser, Louis, 246
altruism, 121–2, 124–5
American Revolution, 259, 261
analytic/synthetic division, 11, 320
analytical philosophy, 11, 108, 318, 320–2
  and European philosophy, 315–27
  as philosophy of science, 321–2
  rationalist assumption, 320
analytical psychology, 217–18, 220
anarchism, 10, 223, 239, 259, 262, 263, 268, 268–72, 286
  and social democracy, 268–73
anarcho-syndicalism, 271
anatomy, 192
  comparative, 72, 79, 82, 111
ancients and moderns, 48–9, 51–2

animals, and human intelligence gap, 116–17
animism, 196
Anschauung see intuition
anthropology, 27, 95, 106, 139, 205
  medical, 207–8
  philosophical, 250, 298, 302
anti-capitalist movement, 274
anti-Semitism, 253
apperception
  immediate, in Biran, 189–93
  transcendental unity of, 55–6
archetypes, 218
Arendt, Dieter, 281
argument, and interpretation, 317, 319–20
Argument from Design, 112
Aristotelianism, 92, 135, 181, 224, 295
Aristotle, 301
  on *kinesis*, 295, 296–7, 298, 299–300, 303
  Metaphysics, 193
Arnim, Achim von, 49
art
  and philosophy, 60, 314–15, 321
  redemption through, 212–13
  and science, 319–20
  unity of self and nature in, 24–6, 36–9
artist
  as individual, 224, 235
  social role for, 62, 64
  as transcendental ego, 55–7
asceticism, 170–1, 172, 182, 213
atheism, 2, 15, 23, 26, 128, 137, 279, 280, 284–5, 292
Atheism Controversy, 279–80
Athenäum, 49, 58
atomism, 162, 321–2
audience, 62, 65
Aufklärung see Enlightenment, German
author
  death of the, 57–8, 61
  role of the, 63–4
authority
  challenges to, 269–70, 281–2, 327
  of criticism, 169
  democratisation of, 271–2
  the nature of, 264–5
authorship, 57–60
  theories of collective, 58
autonomy, 1; *see also* freedom
Avenarius, Richard, 89

Babeuf, François-Noël 'Gracchus', 247, 259–60, 261, 262, 270
  Conspiracy of Equals, 261
Bacon, Francis, 279
Badiou, Alain, 274
Bakunin, Jack, 233
Bakunin, Mikhail, 10, 96, 260, 262, 268, 270–2, 273, 274, 286, 287–8, 289, 290
  'Appeal to the Slavs', 288
Balint, Michael, 218
Bauer, Bruno, 284
Baur, Ferdinand Christian, 146, 156
becoming, 16, 36, 39–42, 44, 124, 136–7, 295–6, 299, 303–9
Begriff see concept
Being, 93, 137, 194–5, 298, 318
Beiser, Frederick, 226, 229
Benjamin, Jessica, 219
Benjamin, Walter, 322
Bentham, Jeremy, 3, 236
Bercovitch, Sacvan, 224
Bergson, Henri, 8–9, 85, 106, 187–8, 196–9, 200
  Creative Evolution, 106
  Matter and Memory, 196–9
  Rapport sur la philosophie en France au XIXième siècle, 196
Bernheim, Hippolyte, 204, 219
Bernstein, Edouard, 10, 230, 262
  The Preconditions of Socialism, 259–60
Bestimmung see vocation
biblical criticism, 145, 156
Bichat, Xavier, 81
Bildung, 226
Binoche, Bertrand, 244
biology, 69, 72, 78–9, 83, 111, 115, 119
Bion, Wilfred, 218
Birchall, Ian, 261
Bismarck, Otto von, 244, 261
Bixby, J. T., *The Ethics of Evolution*, 121
Blackledge, Paul, 10, 259–77, 331
Blake, William, 'Tyger', 281
Blanc, Louis, 10, 260, 269
Blanchot, Maurice, 59, 62
Blanqui, Louis-Auguste, 259–60, 262, 266–7, 268, 270, 272, 274
Blumenbach, Johann Friedrich, 77
Blüntschli, Johann Kaspar, 243
Boccaccio, Giovanni, 50
body
  the habituated, 9, 193–6, 198
  as *le corps propre*, 187–93, 195

the lived, 9, 187–203
  and mind, 307
  and the will, 9, 190–3, 193–6
  see also mind-body dualism
body schema/image, 191
Boehme, Jacob, 52, 93
Boerhaave, Herman, 193
Bolshevism, 289
Bolzano, Bernard, 319
Bonald, Louis de, 247
Bonnet, Charles, 194
Bosanquet, Bernard, 8, 146, 154, 155, 156, 158–64
  'Atomism in History', 162
  Logic, 160–4
  The Principle of Individuality . . ., 159–60
  'Time and the Absolute', 162
Bottomore, Tom, 244
Bourdieu, Pierre, 246
bourgeois state, 10, 274
bourgeoisie, 231, 253, 264, 269
Bourget, Paul, 290
Bouterwek, Friedrich, 49
Bowie, Andrew, 11, 314–29, 331
Bowlby, John, 218
Bradley, A. C., 123
Bradley, Francis Herbert, 8, 105, 154, 155
  Appearance and Reality, 99–100, 155, 156
  Ethical Studies, 155
  The Presuppositions of Critical History, 146, 155–64
  The Principles of Logic, 155, 156
Brentano, Clemens, 49, 60, 281
Brentano, Franz, Psychology from an Empirical Standpoint, 214–15
Breuer, Josef, 204
Brücke, Ernst, 214
Brudney, Daniel, 237
Brunschwig, Henri, 63
Buchholz, Michael, 205
Büchner, Georg, 284
  Danton's Death, 285
Büchner, Ludwig, 89
Buckle, Henry Thomas, 8, 149–50
Buddhism, 278, 281, 290
Bultmann, Rudolf, 142
Buonarroti, Filippo, Conspiration pour l'égalité dite de Babeuf, 261
bureaucracy, 1, 226–7, 264, 284, 324
Burger, Thomas, 150
Burke, Edmund, 229
  Reflections on the Revolution in France, 247
Burrow, John W., 225, 249, 253
Byron, Lord, 48, 51, 56, 281, 282

Cabanis, Pierre-Jean-George, 188
Caird, Edward, 99
Callinicos, Alex, 274
Campbell, Donald T., 119
Camus, Albert, 278
capitalism, 177, 179, 235, 237, 259, 261–2, 265–8, 268–72, 273–4, 326
Caputo, John D., 142
Carlisle, Clare, 10–11, 294–313, 331
Carneri, Bartholomäus von, Sittlichkeit und Darwinismus, 122
Carus, Carl Gustav, 219
  Psyche, 208–9, 211

Cassirer, Ernst, 101
categorical imperatives, 139
Catholicism, 135, 224, 231–2
causality, 77, 97, 118, 181, 306, 322–3
  chain of, 44, 59
  efficient before final, 20–1, 23
  in history, 177–9, 180
  Hume on, 189–93
  and succession, 190
Cavell, Stanley, 84
cell theory, 79
'cell-soul', 117
Cervantes, Miguel de, 49
Channing, William Ellery, 'Self-Culture', 238
Charcot, Jean-Martin, 204, 219
Chateaubriand, René, 63
chemistry, 78, 83
Chernyshevsky, Nikolai, 286, 287, 289, 290
  What is to be done?, 287
Christianity, 3, 98, 172
  and Darwinism, 7, 114, 124
  epistemic status of claims, 7–8
  erosion of authority, 89, 93
  Kierkegaard and, 296, 298, 300–3
  and knowledge, 128–44
  limits on freedom, 301–2
  and metaphysics, 16
  Nietzsche on, 181–2, 290–1, 303
  and nihilism, 279, 280, 284–5
  and Romanticism, 50
Christology, 138, 145, 156
civil society, 227–8, 236, 246, 263–6
class inequality, 10, 231, 265–8, 273–4
cognition, 104, 108, 210, 323–4
  coherentist problem, 323
  scientific, 175
cognitive psychology, 207, 219–20
Cohen, Hermann, 101
Coleridge, Samuel Taylor, 54, 55, 56, 57, 58, 84
  Biographia Literaria, 2, 50
  'Rhyme of the Ancient Mariner', 281
collectivism, 271
Collingwood, R.G., 155, 160–1, 163
  The Idea of History, 156, 157–8, 159
Collini, Stefan, 249, 250
Collins, Henry, 270
Collins, Randall, 245
communication, 320–1
communism, 251, 259, 265, 269, 271, 274
community, ideal, 226–9, 265–6
Comte, Auguste, 3, 8, 85, 89, 95, 149, 154, 237, 244, 246, 250, 253
concept (Begriff), 41, 42–3, 71, 75–6, 78, 131, 136, 176
concept formation, 320
concrete universals theory (Bosanquet), 8, 159–64
Condillac, Etienne Bonnot de, 188, 192
Condorcet, Nicolas de, 243, 247, 248
  Tableau historique des progrès de l'esprit humain, 244
conformity, 9, 236, 239
Connelly, James, 8, 145–67, 331
Conrad, Joseph, 291
consciousness
  continuum of, 195–6, 199

Hartmann on, 210–11
  socialist, 266
  threshold of, 206
  and the unconscious, 205, 208–9, 212–13, 214–18, 219
  and the will, 189–91
consequentialism, 321
conservatism, 228, 244, 246, 247
Conspiracy of Equals, 261
Constable, John, 60
'constellations' of issues, 322
Contemporary, the, 286
Copernicus, Nicolaus, 112
Copleston, Frederick, 245
corporeality, cognitive, 200
corps propre, le see body
'Cosmism', 114
cosmology, and Darwinism, 112–16
cosmopolitanism, 168–9, 171–2, 173–5, 177, 180
Cournot, Antoine, 85
Cousin, Victor, 245
Cramer, Heinrich Matthias August, Dictionary, 280
creativity, 55, 58, 61, 115, 207, 290–1
Creuzer, Friedrich, 49
criticism, 22, 169; see also literary criticism
critique, 172, 174–5, 177
  genealogy as immanent, 168–86
  revolutionary ends of, 179
Croce, Benedetto, 146, 148, 151, 163
  The Philosophy of Giambattista Vico, 158
cultural politics, philosophy as, 326–7
culture, 2, 4, 64–5, 119, 152, 216, 236, 238, 248
  crisis of European, 289–92, 311
Cupitt, Don, 142
Cuvier, Baron Georges, 72
cytology, 117
Czolbe, Heinrich, 89

Dante Alighieri, 48
Darwin, Charles, 103
  The Descent of Man, 120
  The Origin of Species, 3, 89, 111–12, 113, 114, 117
  theory of evolution, 3, 7, 79, 211, 212
Darwinism, 3, 7, 79–80, 83, 85, 100, 173
  and 19th-century philosophy, 111–27
  and ethics, 119–24
Daub, Karl, 131
Davidson, Donald Herbert, 320
de la Mettrie, Julien Offray, 95
De Man, Paul, 54, 58, 61
Debray, Régis, 249
deconstruction, 61–2
Deleuze, Gilles, Difference and Repetition, 294, 310
democracy, 228–9, 232–3, 238, 249
  constitutional, 238
  from above, 261
  participatory, 235–6, 239–40
  social, 268–73
Dennett, Daniel C., 112
deontology, 321
depth psychology, 219–20
Derrida, Jacques, 142, 193, 318, 320

Descartes, René, 22, 30, 69, 128, 188, 208, 214, 279
  cogito, 56, 316, 318
  Discours de la méthode, 205
  mind-body dualism, 187, 189, 197, 205, 316–17
despair, 295, 309
despotism, 235
Destutt de Tracy, Antoine, 188
determinism, 2, 3, 4, 16, 17
  free will issue, 11, 325, 327
  and freedom, 11, 19, 305–8, 311
  Spinoza's type of, 17–18, 323
Dewey, John, 106, 111
d'Holbach, Baron, 95, 103
di Giovanni, George, 5–6, 13–28, 332
dialectics, 245, 263, 299
  Marx's materialist, 177–9, 246
  Schleiermacher's, 319, 320
dictatorship
  of the proletariat, 262–3, 271–2, 274
  'revolutionary', 262, 267, 274
Diderot, Denis, Rêve d'Alembert, 78
difference
  and identity, 40–1
  or indifference and the Absolute, 37–9, 41–2
  quantitative, 38
Dilthey, Wilhelm, 84, 106, 145, 150, 151–2, 154, 251, 252, 253
disciplinary boundaries, 5, 132, 149, 152–5, 315
division of labour, 178–9, 230
Dobrolyubov, Nikolai, 286
dogmatism, 91, 136, 137, 315
  or dogmaticism, 134
Dostoevsky, Fyodor, 10, 288–9, 290
  Crime and Punishment, 288
  Demons, 288
  The Brothers Karamazov, 288
doubt, 133, 134
Draper, Hal, 268, 271, 272
dreams, Freudian intepretation, 204, 213–14
drives, instinctual, 9, 210, 212, 216–18, 218
Droysen, Johann Gustav, 150, 251–2
dualisms
  Bergson, 196–9
  Cartesian, 187, 189, 205, 316–17
  Kantian, 2, 29, 30–3, 34, 103
Dühring, Eugen, 96
Dummett, Michael, 318–19
Dunn, John, 259
Duns Scotus, John, 278
Durkheim, Emile, 244, 246, 253

ecological crisis, 325, 326
economics, 145, 177–9, 230, 237, 252
education
  and politics, 239–40
  religious studies in higher, 142–3
egalitarianism, 232, 238, 239
ego psychology, 218
ego, the, 216–17, 218–19
  relations with the unconscious, 209
egoism, 209, 223–4, 224, 232, 279, 285
  and altruism, 121–2, 124–5
  of civil society, 264–5
Eichhorn, Johann Gottfried, 252
Eigentümlichkeit see individuality

Elias, Norbert, 242
elitism, 266, 272
Ellenberger, Henry, The Discovery of the Unconscious, 204
Ellul, Jacques, 279
embodiment, 5, 8–9, 187–203, 199
embryology, 72, 74, 79
Emerson, Ralph Waldo, 2, 84, 223, 238, 239, 240
  'Self-Reliance', 238
empirical sciences, 1, 2, 3, 78, 153–4
empiricism, 1, 70, 90, 102, 145, 148, 154, 322
  assumptions, 315
  Hegel's critique of, 11, 315, 322
  historical, 149–50
Encyclopédie Nouvelle, 230
Engels, Friedrich, 128, 243, 246, 250, 259, 263, 265, 266, 268, 271, 272–3, 274
  On Authority, 262–3
  The Communist Manifesto, 251
England, 225, 250
  political economy, 231
  revolution, 259, 261
  Romantics, 6, 48, 50–1, 54, 56, 62
Enlightenment, 1, 2, 3, 5, 71, 78, 89, 108, 129, 135, 173, 177, 223, 247, 251, 279, 281
  German, 13–27
  'radical', 13–14, 27
  and Romanticism, 52, 55, 58
  Scottish, 244
  and the unconscious, 205–7, 219
entomology, 84
epistemology, 2, 5, 30, 69, 93, 102, 103, 104–5, 211, 319, 321, 322
evolutionary and mind, 116–19
equality, 1, 2, 9, 180, 232, 242–3, 247; see also inequality
Erdmann, Johann Eduard, 8, 128–9, 137, 139, 140, 142
  Faith and Knowledge, 128–9, 131, 132–7
  History of Philosophy, 132
Erklärung see explanation
Eros, 216
Eschenmayer, Karl August, 92
essence, 38, 40–1, 71
eternal return see recurrence, eternal
ethics, 98
  Aristotelian, 224
  critics of evolutionary, 123–5
  and evolution, 119–23
  and historicism, 148
  and individuality, 224, 301
  and language, 321
  and morality, 122
European philosophy, and analytical philosophy, 315–27
event, 11, 17, 162–3, 179
evil, 209, 282
evolution, 1, 112
  Darwinian theory of, 3, 7, 79–80, 83, 111–27, 212
  and ethics, 119–23
  God and cosmic, 112–16
  moral, 120–1, 122–3
  Spencer on, 7, 85, 112–14, 120
  use of term, 113
existence
  the concept of, 140–1
  and essence, 38, 40–1

and explanation, 18, 19
and individuation, 17
Kant on, 19–20
as meaningless, 279
natural and spiritual, 24
the primacy of, 18–21, 25–6
existentialism, 3, 8, 11, 21, 94, 140–1, 142, 278, 291, 295–303, 310
experimental psychology, 103, 117
experimentation, 43
explanation, 77–8
  and abstraction, 16–17
  empirical, 92, 149, 322–3
  'English' mode of historical, 121–2
  as Erklärung, 8, 145, 150–2
  and existence, 17, 19
  mechanistic, 97–8
  metaphysical limits of scientific, 99–100
expressivism, 224, 321

Fairbairn, W. R. D., 218
fairy tales, 60, 61
faith
  and doctrine, 133–4
  and knowledge, 7–8, 128–44
  leap of, 299–303
  and metaphysics, 1
  and political power, 13
  reflective, 133–4
Fascism, 291
fatalism, 16, 17–18, 21, 22, 307
Fechner, Gustav Theodor, 3, 92, 117, 206–7, 215, 219
  Elemente der Psychophysik, 206–7
Feder, Georg Heinrich, 33
feeling, cult of, 15, 51, 54–5, 78
Ferenczi, Sándor, 218
Ferguson, Adam, Essay on the History of Civil Society, 245
Feuerbach, Ludwig, 7, 83, 139–40, 142, 263, 264, 265, 266, 284, 285, 286, 287, 290
  Principles of the Philosophy of the Future, 139
  The Essence of Christianity, 139
  Thoughts on Death and Immortality, 93
Fichte, Johann Gottlieb, 1, 6, 10, 13, 15, 18, 27, 56, 64, 89, 105, 117, 128, 130, 154, 189, 245, 247, 250, 279–80, 281, 286
  compared with Schelling, 25, 37, 39, 325
  on idealism and dogmatism, 91, 136, 279, 316
  on intellectual intuition, 33–4, 42, 43, 55, 57
  and the ontological Absolute, 30, 33–4, 282, 291, 323
  theory of self-consciousness, 34, 42
  Vocation of Man, 21–4
  Wissenschaftslehre, 23–4, 25, 26, 48
First International, 270, 271
first person, 3, 190–3, 196
Fiske, John, 114
  Outlines of Cosmic Philosophy, 114
Fliess, Wilhelm, 214, 215
Flint, Robert, 158
folksongs, German, 49, 58
Foster, Michael, 163–4
Foucault, Michel, 183
  Les mots et les choses (The Order of Things), 58–9, 248

Fourier, Charles, 248
France, 225, 243, 253
    Constitution (1793), 262
    Ideological school, 188, 192, 193, 247, 248
    July Monarchy, 231
    National Assembly draft constitution (1848), 233
    philosophy, 187–203
    Revolution (1848), 284, 285
    Romanticism, 48, 57, 230
    spiritualist tradition, 5, 8, 187–203
    Universal Declaration of Human Rights, 247
    see also French Revolution (1789)
Frank, Manfred, 56
Frankfurt School, 217
Franz Ferdinand of Austria, Archduke, 291
freedom, 1, 2, 5, 8, 22, 271–2
    of choice, 234–5, 298–303
    in civil society, 263–6
    and communism, 269
    'comparative', 19
    of conscience, 233
    cosmopolitan, 174–5
    and determinism, 11, 325, 327
    historicised, 181
    and individuality, 223, 224, 230, 297, 300
    Kant on, 19, 23, 31, 327
    and morality, 122
    and nature, 23–4, 31, 90–2, 107, 325
    and necessity, 305–8, 311
    or negation, 283–4
    possibility of, 33–4
    power of radical, 286–7, 289–92, 299
    Reinhold-Schmid debate, 18–19, 21
    and repetition, 295–303
    and the subject, 10
    of the will, 194, 306, 325, 327
Frege, Gottlob, 319, 321, 322
French Revolution (1789), 1, 5, 6, 10, 134, 223–4, 228–9, 231–2, 243–4, 259, 261–2, 264, 267, 279
    reactions to, 247–8
    and Romanticism, 48, 51, 52, 53, 62, 63–5, 230
Freud, Anna, 218
Freud, Sigmund, 5, 9, 57, 95, 209
    'Beyond the Pleasure Principle', 216
    clinical theory, 215, 219
    comparison with Nietzsche, 213
    Entwurf einer Psychologie, 214
    'Group Psychology and the Analysis of the Ego', 218
    philosophy of the unconscious, 204, 210, 211, 213–18
    structural theory, 216–19
    Studies in Hysteria, 204
    'The Ego and the Id', 204, 216–17, 218–19
    The Interpretation of Dreams, 204, 214–15
    'The Unconscious', 216
Fries, Jakob Friedrich, 19, 26, 75, 102, 103

Gadamer, Hans-Georg, 253, 314, 316
Galileo Galilei, 69, 279

galvanism, 78, 92
Gardner, Sebastian, 4, 7, 89–110, 331
Garve, Christian, 33
Gasser, Reinhard, Nietzsche und Freud, 204
Gauthier of St-Victor, 280
Gehlen, Arnold, 106
Geist see spirit
Geisteswissenschaften, 149, 151, 178
gender, 82–3, 85
    difference, 180
genealogy, 8, 168–86
    key features of method, 8, 168–9
    Nietzschean, 169–73
    post-history of, 182–4
    prehistory of, 173–5
genetics, 119
Genius, the, 25, 54, 55, 57
Gentile, Giovanni, 163
geometrical method, Spinoza's, 37, 44
Germany, 63–4, 243, 251, 253
    Bismarckian, 244, 261
    Early Romanticism, 5, 6, 10, 24, 323
    Enlightenment, 13–27
    idealism, 1–2, 5–6, 7, 10, 15, 18, 29–46, 145, 316, 320–1, 322
    idealism and naturalism in, 90–2
    materialism, 3
    modern philosophy, 322
    neo-Kantianism, 89, 101–3
    nihilism in, 284–5, 289–91
    Romanticism, 2, 6, 29–46, 48, 56–7, 281, 322
    Social Democratic Party (SPD), 260: Erfurt Programme, 263, 273; Gotha Programme, 272–3
    the unconscious in philosophy and psychology, 204–22
Geschlecht see gender
Gesellschaft, 243
Giddens, Anthony, 247
Gillespie, Michael, 10, 278–93, 331–2
Gleim, W.L., 15
God
    and cosmic evolution, 112–16
    death of, 4, 130–1, 285, 289–91, 291, 292
    as endless nothing, 281
    existence of, 70, 71, 93, 112, 130–1, 136–7, 139, 264, 280, 287–8
    gift of, 11
    love of, 116, 133
    personality of, 132
Gödde, Günter, 9, 204–22, 332
Goethe, Johann Wolfgang von, 14, 23, 25, 63, 64, 69, 92, 224, 282
    Götter, Helden und Wieland, 15
    Conversations with Eckermann, 47
    Das Unglück der Jacobis, 15
    Faust, 284
    and Jacobi, 14, 15, 17–18, 19, 21
    morphology, 72, 73, 79
    Prometheus, 14, 15–16
    on the unconscious, 207
    Wilhelm Meister, 58, 59
Goetzius, F. L., De nonismo et nihilismo in theologia, 279
Gorky, Maxim, 291
Görres, Josef, 49
government
    limited, 227–8, 236
    representative, 235–6

revolutionary, 259–61
    and society, 243
Gramsci, Antonio, 273–4
Green, Joseph Henry, 79
Green, Thomas Hill, 99, 154–5, 156, 158
    Prolegomena to Ethics, 123
Gregory VII, Pope, 231
Grimm, Jacob and Wilhelm, 49
Groddeck, Georg, 218
Guay, Robert, 8, 168–86, 332
guilt, 170, 213
Gusdorf, Georges, 247, 248
Gutzkow, Karl, 287
    The Nihilists, 285
Guyau, Jean-Marie, Esquisse d'une morale sans obligation ni sanction, 121

Habermas, Jürgen, 245, 246, 318, 324
habit, 9, 115, 120, 122, 187, 188–93
    acquisition of, 197, 199–200
    and the body, 193–6, 197
    neurological hypotheses, 194
Haeckel, Ernst, 83, 89, 92, 112, 117, 120
    Die Welträtsel, 112
Hamann, J.G., 207, 320
Hamilton, William, 154
happiness, 21, 22, 95, 120, 236, 237, 260, 301
Hardenberg, Friedrich von see Novalis
Hardt, Michael, 274
harm principle, 227–8, 235–6
Hartmann, Eduard von, 9, 96–7, 99, 104, 219
    Philosophy of the Unconscious, 96–7, 209, 210–11
Hartmann, Heinz, 218
Hazard, Paul, 13
Hazlitt, William, 64
Hegel, Georg Wilhelm Friedrich, 1, 8, 18, 24, 52, 245, 250, 301, 316
    and the Absolute, 29, 30, 39–42, 264, 323
    critique of empiricism, 11, 315, 322
    critique of Schelling, 30, 35, 40–1, 43–4
    on dangers of nihilism, 10, 282–4
    Elements of the Philosophy of Right, 244, 246
    Faith and Knowledge, 7, 128, 129–30, 282–3
    on history, 2, 8, 10, 26–7, 64, 145, 146–9, 154, 155, 179, 181, 252, 264, 291–2, 310, 317
    on Jacobinism, 260, 263–4, 265
    Lectures on Fine Art, 50, 55–6
    legacy of, 89, 93–4, 96–7, 99, 117, 210, 310
    Logic, 41, 91
    Phenomenology of Spirit, 30, 35, 37, 40–1, 75–6, 106, 155, 175–7, 252, 283, 316–17, 322
    Philosophy of History, 176
    and philosophy of nature, 69, 73, 74, 76, 77, 78, 80, 81–3, 85, 91
    philosophy of science, 75–6
    and Romanticism, 55–7
    Science of Logic, 76
    on the social, 245–6

'The Difference Between Fichte's and Schelling's System of Philosophy', 39
Hegelianism, 83, 128, 132–3, 140, 141, 259, 294, 311
  Danish, 131, 295, 299–300
  and the historical model of human nature, 263–8
  rejection of, 137–41, 142, 284, 298, 321, 324
  revival of, 322–4, 326–7
  see also Left Hegelianism; neo-Hegelianism; Right Hegelianism; Young Hegelians
Heiberg, Johan Ludvig, 131, 295, 298
Heidegger, Martin, 278, 279, 304, 306–7, 314, 316, 318, 323, 325
Heine, Heinrich, 50, 284, 285
  English Fragments, 52
Helmholtz, Hermann von, 104, 118, 207, 214
Henrich, Dieter, 322
Henry, Michel, 192, 195, 199
Heraclitus, 303
Herbart, Johann Friedrich, 9, 205–6, 214–15, 219
Herder, Johann Gottfried, 58, 69, 73, 92, 207, 224, 225, 242
hermeneutics, 6, 11, 59, 108, 138, 319, 320
  in philosophy of nature, 69–88
  problems of, 317, 326
  theological, 252
heroic/demonic man, 18, 281–2, 283–4, 291–2
Herz, Marcus, 31
Herzen, Alexander, 230, 286, 290
Hildebrand, Bruno, 252
historical agency, 168, 170–1, 173–5, 177, 180
historical method, 5, 8, 171
historical turn, 2, 4, 8, 135
historical-hermeneutic, 169, 176–7, 179
historicism, 11, 145, 147–8, 246, 248, 251–3, 252–3, 310
history, 1, 2, 4, 5, 8, 327
  critical, 155–64
  as a dialectical process, 146–7
  as a discipline, 145–67
  empiricism and positivism, 149–50
  evidence or testimony, 146, 148, 156–7
  as free actions of individuals, 286–7
  Hegel on, 2, 8, 10, 26–7, 64, 137, 145, 146–9, 154, 155, 179, 181, 252, 264, 291–2, 310
  Marxist theory of, 3, 93, 177–9, 252
  Nietzsche on, 171, 179, 306, 310–11
  philosophising, 145–67
  sources, 146, 148
  transitional/critical age, 231
  see also Methodenstreit; philosophy of history
history of ideas, and philosophy, 315–16
history of philosophy, 11, 210, 314–29
history of religion, 137
Hobbes, Thomas, 264, 279
Hölderlin, Friedrich, 24
  Hyperion, 53, 281
holism, 98, 100, 159, 321–2

homoeroticism, 291
hope, 175
Horkheimer, Max, 217
Hufeland, Christoph Wilhelm, 208
Hughes, Stuart, 253
Hugo, Gustav von, 252
human agency, and responsibility, 17
human nature
  aesthetic vision of, 25
  dangerous instinctual, 209
  heroic/demonic, 18, 281–2, 283–4, 291–2
  the historical model of, 263–8, 271–2, 274
  linguistic, 326
  optimistic view of, 228–9
  pessimistic view of, 236–8, 239
  superhuman, 289–91
  theory of rational self-interest, 286–7
  unity of, 252
human rights, 247, 253
humanism, 18, 27, 131, 140, 265, 279, 311
Humboldt, Alexander von, 92
Humboldt, Wilhelm von, 9, 59, 223, 234, 236, 237–8
  and individuality, 224, 225–9, 232, 235
  The Limits of State Action, 225–9, 246
Hume, David, 8, 91, 95, 105, 171–2, 175, 181, 183, 242, 279
  Dialogues Concerning Natural Religion, 71
  Enquiry Concerning Human Understanding, 189–93
Huneman, Philippe, 6, 69–88, 332
Husserl, Edmund, 106, 133
Huxley, Thomas Henry, 89, 113, 124

'I', and 'Thou', 17, 134–5, 140
id, the, 216–17
Idea, the, 26–7, 41, 42–3, 81–2, 94, 96–7, 130, 139, 179, 194–5, 210
ideal, and the actual, 297
idealism, 132, 139, 149, 245, 294
  absolute, 97–9, 280
  British, 2, 4, 8, 99–101, 112, 145–6, 154–5, 159
  critique of, 83, 303, 307, 310
  critique of post-Kantian as nihilism, 279–80
  German, 1–2, 5–6, 7, 10, 15, 18, 29–46, 64, 85, 94, 145, 316, 320–1, 322
  Italian, 163
  and naturalism, 3, 4, 7, 89–110
  Platonic, 297, 303, 306
  'positivist', 102–3
  reaction v., 2–3, 253
  and Romanticism, 2, 53, 55, 56, 91–2, 285
  transcendental (Kant), 21, 30–1, 90–1, 279, 282
  transcendental (Schelling), 24–6, 30, 36–9
ideas, history of, 315–16
identity, 22, 140, 176
  and genealogy, 169, 171
  the principle of, 29, 40
  thinking (Adorno), 324–6

identity philosophy (Identitätsphilosophie of Schelling), 30, 35–6, 37–44, 194–5
Idéologues, the, 188, 192, 193, 247, 248
ideology, 64–5, 179, 188, 223–4, 231, 232, 248, 269
idiographic, and nomothetic, 152–3
Iggers, Georg, 148
Illuminati, 16, 19
imagination, transcendental, 53, 55–7
immanence, 72–4, 78, 80–1, 177, 183, 299, 301, 308–9
immanent critique, genealogy as, 168–86
impressions, active and passive, 188–9, 192–3, 195
incorporation, 307, 310
individual psychology, 217
individualism, 9, 223–4
  economic, 242
  liberal, 232
  and socialism, 230–4, 265–6
individuality, 1, 2, 4, 5, 9, 25, 124–5, 148, 159–60
  the concept of, 223–5, 238–40
  freedom and, 223, 224, 230, 297, 300
  the ideal of, 232–4, 238–9
  Mill on, 234–8
  and morality, 239
  and radical politics, 223–41
  Romantic idea, 230
  Schelling on, 38–9
  and society, 26, 225, 226, 236, 242–4
  and the state, 230, 233–4, 322
individuation, 17, 124–5
industrial revolution, 1
inequality, 242, 284
  domestic and international, 243
inferences, theory of unconscious, 207
Inquisition, Spanish, 231
instinct, evolutionary theory of, 117
institutions, 171, 173, 177–9, 225, 248
instrumentalism, 111
intellect, subordinate to the will, 210–11
intellectualism, 192–3, 199
intelligence, 194
intentionality, operative, 200
International Working Men's Association see First International
interpretation, 294–5, 306
  and argument, 317, 319–20
  non-rule governed, 319
intersubjectivity, 218–19
  in language, 318–19
intuition, 30–1, 71, 106
  (Anschauung), 6, 20, 24, 25–6, 29
  indefinite awareness (Ahnung), 103
  intellectual, 33–4, 42–4, 45, 55–7, 107–8
  or reflection, 43–5
  sensible, 74
irony, 6, 49, 55–6, 60–1, 65, 173, 181–2
irrationality, 13, 21, 26, 102, 209–10, 212–13, 216–18, 253

Italy
  idealism, 163
  socialism, 273–4

Jacobi, Friedrich Heinrich, 2, 5, 10,
    20–1, 23, 27, 128, 130, 134, 281,
    282, 283, 291, 315, 323
  Concerning the Doctrine of
    Spinoza . . ., 14–15, 17, 18, 20
  David Hume on Faith or Idealism and
    Realism, 19–20
  and Goethe, 14–15, 16, 17–18, 19,
    21
  on Kant, 33
  letter to Fichte, 279–80
  and Spinozism, 14–18, 25–6, 323,
    324
Jacobi, Johann Georg, 15
Jacobinism, 259–63, 268, 274, 280,
    291
Jacyna, L. S., 78
James Sr., Henry, 116
James, William, 117–18, 119, 123
  Pragmatism, 118
  Principles of Psychology, 118
Jameson, Fredric, 248
Janet, Pierre, 204, 219
Jean Paul see Richter, Jean Paul
Jena Frühromantiker, 48, 49, 50, 55, 56,
    57, 60, 62, 280, 281–2, 291
Jenisch, Daniel, On the Ground and
    Value of the Discoveries . . ., 279
Jerusalem, Wilhelm, 215
Jewish community, 14, 16
Journal of Speculative Philosophy, 101
Jowett, Benjamin, 99
Jung, Carl Gustav, 219
  The Archetypes and the Collective
    Unconscious, 217–18

Kant, Immanuel, 1–2, 6, 7, 8, 107–8,
    128, 154, 173, 179, 206, 242,
    316, 319
  Adorno on, 326
  on analytic/synthetic judgements,
    320
  on authorship, 57
  on critical ignorance, 18, 20–1
  Critique of Judgement, 21, 29, 31–2,
    71–2, 73–4, 76–7, 80, 81, 85, 90,
    92, 94, 326
  Critique of Practical Reason, 91
  Critique of Pure Reason, 1, 14, 15,
    29–30, 54, 69, 71, 91, 175
  dualism and monism in, 29–30, 30–
    3, 34, 103
  on existence, 19–20
  on faith and knowledge, 7, 34, 129,
    130, 136
  on freedom, 19, 23
  letter to Herz (1772), 31
  Metaphysical Foundations of Natural
    Science, 69, 72, 73, 91
  Opus Postumum, 91
  and philosophy of nature, 71–2, 73–
    4, 80, 85, 175
  and Romanticism, 53–5, 56, 57
  on the social, 245–6
  Streit der Fakultäten, 244
  and the thing-in-itself, 2, 3, 18, 21,
    29–30, 31–3, 279, 323
  transcendental idealism, 21, 30–1,
    89, 90–1, 279, 318, 323

  on the Unconditioned, 34–5
  will and reason, 19
Kantianism, 53, 252
  biological, 118
  and naturalism, 102–3
  see also neo-Kantianism
Kateb, George, 238
Keats, John, 55, 56, 57, 62
Kernberg, Otto, 218
Kielmeyer, Carl Friedrich, 79
Kierkegaard, Søren, 3, 4, 8, 26, 93, 94,
    105, 131, 140–1, 142, 294–5
  compared with Nietzsche, 309–11
  Concluding Unscientific Postscript,
    140
  Either/Or, 299–300
  on Erdmann, 132
  Fear and Trembling, 295, 302–3
  Johannes Climacus, 295, 297
  The Concept of Irony, 297
  'Open Letter to Professor Heiberg',
    295–6, 298–9, 300
  Philosophical Fragments, 298, 300
  pseudonyms, 295–9, 300–1
  on repetition, 10–11, 295–303
  Repetition, 295–7, 298–9, 300–2,
    310
  The Concept of Anxiety, 295, 298
  The Sickness Unto Death, 295, 298
  kinesis, 295, 296–7, 298, 299–300, 303
Kirkman, Thomas P., 113
Klein, Melanie, 218
Klingemann, Ernst August Friedrich,
    The Night Watches of
    Bonaventura, 281
Knaben Wunderhorn, Des (Brentano
    and Arnim), 49
Knies, Karl, 252
knowledge
  and the Absolute, 30, 31–4, 40–1,
    42–5, 56, 282–4, 323
  and belief, 22
  as cognition based on reason, 135
  critical, 133, 135–6
  and dialectics, 319–20
  empirical, 133, 135, 322
  evolutionary theory of, 119
  faith and, 128–44, 282–3
  the possibility of, 45, 56
  primary and secondary, 191–2
  scientific, 84, 89, 95, 314
  speculative, 133, 136–7
  as Spirit's goal, 175–7
  structures of, 70–1
  as Wissenschaft, 149
Kohut, Heinz, 218
Kolakowski, Leszek, 244
Köppen, Friedrich, 280
Kris, Ernst, 218
Kritisches Journal der Philosophie, 129
Kropotkin, Peter, 272, 290
Kumar, Krishan, 259
Küng, Hans, 143

La Mettrie, Julien Offray de, L'Homme
    Machine, 205
Lacoue-Labarthe, Philippe, 52, 59, 65
Lamarck, Jean-Baptiste, physiology,
    122
Lamprecht, Karl, 148
Lange, Albert, 104
  History of Materialism, 102
  'Standpoint of the Ideal', 103

language, 6, 53, 62, 117, 327
  intersubjective, 318–19
  magic, 320
  mathematical, 72
  non-referential nature of, 59–61
  in philosophy, 57–60, 318–22,
    326–7
  poetic, 54, 58–9
  of religion, 128
  in Romanticism, 57–60
  the 'web' of, 320
Lassalle, Ferdinand, 246, 272
law, German, 252
law and economics, Historical Schools
    of, 251–2, 253
Lebenskraft see vital power
Lebensphilosophie, 84, 106–7, 253
Lebenswelt, 106
Left Hegelianism, 7, 10, 131, 137, 138
  and nihilism, 284–5, 286, 292
legislation, the science of, 248
Leibniz, Gottfried Wilhelm, 20, 57,
    69, 70, 91, 128, 206, 298, 301
  Monadology, 205
  New Essays on Human
    Understanding, 205
Lenin, Vladimir, 289
  The State and Revolution, 273
Lenoir, Timothy, 79
Lermontov, Mikhail Yuriyevich, 281
Leroux, Pierre, 9, 223, 228, 230–4,
    235, 237, 238
  Of Equality, 230
  Of Humanity, 230, 232
  'Of Individualism and Socialism',
    231
Lessing, Gotthold Ephraim, 14, 15,
    16, 17, 18, 20, 279
Levine, Andrew, 260–1
liberalism, 224, 229, 232, 233, 236,
    246, 247, 264–5, 272
  social, 265
libertarianism, 234, 237, 271, 274
liberty, 64, 282
  equality and fraternity, 232, 247
  and power, 270
libido, 216
Lichtenberg, Joseph D., 218
Liebig, Justus von, 79
Liebscher, Martin, 205
life, 73–4, 78–9, 80–3, 85, 113–14
  and consciousness, 195–6
  see also Lebensphilosophie; vital
    power
linguistic turns, 57–60
Linnaean school, 71, 82
Lipps, Theodor, 219
  Die Grundtatsachen des Seelenlebens,
    215
literary criticism, 57
literature
  meaninglessness in, 59–60
  Romantic, 48–9, 60–1, 65
Locke, John, 55, 268
Loewald, Hans, 219
Loewenstein, Rudolph, 218
logic, 76, 91, 115, 160–4, 177,
    299–300, 318, 320
  metaphysics and theology, 70
London, Jack, 291
Lorenz, Konrad, 119
Lotze, Rudolph Hermann, 3, 97–9,
    100, 102, 104, 105, 154

Louis XVI, 267
love
    as *agape*, 116, 307
    metaphysics of sexual, 210
Lovejoy, Arthur, 47, 48, 316
Löwy, Michael, 260
Lüdemann, Gerd, 143
Lukács, Georg, 253
Lukes, Steven, 223
Lunacharsky, Anatoly, 291
Lutheranism, 298, 302, 310
Luxemburg, Rosa, 273

McDowell, John, 11, 322–4, 325
    Mind and World, 322–3
McGann, Jerome, *The Romantic
    Ideology*, 64, 65
Mach, Ernst, 89, 103, 119
    Analysis of the Sensations, 119
    Knowledge and Error, 119
    'On Transformation and
        Adaptation in Scientific
        Thought', 119
machine, metaphor of the, 223–41
MacIntyre, Alasdair, 268
MacLeish, Archibald, *Ars Poetica*, 60
McNally, David, 269
magnetism, 78
Maimon, Salomon, 33
Maine de Biran, Pierre, 8–9, 187,
    188–93, 196, 199
    *Essai sur les fondements de la
        psychologie*, 191–3
    *Influence of Habit on the Faculty of
        Thinking*, 188
    *Mémoire sur la décomposition de la
        pensée*, 189
Maistre, Joseph de, 223, 224, 232, 247
majority, tyranny of the, 9, 233
Malebranche, Nicolas, 188
Manchester, 250
Manent, Pierre, 249
Mannheim, Karl
    Conservatism, 247
    Ideology and Utopia, 247
Mansel, Henry Longueville, 154
Marburg school, 101, 103
Marcuse, Herbert, 246
Marheineke, Philip, 131
Marinetti, F.T., 291
Marquard, Odo, *Transzendentaler
    Idealismus*, 204, 209
Marshall, Peter, 269
Martensen, Hans Lassen, 131, 298,
    299
Marx, Karl, 7, 8, 52, 65, 83, 93, 96,
    105, 129, 131, 183, 238, 239,
    243, 244, 247, 250, 253, 259,
    273, 316
    class analysis, 265–8
    'Critique of the Gotha Program',
        272
    Das Kapital, 112, 178–9, 265
    dictatorship of the proletariat,
        262–3, 274
    on Greek art, 314
    on human nature, 263–8, 271–2,
        274
    materialist dialectics, 177–9, 268
    on morality, 268
    'On the Jewish Question', 249
    on revolution, 260, 261–3, 266–8
    on the state, 10, 246, 271–2, 274

'Conspectus of Bakunin's *Statism
    and Anarchy*', 272
The Communist Manifesto, 251
The German Ideology, 64, 177–8,
    265, 266–8
theory of history, 3, 93, 140, 146,
    177–9, 181, 252, 265–8, 317, 318
on trade unions, 270
Marxism, 245, 246, 247, 249–50
    anarchism and social democracy,
        268–73, 273
    critique of, 259–60
    Hegelianism and the historical
        model of human nature, 263–8
    Russian, 289
materialism, 1, 3, 69, 78, 79, 80, 83,
    84, 89, 90, 93, 95–6, 101, 102,
    140, 211, 214, 216, 231, 232,
    263, 279, 290
    eliminative, 194
    Marx's dialectics, 177–9, 268
mathematics, 70, 92
mathesis universalis, 70–1, 77
Maxwell, James Clerk, 115
Mazzini, Giuseppe, 230
meaning
    of action, 153–4
    objectivity of, 319–20
    shared social, 154
    theory of, 319
meaninglessness, 6, 59–60, 279, 285,
    292, 318
mechanism, 3, 76–8, 97–8, 205, 214,
    223–41
    'psychological', 214–15, 218
Meckel, Johann Friedrich, 79
mediation, 33, 36, 296, 298–9, 311
    'absolute', 176, 183–4
    by philosophy, 326–7
    'infinite', 183
medical science, 97
medicine, Romantic, 9, 207–8
Medicus, Friedrich Casimir, 207–8
Meinecke, Friedrich, 147, 148
memory, 170, 196–9, 205
Mendel, Gregor Johann, 119
Mendelssohn, Moses, 14, 15, 16, 19,
    20, 21, 49, 279, 323
Mengelberg, Kaethe, 251
Menger, Carl, 252
Menninghaus, Winfried, 59
Mercier, Louis-Sébastien, 280
Mérimée, Prosper, 290
Merleau-Ponty, Maurice, 9, 187, 192,
    198, 199, 200
metaphysics, 1, 2, 4, 5, 71, 93, 105
    and Christianity, 16
    criticism by analytic philosophers,
        318, 320–1, 324
    and Darwinism, 111–27
    French, 188–93
    'inductive', 210–11
    Kantian critique of, 69, 91
    logic and theology, 70
    in motion, 294–313
    and natural history, 80
    realist, 206
    and scientific knowledge, 89–90,
        100, 102
    tradition/classical, 4, 16, 20, 27
    of the will, 76, 81, 82, 83–4, 85,
        94–6, 209–10, 212, 213, 216, 219
metapsychology, 214–18, 219

methods
    historical, 149–52, 174, 177–9
    philosophical, 314–17
    verum-factum principle, 150–1
    war of (*Methodenstreit*), 145, 148,
        252
microscope, 78
Middle Ages, 48–9, 50, 52, 65
Mill, John Stuart, 3, 4, 8, 9, 62, 83, 85,
    89, 96, 103, 112, 149, 150, 154,
    158, 244
    Chapters on Socialism, 224
    and the commitments of modernity,
        179–81
    *Considerations on Representative
        Government*, 235
    and individuality, 223, 233, 234–8,
        239
    'On Genius', 238
    On Liberty, 224, 225, 227, 234, 236,
        246
    The Subjection of Women, 179–81
    'Theism', 237
millenarianism, 285–6
mind, 55, 78, 81, 95, 118
    and the body, 307
    and evolutionary epistemology,
        116–19
    and nature, 150–1
    rational model of the, 205
    the thinking, 137
    and vital power, 208
    and world problem, 316–17, 321–4
    see also consciousness; philosophy of
        mind; unconscious, the
Mind (journal), 101
mind-body dualism, 8–9, 187, 189,
    194, 196–9, 205, 316–17
miracles, 129–30, 135, 138, 156, 157
Mitchell, Stephen, 218, 219
modernism, 6
    and Romanticism, 52
modernity, 324–6
    Mill and the commitments of, 179–81
Moleschott, Jacob, 89
monads, 205
monarchy, 228–9
monism, 14, 29, 30–3, 100, 112,
    317
Montesquieu, Charles-Louis, 243, 248
Moore, George Edward, *Principia
    Ethica*, 123
Moore, Gregory, 7, 111–27, 332
moral philosophy, Scottish, 251
morality, 103
    and competition, 237
    and Darwinism, 119–23
    and ethics, 122
    and evolution, 122–3
    happiness, 237
    and individuality, 239
    Kantian, 19, 21, 94
    Marxian, 268
    and nature, 11, 124
    Nietzschean, 4, 8, 104, 170, 172,
        290–1
    and politics, 264–6
    of property, 268–9
    and religion, 120, 228
    slave, 170, 239
morphology, 72, 73, 79
    transcendental, 79

Müller, Johannes, 79
'Münchhausen Trilemma', 315
music, 6, 59, 62
Musset, Alfred de, 47
Mynster, Bishop, 299
mysticism, 133, 134–5, 281
'myth of the given', 322, 324

Nancy, Jean-Luc, 52, 59, 65
Napoleon Bonaparte, 247, 248, 281,
    283
narcissism, 216, 218
Nassar, Dalia T., 6, 29–46, 332
nation, 230, 243
nationalism, 58, 284
Natorp, Paul, 101
natural history, 70, 71–2, 80, 84
natural philosophy, 69, 70–2
natural religion, 71, 129, 135
natural sciences, 8, 69, 70–2, 90–2,
    152–5, 253
    and human sciences, 151–2
    and metaphysics, 100
    and philosophy, 321–2, 326
    relationship with philosophy of
        nature, 74–80
    see also Naturwissenschaften
natural selection, 115, 116, 117, 118,
    120, 121, 124, 211
natural theology, 135–6, 243
naturalism, 3, 25, 27, 138
    criticism of, 4, 322–3
    growth of, 89, 103
    and idealism, 3, 4, 7, 89–110
    and Kantianism, 102–3
    'practical', 89
naturalistic fallacy, 123
nature, 5
    causal influences, 181
    conflict in, 81–2, 85
    and Darwinism, 7
    disenchantment of Romantic, 209,
        326
    divinisation of, 14
    economic-teleological principle,
        325
    economy of, 71–2
    as the entfremdet (self-alienated)
        Idea, 75–6
    and freedom, 7, 8, 23–4, 31, 325
    and gender (Geschlecht), 82–3
    healing power of, 208–9
    hermeneutics of, 72–4, 80–5
    independent of human values,
        152–3
    Kant on, 31–2, 175
    mechanistic and deterministic view
        of, 3, 52
    and mind, 150–1
    and morality, 11, 124
    order of, 71, 80, 82
    and reason, 32, 322–3
    Romantic view of, 2
    and transcendence, 17, 19
    unity of self with in art, 24–6
    versus freedom, 90–2, 107
    see also philosophy of nature
Naturphilosophie see philosophy of
    nature
Naturwissenschaften, 149, 151
    and Naturlehre, 72
Nazism, 291
necessity, and freedom, 305–8, 311

Nechaev, Sergei, 10, 287, 289
    Catechism of a Revolutionary, 288
needs principle, 218, 270
Negri, Antonio, 274
neo-Hegelianism, 151
neo-Kantianism, 7, 89, 101–3, 104,
    151, 245, 253
neo-vitalism, 211
neurobiology, 194
neuroscience, 219–20
Newton, Isaac, Principia, 111
Nicholas I, Czar, 285
Nicholls, Angus, 205
Nietzsche, Friedrich, 7, 9, 52, 59, 63,
    69, 83, 121, 209, 239, 243, 264,
    294–5, 316, 321, 326
    Beyond Good and Evil, 104, 304
    compared with Kierkegaard,
        309–11
    comparison with Freud, 213
    on Darwinism, 112
    Daybreak, 212
    'death of God', 4, 130–1, 285,
        289–91, 291, 292
    doctrine of 'eternal recurrence',
        10–11, 52, 303–9
    Ecce Homo, 304
    genealogy, 168, 169–73, 181–2, 183
    on history, 171, 179, 306, 310–11,
        314, 317
    idealism and naturalism in, 95,
        103–6
    on knowledge, 324, 327
    on nature, 83–4, 85
    on nihilism, 4, 10–11, 95, 278,
        289–91, 292, 306–9, 311, 323–4
    On the Genealogy of Morals, 4, 8,
        104, 105, 168, 170, 173, 182
    On the Uses and Disadvantages of
        History for Life, 124
    Philosophy in the Tragic Age of the
        Greeks, 303, 304
    'positivist phase' (1878–1881), 104
    The Antichrist, 181–2
    The Gay Science, 304
    Thus Spoke Zarathustra, 209, 304,
        305, 308–9
    Twilight of the Idols, 304
    on the unconscious, 212–13, 217,
        219
    on values, 124–5
    Will to Power, 289–91, 304, 308–9,
        318
nihilism, 134, 278–93
    and absolute knowledge, 282–4
    after Nietzsche, 291–2
    as critique of post-Kantian idealism,
        279–80
    dangers of, 1, 2, 4–5, 10, 20, 22, 45,
        324
    European, 303
    in Germany, 284–5, 289–91
    and Left Hegelianism, 284–5
    Nietzsche on, 4, 10–11, 95, 278,
        289–91, 292, 306–9, 311, 323–4
    Romantic, 281–2
    Russian, 10, 285–9, 290, 291, 292
    use of term, 278–9, 280, 281, 286,
        289, 290
    varieties of, 278–9
Nisbet, Robert, 247
Nishitani, Keiji, 278
nominalism, 278

nomothetic, and idiographic, 152–3
nonsense, 6, 59–60, 61, 318
Norman, Judith, 6, 47–68, 332–3
norms, 4, 179, 327
nostalgia, 6, 48–9, 50, 51, 52, 53, 54,
    65, 229
noumenal world, 31, 33, 113, 280, 281
Novalis, 6, 24, 30, 35, 36, 37, 42, 49,
    52, 56, 57, 60, 224, 229, 318
    Heinrich von Ofterdingen, 50, 51
    Hymns to the Night, 281
    Monologue, 58
    Novices at Saïs, 53
Novick, Peter, 149

Oakeshott, Michael, 155
    Experience and Its Modes, 155–6
Obereit, Jacob, 279
object relations theory, 218
objectivity, 323, 326
    of meaning, 319–20
Ockham, William of, 278
Ogden, Thomas, 219
Oken, Lorenz, 69, 79, 80, 92
ontology, 30, 33–4, 108, 115
Ordine Nuovo, L', 273–4
organic, v. mechanical, 2, 76–8
organisms, 71–2, 75–6, 80–1, 94
    evolution of, 114, 120
ought, 22, 136
Outhwaite, William, 9–10, 242–58,
    333
Owen, Richard, 79
Owen, Robert, 266

Paine, Thomas, 243
painting, 60
Pander, Christian Heinrich, 77
pantheism, 15, 16, 112, 280
Pantheism Controversy, 279
paradox, 141
Paris Commune (1871), 262, 271–2,
    274
pathetic fallacy, 54
patronage, 62, 65
Pattison, George, 7–8, 128–44, 333
Paul, Saint, 133
Peirce, Charles Sanders, 3, 114–16
    on evolution, 115–16
perception
    'inner', 215
    and memory, 197–9
    pétites perceptions, in Leibniz, 205
    theory of unconscious inferences,
        207
phenomenal world, and noumenal
    world, 31, 94, 280
phenomenology, 108, 154, 316, 318,
    321
    of embodiment, 9, 187–203
    Hegelian, 175–7
philology, 252
Philosophical Review, 101
philosophy
    analytical and European, 315–27
    Anglo-American, 3, 89, 99–101,
        321, 322
    contextual approach, 317, 324, 327
    as cultural politics, 326–7
    and Darwinism, 111–27
    dialectical, 245
    French, 187–203
    genesis/validation issue, 316

German, 204–22
Greek, 291, 303, 310
mediating role, 326–7
methods, 314–17
nineteenth-century, 1–12
nineteenth-century relations with twentieth, 11, 314–29
real-world test of theories, 317
and the sciences, 101–2, 314–17, 318, 321–2, 325–6
themes, 1, 5
and theology, 132–3
transformation of science through, 74–80
twentieth century and Romanticism, 61–2
twentieth century, idealism and naturalism, 101, 108
see also history of philosophy
philosophy of history, 145, 146–9, 154–6, 173, 177, 244, 249, 252–3
philosophy of mind, 5, 8–9
philosophy of nature (Naturphilosophie), 2, 3, 6–7, 11, 36–9, 42–3, 52, 91–2, 193, 194–6, 280
hermeneutic turn in, 69–88
modern, 325–6
relationship with natural sciences, 74–80, 94–5
Romantic, 207–8, 214
philosophy of religion, 128–9, 137
Hegelian, 129–32
philosophy of science, 75–6, 85, 91, 321–2
physics, 83
physiology, 72, 102, 104, 117, 121–2, 212
Pietism, 134, 135, 279
Pinkard, Terry, 327
Pippin, Robert, 327
Pisarev, Dmitri, 286, 287
Pisemsky, Aleksey, In the Whirlpool, 288
Plato, 108, 301, 303, 314
recollection, 296–7, 298
Platonism, 2, 37, 91, 306, 314
play, 303
Plessner, Helmuth, 106
Plotinus, 278
Pöbel, 243–4
poetry, 48–9, 57, 60, 62, 63–4, 281
political economy, 231, 248, 251, 252, 253, 269
political science, 246, 249
political, the, and the social, 249–50
politics
influence of nihilism on, 291–2
radical and individuality, 223–41
and revolution, 10, 63–5
and society, 5, 96, 243–4
Popper, Karl, 119, 252
positivism, 3, 8, 85, 95, 101, 145, 148, 158, 219, 246, 248, 249–50, 251, 253, 290
in history, 149–52, 154, 252
moral/religious, 26
possibility, 20–1, 174–5, 176, 179, 297, 298, 300–3
post-structuralism, 108
poverty, 1
and inequality, 10, 242, 250, 284
power, 4, 213, 327

demonic, 282
Foucault on, 183
and liberty, 270
political, 13
relations between ego and the unconscious, 209
pragmatism, 111, 114–16, 118, 319, 324
privacy, 242
progress, 1, 3, 302, 309, 314
proletarian state, 10, 274
proletariat, 1, 232, 243–4, 246, 250, 264, 265–6; see also dictatorship of the proletariat
property, morality of, 268–9, 270
Protestantism, 128, 134, 135, 139, 142
Proudhon, Pierre-Joseph, 10, 268–71, 273, 274
Prussia, 63, 225, 226, 231
psyche
apparatus model of the, 216
conflicts within the, 213–14
unity of the, 208–9
psychoanalysis, 204, 213, 219
Freudian, 5, 57, 213–18
intersubjective turn, 218–19
relational, 218
the unconscious in post-Freudian, 218–19
psychology, 5, 78, 103, 104, 108, 116–17, 119, 145, 171–2
explanatory, 206
philosophical, 188–93
the unconscious in German, 204–22
psychophysics, 206–7
psychosexuality, 216
'psychozoölogy', 116
purposiveness see teleology
Pushkin, Alexander Sergeyevich, 281

Quine, Willard Van Orman, 11, 320

Rahner, Karl, 142
random variation, 115, 119
Ranke, Leopold von, 148–9
rationalism, 1, 2, 223, 252, 281, 320, 324
Ravaisson, Félix, 9, 187, 188, 193–6, 198, 199, 200
De l'Habitude, 193–6
realism, 179
medieval, 278
transcendental, 90–1, 101
reason, 1, 2, 5–6, 8, 94–5, 135
as the Absolute, 37–8
crises of, 11, 13–14, 21, 27, 311
dialectical, 136
and faith, 140–1, 142
and intuition, 6
Kantian, 6, 18, 29–30, 32, 69, 174–5, 283
and nature, 32, 322–3
the sociality of, 327
and understanding, 26
will as practical, 94, 105
receptivity, 322, 323
recurrence, eternal, 10–11, 105, 294–313
Rée, Paul Der Ursprung der moralischen Empfindungen, 121–2
reflection, 24–5, 30, 37, 56
or intuition, 43–5

Reformation, 128, 223
reformism, 10, 262, 269–70, 272–3, 285
regress, 315, 319
Reill, Peter Hanss, 74, 83
Reinhold, Karl Leonhard, 15, 33, 56, 57, 63
debate with Schmid, 18–19, 21
relativism, 148, 251, 253
religion, 103
and conception of society, 243
crisis in, 1, 4, 5
critiques of, 279
and Darwinism, 114–15, 124
Eastern, 281
of humanity, 236–7, 250
and knowledge, 128–44
and morality, 120, 228
national, 233–4
natural, 71, 129, 135
and nature of authority, 264–5
positive, 129
privatisation of, 232
and science, 4, 5, 93, 108, 113
see also faith; philosophy of religion
religious studies, in higher education, 142–3
Renaissance, 173
Renouvier, Charles, 246
repetition, 10–11, 52, 294–313
Kierkegaard on, 10–11, 295–303
representation(s), 16–17, 31–3, 131
and association, 206
by association-free class of words, 319–20
by rule, 319
objective, 319
unconscious, 210, 211
repression, 213–14, 215–16
political, 231, 286
republicanism, 63, 228–9, 230
responsibility, and human agency, 17
ressentiment, 63–4
revelation, 128, 304, 323
revolution, 1, 62–5, 259–77
anarchist models, 268–73, 274
bourgeois, 261–2, 274
contested concept of, 10, 259
contradictions and, 178–9
as dictatorship, 262–3
from above, 10, 261, 263–4, 268
from below, 10, 261–2, 267, 268, 273–4
of the mind, 269
nihilism and, 287–8
permanent, 289
proletarian, 244, 261–2, 274
social, 247–9, 267–8
use of term, 259
Revue Encyclopédique, 231
Reymond, Emil du Bois, 79
Reynaud, Jean, 230
Richards, Robert J., 79–80
Richter, Jean Paul, 281, 283, 291
Siebenkäs, 281
Rickert, Heinrich, 145, 151
The Limits of Concept Formation in Natural Science, 152
Riedel, Manfred, 246
Riehl, Alois, 101–2
The Principles of the Critical Philosophy, 101
Right Hegelianism, 7–8, 284, 285–6

Ringer, Fritz, 149
Ritchie, David George, 'The Rationality of History', 155
Ritter, Johann Wilhelm, 78
Robespierre, Maximilien, 10, 231, 259–61, 262, 263–4, 266, 269
Romanticism, 2, 4, 9, 47–68, 228
    as a *Bildungsreise*, 50, 51
    critical self-consciousness of, 50, 53–5, 61, 65
    defining, 6, 47–53
    Early German, 5, 6, 10, 24, 30, 49, 234, 323
    English/British, 6, 48, 50–1, 54, 56–7, 62, 64
    French, 48, 57, 63
    German, 2, 6, 29–46, 48, 50–1, 54, 56, 56–7, 63–4, 322
    Heidelberg group, 49, 50
    and idealism, 2, 53, 55, 56, 91–2
    Jena group, 48, 49, 50, 55, 56, 57, 60, 62, 280, 281–2, 291
    linguistic turns, 57–60
    nihilism, 281–2
    as *ressentiment*, 63–4
    the unconscious in, 207–9, 218, 219
    use of term, 47, 48–9, 50
Rorty, Richard, 317, 326–7
Roscher, Wilhelm, 252
Rose, Gillian, *Hegel Contra Sociology*, 245
Rosenkranz, Karl, 131
Rousseau, Jean-Jacques, 8, 173–4, 175, 179, 263, 269
    general will, 260–1
    On the Origins of Inequality, 173–4, 243
    The Social Contract, 173–4, 260, 270
Royce, Josiah, 111
Rudé, George, 261, 267
Russell, Bertrand, 2, 321
Russia
    materialism, 3
    nihilism in, 10, 285–9, 290, 291, 292
    serfdom, 243
Russian Revolution, 274
Russian Word, 286

Saint-Cheron, Alexandre de, 224
Saint-Hilaire, Geoffroy, 79
Saint-Simon, Claude Henri de, 223–4, 230, 231, 232, 249
    transitional/critical age, 231
sans-culottes, 261
Savage, Rev. Minot J., 120
Savigny, Friedrich Carl von, *History of Roman Law in the Middle Ages*, 252
scepticism, 2, 29, 33, 45, 90, 104–5, 160, 190, 192, 279
Schafer, Roy, 218
Schaller, Julius, 131
Scheler, Max, 106
Schelling, F.W.J., 1, 6, 13, 15, 18, 21, 27, 49, 50, 52, 55, 56, 58, 89, 114, 128, 129, 189, 209, 219, 245, 280, 282, 285, 299–300, 301
    and the Absolute, 26, 29, 30, 35, 36–9, 42–3, 44–5, 64
    Bruno, 80

compared with Fichte, 25, 39, 43, 325
Hegel's critique of, 30, 35, 40–1, 43–4
identity philosophy, 30, 35–6, 37–9, 41–2, 194–5
late 'positivist' philosophy, 93, 97
letter to Hegel (1795), 18
Naturphilosophie, 69, 72–3, 74–5, 76, 79, 80, 81, 83, 325
Philosophy of Revelation, 74–5
'Presentation of My System', 37–9, 44–5
Real-Idealismus, 91
on revelation, 128
'self-critique of idealism', 93–4
System of Transcendental Idealism, 24–6, 30, 36, 208
Von der Weltseele, 73, 77, 80, 81
Schiller, F.C.S., *Riddles of the Sphinx*, 121
Schiller, Friedrich, 24, 48, 103, 225, 228
Schlegel, August Wilhelm, 24, 47, 48, 49, 53, 56, 58
    Vienna lectures, 49, 51–2
Schlegel, Caroline, 49, 63
Schlegel, Dorothea, 49
Schlegel, Friedrich, 6, 24, 30, 35, 36, 37, 49, 56, 58, 61, 64, 65, 281
    on authorship, 57, 58, 59
    Dialogue on Poetry, 60
    'On the Essence of Criticism', 57
    On the Study of Greek Poetry, 48–9
    and Romanticism, 47, 51, 53, 57, 281
    on spontaneity and receptivity, 323–4
Schleiermacher, Friedrich, 11, 19, 26, 30, 36, 37, 49, 132, 136, 234, 252, 324, 326
    Dialectic, 319, 320
    and individuality, 223, 224, 228, 228–30, 239–40
    Monologues, 229–30
Schmid, C. C., 18–19, 21
Schmoller, Gustav von, 252
Schnädelbach, Herbert, 244, 251
    Morbus Hermeneuticus, 317
scholasticism, 128, 134
Schopenhauer, Arthur, 3, 6, 7, 9, 26, 59, 69, 74, 78, 80, 81, 103, 125, 239, 281, 290, 315
    metaphysics of the will, 76, 81, 82, 83–4, 85, 94–7, 209–10, 212, 213, 216, 219
    naturalism, 94–6
    On the Will in Nature, 76
    The World as Will and Representation, 26, 83, 209, 303–4
Schubert, Gotthilf von, 92
Schutz, Alfred, 154
science, 1, 5
    as adaptation, 119
    and art, 319–20
    construction by philosophy, 74–80
    disciplinary boundaries, 152–3
    'finite', 75
    Kant on, 72, 103
    Marx on, 177–8
    metaphysical neutrality of, 116–17
    Nietzsche on, 306
    as paradigm of knowledge, 3

philosophy as, 314–17, 321–2, 325–6
    and religion, 4, 5, 108, 113
    of religion, 132
    Romantic, 52
    see also philosophy of science
scientism, 323, 325–6
Scotland
    Enlightenment, 244
    moral philosophy, 251
Seattle, anti-capitalist movement (1999), 274
Second International, 273
secularisation, 1, 50, 309
'secularism', 1
self
    Freudian theory, 216–17
    and the lived body, 9, 187, 192, 195–6
    loss of the, 301–2
    production of the, 34, 180, 238–40, 298–303
    unity with nature in art, 24–6, 36–9
self psychology, 218–19
self-consciousness, 23, 24, 34, 41–2, 91, 140, 283, 316
    evolution of, 116–17, 122, 123–4
    Romantic, 50, 53–4, 61, 65
    see also subjectivity
self-knowledge, 33–4, 173–4
self-realisation, 9, 123–5, 223, 224, 226, 233, 234, 238
Sellars, Wilfrid, 322
semantics, 321
Sen, Amartya, 243
sensibility, 74, 78
Serres, Etienne, 79
Sewell Jr., William, 249
sexuality, 83, 210
Shakespeare, William, 48, 49, 54
Shelley, Mary, 281
Shelley, Percy Bysshe, 51, 63, 281
Sidgwick, Henry, 'The Theory of Evolution in its Application to Practice', 123
Sièyes, Abbé, *Qu'est-ce que le tiers état?*, 248
Simmel, Georg, 154, 224, 244, 253
sin, 298, 301–3
Sinclair, Mark, 8–9, 187–203, 333
Sismondi, Simon de, 49
Sloan, Phillip, 72
Smith, Adam, *Theory of Moral Sentiments*, 244
Smith, Goldwin, 119
social contract
    Proudhon's, 269, 270
    Rousseau's, 173–4, 260, 270
social philosophy, 242–58
social policy, 244, 251
social psychology, 218
'social question', 1, 242, 244, 250–1
social reform, 10, 96, 251
social science, 10, 148, 153–4, 242, 244, 245–6, 248–9
    'methodological dualist/anti-naturalist' approach, 252
    use of term, 248, 249, 251, 253
social, the
    Kant and Hegel and, 245–6
    and the political, 249–50
    rise of, 242–58
social theory, 217, 245, 253

social welfare, morality and, 121
socialism, 10, 244, 259, 265–6, 273–4,
  309
  democratic, 230–4
  French, 224–5, 234, 243, 271–2
  from above or from below, 268
  German, 262, 285
  and individualism, 230–4, 264
  liberal, 9, 237–8
  modern, 261–2
  Proudhon's critique of, 269–70
  and social science, 251
  state, 268
  through revolution, 266–8
  use of term, 231
  utopian, 223–4
  as working-class emancipation,
    273
sociality, 242–3
society, 1, 5, 9–10
  conception of, 242–4, 249
  and individuality, 26, 225, 226,
    236, 242–4
  and politics, 5
  and the state, 246, 247, 249
sociology, 5, 145, 150, 153–4, 244–5,
  247, 249
  evolutionary, 253
sociology of philosophy, 245
solidarity, 265, 268
Sombart, Werner, 252
Sorel, Georges, 273, 291
Sorley, William Ritchie
  On the Ethics of Naturalism, 123–4
  'The Historical Method', 155
Spalding, J. J., 16, 17, 21–2
'species-being' (Gattungswesen), 93,
  264
speculative theology/philosophy, 131–
  2, 136–7, 138, 139, 141, 142
Spencer, Herbert, 3, 7, 85, 89, 96, 115,
  116, 118, 154, 279
  criticism of his evolutionary ethics,
    123–5
  Data of Ethics, 120, 121
  evolutionary theory, 7, 85, 112–14,
    120–1, 125
  First Principles, 113, 114
  and morality, 120–1
  Principles of Psychology, 117
  Social Statics, 113
  Synthetic Philosophy, 113
Spinoza, Baruch, 2, 5, 10, 20, 21, 22,
  25, 27, 74, 91, 128, 280
  Cartesian Meditations, 20
  geometrical method, 37
  and radical Enlightenment, 13–14
Spinozism, 2, 100
  Jacobi and, 14–18, 25–6, 279–80,
    323, 324
  the new, 13–28
spirit
  as Geist, 8, 40–1, 83, 146–7, 175–7,
    252, 283–4, 318, 324, 327
  Kierkegaard's domain of the, 296
  and nature, 24–5
'spiritualism', 187
spiritualist tradition, French, 5, 8,
  187–203
spontaneity, 322, 323
Staël, Madame de, 49, 50
Stahl, Georg Ernst, 196
Stalin, Joseph, 274

standpoint, 169, 172, 177; see also first
  person
state
  and anarchism, 10, 269–72
  bourgeois, 10, 274
  and civil society, 246
  freedom of the, 272–3
  and individuality, 230, 233–4, 322
  limits to action, 225–9
  negation of the, 179
  paternalist, 226–8, 232, 235
  proletarian, 10, 274
  rational, 284
  redistributive, 9
  reform through the, 269–70
  separate from Church, 228–9, 232
  and society, 246, 247, 249
  subjugation in the, 264–5
  'withering away', 262, 274
  see also absolutism
Steffens, Henrik, 69, 78
Stein, Lorenz von, 243, 246, 247, 250,
  251
Stendhal, 281
Stephen, Leslie, The Science of Ethics,
  121
Stern, Robert, 3
Stewart, Dugald, 244, 247
Stirling, James Hutchison, 112
  The Secret of Hegel, 99
Stirner, Max, 105, 263, 268, 269
  The Ego and Its Own, 239, 264–5,
    284
Stoics, 303
Stone, Alison, 1–12, 333
Strauss, David Friedrich, 7, 124,
  137–9, 146, 156
  Life of Jesus Critically Examined,
    137–8, 284
Sturm und Drang, 14, 207
subject, the, 10, 53–7
subjectivity, 3, 7, 41–2, 53–4, 62, 90,
  93, 96, 198, 294, 310, 323
  absolute, 278–93
  in art, 55–7, 224
  grounding, 318–19
  lived, 11, 196
  and time, 141
  transcendental, 24–5, 54–6, 64, 90,
    107, 318
sublime, the, 54–5
substance, 20
suffering, 7, 172, 304
super-ego, the, 216–17
superhumanity, 289–92, 308–9
supernaturalism, 134, 136, 140
'survival of the fittest', 112, 113
'symphilosophy', 58
syndicalism, 271, 273
Szondi, Peter, 61

Taine, Hippolyte, 215
Taylor, Charles, 224
  'Modern Social Imaginaries', 242–3
Taylor, Mark C., 142
teleology, 3, 71–2, 76–7, 79, 80–1, 85,
  92, 94, 97–8, 101, 102, 107–8,
  112, 150, 173, 211, 223
  in history, 154–5
  Nietzsche's refusal of, 308–9
'teleomechanism', 79
Terror, the, 259–60, 261, 263
Tertullian, 134

Teutscher Merkur, 15
text, literary, 62
  unintended consequences, 57–60
Thanatos, 216
Thatcher, Margaret, 251
theology, 3, 50, 71, 72, 93, 128–9,
  131, 145, 303
  metaphysics and logic, 70
  and nihilism, 279, 280, 284–5
  and philosophy, 132–3, 139
  Protestant, 27, 128
  speculative, 131–2
  status in higher education, 142–3
thinking
  intuitive and discursive, 31–2, 42,
    45
  post-metaphysical, 318–19
Thomas, Paul, 263, 268
Thoreau, Henry David, 2, 6, 69, 84,
  85, 238, 239, 240
  Natural History of Massachusetts, 84
  Walden, 84
Tieck, Ludwig, 49, 57, 60–1, 281
Tillich, Paul, 142
time
  and the Absolute, 162
  as duration, 199
  existential, 311
  in history, 163
  subjectivity and, 141
Tocqueville, Alexis de, 239, 246, 247,
  248, 249, 250–1, 267
  Democracy in America, 246
Tönnies, Ferdinand, 253
Toulmin, Stephen, 119
trade unions, 270
transcendence
  denial of, 280, 298–9, 308–9, 327
  and nature, 17, 19
'transcendental morphology' school,
  79
transcendental philosophy, 2, 24–6,
  37, 55, 59–60, 71, 72, 77, 101,
  104, 108, 136; see also
  idealism, transcendental
transcendentalism, American, 2, 84,
  238–9
transformation, 2, 11, 23, 40–1, 169,
  172, 304–9, 310–11
  social, 265–7, 270–1, 284–7, 292
transition, 298–303, 310–11
Treitschke, Heinrich von, 243
Trotsky, Leon, 273, 289
truth, 4, 18, 20, 32, 40–1, 44, 105,
  118, 136–7, 141, 213, 283, 303
  correspondence theory of, 327
  subjective existential, 297–303
  will to, 170–1, 172
Turgenev, Ivan, 278, 290
  Fathers and Sons, 286–7

Übermensch see superhumanity
Unbewusste see unconscious, the
unconditioned, the, 29–30, 323
  role in textual production, 57–60
unconscious inferences, theory of, 207
unconscious, the, 5, 9, 96–7, 204–22
  cognitive, 9, 205, 207, 216
  collective, 218
  compulsive-irrational, 9, 212–13
  in Freud, 204, 213–18
  origins of conception, 205–7,
    208–9, 215

in post-Freudian psychoanalysis, 218–19
relations between the ego and, 209
Romantic-vital, 9, 207–9
use of term, 204, 209, 217
unconscious will, 209–11
understanding (*Verstehen*), 8, 145, 148, 150–2, 153–4, 163, 251–2
Unitarianism, 136
universal, concrete, 159–64
urbanisation, 1
urea, synthesis of, 83
United States of America
democracy, 247
evolutionary philosophy, 114
historians, 148
idealism, 99–101
individualism, 224
modern philosophy, 322
Romantics, 281
slavery, 243
transcendentalism, 2, 84, 238–9
utilitarianism, 3, 4, 120, 154, 236, 251, 290

Vaihinger, Hans, *Philosophy of 'As If'*, 102–3
Valls, Andrew, 235
value(s)
exchange, 324
labour theory of, 268
modern, 2
in natural science, 152
and naturalism, 4, 103
Nietzschean critique of moral, 124–5, 170, 290–1, 292
Verstehen see understanding
verum-factum principle, 150–1
Vico, Giambattista, 59, 158, 173
New Science, 150–1
Vienna Circle, 315, 318, 320, 321
violence, nihilistic, 291–2
vital power, 207–9, 214
vitalism, 78, 81, 92, 196; *see also* neo-vitalism
Voß, J.J., 49
vocation, 16, 21–4, 175
Vogel, Paul, 246

Vogt, Karl, 89
Volk, 58
Voltaire, 173, 244, 279
von Baader, Franz, 92
von Baer, Karl Ernst, 77, 79
Vorstellung see representation

Wackenroder, Wilhelm, 49
Wagner, Peter, 249
Wagner, Richard, 212, 315
Gesamtkunstwerk, 59
Wallace, William, 99
Ward, James, 160, 161
Weber, Max, 145, 151, 153–4, 244, 251, 252, 253, 279, 324
Wegener, Mai, 204–5
Weiller, Kajetan von, 280
Weishaupt, Adam, 16, 17
Weisse, Christian Hermann, 131
Welchman, Alistair, 6, 47–68, 333
welfare, 121, 227
welfare state, 244
Wellek, René, 47, 48
Weltschmerz, 281–2, 291
Westphal, Kenneth, 73
Wheeler, Samuel, 320
Whewell, William, 83, 85
Whitehead, Alfred North, 85
Whitman, Walt, 238
Wieland, C.M., 15
Wilde, Oscar, 291
will, 3, 7, 286
and the body, 9, 190–3, 193–6
compulsive-irrational, 216–17
consciousness and the, 189
and freedom, 19, 289, 306, 325
general, 260–1, 266
and habit, 194
Hartmann on the, 96–7
Kant on the, 94
metaphysics of the, 76, 81, 82, 83–4, 85, 213
psychology of the, 187, 188–93
Schelling on, 209
Schopenhauer's, 76, 81, 82, 83–4, 85, 94–6, 209–10, 212, 213, 216, 304
to life, 105, 209–10, 212–13, 304

to power, 105, 125, 213, 289–91, 292, 304, 318
to truth, 170–1, 172, 306
the unconscious, 209–13, 216–17
Williams, Bernard, 183
Winch, Donald, 249
Windelband, Wilhelm, 145, 151, 152, 153
'History and Natural Science', 153
Winnicott, Donald W., 218
Winstanley, Gerrard, 262
Wissenschaft, 149; *see also* knowledge; science
Wittgenstein, Ludwig, 317, 318, 319, 321
Tractatus Logico-Philosophicus, 125, 318
Wöhler, Friedrich, 83
Wokler, Robert, 248–9
Wolff, Christian, 128
women
Mill on subjection of, 179–81
status of, 64
Wordsworth, William, 48, 50, 51, 54, 55, 63
Preface to *Lyrical Ballads*, 54
working class, 10, 233, 250, 261–2, 265–8, 270, 271, 272, 274; *see also* proletariat
Wright, Chauncey, 116–17, 119
'Evolution of Self-Consciousness', 116–17
Wundt, Wilhelm, 103, 117, 118
Beiträgen zur Theorie der Sinneswahrnehmung, 207
Vorlesungen über die Menschen- und Thierseele, 117

Young Bosnia movement, 291
Young Germany movement, 284–5
Young Hegelians, 93, 245, 252, 263–5, 324

Zakaras, Alex, 9, 223–41, 333
Zeitschrift für geschichtliche Rechtswissenschaft, 252
Žižek, Slavoj, 274